O - organization
S - sentence structure
D - diction (choice of words)
G - grammar
M - pure mechanics

¶ - paragraph

δ - omit

‖ - parallel construction

- more space

] - move to right

[- left

Must have parallel construction:
1. in a series
2. with correlatives
3. in comparison
4. with a linking verb

Joan Lamar Lesher
2806 Sheila Dr.
Louisville 5, Ky.
GL 8-5170

Writer's Guide

and Index

to English

REVISED EDITION

Porter G. Perrin, *University of Washington*

Scott, Foresman *and Company*

CHICAGO   ATLANTA   DALLAS   NEW YORK

Preface

THIS *Writer's Guide and Index to English* describes our current language in a pattern planned for use in college courses in composition. The aim of these courses is to encourage in students effective communication of facts and ideas, imaginative conception, desires and feelings. This purpose of communication sets the framework of a course and guides the bulk of its activities. Consequently the first chapter of this book is The Activity of Writing, to set in perspective the more detailed topics that follow.

Effective communication must be in the idiom of the day. Familiarity with the language in actual use in the 1950s is a prerequisite for writing. The greater part of this book is devoted to a description of current usage, the language used by educated people in carrying on their affairs. Chapters 4 to 12 and most of the entries in the *Index* describe and comment on our language as it is being used, especially on points on which usage is divided or which for some reason raise questions.

Since usage is described in terms of grammar, the book contains a grammar of current English, not for its own sake but to make it possible to discuss particular items of usage. These topics are under appropriate heads in the *Index* and in Chapter 4, which brings together a number of bothersome points. The type of grammar presented is not prescriptive but descriptive, using wherever possible the categories and terms of scientific descriptive grammar. The book is, then, *a grammatical description of current usage in a perspective of composition*.

Besides information about the language around them, students need guidance in selecting from its wealth and its sometimes confusing variety the expressions that will be effective with readers. Rules can function only for some of the most elementary matters, and even in the most definite of these (agreement of subject and verb, for example), exceptions are numerous. This book meets the problem in Chapters 2 and 3 by describing the varieties of English that are current and by giving principles to guide students in selecting what is appropriate and consequently Good English.

Anyone seeking to improve his expression starts with his material and his purpose for conveying it to a particular body of readers. Then he uses what language he can command to meet the situation before him. He has learned his language by imitation and continues to develop control of it by reading successful examples of communication. A college course can encourage practice and critical examination of the language of students and others. This direct observation can be analyzed and brought into some system by a book such as this.

The essential thing to remember is that our language is not a taskmaster but an opportunity. It offers anyone with material he wishes to convey to others the means for saying it to them. We are its master and not its slave; serious purpose and confidence makes growth possible as worry and fear do not. Curiosity about actual language processes and some feeling of freedom will in the long run produce better writing than a program of prohibition.

The aim of this book is to give students enough information about their living and lively language to help them answer questions about what they should say in a specific situation by applying principles of appropriateness. The core of the approach is understanding why one word or construction is better than another and in what circumstances it is better. In this way students can take much of the responsibility for their expression and for their growth in the natural, confident speaking and writing that constitutes Good English. Both teachers and students find such a relative approach realistic, in keeping with both art and science, and conducive to greater interest and surer growth than a narrower and more negative approach.

The standard of usage the book especially recommends is good Informal English, the English of educated and socially established people as they carry on their everyday work and as they take their part in public affairs. It has a good deal of freedom but is not slovenly and has the widest currency of the various sorts of English. The less widely used Formal English is also described, and academic usage as in research papers. But since few students are to become academic persons—and they really do not need to write as their teachers may—the style recommended is more widely applicable, more democratically based, more flexible to the actual speaking and writing situations they will have to face. For either style, Vulgate, or uneducated, usage is out of place and is duly discouraged.

The two parts of the book are planned for the two approaches necessary in a composition course: the chapters of the *Guide* for comprehensive class discussion of general topics, the entries of the *Index* for individual reference by students while revising papers or correcting them after they have been read by an instructor.

The chapters are arranged in an order that conforms to the principles given in the beginning of this Preface. But it is not necessary to take them in that order if some other emphasis is preferred. It is, however, necessary to be acquainted with the doctrine of Chapters 2 and 3 before particular questions of usage in the later chapters can be successfully discussed. There are brief suggestions at the head of each chapter for its use.

Each chapter has exercises, some for specific application and practice of the principles given, some for further exploration and for writing. Many of them stress consideration of the student's own writing and language habits.

The alphabetical articles in the *Index* are primarily for individual reference (or browsing), for assignment to particular students who need certain points, and for reference by a student at the time of writing or revising his papers. The *Index* also contains some seventy five specific correction entries, reached through the abbreviations listed inside the back cover and identified in the book by the same abbreviations in longhand. Besides the topics the abbreviations refer to, scores of common lapses from Good English can be marked by putting a ring around the word in question (*fiancé, its, however, like, percent, who*, and so on), to show that the *Index* has a specific entry on it. In this way the abstractness of numbers is avoided and both teacher and student can think in terms of the subject itself. The *Index* also serves as a conventional index to the topics treated in the chapters. Its full use is described on page 405.

The doctrine and presentation in this revision are basically the same as in the 1942 edition. The chapters have been rearranged, Chapter 4 now gives a brief résumé of the principal trouble spots in grammar and usage, and Chapter 5 on punctuation has been elaborated. There has been some revision of the doctrine on the paragraph, attempting to get to more basic considerations than the conventional treatment does. More than half of the exercises are new and new materials will be found in those that are retained in form. The chief revision has been intended to clarify statements, to show the relationship between topics, and to improve the articulation between the *Guide* and the *Index*.

Since the *Writer's Guide and Index to English* is based largely on recent linguistic scholarship, it is greatly indebted to linguists of the last two generations. The books most referred to are listed in the Bibliography on pages xi-xiii and more specific books and articles are given at the end of *Index* entries. The first edition was read by the late Leonard Bloomfield and the present one owes much to Russell Cosper. Many specific suggestions have come in the course of a pleasant and fairly voluminous correspondence set in motion by the preceding editions. I am grateful for the many bits of useful advice. The exercises are largely the work of George H. Smith.

Authors and publishers have generously given permission to use the many illustrative quotations. Their aid is gratefully recognized in the list of Acknowledgments.

I hope the book will continue to encourage teachers and students to an active observation of our language as it is used about them and will help them increase their judgment of its use in lively and purposeful writing.

P. G. P.

Contents

The Index contains entries in alphabetical arrangement that fall roughly into these five categories:

a) Entries on particular words and constructions, such as *continual, continuous; fiancé, fiancée; get, got; like—as; route; shall—will; so . . . that; very*

b) Entries for correction and revision of papers, indicated by longhand abbreviations before the entry word

c) Page references to subjects treated in the chapters

d) Articles on English grammar, giving definitions and examples of such matters as *case, conjunctions, plurals, principal parts of verbs*

e) Articles on various facts of language, such as *American and British usage, Foreign words in English, Colloquial and written English, English language, Experiment in English, Foreign words in English, Heightened style, Pronunciation*

ACKNOWLEDGMENTS
LISTS OF WRITERS AND SOURCES QUOTED
CORRECTION CHART (end pages)

Bibliography

THE FOLLOWING WORKS have been the most useful in gathering the material for this book. They are frequently referred to (usually by author's name only) in the chapters of Part I and in the alphabetical entries of Part II, the *Index*.

Aiken, Janet R., *Commonsense Grammar*, New York, Thomas Y. Crowell Company, 1936. An informal presentation of functional grammar

American College Dictionary, New York (text edition), Harper & Brothers, 1948

American Speech, New York, Columbia University Press. A periodical, founded in 1925, containing much direct observation of current American usage, especially vocabularies of particular regions and vocations

Ballard, Philip B., *Thought and Language*, London, University of London Press, 1934. A penetrating and readable discussion of many ordinary problems in language, showing a development in England of language attitudes paralleling that in the United States

Baugh, Albert C., *A History of the English Language*, New York, Appleton-Century-Crofts, 1935. A substantial and readable history of the language

Bloomfield, Leonard, *Language*, New York, Holt, 1933. A basic work on the general principles of language study

Curme, George O., *Syntax*, Boston, Heath, 1931; and *Parts of Speech and Accidence*, Boston, Heath, 1935. A very full grammar of modern English, with much historical material. (Curme's doctrine is more available in *Principles and Practice of English Grammar*, College Outline Series, New York, Barnes & Noble, 1947)

Dobrée, Bonamy, *Modern Prose Style*, Oxford, Oxford University Press, 1934. An illuminating discussion of contemporary prose, English and American

Fowler, H. W., *A Dictionary of Modern English Usage*, Oxford University Press, 1926. Though based on British usage and now dating somewhat, still a readable and often illuminating discussion

Fries, C. C., *American English Grammar*, New York, Appleton-Century-Crofts (NCTE Monograph No. 10), 1940. A fresh approach to a number of points of grammar, discussed with special reference to differences between levels of usage

Goldberg, Isaac, *The Wonder of Words*, New York, Appleton-Century-Crofts, 1938. Readable chapters on current linguistic problems

Hall, J. Lesslie, *English Usage*, Chicago, Scott, Foresman and Company, 1917. Discusses historically 141 locutions on which usage is divided or questioned

Hayakawa, S. I., *Language in Action*, New York, Harcourt, Brace and Company, 1941 (text edition). A readable introduction to "general semantics"

Jespersen, Otto, *Essentials of English Grammar*, New York, Holt, 1933. An abridgement of Jespersen's four volume *Modern English Grammar*, the most important description of English in the light of modern language study

Kennedy, Arthur G., *Current English*, Boston, Ginn & Company, 1935. General linguistic information focused on current English; full bibliography makes possible the further study of most language problems

Kenyon, John S. and Thomas A. Knott, *A Pronouncing Dictionary of American English*, Springfield, G. & C. Merriam Co., 1944. The most reliable guide to American pronunciation

Krapp, George P., *The Knowledge of English*, New York, Holt, 1927. Bridges the gap often left between grammar and style

Kruisinga, E., *A Handbook of Present-Day English*, 5th edition, Groningen, P. Noordhoff, 1931. A comprehensive survey of modern English syntax

McKnight, George H., *English Words and Their Backgrounds*, New York, Appleton-Century-Crofts, 1923. A study of the English vocabulary and its evolution

Marckwardt, Albert H. and Fred G. Walcott, *Facts About Current English Usage*, New York, Appleton-Century-Crofts (NCTE Monograph No. 7), 1938. Includes the data of the Sterling A. Leonard study (1932) of debatable and divided usage, with additional information

Mencken, H. L., *The American Language*, 4th edition, New York, Knopf, 1936; *Supplement I* (1945); *Supplement II* (1948). A mass of material on various varieties of American English, with commentary and references to further sources

Oxford English Dictionary. The great storehouse of information on the meaning and history of English words

Pence, R. W., *A Grammar of Present-Day English*, New York, Macmillan, 1947. A convenient manual of conventional English grammar

Pooley, Robert C., *Teaching English Usage*, New York, Appleton-Century-Crofts (NCTE Monograph No. 16), 1946. Discussion of a number of debatable locutions, with evidence and recommendations for teaching

Rickert, Edith, *New Methods for the Study of Literature*, Chicago, University of Chicago Press, 1927. Suggestions for detailed study of qualities of style

Robertson, Stuart, *The Development of Modern English*, New York, Prentice-Hall, 1934. Gives the background of many points of current syntax

Schlauch, Margaret, *The Gift of Tongues*, New York, Viking Press, 1942. Readable and illuminating discussion of topics in current language study

Summey, George, Jr., *American Punctuation* (New York, 1949). The most thorough and authoritative treatment of punctuation

The University of Chicago Press, *A Manual of Style*, 11th edition, Chicago, University of Chicago Press, 1949. The stylebook of a distinguished conservative publishing house

Webster's Dictionary, Second edition of the New International, Springfield, G. & C. Merriam, 1934; *New Collegiate Dictionary*, 1949

More specific works are cited in the various articles to which they are appropriate.

Part One

Writer's Guide

Part One

Writer's Guide

The activity of writing

In a sense, every kind of writing is hypocritical. It has to be done with an air of gusto, though no one ever yet enjoyed the act of writing. Even a man with a specific gift for writing, with much to express, with perfect freedom in choice of subject and manner of expression, with infinite leisure, does not write with real gusto. But in him the pretence is justified: he has enjoyed thinking out his subject, he will delight in his work when it is done.—Max Beerbohm

Ambition is sometimes no vice in life; it is always a virtue in Composition.—Edward Young (1759)

SUGGESTIONS FOR USING THE CHAPTER: *Since this chapter emphasizes the process of writing, it sets a background for the various activities of a composition course and is a natural starting point for such a course. (Chapters 2 and 3 could be taken first in a program stressing work in language.)*

The chapter can be covered rapidly to give students a notion of the stages in the writing process, and to call their attention to those they are likely to slight, and to remind them of the varied material they have for use in future papers. The various stages then can be stressed in specific exercises and assignments. Or the chapter can be taken more slowly, with exercises and papers to explore the activity of writing, before the work proceeds to the study of current English in the chapters that follow.

F OR MOST PEOPLE who have not written very much, the chief difficulty in preparing any kind of paper is uncertainty as to what they should do. Worry takes more out of them than work. They try to see the completely finished paper at the very start of thinking about it, perhaps even before the topic is definite in their minds, usually before the material has been got together and lined up. Actually at this early stage they cannot even worry intelligently about the paper, much less see their way to working profitably on it.

Writing a paper is work, and it should be gone about in a workmanlike manner. There is no mystery about it (unless you find yourself doing very much better than you expect to do) and, as in all jobs, there is a definite series of steps. Each step has its characteristic problems and makes its characteristic contribution to the finished paper. The beginning of wisdom in writing, and of freedom from loose worry, is in seeing these various stages clearly so that each can be attacked by itself and the paper advanced in an orderly and profitable fashion.

This *Guide and Index* is primarily intended to advise you on the specific problems of writing—paragraphs, sentences, words, phrases, points of grammar and style, and so on. But since these exist only in whole papers, a natural background for their discussion is an account of the process of writing.

RELATED CHAPTERS AND ARTICLES: *Other chapters in this book and articles in the Index give further details about the writing process. Some of these are listed here as a matter of interest.*

Writing a paper can be divided for convenience of discussion into nine stages, shown in the table on page 6. Of course any such analysis is somewhat arbitrary because of the variable conditions involved in a particular article—the writer's habits and background, his purpose, the complexity of the material, the length proposed, and the time at his disposal. In writing a letter to a friend the stages are telescoped and can hardly be separated, but in writing a letter applying for a job each stage may be painfully distinct. Anyone should be able to write a short paper, say of two or three hundred words on a subject familiar to him, without much conscious effort; but writing a long, complex paper will require careful attention to each stage. The problems of all the stages attempted together are enough to swamp anyone, even a professional writer, but if one step is undertaken at a time and disposed of, an orderly, workmanlike process can replace the jumble of worries.

Making due allowance for the telescoping of some of these steps and for the varying weight given each because of the differences between writers and between specific pieces of writing, we may take them as typical of most writing activity. In descriptions of their work made by professional writers, these same steps are indicated more or less definitely. An experienced feature writer described his methods of work in the following way:

First, I fix upon the particular aspect of the particular subject which I wish to treat. Second, I outline the questions which require to be answered in treating this subject. Third, I supply from my own resources what part of the answers I can. Fourth, I complete my answers by additional study and by personal investigations—inquiry from competent persons, or personal visits to whatever places may be necessary. When all the questions are answered satisfactorily, the material is ready to be organized and written out.— PAUL SCOTT MOWRER, in H. F. HARRINGTON, *Modern Feature Writing*, p. 37

Our list of stages applies primarily to the process of turning out an expository article, like a magazine article or course paper, but the steps are not so very different for the "creative" sorts of writing, though the separate stages may be more difficult to distinguish. In stories, for example, the writer usually has an outside stimulus that turns his mind to a theme or person or situation, then a period of gathering

---

Stages in Writing a Paper with the Contribution of Each Stage

1. *The Writer's Background*—A reservoir of general and specific information, habits of expression, etc.
2. *Focusing on a Subject*—Definition of topic, sensing of problems involved and of possible sources of information
3. *Gathering Material*—Notes (in mind or on paper) from memory, observation, interview, reading, speculation
4. *Evaluating and Selecting the Material*—A tested and selected body of information to be presented in the paper
5. *Planning the Paper*—A synopsis or outline of the paper
6. *Writing the First Draft*—Tentative copy of the paper
7. *Revising*—Necessary changes in material, corrections and improvements in the words, sentences, paragraphs
8. *Preparing the Manuscript*—The completed paper, ready for readers or for printing
9. *From Manuscript into Print*—The printed copy

---

material, either from memory, from observation, or (as for a historical novel) from specific research. The material crystallizes into some form, perhaps from the writer's hitting on a climax or a purpose; and then come writing and revision and preparation of copy. In describing the writing of one of his stories, Irvin Cobb shows that the first stage (the writer's background) played a larger part than it would in most factual articles, but he indicates several other steps of the process:

> It will not require many words for me to give you the genesis of my story: *The Belled Buzzard.*
>
> One morning I was returning in a motor-boat to my father-in-law's summer cottage on Tybee Island, Georgia, after a fishing trip to the mouth of the Savannah River. On a sand-pit a flock of buzzards fed on a dead shark. The sight of them, with their ungainly, flopping movements, their naked heads and their unwholesome contours, set me to thinking. My mind went back to the stories I had heard in a country newspaper-office in Kentucky of that hardy annual of rural correspondents, the belled buzzard. To myself I said that here a man might find material for a short story.
>
> That same day I got the notion for my beginning and picked on a name and a personality for my principal character. The following day, I think it was, my climax came to me, all in a flash.
>
> I was busied for the moment with other work but when I returned North, a fortnight later, and went up to the Adirondacks, I sat down and wrote the yarn in about four days of fairly steady grinding. The *Post* printed it and it became perhaps the best known of all my serious stories.—In T. H. UZZELL, *Narrative Technique*, p. 292

It is useful for an amateur writer to look at his writing habits, especially to find the stages that he does best and enjoys most, and to find the stages that give him difficulty. Realizing which these last are (and something of the feelings that accompany them) will show where to work for improvement. One student in a composition course diagnosed her case this way:

1. General interest in some subject.
2. Collecting and reading material or concentrated thinking—expansion.
3. Rest.
4. Deducing some idea.
5. Attacking it any way, some way—to get a start.
6. First draft. Bad, very bad. All sorts of irrelevant ideas crop up. No sense to anything. Despair absolute.
7. Dutifully hanging on to some thread.
8. A sudden inspiration. New viewpoint of the whole thing.
9. Shaping an outline.
10. With outline in mind and in *sight* beginning fresh copy.
11. Gradual and painful progress. Matter of discrimination. Pulling in all relevant material. Arranging material so that it will bear upon a POINT. Translating into language my deductions.
12. Finally an end.

Am in habit of thinking slow (perhaps chaotically)—writing slow—and usually get stuck at points #5 and #6—and very often cut the whole process off right there—result: all sorts of blasphemous statements.

Whatever your present writing habits, a more detailed discussion of the typical activity and of some common problems of each stage may help you prepare to attack your own writing tasks with confidence and a sensible program of work.

1. The writer's background

You don't start writing any paper from zero, and though your background may not be exactly a step in writing, it is so fundamental that it must be considered. Certainly your general attitudes and ways of thinking, as well as the words and habits of expression that you have accumulated, will be put to use in writing any given paper. Out of this background, of course, comes the entire material for a good many papers—accounts of earlier experiences in school, in sports, with books, with people, from travel, hobbies, jobs. From it ought also to come your point of view—the way you look at your subject—without which the paper is likely to be impersonal and dull. Finally, from this source should spring naturally some individual words and personal phrases, illuminating figures of speech and illustrations, incidents, information, bits of color and life that can contribute to the main subject in small but important ways. Your background contributes to every stage in writing a paper.

Your background is steadily growing and the value of new experiences and ideas can be increased if, combing your memory, you bring to light half-forgotten experiences and enthusiasms, consider past and present together, and bring your whole mind to bear on your writing. If you do this, your papers will sound as though they were written by a living person, not by an automaton, and they will, furthermore, sound as though they were written by you, not by anyone else.

2. Focusing on a subject

The first step in producing a particular piece of writing is to focus your attention upon some field of knowledge or experience, or upon some definite topic. This is done almost automatically when you decide to write a letter to someone—Mother, Father, Fred, or Janet. A great deal of the writing in the world is assigned or so closely controlled by circumstances that the writer has relatively little choice. In college some topics are assigned and must be made the best of, but usually you have a list from which to choose, or you are assigned a specified type of paper for which you can select the exact content. If you make yourself write on a distasteful subject, you have handicapped yourself at the start. So far as possible take subjects that you do or could or would like to *talk* about.

2a. Subjects from the writer's experience. Your experience, no matter how limited it may seem to you, will have some elements that are not common to everyone, and at any rate the parts that really interest you can be made interesting to others, in writing as in conversation. Your family, the people you have known either as individuals or as groups or types, your school experiences, your jobs, hobbies, sports, the places you have lived in or visited, your opinions and ideas, all offer material. It will be useful early in a composition course to think over your more interesting experiences and make notes of those that are promising for future use in papers.

Often in college your choice of subjects for writing should grow out of your desire to extend your experience, to know more than you do about something in history, literature, economics, biology, wherever your interest has been aroused. Except in course papers that call for routine summaries of material, choose a subject in which you will not be merely hashing over some stereotyped material or just rewriting something you have read. Take a subject to which you can make some contribution, no matter how small, in attitude or opinion, in illustration or application drawn from your experience.

2b. Subjects for investigation. A good many subjects, especially those dealing with jobs and various social situations, can be investigated by a little reporting—going somewhere to observe, talking with someone. When the paper is to be based on reading, you should choose a subject that you have some curiosity about, that you have some reason for wanting to know about, so that you will feel you are learning something worth your attention as well as preparing a paper. Everyone would like to know more about scores of subjects that come up in conversation (What is the SEC? a sharecropper? electronics? the most successful activity of the United Nations?) or that have been touched on briefly in a college course. There are the whole fields of history, of science, of literature, of social organization to choose from.

2c. Limiting a subject. Sometimes a writer chooses a subject that is too small for the length of paper he is attempting, so that he has to build it out by going into trivial detail or by touching on closely related matters. But ordinarily students choose subjects that are much too large. College papers are short; even one of 1000 words would fill only one newspaper column, or be a quarter as long as the typical

magazine article, or a little over two pages in this book. The purpose
of a paper is to enlighten a reader, to give him some special information or ideas, not just to remind him that the subject exists. Choose
a topic that can be handled adequately in the length expected. There is
not much point in writing 1000 words—or even 5000 words—on Benjamin Franklin, but something could be done in a short paper with
some phase of Franklin's career, his work as postmaster general, his
part in the founding of the University of Pennsylvania, his relations
with other statesmen, his life in Paris, or perhaps with an attempt to
sketch from his letters the great number of things he worked on in a
single year. Similarly "education" or "labor unions" or "Sinclair
Lewis" or "dress designing" are not subjects but fields, within which
a great many possible subjects lie.

Once your attention is fixed on a subject, the material already in
mind begins to gather and to help you foresee what other information
may be needed and where it may be found. For long papers a working bibliography of books and articles that may be of use is part of
this preliminary analysis. Sometimes the subject cannot be definitely
narrowed down until after some material has been gathered. Often
considering the needs or interests of your readers, whether they are the
members of your class or some other group, will suggest a portion of
a field that you can profitably treat. If you are not sure exactly what
the aim of the paper is, try to define it in a sentence or two, or in a
question that will be answered by the paper. This will give you
something to tie to in the later stages of work.

Considering the possible knowledge and interests of your readers
is especially necessary in treating well-known or commonplace subjects. It is not enough to take a general subject like "Learning to Drive
a Car." You have to consider "In these days when almost everyone
knows something about automobiles, what can I write that may possibly be of use or interest to some readers?" The result of such a
question would probably be a narrowed and more specific subject
based on some of the material, perhaps coming down to "Learning the
Traffic Regulations" or "Preparing for Winter Driving." Lack of
some such exact sense of the topic is the cause of many failures
in writing.

At the end of this stage you should know pretty definitely what
the paper is to be about and have some idea of how and where you
will get the material that is to go into it. Obviously the earlier you
decide these questions, the more time you will have for the later stages

of the paper. It is too late to decide what you will write about when you sit down to put words on paper, and waiting for a subject to come to you then wastes valuable time and is completely discouraging.

Focusing early on a subject that interests you and that you believe can interest your readers makes the later ·stages of the writing process easier and the final result worth while.

3. Gathering material

The material for letters and short papers on personal experiences seems to come spontaneously, but often even for this writing a little time given to jogging the memory may be well spent. By far the largest part of the time given to the composition of more elaborate papers will be spent in assembling material. Scientific and scholarly works may represent the accumulations of an author's lifetime. This stage is the most likely to be neglected by a writer in a hurry—and he may wonder why he has trouble in writing a paper when the simple reason is that he hasn't the material to put down.

Material comes from memory, from observation (reporting) and experiment, from interviews with people, from reading and study, from reasoning and speculating on what one has learned in all these ways, and from imagining scenes and actions, as for stories. It is hard to direct one's memory—though thinking about some past experience for a time, then later recalling it again, and so on at intervals, often brings back details that at first were forgotten. Similarly the bits of action for a story can be built up by thinking at frequent intervals of the imaginary people and actions, each time adding some details.

Sources of material outside the writer's mind can be more consciously worked, and skill in handling them can be cultivated. In particular a person's command of the direct sources of original material—observation, experiment, interviews—can be greatly improved by attention and by practice. A writer's chief distinction often comes from small bits of information which he has picked up from his own observation, and the interest and value of many papers rest on the amount of first hand detail they carry. The technique of research in laboratories and in documents and books has been developed by scientists and scholars, and one of the functions of higher education is to teach the methods of research. (See Chapter 13, The Reference Paper.)

Very little of importance can be written without some interpretation or opinion concerning the "facts" assembled, and for critical papers in any field these reflections become the central material. Opinions are by definition less certain than facts, but they can be well grounded in specific information. Common sense and practice in making interpretations and judgments, as well as training in logic and in the methods of various college courses, can improve the reliability of your evaluations and conclusions. At any rate, reasoning and speculation supply an important part of the material of writing.

For short papers on simple and familiar subjects, of course, the material is carried in the writer's head, though often scratch notations are a help—they keep items from slipping away. Voluminous and complex material needs a body of written notes.

4. Evaluating and selecting the material

Since the material when assembled is of varying reliability and of varying importance for the particular paper to be written, it should be gone over, sorted, and evaluated. This is a stage for questions. If your paper is based on personal experience, you may ask if the incidents selected are striking and meaningful. If your paper is based on reading or research, you will need to ask: Is this statement accurate? Is this book reliable—in its facts, in its reasoning? Have I enough material for the paper proposed? Have I tried all the best sources? Can I get more material by talking with someone? Have the important phases been covered? Which are the most important facts and conclusions for my paper? Which are of secondary importance? What is of most interest and possible importance for my readers?

It will help you in visualizing the paper as it will finally stand if you compose a definite statement—not a title, but a sentence—of the subject as you see it after the material has been gathered and thought about. Suppose you are a ham radio operator and are to "write about it." Several different papers could be written in this general field. You could describe various types of equipment; building your own equipment; the legal regulations and procedure of getting a license; C.W. vs. phone communication; the abbreviations and language of ham operators; transmitting as a hobby; its interest and occasional usefulness; and so on. There might be a temptation to say a little something about all of these and so run the risk of being so general that you would tell your readers nothing new: you shouldn't try to cover the field unless the paper is to be very long. A sentence statement would record your choice among the possibilities. It might be:

"Government regulation of amateur radio protects both the public and the ham operator." Such a statement, when considered along with your knowledge of the subject and of the interests of your readers, goes a long way toward helping you decide what material belongs in the paper.

In making this survey of your material, it is helpful to sort out *essential* points that must be included and *contributing* points that may be used or not, perhaps for illustration, depending on circumstances in the actual writing.

The result of this stage should be a sifted body of material with which you are thoroughly familiar, brought in line with the purpose of the paper, and selected after considering its accuracy and importance and interest for your purpose.

5. Planning the paper

While you are criticizing and selecting the material your paper is to present, you are thinking about the order in which the various points should probably stand. The plan—whether an idea in mind, some scratch notes, or a formally prepared outline—is a record of the order in which you expect the material will be arranged. Here you begin to face the reader directly, to consider his expectations, and to see how they can be met.

Primarily the plan grows out of the material you have to present. You get ideas for planning a paper as you gather material, and you probably make one or perhaps several tentative outlines while you are accumulating it, and certainly while you are selecting and evaluating it. These may show gaps in the material that you need to fill in. A narrative paper can be planned early, since all that is required is for you to visualize the climaxes or incidents that will divide it into stages. But drawing up the actual working outline of an expository paper, or revising a tentative outline to use as the working plan, is a relatively late stage in the writing process.

After you have reviewed and selected the material to be presented, the next step is to see the material in a series of blocks or stages. The real process of composing is gathering ideas together, grouping them so that a reader can follow easily. If it isn't easy to see what the main topics are, try listing the various small bits of material and putting the ones that have something in common side by side or in columns or on separate sheets of paper. Some people are helped by drawing squares on a sheet of paper and putting similar or related matters in the same square.

The labels over these squares or the main steps you have seen in the material are the main heads of a plan or outline. Typically a paper will have from three to five main stages or heads within the outline. A paper with only two is likely to break in the middle, unless it is very short. On the other hand, a fairly short paper with five or more heads probably would be overdivided. In a paper of 1500 words or so, five points would average only 300 words apiece—and 300 words does not say very much. Even magazine articles of 6000 words rarely have more than five or six main divisions. Any outline of more than five main heads should be examined carefully to see if the material has really been put together or if perhaps too much isn't being attempted for a short space.

The small special points of the material can next be arranged under the main heads to which they belong. Sometimes these points will in turn form several natural groups, which will stand under subheads in the outline.

After the main blocks are determined, their order can be decided on. There are two principal general plans for expository papers. One, which may be called the *order of support*, begins with a general statement of the subject or idea, which is then developed in a series of specific supporting blocks. The other, the *order of climax*, begins with a specific fact or situation and then goes on unfolding the subject until at the end it stands complete. The first is more com-

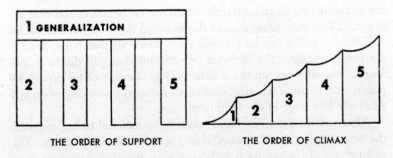

THE ORDER OF SUPPORT   THE ORDER OF CLIMAX

mon in developing scientific and technical subjects and opinions that are methodically substantiated; the second is more common in popular and informal papers. Whichever plan you follow, the last part of the paper should be more important, meaningful, intense, or interesting than the preceding—it should make the point you want the reader to get as the most emphatic. Since most of your papers will be informal, try to see each as a series of waves of increasing height, that is, of increasing value, not necessarily of increasing length. The beginning has the double duty of attracting the reader's interest and getting him really into the subject. The last point is the one he is to carry with him. (See Chapter 7, § 5, "Beginning paragraphs," and § 6, "Concluding paragraphs.") In between, the topics can be arranged according to any reasonable plan that will advance the subject.

The plan that this examination of your material gives can then be compared with your notion of the perfect paper on the subject or with somebody else's idea of how the paper should go—just as a check on the judgment you have shown.

Some written notes, though they do not have to be a formally numbered outline, will be a great help in the actual writing. In fact a good working plan will remove most of your worst worries, for there is nothing more discouraging than to have to pause in the middle of rapid writing to wonder if a certain point really goes there. But it is necessary to remember that a paper cannot always be completely visualized ahead of writing, that any preliminary outline is a working plan—the best way you can see to lay out the material before you begin to write. Even the most perfectly numbered outline should be changed in the process of writing if there is good reason to change it.

After the paper is written, the outline should be adjusted to the actual development of the paper if it is to be made a part of the submitted manuscript, and it should be cast in one of the standard forms described in the *Index* article *Outline form.

6. Writing the first draft

Of course some writing has been going on in the last three steps, but actual consecutive writing ordinarily takes place as the sixth step in developing a paper. If the preliminary stages (whether they took only a few minutes of concentrated thinking or weeks of reading and study) have been well done, the writing should be free from worry, perhaps even a pleasure.

Most papers that a person is taking seriously need to be written out in a first draft and then revised and written over. After the material has been gathered and a plan made, either in rough notes or in an outline, you can concentrate all your energies on expression. A long paper can be broken up into stages and each stage concentrated on and written more or less by itself. This removes the strain of trying to keep a great deal of material in mind at once. If the writing is done at various times you should read over what you have previously written before continuing.

You shouldn't wait too long to get an ideal opening—this is really a sort of procrastination. The paper must be started some way if it is to be written, so that it is better to make a tentative start, the best that suggests itself at the moment, and change it later if necessary. After a few pages you will find that you are writing better, and many times a good opening will be found by simply crossing out the first paragraph or two.

For most people the first draft should be a rather rapid writing down of the material of a paper. The paper will have more life and will represent your sense of your material more closely if you write it rapidly than if you pause to perfect each sentence before going on to the next. Don't stop to look up spelling or to check mechanics as you write the first draft, but save a little time for revising so that you can tend to such small matters in one operation after you have written the paper. Leave plenty of space in a first draft between lines and paragraphs and in margins to allow for this working over.

It is probably best to make the first draft a full telling of your material, since it is always easier to take out unwanted matter than to fill in topics that have been done too sketchily.

Besides a good stock of material, the feeling of *being ready to write* is the best guarantee of a good paper. This is the prime result of careful work in the early steps.

7. Revising

Few people work so precisely that their first draft will represent the best they are capable of. Freed from the problems of actual composition, you can go over your work and bring it up to a desired standard. This criticism and reworking should bring the paper to an accurate expression of your view of the subject and prepare it for a reader.

In revising, the writer takes the point of view of a reader or critic as far as he can and looks at his work to see how it will read or, if it is a speech, how it will sound. This means testing for material, for plan, and for style and the mechanics of writing.

7a. Material. A check for material is necessary to make sure that enough has been put in the paper to gain its intended purpose. Occasionally there will be too much included, but not often. Usually the writer is so familiar with the topic that he forgets to put in enough details to inform or interest the readers. The first questions then are, Is the material complete enough for my purpose? Does it need more examples, details? Do the facts given need more interpretation? The accuracy of the statements should be checked; if the writer is uncertain about anything, the uncertainty should be acknowledged by words like *perhaps, probably, I think.* The interpretations and opinions should be examined once more for their reasonableness and convincingness.

Trying to take the reader's point of view will result in sounder and more illuminating papers. A writer should always think, Would I like to read this paper? Could I profit from reading it?

7b. Plan. Reading the almost completed paper will test its plan. Is space wasted at the beginning? Will the first few sentences appeal to a reader and make him want to continue? Is it clear what the subject is from the beginning (or near the beginning)? Is the subject advanced by clear-cut stages, and is the relation between one stage and the next clear? That is, can a reader pass from one paragraph or group of paragraphs to the next without losing the thread? A paragraph which sounds like a new start, sounds as though nothing has been said already, obviously needs attention. Does the conclusion leave the reader with the point the writer wants him to carry away? Is it distinctively written? Many times irrelevant matters are brought in at the last, or the writing goes flabby or shows signs of haste. The beginning and ending of any paper need special attention in revision.

7c. Mechanics and style. Finally the paper should be examined for the small matters that can so easily mar what is fundamentally a good job. Are the sentences direct and effective? Is the style fairly consistent, that is, either dominantly formal or informal, the colloquialisms (if there are any) appropriate? Is there any deadwood to be removed? Are the words as exact and meaningful as possible? Finally, the accuracy of spelling, punctuation, and other mechanical matters should be checked.

Reading a paper aloud is a particularly good investment of time. In reading aloud the writer must read more slowly than in silent reading and not only will catch unhappy phrases and sentences but also will see more of the details, especially of punctuation and spelling. A person who makes a good many mistakes will sometimes find them more surely if he reads with a pencil point running just below the line of writing to help keep his eyes focused. It is a good idea for a writer to give a paper a special reading, looking just for his known weaknesses—the joints between paragraphs, or spelling, or meaning of words, or whatever he has been criticized for. Such concentration in revision will go a long way toward clearing up special difficulties.

A good dictionary and the *Index* part of this book should be especially useful in revision, since they will help answer many particular questions.

On page 19 is the beginning of the first draft of the radio speech given by Franklin D. Roosevelt on the evening of April 14, 1938.[1] It shows the care with which a writer revises his copy and how a speech or an article may grow in revision. Some of Mr. Roosevelt's changes are stylistic, as when he changed the formal and distant "to add certain observations by way of simplification and clarification" to "to talk with you about them," or when he changed the abrupt "has received a setback" to "has received a visible setback."

Others are elaboration of points. Between the original first and second sentences he made an addition (indicated by *A1*) of two brief paragraphs on the appropriateness of his theme to Holy Week, ending ". . . and that it is not inappropriate to encourage peace when so many of us are thinking of the Prince of Peace." This adds a note of feeling and leads indirectly to the main topic. Other changes are in the direction of accuracy, as the "six" to "seven," and others are defensive, as changing "Spring of 1933" (when he was President) to "beginning of 1933" (when Herbert Hoover was still in office). Insert B, about 200 words, elaborates and makes more personal the reasons for the government's delay in undertaking relief measures, and includes the material crossed out at the bottom of the page:

> But I know that many of you have lost your jobs or have seen your friends or members of your families lose their jobs, and I do not propose that the government shall pretend not to see these things.
> I know that the effect of our present difficulties has been uneven; that they have affected some groups and some localities seriously, but that they

[1] This speech will be found in newspapers of April 15, 1938. There is a discussion of the style of this and others of Roosevelt's speeches by S. T. Williamson in *The New York Times Magazine* of May 1, 1938. Elmer Adler, *Breaking into Print* (New York, 1937), reproduces a number of manuscript pages by well-known writers, showing their revisions.

DRAFT #1

RADIO SPEECH

Five months have gone by since I last spoke to the people of the Nation about the state of the Nation. *Hait* Five years ago we faced a very serious problem of economic and social recovery. For four and a half years that recovery proceeded apace. It is only in the past *seven* ~~six~~ months that it has received a *visible* setback. *HA2.*

This recession has not returned us to the disasters and suffering of the ~~Spring~~ *beginning* of 1933, *B* ~~but it is serious enough for me to talk with you about it tonight in the same spirit and with the same purpose which I employed in talks from the White House in the earlier years.~~

Therefore Today *I have* *shown* sent a Message of far-reaching importance to the Congress. I want to read to you tonight certain passages from that Message, and to ~~add certain observations~~ *talk with you about them* by way of simplification ~~and clarification.~~

~~Each of you is conscious of some aspect of the present recession; it has affected some groups and some localities seriously; it has been scarcely felt in others. And let us agree at the outset that this recession is not to be compared in fundamental seriousness with the great depression of 1929 to 1933.~~

The beginning of the first draft of the radio speech given by Franklin D. Roosevelt. April 14, 1938.

have been scarcely felt in others. But I conceive the first duty of government is to protect the economic welfare of all the people in all sections and in all groups. . . .

The page offers an excellent example of revision that improves style, adapts the material and the presentation more definitely to the audience, and carries out the writer's purpose more accurately.

8. Preparing the manuscript

The final step in writing a paper is preparing the manuscript for another person to read. This may be simply making a fair copy of a first draft, or, as in research papers, it may involve footnotes and a bibliography. Whether it is a letter, a class paper, or an article or book for publication, the aim is the same, to make a manuscript that reads easily and represents the writer's decent pride in his work.

8a. Materials. The materials for copy have now been pretty well standardized. Paper 8½ by 11 inches is almost universally used, except in legal documents. For longhand copy the conventional "theme paper" having lines about half an inch apart is best. Odd sizes do not handle or file well, and narrow-lined notebook paper makes hard reading. For typewritten copy use a fair grade of bond paper. Certainly using paper that allows the writing to show through is discourteous to readers. Handwritten manuscripts should be in ink. Pale ink is often illegible, and colored inks are regarded by many as in bad taste; black or blue black is the best. A good black typewriter ribbon and clean type make a readable typed page.

8b. The page. (1) Leave comfortable margins on all pages. A good right margin not only will improve the looks of a page but will reduce the number of words that have to be divided at the end of lines. An inch and a half at the left, an inch at the right, an inch and a half at the top, and an inch at the bottom are typical margins. Very short papers should be centered on the page.

2) Typewritten copy should be double spaced. An extra space can be left between paragraphs but is not necessary. More useful is an extra line left between the main stages of a paper.

3) In longhand copy the ascenders and descenders of letters like *b, l, f, g* should not be allowed to cut across letters on the line above or below, and letters easily confused (*a-o, n-u*) should be made clearly. The letters of a word should be held together so that the reader's eye can grasp the word at a glance.

4) Paragraphs are indented about an inch in longhand and from five to eight spaces in typescript.

5) Only one side of the sheet should be used.

6) Pages should be arranged in their proper order (it is surprising how many times they are not in order), and pages after the first should be numbered, preferably in the upper right hand corner and in Arabic numerals (2, 3, 4).

7) The title should be centered on the top line in longhand manuscript and about two inches from the top in unlined paper and the text should begin about an inch below. On lined paper leave the line below the title blank. A title should not be underlined or set in quotation marks unless it is an actual quotation. No end punctuation is necessary unless the title is a question or exclamation. Since the title is not a part of the body of the paper but is rather a label put upon it, the first sentence of the text should usually be complete in itself and not refer back to the title by a pronoun. (See *Titles of themes.[1])

8) Common practices that should be avoided are: (a) Indenting the first line on a page when it is not the beginning of a paragraph; (b) Leaving blank part of the last line on a page when the paragraph is continued on the following page; (c) Putting punctuation marks, other than quotation marks, at the beginning of a line. A mark belongs with the word that it follows, not at the beginning of the next construction.

8c. Endorsing manuscript. Manuscript to be submitted for publication carries the writer's name and complete address in the upper left hand corner of the first page.

Most course papers in college are folded vertically and endorsed near the top of the outside front fold, as the instructor may direct. Most teachers want to have available:

> Student's name
> Topic, title, or assignment of paper
> Date submitted

Other facts, such as the number of the paper, the name and section of the course, or the instructor's name, may be put below these three lines. Clear and uniform endorsement is a real convenience to the teacher who must handle the papers.

If the papers are to be handed in flat, this endorsement should be on the back of the last sheet or on a special title page as the teacher

---

[1] Starred items are discussed in the *Index* part of this book.

directs. Sheets should be held together by paper clips that can be slipped off, not by fasteners that pierce the paper or by pins, hairpins, or string.

8d. Corrections in copy. The final copy should be made as accurate as possible, but later corrections are sometimes necessary. If there are many or if they are complicated, the page should be done over. If they are relatively small, involving only inserting a letter or a word, or substituting a single word, they can usually be done neatly without damaging the page.

Words that are to be struck out should have a line drawn through them. (Parentheses have other uses.) Words to be added can be written in the margin or between the lines, and a caret ($\wedge$) inserted at the place where they belong.

The goal is a clean, legible copy that can be read by another. Reading this final copy aloud rather slowly will be a good last check to make sure that mistakes have not slipped in in the copying.

9. From manuscript into print

The manuscript form is the final state of most college writing, but some of the papers in composition courses find their way into campus periodicals. Anyway, since the goal of much writing is publication and since a college graduate is almost certain to write something that will see publication of some sort, he should know something of this last stage. It may be merely a final check preparatory to mimeographing or some other informal sort of publication. Or it may be an elaborate process of editing, revision at the suggestion of an editor, and proofreading, before the words are finally published. (See *Proofreading, *Submitting manuscripts, *Type.)

10. Craftsmanship in writing

Perhaps our sketch of the writing process doesn't seem to pay much attention to the gliding of the pencil on paper or the click of typewriter keys. The actual work of putting words on paper is a result of other effort and its success depends completely on the earlier steps. The ideal of a writer at each step and in the activity as a whole can best be put in terms of the craftsman's ideal, of handling tools and materials well. The *materials* in writing are the facts, opinions, ideas, imaginings, and feelings that you want to put in readable shape for others. The *tools* are the words and constructions of the English language. The materials for the most part lie outside the scope of this book, which presents a description of the tools and some suggestions for their handling.

In handling these tools we can't do better than stress the craftsman's ideal of good materials worked upon honestly with the right tools. Sherwood Anderson presents this ideal as it applies especially to writers of fiction but in a way that can be extended to all writers:

> Consider for a moment the materials of the prose writer, the teller of tales. His materials are human lives. To him these figures of his fancy, these people who live in his fancy should be as real as living people. He should be no more ready to sell them out than he would sell out his men friends or the woman he loves. To take the lives of these people and bend or twist them to suit the needs of some cleverly thought out plot to give your readers a false emotion is as mean and ignoble as to sell out living men or women. For the writer there is no escape, as there is no real escape for any craftsman. If you handle your materials in a cheap way you become cheap. The need of making a living may serve as an excuse but it will not save you as a craftsman. Nothing will save you if you go cheap with tools and materials. Do cheap work and you are yourself cheap. That is the truth.—SHERWOOD ANDERSON, *The Modern Writer*, p. 39

This applies equally to writers who may be simply reporting what they have seen or sketching their ideas or giving their opinions.

In many of the pages that follow we may seem to be rather far from ideals. But in discussing the meaning of words, the patterns of English phrases, even relatively mechanical matters like punctuation and spelling, our motive is to help you present your materials more effectively, to help you in your work as a craftsman in writing to satisfy the craftsman's ideal of a good job well done.

Suggested study and writing

These exercises are to acquaint you with successful and unsuccessful features of student writing; to give you opportunity to analyze your own writing habits and needs; and to help you select topics and gather material for writing papers. The first three exercises may be used for classroom discussion; exercise 4 for preparation and discussion in individual conferences; exercises 5, 6, 7, 8, 9, and 10 as the basis for writing assignments.

1. The following student themes are explanations of activities about which the writers had special, first hand knowledge. Read each paper through once to get a general impression of its material and arrangement. Then using the correction symbols in the *Index* of this book, make a list of all the ineffectual passages or errors that you find—spelling, punctuation, diction, repetition, sentence structure, paragraphing, or anything else that you think might be improved. Identify the passages by the line numbers, as in the first paper:

Line 5   succesful Sp   Correct: successful

When you have finished your lists, write a statement commenting on the successful as well as the unsuccessful qualities of each paper. Which papers do you think are too long, too short, or perhaps too technical for a general classroom audience? Is the writer's background in each instance adequate for the activity he is explaining? Is his paper well organized, or does it bear signs of hasty revision? Assign grades to the papers to show your opinion of their relative merit.

1. *Break Your Own Horse*

1   There was a day when horse-breaking was a simple, everyday affair. All
2 you needed was a horse, saddle, halter and buckrein, or hackamore, and
3 enough courage to climb on. However, times have changed, the methods
4 of horsebreaking have changed with them. There are several methods now
5 in use, but this is the one I have found to be most succesful.
6   The best time to start breaking a horse is while he is still a colt, not over
7 three or four years old, although a horse older than this may be broken,
8 but it is much more difficult. If the horse has been raised in a barn this
9 first step has probably been completed, but if it is a range pony the first step
10 in his training is breaking him to lead and gaining his confidence. Never
11 yell or make any quick movements around a green horse for it is all new
12 to him and he'll scare easily. Talk to him in a low gentle voice and pet
13 him around his neck and shoulders. To break him to lead, take an extra
14 piece of rope and run it around his rump or around a fore-foot and pull on
15 this rope and the halter rope at the same time. If you run the rope around
16 his rump don't pull too hard or he may be on top of you before you know
17 whats happening. Never use a halter rope alone when your first breaking
18 a horse to lead because he'll just pull against you, and you'll have a hard
19 time breaking him of this habit.
20   After the horse leads well, the next step is breaking him to the bit. The
21 best type of bit to use for this bitting up is a broken snaffle or a straight
22 buggy or work bit. This part of the training aquaints the horse with the
23 feel of the bit in his mouth, and the horse will hold his head up where it
24 belongs when you start to ride him. To bit him up tie the reins to the
25 saddle, or driving harness is used, and apply a small amount of pressure
26 against the bit. Leave this on for about fifteen minutes the first day, half
27 an hour the second day, and so on until it can be left on for about two
28 hours a day.
29   After the horse has been bitted-up for about a week it is time to start
30 ground driving him. This is to train the horse to stop and turn in each
31 direction. A driving harness may be used for this but I prefer a saddle, be-
32 cause the horse gets use to the saddle and the flapping of the stirrups, and
33 it makes things easier when the time comes to ride him. If the saddle is

34 used it is wise to attach a ring, at least one inch in diameter, too the dee
35 ring on each side of the saddle, and run your reins through these. They will
36 keep the reins free from the saddle, and pressure will be applied from the
37 proper direction. You should also have a pair of reins about thirty feet long,
38 a buggy whip, and a circular corral about fifty feet in diameter.
39 If you don't have leather reins a length of clothesline will do, and if a
40 circular corral is unavailable a square one will serve you just as well. Drive
41 the horse in a walk, trot, and lope, stopping him now and then to reverse
42 his direction.
43 After the horse has been ground driven for a week it is time to mount
44 and ride him. I prefer to ride a green horse snubbed the first two or three
45 times, for, although he should be used to a saddle by now, the extra weight
46 of the rider and having a man on his back may cause him to buck, and I
47 believe a horse is better if he doesn't know what a buck is. Also, you should
48 mount and dismount several times at the beginning and end of each ride to
49 get him use to it.
50 After the third day it is safe to ride him unsnubbed, and it is time to
51 concentrate on his reining again. The ground driving was the ground work
52 for this part of the training. When the horse becomes so bridle-wise that he
53 responds to a gentle pull on the reins it is time to break him to neck-rein.
54 The easiest way to do this is to cross the reins under his neck. This will
55 cause pressure on the bit as well as his neck at the same time, and he will
56 soon associate the two and the reins may be uncrossed.
57 If a person has a slight knowledge of horsmanship, and a great deal of
58 patience, and follows these directions it is not at all difficult to break a horse
59 to ride, and the personal satisfaction of riding a horse you have broken
60 yourself is well worth the time and effort used in the process.

2. Whaling Processes

1 Most people do not know anything about whales and the whale industry,
2 but as the whale oil is rather important in the chemical industry, I would
3 like to introduce the whaling processes very briefly to you as it is now in
4 Iceland.
5 For capturing whales we use steam boats, 150 to 200 tons in weight. They
6 are provided with a harpoon gun in the bow. The gun looks similar to the
7 big machine guns which, in the last war, were used on corvettes and
8 small armed ships. The harpoon is put into the barrel, and to it is tied a
9 500 fathom rope, 2 inches in diameter. The ship goes to the ground on
10 which the whales are expected to be, and there the crew searchs for a
11 whale. Usually the whales are under sea level for 15-20 minnits. Then
12 they come up to breath. This they do two or three times with a short inter-
13 val, but then they go down again. When the crew hears the first exhale,
14 they try to see the whale and in what derection it is going. Then they turn
15 the boat into that derection; and when the whale exhales the next time,
16 the gunman tries to harpoon it. If the harpoon hits, the whale usually takes
17 the boat for a wild ride, unless the backbone is broken. It can take up to
18 8 hours to exhaust a whale, but sometimes they are killed instantly. When
19 the whale is dead, it is taken alongside the boat and towed in to the factory.
20 The factory, usually, is a low house with a flat roof, 100 feet long and 60
21 to 70 feet wide. On each side of the roof there are openings to the boilers
22 which are underneath. Each boiler takes up to 25 tons of meat and bones.
23 Near the openings to the boilers are winches that are used to help in cut-
24 ting the whales and also to drag the meat and bones into the boilers.

²⁵ When the whale has been towed up to the roof, the land crew begins
²⁶ cutting it into pieces small enough to be handled easely. First they skin
²⁷ the whale. They begin on the head where they hook in a wire and then
²⁸ tear the hide off with a winch. Usually the hide is taken off in four long
²⁹ pieces. Then the head is cut off. For that purpose a powerful winch is used,
³⁰ for the tendons that lead to the head are very strong, and it is difficult to
³¹ cut them. Next the back muscles are cut off. They are the only muscles
³² that are eaten. From a medium sized whale, 70 to 80 feet long, the meat
³³ of the back muscles weights 12 to 15 tons. When this has been finished,
³⁴ the thorax and the abdomen are opened and the organs in there are taken
³⁵ out. Now the most difficult job is left e.g. to disjoint the backbone and the
³⁶ ribs. As the bones are very large, winches have to be used to make it pos-
³⁷ sible to disjoint them. In some cases it is possible to use a large steam saw
³⁸ to saw the bones, but, for the most part, the steam saw is used to saw bones
³⁹ that are too big to go down into the boilers.
⁴⁰ Now the whale has been cut, and down in the factory the boilers are cook-
⁴¹ ing the meat and the bones. As they cook they rotate and grind the bones into
⁴² small pieces. From the boiler the products goes into a press that presses
⁴³ out most of the moisture. The fat is separated from the moisture by cen-
⁴⁴ trifuges, but the pressed product is dried and ground into meal, which is
⁴⁵ used for cattle fodder and also for fertilizer.

3. *It's Not as Bad as You Might Think*

¹ Most people have seen an auto-trailer, but because the majority have never
² lived in one or have never even had a good look at the inside of one, the
³ feeling is that they contain only a few things, and that only those who have
⁴ little money ever travel in them. In attempting to clear up or correct this
⁵ erroneous thinking, I will try to paint a picture of the inside of one of these
⁶ streamline covered wagons, and then give some of the benefits derived
⁷ from owning one.
⁸ Using as an example a trailer that sells for about three thousand dollars,
⁹ we'll see what they jam into this small space. In the rear, immediately after
¹⁰ coming through the backdoor, we would find the kitchen, a unique arrange-

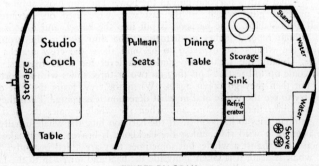

TRAILER DIAGRAM

¹¹ ment in that everything is in an arm's reach. There is no walking from one
¹² cupboard to another or back and forth from the sink to the stove, as is
¹³ necessary in most houses. In a trailer everything is compact, and yet all the

14 kitchen necessities are there. We find a table-high combination cooking and
15 heating stove across from the porcelain sink. On the walls are cup-boards,
16 and two twenty-gallon steel water tanks are stored away in the rear wall. To
17 the right of the backdoor, small I will admit, is a toilet, but although there is
18 a mirror and a shelf in the room also, there is no wash basin, for the sink in
19 the kitchen is used for bodies and dishes alike. The modern trailers will
20 have a small electric refrigerator, however you'll still find many that have
21 only a box-like affair that uses ice.
22 Coming forward a little we will find a compartment, comprised of closets
23 and pullman seats, that is used as a sitting-room in the daytime. This same
24 room, during meals, can be converted into a dining-room by moving the
25 seats forward and by pulling down a table which lies flat against the wall
26 that separates this room and the kitchen. These seats make up into a six foot
27 double-bed, as does the studio couch that is in the next compartment. Both
28 of these couch-bed affairs run crosswise and just fit into the space allotted to
29 them. Also in this third compartment, to the side, is a small table and a
30 straight chair for writing.
31 The trailer is equipped with electric lamps and wall connections, a radio,
32 from six to eleven safety-glass windows, and two roof ventilators. In every
33 available space there are closets or small shelves, the latter being connected
34 to the walls in such a way that they can fold back and lay flat—as does the
35 table in the middle compartment, out of the way—when they are not in use.
36 The majority of trailers, by the way, are now constructed of steel, with about
37 an inch and three-quarters of dead-air space in the walls for insulation. Also
38 I should mention that a trailer in the price-field that I have been speaking
39 of, is about twenty feet long, a little over six feet wide, and a good six
40 feet high.
41 Of course this description has been of the enumerating type, but what
42 I'm trying to stress to the reader is that a great deal is contained in this little
43 space, in this house-on-wheels. In fact, almost everything that is needed for
44 a couple of weeks vacation is included in some nook or corner.

4. Used Car Lot

1 A long white arbor covered with a gaudy yellow-and-black awning; a
2 little shanty off to the side, with a mammoth sign overhanging its provincial
3 whiteness— Smoky traffic roars by, leaving trailing wisps of stinking smoke.
4 Dribbles of pedestrians slowly stroll along and idly gape at the shining stock
5 on hand of Bradley's Used Cars.
6 Beneath the protecting canvas, the front line or "show cars" waited for
7 prospective customers. Late Cadillacs, sporty Fords, Buicks and other popular
8 makes showed off their merits here. Back of these stood late model cars,
9 not as expensive as their brothers in front. The rear line had the "bargains,"
10 cars that any salesman would be glad to get rid of for fifty or a hundred
11 dollars.
12 George, a conservative, well-dressed college man, disposed of the first line
13 stock for prices ranging from $500 to $1000 or more. Fisher's stand was the
14 middle line. Hard-bitten and a good business man, he could handle the
15 toughest prospects easily. Hagar, a flashy, loud, fellow took care of the last
16 line, commonly called "jalopy row."
17 The cars of the first two lines received 15 or 20 repair operations. Motor
18 work, fender straightening and touch-up jobs were necessary on all. New
19 tires were never put on. Instead, the originals were retreaded by a vulcaniz-

20 ing process which cost about $6 and lasted for 10,000 miles. Tires not badly
21 worn had their treads regrooved by a red-hot cutting tool. Retreads looked
22 like new tires and regrooves seemed slightly worn to the suckers. To com-
23 pensate for the seeming paradox of a 15,000 mile car riding on excellent
24 tires, the mileage would be cut down to six or seven thousand. Every car
25 in the lot had its mileage turned down at least 1/3 of its original distance.
26 Sharp-eyed mechanics always made mileage and tire conditions agree. Turn-
27 ing mileage down is a common practice in businesses of this sort, despite
28 stringent laws to the contrary. It was a "well-if-he-does-it-I-can-do-it" situa-
29 tion. Other operations were merely check-ups. Wheel alignment, windshield
30 wipers, upholstery and pedal pads came under this heading. At an expense
31 of 15 cents, new pedal pads could be put on, checking any possibility of
32 the prospect's guessing how far or how hard the car really was driven.
33 Inexpensive checking of small points paid profits in the end. The last line
34 of cars received only a motor tuning and a polish, but surprizing enough,
35 were a lucrative investment. The company's price policy answers this pos-
36 sible inconsistency.

37 Salesmen were paid $25 straight salary plus a 2% commission on sales.
38 On the front of every car was a cardboard tag supposedly bearing the car's
39 record number for the company's books. It was, however, a code by which
40 the salesmen could determine the price they should get and the price they
41 could take for that particular car. A number such as 665705 meant: get
42 $675 but take $650, the second, fourth and sixth numbers being the "get"
43 price; the first, third and fifth, the "take" figure. If a salesman sold over the
44 top asked figure, the difference was split between him and the company.
45 Therefore, on the third line of cars, where running condition instead of age
46 was a prime necessity, prices wholly out of line from the true value were
47 received. Because of a great turn-over of third line cars, the company real-
48 ized a larger percentage of profit on the "jallopies" than on the first line
49 automobiles.

50 This used-car lot was sponsored by an organization which sells over a
51 million cars a year, so it was by no means a fly by night affair. Although
52 no sloppy repairs were done, and no highly crooked deals were tolerated,
53 there was just a slight suspicion that the company was getting the best of
54 the customer on every deal. This company, however good or bad, is repre-
55 sentative of many similar organizations in the United States.

5. Electrolysis in Cosmetology

1 In studying the structure of hair we find that it grows thru the skin in a
2 tube like pore, technically known as the follicle. At the bottom of the follicle
3 are the hair papilli cells, and it is from the papilli that the hair gets the
4 nourishment that causes it to grow. Since the papilli is the only source of
5 nourishment it is logical that only by completely destroying it that the growth
6 of the hair can be stopped permanently.

7 For this purpose in a beauty shop, a multiple electrolsis machine, that is
8 many needles, usually twelve, is used. The needle is made of platinum
9 about three-quarters of an inch long and a slightly bit thicker than a hair.
10 The source of electrical current is a dry cell battery and the wiring is such
11 that the needles carry a negative charge, which as we know will disintegrate
12 body tissue. A single red wire carries a positive charge and is used to com-
13 plete the circuit.

14 The first step in use of this machine is sterilization not only of the needles
15 but of all objects that come in contact with the patient. A sterilizing lotion

16 other than alcohol is used for this purpose. Alcohol will retard the chemical
17 decomposition and also causes the pores to contract making it difficult to
18 insert the needles.
19   It is essential that the patient is in a comfortable position so that the
20 muscles and nerves are relaxed. Taunt muscles make insertion of the needles
21 difficult and it is impossible to work on a patient under nerveous strain. The
22 operator, too, must be in a comfortable position as standing and bending soon
23 becomes very tiresome.
24   Placing the needle into the follicle is not a difficult task as one uses a
25 derma-lense and gives consideration to the natural growth of a hair. Hair
26 follicles naturally grow at a slant of twenty-five to forty degrees. The needle
27 is inserted in a straight line along the angle of growth. Pressure is not used
28 at anytime to force the needle as such action will cause the needle to pierce
29 the follicle, enter the skin tissues, cause pain, and miss the papilla. The needle
30 will slide easily into the follicle, so that when placed at the wrong angle it
31 will pierce the skin warning the operator of incorrect insertion. There will
32 always be a slight resistance when the needle reaches the papilla thereby
33 signifying to the operator that the proper designation has been reached. After
34 the first needle has been placed the second is then inserted, not to close to
35 the first as this would centralize the disintegration and cause a slight pain.
36 As other needles are inserted the current is stepped up.
37   When the last needle is inserted the first hair treated is usually ready to
38 be removed. Never allow a needle to be inserted over two or three minutes.
39 The hair is lifted out with a tweezer and if the disintegration is complete
40 the hair will come out freely. If there is any resistance it is a sign that the
41 follicle has not been completely destroyed and the needle should be rein-
42 serted to continue the action.
43   After removing a needle a substance will come to the surface, this is the
44 decomposed cells, it should be removed immediately as it will become hard
45 upon reaching the air and form a scab called an *escher*. Formation of eschers
46 will prolong healing and if picked off by the patient will most likely leave
47 a scar. The liquid will also be on the needle and should also be wiped off
48 immediately or it will crystalize and make reinsertion impossible. This
49 liquid trapped under the skin will be carried off through the body's waste
50 system.
51   After the treatment hot towels should be applied in order to open the
52 pores allowing most of the liquid to escape thru the skin and to stimulate
53 circulation and in that way carry off the trapped waste. Cold towels should
54 follow the hot ones to insure a cleansing and rapid closing of the pores so
55 that eschers cannot form. An astringent lotion should be applied after the
56 cold towels to complete the action.

6. Logging

1   There is a great deal which must be done before actual logging operations
2 can commence. Roads must be built, a landing cleared, and a spar pole
3 constructed. Logging is often done in swampy places, and building roads
4 strong enough to support a heavy truck with a load of logs can constitute
5 quite a problem. These roads are laid to the center of the area to be logged,
6 and there the landing is prepared. The landing is a cleared area large enough
7 for a truck and cat to manuever and must also have a space for the log pile.
8 The spar tree is constructed in the middle of the landing. This is the center
9 of all operations. The logs are pulled to this tree and then loaded on to
10 trucks to be sent out. It consists of a tree which has been topped and limbed

11 and has four guy lines rigged out from the top to give extra support. By
12 means of a cable through a pulley at the top of this tree the logs are lifted
13 onto the trucks.

14   The job of falling the trees has changed a great deal in the past ten years.
15 It used to be a job requiring an axe, bucking saw and a great deal of hard
16 work. The axe is still used for making the under cut and limbing the tree,
17 but the bucking saw has been replaced by the modern power saw. This
18 speeds up the fallers part of the operation, and it also eliminates a lot of
19 the work. Fallers are now usually special crews hired solely for the purpose
20 of falling the allotted number of trees. When this is done their job with the
21 organization is finished.

22   Getting the logs from the woods to the spar tree requires a lot of coopera-
23 tion between the cat driver and the choker. The cat driver, first of all,
24 manuevers as close as possible to the downed trees. The choker then drags
25 the main line, which is on a drum at the rear of the cat, to the logs.
26 He connects this line to the chokes which he has previously secured to the
27 ends of the logs. The cat driver then snakes them out. If the downed trees
28 are behind standing trees or stumps, it is sometimes necessary to change the
29 position of the chokes a number of times. It takes much experience to be a
30 good choker.

31   Loading the logs onto trucks is the most dangerous of the jobs connected
32 with logging. One end of the hoisting cable is divided into two sections.
33 These sections are each about twenty feet long and have a hook at the end.
34 They are held at the end of the log. When the cable is raised they tend to
35 bury themselves in the wood. These hooks sometimes break and the loose
36 end of the cable acts like a giant scythe as it whips through the air. It
37 could easily cut a person in half. When the log is raised into the air, the
38 truck backs in under it, and it is then lowered onto the trailer. When
39 the trailer is completely loaded, the load is secured and then taken to the
40 mill pond or to the log dump.

41   These are the main divisions in a logging operation. To have an efficient
42 organization, and to obtain the greatest amount of safety, each division must
43 work in close cooperation with the rest.

2. For each of the following subjects formulate one or more topics which could be treated adequately in themes of approximately 600 words. "Clothing" for example might suggest "Planning a College Wardrobe for $150," or "Why Men Won't Wear Hats."

Books	Movies
Clothing	Music
Comics	A Profession
Dormitories	Sports
Honor Systems	Student Government

3. Which of the following topics do you believe would be appropriate for 750-word themes? How would you limit those topics that seem too broad as they stand?

Classical Music	A Solution for Campus Parking Problems
My Home Town	Scientific Progress in the Twentieth Century
Socialism	Hitchhiking from Chicago to New York

Experiences of a Baby Sitter   Propaganda in World War II
Divorce in the United States   How a Drive-in Theater Operates

4. Answer these questions concerning your writing experiences:

a) About how much writing have you done both in school and outside? What writing assignments have been most difficult for you? What kind of writing have you most enjoyed doing?

b) What type of subject matter do you prefer to write about? Personal experiences (My Trip Through the Grand Canyon, Learning to Ski)? Topics of current interest (What Is Wrong with Radio Commercials, Federal Aid for Deserving College Students)? Subjects closely related to courses you are taking (Chemistry in Cooking, Geology as a Hobby)?

c) For what kind of writing have you found outlines most useful? What form do you generally use: sentence outline, topical outline, or informal notes?

d) How do you go about revising papers? Discuss typical changes you have made, including material (adding, omitting), plan, paragraphing, grammatical and mechanical matters (spelling, punctuating, sentence movement). Which of the specific weaknesses corrected are generally characteristic of your writing? Can you think of any specific ways to eliminate them?

e) What different kinds of writing will your college courses probably require? What writing may you be called upon to do after graduation? Considering these demands, what particular writing skills do you need to develop?

5. Make outlines of two expository articles, one of which seems to illustrate the "order of support," and the other, the "order of climax." Include with your outlines a statement evaluating the relative effectiveness of each method of development.

6. Consider your past experience as subject matter for papers. Do not plan an autobiography, but draw up a list of specific matters that you would like to write about and that might interest others. Make an inventory of places you have lived in or visited; people you know; jobs you have had; sports, hobbies, reading, plays, movies; subjects you like to talk or argue about.

7. Prepare a list of subjects for investigation, on matters that interest you and about which you would like to know more. Your subjects may range from some aspect of aeronautics to voodoo practices in the West Indies. When your list is completed, select two subjects which you think would make good papers of 500 words each; two that would make papers of 1200 words each; and one that would be suitable for a paper of 2500 words.

8. Compare the process of writing papers in class with that of writing papers at home. Consider such features as the time at your disposal and the effect of the surroundings, the selection and organization of the material, the opportunities for revision. What advantages and disadvantages do you find in each kind of writing?

9. From your lists in exercises 6 and 7 select a few particular topics and write down what you would need to do in the various stages of writing a paper on each. Indicate what sources of material you might use for the investigative papers.

10. Write an analysis of a magazine article or a newspaper editorial that deals with some current national, regional, or local problem in which you are interested. How much of the material seems to you to be reporting and how much is based upon opinion and interpretation? What facts are emphasized and what facts, if any, seem to be omitted?

Varieties of English

The circle of the English language has a well-defined centre but no discernible circumference.—Oxford English Dictionary

Formal written English is not the language; it is merely one type of English. Its rules are pertinent only to people studying or writing formal written English; other types of English have their own rules.—James B. Macmillan

It takes a great deal of experience to become natural.—Willa Cather

SUGGESTIONS FOR USING THE CHAPTER: *The chief purpose of this chapter is to lay a foundation for a realistic consideration of our language today, to encourage observation and evaluation of usage, and to bring the "English" of a composition course into relation with the "English" of people carrying on public affairs.*

Chapter 2 is necessary for understanding the approach to language in this book and for understanding the recommendations on particular points of usage. It should be read, followed immediately by Chapter 3, before a course gives attention to specific matters of language, though obviously it need not come first in a course. Chapters 2 and 3 could be read rapidly to get the point of view and returned to later for details and for practice.

WE BEGAN TO LEARN our language by imitating what our parents and others around us said, and very soon we picked up enough words to make our wants known and then to talk with others. When we got beyond the stage of wailing and grabbing, our parents were so pleased to have us talk that they accepted some of our own infantile contributions to the English vocabulary. In one family milk was *nuck*, a hammer an *agboo*, an elephant an *umpy-dump*, a screwdriver a *toodle-oodle-da*. We used our own forms of words and our own syntax: One youngster, struggling with irregular verbs, said, "Mother did gave me a lot of pants. She shouldn't have gaven me so much pants this summer." For a while the grown-ups thought this sort of language was cute and perhaps they even went so far as to use it themselves when talking to us. But by the time we were four or five, they began to laugh at our childish sounds, childish words, and childish constructions and in other ways gave us to understand that they expected us to talk about as they talked. So far as we could talk that way, we did.

In school we added to the skill in using the language that we had picked up at home by learning to read and to write. We studied "grammar," which told us that "It is I" and other expressions were correct and "It is me" and a lot more were not, without telling why or with some such reason as "the verb *to be* is followed by a predicate nominative." Most of us did our lessons, as lessons, and though we

RELATED ARTICLES: *A number of articles in the Index part of this book give further details of language and language processes. The most important are listed here as a matter of interest.*

*Academic writing
*American and British usage
*Business English
*Change in language
*Colloquial and written English
*Conversation
*English language
*Experiment in English
*Foreign words in English

*Grammar
*Heightened style
*Latin and English
*Legal language
*Newspaper English
*Origin of words
*Pronunciation
*Scientific and technical writing
*Style

---

tried to follow this grammar while in the schoolroom, outside we talked about the same way we always had. But some of us began to realize that English, which we supposed we just talked naturally, was a pretty complex matter and that opinions about it differed, sometimes violently.

1. General English and varieties of English

Those of us who reach college and find that we are almost ready to take our places in public affairs realize, whether we pay any special attention to our English or not, that we have a double concern for our language. One is a desire for confidence, often a wish to overcome an unpleasant feeling acquired from "corrections" we have received or from fun made of our "accent" or our choice of words. More positively this concern is a hope for control of language, an assurance that when we sit down to write something it will come readily and presentably. The other concern is a desire to extend our ability to discuss the new matters we are learning and to write for other people, even to reach people we do not know—to meet the more varied and more mature communication situations that increasingly face us.

Most of the time of course we are unconscious of our words and constructions, unless some expression puzzles us or attracts our particular notice. But when meeting new people, or people from a different social circle, or when we have to "give a talk" or write an important letter or something that will be printed, we may become acutely conscious of *how* we are speaking or writing.

Confidence comes from a practical, realistic knowledge of the possibilities of English usage, of what successful speakers and writers do with words. We need an understanding of how to choose the most effective forms of expression for ourselves, and sufficient practice so that the sort of English we wish to use comes to us easily and naturally. We can gain such habits of expression not by memorizing rules and trying to apply them but by reading the work of good writers and listening to good speakers and occasionally pausing to examine how they gain their effects. To do this profitably we need some general knowledge of how language works. A first hand, realistic study of our language can raise discussion of what is appropriate and can help us to answer questions in a businesslike way.

Fortunately the greater part of our language at any given time raises no questions; we use it automatically. Differences do exist, however; choices among forms and constructions have to be made, and because the choices we make contribute so much to the tone of a speech or a piece of writing, they are important. But we should not forget that much of our language can be used at any time, under any circumstances: the ordinary names of things (*apples, trees, paint*) and of acts (*dance, buy, drive*) and thousands of other words are in the central, general vocabulary; most of the forms of words, the plural of nouns in *-s*, the possessive, the present indicative third person singular in *-s*, the forms of pronouns (though these show some variety) are pretty largely standard along with the word order in phrases and sentences and so on.

Such words and expressions that would not attract special attention in any sort of speaking or writing are labeled *General* usage in this book. General usage makes up a considerable part of what is spoken or written in everyday affairs and, when somewhat tidied up from our typical conversation, of literature as well. In this passage from a short story, for example, the language is simply a compressed form of what we might all use (except perhaps the expression "the world leaps into proportion"):

> The man who expected to be shot lay with his eyes open, staring at the upper left-hand corner of his cell. He was fairly well over his last beating, and they might come for him any time now. There was a yellow stain in the cell corner near the ceiling; he had liked it at first, then disliked it; now he was coming back to liking it again.

He could see it more clearly with his glasses on, but he only put on his glasses for special occasions now—the first thing in the morning, and when they brought the food in, and for interviews with the General. The lenses of the glasses had been cracked in a beating some months before, and it strained his eyes to wear them too long. Fortunately, in his present life he had very few occasions demanding clear vision. But, nevertheless, the accident to his glasses worried him, as it worries all near-sighted people. You put your glasses on the first thing in the morning and the world leaps into proportion; if it does not do so, something is wrong with the world.—STEPHEN VINCENT BENÉT, "The Blood of the Martyrs," *Thirteen O'Clock,* p. 23

It is obvious that the tone of a passage may be set by a relatively small number of words or constructions because they stand out, are not in general usage but are appropriate to a particular situation. A few contractions and shortened constructions, for example, might make a passage seem distinctly informal though it was made up otherwise of words in general use.

The "problems" of English usage arise chiefly from the presence of differing strands of the language that cannot be used with equal effectiveness in every situation. Our language, like every widely used language, is not one single group of words and constructions, everywhere the same, but a variety of such groups that have much in common but are still far from uniform. There are two reasons for stressing these varieties: one is to show the immense resources our language offers and the other is to help form habits of easy and automatic adaptation of a person's actual usage to the varying communication situations he faces. A mature use of English means speaking and writing the sort of English that is appropriate to the situation in which we find ourselves, *for English is not just "good";* *it is good under certain conditions.*

The three principal sources of variations in a language are time, place, and circumstances of use. Any of these may give rise to expressions that are not in general use. As the basis for a complete picture of current English, looking toward a realistic approach to Good English, we shall now consider these variations, beginning with the most important, those due to circumstances of use.

2. Variations due to use

Many words of similar meaning that are in current use and that are not affected by difference of place cannot be used interchangeably in all situations. Consider the following groups:

indigent, impecunious, underprivileged, in want, penniless, poverty-stricken, *poor,* hard up, broke, flat

spent, fatigued, weary, exhausted, *tired,* worn-out, played out, used up, dog tired, all in, pooped

lunatic, demented, mentally ill, mad, psychopathic, *insane,* crazy, out of his mind, bughouse, nutty

stripling, youth, lad, *boy,* youngster, kid, punk

Similarly, there are many idioms and constructions carrying the same idea but suggesting different sorts of speech:

dare not, daren't, do not dare, don't dare, dassent

were it not for, if it were not for, if it was not for, if it wasn't for, if it wan't for

Poor, tired, insane, and *boy* certainly belong to the General language, and so do some of the words near them in these series; we all use them. But as we move away from these central words, the terms become somewhat more limited, until those at the ends are definitely restricted to formal writing or to slang.

Probably most of us would not use *indigent, spent, stripling*—they suggest old-fashioned or rather pedantic usage. And we would probably all use *broke, all in, nutty* in casual company, but not in more formal situations, not when we were talking to someone on whom we wanted to make "a good impression." These differences are due not to the meaning of the words but to the circumstances in which they have been generally used and which they suggest. That is, language differs according to the education, occupation, and social standing of the people who use it; and words and constructions suggest and carry with them traces of the situations in which they are habitually used.

There is no universally accepted system of naming these different levels of usage, but considerable progress has been made in describing various types of English.[1] In this book three principal levels are presented, *Informal* English, *Formal* English, and *Vulgate* English, along with subordinate varieties like *Shoptalk, Familiar* English, *Academic* English, and others shown in the table on page 40. Although hard and fast lines cannot be drawn between the levels, and people's judgment of their boundaries will differ somewhat, the

---

[1] Bloomfield, p. 52, 149 ff.; Fries treats current American usage according to levels in *American English Grammar;* Kennedy, § 7; John S. Kenyon, "Cultural Levels and Functional Varieties of English," *College English,* 1948, 10: 1-6; G. P. Krapp, *A Comprehensive Guide to Good English* (Chicago, 1927), pp. xii-xix; Marckwardt and Walcott; Pooley, ch. 3. (Full titles for works mentioned by author only will be found in the Bibliography, pages xii-xiv.)

principal characteristics of the levels are pretty clear and the illustrations in the following sections will make it possible for anyone to distinguish them.

2a. Informal English. Here is the opening paragraph of Miss Willa Cather's novel *O Pioneers!*

> One January day, thirty years ago, the little town of Hanover, anchored on a windy Nebraska tableland, was trying not to be blown away. A mist of fine snowflakes was curling and eddying about the cluster of low drab buildings huddled on the gray prairie, under a gray sky. The dwelling-houses were set about haphazard on the tough prairie sod; some of them looked as if they had been moved in overnight, and others as if they were straying off by themselves, headed straight for the open plain. None of them had an appearance of permanence, and the howling wind blew under them as well as over them. The main street was a deeply rutted road, now frozen hard, which ran from the squat red railway station and the grain "elevator" at the north end of the town to the lumber yard and the horse pond at the south end. On either side of this road straggled two uneven rows of wooden buildings; the general merchandise stores, the two banks, the drug store, the feed store, the saloon, a post-office. The board sidewalks were gray with trampled snow, but at two o'clock in the afternoon the shopkeepers, having come back from dinner, were keeping well behind their frosty windows. The children were all in school, and there was nobody abroad in the streets but a few rough-looking countrymen in coarse overcoats, with their long caps pulled down to their noses. Some of them had brought their wives to town, and now and then a red or a plaid shawl flashed out of one store into the shelter of another. At the hitch-bars along the streets a few heavy work-horses, harnessed to farm wagons, shivered under their blankets. About the station everything was quiet, for there would not be another train in until night.—WILLA CATHER, *O Pioneers!* pp. 3-4

None of us could keep his eyes quite so firmly fixed on a street in describing it to a friend. We would probably take several sentences to say "The main street was a deeply rutted road, now frozen hard, which ran from the squat red railway station to the grain 'elevator' at the north end of the town to the lumber yard and the horse pond at the south end"; and perhaps most of us would not say "eddying" or "abroad in the streets." But the general tone is of the natural speech of educated people, conversation refined. Many of the phrases sound like conversation: "moved in overnight," "headed straight for the open plain," and "there would not be another train in until night." Through this direct and informal writing we come to see the village of Hanover—and to have a feeling of confidence in the writer.

This passage is typical of informal English in writing.[1] It is the

---

[1] For discussion of informal written English, see Ballard, Chapter 10, "Toward Simplicity"; Dobrée, Part 4, "The New Way of Writing"; Rudolph Flesch, *The Art of Plain Talk* (New York, 1946).

LEVELS AND VARIETIES OF ENGLISH USAGE

Principal Levels	Typical Varieties	Characteristic Uses
		Chiefly spoken
VULGATE	Regional dialects	Conversation of many people in their work and personal relations
Not much touched by school instruction; not appropriate for public affairs or use of educated people		Local color radio programs; some comic strips
		Conversation in plays, stories
		Spoken and written
	Shoptalk	Talk in factories, garages, shops, offices; articles in trade journals; stories dealing with jobs
	Slang	Easy or flashy conversation; humorous, sporty or informal writing
	Familiar English	Talk and letters between intimates; diaries; some informal writing
INFORMAL		Conversation of educated people
		Talks to general audiences
Speaking and writing of educated people in their private or public affairs	Typical informal English	Most news stories, features, columns
		Business letters, advertising
		Magazine articles and books on subjects of general interest
		Most fiction
		More often written than spoken
	"Literary"	Addresses and lectures to restricted audiences
		Some editorials and special class business writing
FORMAL		Literature of somewhat limited circulation: essays and criticism, much poetry, some fiction
Speaking and writing for somewhat restricted groups in formal situations	Scientific and technical writing	Books and articles dealing with special subjects for professional audiences, impersonal reports, etc.
	Academic	Reference works, dissertations, some textbooks
	"Gobbledygook"	Pretentious and unnecessarily abstruse treatments of simple matters: legal documents

COMMENTS ON THE LEVELS AND VARIETIES

1. The three main levels described in the table are *Informal, Formal,* and *Vulgate.* The Informal and Formal levels make up what is commonly referred to as "Standard English"; the Vulgate level, "Substandard." The labels Standard and Substandard (or any of the other epithets frequently applied to the latter—"illiterate," "popular," "vulgar") are not used in this book because the aim is first to be descriptive, and then to suggest how to select from the kinds of English described what is appropriate to a given situation.

2. The term *General* usage is applied to words and constructions that appear at all levels. It is language that will not attract special attention wherever it is used.

3. Although differences are observable between the levels and the varieties, they must not be thought of as mutually exclusive but as relatively different. A speech or passage, for instance, might be placed in one or another level because of its having several strong traits characteristic of the level, and thus the "feel" or "tone" of that level, even though the greater part of the passage was in General usage.

4. The three levels are characterized by traits of pronunciation, by choice of words and constructions, and by the avoidance of certain locutions (as Informal and Formal English avoid double negatives). The chief differences between the varieties (named in the middle column) are in vocabulary (the easiest trait to distinguish and discuss), but they usually show increasingly the other traits of their level as they move toward the top or the bottom of the table.

5. *Colloquial* means "spoken" and consequently is not a level of usage. Spoken language differs among the levels, and frequently shows more clearly than written examples the characteristics of the level. Within each level, of course, the spoken language differs from the written.

6. *Literary* is not an accurate word for a variety of language, since we have literature in both Informal and Formal English. It is used here in quotation marks at the point where it is sometimes applied.

7. In this book, labeling a locution as any one of the varieties is meant to indicate that it is characteristically used as the description of that variety suggests, that its connotation comes from this use, and that it is not characteristic of another variety. Obviously words are borrowed from one variety to another (for example, Shoptalk occurs in many informal articles). Such labeling is not intended to prevent a word's use under other conditions but does suggest that it may be conspicuous in another level, and that its connotation should be intended.

language of an educated person as he goes about his everyday affairs or takes part in public affairs—in business or politics, for example. It is the language of most newspaper and magazine articles, of the bulk of plays and novels—in short, of most of what we read. Informal English has a considerable range, from casual speech to writing that has been carefully edited, but it lies between the vulgate on one side and the more restricted formal level on the other. It is put first in this discussion because it is the most generally useful level, without the limitations of the other two, and because, since it has such wide currency and in fact can reach everyone, it is the most necessary and so is the proper goal of school instruction.

Within the last generation informal English has come once more to dominate writing in English, partly in reaction against the more elaborate style of the nineteenth century. Informal English has a long and honorable tradition, for it is characteristic of the pamphleteers and popular storytellers of Elizabethan literature, of the plainer portions of the English Bible, especially the direct narratives of the New Testament, and of such writers as Defoe and Fielding and, to a large degree, of Swift.

Informal English lies close to current speech, but it is not, when written, speech exactly reproduced, partly because the written vocabulary is larger and somewhat more precise than the spoken. But its movement is largely colloquial, the movement of spoken English refined, tidied up, shorn of its looseness. Whenever they are exact enough to convey the intended meaning, informal English uses colloquial words, or at least words from the general vocabulary; such words are likely to be concrete, close to experience, and familiar to a large number of readers. The sentences are likely to be rather short and to have a simple, direct movement, as contrasted with the more elaborate sentences of formal English. The allusions are more to living people, places and things of current interest, than to literature or history.

Informal English is especially appropriate to personal narrative, since most people are informal except on special occasions. In fact, formal English may suggest pretentiousness or lack of sincerity. In this passage from *Life With Father*, the sentences even outside the dialog have a conversational movement, and some of the expressions (*pretty things, She didn't like it a bit, his blood pressure and everything*) are definitely colloquial. Even contractions are used, to carry out the natural rhythm.

Mother used to go to the cemetery in Woodlawn with her arms full of flowers, and lay the pretty things by some headstone, as a sign of remembrance. After a while she bought a cast-iron chair and left it out there, inside the square family plot, so that when it took her a long time to arrange her flowers she could sit down and rest. This was a convenience, but unluckily it was also a worry, because absent-minded visitors to neighboring graves began to borrow that chair. They dragged it off across the grass to sit and grieve in, and forgot to return it. Mother then had to hunt around for it and drag it back, which made her feel cross, and thus spoiled the mood she had come out in. She didn't like it a bit.

One Sunday when she herself was past seventy, and when Father in spite of his blood pressure and everything was nearly eighty, she asked him if he wouldn't like to drive out with her to Woodlawn. She hadn't any flowers to take, but she had happened to think of that chair, though she didn't say so to Father. She merely said that it was a beautiful day and it would do him good to go out.

Father refused. Positively. He winked robustly at me and said to Mother, "I'll be going out there soon enough, damn it."

Mother said that he ought to come because one of the headstones had settled and she wanted him to tell her whether he didn't think it needed attention.

Father asked whose headstone it was, and when Mother told him, he said: "I don't care how much it's settled. I don't want to be buried with any of that infernal crowd anyhow."

Mother of course knew how he felt about some of the family, but she said that he wouldn't mind such things when it was all over.

Father said yes he would. He became so incensed, thinking of it, that he declared he was going to buy a new plot in the cemetery, a plot all for himself. "And I'll buy one on a corner," he added triumphantly, "where I can get out!"

Mother looked at him startled but admiring, and whispered to me, "I almost believe he could do it."—CLARENCE DAY, *Life With Father*, pp. 257-58

In presenting information and discussing ideas, formal English is often used, because the material is likely to be intended for a rather restricted group of readers. But more and more, information and ideas are being presented in a style which is basically informal. Certain precise or technical words not in the usual colloquial vocabulary are necessary (as *shaman*, *ethos*, *possession* in the selection that follows from a book on ethnology), but the pattern of sentences and most of the writer's vocabulary may be informal and so increase the readability and often the influence of the book or article.

A chief of the Digger Indians, as the Californians call them, talked to me a great deal about the ways of his people in the old days. He was a Christian and a leader among his people in the planting of peaches and apricots on irrigated land, but when he talked of the shamans who had transformed themselves into bears before his eyes in the bear dance, his hands trembled, and his voice broke with excitement. It was an incomparable thing, the power his people had had in the old days. He liked best to talk of the desert foods they had eaten. He brought each uprooted plant lovingly and with an unfailing sense of its importance. In those days his people had eaten "the health of the desert," he said, and knew nothing of the insides of tin cans and the things for sale at butcher shops. It was such innovations that had degraded them in these latter days.

One day, without transition, Ramon broke in upon his descriptions of grinding mesquite and preparing acorn soup. "In the beginning," he said, "God gave to every people a cup, a cup of clay, and from this cup they drank their life." I do not know whether the figure occurred in some traditional ritual of his people that I never found, or whether it was his own imagery. It is hard to imagine that he had heard it from whites he had known at Banning; they were not given to discussing the ethos of different peoples. At any rate, in the mind of this humble Indian the figure of speech was clear and full of meaning. "They all dipped in the water," he continued, "but their cups were different. Our cup is broken now. It has passed away."

Our cup is broken. Those things that had given significance to the life of his people, the domestic rituals of eating, the obligations of the economic system, the succession of ceremonials in the villages, possession in the bear dance, their standards of right and wrong—these were gone and with them the shape and meaning of their life. The old man was still vigorous and a leader in relationships with the whites. He did not mean that there was any question of the extinction of his people. But he had in mind the loss of something that had value equal to that of life itself, the whole fabric of his people's standards and beliefs. There were other cups of living left, and they held perhaps the same water, but the loss was irreparable. It was no matter of tinkering with an addition here, lopping off something there. The modelling had been fundamental, it was somehow all of a piece. It had been their own.—RUTH BENEDICT, *Patterns of Culture,* pp. 21-22

Besides the serious uses of informal English, there is of course its lighter vein, a sort of informal informality. This shows usually a wider range of language in both words and constructions, from appropriate slang and colloquial expressions to nearly formal usage, and moves with enough force to fuse these varied elements into one pattern of expression. It is especially useful for brief comments, which, like the one that follows, are serious enough, but which at the moment the writer is treating in a far from earnest tone.

One scientist has an idea that it might be fun to dig a hole down into the earth deeper than anybody has ever gone before, and poke around down there. He says there's some swell gas in the earth's core and we ought to let it out because it would be such a great supply of power. Well, pardon us, but we have a counter-plan calling for the formation of a non-power-loving organization called the Society for Letting Well Enough Alone. The S.L.W.E.A. would be founded on the notion that Science is a busybody, and that some day, thanks to Science, we'll hear a loud noise, see a stream of yellow flame in the sky, and zippo, there won't be any more earth, any more sky, any more science, or any more coconut oil. Hereafter, any scientist who wants to try an experiment involving the whole earth is going to have to get permission from the S.L.W.E.A. That goes for side trips into the stratosphere, chemical twiddling of all sorts, and boring holes into the center of the works. The earth is the property of all of us; scientists have got to quit claiming her as their oyster. The earth, just as she stands, has a lot of qualities which we cherish: we like the climate, we like the food, and we like the view from the porch. Nobody is going to let the gas out of her if we can prevent it. If scientists have to let the gas out of something, let 'em buy a nickel balloon.—*The New Yorker,* June 30, 1934

Little would be gained by trying to discriminate a large number of subtypes of informal English, but three of the informal sorts call for a little comment: familiar English, shoptalk, and slang.

1) FAMILIAR ENGLISH. When we write for our own convenience or amusement, and when we talk or write to members of our family or to intimate friends, we use English more casually than when addressing strangers or people with whom we are only slightly acquainted. The basis of this familiar English is our natural speech, and the colloquial traits are carried over into writing in letters and diaries. Contractions, abbreviations, *clipped words, nicknames, and short constructions are characteristic. *Localisms, shoptalk, slang, various sorts of play with words (from babytalk to *blends like *tantrumental*) are likely to appear. Since usually writer and reader have a good deal in common, much can be taken for granted, in material, in allusion to common experiences, and in the special connotation of words. A word may set a group of friends to laughing in a way quite mystifying to a stranger, just because it has some special association in their common experience.

The sloppiness we sometimes permit ourselves in writing letters is not a legitimate characteristic of familiar English; it is really insulting to our readers. But familiar English has its proper place in using the small bits of language we hold in common and in drawing upon our individual stock of words and constructions—to make the communication on paper come as close as possible to what we would say in conversation. In what we write for unknown readers we shall have to be somewhat more impersonal and go further toward meeting their expectations.

2) SHOPTALK. *Shoptalk* is the offhand talk of people in various occupations, from medicine and law to ditchdigging and panhandling.[1] It varies with the social class and personal taste of its users, from the talk of a garage hand, to that of an automotive engineer, or

---

[1] *American Speech* has many articles dealing with the vocabularies of particular occupations.

a professor of physics. Its distinguishing feature is vocabulary. Many of its words are the necessary names for materials and processes and tools and other objects and people—for everything that is commonly referred to in a line of work—like *em, en, pica, pi, spreaders, platen, rule, chase,* and so on, from a printing shop. Workmen need names for thousands of things the laymen don't know exist. These words would be regarded as a part of the general informal vocabulary of English if they were needed outside the vocation. Shoptalk may often include formal technical and scientific words, as in the conversation of internes and nurses, but it is set off from formal technical and professional writing by the colloquial (or even vulgate) tone and by the presence of the slang of the field, which would not be found at the formal level.

Shoptalk uses all the freedom of slang in forming words and putting them together, making a vigorous and figurative vocabulary, often shocking to polite ears. Especially convenient are short substitutes for long technical words formed from the ancient languages, like *TNT* for *trinitrotoluene.* A *mike* may be a microphone in a radio studio, a microscope in a laboratory, a micrometer in a shop; *hypo* is a fixing bath to a photographer, or a hypodermic injection in medical context; *soup* is the name of a pourable mixture in scores of manufacturing processes. Racing has *place, show, on the nose, tipster, bookie;* unlisted securities are *cats and dogs;* football men have *skull practice;* a student pilot must *dual* for many hours before he is allowed to *solo;* a *gagman* makes up the comedian's lines; the announcer's advertising speech is a *plug;* and so on.

Shoptalk is appropriate and necessary in informal speaking or writing about the particular occupation in which it is used. It is usually out of place in formal writing. Some of it is useful in discussing other subjects, like *fade-out* (from the movies), and may become colloquial, like *juice* (electricity) or part of the general vocabulary, like *third degree.* The suggestion of different shop vocabularies varies, as the suggestion of business terms (**contact, *proposition, in the red*) is unpleasant to many people not in business, but the words from sailing (*aft, amidships*) seem romantic and have more popular appeal. Shoptalk constitutes one of the liveliest parts of the language and is contributing more and more to the general vocabulary of English.

3) SLANG. It is hard to draw a line between slang and colloquial or informal English. The central trait of slang comes from the mo-

tive for its use: a desire for novelty or for vivid emphasis.[1] Other varieties of the language have ways of expressing the ideas of slang words, but their tone is quieter, more conventional. Young people like novelty, and so do fashionable and sporty grown-ups. Slang is especially common in talking about sports and all sorts of amusements and for all kinds of everyday activities—eating, drinking, use of money, traveling, and relations between people, for which the ordinary terms have worn thin. For racy discussion ordinary English words do not seem colorful enough for some sprightly spirits and they adapt words to suit their moods—and other people take up their inventions.

Slang words are made by natural linguistic processes. The slang quality may lie in the stress of a word (*positive'ly,* that was *some'* party), or in intonation, as in the variations on *Oh yeah.* A slang expression may be a fashionably overused expression, without any essential change of meaning from the ordinary use of the words: *so what,* or *what have' you?* or *you and who else?* Slang abounds with clipped words: *bunk, razz, goo;* and with compounds and other derivatives of ordinary words: *screwball, sourpuss, tough break, ritzy, cockeyed.* Many slang words are borrowed from shoptalk, especially from the shoptalk of sports, of criminal activities, and of popular lines of work like movie production, and used in more general situations: *punk, scram, close-up (klōs' up'), behind the eight ball.* And a great many are figurative uses of words from the general vocabulary: *a mean swing, lousy, a good egg, a five-minute egg, drugstore cowboy, pain in the neck, a bird, a peach, drop dead.* To *park* a car is general English; to *park* a hat or a piece of gum is slang.

Many slang words have short lives—*skiddoo, twenty-three, vamoose, beat it, scram, hit the trail, take a powder* have succeeded each other within a generation. Words for being drunk and for girls, and words of approval (*tops, a wow, neat*) and disapproval (*wet, screwy*) change almost from year to year. Many slang words prove more permanently useful and become part of the general colloquial and familiar vocabulary (*date, boyfriend, shebang*), and others become general English (*highbrow, lowbrow, ballyhoo*). In this way slang contributes words to the general English vocabulary. Dictionaries

---

[1] Most books dealing with language or with English have sections on slang. See Lester V. Berry and M. V. Van den Bark, *The American Thesaurus of Slang* (New York, 1942); J. S. Farmer and W. E. Henley, *Dictionary of Slang and Colloquial English* (New York, 1929); Mencken, Chapter 11; Eric Partridge, *A Dictionary of Slang and Unconventional English,* rev. ed. (New York, 1950).

tend to be conservative in their treatment of such words and mark as "Slang" many that are actually regular colloquial words, in quite general use.

Slang belongs primarily to familiar and rather flashy speech, to which it can give a note of freshness. This freshness wears off after some hundreds of repetitions so that the prime virtue of the words is lost. In writing, slang is less often appropriate, partly because of triteness and partly because many of the words name general impressions instead of specific ones, so that they rank with *nice* and *good*. (See *Counter words.) Slang is generally out of place in formal writing (as in "The Jews have experienced many *tough breaks* since the War"), and if used for some special purpose would ordinarily be put in quotation marks. In informal writing, slang is often appropriate, as in discussions of sports, of campus affairs and familiar subjects, though even with such subjects appropriateness to the expected readers should be considered. If slang expressions are appropriate, they should be used without apology (that is, without quotation marks), and if they are not appropriate, they should not be used. The chief objections to them, aside from their flashiness, are to their overuse and to their use in place of more exact expressions. Chiefly they are valued for their lively connotation.

The dangers of these conspicuously informal varieties of English have just been mentioned. The dangers of the more typical informal level are perhaps flatness and a lack of exactness of statement, both resulting from not using the full resources of the language. But its advantages are obvious. Informal English is appropriate to most subjects, and it reaches a wide reading public, since it can appeal to general readers as well as to those who may also belong in the restricted group to which formal English is customarily directed. ("Tell it to Sweeney, the Stuyvesants will understand.") It is the necessary English for everyday writing and is equally effective for literature. Above all, it is appropriate to most writers, since it allows them to write with a good deal of naturalness, to base their writing on their speech instead of on a less familiar idiom. George Herbert Palmer said of English literature, "Its bookish times are its decadent times, its talking times its glory."

2b. Formal English. Formal English bears somewhat the relation to informal that formal dress or a uniform does to the clothes worn at everyday work in office or store and at informal social gatherings. It is usually found in books and articles of mature interest, intended for circulation among a rather restricted group, among teachers, ministers, doctors, lawyers, and others of specialized intellectual interests. It is one of the major levels of usage, characteristic of many speakers and writers whose interests or work have involved a good deal of reading. Such a person's conversation would probably also be rather formal, though less so than his writing, for the background of this strand of language is writing or formal (platform) speaking.

Formal English appears in two different types of writing. One is impersonal, as in academic and scientific writing—textbooks, dissertations, reports of experiments, legal papers; the other is more personal, as in literature—literary and other criticism, a good deal of poetry and poetic drama, and the less popular fiction. These two types of formal writing make quite different appeals, but the traits of their language have a good deal in common.

Formal English is distinguished by its vocabulary and by certain grammatical traits. In vocabulary it uses words that belong to the written rather than to the commonly spoken language. Such words are likely to be used little in colloquial English, to be associated with the literary, or scholarly, tradition (*nonchalant, invidious, congenial, habitable*). They are also likely to be more exact in meaning, especially those in scientific writing, than words whose edges have been worn by everyday use. For people familiar with them they often carry a great deal of suggestiveness (*ceremonial, eternity, dogma, fated*) and often have some charm of sound or rhythm (*quintessence, immemorial, memorable*).

In formal English the constructions are usually filled out: short cuts characteristic of colloquial and informal English are not taken. Relative pronouns are not omitted, prepositions and conjunctions are repeated in parallel constructions, and so on. Sentences are likely to be of the aggregating type, somewhat longer than in informal writing, binding more ideas together. They may be more elaborately constructed, with parallel and balanced clauses, and are frequently periodic; that is, the complete meaning is suspended till the end. Items are often put in series of three. Modifiers often interrupt the usual word order. Allusions to literature and to events of the past are more common than allusions to current affairs.[1]

---

[1] For further discussion of some of the traits of formal English see Chapter 10, § 1b, "Aggregating sentences," § 2e, "Parallelism and balance," and § 3c, "Long and short constructions."

This does not mean that formal writing is weak or dull, though its dangers lie in that direction, but that, from the nature of its language, its appeal is necessarily somewhat limited. Unless the average reader is considerably interested in the subject, he is likely to turn aside. But the special audience which is aimed at will not only follow the material but, if it is really well handled, appreciate the style as well. To some readers, one appeal of formal writing is its very difference from the ordinary and everyday expression.

Many examples of formal or somewhat formal writing are scattered through this book. Here two are given to emphasize the traits that have just been mentioned. In the first, from a novel, there are a few definitely formal words (*bejewelled, symposium*), a few formal idioms (*after the manner of, that longed always, there would ensue*), a literary use of adjectives (*dry regret, wise sad anecdotes*). There are several triads, many words with literary associations, and a conspicuous use of parallelism, balance, and climax.

> Generally the reunion had been several hours under way before Camila was able to join them after her performance at the theatre. She would arrive towards one o'clock, radiant and bejewelled and very tired. The four men received her as they would a great queen. For an hour or so she would carry the conversation, but gradually reclining more and more against Don Andrés' shoulder she would follow the talk as it flitted from one humorous lined face to the other. All night they talked, secretly comforting their hearts that longed always for Spain and telling themselves that such a symposium was after the manner of the high Spanish soul. They talked about ghosts and second-sight, and about the earth before man appeared upon it and about the possibility of the planets striking against one another; about whether the soul can be seen, like a dove, fluttering away at the moment of death; they wondered whether at the second coming of Christ to Jerusalem, Peru would be long in receiving the news. They talked until the sun rose, about wars and kings, about poets and scholars, and about strange countries. Each one poured into the conversation his store of wise sad anecdotes and his dry regret about the race of men. The flood of golden light struck across the Andes and entering the great window fell upon the piles of fruit, the stained brocade upon the table, and the sweet thoughtful forehead of the Perichole as she lay sleeping against the sleeve of her protector. There would ensue a long pause, no one wishing to make the first move to go, and the glances of them all would rest upon this strange beautiful bird who lived among them.—THORNTON WILDER, *The Bridge of San Luis Rey*, pp. 179-80

The second paragraph shows a full and careful development of an idea, a comparison between the French and the Russian revolutions. It is from a lecture before a university audience (at Yale) and shows some traits of academic English though it is more forceful and more graceful than most academic prose. (Note the rhythm of the last sentence.)

And now, in our day, the first act in the social revolution, accompanied and sustained by the communist faith, has just been staged in Russia. Between the Russian and the French revolutions, as between the democratic and the communist faiths, there are no doubt many points of difference; but what concerns us is that the differences, in the long view, are probably superficial, while the similarities are fundamental. If we, the beneficiaries of the French Revolution, fail to note the similarities, it is because we are easily deceived by a slight difference in nomenclature (for "people" read "proletariat," for "aristocrats" read *bourgeoisie*," for "kings" read "capitalistic government"); and we are more than willing to be deceived because we, the beneficiaries of the French Revolution, would be the dispossessed of the Russian Revolution should it be successful throughout the western world. Like Diderot's Rameau, we are disposed, naturally enough, to think, "The devil take the best of possible worlds if I am not a part of it." But whatever we think, the plain fact is that the Russian Revolution which menaces us, like the French Revolution which destroyed the possessing classes of the *Old Régime* that we might succeed them, is being carried through in behalf of the dispossessed classes. It aims at nothing less than the establishment of liberty and equality ("true liberty and equality" this time, of course) in place of tyranny and exploitation. For the accomplishment of this object it employs, deliberately, as a temporary but necessary measure, a dictatorship of the faithful similar to that which functioned in '93. And the Bolsheviks who control the Council of Commissars, like the Jacobins who controlled the Committee of Safety, regard themselves as the fated instruments of a process which will inevitably, in the long run, break down the factitious division between nations by uniting all the oppressed against all oppressors. "If cabinets unite kings against the people," exclaimed Isnard in 1792, "we will unite peoples against kings." Similarly, the Bolshevik leaders, following Karl Marx, call upon the "proletarians of all countries" to unite against all *bourgeois*-capitalist governments. The Russian is most of all like the French Revolution in this, that its leaders, having received the tablets of eternal law, regard the "revolution" not merely as an instrument of political and social reform but much more as the realization of a philosophy of life which being universally valid because it is in harmony with science and history must prevail. For this reason the Russian Revolution like the French Revolution has its dogmas, its ceremonial, its saints. Its dogmas are the theories of Marx interpreted by Lenin. The days which it celebrates are the great days of the Revolution. Its saints are the heroes and martyrs of the communist faith. In the homes of the faithful the portrait of Lenin replaces the sacred icons of the old religion, and every day the humble builders of a new order make pilgrimages to holy places.—CARL L. BECKER, *The Heavenly City of the Eighteenth-Century Philosophers*, p. 163

Corresponding to the shoptalk and slang of informal English, there are conspicuously formal types within formal English. There are some highly individual styles in literature that require detailed study for their understanding because of unusual use of words and uniquely personal associations of the words and various departures from the typical patterns of current English. There are the quite different styles characteristic of scholarly and scientific writing, in which a precise and specialized vocabulary is employed (at its best) in a compact and impersonal form of statement. And beyond these are two sorts of abuses of formal English: the cumbersome, archaic, and highly repetitious language of most legal documents; and the pretentious, abstract, and equally repetitious style of some bad academic writing and of much of the official writing of government and business, popularly and appropriately known as gobbledygook. *Big words and pompous statement of simple matters do not constitute proper formal English but only an abuse of it.

The usefulness of formal English, as of other levels of English, depends upon appropriateness—appropriateness to the writer, to the subject, and to the reader. Students, like their elders, often write more formally than their subjects require, but they need to remember that formal English is appropriate for much mature writing and that as educated people they should be able to understand and to appreciate its qualities, and on occasion to use it. Especially those who are going into the professions of law, ministry, medicine, teaching, and science and those who are going to play a part in public affairs as editors, as publicists, or as intelligent and influential citizens need to be able to write with sufficient dignity to reach their colleagues.

2c. Vulgate English. The two previous levels of English are used in carrying on public as well as private affairs and are characteristic of people of some education or at least of those who accept as standard the usage of editors and public speakers, which is the basis of school instruction. The everyday speech of many people, relatively untouched by this tradition, makes up the third "level" of English, which we are calling vulgate English, the name popularized by H. L. Mencken in *The American Language* and given in *Webster's International Dictionary* as the third sense of *vulgate*, "vulgar speech or language."[1]

This speech level is a very real and very important part of the English language and is studied by linguists with the same seriousness with which they study the formal and informal levels. It is not made up of lapses from any brand of reputable or standard English but is a different development from the same language stock, representing a selection of sounds, words, forms, constructions made under differ-

---

[1] See Leonard Bloomfield, "Literate and Illiterate Speech," *American Speech*, 1927, 2: 432-39; Fries; Mencken.

ent social conditions. It works very well in carrying on the private affairs of millions of people and is consequently worthy of study and of respect. That it is not used in business, government, or literature is due to social rather than to linguistic causes. It is not ordinarily printed, since, for various historical and social reasons, the printed language is a selection of words, forms, and constructions now considered appropriate to public affairs.

Vulgate English is in many respects different from formal and informal English, most conspicuously perhaps in the use of pronouns and verb forms and in the free use of localisms. Many of its words have a longer history in English than the more genteel words that have replaced them in "society": *stink* (instead of *stench* or *smell* or *odor*), and the like. Many of the forms and constructions have a continuous history back to a time when they were reputable: Chaucer could use a *double negative occasionally; *ant* (*are not*) and *you was* were reputable in the eighteenth century; what is wrongly referred to as "dropping the *g*" in words ending in *-ing* is a continuation of an original participial ending. Many other features of vulgate English are equally natural developments of the language that by some accident of dialect or other circumstance did not become adopted in more formal English.

Vulgate English is of course primarily spoken. Its forms (like *dassent, scairt, he don't*) are not particularly conspicuous when we hear them spoken rapidly and with appropriate, not exaggerated, emphasis. It appears in many radio programs, in plays, and in the conversation of stories. It is used in many comic strips, where it is often intensified, for genuine speakers of vulgate would not use so many double negatives, for instance, as some comic-strip characters are made to. Occasionally a vulgate proverb or formula is drawn on in informal writing:

> Them's hard words, Mr. Hutchins. They won't appeal to the fathers of two-hundred-pound, six-foot-two halfbacks.—JOHN R. TUNIS, "Who Should Go to College?" *Ladies' Home Journal*, Sept. 1938

The monolog of the barber in Ring Lardner's story "*Haircut*" is a fairly accurate representation of vulgate. A few traits of pronunciation are shown (though the *of* in "she'd of divorced him" has no relation to the preposition *of* but is a spelling of the normal contraction of *have*—"she'd've divorced him"), adverbs without the *-ly* ending, *seen* for *saw*, *beat her to it*, and so on.

Jim didn't work very steady after he lost his position with the Carterville people. What he did earn, doin' odd jobs round town, why he spent pretty near all of it on gin, and his family might of starved if the stores hadn't of carried them along. Jim's wife tried her hand at dressmakin', but they ain't nobody goin' to get rich makin' dresses in this town.

As I say, she'd of divorced Jim, only she seen that she couldn't support herself and the kids and she was always hopin' that some day Jim would cut out his habits and give her more than two or three dollars a week.

They was a time when she would go to whoever he was workin' for and ask them to give her his wages, but after she done this once or twice, he beat her to it by borrowin' most of his pay in advance. He told it all 'round town, how he had outfoxed his Missus. He certainly was a caution.— Ring Lardner, "Haircut," *Roundup*, p. 25

Schools carry on their work in the language of the upper social classes, formal or informal English. Students who go into the professions, into many branches of business, and into most white-collar jobs continue to use more or less consistently the more formal language. Those who go into manual labor and the less well paid and less socially elevated jobs return to the use of vulgate English. Naturally and necessarily, though, their speech is gradually losing many of its vulgate traits because of the increased number of white-collar jobs, the greater number of contacts between white-collar and other workers, and the increase of education.

In the lower schools where the pupils are likely to be in daily contact with vulgate speech, it forms a serious problem. At the college level it is seldom a problem, though the speech of many college students is more crude than their social standing would warrant and is consequently a poor background for their writing.

The objection to this level of speech should be clear. It is not that its grammar is "bad," but that vulgate words and constructions are not appropriate to the readers for whom college students and college graduates try to write or to the subjects they are handling. Complex ideas and dignified subjects cannot be discussed adequately in the relatively limited vocabulary of vulgate English. Vulgate is necessary in writing the conversation of many characters in stories, or at least it should be approximated, and it should be used occasionally to give a note of realism to portraits of real people who naturally speak it. But any other use of it must be judged by fitness. When a locution in this book is marked "vulgate," it should not be used except for good reason.

A realization that current English is made up of these principal "levels" and their varieties is the basis of a realistic approach to our language. Observation both by listening and by reading will develop further the outline given here and serve as a background for determining what is Good English as discussed in Chapter 3. It is of course necessary to remember that a good deal of the language is in general use in all levels and that though the levels have identifiable characteristics, they are not mutually exclusive. The language of a person tends to fall into one level or another, but he usually has a considerably larger range, and certainly an educated person should draw on as large a part of the total language as his experience permits.

3. Variations due to time

The variations in our language due to time are less of a problem in speaking or writing than those due to circumstances of use. It is natural that a language used by millions of people over centuries should change, slowly and perhaps imperceptibly. We know from reading older literature that our language has changed a good deal in the centuries during which it has been written down.[1] A play by Shakespeare needs a good many notes to tell us what the words meant to the people who heard them over three hundred years ago. If we go back far enough, English seems like a foreign language, though we recognize in the older forms the ancestors of some of our current words. Language changes as naturally as other customs do—in clothes, food, literary fashions, government.

The forms and meanings of words, pronunciations, and grammatical constructions can be classified in four groups according to their standing in time from the point of view of the present:

> *Obsolete:* Once current but no longer in use
> *Archaic:* Disappearing from use; used occasionally or under certain circumstances
> *Current:* The great body of English that can be used without attracting attention as being either new or old
> *New:* Newly coined words, popular or scientific; new meanings of old words; fresh slang; recent borrowings from other languages; revivals of old words; new idioms

Obviously these groups are relative—it is hard to draw a definite line between obsolete and archaic, or to tell when a word or construc-

---

[1] For further discussion, see histories of the English language, especially Baugh, and Robertson; Otto Jespersen, *Growth and Structure of the English Language* (various editions); Kennedy, § 13; McKnight, Chapter 27; *Oxford English Dictionary*.

tion is sufficiently uncommon to be called archaic. But about the great majority of words, the current words, there can be no question.

3a. Obsolete expressions. Turns of expression that have completely disappeared from use offer little trouble. There is no temptation to refer to a *bottle* of hay, or to use *can* in the sense of "know," or *kind* for "family" or "blood-relationship." Dictionaries contain many obsolete words to help us read older literature or enter into the life of past times. But since Webster's *Dictionary* marks "Obsolete" only words for which no evidence of use since 1660 could be found, obviously it includes and marks as "Archaic" many words which are practically obsolete.

3b. Archaic English. Words are disappearing from use continually, in part because of changes in living that make them no longer necessary—as people no longer travel by the method that used to be known as *ride and tie;* men no longer wear *ruffs* or even *dusters;* few people easily understand "The proof of the pudding is in the chewing of the pudding string" because *proof* is not generally used in the sense of *test* and puddings are seldom made in bags now. Fashion or taste drives out some words or some senses of words, as *betrothed* has given way to **fiancée, jape* to *joke; admire* is no longer used in the sense of "wonder." And some words become less expressive as they lose their suggestiveness, like *parti-colored.* Constructions change as well as words, as in the use of **infinitives* and **participles* and the **subjunctive* mood. Changes in pronunciations sometimes affect phrases, as the pronunciation of the *h* sound in *historical* leads to the use of *a historical* instead of *an historical.*

Archaic language survives in certain situations, conspicuously in church services which still employ *thou,* and in many words from the Bible and the Book of Common Prayer. Some words have been associated with a certain tradition of poetry, but recent poets of importance have been able to express themselves in the current language (or have even experimented beyond the typical current vocabulary). Beginners in verse need to be warned against *yesteryear, olden, o'er, wight,* and other archaic words which often stamp their work as amateur.

A few archaic or even obsolete words survive in set phrases, such as "much *ado*," "in good *stead*," and many are preserved in uneducated speech after they have disappeared from more general English. *Eat* (et) for the past of *eat* (ēt), *you was* in the singular, *accept of,* and the **double negative* were all once in general and reputable use.

A good many words replaced by genteel expressions in polite speech survive in uneducated English, and many used only in a definite locality are archaic (*unbeknownst, cheapen* in the sense of "bargain for").

In conspicuously formal style many older locutions are found—*twain, deem, therein, wherein, whereupon, whosoever, methinks, erstwhile, albeit,* and so on. By no means all of these are labeled "Archaic" or "Rare" in dictionaries, though they have passed out of the main current of English. Their use is not one of the essential or even agreeable features of formal English.

Archaic words are still thought by some to be an easy form of humor—so that writers for college comics and some others fall back on *quoth* and *wight* and *steed*. This is part of the elephantine levity that leads to pompous and boring writing, and fortunately the style is disappearing.

In college writing there are few excuses for archaisms, except occasionally to preserve the flavor of a past time, as in a historical paper. English majors especially need to remember that though their reading may be in the sixteenth or the nineteenth centuries, they are speaking and writing for the twentieth. The archaic style of their reading may pass over into their writing if they do not keep in close touch with current literature.

3c. Current English. Whether or not words and constructions are current rarely raises any question. They are the expressions we hear around us daily, that we find in reading magazines and recent books. Observation of current speech and present-day writing is a safer guide to which words are current than are dictionaries, because a great many words that the dictionaries do not label "Archaic" or "Rare" actually are used very seldom in writing, and almost never in conversation. Words, constructions, and "style" change somewhat even from generation to generation. The last forty years has seen the addition of many words, the dropping of many from general use, and a tendency toward more concise idioms and constructions, as compared with nineteenth-century style. This *Guide and Index* describes our current language. It can help develop your observation of the usable body of English and perhaps help increase your sensitiveness to what is best in contemporary usage. When you write naturally, from your observation of language, you usually write current English, and you should aim for no other kind. In the 1950s write for the 1950s.

3d. New words and constructions. People used to shy away from new words until they had "proved themselves a permanent part of the language." Dictionary editors watch new words in books and magazines and include them if they continue to be used. But users of the language need not be so hesitant. The use of a word should depend on its fitness rather than on its passing a probationary period, and acceptance by a dictionary should be a result of use. Obviously the name of a new invention or of a new social situation is needed immediately and should be freely used, though there may be a question of its exact form, as in *airplane—aeroplane*.[1] There need be no hesitation about words like *televise, blitzkrieg, draftee, sit-down strike, candid camera, newscast.* Such words come from a need to name something. Some words for a time are overused, like *streamlined* and *stockpile* at present, but their life is usually short. It is wise to hesitate before adopting new words for things that have already been named. This is especially true of the large number of abstract words that higher education and specialization in occupations seem to be substituting for common activities and situations, such as *recreational facilities, urban area, causal factors.* (See Chapter 12, § 1c, "Big words.")

New words make their way rather slowly into more formal literary usage. But most writers today take a new word whenever it fits their meaning of it and is appropriate to their type of writing and will not trouble their readers. Occasionally they may even coin a word to serve their purposes. A number of the articles in this *Guide and Index* treat specific points from the frontiers of usage, especially in the written language.

4. Variations due to place

In describing variations of language due to time it is easiest to draw illustrations from written words; in describing variations due to place we can also give examples of pronunciation and idioms, since we can observe them in the speech of people we meet.

No language is spoken exactly the same way in all parts of the country or countries in which it is used. We can easily spot an Englishman because some of his sounds and some of his words and constructions are different from those that we are used to in the

---

[1] *American Speech* keeps track of new words, and each year *The Saturday Review of Literature* has an article on them by Allen Walker Read.

United States. We can also tell very often what part of our country a person comes from by listening to him talk, or at least we can be sure that he comes from some other region than our own. These differences in words, sounds, stress, phrasing, and grammatical habits that are characteristic of fairly definite regions are called *dialects*, or more accurately, a dialect is speech that does not attract attention to itself among the residents of a region. Every one of us speaks a dialect, or several dialects. A pronunciation, a word or meaning of a word, or an idiom that from natural and usually traceable historical reasons is current in one region and not in others is called a *provincialism* or a *localism*.[1]

Dialects exist because of the separation of groups of speakers. They are not peculiar to backward regions, for the "Oxford accent" forms a minor dialect and the people of Boston and of New York speak differently from their neighbors. Nor do dialects depend upon lack of education or social standing. An educated, as well as an uneducated, Westerner will speak somewhat differently from a Southerner or New Englander of a similar degree and quality of education. A dialect may show traits of differing British dialects spoken by early settlers or of foreign languages spoken by large numbers of people in the region, as in sections of Pennsylvania or in the Scandinavian sections of the Middlewest. It may show traits of a neighboring language or of earlier settlement: the dialect of the Southwest contains Spanish elements; New Orleans, French elements; and New York and the Hudson Valley, Dutch elements. Such dialects of course may be spoken by the people of the region regardless of their own ancestry.

4a. Dialects in the United States. There are recognizable dialects in the United States, but we should realize at the outset that they show fewer differences than would be expected in a country of such size, many fewer than are shown by the dialects in much smaller Great Britain. The relative freedom of movement of the American people, transportation facilities that have prevented even the Rocky Mountains from marking a linguistic boundary, the educational system, the circulation of national magazines and of books, and more

---

[1] See Baugh, Chapter 11, especially § 250; Bloomfield, Chapter 19; *Dictionary of American English;* Otto Jespersen, *Mankind, Nation and Individual from a Linguistic Point of View* (Oslo, 1925); G. P. Krapp, *The English Language in America* (New York, 1925), pp. 225-73; *Linguistic Atlas of the United States and Canada* (in progress); Mencken. Many articles in the magazine *American Speech* record facts of various American dialects. Linguaphone album L-19 has recordings of twenty four American dialects.

recently the radio—all keep people who are thousands of miles apart speaking substantially the same language.

Three major American dialects are recognized: *Eastern* (New England and a strip of eastern New York), *Southern* (south of Pennsylvania and the Ohio River, extending west of the Mississippi, into Texas), and *Western,* the most extensive of the three, sometimes called *General American* (or *Northern* in Kenyon and Knott). Minor dialects exist within these three main dialects, as in the Ozarks, or in New York City, but the differences between the speech of California and Illinois are fewer than the differences between either of these and, say, Virginia or Massachusetts. As a result of the work being done on *The Linguistic Atlas of the United States and Canada,* the boundaries of these dialects are being more exactly drawn, subdivisions indicated, and lines of influence between areas shown. Roughly one twelfth of the population speaks Eastern, one sixth Southern, and three fourths Western or General American.

A professional student of the English language observes many differences in pronunciation, words, and idioms between these regions that the ordinary person might miss, but some traits are obvious enough to be sensed by anyone. Some eastern New Englanders use a broad *a* (äsk, gräss, päst) where most Americans have short *a;* they usually slight *r* (bän for *barn*), though they may sound an *r* where there is none in the spelling (idear of). A Westerner has a distinct, perhaps even a prolonged, *r* and usually says ä in words spelled with *o:* pänd—*pond,* hät—*hot,* and so on. A Southerner usually omits his final *r* (as in *suh,* the popular spelling of *sir,* and in words like *door*—dō, or dō′ə). His long *i* has an ä quality as in the popular spelling *Ah* for *I.* East Side New York has its distinctive sounds, as in *goil* (*girl*). And so on. Besides these typical vowel sounds, the regions have their characteristic stress and speech rhythm.

In vocabulary, different words will be found for many common objects. Which of the following is used in your locality, or is some other word used?

    bag—sack—poke
    piazza—porch—stoop—veranda
    griddle lifter—lid lifter—stove handle—stove hook—stove lifter
    doughnut—fried cake—cruller—fat cake
    gumshoe—overshoe—rubber
    sour milk—clabber—clabbered milk—loppered milk
    see saw—teeter totter—teeter board

The accompanying map shows several words that are used within

the relatively small limits of New England for the common earthworm: *angleworm, angledog, easworm* (for *eastworm*), *fish worm*.
In other regions it is known by some of these names and by others
as well.

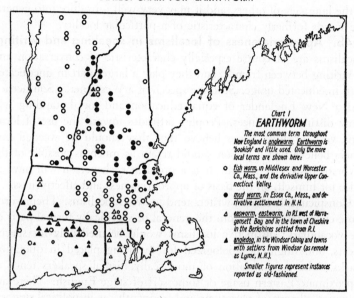

Chart 1
EARTHWORM

The most common term throughout
New England is *angleworm*. *Earthworm* is
'bookish' and little used. Only the more
local terms are shown here:

○ *fish worm*, in Middlesex and Worcester
Co., Mass., and the derivative Upper Con-
necticut Valley.

● *mud worm*, in Essex Co., Mass., and derivative settlements in N.H.

△ *easworm, eastworm*, in R.I. west of Narra-
gansett Bay and in the town of Cheshire
in the Berkshires settled from R.I.

▲ *angledog*, in the Windsor Colony and towns
with settlers from Windsor (as remote
as Lyme, N.H.).

Smaller figures represent instances
reported as old-fashioned.

From *Handbook of the Linguistic Geography of New England*, p. 38

Besides these varying names for common objects, each region has
special words for local features of the landscape or for occupations
that are more or less local: *coulee, hogback, sierra, mesa; mesquite, loco*
(*weed*), *piñon, shang* (*ginseng*); *mule skinner, vara* (a surveyor's
measure in the Southwest), *rodeo, fattening* (food for hogs).

Besides pronunciations and special words, there are a good many
local idioms, like the Southern "I would *like for* you to do it." Conspicuous are those that show the influence of foreign languages, like
"I'm going to catch me some supper" and those of Pennsylvania
German-English: He is going away, not? The potatoes are all. Never
mind, it don't make [doesn't work]. The paper wants rain tomorrow.

Increased travel, education, and reading are probably reducing the
dialects of the United States just as they are blotting out the dialects of
Great Britain. Words peculiar to a local terrain or to local occupations will probably survive, since they fill a real need and usually have

no equivalents in other dialects. The vogue of plays and stories with strong local flavor and of radio programs that grow out of homely New England, Southern, or Western backgrounds is familiarizing all parts of the country with a great deal of local usage. It may be that this public use of localisms will make one region more tolerant of the language of others, and it may very well introduce into general use words formerly characteristic of a particular locality.

4b. Appropriateness of localisms in speaking and writing.
Localisms are of course especially characteristic of conversation and of writing between friends, and they play a larger part in uneducated than in educated usage. Still, the speech of a Westerner, a Southerner, and a New Englander of equal education and social standing will show distinct differences. People's attitudes toward the use of localisms vary greatly. Some believe that they should be weeded out, others believe that a person should retain as much as possible of the flavor of his native speech. It is a problem each person will have to settle for himself, on the basis of appropriateness and effectiveness.

Conspicuously formal writers tend to avoid localisms. Their words come characteristically from the general or specifically formal parts of the vocabulary; distinctive localisms would be used only for special effects, and might be apologized for by being placed in quotation marks. The pronunciation of most really formal speakers tends to approximate Eastern usage or some sort of stage English. There are of course all sorts of variations and frequently, as in political oratory, the style may be formal and the pronunciation local.

In informal English, of course, localisms have more place. An educated person will tend to shed the more conspicuous local pronunciations of his youth and he may have little occasion to use purely local words. But conscious effort to change his speech to a different pattern will often result in an unhappy combination of elements from both. Natural, gradual, unconscious change is best.

Localisms are necessary to narrative, both in histories and in stories and plays. Consider this description of a meal from a novel of Florida:

> There were poke-greens with bits of white bacon buried in them; sand-buggers made of potato and onion and the cooter he had found crawling yesterday; sour orange biscuits and at his mother's elbow the sweet potato pone. He was torn between his desire for more biscuits and another sand-bugger and the knowledge, born of painful experience, that if he ate them, he would suddenly have no room for pone. The choice was plain.—
> MARJORIE KINNAN RAWLINGS, *The Yearling*, p. 12

Localisms often bring a fresh, personal note into discussions of ideas. Obviously in speaking or writing for a definite audience, local terms are appropriate if they are used naturally.

In college writing the same test of fitness applies. Many young people first become conscious of their native speech when they go away to school or college. They should study their speech if it attracts attention, but they should not abandon it just because classmates remark about it. They should try to find what in it is appropriate and effective and what seems to defeat easy communication. But we should hate to see everyone's speech smoothed to the colorless, place-less tones of a chain radio announcer. Localisms are usually out of place in strictly academic writing, term papers, and so on, but in more personal papers, as in a composition course, they may help give a pleasing individual note. Their expressiveness and appropriateness will be sufficient reasons for their use.

Even this brief sketch suggests something of the range and the tremendous resources of the English language available to anyone speaking and writing today. It offers the means for conveying any subject to any desired readers—but the language itself does not do the job. The individual speaker or writer—either automatically or consciously—chooses the sort of language he will use and handles it with what skill he may have. No one speaks or writes the same way at all times. He faces different situations and has different purposes and adapts his language to them.

Because of the social pressure, especially on young people, for using a certain standard of language as it is crystallized in school, it is easy to become too conscious of the form of our expression and even to lose confidence. One sort of defense, especially common in school work, is to play sage, to turn our backs on our natural speech and to use English that we think is better because it has "bigger" words and more formal constructions than we ordinarily use. Granted that we can all improve our powers of communication, we are likely to do so not by assuming a quite different way of talking or writing but rather by capitalizing on and extending the successful qualities we already have, bringing them more in line with general usage if necessary.

We all use English now with a good deal of effectiveness in the situations in which we feel most at home. The reason for studying English further is to increase our confident control, first in the broad informal area of the language and then in any other strands for which we may have a concern or a practical use. It is a simple process of continuing a natural growth begun in infancy, one that will continue as long as we have any lively contact with other people.

Suggested study and writing

These exercises are to give you practice in observing and describing the varieties of English with which you come in contact. The first six exercises may be used for classroom discussion; exercise 7 for preparation and discussion in individual conferences; and exercises 8, 9, and 10 for written assignments.

1. Analyze the language in each of the following sections. Comment in detail on the use of words: localisms, dialect, foreign words, or standard American; formal, informal, or vulgate. Indicate any expressions that seem unusual to you or that are not in keeping with the tone of the rest of the passage.

1. We shall all agree that the fundamental aspect of the novel is its story-telling aspect, but we shall voice our assent in different tones, and it is on the precise tone of voice we employ now that our subsequent conclusions will depend.

Let us listen to three voices. If you ask one type of man, "What does a novel do?" he will reply placidly: "Well—I don't know—it seems a funny sort of question to ask—a novel's a novel—well, I don't know—I suppose it kind of tells a story, so to speak." He is quite good-natured and vague, and probably driving a motor-bus at the same time and paying no more attention to literature than it merits. Another man, whom I visualize as on a golf-course, will be aggressive and brisk. He will reply: "What does a novel do? Why, tell a story of course, and I've no use for it if it didn't. I like a story. Very bad taste on my part, no doubt, but I like a story. You can take your art, you can take your literature, you can take your music, but give me a good story. And I like a story to be a story, mind, and my wife's the same." And a third man he says in a sort of drooping regretful voice, "Yes—oh, dear, yes—the novel tells a story." I respect and admire the first speaker. I detest and fear the second. And the third is myself. Yes, oh, dear, yes—the novel tells a story. That is the fundamental aspect without which it could not exist. That is the highest factor common to all novels, and I wish that it was not so, that it could be something different— melody, or perception of the truth, not this low atavistic form.—E. M. FORSTER, *Aspects of the Novel*, pp. 44-45

2. It ain't that he's surly. I seen him kindhearted often. One time I had to climb in the hack, run an errand around Fifty-ninth. It was about seven P.M. and when I got into the cab what was in the seat but a scooter, two dolls, and three tops. "What the hell is this?" I says to Grady. "Oh, never mind them," he says, "the McNally kids were playing house in the cab, leave the kids' things alone." Grady wouldn't stop kids playing house in the cab. He's kindhearted.

8 But Grady's even worse than I told you about regarding the cab as a
9 private affair of his own and not something for every Tom, Dick, and
10 Harry to get into that's got a couple of bucks and wants to be taken some-
11 place. I've seen guys get into the cab while Grady was sitting in it, dopey,
12 and not seeing them get in, and you ought to see Grady then. He steps on
13 the starter without turning on the switch and it makes a discouraging noise,
14 whirrrrrrr, and of course the engine don't start. Grady looks around his
15 shoulder at the stranger while he does this a few times and the stranger
16 finely gets out and looks for another cab. Grady's tickled to death and
17 turns back to reading the intelligence test in the *News*. The intelligence
18 test is a favorite of his, especially if it's got geography in it.—JOHN Mc-
NULTY, *Third Avenue, New York*. Originally published in *The New Yorker*

1 3. In research centers, individual wishes for recognition are implemented
2 by administrative imperatives, so that the intensity of competition and the
3 large number of competitors multiply enormously the real and alleged con-
4 tributions to the advancement of learning. That a strong emphasis upon
5 scholarly productivity results in tremendous positive values from leading
6 universities is generally known. That it also interferes with the performance
7 of other functions and in marginal cases produces flamboyancy, exhibi-
8 tionism, quantitativeness without regard for quality, and other results in-
9 directly inimical to knowledge itself is not so generally acknowledged.
10 The patterning of higher education is such that even for those (the major-
11 ity) who will engage primarily in teaching, graduate training means research
12 training. When the social structures, functions, and evaluative methods of
13 leading universities are indiscriminately copied in all sorts of institutions,
14 chaotic consequences are inevitable. Equally productive of personal and
15 institutional disorganization are the unstudied procedures imposed by ad-
16 ministrative whim or faculty sentiment. To offset the wasteful division of
17 labor and haphazard evaluative methods found in the present anarchic
18 state of affairs, it is unquestionably high time that faculty committees as
19 well as administrative officers should base their proposals and actions upon
20 a more objective knowledge of social organization.—LOGAN WILSON, "The
Functional Bases of Appraising Academic Performance," American Association of University Professors *Bulletin*, Oct. 1941, 27:449

1 4. Well, right in front of me, in the grand stand that day, there was a
2 fellow with a couple of girls and they was about my age. The young fellow
3 was a nice guy, all right. He was the kind maybe that goes to college and
4 then comes to be a lawyer or maybe a newspaper editor or something like
5 that, but he wasn't stuck on himself. There are some of that kind all right
6 and he was one of the ones.—SHERWOOD ANDERSON, "I'm a Fool," *Horses
and Men*

1 5. I was on the fattish side as an infant, with a scow-like beam and
2 noticeable jowls. Dr. C. L. Buddenbohn, who fetched me into sentience at
3 9 P.M., precisely, of Sunday, September 12, 1880, apparently made a good
4 (though, as I hear, somewhat rough) job of it, despite the fact that his
5 surviving bill, dated October 2, shows that all he charged "to one confine-
6 ment" was ten dollars. The science of infant feeding, in those days, was as
7 rudimentary as bacteriology or social justice, but there can be no doubt that
8 I got plenty of calories and vitamins, and probably even an overdose. There
9 is a photograph of me at eighteen months which looks like the pictures the
10 milk companies print in the rotogravure sections of the Sunday papers,

11 whooping up the zeal of their cows. If cannibalism had not been abolished
12 in Maryland some years before my birth I'd have butchered beautifully.

13 My mother used to tell me years afterward that my bulk often attracted
14 public notice, especially when it was set off dramatically against her own lack
15 of it, for she was of slight frame and less than average height, and looked,
16 in her blue-eyed blondness, to be even younger than she actually was. Once,
17 hauling me somewhere by horse-car, she was confronted by an old man
18 who gaped at her and me for a while with senile impertinence, and then
19 burst out: "Good God, girl, is that baby *yours?*" This adiposity passed
20 off as I began to run about, and from the age of six onward I was rather
21 skinny, but toward the end of my twenties my cross-section again became a
22 circle, and at thirty I was taking one of the first of the antifat cures and
23 beating it by sly resorts to malt liquor.—H. L. MENCKEN, "Introduction to
the Universe," *Happy Days, 1880-1892*, pp. 6-8

Additional passages for analysis may be found in the illustrative
paragraphs throughout the *Guide*.

2. Arrange the following words in groups according to your
judgment of the level in which they are characteristically used. Refer
to a dictionary if necessary. (Study table showing levels of usage
on page 40.)

allocate	flashback	photon
albeit	goon	picayune
baby sitter	gotta	quest
bail out	hostelry	scads
cinema	hellion	side meat
corny	home	smog
coulee	huckster	soap opera
cram	invertebrate	spheroid
cultus	jalopy	teleran
dicker (verb)	kibitz	tort
esoteric	k.o.	utopian
fellow-traveler	monetary	victuals

3. Classify the following words as formal or informal. List an
appropriate synonym for each word in the *other* level.

ad lib	dipsomaniac	often
autumnal	dirt-cheap	onus
blurb	gloaming	poliomyelitis
bobby soxer	gnarled	scared
bovine	job	swank
coöp	little	tycoon

4. You might say any of the following in talking. How would
you write the equivalent idea more formally?

1. The man's here to fix the radio.
2. Most always she does what she's told.
3. Who do you want to talk to?

4. Engraving is when the letters are raised up so you can feel them with your fingers.
5. Hold on tight when we hit the curve.
6. You can't help but like our neighbors.
7. He was crazy about fishing, but never seemed to catch one.
8. "By gosh," the coach chuckled, "it's him again."
9. Come any time you want to.
10. The catcher stands in back of the home plate.

5. Study the following *Index* articles and be prepared to discuss the positions these words hold in our language.

*can't help (but)	*inside (of)
*depot	*let (leave)
*drunk	*like (as)
*due to	*no account
*either (pronunciation)	*pants
*enthuse	*plenty
*faze	*put in—put across
*fix	*show up
*height—heighth	*try and—try to

6. The following poem, reprinted from Hyder Edward Rollins' edition of *Tottel's Miscellany*, was written in the sixteenth century. Read it through first to get the meaning; then point out word forms that differ from modern usage. Notice differences in spelling. Consult an unabridged dictionary for the meaning of "feater" (line 5) and the *Oxford English Dictionary* for the sense in which "iuglying" (jugling) (line 6) and "knittying" (line 7) are used.

Of a new maried Student

A student at his boke so plast,
That welth he might haue wonne:
From boke to wife did flete in haste,
From wealth to wo to runne.
Now, who hath plaied a feater cast,
Since iuglying first begoon?
In knittying of him selfe so fast,
Him selfe he hath vndoon.

7. Answer these questions indicating the bearing they may have on your present use of English:

a) Where did you grow up?

b) What places have you lived in long enough to have some impression of the language used in them?

c) Are you conscious of any specific influences on your speaking and writing—particular people, teachers, books, English courses, work?

d) Characterize your typical speech and your typical writing in terms of regional English and in terms of levels of usage. If your speech deviates from general usage, give examples of words, pronunciations, and constructions which you habitually use.

e) What foreign languages, ancient or modern, do you know something of (and about how much)?

f) What kind of books and what writers do you read from preference? What periodicals?

g) Do you regularly read a newspaper? What sections (including comic strips)?

8. Copy from a book or magazine, giving full reference to its source, a good paragraph showing either formal or informal usage. In the margin comment briefly on any distinctive words or constructions.

9. See *Newspaper English. Write an analysis of the language used in different sections of a large metropolitan newspaper: in the editorial, financial, and sports pages, in the women's sections and amusement pages. List examples of journalese, technical terms, shop talk, slang. What different levels of usage do you find in the letters to the editor? Among various comic strips?

10. Keep a speech notebook and write down characteristic campus expressions, slang, phrases, pronunciations. A method of recording usage is illustrated in the Index article *Linguistics, § 2. When you have gathered sufficient material, write a paper on the student speech at your college. Comment on differences you have observed between the levels of speech used by college students inside the classroom and outside.

Good English

. . . standard English is an ever-changing and never-fully-attained ideal toward which the entire English-speaking race is steadily striving, but good English—or may we change the term to better English—is the aim and goal of every intelligent speaker of the language, just as better thinking is always the desire of such a person.
—Arthur G. Kennedy

Our language is a sulky and inconstant beauty, and at any given moment it is important to know what liberties she will permit.—Cyril Connolly

To a student of language, all varieties of English are equally a part of the language, and one variety is to be observed and studied as much as another. But to a *user* of English, as some of the comments in Chapter 2 suggest, the varieties are by no means equal. They differ in the impression they make on people and in the sort of ideas they can communicate.

Every educated person naturally wants to speak and write what may be called "Good English," just as he wants to "make a good personal appearance" and to "be intelligent." But the great range and diversity of the English language raise numerous questions about usage. Realizing that there are differences in usage is the basis of a realistic and sensible approach to Good English, for then it becomes a matter of selection, of choosing the expression that is best for a speaker's or writer's specific purpose. *English is not just good; it is good in a particular situation.*

1. Language as behavior

We can begin by looking at language as something we do, a part of behavior. It is much like the problems which face us in almost everything we do that comes under the eyes of others, in our manners, in the jokes we tell, in our food, in our living quarters, in our political ideas. In dress, to make the most convenient parallel, we gradually develop something we call taste or judgment, in part by imitating others, consciously or unconsciously, in part by consulting people who are supposed to know what is good form, in part by following our own preferences in design and color and fabric.

Dress varies according to the taste of the individual; it varies among classes of people and with their occupations and activities. Overalls are appropriate and necessary for a good deal of work. Clothes that would be out of place in an office or a classroom are quite in order on a tennis court, at a beach, or on a hike. For some occasions formal dress is definitely prescribed—at least for men, and for women, too, although their choice is less limited. But usually dress lies between the extremes of work or sport and formal clothes. It is comfortable; it reflects something of the taste of the person who chooses it; it is in good taste and does not attract attention; it is appropriate to going about personal affairs, to work in stores and offices, to college classes, to informal social affairs. The attractive possibilities of everyday costume offer much opportunity for individual choice and judgment. A person needs to have and to be able to wear several kinds of clothes, and he needs to know for what occasion each is appropriate.

In language as in dress there are general expectations, conventions to be taken into account in speaking and writing, but there is also great leeway for personal choice. Anyone who is going to take his place in public, business, or social affairs needs to know the resources of the various sorts of English and when they can be profitably drawn on. On questions of English usage, we often consult books that can answer questions about language, especially dictionaries and handbooks. We can ask people who write well, and we can ask teachers who have made the study of our language part of their professional training. And we can always be watching what effective writers do, how the language is handled in the better books and magazines. This observation is especially important, because as in dress and in manners, more or less conscious imitation of those we like and approve of or wish to be associated with will bulk large in forming our own habits. Few will ever write with real ease unless they listen and read a good deal and so unconsciously absorb the ways of their language by direct experience.

2. The basis of Good English

There are, luckily, principles to help develop judgment in the use of Good English and to guide in forming habits of effective speaking and writing.[1] Because we do not have a series of rules and prohibitions does not mean that "anything goes" or that there are not fairly definite goals toward which we can constantly move.

2a. Limits of Good English set by the purpose of communication. Of course anyone may talk to himself or write for his own amusement or relief or he may wish to deceive or puzzle, and then his usage is his own affair. And a writer may experiment as much as he wishes, as James Joyce and Gertrude Stein and others have done, creating for themselves a limited audience or cult that is willing to study out their meaning in spite of handicaps. But the ordinary and principal function of language is effective communication, making someone understand or feel something that we want him to, or getting him to do something that we want him to.

This fundamental purpose in speaking and writing prevents usage, complicated as it is, from falling into chaos and so sets the broad limits of Good English. We use words in the meanings they have acquired from their past use, and we try to make our statements in understandable patterns. The language itself, says Professor Jespersen, "has developed through an infinite number of solutions of such problems of communication as arise every instant of our daily life." From this point of view, Professor Fries defines the basis of Good English:

> . . . language is a means to an end, and that end is specifically to grasp, to possess, to communicate experience. Accordingly, that is good language, good English, which, on the one hand, most fully realizes one's own

---

[1] Ballard, Chapters 9, 10, 11; Fries, Chapter 1 (an unusually good statement); Fries, *The Teaching of English* (Ann Arbor, 1949) Chapter 5; Otto Jespersen, *Mankind, Nation and Individual from a Linguistic Point of View* (Oslo, 1925), Chapter 5; Krapp, Chapter 13, The Morals of Good English and Chapter 5, A Touchstone for English; Pooley, Part I.

impressions, and, on the other, is most completely adapted to the purposes of any particular communication.—C. C. FRIES, *What Is Good English?* p. 120

In other words, so far as the language used furthers the writer's intended effect, it is good; so far as it fails to further that effect, it is bad, no matter how "correct" it may be.

2b. Further limits of Good English set by social attitudes. A person can make his meaning clear—at least if he doesn't try to convey too complex matters—in any of several varieties of English, but, in any variety of English, he cannot meet on an equal footing all levels of society. For various historical and social reasons vulgate is frowned on in many quarters, though it works well enough in others. The use of what we have called informal and formal English is one of the requirements for admission to the "upper" social classes, along with certain expectations in income, living quarters, dress. A person of sufficient intelligence and experience may be laughed at or snubbed because his speech is not quite what is expected in a social circle in which he wishes to move.

Informal and formal English is the language of business, science, and literature, of public affairs in general. It deserves perhaps to be called "standard English," as Professor Fries defines it:

> On the whole, however, if we ignore the special differences that separate the speech of New England, the South, and the Middle West, we do have in the United States a set of language habits, broadly conceived, in which the major matters of the political, social, economic, educational, religious life of this country are carried on. To these language habits is attached a certain social prestige, for the use of them suggests that one has constant relations with those who are responsible for the important affairs of our communities. It is this set of language habits, derived originally from an older London English, but differentiated from it somewhat by its independent development in this country, which is the "standard" English of the United States. Enough has been said to enforce the point that it is "standard" not because it is any more correct or more beautiful or more capable than other varieties of English; it is "standard" solely because it is the particular type of English which is used in the conduct of the important affairs of our people. It is also the type of English used by the *socially acceptable* of most of our communities and insofar as that is true it has become a social or class dialect in the United States.[1]

The attention given to eliminating vulgate expressions and encouraging the formal and informal levels of usage in schools and colleges is intended to help young people prepare themselves to take

[1] C. C. Fries, *American English Grammar*, published by Appleton-Century-Crofts, Inc. Copyright, 1940, National Council of Teachers of English and Charles C. Fries.

their part in public affairs, to speak and write for people who are more or less educated and so to continue or broaden their range of possible social contacts. Writing in composition courses is practice for later work in college and after college.

At the lowest level this social pressure means conforming to the conventional grammar of those who carry on public affairs, especially as it appears in books and periodicals. Even if students have not been in the habit of using this sort of language at home, they have had by the time they enter college several years of school instruction in the words and forms and constructions expected in "standard English." The instruction may vary among schools, and some of it may be antiquated, but no college student can truthfully say that he hasn't been exposed to it. If he doesn't write complete sentences, if he doesn't make his pronouns match their antecedents, and if he is guilty of other elementary lapses from the language of educated people, he should realize that the fault is principally his. He should take the responsibility for overcoming this handicap—not rely on a teacher to take it for him—so that he can enter the more or less educated class without attracting unpleasant attention to his speaking and writing. If he has already mastered these "minimum essentials," he can go on to the more interesting and important considerations involved in speaking and writing reputable English.

2c. Personal, editorial, and puristic standards. Since people write under varying conditions and for varying purposes, there are different standards, or approaches to answering questions about particular words or forms or constructions.

1) PERSONAL. In writing for himself or for intimates, a person follows pretty much his own impulses, adapting general usage to his needs of the moment. In notes and other private papers, economy and convenience are usually of prime importance; individual and standard short cuts (abbreviations and symbols, dashes for punctuation) can be used if they do not make later reference difficult. In a familiar letter the writer may employ the usual short cuts or invent ones of his own, use his favorite words, experiment with any aspect of language—even to the point of mystifying his correspondent. The writer may prefer British spelling or super-simplified spelling; colloquial expressions may appear side by side with formal, elegant words.

Such writing reflects the writer himself, or at least the sense of himself that he wishes to project. Individual experiment is one of the ways in which language is refreshed (as by James Joyce). But obviously it is not necessary to write handbooks or plan composition courses for the exercise of individual whims, nor is it possible to train for any basic individuality. While no specific advice can be given, perhaps one word of caution should be spoken. We should watch, even in our personal writing, that we don't become careless and sloppy to the point of handicapping our use of our materials and perhaps of treating our best friends and closest relatives with a carelessness they do not deserve. Immediate needs, one's self-respect, and consideration for others, then, are the guides in personal usage.

2) EDITORIAL. The "standards" for writing that is to go to strangers or to a public are set by editors and publishers who hire copy and proofreaders to enforce these rulings. Since publishers set great store by consistency, they select, sometimes arbitrarily, one practice from among those current and "edit" manuscripts to conform to this "style," no matter how reputably written they may be. There is considerable range in printed styles, newspapers generally being the most simple and informal and (according to Norman Lewis in *Harper's Magazine* for March 1949) the women's magazines the most puristic. Book publishers vary a good deal and now frequently follow a writer's preference in usage; fiction is likely to be freest in style and academic books the strictest.

The range, then, of written usage is set by what is found in reputable periodicals and books. This usage is reported in dictionaries, stylebooks, and other reference books on language, though these tend to present the more formal practices. This *Writer's Guide and Index* takes the position that any edited style is suitable for college writing, but that some styles are more appropriate to certain conditions and subjects than others: informal practices for narratives of personal experience and most communications of young people; more formal usage for academic work like term papers. The statements in this book about particular items of usage are intended to help a writer select among forms that are current in edited matter.

3) PURISTIC. There has been a tendency for textbooks to repeat each other and so keep alive recommendations for a usage after it has become outmoded (for example, the use of *shall* and *will*, or the subjunctive); and some people tend to remove speech and writing from the realm of natural behavior by giving precedence to "rules." It is of course an individual's right to assume for himself any conception of the language that he may wish, no matter how limited, but it is not his right to insist on his own choice for others when

it differs from the prevailing patterns of educated usage. A good deal of academic instruction in the past and some published writing seem to be in a dead language. This ultraformal usage is not the proper basis for course instruction, and its method of stressing rules is contrary to language practice. It is consequently discouraged in this book. Good usage in a composition course is the same as good usage outside.

Standards of writing are not a mystery nor a matter of prejudice; they have a history and a definite and discernible source in public practices. Any particular point regarding usage can be investigated and a choice made among any variations found. Even when limited to published usage, English offers considerable variety and plenty of opportunities for choice. Since Good English is English that serves the definite intention of a person to communicate something to a certain person or group, the answer to most questions of usage can be found by considering the appropriateness of the word or expression to the immediate purpose. This appropriateness is threefold: to the purpose and situation, to the expected listeners or readers, and to the speaker or writer himself. Considering these will yield *principles*, rather than *rules*, to guide the actual writing.

3. Appropriateness to purpose and situation

In conversation we automatically adjust our language as well as our topics to the situation in which we find ourselves. Similarly, talks and papers take on a tone, whether they are assigned or voluntary. The language of an informational paper for a general audience will be somewhat different from that of the discussion of an idea, or from that of a plea for action. The tone of the language depends chiefly on the *level of usage* and on the *personal* or *impersonal* quality of the style.

3a. Choice of level of usage. In Chapter 2 we noted several typical uses of formal, informal, and vulgate English. Good judgment in choice of the appropriate level is one of the signs of a practiced and mature writer.

1) IN GENERAL SPEAKING AND WRITING. Slang may fit in a letter or in a popular newspaper column; it is probably out of place in discussing a serious or elevated subject. A talk to a general audience would usually be informal. Most fiction is informal. Writing by and

for people in the professions (teachers, doctors, lawyers, various scientific and scholarly workers) is more likely to be formal. Textbooks have been dominantly formal, though now that they are being written more with the student readers in mind, they are somewhat less so. The language of a church service and of religious and philosophical discussion is formal, though some revivalists and others capitalize on obvious contrast with the usual tone. A political talk may be full of words that appeal to feeling and perhaps to prejudice and may show an elaborate "oratorical" style of sentence that has been abandoned in most situations.

Obviously a person needs to know the styles that are typical of the sort of speaking or writing that he is to do. He shouldn't try to write for a magazine he has never read, or try to write a technical report without having seen one, or try any type of speaking or writing with which he is unfamiliar. If he is faced with such a task, he should try in every way to find what is typically done—and follow that as a general suggestion unless he has good reason for some other usage. This means that part of the preparation for a new sort of writing is attentive reading of some good examples of that writing.

2) IN A COMPOSITION COURSE. Students in a composition course face a slightly different problem from that of a writer for publication, since most of their writing is primarily for practice. The language of both the teacher and the students in a college classroom is naturally somewhat more formal than the language of either is outside. The level of usage expected in themes will generally be defined by the instructor, in line with the practices and purposes of the institution. Usually the tone, as well as the method of work and the type of content, will be illustrated by readings, which can set an example for the usage expected. Unless the nature of an assignment specifically calls for formal style, as in a research or term paper, the usual goal in a composition course is informal English, because it is the most generally useful type of English.

For students (for all writers, for that matter) the chief consequence of paying attention to appropriateness to situation is the resolve *to treat simple subjects simply*, or, in terms of our levels of usage, to treat them informally. Most subjects are relatively simple, or at least the writer is going to give only a simplified version of them. Their interest and their importance are quite lost when the language is too formal. Amateur writers are often not content to be themselves but assume a dialect that is really foreign to them, too formal to be appropriate to them or to their subjects. A boy with a few shrewd remarks to make on modern suicides began this way:

> Through the ages, people have been accustomed to making a premature departure from this "vale of tears" by manifold means. Some favored hanging or a certain type of strangulation; others have been partial to poison, gunshot, or any of a variety of other methods.
>
> However, during recent years a radical change has occurred in the gentle art of self-elimination. This has been due in a large part to the advent of tall buildings. They are seemingly attracted by a strange fascination for the height in combination with a desire to put a spectacular end to their relations with this world.

He may seriously have believed that this kind of writing was better than saying in some simple way that hanging, poisoning, and shooting have given way to jumping off tall buildings, and then going directly into his subject. He might even object to being told that his sentences were bad English, worse perhaps than if they had contained actual vulgate expressions. The errors could be quite easily corrected, but these inflated and pompous paragraphs must be completely rewritten to be acceptable.

Perhaps the influence of teachers led a student to write:

> No more did I have to answer the demands of motorists, nor come home tired, dirty, and filled with pent-up emotions which I dared not loose during the day.

He will soon see that such formal idioms as *no more did I have to answer* (perhaps for *I no longer had to answer* or *Now I didn't have to wait on cranky motorists*) and *which I dared not loose* are too formal for a typical young person's account of a summer's work in a gas station.

Teachers and students will not always agree in their judgments of particular passages, though they will agree on a surprising number of them. But once students understand the principle of appropriateness, they will never return to such unnecessary pomposity. It will be as natural to write informally about a personal experience as it is to talk informally about it. They will soon come to appreciate the simple appropriateness of this account of an interview with a dean:

> "I guess you're next, son," he said, motioning me into his office. Walking to a chair he had pointed out beside his desk, I sat down. "Well," he said, leaning way back in his swivel chair with his hands folded across his waist, "what seems to be your trouble?" "The trouble, sir, is that I have a couple of Fs as you already know." He didn't smile so I'm sorry I said that. Pulling out my deficiency report from a pile on his desk he read it with

frowning eye-brows. Looking up at me he said, "How much studying have you been doing?" "Practically none, sir," I said in a weak cracking voice. Laying down the report he started in on a long speech on studying. He looked me straight in the eye and I tried to glare back at him but couldn't. I shook my head every once in a while and said "That's right," to show him that I was listening. He went on to explain how I should make out a time schedule and stick to it, how I should write out notes on little cards and carry them around with me so that I could review them at spare moments, outline this and outline that. Go to your professors and ask them for suggestions—they'll tell you how and what to study, get your tutor to help you. After he had finished, he got up, slapped me on the back and said, "So, son, get down to work and you'll pull through all right." "Thank you, sir, and good-day," I said as I rushed out of the office. Back to my room I slowly plodded, hands shoved deep in my pockets, chin on my chest, feeling very guilty indeed. Slumping into my chair I lit my pipe and began to think. "Gotta get down to work," I thought. "Guess I'll start—next week."

In a composition course, and out of one, keep a formal style for complex and elevated subjects; write naturally and informally of ordinary matters. If you know the tone and level that are appropriate for the piece of writing you are doing, this advice is relatively easy to follow. You can settle most problems of appropriateness to subject and situation for yourself simply by considering what the usual tone is in such articles.

3b. Choice between personal and impersonal styles. Somewhat related to the level of usage is the degree to which a speaker or writer includes himself in his communication. This is more than the presence of *I*, for a personal style, at least in these days, tends to be informal and to include more individual traits of language, and an impersonal style tends to be more formal.

Obviously conversation among friends, accounts of personal experience, and "personal essays" involve the speaker or writer directly, and any attempt to avoid using *I* or to take out turns of expression with personal associations will make the style distant and dull. Much of the production of writers who have a regular following of readers, such as newspaper columnists and regular reviewers of books, plays, and movies, will be distinctly personal. Conceited people will overuse *I*, but anyone with only an average concern for himself needn't worry about this tendency, even when he is talking about himself.

The types of writing that are usually impersonal include editorials, most serious discussions of situations and of ideas, and all sorts of academic and professional writing, compilations of facts, reports, term papers, dissertations. Students usually do rather well in personal writing, but need practice in impersonal phrasing. It seems easier to begin a research paper on cancer with a personal note:

> I have chosen cancer for my subject because I have decided to make medicine my life's work, and because cancer is one of the most dreadful and baffling diseases known to the medical profession. Several of my family have died of cancer and I didn't know whether it was hereditary, so I decided to find out. A positive cure has not been found as yet, nor has a positive cause . . .

In an impersonal paper, points such as those in the first two sentences in this example, if they are to be given at all, should be in a prefatory note. The paper should begin with some striking and important fact about the subject itself. The reader knows that the writer has gathered the material and selected what suits his purpose (as, for example, in this book). That can be taken for granted, and if the statements are reasonable, if they do not outrun the evidence, no objections will be raised.

Some conventional devices are handy in impersonal writing, like the editorial "we," "the writer believes," "in the opinion of the writer." These should not be used when a more personal expression would be appropriate, but if they cannot be easily avoided they are better than weak passive constructions or the colorless "one," or subterfuges like "many believe," "it seems." In a typical formal and impersonal fashion, the following paragraph gives the writer's conclusions from a study of the spelling bee. (Footnotes giving evidence for facts are omitted here.)

> In the first half of the nineteenth century, spelling bees developed naturally to meet an educational need felt by the populace, and they may be counted as a genuine folk institution. The community participated without social barriers, in a fashion typical of democratic American social conditions. The revivals in recent years have often had an artificial, nostalgic quality, as when Webster's "Blue-Backed Speller" is selected as the authority and the caller of words is referred to as the "schoolmaster." From the educational point of view, the bees have had severe critics and few defenders. Nevertheless, they are significant not only socially but linguistically. They take rank among the conservative influences in American speech. They are a factor that helps to account for the prevalence of spelling pronunciations in the United States and for a central body of speech that does not yield to passing fashions. Spelling bees have been not only a mechanism of adjustment to the heavy burden of arbitrary English spelling, but also a determination of the course taken by the language.—ALLEN WALKER READ, "The Spelling Bee," *PMLA*, June 1941, pp. 511-12

3c. Consistency in tone. It is obvious that the tone of a passage should be consistent unless the writer has special reason for departing from it. The lines between the levels of usage cannot be drawn precisely, but a conspicuous lapse from formal to informal or from informal to formal should ordinarily be avoided. The next two examples illustrate obvious and awkward lapses:

Formal to informal: If our Concert and Lecture program this year is not superior to that of any other college in the country, *I'll eat every freshman lid on the campus.*

Informal to formal: *I was quite bowled over* by the speed with which the workmen assembled the parts.

A characteristic of vigorous styles is a wide range of usage, in both words and constructions. H. L. Mencken and *The New Yorker* and many columnists often fuse slang and colloquialisms with formal and even distinctly bookish words. The expressions are unified by the vigor and naturalness with which they are brought together, and are not lapses from appropriateness. Consistency is not so important as the fundamental appropriateness to the situation. But, in general, informal writing should be kept informal, and personal too, if it is personal; and formal writing should be kept formal, and impersonal if it is impersonal.

4. Appropriateness to listener or reader

If you are trying to reach a particular type of reader, you will adjust both your subject matter and your expression to him. To reach him, really to get your points across, you have to be more than merely intelligible; you have to meet him pretty much on his own ground. You already do this automatically in your letters, writing in somewhat different ways to different persons. You no doubt adjust your expression to the expectations of different teachers. Certainly in many other situations you pay some attention to the language you believe is expected of you, as you do to the dress and conduct you believe are expected of you in meeting certain people.

Certain types of writing are in theory completely adjusted to their readers, notably newspaper writing and advertising. Although we realize that both often fail, either from cheapness or from dullness and unintended formality, in a general way they do meet their readers. An advertisement for an expensive car is not written in the same style as one for a cheaper make, and the same product is presented differently in magazines of different appeal, especially if the appeals are to different income groups.

Trying to write without knowing who will read your words is discouraging. That is one reason why themes are sometimes difficult to write and why it is better for a student to try to visualize some particular audience, to direct his paper to some magazine, or, more commonly, to write for the class of which he is a member. Directing his paper to the members of his class will help him select material that will interest and inform them or at least will appeal to a certain part of the group, and it will help him judge what words and what kinds of sentences are appropriate. Remember that you are not writing for everyone, but for a selected audience. Novels are for readers of differing tastes, and even the audiences of best sellers like *The Robe* and *The Wall* are not identical. For practice work in which you can choose your level of style, a firm informal style is probably best, for many people prefer it and anyone can be reached through it.

Considering the listener or reader leads to language that is clear, correct, and lively.

4a. Clearness. Since your aim is to convey some fact or opinion or fancy or feeling to a person or a group, appropriateness to a reader means clear expression. This means clear, exact words, and for the most part words that lie within the knowledge of the person you are addressing. If the subject requires words that may not be familiar to him, their meaning can usually be made clear from the way they are used, or you can throw in a tactful explanation, or in extreme instances resort to formal definition or even a glossary. Words whose suggestion may be unpleasant to a reader should be avoided, as a matter of tact: *contact, *proposition in situations outside business, slang in formal contexts, and so on. Keeping in mind what courtesy demands will settle many questions.

Clarity also requires careful sentence construction. Readers of more education or at least of more experience in reading can take more elaborate sentences than those who read little or who will read hurriedly. But anyone will be pleased with direct, straightforward sentences.

4b. Correctness. A large part of a beginning writer's adaptation to a reader is avoidance of errors and of other matters that might offend. People tend to judge us by superficial traits, in language as in other matters. Spelling, for example, bulks larger in most people's judgment of writing than it reasonably should. Certainly many people take delight in finding what are (or what they consider are) errors in language, especially in the writing or speech of those supposed to be educated or of anyone who is soliciting their favor. Again courtesy demands that a writer does his best in anything he is submitting to another; small slips show carelessness that is a sign of discourtesy. Soiled manuscript, many interlineations, confusion of common forms like *its* and *it's*, *they're* and *their*, *affect* and *effect*, misspelling common words (*similiar* for *similar*) are ordinarily the result of carelessness or thoughtlessness. They show that the writer just isn't bothering, that he is not doing as well as he easily could, and so they are really an insult to his reader. A teacher has sympathy for honest confusion and for real lack of knowledge, but he will seldom bother to read beyond a few lines of a manuscript that is conspicuously careless. The chief reason for mastering the "minimum essentials" of English forms is to meet the expectations of educated readers. You should not worry about these small matters as you write but reserve some time for revision to bring the paper to the best state you are capable of.

4c. Liveliness. There is so much unavoidable dullness in the world that any reader (and especially any theme reader) will appreciate some liveliness in writing, in the expression as well as in the material. Striving for novelty is dangerous and its results are often offensive. But frequently students in their teens hide behind a flat sort of language, squeeze all the life out of their writing until it sounds as though it was written by someone three times their age (and asleep at that). The words do not need to be out of the ordinary but just those that might be used in a reasonably active conversation. The sentences should not be formless or allowed to drag but should suggest an alert interest. Reference to things people do and say, plenty of lively detail to demonstrate ideas fully and to keep up interest, all help. Interest is especially important in beginnings and endings. A plan that gains attention at once and carries on the subject by natural stages is merely an extension of the smaller considerations for a reader.

Some professional writers have set themselves this rule: "Don't write anything you couldn't read yourself." Following this rule means that you will choose your best available material, write it as interestingly and as carefully as you can, make it as genuinely readable as you can. If you promise yourself that you will not turn in a paper that you couldn't read yourself with interest and perhaps profit, you will be taking the responsibility for your work, doing composition of actual college grade—and you will be permanently improving your control of expression, laying a sure foundation for continued growth in Good English.

In general, satisfy your reader's expectations insofar as you believe they are worthy of respect. One warning is needed: Don't aim at your reader's worst, compromising yourself and insulting him. Visualize him in his better moments and write for him as he is then.

5. Appropriateness to speaker or writer

In the speaker-listener or writer-reader relationship, the speaker or writer actually dominates. He makes the choices; his judgment or unconscious sense of fitness finally controls.

> The speech-usage of each one of us is constantly swinging backwards and forwards between the demands of society, and an individual expression of his momentary needs. . . . The more commonplace a person is, the more will his language bear the stamp of the community in which he lives: the more unique his nature, the more peculiarly his own will be the colouring of his language.—OTTO JESPERSEN, *Mankind, Nation and Individual from a Linguistic Point of View*, pp. 131, 204

This quotation points up the fact that a person's language in the long run represents his personality, and it also suggests that the individual is finally responsible for the language he uses. To take this responsibility he first needs to make every effort to inform himself of the possibilities of English, by observing what is actually spoken and written, by using dictionaries and other reference works, by consulting people who have studied English as a language. Then he can apply this information in his own work according to his best judgment. There is nothing mysterious about the matter; it is just a natural process of learning and applying what is learned.

The most important step in the early stages of considering how to improve your language habits is to watch your own speech and your own writing to see what their good qualities are and what shortcomings they may have. Do you feel the need for more information about language? Can you pronounce with confidence the words you need in conversation? Do you have trouble with any of the mechanics of writing—spelling, punctuation, sentence structure? Does your language tend to be formal or is it predominantly informal? Do you rely much on slang or on trite words, or do you lapse into vulgate expressions? When you talk or write to someone older than yourself, or when you write a paper for a college course, do you choose the best part of your natural language or do you assume an entirely different sort of English?

And finally, is the language you use consistent with the rest of your conduct? Does your language in conversation represent your better self, or do you on occasion speak beneath yourself, or on other occasions affect a more pretentious speech than is natural to you? If you are a rather casual person, informal in dress and manner, we should expect your English also to be informal; if you are conventional in dress and manner, we should expect your English to be more formal. It is necessary for you also to realize the direction in which you are moving, for young people, especially in college, are changing, becoming more flexible in their ideas and manners or becoming more positive and conventional, or making some other change. Their language should be moving similarly. In a student's first papers in a composition course he should write as naturally as he can, so that both he and his teacher can see the present state of his language and so that they can decide together on the direction his growth should take. Such growth will be in the direction of increasing sincerity, of greater appropriateness to himself.

This sincerity in usage and style is one of the conspicuous traits of the better contemporary writing. The English that we find in print is the English the writer would use in talking with his friends, tightened up a little and shorn of the irregularities that usually creep into talk, but still fundamentally informal. He does not appear at a distance, on a platform delivering an oration at us, but seems rather to be talking with us. We can come close to his mind as it actually works. In discussing "The New Way of Writing," Mr. Bonamy Dobrée, an English critic, says: "One would like to think that all of us will come to the stage of refusing to write what we would not, indeed could not, say, though that, of course, is not to limit our writing to what we actually do say." (*Modern Prose Style,* p. 229.)

As a result of this approach to Good English you should have confidence in writing. The greatest handicap in writing is fear—fear of pencil and paper, fear of making a mistake, fear of offending the reader's (teacher's) taste. The opposite attitude, cockiness, is a nuisance and equally prevents good writing, but not so many students suffer from that as from inhibitions about their language. Psychologists can't tell us much about the mental activity involved in thinking or writing, but some of them believe that the fundamental condition for effectiveness is a positive feeling of readiness—which amounts really to a sort of faith that when we open our mouths or prepare to write, something appropriate to the occasion will come. A wide knowledge of the possibilities of current English, backed up by sufficient practice in writing for definite readers, should increase your confidence. Only with some such courage can you write your best and give that extra something that places your writing above bare competency, that makes it really Good English.

It is obvious that the three sorts of appropriateness here suggested for arriving at good English will not always be in harmony. When they conflict, the solution will have to come through the writer's judgment. The subject may seem to demand words that are not appropriate to the reader. The writer can usually solve such a problem, either by finding simpler words or by explaining the necessary but unfamiliar ones. The reader's expectation and the writer's natural manner of expression may be different. Such a conflict can be solved only by the writer—deciding how essential to his purpose his own turns of expression are, whether he can gracefully yield to the reader's expectation or whether his usage is so necessary to his sense of his subject that compromise is impossible. In the long run the writer's sense of fitness, his pride in his work, a craftsman's pride, will resolve most such conflicts.

Good English, then, is not primarily a matter of rules but of judgment. A speaker or writer is not struggling up under a series of prohibitions but is trying to discover among the magnificent resources of modern English what best suits his purposes. His desire to communicate something to another is fundamental; it sets the limits beyond which he will not ordinarily go. This general limitation is made more specific by considering whether the level of usage and the particular expressions are appropriate to the subject and the situation, to the expected readers, and finally and most important, to the writer himself.

Suggested study and writing

These exercises provide additional practice in observing usage and style, and opportunity to judge the appropriateness of different kinds of writing. Exercises 1 through 4 may be used for discussion in the classroom; 5 and 6 for individual discussion with the instructor; and 7, 8, and 9 for written assignments.

1. Copy a passage of 400-600 words which you would like to have your own writing resemble. Be prepared to comment on its use of words, its sentence length and sentence movement, its level of language, and any other qualities which strike you. One good way to improve your writing is to copy writing you like and also to read it aloud.

2. The following paragraphs are from themes written at the beginning of a freshman composition course. Read them carefully to determine the level of usage and the appropriateness of the language in each passage. Point out specific flaws, including changes in style or tone within the paragraphs, and revise unsatisfactory passages for greater clarity and effectiveness. Which paragraphs seem to you most effective? Which seem least satisfactory? Would you say that bad English is something besides "mistakes" in spelling and grammar?

1. While perusing the text assigned for this course, the writer was looking for some unforeseen specific study aids that would assist him in his educational endeavors. For, by the time a student has reached the age of maturation which allows him to compete in higher scholastic endeavor, he must realize and be acutely aware of his innumerable poor study habits and weaknesses. It is this correspondent's impression, therefore, that much of the material and space of the present text under consideration was wasted in orientating the reader to the very obvious facts of his own already known inadequacies.

2. Although I believe in work, I do not believe in labor for the sake of labor. Life, in reality, is extremely short. I feel that it should be spent in taking as much pleasure from existence as possible. I am not attending college because I desire to become an intellectual; instead, I am here to increase my earning capacity so that I may lead a successful and happy life. Hence one can see why I don't go for this esthetic stuff. It's great to know Dante, Goethe, Kant and Spinoza, but how far will it get you in a tennis match or a business office? Schopenhauer may have been brilliant, but he died crazy. His name lives after him, sure, but what is that to Arthur, who isn't around to enjoy his fame?

3. I had the opportunity, while working at a resort last summer, to observe the practice of tipping and to talk with people who tipped and those who didn't. During this time I made some interesting discoveries, including the fact that the wealthiest people aren't necessarily the ones who leave the biggest tips. From my experience, I think tippers may be divided into four main classes: the No-tip type, the Ten-center, the Straight Ten-percenter, and the High tipper. The people who fall in these various groups show remarkably similar characteristics.

Take the first type for instance, the No-tippers. These people are of two kinds: those who forget to tip and those who can't afford it. In the first group are apt to be successful business men with a great deal on their minds, who simply fail to remember to tip. And the second kind, the ones who can't afford it, are mostly high school youngsters, or young married couples who happen to be a little short on cash.

4. As viewed through the eyes of a premedical student and potential doctor, the definite disadvantages of specialization in education in college far exceed any possible advantages. This viewpoint is no doubt brought about by the fact that medical schools in general prefer a well-rounded premedical course, rather than one that is characterised by excessive specialization in the sciences. Perhaps too, if the student has an analytical mind, he will see that extreme specialization while he is attending college will not only deny him a general knowledge of other subjects equally important, but it will also, at the same time, tend to limit his viewpoint toward his scientific subjects.

5. Frequent parties and new faces filled most of my daily existence, but being a simple soul at heart, I soon began to tire of these things, but to whom could I turn? Everyone else was too engrossed in monetary activities to give me any diversion. At this point I would like to state that I am not what is commonly known as a party "pauper" or a "kill-joy"; however, there are times when something else besides the wild life of the care-free fraternity "play-boy" should be taken up.

6. As I sit here this evening, with my tomes of learning stacked six deep around me, I come to the conclusion that my inadequate mind hasn't the wisdom to construct a manuscript of literature on the topic assigned for this composition. Consequently, I sit here thinking incoherently, wondering whether the consequences will be for the better or worse, if I turn over this masterpiece(?) to the English Dept. In the last page and a half I have wandered precariously from Greek philosophies to feeble-minded school girls. When this you read, you will realize that the writer of this theme will progress upwards as there is no other way to go.

7. One of the greatest mistakes parents can make in bringing up their children is to bestow upon them an overabundance of material substances, meanwhile gravely neglecting personal sacrifices. By this I mean that a person who gives his offspring everything that wealth can buy and yet is too selfish to spend any time on love or on the child, has missed the boat completely.

3. Select one or two of your textbooks and make a study of the way in which they are written. Discuss the merits or defects that you find in the writing of each text. Do the authors seem to be writing for students of your educational level, or for readers whose knowledge of the subject is greater than yours? Bring in passages you find hard to understand, and try to decide whether the difficulty is due to the style of writing, to the language used, or to the complexity or unfamiliarity of the ideas. Comment also on passages you consider well written.

4. Read *Foreign Words in English. Keep a list of foreign words and phrases that you encounter in your reading or that you hear in classroom lectures and elsewhere. Notice particularly those terms italicized in print or pronounced as foreign words. With each entry, describe briefly the context in which the word occurred: *couturier*, for example, might appear in an ad for women's fashions; *décor* in an article on interior decorating; *sauté* in a cookbook; *laissez-faire* in a history lecture; *déjà vue* in a psychology textbook. When you have gathered sufficient examples, prepare to discuss the appropriateness of the expressions with reference to the situation in which they occurred and to the intended audience. What English equivalents would you suggest for the foreign words that seem inappropriately used?

5. Analyze and prepare to discuss your speaking and writing habits on the basis of the following questions:

a) What different levels of English do you use and under what circumstances do you use each—in the classroom, on the campus, at home; in writing done for different courses; in formal letters and in personal correspondence?

b) At what language level do you feel most successful in speaking? In writing? When you are obliged to use other levels, do you find it easy or difficult to make the shift?

c) How would you describe your characteristic level of usage? Is it appropriate to your personality and temperament?

d) What comments and criticisms have you received on your writing? Of these comments, which have been most valuable and helpful to you? Have you ever been corrected in your speaking, and do you ever correct others?

e) What in your opinion are the characteristic marks of "Good English"?

6. On your next paper put a concise but definite statement of the audience it is intended for. Do not generalize; word your statement to indicate clearly the readers' backgrounds or special interests, putting it, for instance, in terms of a specific periodical. Discuss the usage and style you employ in the paper under the heads of the three sorts of appropriateness. Your instructor, in correcting your paper, will take into account two points: the soundness of your purpose and the extent to which you have carried it out.

7. Select one magazine from one of the groups below—your instructor may suggest alternatives to the publications listed—and prepare a report on the usage and general tone of the magazine. Determine whether the usage is predominantly formal or informal. Comment on any variations in usage you may find in the magazine, the educational and social levels of the audience for which the magazine is intended, and the appropriateness or inappropriateness of the writing both to the subjects discussed and to the readers of the magazine. Do you find any evidence to support Mr. Lewis' statement on page 75 about the puristic editorial standards in women's magazines?

    1. Magazines of general interest: *The Atlantic Monthly, Coronet, The Saturday Evening Post, Time.*
    2. Women's magazines: *Good Housekeeping, Harper's Bazaar, Mademoiselle, Ladies' Home Journal.*
    3. Magazines written primarily for men: *Field and Stream, Fortune, The Nation's Business, Scientific American.*
    4. Professional or semitechnical publications: *Architectural Forum, Étude, Today's Health, College English.*

8. Analyze the writing of a well-known columnist: H. V. Kaltenborn, Walter Lippmann, Drew Pearson, Westbrook Pegler, Mrs. Eleanor Roosevelt, Robert Ruark, Dorothy Thompson, Walter Winchell, or any other your instructor may suggest. Characterize the level of usage and the style of writing, the columnist's attitude toward his readers, and the appropriateness of the language to the subjects discussed. What are your impressions of the columnist's personality as it is reflected in his writing?

9. Compare full length reviews of a recent book in several magazines and newspapers. If necessary, consult the *Book Review Digest* for names and dates of the publications in which the reviews appeared. Describe in each instance the general tone of the review (it might be flippant or sympathetic, witty or serious), the attitude of the reviewer toward the book, and the type of audience for which the review was written. Comment on any differences of opinion among the reviewers about the author's style.

Problems in English grammar

English grammar is the English way of saying things.—George O. Curme

Mrs. Nettie M. Weismeyer said that one reason why she had shot her husband was that he used bad grammar.—Time Magazine

It is, methinks, a very melancholy consideration that a little negligence can spoil us, but great industry is necessary to improve us.—Sir Richard Steele

C OLLEGE STUDENTS and the great majority of college graduates find themselves in situations in which Good English (in the terms of Chapter 2, the formal and informal levels rather than vulgate) is generally used. They intend to speak and write as their social circumstances warrant, and in general they succeed in doing so. They hope to use "Correct English," which means actually expression that conforms to editorial expectations, that is appropriate to communicating with more or less educated people, appropriate to carrying on "public affairs" of business, government, literature, education, and so on.

But because of the varied usage within the broad extent of the English language a good many choices exist, and there are a number of forms and constructions that are especially likely to raise questions —among professional writers as well as among college students. The greater part of our language raises no questions at all—fortunately— but the part that does is likely to be conspicuous and easily spotted by others. We are not speaking here of mere laziness or carelessness, like writing *to* for *too*, *quiet* for *quite*, or the omission of let-

RELATED CHAPTERS AND ARTICLES: *Other topics treating elementary correctness are discussed in:*

ters or little words in writing. Nor are we speaking of genuinely *divided usage, in which alternate reputable forms of expression exist within the area of Good English: spellings like *cigaret—cigarette, traveler—traveller,* or verb forms like *dived—dove,* or the choice between verbs in "If we go tomorrow"—"If we are going tomorrow," or in "If he was only a little taller"—"If he were only a little taller." These choices are matters of style rather than of correctness and depend on appropriateness to the writer's own usage in a particular piece of writing.

But our "mistakes" also come because of differing usage that exists within our language—we invent very few of them. They occur when we use a word or construction that is generally regarded as out of place in educated writing. They occur because of the differences (1) between spoken and written usage; (2) between different levels of usage; and (3) between hypercorrect and ordinary forms.

1) *Between spoken and written usage:* Usage often varies even between informal speech and informal writing. For example, the reference of pronouns is less precise in spoken language than in the

written; most "run-on sentences" are held together by the tone of voice in speaking but conventionally in writing they are "corrected" by the use of conjunctions and punctuation.

2) *Between different levels of usage:* The vulgate verb forms (*was* in the plural of the past tense, past tense forms like *he begun*, and so on) frequently differ from those of formal and informal English; there are some differences in vocabulary between the levels; and some constructions differ, as Good English avoids double negatives, vulgate makes freer use of double prepositions (*outside of, off of*), and all three levels differ from each other in pronoun forms in various constructions and in a number of idioms.

3) *Between hypercorrect and ordinary forms:* Occasionally an unacceptable expression comes as the result of overdoing the effort to be correct, as in the use of *shall* when it is uncalled for, and perhaps even of the *I* in "between you and I," or of the subjunctive in a simple condition.

If you have reached college without forming the habit of using easily and regularly the language expected of you, your first responsibility in a composition course is to make up for lost time. No one can take the responsibility for you—a teacher can only indicate what you should do. You cannot plead ignorance of the more elementary matters, for they have been drilled on in your earlier schooling. A desire to take a proper place in society, or pride in accomplishment, or even a desire for college grades can lead you to do now what you could have done long ago. (Discovering why you did not is perhaps useful, too.)

The steps to becoming sure in these "minimum essentials" (and in more complicated matters, too) are definite and simple:

1) *Be sure you know what is appropriate to Good English; know the form or phrase or construction that is most generally used by educated people.* You learn what is appropriate by listening to conversations and to talks, by reading in books and magazines, by looking points up in a good dictionary or in a reference book such as this. If for some reason you have difficulty with the trouble spots discussed in this chapter, you should concentrate on them and not worry about more complicated matters in which practices may differ, like the use of hyphens, or of the subjunctive. And don't worry about matters that are no longer considered so important as they once were, like the *split infinitive or a *preposition at the end of a sentence. Keep your eye on the practices that are really important, that will attract unpleasant

attention almost anywhere, and know what is expected of you in those.

2) *Practice on the points that you have not mastered* as you would practice a play in a sport or the use of a tool that you want to become skillful with. Exercises in textbooks give some opportunity for this practice. More important is revising your papers according to the corrections and criticisms made on them. Most important of all is revising your papers for all courses before they are handed in. If you know that you are not sure of some particular points—reference of pronouns, spelling, run-on sentences, for example—go over your paper once looking for those particular points alone. Careful proofreading will cut down the number of mistakes surprisingly, for most college students know (or at least suspect) what good usage calls for. Taking the responsibility for your own usage in this way is the quickest road to genuine improvement, and to getting full credit for your progress.

In any systematic effort to cultivate acceptable habits of expression, as in a college composition course, grammar plays a useful if not very large part. The chief aim is improvement in natural and effective communication, in conveying information, opinion, imagination to others. This is the background, the main work of the course, consisting in actually writing papers—*composition*. These papers are to be written in appropriate current *usage*. When it is necessary to group or to discuss these matters of usage we do so in terms of *grammar*, the systematic description of language. This chapter discusses the most common trouble spots of usage in a grammatical setting.

1. Word forms

One way in which the relations between the words within a sentence may be indicated is by the forms of the individual words, in our family of languages chiefly by means of endings (a sound or syllable like *-s* or *-ed*) added to the simple word. Some languages, such as Latin or German, make a great deal of use of such endings, but for centuries English has been simplifying its forms: there are now only four distinctive forms of most verbs (*ask, asks, asking, asked*) where once there were forty. This trend toward simplification is still continuing, in spite of the influence of the schools and of editors.

The relations once indicated by the forms of words are now shown chiefly by other means, especially by a definite *word order and by *function words (prepositions, function verbs like *have, was*). Of the word forms that still change to show relationships, we learn the dominant ones by imitation when we are children and use them later without effort. The few questions we have come because some irregularity has developed in a word's history or because vulgate continues an old form or has developed a different one that is not used in Good English. Some twenty pronoun and verb forms are among the more conspicuous traits of uneducated usage, and consequently great stress is laid on the "correct ones" by educated people.

This section presents chiefly the forms that frequently raise questions. Further details will be found in the *Index* articles indicated by asterisks (*).

1a. Nouns. English nouns—conveniently for us—no longer distinguish in their form between subjects and objects (*Case), so that the only distinctions are for the possessive (genitive) and for plurals.

1) PLURALS. The dominant plural is an *s* or *z* sound added to the singular, spelled *-s* (*books, trees*) or *-es* (*buses, dishes, *Joneses*). Almost the only questions that arise in the *-s* plurals are in their spelling:

a) *Nouns ending in -y* following a consonant have plurals in *-ies* (*babies, cities, companies, ladies*); but if the *-y* follows a vowel the usual *-s* is added (*attorneys*).

b) *Words ending in -o* are a nuisance because their plurals may be spelled *-os* or *-oes* and so have to be remembered individually or looked up: *Filipinos—Negroes, pianos—heroes, sopranos—potatoes.*

c) *Plurals of compound words* are usually normal (*sideboards, player pianos*), although a few in which the key word comes first add the *-s* to that (*heads of state, daughters-in-law*).

d) *The plurals of figures, letters, or words* are written with *-s* or *-'s*, increasingly the first way: *several Fs* (or *F's*), *four 7s* (*7's*), *two thats.*

e) *A few words keep the same form* for both singular and plural: all words in *-ics* (*athletics, politics*) and some others ending in *-s* and rarely used in the singular (*means, measles*); some names of animals (*fish, sheep*); some nouns of measure and number when used as modifiers: *foot* (a six foot wall), *ton* (a two ton truck).

f) *Some plurals surviving from older English* are made by a change of vowel or the ending *-en*, but the words are so common that they cause no trouble except in hasty or careless writing (*man—men, foot—feet, child—children*).

g) Some problems are offered by the *plurals of words borrowed from foreign languages* for which English keeps the foreign forms. The great majority of borrowings have typical plurals (*bureaus, circuses, quotas*) and others are in the process of change, having two forms (*indexes—indices, *formulas—formulae, beaus—beaux*). The Latin forms of a good many words are kept in scientific usage (*antennae* in zoology but *antennas* in radio). **Alumnus* is one of the chief nuisances because both masculine and feminine forms are kept:

For men: Singular, *alumnus;* Plural, *alumni* (ə lum′ nī)
For women: Singular, *alumna;* Plural, *alumnae* (ə lum′ nē)

Further details about plurals and some lists of words will be found in the *Index* article *Plurals.

2) Genitives (Possessives). The other form change in nouns is the addition of -'*s,* or the apostrophe alone if the word already ends in *-s,* to form a genitive case that indicates possession (the *doctor's* medicine case) and some other relations (as in *the first day's hike, the secretary's report, his brother's efforts*). The only problems here are a tendency to forget the apostrophe (which historically represents the *e* of an older ending *-es,* which was added to some nouns); or to be uncertain which side of the *s* the apostrophe goes on; or to hesitate between this *-s* genitive and the alternative one made with the function word *of* (*the rock's face—the face of the rock*).

Only habit and continual watchfulness in proofreading will get the apostrophes all in. The forms themselves are simple:

a) When the word is pronounced with an added sound (*s* or *z*), the spelling is '*s:*

man's   horse's   shirt's   George's

b) When there is no added sound, the apostrophe alone is used. This includes all regular plurals ending in *-s:*

horses'   shirts'   automobiles'   the Barkers'

Increasingly words ending in an *s, sh,* or *z* sound, especially those of one syllable, are written with '*s* to represent the pronunciation of an extra syllable:

Alice's (al′ i siz)   dish's (dish′ iz)   Fritz's (fritz′ iz)

c) The choice between '*s* and the *of* forms depends principally on the sound of the expression and sometimes on the emphasis or on the part of the idea from which the statement is approached. The apostrophe form is somewhat more common with names of and for people and other living things and also when actual possession is indicated, but the *of* form is also used for them, and both forms are used for inanimate objects:

> Professor Schantz' office—the office of Professor Schantz
> the mink's tail—the tail of the mink
> the cupboard's shelves—the shelves of the cupboard
> We finally reached Lawyer Hodge's house.—We finally reached the house of Lawyer Hodge.
> The rock's face was sheer.—We climbed the sheer face of the rock.

A slight preference for one form or the other will usually emerge from a natural reading of a sentence in its context. Often the form used makes no appreciable difference.

Further details of form and use of the genitive will be found in *Genitive case.

1b. Pronouns. Some types of pronouns are quite different from nouns. These differences make up most of our problems in pronoun forms. The large number of "indefinite pronouns," including *all, any, each, everybody, someone* (see *Pronouns, types and forms), are like nouns in that they have no separate form as objects (*Everybody* came. They invited *everybody*.) and are written with *'s* in the genitive (*everybody's, someone's*) or with an *of* form (*of any, of each*). But the very commonly used "personal" and "relative" pronouns have special object and genitive forms.

1) OBJECT AND SUBJECT FORMS. We know the object forms (*me, us, him, her, them, whom*) well enough but sometimes forget to make the distinction between them and the subject forms in a few constructions. One reason for this is that vulgate and even educated conversational usage do not always make the distinction.

a) When a pronoun (usually the first person plural, *we*) is directly joined with a noun, the proper case form should be used:

> Subject: *We children* used to make a wide circle around all the cemeteries.
> Object: They used to terrify *us children*.

b) After forms of the verb *to be*, formal English usually has the subject form, informal English frequently the object form:

> Formal: I was hoping it would be *she*.
> Informal: I was hoping it would be *her*.

Much fuss has been made over the *It's I—It's me* construction. All authoritative grammars now say *It's me* is the usual form, and since it can occur only in a conversational setting, there is no point in trying for the subject form. (See *it's me.)

c) Usage of *who* or *whom* as an object when it precedes the verb or preposition is divided. *Whom* has practically disappeared from the spoken language, so that we naturally and regularly say, "*Who* were you with?" In writing, some editors and teachers try to keep the object form, "*Whom* were you with?" In informal writing the subject form is proper in this kind of construction; in formal writing the object form is preferred. (See *who, whom.) This is one of several small matters of usage that make it important to know in what level you are writing.

d) After prepositions the object form should be regularly used:

> with him and her   *between you and me

2) GENITIVE FORMS. The chief point to remember in the use of genitive forms is that *ours, yours, his, hers, theirs, whose,* and especially *its* are written without an apostrophe. The temptation to use one in *its* is especially strong because *it's,* the contraction of *it is* and *it has,* is also a common word. Getting these spellings straight is a matter of proofreading.

For the genitive of *which, whose* is quite generally used, as well as the more cumbersome *of which*:

> General: A book *whose* author is unknown is less likely to succeed.
> More formal and less usual: A book the author *of which* is unknown is less likely to succeed.

(See *Pronouns, types and forms.)

1c. Adjectives and adverbs. There are few problems of form in adjectives and adverbs, though some adverbs without the typical *-ly* ending and the forms of comparison are worth noting.

1) The typical English adverb is made by adding the *suffix *-ly* to an adjective: *dim, dimly; hurried, hurriedly.* There are some common adverbs, however, which have the same form as the adjective, and have had for centuries. We can say either "Go slow" or "Go slowly"; "Don't talk so loud" or "Don't talk so loudly." In informal English the shorter form is usually preferable unless the phrase sounds better with the *-ly* word.

Vulgate and familiar English tend to drop the *-ly* from adverbs that have not developed reputable short forms, and use such words as *easy* and *real* when written English has *easily* and *really. Special* and *considerable* are found for *specially* and *considerably.* In careful writing use the *-ly* form of these adverbs and others that do not have accepted short forms. A list of the more common of these will be found in *Adverbs, types and forms.

2) There are two standard ways of comparing adjectives and adverbs to show a greater degree of the quality named: by adding *-er* and *-est* to the simple adjective or adverb or by preceding it with *more* or *most*. Short words use either way:

Positive	Comparative	Superlative
crisp	crisper	crispest
	more crisp	most crisp
even	evener	evenest
	more even	most even

Words of three syllables and many of two use only *more* and *most*: *more beautiful, most beautiful; more easily, most easily; more childish, most childish*. When both forms are possible for a word, the choice will ordinarily depend upon sound, though there is a slight difference in emphasis. In the *-er* and *-est* forms the stress tends to be on the quality: *kind*er, *dull*est; with *more* and *most* the emphasis falls more on the degree: *more* kind, *most* dull.

1d. Verbs. The forms of our verbs have been so reduced in number (*ask, asks, asking, asked*) that they raise very few questions, and not many problems occur with verb phrases (*have gone, may go, did see*, and so on) that have replaced old special forms. Even the most irregular ones, **be* and **go*, are so common that we easily get control of them. In writing verbs, the few problems that arise, except for some noted in §1 below, are mostly from careless spelling—misspelling *does* and *doesn't;* or not getting the apostrophe between the *n* and the *t* of the contracted negative forms—*doesn't, shan't, won't;* or using the colloquial *he don't* for *he doesn't*. This section notes a few debatable points and gives some definitions for use later in the chapter.

1) PAST TENSES AND PAST PARTICIPLES. An overwhelming number of English verbs make their past tense and past participle by adding a *d* or *t* sound to the simple (infinitive) form. This sound is ordinarily spelled *-ed* (*asked, hunted, beautified*), but in a few verbs *-t* (*kept, slept, wept*); with some verbs both forms are used (*dreamed— dreamt, kneeled—knelt, spelled—spelt*). In these last examples the *-ed* forms are now the more common. The same form is used for all persons of the past tense (I, you, he, we, you, they *asked*), and vulgate is so consistent in this that it ordinarily uses *was* for both singular and plural, where educated usage is careful to preserve the singular *was* and plural *were*.

A number of "strong verbs" continue to make their pasts by an older method of changing the vowel. Some of these have two forms, either because they are changing to the typical past in -ed or because two forms are current. A few of the more common verbs with some irregularity are:

Infinitive	Past tense	Past participle
awake	awoke—awaked	awoke—awaked
begin	began	begun
*burst	burst	burst
choose	chose	chosen
dive	*dove—dived	dived—dove
drink	drank	*drunk
*eat	ate (eat—pron. et)	eaten (eat)
fly	flew	flown
*get	got	gotten—got
lead (lēd)	led	led
see	saw	seen
shine	shone—shined	shone—shined
sing	sang—sung	sung
slide	slid	slid—slidden
swim	swam—swum	swum
throw	threw	thrown
write	wrote	written

A fuller list of verbs with irregularities will be found in *Principal parts of verbs.

2) SHALL-WILL AND OTHER AUXILIARY VERBS. English expresses future time in a variety of verb constructions: *I am to go, I am going to go, I am about to go, I go* (tomorrow), *I shall* or *will go.* There has been a great deal of argument about the last two forms, the use of *shall* or *will.* All authorities now agree that *will* is in general use with *I* and with all persons, and has been for centuries, but formal usage (enforced by some editors) tries to hold to *I* and *we shall—you, he, they will.* College students should be aware of this distinction, but they do not need to follow the formal usage unless it appeals to them or unless they are expressly told to follow it. (See *shall—will, should—would.)

Similarly formal usage tends to preserve a distinction between *may* (indicating permission) and *can* (indicating ability): You *may* do it if you *can.* But as the dictionaries all record, the distinction has largely been abandoned in actual usage, so that the difference between the two words is largely one of emphasis. (See *can—may.)

By use of a number of other "auxiliaries" or "helping verbs" which are used with the infinitives of particular verbs, English is able to express a considerable variety of shades of meaning or emphasis: consider the series *may, might, could, should, ought, must.*

3) INFINITIVES, PARTICIPLES, GERUNDS. These three forms of verbs combine some verb functions with those of other parts of speech and are here defined for use in discussing various constructions in later sections of this chapter.

a) The *infinitive* is the simple or basic part of a verb, the same as the present tense form: *ask, hide, manipulate.* With or without *to* it combines with auxiliaries and other verbs for a variety of relations: I can *go*, I have *to go*, I would like *to go*. It is used as a noun, still taking an object (*To spear* flounders takes a quick eye and a quick hand). It is used as an adjective or adverb modifier (He had money *to burn*. The feature writer came *to get* material for his story). It also makes a sort of clause with its "subject" (if its "subject" is a pronoun it is in the object form): They were finally getting *him to talk English like a native.*

b) The *present participle* ends in *-ing* and is used in many verb phrases (he *was trying*, he *had been trying*) and as a modifier of a noun or pronoun: *Trying* as hard as he could, *he* still couldn't make it; *Looking* over the whole region, the first *settlers* chose this site for their town. These phrases are often used "absolutely" (as the equivalent of clauses): *Judging by the looks of the floor*, no one had swept it for months. The present participle is also used singly, like an ordinary adjective: the *leaping* deer.

c) The *past participle* ends in *-ed* or occasionally in *-t* (*tried, slept, fabricated*) or shows a vowel change in the strong verbs (*chosen, swung*). It combines with forms of *have* for the past tenses (*has sung, have chosen, had died*) and with forms of *be* for the passive (*was sung, were chosen*). It is used as an adjective (an *overworked* horse; Completely *turned about* in the dark, he floundered in the woods for hours). It makes an abridged clause: His name *linked* too long with shady characters, he couldn't clear himself with words alone.

d) The *gerund* or *verbal noun* ends in *-ing* and is used in all the functions of a noun, though frequently keeping the verbal habit of taking an object: *Sleeping* in that racket was impossible; His habit of *saving* money tided him over; He would not go *fishing*; a *swimming* suit (that is, a suit for swimming, not a suit that swims).

We use these verb forms constantly, whether we can name them or not, and in fact need to name them only when discussing the pattern of the language we are using. When they are used in constructions involving their verb function as well as their adjective, adverb, or noun function, they are frequently called *verbids.

4) SUBJUNCTIVES. A subjunctive form is recognizable in English verbs only in the third person singular present, when the usual -s does not appear (They suggested that he *take* [instead of *takes*] the earlier train) and in forms of *be* (He said it was important that you *be* there). There are only two constructions in which the subjunctive is likely to be used today:

a) *In certain conditions, cautiously made or "contrary-to-fact"*: He wanted to find out whether this condition *were* true; It would be complete if he *were* here [he isn't]; If I *were* you.

b) *After verbs of requesting, suggesting, etc., and impersonal constructions like "It is necessary . . ."*: He requested that everyone *be* in his place five minutes before the bell; It is necessary that a boy *have* some initiative.

The subjunctive, however, is not regularly used in these constructions, even by formal writers. The usual indicative form is used (It would be complete if he *was* here) or an auxiliary (It is necessary that a boy *should have* some initiative) or an infinitive (He requested everyone *to be* in his place five minutes before the bell). In fact, it is quite possible to lead a useful and busy life without ever using a subjunctive, except perhaps in some old formulas like "Heaven help us." (For further details see *Conditions, *Subjunctives.)

5) VERB-ADVERB COMBINATIONS. An important and apparently increasing development in English verbs is the use of a verb plus an adverb to express a meaning not belonging to the two separate words. In *"run down* a hill" the meaning is a literal combination of *run* and *down;* in *"run down* to the store" the *run* and *down* may still be literal, though the running may not be *down* at all; but in *"run down* a pedestrian" or "the clock *ran down*" they are equivalent to different words—to *hit* and to *stop*. Similar combinations are *look into, take over, plug in*, and scores of others. They are especially characteristic of vigorous speech and writing and offer one way to avoid some longish or formal words (as *look into* for *investigate*).

In these constructions the noun following and linked to the verb is the object of the two word verb: *pedestrian*, for instance, is the object of *run down*, not just of *run* or of *down*. The adverb is frequently separated from the verb, and often goes to the end of the construction: There was no outlet to *plug* the heater *into*. (See *Verb-adverb combinations.)

6) LIE—LAY, SIT—SET. These two pairs of verbs are an instance of the tendency of educated or at least written usage to hinder or deny a natural language change. The verb *lie*, to "recline," is going out of use—even in the conversation of educated people—and the verb *lay* is taking over its work, so that it, like so many English verbs, is being used with an object (*Lay it* on the table) and without (He let it *lay* there). But since a good many people are sensitive about keeping the older distinction, it is safer for students still to follow it in their writing:

> Intransitive (without an object): *lie, lay, lain*
> He let it *lie* there. She *lay* down for a nap.
> The boards *had lain* in the sun for months.

> Transitive (with an object): *lay, laid, laid*
> You can *lay it* on the table. They *laid the linoleum* the following week.
> She had *laid it away* for some future use.

(See *lay—lie.)

Much the same situation exists with *sit* and *set*. The formal distinction in their commonest meanings is:

> Intransitive (without an object): *sit, sat, sat*
> Let's *sit* down. They *sat* for over an hour without moving. They *had sat* that way every Sunday morning for years.

> Transitive (with an object): *set, set, set*
> *Set the box* in the corner. He *set out a dozen tomato plants*. They *had set one too many places* at the table.

(See *set—sit.)

Some further details on verb forms, in addition to the articles listed in the text above, may be found in *Index* articles: *Auxiliary verbs, *Linking verbs, *Passive voice, *Split infinitives, *Tenses of verbs, *Transitive and intransitive verbs, *Verbs, *Voice.

2. Subject—verb—object

The larger part of grammar deals not with word forms but with *syntax*, the relations between words in sentences. The verb is the key word in the typical English sentence, with the subject and object or complement the words most closely related to it. Though some pronouns have special forms for the object, the relation between these three elements is shown by their position, by word order. In the typical sentence the subject precedes the verb and is the starting point of the statement (not necessarily the "doer"; see *Passive verbs). The

object ordinarily follows the verb, or if both subject and object precede, the first noun is the object (This *book* [object] *he* [subject] had
written first). In some constructions the order is inverted:

> In questions: *Have you* any kerosene? *Does* [the form-part of the verb]
> *he* expect us to read all that?
> In some conditions (a formal construction): *Had he* known then what
> he knew now, he would have hesitated.
> After emphatic adverbs: Never *have I* seen such a mess.

All these basic matters we pick up early and without conscious
effort. The few trouble spots come from slight complications in a few
particular constructions and from the fact that in several of these,
English tends to make the verbs agree with the meaning rather than
with the form.

2a. Compound subjects. Two or more words, usually connected by a conjunction, are frequently subjects of one verb.

1) Usually the verb with a compound subject is plural:

> *Pat* and *Stan have* the same colored eyes.
> Both the *grammar* and the *style* of advertising *vary* considerably from
> Formal English.

2) When a singular subject is joined by a preposition (*with, together with, as well as*) to a related noun, the agreement depends on
the closeness of the relation. When the added phrase seems closely
related, it is treated as part of a compound subject, and the verb is
plural; when it is loosely related, especially when set off by commas,
the verb is singular:

> Loosely related: That *decision,* as well as other precedents, *was* the decid-
> ing factor in the trial.
> The *lack* of rain, together with late frosts, *is* cutting down the yield.

> Closely related: *The captain with these three teammates were* given the
> credit.
> *The lack of rain together with late frosts are* cutting down the yield.

Formal usage more often than informal uses the singular.

In most sentences of this sort *and* will ordinarily seem a more
natural connective and simpler to handle (taking a plural verb) than
the preposition.

3) When the two words of a compound subject refer to the same
person or thing or otherwise form a unit, the verb is usually singular:

> *The philosopher and scientist was* in unusually good spirits that day.
> (But the verb is plural if the idea is not single: *The philosopher and the
> scientist* in Professor Werner's makeup *were* at odds on this question.)

New York City and vicinity was suffering from a strike of delivery truck-men.

Silver cuts like wood when the proper *tool and technique is used.*

4) Singular subjects connected with *or* or *either . . . or* have a singular verb when the idea is clearly singular:

> *Either a dentist or a doctor is* to treat such cases.

Frequently the idea is felt to be plural (especially in questions, where the verb precedes):

> If *you or anyone else want* to come, there is plenty of room.
> *Are your father or mother* at home?

With negatives (*neither . . . nor*) the situation is similar, with the plural the more common:

> Since *neither chemistry nor physics were required* [more formal: *was required*], most students had no basic physical science.

5) When the two elements of the subject are pronouns in different persons, the verb is usually plural in spite of some temptation to use the form associated with the nearer:

> *You and I are* sure to go, anyway.
> *Either you or he are* likely to go. (*Is* is possible here to emphasize the singleness of the choice.)
> *Neither you nor I are* fit for that job.

2b. Collective subjects. Collective nouns are singular in form but refer to a group of objects or persons or acts: *army, athletics, committee, jury, public, team.* When the group is meant as a unit, the verb is singular; when the individuals are meant, the verb is plural:

> *The jury* [as a group] *has been out* five hours.
> *The jury* [i.e., the individual members] *have been arguing* for hours.

A number of terms of amount and measure have collective agreement with the singular the more common:

> *Sixteen and a half feet makes* a rod. (Or: *make* a rod)
> *Six tons was* all we used to get.

2c. Blind agreement. When a construction with a plural noun comes between a singular subject and its verb, there is a temptation to make the verb plural. Formal English tends to keep the agreement strict, but spoken and informal English often have the plural.

1) Long intervening phrases or clauses containing plural nouns often conceal the real subject:

The state has hired men to see that *everything* that has the least contact with the milk, from the milker to the caps on the bottles, *is* spotless.

Here and there a *man* such as Columbus, Galileo, and others *has* ventured into the unknown physical and intellectual worlds.

Occasionally a *blitzkrieg* of apples and pillows, followed by water fights, *disturbs* our floor until early morning.

2) A short dependent phrase, especially an *of* phrase closely related to the singular subject, frequently causes trouble:

I decided to go and see exactly how *one* of these present day cars *is* put together.

Memory of summer heat and summer friends soon *fades* in the first exciting days of the college year.

Words like **type*, *part*, *series*, likely to be followed by a plural phrase, are a special temptation:

The greater *part* of their inventions *has* no particular economic importance.

The last *type* of clouds *is* those of vertical development.

A *series* of articles *was* planned, written, and published.

In spoken usage and in a good deal of informal writing a plural verb is found after these closely knit phrases because their sense is plural. With *kind* and *sort* the plural is frequently found (and explained naturally by grammarians—see *kind, sort):

This *kind of people make* [Formal: *makes*] me nervous.

This *sort of pictures have* [Formal: *has*] *attained* a considerable vogue in recent years.

Appropriateness to your level of writing is important in such constructions, though of course in college writing it is perhaps best to play safe and follow formal usage.

3) Relative clauses introduced by *who* or *that* or *which* have verbs agreeing with the pronoun's antecedent:

A skunk *that has been captured* young makes a good pet.

Skunks *that have been captured* young make good pets.

In sentences containing the construction *one of those who*, formal usage has a plural verb for *who* because its antecedent (*those*) is plural; informal usage more often has a singular because the main idea is singular:

Formal: Dad is one of those folks *who see through* people at the first meeting.

Informal: Dad is one of those folks *who sees through* people at the first meeting.

2d. Subject—complement. When the subject and the complement after some form of *be* are of different numbers, there is a temptation to make the verb agree with the following noun (the complement) rather than with the preceding one (the subject):

> Our chief *trouble was* [not: *were*] the black flies that swarmed around us all during the trip.
> The *material* for a good story *is* the experiences of the early settlers.
> The territory comprised *what is* [not: *are*] now Texas and Oklahoma.

(Compare *there is, there are.)

2e. Gerunds. The subject of a gerund (a noun form of a verb, ending in *-ing*) is either in the genitive or the objective form. The genitive is more common with pronouns. With nouns formal English uses the genitive form, but the objective (the common noun form) is more usual and is the regular informal usage:

> They had never heard of *his asking* for such a privilege.
> They had never heard of a person [less common: *a person's*] asking for such a privilege.

Ordinarily use whichever seems the more natural. (See *Gerunds for further distinctions.)

3. Pronouns

The chief reason why pronouns are a problem is that a greater exactness is expected in writing than in speaking. In conversation the pronouns are inconspicuous words, casually serving various grammatical functions. In writing they can be scrutinized, and the schools and publishers have traditionally given them considerable emphasis, even more than they deserve. A fairly careful use of pronouns is then not so much a matter of exact meaning—they are rarely ambiguous —as of tidiness and conforming to the expectations of educated readers. Checking the use of pronouns is one of the jobs of revising a paper.

3a. Agreement in number. Frequently we forget whether we are using a singular or plural notion, as this student did:

> The value that *a person* can receive from understanding such give and take methods will stand *them* in good stead for the rest of *their* lives.

This sentence could be tidied up by making the whole consistently singular: will stand *him* in good stead for the rest of *his life*. But the notion seems actually plural—a statement of general application

—so that a slightly better revision would be to change *a person* to *people*. It is not always the pronoun that should be changed.

3b. Misleading or vague reference. Sometimes an amateur writer's pronouns seem to just happen, as in this:

> We pulled out our spare, which was under the seat, and put *it* on. *It* sort of dampened our spirits but we decided to try *it* again.

The first *it* refers to the spare tire, the second to the operation of changing tires, and the third to the road or trip. Rewriting is needed for such sentences.

Usually the situation is simpler:

> Students and teachers are working at the same job but sometimes *they* don't seem to realize it and seem to be competing with *them*.

The *they* seems to refer to both students and teachers but by the end of the sentence we see it should refer to students only. The sentence could be revised:

> Students are working at the same job as the teachers, but sometimes *they* don't seem to realize this and seem rather to be competing with *the teachers.*

But readers should not be perverse and pretend there is misunderstanding when none is necessary. In this sentence the context keeps the meaning of *he* and *him* straight even though two people are intended:

> *He* hoped *his* grandfather wasn't in because *he* made *him* mad and then *he* would be sure to cry.

Sometimes a statement including two nouns can be kept clear by making one of them plural:

> One way to approach criticism is to compare *an inferior work* with *good ones* to see what *it* [the inferior one] lacks that *the others* [the good ones] have.

The most common reference fault in amateur writing is using a pronoun to refer to a noun that is only implied in the statement:

> The actual sport of sailing has changed very little from the time when only the wealthiest had the pleasure of owning *one* [Better: of owning a sailboat].
> The other fellow enlisted about two years ago and had spent a year of *it* in Persia. (Better: The other fellow, who had enlisted about two years ago, had spent a year of his service in Persia.)

3c. Collective pronouns. A collective noun may be taken as singular *or* plural. (See § 2b, "Collective subjects.") In conversation if we have a collective noun as subject we frequently make its verb singular and make a later pronoun referring to it plural. This shift in number is frequently found in writing too, especially when the meaning is clearly plural, but it is avoided in careful writing.

> If the University *wants* to play big time football, why *don't they* go out and get big time teams? More accurate: why *doesn't it* go out . . .
> Sometimes there is a lot to do and the crew *is* not allowed to run things to please *themselves*. More accurate: and the crew *are* not allowed . . .

A shift in number is especially likely to arise in referring to the collective pronouns: *anyone, each, everybody, everyone*. In speech these are almost universally referred to by plural pronouns; in formal writing the singular is used or the subject changed to a plural:

> *Anyone* who has spent part of *their* [Formal: *his*] time abroad can see *their own* [Formal: *his own*] country in a different light. (Or, the *anyone* could be changed to *people: People* who *have* spent part of *their*. . . .)
> It is a rule that before entering an operating room everyone must scrub *their* hands thoroughly. (Formal: change *their* to *his* or change *everyone* to something like *all doctors and nurses*.)

(See *Collective nouns and *every and its compounds.)

3d. Reference to an idea. *This, that*, and *which* are regularly used to refer to the idea of a preceding statement:

> The mud was eight inches deep, *which* made the road to Edward's Bay impassable.

Care should be taken in such a construction not to use a pronoun that may seem to refer to a particular noun:

> I proceeded to go to the phone, *which* decided my fate for the rest of the summer. Better: Answering that phone decided my fate for the rest of the summer.

3e. Indefinite reference. English lacks a pronoun like German *man* or French *on* to refer to people in general. Since *one* is definitely stiff and formal, we use *they*, or *we*, or *you*. The only problem is in being consistent in the use of whichever pronoun seems most natural in a passage and not shifting from one to another unless there is a genuine shift in point of view. (Compare *he or she.)

Because of these small problems in their use, some students (and some journalists) tend to avoid pronouns; but they are necessary for easy and clear writing. Keeping an eye on them in revising a paper and occasionally recasting a sentence will bring them out all right. Remember that it is not always the pronoun that needs to be changed but sometimes another part of the sentence. (For other examples, see *Reference of pronouns.)

4. Modifiers

Next to the subject-verb-object relation, the most important grammatical relationship is of *modifier* to a principal (called the *head* or *key* word or words). We distinguish modifiers of nouns and pronouns (*adjectives*) and of verbs, adverbs, and other modifiers, and of complete statements (*adverbs*). Since our adjectives do not have distinctive forms, except in comparatives, their relation is shown by position, single word modifiers usually preceding the key word (the *tallest* buildings) and groups of words usually following the key word (the buildings *of the new plant*, the buildings *that are tallest*). The position of adverbial modifiers is somewhat less definite. Those modifying specific words are usually near those words (He drove *fast;* an *almost* imperceptible breeze) and those modifying the whole statement tend to stand first or last in the sentence (*Certainly* you know who did it; *Since the trolleys had given way to buses,* most of the tracks had been torn up; It was impossible to keep up with them *because the traffic was so heavy*).

4a. Single word modifiers. Very few single word modifiers cause any trouble, but a few facts may be noted about them.

1) PREDICATE ADJECTIVES. *Be* and a number of other verbs (*become, feel, grow, taste*) are used as *linking verbs (or copulas). A modifier following one of these is related to the subject and so is an adjective rather than an adverb:

> The train was *slow.* He became *silent.*
> He felt *bad.* The tree grew *straight.*
> This tastes *flat.* The picture looked *real.*

Such predicate adjectives should be distinguished from the adverbs that modify these same verbs or other verbs:

> He felt the edge *carefully.* She looked *sadly* out of the window.

(See *Linking verbs and *Adjectives, types and forms.)

2) ADVERBS. Many times there is a choice of position for an adverb, allowing for variety and a little different emphasis:

> He turned the dial *slowly.* He *slowly* turned the dial. *Slowly* he turned the dial.

A good deal of useless effort has been spent over the placing of *only*. Formal usage tends to put it directly before the element it modifies but more general usage tends to place it next to the verb:

> There have *only* been four presidents people in general know of and admire. (Formal: There have been *only* four presidents . . .)

But adverbs should not be carelessly placed so that they are misleading or seem to belong to words they are not intended to modify:

> Not: Using several pen names, the two editors had *almost* written every article in the magazine. (But, since the *almost* belongs with *every:* Using several pen names, the two editors had written *almost* every article in the magazine.)

Section 1c of this chapter calls attention to a number of adverbs without the characteristic *-ly* ending. But most have the ending: *hurriedly, moodily, rapidly.* (See *Adverbs, types and forms.)

3) NOUNS. A conspicuous trait of English is modifying nouns by other nouns: a *pen* knife, *hospital* zone, *gasoline* buggy, *teachers* college. This construction (the attributive use of nouns) occasionally becomes awkward, as in some newspaper headlines, but it is a natural and useful locution.

4b. Noun phrases. Nouns occur typically in phrases, either with or without prepositions:

> Modifying nouns: The white house *in the next block* was built in 1842. His paper, *a sloppily typed manuscript,* was obviously done in a hurry.
> Modifying verbs: He walks *in his sleep.* The box was kept *right side up.*
> Modifying statements: He learned more *in those first days* than he ever had before. He studied harder *the first semester* than the second.

4c. Verbid phrases. The verbid constructions made with participles, infinitives, and gerunds are usually modifiers, either of individual words or of a whole statement:

> Infinitive: The easiest way *to loosen a screw top on a jar* is to thump it a few times on the floor. (Modifies *way*)
> Participle: *Coming suddenly to a dead end street,* we had to start all over again. (Modifies *we*)
> Gerund: *In painting four of these pictures,* he used his wife as model. (Modifies the main clause.)

1) MISRELATED MODIFIERS. In the examples just given, the phrases are closely related to the rest of the sentence, usually because the doer of the action expressed by the verbid is also the subject of the main construction. When the relationship is faulty, as in the crude and

even humorous sentences in which the phrase seems to modify a word that it cannot sensibly apply to, the phrase is *misrelated:*

> *By darting through clouds and keeping themselves well hidden,* the enemy battleships are taken by complete surprise. (The phrase actually refers to the airplanes mentioned in a preceding sentence.)
> *Hit in the neck by a squashy snowball,* memories of those distant winters in Wisconsin came crowding back to him.
> He knew what to do when the first frost set in *to prevent the walls from cracking.*

The difficulty may come from the position of the phrase, as in the last sentence; or it may be that a different construction, such as a clause, would be more natural, as in the second example (When he was hit in the neck by a squashy snowball); or the trouble may arise from an unfortunate choice of subject for the main clause, since the second sentence would be all right if the main clause was "he remembered those distant winters in Wisconsin."

The verbid phrases that attract the reader's attention, puzzle him even briefly, or obviously break a sentence into two parts instead of making it a unit, are misrelated and should be rewritten.

2) "ABSOLUTE" USE OF VERBIDS. Between the perfectly related and the obviously misrelated verbid modifiers are many that, though objected to by those following strict "rules" of agreement, are natural and not misleading. They really rank as subordinate clauses. A number of verbs for mental activity are generally so used, especially when no actual "doer" of the action in the main clause is named (as in the first example below), and frequently when an added detail is in an independent verbid construction (as in the second):

> *Considering that they were handmade,* the price was reasonable enough.
> The two men strolled unconcernedly down the street, *their outlandish costumes making everyone turn his head to look at them.*

These constructions are one of the several phases of usage that require judgment. Some will find adhering to strict agreement the easiest way, but most will use the natural expressions when they are not misleading or awkward. (See *Misrelated modifiers and *Absolute phrases.)

4d. Clauses. The relationships of subordinate clauses to other words of sentences are the same as those of single words:

> Subject (a rather formal construction): *That he could be wrong* had never occurred to him.
> Object: We thought *they had more sense than that.*

Modifier (adjective): The first person *who arrived* got a door prize.

Modifier (adverb): *When the first snow came,* there was still much out-door work to be done.

1) ADJECTIVE CLAUSES. Clauses modifying nouns are introduced by *that, which* (of things and ideas), *who* (of people), by *where, when, why,* or without connective:

1. People *who live in glass houses* shouldn't throw stones.
2. These people, *who had hardly had a full meal for three years,* just looked at the table piled with food.
3. The man *I saw watching from across the street* [or, *whom I saw watching . . .*] had moved on.
4. He brought out the musket *that* [or *which,* or no connective] *his great-great-great-grandfather had used in the Revolution.*
5. The tractor, *which* [less common, *that*] *his wife and daughter also drove,* was going all the time.
6. Do you remember the time *when Dad caught him smoking?*

The clauses in sentences 1, 3, 4, and 6 are close modifiers, setting off their noun from other similar things; they are called *restrictive clauses* and are not set off by commas. Those in 2 and 5 are less close, giving an added fact about the noun they modify; they are called *nonrestrictive,* and *are* set off by commas. (See *Restrictive and nonrestrictive, and Chapter 5, § 8.)

2) ADVERBIAL CLAUSES are introduced by a number of subordinating conjunctions (including *after, although, as, because, if, since, so, so that, when, where, why*) and indicate a number of relationships—time, place, cause, condition, and so on. It is important to see that they are related to the rest of the sentence by the conjunction that expresses the most exact relationship.

A few adverbial clauses modify verbs (He rows exactly *as his father used to*) or other adverbs (It was farther away *than we thought*), but the greater number modify a whole statement: *When the fog lifted,* everyone started taking pictures furiously (The clause can't belong sensibly to *started* alone). The position of clauses modifying single words is fairly well fixed—close to and usually following them—but modifiers of statements usually can either precede or follow. (See *Conjunctions in use and *Clauses.)

5. Idiom and idioms

Natural and effective English involves many constructions of less frequent and less widespread use than those we have been discussing.

It is impossible to present them all in any book, and certainly not in a brief chapter. But the following sections touch on a few types of expression that sometimes raise questions.

5a. Particular idioms. Every language has a number of expressions that do not fit easily into its grammatical categories and yet are in good use. Some of these are survivals of early patterns of expression: *methinks, many is the time, come fall, good bye.* Others are made for convenience or to fill some need: *Let's don't, to make good, Easy does it.*

Proponents of formal English have sometimes discouraged such idioms, even some in widespread use, like "*I don't think* so and so" instead of "*I think that* so and so *is not.*" Another idiom of long standing is *try and* do something, *go and* get something, instead of the more conventionally formed *try to, go to.* Not all unconventional phrasing works, but writing is impossible without such widely used idioms, and straining to avoid them results in stilted style.

5b. Idiomatic prepositions. A number of words are conventionally related to other words by a specific preposition:

> belief *in* technocracy
> conform *to* public opinion (but: in conformity *with* public opinion)
> conscious *of* his position   interest *in* mathematics

If we learn these words naturally, we pick up the idiom; in learning new words we should see them in use, see how they fit into sentences, not learn them as isolated "vocabulary."

A word may occur in idioms with different prepositions, like *agree on* a plan, *agree with* a person, *agree in* principle; in some there has been confusion, as with *different.*

When two words which conventionally call for different prepositions are used with a single object, both prepositions should be given:

> We know for a fact that most of our players lost a great deal of respect *for* and confidence *in* the coach.

Probably most mistakes in the use of prepositions come from the confusion of two constructions of similar meaning: "I was *informed to* report to the branch office in the morning" might be a confused blending of "I was *informed that* I should report . . ." and "I was *asked to* [*ordered to*] report. . . ."

5c. Infinitive or gerund. Some words are followed conventionally by an infinitive and some by a gerund as illustrated by the following examples:

Infinitives	*Gerunds*
able *to work*	capable *of working*
take pains *to tell*	the idea *of writing*
the way *to cut*	this method *of cutting*
neglect *to say*	ignore *saying*

With a number of words either is used:

a chance *to learn*—a chance *for learning*
the privilege *to live*—the privilege *of living*

Gerunds may be used so that their noun aspect is emphasized (The *trusting* of women is a mark of a gentleman.) or their verb aspect (*Trusting* women is the mark of a gentleman.). The latter construction is the more active and is increasingly used in current writing. (See *Gerunds.)

5d. Idioms for comparisons. The idioms for simple comparisons are not troublesome: He is *younger than* I thought; It was the *hardest* fight of his career. But when other elements are involved, there are some questions of idiom.

Most people say "The summer was *as* dry if not *drier than the last.*" Formal English would complete both constructions: "The summer was *as* dry *as* if not *drier than* the last" or "The summer was *as* dry *as* the last, if not *drier.*"

Other is used in a comparison between things of the same sort but not between things of different sorts:

This picture is a better likeness than the other portraits.
This portrait is a better likeness than the bust.
There is not a more enjoyable light novel by any writer. [Not: by any other writer.]

The two terms of a comparison should be actually comparable. This means using a possessive if the main term is not repeated:

His muscles were firm, like an athlete's. [Not: like an athlete].
The president's recommendations were more practical than the committee's. [Not: than the committee.]

(See *Comparison of adjectives and adverbs.)

6. Consistent constructions

Finally, a number of matters of tidiness can be grouped under the head of consistency. In general, notions of the same value in a statement would be in grammatical constructions of the same sort and the same value; that is, they would be "in parallel constructions." A beginning writer is sometimes not sensitive to little shifts in construction but with practice cultivates a sensitiveness to his words as words. Formal writing is more insistent on parallelism than conversation or informal writing; but similar expressions for similar notions help hold a sentence together and make for clear and easy understanding.

Several matters of consistency have been treated in earlier sections of this chapter. Here two general sorts are brought together.

6a. Shift in approach to the idea. Although it is not always necessary for the two clauses of a compound or a complex sentence to be of the same pattern, frequently shifts keep them from being a neat unit.

1) SHIFT IN SUBJECT

Not consistent

Perhaps *one* should not complain, but *I* would like a little more recognition.

Consistent

Perhaps *I* should not complain, but I would like a little more recognition.

Tires should be checked for pressure at least once a week, and *you* should move them to different wheels every few months.

Tires should be checked . . . and moved . . .; or: You should check tires . . . and move them . . .

2) ACTIVE—PASSIVE VERB

Therefore the group does not work together [active] and a minimum of accomplishment is expected [passive].

Therefore the group does not work together or expect to accomplish anything.

3) PERSONAL—IMPERSONAL

He immediately told his companions of the vast amount of water power these falls represented, and since they were a thrifty lot, it was decided to import a herd of sheep and manufacture woolen blankets.

. . . and since they were a thrifty lot, they decided to import a herd of sheep and manufacture woolen blankets.

6b. Shift in grammatical rank. In longer pairs or series of constructions having the same relation in a sentence, the grammatical value and usually the parts of speech should be similar.

Dad took us aside and gave us a pep talk on sportsmanship [noun] and to remember [infinitive] that even on opposing teams we were still brothers.

. . . and told us to remember. Or: . . . a pep talk on sportsmanship and on remembering [verbal noun] . . .

Unity is impossible in this world of domination, imperialism, and na-

Unity is impossible in this world in which nations are seeking dom-

tions seeking alliances to keep themselves powerful.

ination, imperialism, and alliances to keep themselves powerful.

I noticed that I was sweating very freely, not because of the climate, but because of being nervous.

. . . but because of nervousness.

By employing these various methods—combination, predatory competition, rebates from railroads, and having influential friends where they were needed—John D. Rockefeller in 1878 came to control 95% of the petroleum industry of the country.

. . . and the use of influential friends where they were needed . . .

An illustration of politics in the service is in the experience of two brothers from my home town, one with no education after high school and the other has a doctor's degree.

. . . and the other with a doctor's degree.

Any young man who likes a little adventure and to save money at the same time will find working on an ore freighter ideal.

. . . who likes a little adventure and who wants to save money . . .

(See Chapter 10, § 2e, "Parallelism and balance," and *Shifted constructions.)

When the trouble spots of our language are isolated as in this chapter, writing English looks a great deal harder than it really is. Putting undue emphasis on these matters makes people too self conscious as they write, and perhaps scared. The proper use of this material is to help students prevent some errors they may have been in the habit of making. By studying certain specific constructions, seeing realistically what experienced writers do with them, and perhaps practicing some improvements in exercises, students can do much to eliminate habitual errors. But in their own writing they shouldn't be concerned especially for these details of language until the revision stage. They should give their papers a careful check for such errors as they are likely to make and give the final copy a last reading to make sure it represents their best present use of English.

Suggested study

The exercises in this chapter are arranged in the same order as the main topic headings in the preceding discussion, with emphasis placed upon the trouble spots most frequently encountered in freshman writing. Wherever levels of usage are involved, students should be encouraged to discuss the reasons for their choice of one word form rather than another. For practice in the recognition and correction of errors as they occur in student writing, two themes are included, one as a pre-test at the beginning of the exercises, and the other at the end as a review.

Pre-test

The following theme was written by a student whose powers of observation were good, but whose background in English was weak. Read the paper through to see how incorrect wording and faulty constructions detract from the merits of the theme; then point out and revise each instance of faulty usage that you find, including spelling and punctuation mistakes.

"Trail Eating" in the Olympic Mountains

Have you ever carried a heavy pack up a trail that seemed vertical? Have you ever trudged along a trail with a dollar sized blister burning your heel? Have you ever breathed in to your lungs thin, dry mountain air? I have and I am going to enjoy those pleasures of mine again. To my comrades and I, following a new trail into those beautiful Olympic Mts. is sport which ranks first with us. It leads us to mountain meadows which make the finest kind of a camping place. It leads one through trees made only by God. A person does think more of ones God when out "packin' in."

Grazing on the other side of some valley, peaceful like cattle, we see herds of Roosevelt Elks. At night we go to sleep listening to the Marmot whistle and awake listening to them whistle also. They generally are the first little animal we learn to love in the Oympics. Of course there is another little fellow who we meet, he is the sly old pack rat. If we aren't careful to tie our supplies safe in a tree out from his reach, he is sure to steal all or part of them. We are "clicking" with our cameras continuously lovely views and sites we wish to take home with us. It is fun to open up a photo book in front of the old fireplace at home and look over the wonderful wonderful places you've been to and of course should go to some time again.

Being real mountaineers, climbing to the summit of one of the huge peaks all around us is something we can't resist. We found the view from the top terrific. After a hot and dangerous climb, it is always fun to take a dip in a cool mountain lake. All of our party who enjoys this dip is admitted to the Old Honorable Organization of Polar Bear's. Often we come across neatly kept forest ranger stations usely occupied by the most interesting kind of a fellow. In the cool evenings its fun to listen to them relate there stories of the mountain which have fascinated my comrades and I so much. Again one often meets old prospectors, whose wirey bodies hardened by their healthy surroundings seems to keep them alive for ever. We who know we must go back to the city envied them very much.

Although we don't want to be a travelling library, we always found room in our packs for a bird book, it is the easiest way to settle disputes in regards to birds and their names. After many days of outing we go back home with the immovable idea in our head that we should never care to pack and climb those steep trails again. Yes Sir, it is funny, but the next Season we are altogether again back in those Olympics "trail eating."

1. Word forms

a) NOUN FORMS. Select the proper form of the words in parenthesis. If more than one form is permissible, explain under what circumstances each might be used.

1. Our straight-line, all-band television (<u>antennas</u>, antennae) with either five- or eight- (<u>foot</u>, feet) steel masts are no more difficult to install than are aerials for most (<u>radios</u>, radioes).

2. Go down to the (wharfs, <u>wharves</u>) when the fishing boats come in, and you'll see (basketfuls, basketsful) of (fish, <u>fishes</u>) of every variety.

3. There are more (woman, <u>women</u>) doctors practicing today than there were twenty years ago.

4. It is not difficult to get (synopsis, <u>synopses</u>) of the classics, but it is better to read the works themselves, if you wish to have adequate (basis, <u>bases</u>) for critical judgment.

5. Women interested in home (economic, <u>economics</u>) research may follow one of two (curriculums, <u>curricula</u>).

6. The girls were cutting graceful figure (eight's, <u>eights</u>, 8's) on the ice, their (scarfs, <u>scarves</u>) whipping like pennants.

7. The (<u>brothers</u>, brethren) in the fraternity scanned all (<u>passers-by</u>, passerbys) with close attention.

8. The bus line was but a two (minutes, minutes', minute's, <u>minute</u>) walk from the house, but the (buses, <u>busses</u>) never came by when you needed them.

9. The (hanger-ons, <u>hangers-on</u>, hanger's-on) down at the City Hall this time of year are thick as (<u>leaves</u>, leafs) in fall.

10. Two of his (brother-in-laws, <u>brothers-in-law</u>) are (alumnuses, <u>alumni</u>, alumnae) of this school.

11. This handwriting is obviously (someone else, someone else's, someone's else).

12. The sudden flowering of countless varieties of (cactuses, cacti) is a (phenomena, phenomenon) that never fails to delight those who visit the Southwest desert in spring.

b) PRONOUN FORMS. Choose an appropriate form in each sentence. If you believe that more than one form could be used, indicate a suitable level for each.

1. Do these rules apply to (we, <u>us</u>) freshmen?

2. (<u>Who</u>, whom) do you think it could be?

3. (<u>It's</u>, its) easy to see that the team has lost (it's, <u>its</u>) will to win.

4. No wonder she objects to (you, <u>your</u>) singing first; you sing so much better than (<u>she</u>, her).

5. They decided that two of us should attend the convention—John and (<u>I</u>, me).

6. (<u>We</u>, us) men are chiefly concerned with protecting what is (our's, <u>ours</u>).

7. They are awakened by (him, his) crying out in his sleep.

8. A heavy penalty is imposed upon (whoever, whomever) disobeys the ordinance.

9. All three of us—Mary, Dick, and (I, me, myself)—climbed into the front seat.

10. (Who, whom) are you waiting for?

11. After the schooner set sail, there were only (we, us) two on the little island.

12. Father decided that it was time for (we, us) older girls to help out in the kitchen.

13. (Who, whom) do you think plays better bridge, Dorothy or (I, me)?

14. In our quarrels with others, it is usually not (we, us) who are at fault, but (they, them).

15. I think (he, his, him) taking charge prevented a panic.

16. The teacher had no right to talk like that to (we, us) girls.

17. Between (we, us) and the old man, who loved his grapes better than (we, us) children, a hot feud broke out every season.

18. Don't let him in, (whoever, whomever) he may be.

19. We heard many rumors about (who, whom) the culprit really was.

20. When four of (we, us) boys reached camp, we found our visitors had taken our bedding and left (theres, their's, theirs).

c) ADJECTIVES AND ADVERBS. Choose the adjective or adverb form that seems appropriate to you in each sentence, and give reasons for your choice.

1. The dog barked, the phone rang, and the baby cried (louder and louder, more and more loudly).

2. Confronted by the same temptations, a less conscientious person might have acted (different, differently).

3. Does any flower smell (sweeter, more sweetly) than the rose?

4. Without any additional machinery, the factory can turn out parts much (quicker, more quickly) than it has been doing.

5. You don't look as if you felt very (good, well).

6. Each experiment assigned in the course must be done (accurate, accurately).

7. If you want to enjoy some fine mountain scenery, drive (slow, slowly) when you come to the canyon.

8. With deft fingers, the cowboy rolled the cigarette (tight, tightly).

9. The ranger's station is built on (private, privately) owned land.

10. With high octane gas the motor starts (easy, easily) and runs (good, well) even in sub-zero weather.

11. Your arguments always sound (convincing, convincingly) even though there is usually a catch in them.

12. While cutting out the neckline, Grace (accidently, accidentally) cut her finger and stained the material with blood.

13. The temperature in the room dropped (considerable, considerably) when night came on.

14. The office staff were quick to volunteer that they had been treated (fair, fairly).

15. As the motor warmed, it stopped popping and began to run (steadier, more steadily).

d) VERBS. In each of the following sentences, supply the proper form of the verb in parenthesis. If more than one form is acceptable, explain under what circumstances each form might be used.

1. I wish now I had (choose) my history and political science courses more wisely than I did.
2. When the child was at last found, the news was immediately (broadcast) by every radio station in California.
3. If you (take) more pains with your work earlier in the term, you might have (get) better grades.
4. No one was allowed to visit the condemned man before he was (hang).
5. The child (blow) until his face was scarlet; then suddenly the balloon (burst), scattering fragments of rubber all over the room.
6. Long before the class bell (ring), everyone was restless and eager to leave the room.
7. When feeding time came, the seal (dive) off the rocks and with effortless grace (swim) the length of the pool to his dinner of fish.
8. No sooner had the cards been (deal) than he (lay) his hand upon the table, claiming a misdeal.
9. If we hadn't been close to shore, we might easily have (drown) when our boat (spring) a leak.
10. When they returned home, after having (sing) carols in front of every sorority house, they were nearly (freeze).
11. I would like to get some of that money back that I (lend) so freely last year.
12. A roaring fire was (light), toasts were (drink), and all cares were for the time (forget).

e) VERBS. Rewrite the following sentences, adding an auxiliary *have* or *has* to the italicized verb in each sentence below and making any other necessary changes.

1. From three to five persons *swim* the English Channel each summer.
2. Ten seconds after the alarm rings the big truck *slides* out of the fire station.
3. Mumps and chicken pox *broke* out in camp.
4. The two old spinsters *cling* to each other for support year after year.
5. See that the children *wring* out their bathing suits and *hang* them out to dry before they eat.
6. By the time the cast memorize their lines, the jokes *begin* to wear thin.
7. Mrs. Madison *bears* her many trials with a degree of fortitude amazing to her neighbors.
8. They *drank* cup after cup of coffee but finally they grew sleepy.
9. Each morning of the week for the past five years she *rises* promptly at six-thirty.
10. Man did not *spring* from the apes, but both presumably came from a common ancestor.

f) VERBS. Choose the forms of the verb in parenthesis appropriate to formal usage, remembering that *lie*, *sit*, and *rise* are intransitive, *lay*, *set*, and *raise*, transitive. If you are in doubt about certain idiomatic usages of these verbs, consult the *Index* or a dictionary.

1. The route to Key West (lays, lies) almost straight across the shallow sea on a series of fills and bridges.
2. The excavation was abandoned, and the tomb was left (laying, lying) open and empty.
3. The Mayan pyramids had (lain, laid) buried in the jungles for uncounted centuries.
4. The rank jungle growth had tried to thrust the stone apart, but the great blocks were so closely set that it could only (lay, lie) a cover of humus over them.
5. Before their astonished eyes the barren little valley (laid, lay) as empty as a cup.
6. The men worked throughout the night (raising, rising) a barrier of sand bags to stem the (rising, raising) river.
7. As soon as the dough (rises, raises), (set, sit) it in a warm place for one-half hour.
8. For seven innings, the Cleveland batters were (set, sat) down without a hit.
9. Many a time I have (sat, set) in a duckblind for hours without seeing a single duck.
10. (Sitting, setting) hens should not be disturbed.

2. Subject-verb-object

a) Rewrite the following sentences, making the indicated changes and any others which you think necessary. Be prepared to give reasons for your choice of verb forms.

1. Change *The four* to *A series of:* The four articles on juvenile delinquency that appeared in the *Times* last month are still being discussed by parents and teachers.
2. Change *in addition to* to *and:* The state sticker in addition to the federal revenue stamp brings the total tax to eight cents for each medium-sized package.
3. Change *Most* to *A large portion:* Most of the Christmas trees cut in this area are shipped to Southern California.
4. Change *Sociology* to *Economics:* Sociology is now the most popular course in the University.
5. Omit *a collection of:* There was a collection of forty French moderns in the exhibit.
6. Change *its* to *their:* The orchestra responds perfectly to its leader's direction.
7. Change *One* to *Two:* One dollar seems too much to pay for a single concert.
8. Change *Northwest* to *Oregon, Washington, and Idaho:* The Northwest, with all its vast area, comprises only one division of the Bureau.
9. After *He* add *is one of those people who:* He hates green salads and vegetables.
10. Begin with *Neither:* The President and the Vice-President are in Washington this week.

b) Follow here the directions given for the preceding exercise.

1. Change *lighting* to *acoustics:* Several speakers have suggested that the lighting in our auditorium is not what it might be.
2. Change *All* to *None:* All of the subjects I am now taking are related, directly or indirectly, to my major.
3. Change *The whole family* to *Everyone:* The whole family were gathered in the kitchen.
4. Change *All* to *Each:* All the ushers have little red badges on their caps.
5. Change *Various* to *A variety of:* Various suggestions have been offered for simplifying the parking problem downtown.
6. After *always* add *a pile of:* There were always books by the bed.
7. Change *or* to *and:* What you want or what you think you can get is a question you must settle in advance.
8. After *crowd* add *of cadets:* There is always a crowd around the soda fountain.
9. Change *money* to *riches:* Too many people still think that money is the sole standard of success.
10. Begin with *Every motorist* instead of *Motorists:* Motorists who do not have new license plates by the first of January are liable to arrest.

c) Select the verb form that agrees in number with the subject or the pronoun form that indicates the proper case.

1. The chief attraction of Glacier Park for many tourists (is, are) the numerous bears that roam the highways begging food.
2. How much (do, does) a good set of golf clubs cost?
3. In recent years the study of Latin has attracted so few high school students that many teachers are fearful of (its, its', it's) becoming in truth a "dead" language.
4. Unfortunately, neither Robert nor I (am, is, are) capable of playing the leading role.
5. When the intermission ended, the audience came back singly and in pairs and took (its, their) seats.
6. The people who laughed when Hitler rose to power were unable to foresee the possibility of (he, his, him) becoming virtual ruler of all Europe.
7. A small kit of hand tools (is, are) furnished with each machine.
8. It is not difficult to imagine (oneself, oneself's) falling into a similar predicament.
9. The total number of hogs sold this year (was, were) less than the number sold last year.
10. Despite what one occasionally reads to the contrary, there (is, are) prosperity in this country of ours, and happiness, too.

3. Pronouns

a) The student who wrote the following paragraphs on the advantages of swimming had more than the usual amount of difficulty with pronouns. Point out every instance of faulty agreement, misleading or vague reference, shifts in person or number, and whatever other errors you detect. Then revise the passage for greater clarity and consistency.

> I think that every person should learn to swim when they are young, because it is one of the most healthful and inexpensive sports there is. You don't have to spend a lot of money or weeks of time on expensive lessons. Almost everybody can learn to swim by watching others and then trying it themselves. Of course they may have a little trouble at first, but in swimming, as in most other sports, we only learn to do by doing. It is important for the beginner to master the proper method of breathing as well as the strokes and kicks. One must breathe in rhythm with the stroking, because you turn your head to get a breath on each alternate upward stroke.
> Once you have mastered the fundamentals, you will find that it is a very inexpensive sport. If you don't happen to own a suit of your own, at most pools they will furnish you one for a very small fee. Girls are required to wear caps at some pools I have visited, such as the Y.W.C.A. and University pools, but these are inexpensive, too. Since the cost is small and it can be enjoyed indoors as well as out, everyone should visit a pool or a swimming beach as often as they can.
> It has been said that if you swim regularly in the winter time, you are less liable to get a cold than those who do not, which proves that it builds up a person's resistance. And in the summer time, one can swim outdoors as well as indoors, so no matter what the weather, the age or type of person, or the size of your bank account, swimming is a wonderful all-around sport.

b) Rewrite the following sentences changing each subject to the singular. Make all other changes which naturally follow, taking particular care that all pronouns are appropriate to their antecedents. In any cases of divided usage, give both and indicate the level you think appropriate for each.

> 1. Both teams have their minds made up to win.
> 2. All you men will receive your notifications in the morning mail.
> 3. We have all had our feelings deeply stirred by this unprovoked attack. (Use *Everyone*.)
> 4. Both species of plants will thrive indoors if their leaves as well as their stalks are watered. (Use *Either*.)
> 5. The company were lined up behind their captain.
> 6. First come two groups of novels, and all of them are on the same theme.
> 7. All parents favor their own children.
> 8. The audience were pleased and gave their applause generously.

c) Revise any of the following sentences in which the reference of pronouns seems to you ambiguous, misleading, or otherwise incorrect. If you leave a sentence unchanged, explain why you think it satisfactory as it stands.

> 1. I saw a waitress wipe lipstick off the water glasses with her fingers, and, without washing them, put them into a revolving steam sterilizer.

2. My father and my uncle are both professional photographers and I intend to make it my career too.

3. Yesterday he passed the Dean on the campus, but he failed to recognize him.

4. Some students think the library is a place to discuss the latest campus gossip, which makes it almost impossible for other students to study.

5. When the cake is taken out of the oven, let it cool for at least five minutes before frosting it.

6. Few people have tasted buffalo meat because they are now almost extinct, except on one or two reservations.

7. How can people expect freshmen to take a real interest in their subjects when they put so much emphasis on grades?

8. International law has been profoundly affected by the recent war in all its phases.

9. My liking for my new roommate soon developed into friendship and today he is one of the best I have.

10. There are also rubbing tables in the gym for any athlete who may need it.

4. Modifiers

a) Rewrite any of the following sentences in which modifiers, whether single words, phrases, or clauses, obscure the meaning or make for ambiguity. Be careful to distinguish between "dangling modifiers" and modifiers used absolutely (see § 2, page 113). If you leave any sentence unchanged, explain on what level or levels of usage it would be considered correct.

1. If left alone night after night, how can parents expect to know what their children are doing?

2. Accidents are frequent in the coal mining industry, and sometimes even miners get killed.

3. Students who cheat in the end harm nobody but themselves.

4. By this time everyone knows that Bill only works when he has to.

5. Taking everything into consideration, my first year at college has been a happy one.

6. While at liberty on bail the prosecuting attorney told the court that Carter took a watch valued at $200 from a local store.

7. After spending hours poring over school books, it is very pleasant to take a little time out for relaxation.

8. If the straw on the floor of the chicken coop becomes wet, it should be taken out and put in fresh.

9. Didn't she even write one letter to you while you were away?

10. To return a backhand shot, the grip should be changed by moving the hand counterclockwise on the handle about 45 degrees.

b) Follow the instructions for the preceding sentences.

1. Assuming the prisoner to be guilty, should he not be given a fair trial?

2. The first medical schools in the United States were exclusively for men, but at least one school today in this country only admits women.

3. There is a complete record of all fires started by saboteurs in the fire marshal's desk right now.

4. John apologized to his friend, convinced that he was wrong.

5. The election officials did not notice that some of the ballots were missing until they were counted.

6. Climbing a ladder and taking off the shade, the trouble turned out to be only a burned-out globe.

7. Flattered, although he had done nothing to be proud of, George began to swell out his chest and show off.

8. Looking at Williamsburg, now so perfectly restored, the past seems very close.

9. Nonchalantly smoking a cigarette, his hands automatically found the chords and beat out the rhythm.

10. The company was looking for a man with a car to interview rural clients.

c) Read the directions for each sentence carefully and write the revised sentence, making the change asked for and any other alterations that are necessary, but do not make unnecessary alterations.

1. Add the idea of *to fly safely* at the end of the sentence: Cadet Franklin's training is still insufficient.

2. Begin *Coming out of the subway:* A solid row of skyscrapers faced us.

3. Begin *Fresh from the tropics:* The intense cold made him suffer.

4. Add *to float:* A ship's volume must be greater than the volume of an equal weight of water.

5. Show that the pistol belonged to the guard on duty: The guard's pistol had a broken firing pin.

6. Begin *To arbitrate fairly:* Local standards of living and wage scales must be studied.

7. Begin *To save themselves work:* Many inventions have been developed in the textile industry.

8. Begin *Entering the airlock:* The air pressure which has filled the diver's blood with abnormal amounts of oxygen is gradually reduced.

9. Begin *Fishing off Florida:* A big sailfish struck the hook.

10. Add *to get cold in the water:* The layers of fat on his body are too thick.

5. Idiom and idioms

a) Some of the expressions in the following sentences from student papers are not idiomatically correct; others might be appropriate in certain levels of usage. Revise the expressions that seem incorrect to you, and explain under what conditions the others might be considered appropriate.

1. The book on proper study habits created a false illusion to the value of tests and grades.

2. A student studying in the library on the afternoon of the homecoming football game is something you seldom or ever see.

3. If a young woman attending college plans on marrying before she graduates, it is of my opinion that she should take several domestic science courses.

4. Our teacher took great pains in seeing that we got a lot out of the course.

5. I soon found out, after that first hectic week, that college was no different than high school in many ways.

6. The author presented his characters well, and succeeded to make each one interesting and unforgettable.

7. Now that I have finished the book, and have had a chance to think about it, I can't help but feel that the plot would be better for a movie than for a novel.

8. It isn't easy to give that first three-minute talk in speech class, because the members of the class don't hesitate in making criticism aloud.

9. There are many advantages and disadvantages in a specialized education in comparison to an education that is not specialized.

10. During my first two years in high school, I seldom made the grades my parents expected, due to my interest in basketball and football.

b) IDIOMATIC PREPOSITIONS: In each sentence a blank represents an omitted preposition which would complete the idiom. Fill in the preposition.

1. Johnson vowed to himself that if he were acquitted . . . this charge, he would never again meddle . . . his neighbor's affairs.

2. They spent the whole morning in a glass-bottomed boat, fascinated . . . the marine plants, the coral formations, and the brilliantly colored fish.

3. Some students have trouble adjusting . . . college because it is fundamentally different . . . high school.

4. Six Justices concurred . . . Justice Robinson's opinion.

5. Since he was not opposed . . . the idea, he said he would comply . . . my request.

6. After the prize was awarded, it was discovered that whole pages of the winning essay were identical . . . a pamphlet published ten years before.

7. The old heating system was not adequate . . . both the original building and the new wing.

8. The union will not agree . . . the proposition offered by the management.

9. The partners entered . . . an agreement whereby neither would dispose . . . his holdings without the consent of the other.

10. He developed a strong distaste . . . publicity after his home was overrun . . . newspaper reporters and curiosity seekers.

c) IDIOMATIC COMPARISONS: In each sentence make the change suggested and any other alterations made necessary by this change.

1. Change *three* to *two*: *Afterglow* is the most subtle of Travers' three novels.

2. Add the idea that flying may be safer: Transatlantic flying is just as safe as steamer travel.

3. Give Al more than one opponent: Al will be the more dangerous in the final sprint because he has greater endurance than his opponent.

4. Make the mule more adept than a horse: A good mule is just as strong and adept at applying his weight as any horse.

5. Change *unusual* to *unique:* This novel has one of the most unusual settings in American fiction.

6. Make the adjectives superlative: Of the four puppies, Timmy was always sleepy and indolent.

7. Make the adverbs comparative: Because he was excited, he drove fast and recklessly.

8. Make Morse even more vicious than a snake: This gunman, Morse, is as sly and vicious as a snake.

9. Make Tommy the most intelligent: Tommy stands out as intelligent in a group of remarkable children.

10. Begin with *not only:* She is the last one to arrive at the office and the first one to leave.

6. Consistent constructions

Recast the following sentences to get rid of shifted constructions and to make elements parallel in idea parallel in form.

1. A person's education should be a cross-section of as many subjects as can be taken.

2. Many times I have bought a textbook and from its size alone either dreaded the course or else comforted; however, one soon discovers that the cover of a book means nothing as far as the course is concerned.

3. The war brought about a revolution in the general attitude toward women doctors, and from being merely tolerated, private institutions as well as governmental agencies eagerly sought their services.

4. Problem drinkers are actually sick people and to threaten them, plead with them, or, as is most commonly done, sending them to jail, is wasteful and ineffectual.

5. Perhaps one should not report bus drivers, but I am tired of their rudeness.

6. Listening to an opera in the dark is certainly less strain on the culture seeker than to stand uncomprehendingly in the bright light and on the hard floors of an art museum.

7. One should buy all the savings bonds he can afford, and they can be bought almost anywhere.

8. Actually, the effect of cigarette smoke on the human system is not thoroughly understood; doctors have blamed all sorts of disease on it, it has been denounced by reformers, but science has been able to prove little about it.

Review

You will find in the following student theme examples of many of the trouble spots taken up in the preceding exercises. As you read the theme, characterize the level of usage, and notice any departures from this level. Revise unidiomatic expressions, or those that seem to you questionable, correct any unnecessary shifts and any grammatical, spelling, or punctuation errors.

The Emancipation of Women

The life of the American woman is becoming nearer as an equal to the life of the American men. As each generation passes, we find the American women are becoming more independent and they are receiving equal opportunities to the American men.

In our past history, the women's duties and privileges were bound by tradition as established by the generation before them. The women were educated to respect these traditions. The main reason she had little opportunity for a career was because this practice was against tradition, also a woman had little or no chance for an education. On entering marriage, she was expected, in various ways, to reduce her attractiveness by adopting a kind of a dull, uniform hairdress and costume. She was unable to appear superior to the master of the household. The women were subject to the dull household routine that wore her character and appearance to that of a middle-age woman before she reached the age of twenty-five. She became an unhappy woman unless she forced herself to accept these traditions and take her place in life where it is expected of her.

The American women today are closer to being on a par with the American men. For more than a century women have engaged in a drive to gain emancipation from the traditional restrictions and also hopeful of gaining equal opportunities with men. In the second half of the nineteenth century they succeeded in opening the doors to higher education. Careers were opened, mostly monopolized by women, such as the stenographers and secretaries. The women could be educated into a specialized field and be respected and admired for her position in the business world. Some women have proved themselves even superior to men in certain specialized work. They infiltrated into many kinds of occupations, particularly during warfare. The Women's Suffrage Act was passed in 1920, which enables the women to vote, to serve on juries, and some even held governmental positions. Her home has become increasingly mechanized which has permitted her more time for outside functions, such as bridge clubs, sewing circles, and other social and political clubs she is able to perform without her husband.

Even in the home she has aquired new rights and privileges. In an equalitarian home she is able to voice her opinions on matters in and outside the home. She has aquired the privilege of smoking, drinking, and traveling alone without incurring moral disrespect. Along with this social revolution by the women, they have broken the traditional costume. They now dress in more appealing (or revealing) garb and keep in the latest fashions in dress and hair-do. They have openly aquired coquettish mannerisms, which was definitely against the traditions of the past generations. Making their own decisions and forming the life they wish to live, a great opportunity for happiness and success is assured them.

In general, we see a very bright future for the women. In another generation they can't help but aquire the rights and privileges equal with the men, as they will be making their own decisions.

Punctuation and other conventions of writing

Good punctuation is possible only in good writing. If sentence structure is lame or stiff, punctuation is only patchwork, helping after a fashion but also showing how bad the word pattern is.— George Summey, Jr.

mister printer the Nowing ones complane of my book the fust edition had no stops I put in A Nuf here and thay may peper and solt it as they plese.—"Lord" Timothy Dexter

*An experienced writer means a point as definitely as he means a word.—*Arlo Bates

SUGGESTIONS FOR USING THE CHAPTER: *This chapter presents a general approach to punctuation and reviews the principal uses of the various marks. Further examples and some less important uses will be found in the Index article on each mark. The teacher should look at these and decide whether a given class would profit from reading them also.*

The chapter does not depend directly on any other, though in presenting a realistic view of punctuation instead of an approach from fixed rules, a sense of the general characteristics of formal and informal English (Chapter 2) is necessary as a guide to the choices in practice offered. The chapter could be taken up at any time during a course when specific work on punctuation seems profitable.

Punctuation marks are one aid toward getting our exact meaning on the page. They do more than mark such obvious facts of language as "This is a sentence," "This is a question." They help us separate both words and thoughts and so present them distinctly to a reader; they help group and keep together related ideas; they set off certain words for emphasis. Their use affects the tempo of writing: Too many marks may slow the reader to the point of exasperation, and too few may make him go over a passage two or three times to get its probable meaning. The writer who wishes his work to appear to the best advantage will give close attention to its punctuation.[1]

[1] The most thorough study of current punctuation practices (and the only one with any "authority") is George Summey, Jr., *American Punctuation* (New York, 1949). There is a useful survey of practice and discussion of principles in S. A. Leonard, *Current English Usage* (National Council of Teachers of English, Monograph No. 1; Chicago, 1932), pp. 3-92.

There are a number of articles on general principles, such as Constance M. Rourke, "The Rationale of Punctuation," *Educational Review*, 1915, 50: 246-258 and Sterling A. Leonard, "The Rationale of Punctuation: A Criticism," *Educational Review*, 1916, 51: 890-92.

The stylebooks of publishing houses treat punctuation. The University of Chicago Press, *A Manual of Style*, 11th Ed. (Chicago, 1949) is thorough, representing the usage of a conservative house. John Benbow, *Manuscript & Proof* (New York, 1937), which gives directions for writers and compositors of the American Oxford University Press, is brief but perhaps the most sensible of the stylebooks.

RELATED CHAPTERS AND ARTICLES:

Most marks come naturally. Even in a hastily written first draft the writer will feel the natural grouping of his ideas sufficiently to mark the sentences and most of the subordinate elements in some reasonable way. But punctuation is not completely automatic, even with practiced writers. The boy who put at the end of a class theme "Not time to punctuate" was partly right, for punctuation needs careful checking in revision. By far the largest number of slips in punctuation in student papers are from carelessness—omission of end quote marks, period after a question, a comma or an apostrophe forgotten. Most of the suggestions about the use of particular marks made in this chapter and in the alphabetical articles in the *Index* are to be applied in revising papers rather than in writing the first draft.

The practices of punctuation are set by the editors of books and periodicals, who draw up statements of their usage in stylebooks and change the manuscripts they print to conform to these rules. Though the practices vary somewhat between publications, they agree on most points. English teachers try to encourage students to follow the more important and commonly accepted uses. Since readers have come to understand punctuation marks as signals in interpreting what they read, it is to a writer's interest to know and to follow the usual conventions and also to know where he has a choice.

1. Appropriate punctuation

Effective punctuation depends on a knowledge of the meaning and function of the various marks, summarized in the table on the opposite page, and on a knowledge of their actual use in current writing. Some uses are so fixed in typical writing and printing that they serve as definite signals to the readers, and because they are so widespread and definite, they offer no problem for a writer: he uses them automatically and if he neglects them it is from carelessness or haste. The marks at the ends of sentences, for example, are fairly well standardized; the uses of other marks, such as the period after abbreviations, the colon, and quotation marks, are quite definite.

But in a number of punctuation situations, especially in pointing the parts of sentences ("internal punctuation"), a writer has a choice. The basic aim of course is to make his statements easily grasped by a reader—remembering that strangers coming cold to his matter may need a little more guidance than does the writer, who is already familiar with it. The readers' minds may not run in the same grooves as the writer's, but they can be guided so that they will follow him. The clues to the choices that do exist are in appropriateness to the writer's intention and to the other qualities of his style.

Two series of marks that are related can illustrate the range of choice. The first series—the comma, semicolon, and period—may be used to separate elements or statements, differing in degree of separation indicated. A comma makes a slight separation, a period a complete separation, and a semicolon a separation that is between the other two but much nearer the period than the comma. Look at these versions of the same statement:

1. The person, the time, the place, the purpose, the preliminary assumptions—these enter into all discussions of human affairs; it seems impossible to conceive of any discussion without these features.
2. The person; the time; the place; the purpose; the preliminary assumptions: these enter into all discussions of human affairs. It seems impossible to conceive of any discussion without these features.
3. The person. The time. The place. The purpose. The preliminary assumptions. These enter into all discussions of human affairs. It seems impossible to conceive of any discussion without these features.

The first is obviously the most rapid, holding the elements most closely together; the second is more emphatic and slower; the third gives still more emphasis to each element but moves more rapidly than the second. Professor C. A. Beard actually wrote it the third

The Principal Punctuation Marks

1. SENTENCE MARKS. Used principally to mark the end of sentences:

.   *Period*, at the end of statements (and after abbreviations, in decimals, dollars and cents, and so on).

?   *Question mark* (interrogation point), at the end of questions: He said, "Do you want to come?"; not used after indirect questions: He asked if we wanted to come.

!   *Exclamation mark* (exclamation point), at the end of an exclamation or vigorously stressed sentence.

—— *Long dash*, after a statement that is interrupted.

. . . *Ellipsis*, after a statement that is left uncompleted, or a speech that is allowed to die away. *there dots only* *Used if quotes are not* *mally a period after it* *finished*

2. INTERNAL MARKS. Used to separate or to indicate the relation between elements within a sentence:

,   *Comma*, the most common mark, is basically a mark of slight separation between words, phrases, or clauses. It has a number of routine uses, as in *dates.

;   *Semicolon*, indicating a degree of separation between constructions greater than that marked by a comma and slightly less than that marked by a period.

:   *Colon*, a mark of anticipation, pointing to what follows. It is used after the salutation of a business letter, and to introduce formal quotations, explanatory statements, or series too long or too heavy to be prefaced by commas.

—   *Dash*, a mark of separation more intense than a comma. It is used when the construction of a sentence is abruptly broken and when a note of surprise or feeling is indicated. Two dashes may set off a parenthetical expression.

( )   *Parentheses*, or curves, used to inclose explanatory statements not built into the construction of a sentence.

[ ]   *Brackets*, used to inclose matter that has been inserted in quotations and as parentheses within parentheses.

3. QUOTATION MARKS " " Used to inclose speeches in real or imagined conversation and any short quoted words or statements.

way (*The Discussion of Human Affairs*, p. 14), giving the statements still more emphasis by having them stand as a complete paragraph. In a somewhat less emphatic style the first would be equally good, but it would fit only in a more informal style than the book was written in.

1. The classroom is sparsely populated because the assignment had been a long one and many of the smart boys are in their rooms still sleeping.
2. The classroom is sparsely populated, because the assignment had been a long one, and many of the smart boys are in their rooms still sleeping.
3. The classroom is sparsely populated, because the assignment had been a long one; many of the smart boys are in their rooms still sleeping.
4. The classroom is sparsely populated, because the assignment had been a long one. Many of the smart boys are in their rooms still sleeping.

Any of these four versions is possible, and which is best could be determined only by knowing the general style of the paper. The first would be appropriate in an informal, rapidly moving paper; the third in one distinctly more formal; the fourth gives more emphasis to the individual statements and comes between the first and third in ease and speed; the second follows a rule often found (to put a comma between the two clauses of a compound sentence) but seems perhaps the least satisfactory of the group.

A second series of marks that have much the same meaning but different tone is two commas, two dashes, or parentheses used to "set off" a casually included or parenthetical part of a statement. Consider the emphasis on *but actually turns out to be a help* in these four versions of the same sentence:

1. One thing which at first seems to be an obstacle for an athlete but actually turns out to be a help is the fact that he usually has less spare time than a non-athlete.
2. One thing which at first seems to be an obstacle for an athlete, but actually turns out to be a help, is the fact that he usually has less spare time than a non-athlete.
3. One thing which at first seems to be an obstacle for an athlete—but actually turns out to be a help—is the fact that he usually has less spare time than a non-athlete.
4. One thing which at first seems to be an obstacle for an athlete (but actually turns out to be a help) is the fact that he usually has less spare time than a non-athlete.

The first version could go in an informal style that was using as few marks as possible; the second, with commas, throws more emphasis on the *but actually turns out to be a help*, the idea that is to be developed in the rest of the paper; the dashes emphasize the phrase still more; the parentheses depress it, make it less essential than the writer would want it to be. Whether he chose the second or third would depend on whether the general style was more or less emphatic.

Consider the following set of sentences:

1. When writing presents the great human emotions common to all people of all civilizations, jealousy, love, pride, courage, etc., it may be said to have "universality."

2. When writing presents the great human emotions common to all people of all civilizations (jealousy, love, pride, courage, etc.), it may be said to have "universality."

3. When writing presents the great human emotions common to all people of all civilizations—jealousy, love, pride, courage, etc.—it may be said to have "universality."

The first of these seems awkward, largely because there are several commas within the element that is to be set off (, *jealousy, love, pride, courage, etc.,*); the second is too formal, even though parentheses are common in such a reference book as the quotation is from; the third, which actually occurs in Thrall and Hibbard's *A Handbook to Literature* (p. 452), is the best solution. Ordinarily dashes would indicate a more emotional note, but here they serve as enlarged commas.

These short examples show that when there is choice, decision rests on the writer's intention, the reader's convenience, and the tone and other characteristics of the style. More complex (not necessarily longer) sentences need more and heavier points (semicolons for commas, perhaps) to guide the readers; shorter and more direct sentences need fewer. Many of the "rules" ordinarily given for punctuation are based on nineteenth-century style, in which the sentences were longer, averaging about 40 words, and contained more constructions; sentences in current writing tend to average nearer 20 words, have fewer constructions, are more direct, and so need fewer marks.

The present practice is for rather informal or "open" punctuation, using the marks conventionally required and only as many more as the readers will require for ready understanding. More formal writers tend to use more marks, often required by their more elaborate sentences but often also because they follow a tradition of formal or "close" punctuation. The following passage, given with the formal or "close" punctuation and with the informal or "open," illustrates some of the differences between the two styles:

Formal (Close)	*Informal (Open)*
Now, the chief literary and dramatic vice of the scientists and philosophers, is that they seldom begin at the point of the reader's or hearer's interest. Here, for example, is a book on botany. It begins with a long account of the history of botany, and continues with an even longer account of the general principles of the science. But what do you, or what do I, want to know about the feeble beginnings of botany? We want to know—provided, of course, that we want to be something more than the ladylike botanists who know only the names of flowers— we want to know what the problems of botany are; in what direction botanical research is tending; what differences all this botanical research makes anyway; why it is worth studying.	Now the chief literary and dramatic vice of the scientists and philosophers is that they seldom begin at the point of the reader's or hearer's interest. Here for example is a book on botany. It begins with a long account of the history of botany and continues with an even longer account of the general principles of the science. But what do you or what do I want to know about the feeble beginnings of botany? We want to know, provided of course that we want to be something more than the ladylike botanists who know only the names of flowers, we want to know what the problems of botany are, in what direction botanical research is tending, what differences all this botanical research makes anyway, why it is worth studying.

Since most writers today, and certainly most student writers, write in rather simple sentences, they generally are encouraged to follow the more informal custom. With simple, direct phrasing this is natural. The direct movement of this 36 word sentence from a brief review of a novel in the *London Times Literary Supplement* shows how directness removes the need for internal marks:

> Cardiac failure has been so often used as a device that the reader's own heart sinks slightly on learning in the first chapter that John Raymond was given six months to live by a Harley-street specialist.

Modern fiction writers, for whom straightforward movement is important, have more leeway in punctuation than factual writers and also tend to use fewer marks than their predecessors. A passage from John Dos Passos' *The Big Money* shows how open punctuation tends to help the impression of movement; more marks would make the passage appear more formal and make it move less swiftly:

> Margo felt funny driving out through the avenues of palms of Beverly Hills sitting beside Sam Margolies. He'd made her put on the old yellow eveningdress she'd bought at Piquot's years ago that Agnes had recently had done over and lengthened by a little French dressmaker she'd found in Los Angeles. Her hands were cold and she was afraid Margolies would hear her heart knocking against her ribs. She tried to think of something funny to say but what was the use, Margolies never laughed. She wondered what he was thinking. She could see his face, the narrow forehead under

his black bang, the pouting lips, the beaklike profile very dark against the streetlights as he sat stiffly beside her with his hands on his knees. He still had on his white flannels and a white stock with a diamond pin in it in the shape of a golfclub. As the car turned into a drive towards a row of bright tall frenchwindows through the trees he turned to her and said, "You are afraid you will be bored. . . . You'll be surprised. You'll find we have something here that matches the foreign and New York society you are accustomed to." As he turned his face towards her the light glinted on the whites of his eyes and sagging pouches under them and the wet broad lips. He went on whispering squeezing her hand as he helped her out of the car. "You will be the most elegant woman there but only as one star is brighter than the other stars."—John Dos Passos, *The Big Money,* p. 407

All this suggests that before one can worry intelligently about a specific mark of punctuation in his writing he needs to know something about his style in general, whether it is rather involved and formal, requiring the support of a number of marks, or whether it is straightforward and relatively simple, not needing them. A theme reader's experience is that most college students write rather directly, or soon learn to, and that they come to college with a tendency to close punctuation that is not appropriate to their writing. Most of them should probably follow a rather open style, using marks—except in a few stereotyped places where readers will expect them—only to emphasize the structure and meaning of the sentence. Benbow's advice (*Manuscript & Proof,* p. 85) is sound: "In general, omit all punctuation which does not add to clearness."

2. Sentence marks

The sentence marks are among the most fixed and least troublesome to use: a period after a statement, a question mark after a question, an exclamation mark after an exclamation or emphatic command or especially vigorous statement. In the great majority of sentences no question arises about the end punctuation.

2a. Period. Besides marking statements, the chief conventional uses of the period are:

1) ABBREVIATIONS: Dec. N.C. e.g. vol. When the letters of the abbreviation are frequently spoken instead of the words they stand for, the period is often not used: CIO, ECA, TVA, USSR (but it should usually be kept in U. S.). See *Abbreviations § 3.

2) DOLLARS AND CENTS: $14.28 $.87 (but not in 87 cents, 87¢). See *Money

3) DECIMALS: .4 .04 14.33 1/3 (but 4%, 4 per cent).

2b. Question mark. A question mark is used after a clear cut question: Did you know that he had been to Alaska? It stands immediately after the question if it is included within a sentence: What do all these facts prove? you may ask. (A comma might be used here, giving a good deal less emphasis to the question: What do all these facts prove, you may ask.) A question mark is not generally used after a request phrased as a question (Will you please give this your immediate attention.), though it might be used in rather formal style. A question mark is not used after an indirect question: He asked if we wanted to play tennis. He asked his mother why he could not leave the house on Saturday.

In formal exposition and reference works a question mark indicates an uncertain fact: the Venerable Bede, 673?-735, or 673(?)-735.

2c. Exclamation mark. Whether or not a word or statement is regarded as an exclamation depends on the stress it receives. In this, writing is largely a representation of speech. The one word exclamations range from ones like *Ouch!* which would almost always carry an exclamation mark to mild ones like *Oh* that might warrant one or might deserve only a comma. In general, exclamations (You! You there with the glasses!), vigorous commands (Don't you dare say that again!), and occasional emphatic statements (This was a markup of 300%!) have exclamation marks. But they are less used than formerly, except in advertising and in some excited personal writing that deserves to be called the *schoolgirl style.

3. Commas

Over two thirds the total number of punctuation marks used in writing are commas and probably the question "Should there be a comma here?" is the most common question we ask in revising our manuscript. The question is hard to answer because the comma is a light mark without any special tone or meaning of its own, as the colon and dash so conspicuously have, and yet it is tremendously useful in clarifying our meaning.

Fundamentally a comma is a mark of slight separation. The separation is very slight indeed in the conventional uses (as in dates), but in most instances it is just sufficient to keep words or phrases distinct and so make them more easily understood, and often to throw a slight emphasis on what follows or on what precedes. The following passage shows typical modern practice in use of commas. At the end the reason for each comma is noted, and some places are pointed out where commas might have been used but were not.

> Just as we were leaving [a paper factory], [1] I saw two little boys sweeping an immense, [2] dusty litter down a long corridor. They must have been fourteen, [3] which is the age for leaving school in England, [3] but they were small enough to be taken for nine or ten. They glanced at us apathetically [4] and then went drearily on with their sweeping. Their faces were almost blotted out with fatigue [5] and they moved like sick old men. I touched Mr. Higginson on his pin-striped sleeve [6] and asked him how many boys of that age were employed in the plant, [7] but either he did not hear me over the noise of the machinery [8] or he pretended not to. There is a curious distinction, [9] incidentally, [9] between English and American conservatives. It lies in their hearing. If an American reactionary has his attention called to subhuman living conditions, [10] he answers with great heat [11] that those people spend all their money on radios and fur coats. The British Tory, [12] on the other hand, [12] smiles radiantly and replies, [13] "We *have* been having frightful weather, [14] haven't we?" That is the principal difference, [15] I think, [15] between the two civilizations—Americans make an unconscionable noise and clatter in their running away from life, [16] whereas the English have been running away from it for so long, [17] they do not even know that it is there.—MARGARET HALSEY, *With Malice Toward Some*, p. 226

  1 Comma separating an adverbial clause that precedes the main clause
  2 Comma between two parallel adjectives, both modifying *litter;* contrast *sick old men* below
  3 Two commas setting off a nonrestrictive adjective clause
  7 Comma separating coordinate clauses connected by *but*
  9 Two commas setting off the parenthetical modifier *incidentally*
  10 Comma separating an adverbial clause that precedes the main clause
  12 Two commas setting off the parenthetical *on the other hand*
  13 Comma preceding a quotation
  14 Comma separating two clauses of a compound sentence
  15 Two commas setting off the parenthetical *I think*
  16 Comma between two coordinate clauses of a compound ·sentence; formal writing would have a semicolon here because *whereas* is a *conjunctive adverb.
  17 Comma separating the main clause from a following subordinate clause. If the connective *that* had been written introducing the subordinate clause, probably no comma would have been used.

A writer using close punctuation, that is, using as many marks as he could, would probably put commas at 5 and 8, separating pairs of coordinate clauses, but since the clauses are short and closely connected in thought, the comma is not necessary and is properly omitted here. Some writers might put a comma at 4 and 6, separating the coordinate verbs that have *they* and *I* as subjects. Unless the parts of the compound predicate are very long, it is better to omit such a comma. Open punctuation rightly omits a comma at 11, though one might be used in close punctuation.

The examples on pages 134, 136, and 137 suggest that though rules can be given for the use of some commas the actual practice of writers varies considerably. Except for uses that are quite conventional, writers go largely by the feel of the sentence, its movement and emphasis. Studying the punctuation of good recent prose that has about the same movement that you would like your writing to have is quite useful in getting the right feeling for placing commas.

As a general thing college students use too many commas, more than the simple material and the direct movement of their sentences need. Most textbooks and most teachers have tended to encourage close punctuation, and students sometimes, especially the more conscientious students, seem to see how many commas they can put in and so give their writing a slow movement that it doesn't deserve. The boy who wrote this sentence was taking no chances:

> Naturally, the first thing he does, after his interest is aroused, is to attempt to construct a small receiving set of his own.

No one of those commas is wrong but no one of them is necessary, and without them the sentence moves more easily—and more appropriately to a simple account of experiences in amateur radio:

> Naturally the first thing he does after his interest is aroused is to attempt to construct a small receiving set of his own.

The general advice of this book, then, is to use commas where the reader will expect or need them, but beyond this to use them only when they actually contribute to the understandability of the sentence. Where choice is possible, the final decision will often depend on the rhythm and meaning of the individual sentence and on fitness to other factors of style: The formal writer will always tend to use more commas than the informal. Partly because the use of commas depends on the movement of a passage, it is better not to pause in writing the first draft to decide about putting in a comma. Commas should be attended to in revision, when the context can help decide questions of appropriateness.

The following sections on uses of the comma are given to help you decide what uses are appropriate in your writing.

3a. Conventional uses. Commas are used in a number of standardized situations:

1) IN DATES, between the day of the month and the year: May 20, 1951. When only the month and year are given, a comma is not necessary (May 1951), though it is frequently found (May, 1951).

2) IN ADDRESSES, between town and state or city and country when they stand on the same line: Waco, Texas; Seattle, King County, Washington; Casablanca, Morocco.

3) After the salutation of informal letters: Dear Fred, Dear Aunt Dorothy,

4) In figures, grouping digits by threes: 6,471,063.

5) After names followed by titles or degrees: A. H. Hazen, Ph. D.; Arthur Garfield Hays, Esq.; J. F. Forsythe, Jr.; Annie T. Bowditch, Secretary.

6) After weak exclamations, like *well*, *oh*, *why*, when they are not emphatic.

3b. In series. Commas separate the items of a series of three or more short elements:

> The typical freshman's program includes English, social studies, a language, and some sort of science.
> When to get up, when to eat, when to work, when to have fun, when to go to bed were all laid down in the regulations.

Commas are not used when the items are joined by connectives:

> Fire insurance and life insurance and accident insurance and car insurance and all other forms of insurance are bets placed on odds more or less scientifically determined.

Formal usage regularly retains a comma before the last member of a series when it has a connective (literature, painting, sculpture, music, and drama); informal usage does not (literature, painting, sculpture, music and drama) unless some misinterpretation would result, as when the last item itself contains a connective (tired, dirty, and black and blue). A writer should be consistent in this use or non-use of the final comma, but he has the option of choosing whichever practice is more consistent with the other traits of his style. (See *Series.)

Commas are used in a series of adjectives modifying a single noun if each separately modifies the noun: this short, clear, illuminating account. Commas are not used when one adjective qualifies the total expression following it: in the good old New Deal days. Actually the commas tend to be used in a literal, expository tone and not to be used in more emotional tones. The difference is seen in these two versions:

> glowing, deepset, fanatical, brown eyes (literal, descriptive)
> glowing deepset fanatical brown eyes (more moving)

3c. Between clauses. The use of a comma between the clauses of a compound or complex sentence depends in general upon the length of the clauses and upon the closeness of the relation between them: the less close the relation the more need for a comma.

1) BETWEEN COORDINATE CLAUSES. In informal writing two co-ordinate clauses closely related in meaning and joined by a conjunction have no punctuation, though formal writers usually have a comma. If the clauses are long and not very closely related, especially if they have different subjects, there is more often a comma. There is usually a comma if the connective is *but* or *for*.

> They read novels by the dozen and they write a report on every one.
> Informal: Most textbooks have tended to encourage close punctuation and students sometimes seem to see how many commas they can put in.
> Formal: Most textbooks have tended to encourage close punctuation, and students sometimes seem to see how many commas they can put in.
> These increased orders meant a demand for labor, [Informal, no mark] and workers began to stream in from all parts of the state.
> There are recognizable dialects in the United States, but they show fewer differences than would be expected in a country of such size.
> Yet this is not a characteristic test, for the same reaction is given by several other aromatic compounds.

2) WITH PRECEDING SUBORDINATE CLAUSES. Short, preceding subordinate clauses are usually not punctuated; longer clauses or phrases, especially if they modify the whole statement, are usually set off. As usual, formal style is more likely to use a comma.

> Comma not necessary: As soon as they register they must pay their fees.
> Comma optional: When we lost the fourth of the six games, [or no mark] we just about gave up.
> Comma likely: Because so much of the land has been taken for farms, regions where birds and wild animals can live have been greatly reduced.
> Comma with long phrase: In a society without hereditary social standing, a person's job is the chief sign of his status.

3d. With close and loose modifiers. The punctuation of words, phrases, and clauses modifying words that precede them depends on the closeness of the relationship between modifier and key word.

1) CLOSE OR RESTRICTIVE MODIFIERS—no commas. A modifier that closely limits or restricts the meaning of its key word is not set off by commas. The principal type is the restrictive adjective clause:

> Boys *who are supposedly wild* should not be sent to a strict preparatory school. (Not all boys are supposedly wild.)
> The man *who had the aisle seat* had to get up four times.
> The house *that burned* was pretty well gone to pieces anyway. (Most adjective clauses beginning with *that* are restrictive.)
> The first three cars *we saw* were going the wrong way. (All adjective clauses without an introductory pronoun are restrictive.)

Other close modifiers are appositives and epithets that are treated as part of a name (Charles the Good, Lang the baker) or that obviously limit a noun (His friends Jock and Harry were the first to arrive) and adverbial clauses that would be spoken without a pause:

He must have left *because he had another appointment.*
A freshman has a chance to see all that is going on at a fraternity *when he receives an invitation to dinner.*

2) LOOSE OR NONRESTRICTIVE MODIFIERS—commas. Loose modifiers —added descriptive but not limiting details, nonrestrictive or parenthetical—are usually set off by commas:

A. T. Fowler, *assistant professor of zoology,* teaches the course.
Another time Frank spent an unforgettable week with his father, *who had broken a leg and was unable to go to the office.*
His best friend, *Jock,* was the first to come.
Old Nat, *who had been a great fisherman in his day,* wouldn't believe our story.
He must have left, *because his coat and hat are gone.*

In saying or reading sentences like this there is usually a slight change of tone and a very brief pause before the modifier.

Note that if the loose modifier is not at the end of the sentence two commas are necessary.

Frequently a writer has a choice of using or not using commas with a loose modifier, using them if he wants to emphasize a slight relation, not using them if he wishes them to seem more closely related. There is often no difference in meaning, only in tone and movement. The tendency to open punctuation has resulted in fewer marks around modifiers. In sentences like the following, commas might or might not be used around the italicized expressions, depending on the tone and emphasis desired:

The man *who had previously glanced at us* now really stared.
We must *of course* face the facts.
This atmosphere is completed when you are greeted by the doorman *dressed up like a vaudeville admiral.*

The best test is reading the passage aloud, using commas if you change your voice and pause slightly before the modifier, not using them if you naturally read without change.

3e. To prevent confusion. A comma is used to prevent any probable confusion or hesitation in reading:

After all, the students had gone quietly.
They had to hurry, for their dinner had been long on the table.

He came up sputtering and blubbering, as usual looking like nothing but an overgrown baby seal.

As this shrewd fellow knew, nothing makes food cook like a good fire.

3f. Commas to avoid. There is a temptation to put commas in some places where they actually interfere with reading, that is, where they keep apart elements that should run consecutively.

1) Do not separate a subject from its verb, or a verb from its complement, or a preposition from its object, or the two verbs of a compound predicate.

Boys who are supposedly wild [no comma] should not be sent to a strict preparatory school.

All my hobbies and inclinations [no comma] came at last into their own.

Everyone is crying [no comma] "Economize." ("Economize" is a direct object, not a quotation formally introduced by a verb like *He said*.)

He would not have done it except [no comma] that everyone was daring him to.

When teeth are extracted [no comma] and not replaced immediately, there is nothing to prop the jaws apart.

Another way in which the schedule should be rearranged is [no comma] so that the games in the last week should be at home.

If a loosely related element comes within any of these constructions, it should be set off by commas ("Two commas or none"):

All my hobbies and inclinations, *acquired slowly in the past ten years*, came at last into their own.

Another way in which the schedule should be rearranged is, *in my opinion*, so that the games in the last week should be at home.

2) Do not separate a short adverb from the words it modifies:

Soon [no comma] we were at the gym and in less time than usual [no comma] were in our uniforms.

Women also [no comma] are interested in sports and even in business.

3) Do not separate a conjunction from the clause it introduces:

The girls almost always did the assignments, but [no comma] the boys usually tried to bluff.

4. Other internal marks

The other marks used within sentences are much less frequent than the comma and raise fewer questions, partly because each has a fairly definite meaning or tone.

4a. Colon and semicolon. The distinction between the semicolon and colon is simple. The colon points to what follows, introduces or anticipates something, as the text of a letter following the salutation *Gentlemen*:, or a long or formal quotation (Mr. Bristow said in part:).

> Then come the fellows in charge of the various departments: the soda fountain, ice cream, the grill, and the clams.
> There is one thing that I am very sure of now: at this stage of his experience he should have followed my advice.

A semicolon, on the other hand, is a mark of separation, almost as full as a period. It is not needed except in rather long and complicated sentences; or when one or more of the elements have commas within them; or when coordinate clauses are not closely connected, either with or without a connective or with a *conjunctive adverb (*however, consequently*, etc.); or, occasionally, because the writer wants to make his clauses especially distinct and yet hold them in the same sentence.

> Most words need modifiers to make their meaning more exact; they need connectives to tie them to other words.
> For *pumpkin*, two levels of pronunciation are recognized: formal, pump′kin; informal, pung′kin.
> In formal papers for college courses and in theses formal usage should be followed; in informal college papers, like many themes, either style may be used, as the instructor prefers.

In current direct style semicolons are much less used than formerly. Students tend to overuse them, in part because they have been encouraged to use the heavy connectives, which are ordinarily not appropriate to the other traits of their style.

> Heavy: Medical schools keep requesting the colleges not to teach "medical subjects"; however they still give the advantage in admissions to students with lots of chemistry and zoology.
> More natural: Medical schools keep requesting the colleges not to teach "medical subjects," but they still give the advantage in admissions to students with lots of chemistry and zoology.

Semicolons should not be used to set off subordinate clauses or verbid phrases:

> Because learning to live together is so much harder than learning to fight each other, [not ;] the nations of the world make little progress toward peace.
> It takes quite a bit of courage to start *War and Peace*, [not ;] because it is not only long but has a lot of characters with curious Russian names.
> It is a wonder that these people got along as well as they did, [not ;] coming from all corners of the United States and even from most of the countries of Europe.

Remember a semicolon is not so much a large comma as it is a small period.

4b. Dash. A dash has the value of a vigorous comma and when sparingly used may contribute a tone of liveliness. It is very easy to overuse dashes, especially in ordinary expository writing; they should be kept for special spots where they can add something rather than be indiscriminately used for other marks.

The more common uses of the dash are: (1) to mark a sharp turn in the thought or construction of a sentence; (2) to indicate that a word or phrase summarizes or repeats in other words what has just been said; (3) to make an abrupt separation between clauses; (4) to inclose a parenthetical expression, more sharply marked off than by commas and less formally than by parentheses. These uses are illustrated by number:

> 1. How many times she must have said this before—I shuddered at the simple thought.
> 2. The characters, plot, theme, the scene—all are trite in this play.
> 3. It was the best one made—and it still is.
> 4. They think they are the last radicals—and the greatest—and that their ideas and their works will live forever.

Commas could be used in all of these sentences except the first one, but with a difference in emphasis and tone.

4c. Parentheses. Parentheses are used to inclose added details or illustrations not built into the construction of a sentence or for depressing an aside or an obvious fact. They are more appropriate for businesslike or slightly formal exposition and should be used sparingly in more general sorts of writing.

> The few verb endings that English now retains (*-s, -ed, -ing*) are being still further reduced in ordinary speech.
> The horse (sold and re-sold at auctions all over the county) had finally come to its present owner as the result of a bet.
> The largest additions to the territory of the United States (the Louisiana Purchase and Alaska) were gained by purchase.

Other typical expository uses are illustrated in the text of this chapter. (See §1, p. 136, for comparisons with the comma and dash.)

Square brackets ([ ]) are used chiefly as parentheses within parentheses or for an interpolation in a quotation:

> Each pronunciation of *process* (pros′es and [much less commonly] prō′ses) has a history.
> "It [the institution of private property] is in our time under attack in most parts of the world."

4d. Marks in combination. Occasionally questions arise over the order of two marks of punctuation that follow the same word.

Most publishers put a comma or a period inside the closing quotation mark, regardless of whether it belongs to the quotation or to the sentence as a whole:

> "In the beginning," he said—probably meaning "two years ago."

Exclamation points and question marks stand inside the quotation marks if the quotation is an exclamation or a question, outside if the including sentence is the exclamation or question:

> Then suddenly he shouted, "Get out of here, all of you!"
> You don't mean that he actually said "You're another"!
> She asked, "Won't you please try to do it for me?"
> Did she say, "Please try to do it"?

A punctuation mark belonging to a part of a sentence that includes a parentheses comes *after* the second curve:

> There are several words of foreign origin that keep their original plural forms (like *alumnae, alumni, analyses*), and many that have two forms (like *appendix, cactus, formula*).

It is not usual now to use a comma and a dash together.

5. Quotation marks

Quotation marks are used to inclose speeches of real or imagined conversation and short excerpts from printed matter.

    " " Double quotation marks   ' ' Single quotation marks

Either may be used as the mark of quotation, though the double are still much more common. If there is a quotation within a quotation, the marks are alternated:

> "The first eight I called on answered, 'Not prepared,'" Miss Stoddard complained.
> Or: 'The first eight I called on answered, "Not prepared,"' Miss Stoddard complained.

In expository matter now, formally introduced quotations of more than one sentence are indented and printed in smaller type without quotation marks—as frequently in this book. In longhand manuscript simply indent such quotations about half an inch; in typed copy, indent and single space.

6. Capitals

The principal uses of capital letters in English are well standardized and give very little trouble. These are: the first word of a sentence, names of people and places, proper adjectives derived from these names, days of the week, months, the important words in *titles, ordinarily the first word of a line of verse, the pronoun *I and the exclamation *O*, nouns and pronouns referring to Deity, names of companies and organizations.

Some items formerly capitalized no longer are: the seasons, points of the compass (but capitalized when they refer to a region, the *Southwest*), common nouns derived from proper names when they have lost the suggestion of the name (*paris green, jersey, macadam, volt, fedora, shrapnel*).

Many class nouns are capitalized when they refer to an individual thing or person: I dislike all professors—I dislike Professor Weems; He was taking geography—He was taking Geography 106. If a person wishes to capitalize names of members of his family (*Father, Brother*, and so on), he may do so as a sort of courtesy but it is not necessary. A title standing for a particular person may be capitalized, especially if the position is eminent: *the Senator, the Principal.*

The first and last words of the title of a book, article, play or movie and all words except articles and the short prepositions and conjunctions are capitalized: *The Brothers Karamazov; Yesterday, Today and Tomorrow; No Place to Hide; The Bible in Spain.*

Magazines and books use capitals on words like *street, river, church, hotel*, when they are parts of proper names, although newspapers do not. Most general writers follow book conventions (*Bond Street, Potomac River, First Methodist Church, Drake Hotel*).

Capitals may be used for stylistic reasons, as for emphasis, especially in formal writing: Her precious Intuition, I suppose. This practice is not recommended unless other traits of style make it appropriate.

7. Underlining for italics

Words or statements that would be printed in italics are underlined once in manuscript. Formal, especially academic, writing follows the conventions of book publishing, which uses italics in a number of standardized places; informal and personal writing is more likely to follow newspaper usage, which has largely given them up. The principal uses are:

1) To indicate the titles of books, plays, motion pictures, and other complete works. (Article titles are usually quoted.) Newspapers and many magazines usually put such titles in quotation marks.

2) To indicate the titles of periodicals and newspapers: *Harper's Magazine*, New York *Times*.

3) To mark words and expressions considered as words rather than for their meaning: There is a shade of difference between *because* and *for* used as conjunctions.

4) To mark words from foreign languages that are not regarded as English: *persona non grata, mon vieux, coup d'état, Götterdämmerung;* but not "chassis," "coup," "blitzkrieg." (For a list see *Foreign words in English.)

5) To emphasize words or statements, especially in expository matter. Spoken emphasis may be represented, though this device is best used sparingly: It was *his* night, all right.

8. Indention and display

The attractiveness and the ease of understanding of a good deal of print depends in part on the spacing of parts, on eye appeal. Manuscript does not need to ape the appearance of printed copy but some of its devices are useful. Besides neatness and legibility, placing on the page is important—good margins, not crowding the right side, space between title and text, and easily noted indention of paragraphs are a help to reading. (See Chapter 1, "Preparing the Manuscript," p. 20.) In long papers the use of subheads, centered in the line, may be a guide to readers.

No punctuation marks (except question and exclamation marks required by the sense) are used at the end of titles or other display lines. The white space remaining at the end of the line serves as punctuation, as it does in the address lines of *letters or in formal *social correspondence such as wedding invitations or announcements, which use no marks at the end of lines.

Closely related to this display is the use of *tabulations for series of short facts that are often concealed when run in consecutive sentences, as well as charts, graphs, *diagrams, and illustrations.

These devices do not take the place of the written words but support them. Their usefulness, like the usefulness of punctuation, is in making understanding more easy. It is the mark of a good writer to follow through with these devices and to make his copy in all possible ways clear, attractive, totally effective.

Suggested study

1. Read the following passages from student themes and discuss the punctuation in each selection. Is the punctuation appropriate to the level of usage and to the subject matter? Do you find any inconsistencies within the individual passages? What marks of punctuation would you omit or add? Give the reason for each change you make.

1. While working for a large national organization I found it necessary many times to write a business letter to one of the factories or to our customers. My first attempt, due to a lack of schooling for a good many years, I'm afraid was a tedious job for the secretary. Thanks to her many years of experience however we managed somehow to get the letters written. I supplied the necessary information in rough form and I use the word rough loosely, and she transcribed it into a business letter. She enjoyed doing this for me I'm sure, as she was the sort of person that enjoyed doing things for other people, but how will my luck hold out in later years. I won't always run into a secretary with such knowledge and such a pleasing disposition as this one had. The alternative then would be for me to learn the fundamentals of writing a good business letter. I don't believe there are many people, even those with the proper education, who can write good business letters, until they have had some practical experience, especially if they hold positions in specialized fields.

2. My first job, as an elevator operator, was the most thrilling job, as it is with most people. To me it was almost as if I was an actor, waiting my cue to speak and move! My audience responded! (How could they help it? They had to get off!!) But I thought myself a person of great authority and recognition—however false that feeling turned out to be!

3. I think Life is the best magazine of its type for several reasons. For one thing the subjects are dealt with almost entirely by means of pictures with the minimum of printed material, whereas the magazine Look, has almost as much explanatory matter as pictures. Naturally each picture in Life has a short explanation accompanying it, if the editors tried to describe each and every minute detail that the cameras eye records, they would need a page for each illustration or in some cases several pages. The truth of the saying "One picture is worth 10,000 words" can readily be seen if one compares a written account of a disaster—or any other notable event, with a good picture of the same incident. And Lifes pictures are I think, much more vivid and lively than those in Look.

4. As I was reading this story I was impressed with the power of observation which the author seemed to have. I felt that he surely must have experienced some of the incidents sometime, (perhaps during his youth,)

for he painted a clear true picture in words of the incidents which he was describing. In order to give a vivid account one has to be accurate in his observations. Isn't it true I thought when I finished the story, that very few of us observe accurately.

2. The punctuation marks have been removed from the following passages, and you are asked to put in marks that will make them meaningful. First glance through a passage to get an idea of its content and general movement. Decide whether formal or informal punctuation is appropriate to it, and what your own tendency is in punctuation. Then copy the passage, inserting punctuation marks, capital letters, and paragraph symbols but making no other changes. Be prepared to tell why you used each mark.

1. and for my part i will try to punctuate this book to make it easy for you to read and to break it up with spaces for a pause as the publisher has asked me to do but this i find very extremely difficult for this book is the talking voice that runs on and the thoughts come the way i said and the people come too and come and go to illustrate the thoughts to point the moral to adorn the tale oh talking voice that is so sweet how hold you alive in captivity how point you with commas semi colons dashes pauses and paragraphs—STEVIE SMITH, *Novel on Yellow Paper*, pp. 37-38

2. thus then on the night of the tenth of may at the outset of this mighty battle i acquired the chief power in the state which henceforth i wielded in ever growing measure for five years and three months of world war at the end of which time all our enemies having surrendered unconditionally or being about to do so i was immediately dismissed by the british electorate from all further conduct of their affairs during these last crowded days of the political crisis my pulse had not quickened at any moment i took it all as it came but i cannot conceal from the reader of this truthful account that as i went to bed at about 3 a m i was conscious of a profound sense of relief at last i had the authority to give directions over the whole scene i felt as if i were walking with destiny and that all my past life had been but a preparation for this hour and for this trial eleven years in the political wilderness had freed me from ordinary party antagonisms my warnings over the last six years had been so numerous so detailed and were now so terribly vindicated that no one could gainsay me i could not be reproached either for making the war or with want of preparation for it i thought i knew a good deal about it all and i was sure i should not fail therefore although impatient for the morning i slept soundly and had no need for cheering dreams facts are better than dreams—WINSTON S. CHURCHILL, *The Gathering Storm*, pp. 666-67

3. accuracy is the first requirement in galley reading the next is to carry out faithfully the copyreaders intention in typography if the copy has not been edited the proofreaders task is much more difficult it then requires thinking quickly exercising careful judgment and weighing the cost of change against the values of appearance and correctness contradictions duplications errors of fact anachronisms imperfect sentences solecisms barbarisms and so on are to be detected by the reader and pointed out such corrections are very costly if made in the type therefore most printing houses whose

work must be of very good quality employ editors and copyreaders to prepare their copy before passing it to the compositor when this is not done the proofreader must assume responsibility if the copy has been edited the galley reader has but to prove that the printer has interpreted the copyreaders marks correctly this task is not an easy one under the best conditions the best galley reading consists of two operations a preparatory silent reading for purely typographical errors and a reading with the copyholder for accuracy sense and all possible errors of consistency in preparatory reading the proofreader should note the condition of the copy so that he can time the first reading to a speed that will insure perfect accuracy—*A Manual of Style*, Tenth Edition, The University of Chicago Press, pp. 183-84

4. it was the phthisic killed your pap ma said she overflowed the chair she sat on being big hipped like an old squaw but wizened from the waist up and not strong and quick in her movements as a squaw would be you told me that it was his sinnin killed him cora put in while she wiped a pan it was the lord in his wrath it aint becomin to talk that way not about your mans pa all the same it was boone sat in the doorway only half hearing what the two women said it struck him again though that dans wife was a fool laying everything to god or the devil if it was the lord he said while he watched dans two boys climbing a black oak tree he was late gettin around to it he shouldve kilt him sooner your paps dead boone ma said thats what i heerd it was the phthisic done for him boone didnt say anything to that ma was getting old and mixed in her mind so that she didnt remember from one word to the next what it was she had said it aint for us to pass judgment on the dead she went on pap had good in him.—A. B. Guthrie, *The Big Sky*, p. 409

3. Copy and bring to class for discussion two or three examples each of conspicuously formal and informal punctuation. Look for these examples in textbooks as well as in magazines and newspapers and notice particularly passages you find difficult to grasp at first reading either because of too many or too few marks. Comment on the effectiveness of the punctuation, and its appropriateness to the subject matter and the general tone of the writing.

4. Characterize your punctuation after you have examined several of your recent papers. Is it consistently formal or informal, or a mixture of both? Is it appropriate to other qualities of your style of writing?

5. What comments have been made about the punctuation in your written work? Study the corrections you have been asked to make on your papers to see if you have any recurring problems in punctuation. Before revising your next paper refer to appropriate articles in the *Index* of this book to see how far you can go toward settling these problems.

Spelling

TOPICS OF THE CHAPTER

I came beneath a pine tree bough
When I was searching for my cough.
I could not reach the pine cones, though,
The branch was high and I was lough.
"Ah, me," I cried, with rueful laugh,
"Would that I were a tall giraugh."
Just then a wind came hurtling through,
The branches cracked, so fierce it blough.
This blast, so shrill it made me cough,
Dislodged the cones, which tumbled ough,
And on it went with angry sough;
I put my treasure in my mough
And started home across the slough
Forgetting what I'd come to dough.
Bossy was standing by her trough;
Did I mistake, or did she scough?
—By Katherine Buxbaum, from *Word Study,*
copyright, 1945, by G. & C. Merriam Co.

SUGGESTIONS FOR USING THE CHAPTER: *Since spelling is pre-eminently an individual matter, not very much can be done in class instruction. This chapter could be used to call attention to the problems, to encourage a realistic and reasonable attitude toward them, and to make some concrete suggestions for increasing accuracy and confidence. It might be taken up with poor spellers in conference.*

The "spelling list," given in the Index article *Spelling, contains a considerable number of words rather frequently misspelled in college. It can't take the place of a dictionary, but it may serve for a quick check of individual words.

G ETTING A LANGUAGE down on paper is not easy. A language exists first and fundamentally as speech, and for the most part, writing is a representation of what we say. In English we try to represent our speech with an alphabet of twenty six letters, three of which—*c* (or *k*), *q*, and *x*—merely duplicate the work of other letters. The twenty three active letters singly and in combinations like *th*, *ea*, *sh* have to record words employing some forty sounds. The difficulty is greatest in the vowels: *a*, for instance, spells the vowel sounds of *lay*, *lap*, *far*, *fare*, *was*, not to mention untypical words like *many* and neutral sounds like the second *a* in *comparative*. This means that one may with very good reason be uncertain of the conventional spelling of a word that is familiar in his speech.

1. The difficulty of English spelling

Besides the limitation of the alphabet there is also difficulty because spelling fails to keep pace with gradually but steadily changing pronunciation. English spelling was stabilized chiefly by the printers of the fifteen and sixteen hundreds, and though it has changed considerably since then, it has not kept abreast with the spoken forms. This fact accounts for many of the strange English spellings: *meat* and *meet* once represented different sounds; *colonel* was a word of three

---

syllables, col-o-nel; the *gh* in *night, though,* and other words was sounded, as it still is in Scotland. The curious group including *bough, cough, though,* and *through* is largely explained by different pronunciations in different English dialects—the pronunciation of one word comes from one dialect, of another from a different dialect, but the original spelling is kept.

The English habit of borrowing words generously from other languages is responsible for such groups as *cite, sight, site,* and for hundreds of words that do not follow conventions of English spelling— *bureau, croquet, hors d'oeuvre, khaki, onomatopoeia.* We have even borrowed foreign tricks of spelling some sounds, as in *gu*ard and *qu*een.

These facts suggest that though English spelling cannot be defended, both its general confusion and the form of a particular word can be explained by reference to the history of the language.[1] This does not help us spell a given word, but it does help us understand why the difficulties exist, why our spelling can be made the butt of so many jokes and furnish curiously spelled rhymes for limericks.

[1] Henry Bradley, *Spoken and Written Language* (Oxford, 1919); W. A. Craigie, *English Spelling* (New York, 1927); Kennedy, Chapter 7 and section 128; Thomas R. Lounsbury, *English Spelling and Spelling Reform* (New York, 1909); Robertson, Chapter 8. The section "Orthography" at the front of the Webster dictionaries, especially the International size, contains a great deal of information about English spelling.

1a. The demand for uniformity. The present emphasis upon uniformity and correctness in spelling is due partly to historical and partly to social causes. In the eighteenth century there was a special drive for uniformity in various matters of language. After the appearance of Samuel Johnson's dictionary and later of Noah Webster's, spelling received special emphasis. In the United States Webster's blue-back speller—over 60,000,000 copies of which were sold in the nineteenth century—helped make spelling one of the main jobs in school. The spelling lesson was something definite; the goal was well defined in the dictionary and spelling book; progress toward it could be marked. There is now over a century of this school pressure behind the desire for uniformity in spelling.[1]

Another enforcement of uniformity has come from printers and publishers, who naturally wish for consistency in what they print and so usually revise manuscripts according to the dictionaries or according to their own stylebooks based on the spellings of the dictionaries. Dickens and others of our celebrated writers were "poor spellers" whose copy was corrected by editors. Recently book publishers have come to allow a writer a little freedom in his choice of spellings, but periodicals normalize the spelling in the manuscripts they print. Our spelling is the most conspicuous example of the influence of editorial standards.

Back of the schools and the editors there is a more general social demand for uniformity. Mistakes in spelling are easily noticed, even by people who would have difficulty with some of the more complex matters of language. Consequently spelling is a convenient test of literacy and even of respectability. "English orthography [spelling]," says Thorstein Veblen, ". . . is archaic, cumbrous, and ineffective; its acquisition consumes much time and effort; failure to acquire it is easy of detection. Therefore it is the first and easiest test of reputability in learning, and conformity to its ritual is indispensable to a blameless scholastic life."

The real reason for "learning to spell" is that educated readers expect to see words in the standard forms and are likely to undervalue a person who does not use them. Employers of college graduates frequently complain that "they can't spell," implying that they do not meet a minimum requirement of education. Good spelling is an important—if the most superficial—trait of Good English.

---

[1] Allen Walker Read, "The Spelling Bee: A Linguistic Institution of the American Folk," *PMLA*, 1941, 56:495-512.

1b. Choice in spelling. Students of the language are united in their belief that spelling should represent our spoken words more accurately. Forty years ago Professor Lounsbury wrote his *English Spelling and Spelling Reform* in the belief "that the English race will not be content to sit down forever with a system of spelling which has nothing to recommend it but custom and prejudice, nothing to defend it but ignorance, nothing but superstition to make it an object of veneration." A completely phonetic spelling is unlikely, and even if one was set up, it would soon become antiquated, because pronunciations (the real forms of words) would continue to change. But many of the inconsistencies would be removed and many silent letters dropped. Laymen who have mastered the present spelling object to change. They feel that it would be tampering with our literary heritage—not realizing, for example, that the spelling of the current Shakespeare texts has been modernized by editors. The sweeping changes suggested by devotees of "spelling reform" have naturally made a good many people afraid of even moderate change.

But in spite of opposition many changes in spelling have taken place and are taking place. The *u* has been dropped from words ending in *-our* (*colour—color*) in the United States, and it is being dropped in England. *Economic, public, poetic* once ended in *k;* words with *ae* are being spelled with *e* (*anaesthetic—anesthetic*), and so on. These gradual and almost imperceptible changes are more in keeping with the spirit of the English speaking people than a wholesale "reform" would be.

A writer now has a choice of simpler spellings in some hundreds of words. The choice he makes between forms will depend upon his feeling of appropriateness. Formal writers are consistently conservative in spelling. Informal writers make use of the shorter forms more readily. At present scientific and business English are most open to changes in spelling. In familiar writing many people are more adventurous than in writing intended for strangers. Most professional writers will be conservative, as most readers will expect them to be. But anyone seriously interested in furthering the gradual simplifying of English spelling will find many occasions on which he may appropriately exercise his mite of influence by using simpler spellings and familiarizing readers with such forms. These will be more widely accepted, as readers become accustomed to seeing them.

The essential point is for a person to realize how generally the shorter form is used and then to decide whether he wants to use it or not. *Altho, tho,* and *thru* are in general use in advertising and in familiar correspondence and have been adopted by enough periodicals so that they are included in recent dictionaries as alternate forms. *Nite* and *naborhood,* on the other hand, are not found outside advertising and familiar writing, and *brot* or *thot* have hardly reached the advertising columns. In many words (*catalog—catalogue, program—programme, esthetic—aesthetic*) usage is divided, and the shorter forms are becoming the more usual.

When usage is divided in spelling a given word, ordinarily choose the simpler or more natural form. For a surprising number of words, two spellings are current and are recorded in dictionaries. Most people writing today, and certainly anyone who has difficulty with spelling, will ordinarily prefer:

1) The more modern of two equally reputable spellings of common words: *catchup, mold, sirup,* rather than *catsup* (or *ketchup*), *mould, syrup.*

2) The simpler form of a specialized word if it has attained currency among the people who use it most: *anesthetic, catalog, medieval, program, sulfur* rather than *anaesthetic, catalogue, mediaeval, programme, sulphur.*

3) American rather than British spellings (though both spellings are usually current to some extent on both sides of the Atlantic): *center, color, labor, pajama, story* (of a building), *traveler,* rather than *centre, colour, labour, pyjama, storey, traveller.* Of course in spelling British proper names or in direct quotation, British spelling should be kept, as in "the Labour party."

2. Suggestions for improving spelling

It is social insistence, then, rather than any fundamental linguistic requirement that makes accurate spelling a requirement of Good English. And in spite of its admitted difficulty, fairly correct spelling is possible for anyone, though if he has reached college age without having acquired the knack, it will mean work. The goal for a "poor speller" is not to spell perfectly but to spell well enough so that his copy will not attract unfavorable attention—and to know how to check possible errors. The fatal mistake is to give up, to enjoy poor spelling as a hypochondriac enjoys poor health.

If you have really serious difficulty with spelling, it will pay to do some general reading, focusing on the individual words. Keeping lists of your own spelling problems and working on them is more important than using lists made up by others. Copying short passages that contain words you need to use helps fix them in mind, and writing down from dictation is even better. This lets you write the word in its context and so helps accustom you to putting it in a natural setting.

There are rather obvious reasons for many of the commoner misspellings—overlooking for the moment the commonest one, carelessness—that can suggest some ways of improvement. These general suggestions are followed in § 3 by more specific ones on particular groups of words.

1) *Confusion between similar forms.* Two closely related words sometimes show differences in spelling that are hard to keep separate: *four—forty*, *comparative—comparison*, *curious—curiosity*. A vowel may be dropped or changed when an ending is added to a word: *enter—ent[ ]rance*, *disaster—disast[ ]rous*, *maintain—maintenance*. Or the vowel may be retained: *temper—temperament*, *mountain—mountainous*. As a rule such words do not show any difference in sound and so have to be remembered.

One of the greatest nuisances in our language is a group of prefixes and suffixes with two different forms: **en- in-*; **in- un-*; **-able -ible*; **-ance -ence*; **-er -or*. The meaning of each pair is the same; the differences in spelling have histories, most of them going back to distinctions in Latin. Preserving them today is a waste of mental effort but still constitutes one of the chief spelling hurdles, one that only practice in actual use of the words can surmount. The following samples show how common and necessary these groups of words are (more examples are in the *Index* articles on each):

en-(or em-): embark, enable, encourage, enforce
in-: inclose (or enclose), infuse, inquire, insure (or ensure), instruct (During the war, the Navy used *inclose*, the Army *enclose*.)

in-(not): inactive, incompatible, infrequent, impractical
un-: unacceptable, uncontrollable, unrecognizable

-able: advisable, changeable, desirable, laughable, usable
-ible: audible, credible, eligible, flexible, irresistible, legible, visible

-ance (noun) -ant (adj.): attendance—attendant, intolerance—intolerant, resistance—resistant
-ence (noun) -ent (adj.): confidence—confident, independence—independent, persistence—persistent

-er: advertiser, consumer, manufacturer, subscriber
-or: administrator, conqueror, editor, proprietor, ventilator

Similar as a spelling problem is the group: *precede, proceed* (but *procedure*), *recede, supersede*.

English is rich in *homonyms, pairs of words pronounced alike but often spelled differently: *pair—pare, piece—peace, plain—plane, stationary—stationery*. The context keeps their meaning clear. Most of them are in common use, so their confusion is usually because of carelessness. If you have trouble with any of them, try writing them in phrases or sentences that will show their meaning:

> The *capital* of California is Sacramento.
> The *capitol* has a gilded dome.
> the city *council—counsel* for the defense—good *counsel*
> the *principal* of the school—4% on the *principal*—a man of *principle*

Affect—effect, weather—whether are homonyms in most people's speech and so belong in this group.

2) *Misspellings due to pronunciation.* Curiously enough the discrepancy between pronunciation and spelling is not such a common cause of misspelling as might be expected. We usually remember the words that seem furthest from the sound, like the *-ough* words and those with silent letters (de*b*tor, *p*sychology, sa*l*mon). The trouble comes in words like *arctic* (or *Arctic*), since few people pronounce a *k* sound in it, and *used to*, since we make only one sound for the *d* and *t* (and so are tempted to write *use to*), and in words like *accidentally* and *occasionally*, where we may fail to remember the *-al*.

Frequently a common but not "accepted" pronunciation is represented. An extra *e* or *a* gets in *athlete* because of the tendency to say it in three syllables; the second *e* in *every* and the second *o* in *sophomore* are dropped because they are almost never spoken; *disgust* appears with a *c* for the *g* and *significance* with a *g* for the first *c*; *quantity* without its first *t* and *undoubtably* for *undoubtedly*. Perhaps more attention to pronunciation would help in such words, though more important would be a clear picture of their written form.

3) *Failure to visualize the letters of a word.* In reading we do not see all the letters of a word, only enough to identify it, and then usually as part of a phrase. In recent years the speed of reading in schools has been greatly increased, with very real gain but with even less clear images of individual words. The vowels especially are not seen—and almost all spelling mistakes are in vowels. Failure to have a clear visual image is probably back of most commonly misspelled

words, such as *physicist, quiet, quite, separate, similar.* Some words spelled with vowels for which the word's sound is no clue (*Slurred vowels) can be remembered by associating them with derivatives in which the vowel is clearly sounded:

comp*a*rable—com p*a*re′   comp*e*tition—com p*e*te′
hypocr*i*sy—hyp o cr*i*t′ i cal   priv*a*te—pri v*a*′ tion
stab*i*lize—sta b*i*l′ i ty

Dormitory can be associated with the French *dormir.* Any device that can help fix a vowel in mind will help.

3. Groups of words

Much sheer memory is necessary to attain accepted spelling, but there are a few rules that apply to several hundred fairly common words. You've heard them since the fourth grade but for the record, and your convenience, here are four with the widest application.

3a. Doubling final consonants. (See *Doubling final consonants.) Words of one syllable ending in a single vowel followed by a single consonant (*hit, log, sit*) double the consonant before an ending beginning with a vowel (*-able, -ed, -er, -ing, -y*):

hittable, hitting   sittable, sitter, sitting
logged, logger, logging

The consonant is not doubled if the word has two vowels (*float, floating; shout, shouting*); or if it ends in two different consonants (*ask, asking; duck, ducked*).

This convention keeps apart a number of pairs of somewhat similar verbs, those with short vowels and those with long, the latter usually spelled with a final *-e:*

bat (băt): batting, batted, batter
bate (bāt): bating, bated, bater
din (dĭn): dinned, dinning
dine (dīn): dined, dining (But: dinner)

Words of more than one syllable ending in a single vowel followed by a single consonant and stressed on the last syllable double the consonant before an ending when the stress remains on the same syllable:

e quip′   e quipped′   e quip′ ping (But: eq′ ui page)
pa trol′   pa trolled′   pa trol′ ling

re fer′ re ferred′ re fer′ ring (But: ref′ e ree ref′ e rence)
ben′ e fit ben′ e fit ed ben′ e fit ing

There are some variations in these words (see *Doubling final consonants), but the rule generally holds.

3b. Ei and ie. The *i* comes before the *e* to represent the sound ē except after *c* (see *-ei-, -ie-.):

belief	believe	chief	companies	fiend
hygiene	niece	piece	priest	siege

After *c* and to spell the sound ā, the *e* comes before the *i:*

After *c:* ceiling   conceive   receive
Long *a:* eight   freight   heinous   neighbor   sleigh   weight

The few exceptions are rather common:

Long *e:* either   neither   seize   weird
Other sounds: counterfeit   heir   height

3c. Ce, ge. A word ending in *-ce (pronounced s) or -ge (pronounced j) keeps the *e* before endings beginning with *a, o,* or *u,* to represent the pronunciation:

courageous   noticeable   peaceable

Before an ending beginning with *e* or *i* the *e* is dropped:

encouraging   noticing   spliced

3d. Final e. Most words spelled with a final unpronounced *e* drop the *e* before additions beginning with a vowel and keep it before additions beginning with a consonant (see *E § 5):

change: changed, changing; changeless (But: changeable [see § 3c])
like: likable, liking; likely, likeness
love: lovable, loving; lovely
please: pleasant, pleasing, pleasure
use: usable, used, using; useful, useless

Some other groups of words having some spelling trait in common are listed on page 157 at the beginning of this chapter.

4. Learning new words

In learning new words, get both the spoken and the written forms at the same time. Making a word your own is chiefly a matter of attention to its sound and its looks. Pronounce a new word distinctly, visualizing it in syllables: *Han-se-at-ic, he-mo-glo-bin, u-ni-cel-lu-lar.*

If you have any doubts about its meaning or pronunciation, consult a dictionary. If the word is at all difficult, study it carefully and then say it without looking at it; then write it down, and compare with its printed form. Then continue saying and writing it a few times until you are sure of it. Focus on the word's appearance by holding a pencil point under it. Underline new words, if they are going to be important to you, so that they will stand out on the page and thus help you remember their exact form. At times it is necessary to counteract the habit of rapid reading so as to really *see* the individual words and even the letters of the words, to fix them in mind.

This method of learning the spelling of a new word holds also for correcting errors you may have fallen into. But it is important not to add to that collection of errors. Paying careful attention to the sound and the sight of a word will in time fix it in your memory so that it will always come right.

5. Proofreading

Students really know how to spell a good proportion of the words they miss on papers. In conference they will frequently spell right a word that had to be marked on a theme. To close the gap between knowledge and performance, careful proofreading of the final copy is necessary.

Spelling is to be attended to in revision. This is the most important general advice to remember. Don't stop when you are writing to look up a word or even to worry about it. You will almost certainly lose something more important if you do—the trend of your thought, the movement of your sentence at least. Mark it in some way (with a ? or √) if you are suspicious of the way it looks, and then check up on all spellings together while working over what you have written. Scrutinize the final copy for careless spellings. A teacher can sympathize with misspelling difficult words or new words, but hardly with *quiet* for *quite* or *their* for *there*. Careful reading of a paper just for the spelling is the best advice for anyone who is likely to make mistakes. To make your eye slow down, if you need to, read with a pencil point just below the line so that you will see every syllable.

Make it easy for yourself to look up the spelling of words you are not sure of. A moderate sized dictionary, the "college" size in most makes, will have all the words you will need, and it is not so full as to make searching hard. Some word lists, if large enough, may help with common words. One of the most compact is the index to Roget's *Thesaurus of English Words and Phrases*, which is especially easy to use because it has several hundred words on a page and no extraneous material to get in the way.

Above all, don't rely on roommates or other persons who may happen to be around. Their guesses are often no better than yours.

Suggested study and writing

1. The following theme was written by a student who had more difficulty with spelling than most college freshmen. Is his spelling consistent with the simplified usage which he defends? Point out every misspelled word you can find and then write each word correctly. Which misspellings would you attribute to faulty pronunciation? To confusion with similar word forms, or inability to visualize the word correctly? To carelessness?

Why Spelling Reform Has Failed

Before I began reading about the spelling reform movement in America, I had often wondered why nothing definate had been perscribed to alleviate the serious problem which nearly every one acknowleges. This problem of twenty-six letters trying to do the work of fourty-two has been branded as ridiculous by editors of the leading dictioneries and encyclopaedias, and by other emenent men from Theodore Roosvelt up to the present time.

Why, then, does this problem remain with us? All the sources I have read have emphasized the seriousness of the problem in differnt ways, but never-the-less not one has given it the through attention which it undoubtedly deserves.

Learned people say that the most practical way of writing "through" is "thru." Then why not write "lamb" as it actually sounds, "lam"? Or "ghost" as "gost"? Some opponents of simplified spelling say that "gost" is not as ghostly as "ghost," and that "lam" doesn't communicate the same association as "lamb." They state that the word originated as "lamb" and that is the way it should remain.

It has been said that the English language offers an almost unparalelled freedom of expression because so many of it's words have been derived from other languages; and that the aesthetic value of the language would therefor be lost if a new system of spelling were adapted. This arguement doesn't take into consideration the fact that such beauty in a language is only skin-deep, and that efficiency counts for more. Many advantages of a new system of spelling have been pointed out, but dispite the optomistic pictures, I don't beleive a complete and thorough reform will ever come about.

If a person indicates a preference for simplified spelling, he is considered by many as ignorant or even illiterate. Consider for instance those who have the greatest influence on education—the teachers. Would any teacher or proffessor jeopardize his position or risk being called illitrate by advocating a sensible system of spelling? Would any editor of a newspaper or a magazine risk irritating his readers by using reformed spelling?

The faults of our present system of spelling are due mainly to illogical public opinion. Each generation has willed to the suceeding generation the ineffective, irratating, and wastefull system with which we still have to struggle; and always with the sympathetic words, "Well, we learned it; why shouldn't you?"

2. Here is a short list of common words that are frequently misspelled. Each word is divided into syllables so that you may visualize more clearly how it is put together. Go through the list carefully, checking those words which you are not absolutely certain you can spell correctly. Then write out each doubtful word four or five times, pronouncing each syllable as you do so.

ac-com-mo-date	ex-is-tence	prej-u-dice
ac-cus-tom	ex-pe-ri-ence	priv-i-lege
ac-quaint-ed	fa-mil-iar	pro-ce-dure
a-cross	fas-ci-nate	pro-fes-sor
ad-o-les-cence	for-ty	pro-nun-ci-a-tion
a-nal-y-sis	gen-er-al-ly	pro-por-tion
a-pol-o-gize	gov-ern-ment	psy-chol-o-gy
ap-pear-ance	gram-mar	re-ceive
ar-ti-cle	hav-ing	rec-om-mend
as-so-ci-a-tion	hin-drance	re-fer-ring
ath-lete	hun-dred	re-pe-ti-tion
at-tend-ance	in-ci-den-tal-ly	re-sem-blance
be-lieve	in-de-pend-ent	sac-ri-fice
ben-e-fit-ed	in-struc-tor	sen-si-ble
Brit-ain	in-ter-pre-ta-tion	sen-ti-men-tal
bus-i-ness	ir-rel-e-vant	sep-a-rate
can-di-date	lab-o-ra-to-ry	sim-i-lar
change-a-ble	lei-sure	suc-ceed
com-par-a-tive	li-brar-y	suc-cess
con-tin-u-ous	lik-a-ble	sur-prise
cu-ri-os-i-ty	main-te-nance	sym-pa-thize
cur-ric-u-lum	med-i-cine	tem-per-a-ment
def-i-nite	mis-spell	tend-en-cy
de-scrip-tion	mo-not-o-nous	trans-fer-ring
de-vel-op	nine-ty	tru-ly
dif-fer-ence	no-tice-a-ble	un-doubt-ed-ly
dis-ap-pear-ance	nui-sance	un-nec-es-sar-y
dis-ap-point	oc-ca-sion-al-ly	un-til
e-lim-i-nate	oc-cur-rence	val-u-a-ble
em-bar-rassed	o-mit-ted	vis-i-ble
en-coun-ter	op-ti-mis-tic	whol-ly
ex-ag-ger-ate	par-tic-u-lar-ly	writ-ing
ex-er-cise	plan-ning	writ-ten

For further practice, see the longer list of words in the *Index* under *Spelling. Either list may be used for class dictation.

3. The following pairs of words are frequently confused in writing. Distinguish between them by using each correctly in a sentence:

advice—advise	loose—lose
affect—effect	moral—morale
already—all ready	principal—principle
beside—besides	quiet—quite
capital—capitol	site—cite
choose—chose	stationery—stationary
complement—compliment	than—then
conscience—conscious	there—their
emphasis—emphasize	waist—waste
formerly—formally	whether—weather
its—it's	whose—who's

4. Plural and possessive forms constitute another common source of spelling errors. Write out for each of the following words the singular possessive, the plural, and the plural possessive forms.

attorney	city	lady	Negro
baby	class	library	puppy
boy scout	country	man	state
bridesmaid	hero	mother-in-law	wife
child	hour	mouse	woman

5. In your spelling notebook keep a list of words encountered in your reading that you will have to use when writing for different courses. To fix the spelling more definitely in your mind, divide the words into syllables as you enter them; consult your dictionary for this purpose. Use the names of your subjects for headings and whatever other classifications you may need, in this manner:

> Economics: guar-an-tee; de-ben-ture; per-son-nel . . .
> History: me-di-e-val; Med-i-ter-ra-ne-an; ren-ais-sance . . .
> Psychology: ap-per-cep-tion; cor-re-la-tion; he-red-i-tar-y . . .
> "General": dor-mi-to-ry; soph-o-more; sched-ule . . .

Writing paragraphs

No, paragraphs are not made by spacing or pausing. The spacing or pausing merely indicates where they are after they are made. . . . A paragraph is planned, therefore, before it is written. It is not yet a group of sentences; it is a group of ideas or facts in the writer's mind. It is going to be one of the little compositions which he will build up into his single whole composition. He does not yet know in what words he will express it; but he knows exactly what ground it will cover.—Charles Sears Baldwin

SUGGESTIONS FOR USING THE CHAPTER: *Since this chapter is centered on actual writing, it should probably come early in a composition course, perhaps directly after Chapter 1, The Activity of Writing, or even before it. It can be used as background for short early practice papers. In order that students clearly understand the doctrine, it is important for them to read the illustrative paragraphs, in spite of the natural tendency to skip lightly over reduced type.*

A PARAGRAPH is a group of related statements that a writer regards as a unit in the development of his subject.[1] To the eye it appears as a unit because of the indention of its first word, sometimes because of its incomplete last line, and perhaps because of spacing. More essentially a paragraph appears to the mind as a unit because of the relation that exists between the statements it contains. These related statements represent a stage in the flow of the writer's thought, for his thought is continuous, even though it may not be consecutive in a logical sense. By the mechanical device of indention and by the inner connection between his statements, he indicates small stages in his material to help his reader see the movement of his thought as nearly as possible as he sees it. A paragraph is consequently a punctuation mark indicating a unit of thought larger than a sentence and smaller than a whole article or chapter. It is an indication that the writer's natural, rapid, more or less helter-skelter thought has been prepared, arranged, organized, *edited* for a reader.

Looking at a single paragraph, the continuity of material is its most important feature; it is a handful of related statements. Considering a series of paragraphs, the obvious fact is that though each one relates to the subject of the paper, each develops a little different phase of it. That is, paragraphs separate as well as join. The indention is a sign to a reader that the thought is going to shift slightly, and he adjusts his attention automatically. (Can you imagine trying to read this chapter not divided into paragraphs?) Paragraphing also

---

[1] E. H. Lewis, *The History of the English Paragraph* (Chicago, 1894); Herbert Read, *English Prose Style* (New York, 1928), Chapter 5. All rhetorics and handbooks have discussions of paragraphs.

helps the writer separate his material into units that can be grasped easily by the reader and that will let the writer place emphasis where he wants it.

1. Materials of paragraphs

When we look into what we call our "minds," we find a continuous succession of images—the remains of sights, sounds, even smells that we have experienced—and of words, some of them names for images and experiences, some less specific. We can speak or write the words that come to mind, but even our most rapid speech does not represent the full stream of what passes in our minds, and writing, slower, more "conscious," is a still smaller selection from what we are thinking. Since each person's thought depends on his own make-up and experience and attitudes, we do not think entirely alike; but since our make-ups and our experiences and our culture (as represented by what we see and hear and read) have a great deal in common, we can communicate pretty well with each other if we really want to.

The immediate material for our writing is this continuous flow in our minds, but its natural course is so irregular, even in the most systematic thinkers, that it needs to be sorted and shaped, put in an order that can be followed by others who will read it. No one is able to tell just how this is done, but by practice in thinking about a subject and in shifting and revising what we first put down on paper we become more and more skilled in conveying our notions to others. The job of writing is representing on paper the natural flow of our thoughts, keeping as close to them as possible, and still shaping them in words so that other people can follow them.

To make a point for a reader, to present it and to make it clear and interesting, we need to draw on all the resources of our minds, to use whatever sorts of material are pertinent and appropriate. There is no scientific classification for these sorts of material, but for convenience we can distinguish a few. Since we can't capture for presentation the thought itself, we will use paragraphs that are made up principally of the sort of raw material being discussed.

1a. Details. Probably the bulk of writing consists of details, words for sensations, images, particular facts. They are the basis of description, of narrative scenes, both factual and imaginative, and of explanations of objects, processes, situations; and they are the evidence, the foundation of general ideas. All sorts of writing show the use, sometimes the massing, of such particular bits of data. This "conception of the difficulties travelers met" in New York's great blizzard of 1888 seems to consist almost solidly of "details":

> The actual fall in 53½ hours was 20.9 inches, or more than twice as much snow as had fallen all that winter, but this figure gives no conception of the difficulties travelers met. For the wind continued high, and the soberest observers reported drifts of fifteen and twenty feet. It was almost impossible to walk. A few hacks took to the streets, the drivers charging anything they could get and in some cases forcing whiskey down the throats of their horses in order to keep them alive. Surface cars struggled for a little while, and then stopped; many of them were literally buried. The Third Avenue Elevated Railway, not then electrified, ran a few trains downtown—one car each, with two or even three dinkey engines pushing it—but these too were stalled. In one of them, helpless between stations, were thirty men; but though they could not get down, they were so fortunate as to be in front of a saloon, and hot toddies were hoisted to them by means of a pail and a length of cord, so that the men remained tolerably happy for the fifteen hours of their captivity, and even were heard to sing. Sturdy little boys with ladders went from place to place letting people down out of second-story windows; generally they charged (this being in the days before Boy Scouts) fifty cents for the descent.—DONALD B. CHIDSEY, *The Gentleman from New York: A Life of Roscoe Conkling*, pp. 381-82

The details in Sherwood Anderson's amusing (or tragic) analysis of the "things that can happen to a chicken" depend on the first sentence and are again bound together at the end of the paragraph.

> One unversed in such matters can have no notion of the many and tragic things that can happen to a chicken. It is born out of an egg, lives for a few weeks as a tiny fluffy thing such as you will see pictured on Easter cards, then becomes hideously naked, eats quantities of corn and meal bought by the sweat of your father's brow, gets diseases called pip, cholera, and other names, stands looking with stupid eyes at the sun, becomes sick and dies. A few hens and now and then a rooster, intended to serve God's mysterious ends, struggle through to maturity. The hens lay eggs out of which come

other chickens and the dreadful cycle is thus made complete. It is all unbelievably complex. Most philosophers must have been raised on chicken farms. One hopes for so much from a chicken and is so dreadfully disillusioned. Small chickens, just setting out on the journey of life, look so bright and alert and they are in fact so dreadfully stupid. They are so much like people they mix one up in one's judgments of life. If disease does not kill them they wait until your expectations are thoroughly aroused and then walk under the wheels of a wagon—to go squashed and dead back to their maker. Vermin infest their youth, and fortunes must be spent for curative powders. In late life I have seen how a literature has been built up on the subject of fortunes to be made in the raising of chickens. It is intended to be read by the gods who have just eaten of the tree of the knowledge of good and evil. It is a hopeful literature and declares that much may be done by simple ambitious people who own a few hens. Do not be led astray by it. It was not written for you. Go hunt for gold on the frozen hills of Alaska, put your faith in the honesty of a politician, believe if you will that the world is daily growing better and that good will triumph over evil, but do not read and believe the literature that is written concerning the hen. It was not written for you.—SHERWOOD ANDERSON, "The Egg," *The Triumph of the Egg*, pp. 47-49

And particular facts are the chief content of technical and scientific writing:

When a volume of air saturated with water vapor is cooled, it condenses in either the liquid or solid form, depending upon whether the temperature is above or below 0° C. This condensation does not occur throughout the entire mass of humid air, but around small condensation nuclei, chiefly sea salts, which are constantly present in the atmosphere. A cloud then is composed of a great number of small water droplets, ice crystals, or both, which are separated from each other but yet limit the visibility. The diameter of the water droplets is very small, ranging from 1 to 70 microns with the most frequent diameter being 12 microns. There are about 50 to 500 of these particles in a cubic centimeter of cloudy air. The rate of fall of these droplets is so small, a few millimeters per second, that the slightest ascending air current is sufficient to hold them aloft. Rain drops, on the contrary, which are composed of an accumulation of small droplets, are comparatively large and fall with appreciable velocities.—*Weather Manual for Pilots* (War Department, TM 1-230), p. 69

Frequently the details are *evidence* or *reasons* for a general statement, as in this from a discussion of the relative positions of nations, written during the war:

We can say that nations have in the past been conclusively defeated [the general statement]. Spain was so conclusively defeated in the sixteenth century that it never again was a great power. France was so conclusively defeated by Russia and Britain in 1812-1814 that it was never again able to seek a Napoleonic Empire. The Spanish nation did not cease to exist. The French nation continued to play a great part in the world, and the ghost of Bonaparte walked again in Napoleon III. Nevertheless, the retreat from Moscow and the defeat at Waterloo were conclusive. What made them conclusive? It was that in the nineteenth century the French potential for war declined first in comparison with Britain's, and then in comparison with the war potential of a unified and industrialized Germany with its rapidly growing population.—WALTER LIPPMANN, *U. S. Foreign Policy*, pp. 144-45

Or the details may be *illustrations* of a statement, like the brief references to specific situations in these paragraphs:

> Assuming that relations exist between events, indeed convinced by common sense and consensus, that they do exist, it follows that in tracing relations we are led afar in space and backward in time. This rule applies even to personalities and occurrences apparently trivial in influence. The building of rayon factories in the United States affects the living standards of Japanese engaged in producing silk worms. The simplest words used by a mountaineer suggest the distant origins of the language he speaks. Every personality, no matter how humble, every human occurrence, however slight, has relations with other personalities and occurrences contemporary and past.
>
> Some of the relations are clear and can be easily traced to a certain extent; for example, the relationships of family and race. Others are complicated and elusive; for instance, the influence of interested propaganda upon government policy and action. But whether clear or elusive, we can never find a stopping place when we try to trace them. A Baptist sermon in Atlanta, if we seek to explain it, takes us back through the Protestant Reformation to Galilee—and far beyond in the dim origins of civilization. We can, if we choose, stop at any point along the line of relations, but that is an arbitrary act of will and does violence to the quest for truth in the matter.—C. A. BEARD, *The Discussion of Human Affairs*, pp. 68-69

The principal weakness of amateur writing is not presenting enough details, failure to bring forth enough particulars to make the subject clear, convincing, and interesting. A little time spent in consideration before writing to bring into mind people, things, incidents, anything specific that belongs to the subject will make the writing easier and will do more than anything else to bring the reader to an understanding of the subject.

1b. Opinions and generalizations. Besides this mass of details, we have in our minds a vast amount of less specific data, which for convenience can be called "generalizations." Most of them we have acquired in words from other people or from reading, but some we have built for ourselves by putting two and two together. We don't need to be told that we have "ideas" as well as "facts," but it is important to try to see the differences between them. Here are a few samples of material more general, more abstract than that illustrated in the preceding section.

First is a simple summary of particulars, a classification of a great many instances, in a description of three methods in education:

Let me explain. The three basic ways are the lecture, the discussion group, and the tutorial hour. In a lecture, a silent class is addressed, more or less like a public meeting. In a discussion group, comprising from five or six to not more than thirty students, the members of the class speak freely, putting or answering questions on points which the teacher organizes so as to form a coherent account of some topic. It may be that for this purpose discussion by the class is broken at intervals by lecturettes from him. In a tutorial hour, the instructor is really holding a conversation, usually with one student, certainly with not more than three or four. This is in the best sense a free-for-all and it presupposes a good stock of knowledge on the part of the students. I may seem to have left out the recitation class, common to the lower schools, in which every pupil in turn answers a part of the day's lesson. But this is really a form of examination. Its teaching value is that of any good examination and I shall speak of it later under that head.—Jacques Barzun, *Teacher in America*, p. 37

Another point about education is more inclusive, offering an interpretation of and the writer's opinion about a matter of general educational and social policy:

The country has become much more socialistic than most people realize. Theoretically it is committed to a policy of free medical advice, and free mental training in the public schools. This program is partly logical and partly illogical. It is logical in that every citizen should be given the opportunity to realize on every physical and mental asset he possesses. It is illogical in that we treat all individuals as if they were Boston terriers, trimming their ears and teaching them identical tricks, so that they will fit a single given standard. It would be much better, would it not, after patching up such physical disabilities as we may, to give each child all the education he can assimilate of the type for which he is fitted? There is no point in trying to teach our twenty million morons to read and write. It is hardly worth while to prod another twenty million dullards through grammar school. It is foolish to lower high-school and college standards so that everyone who has a mere social urge for educational gloss is able to obtain it. It would be a much better policy to reorganize the whole educational system in a way which would permit the establishment of specialized schools fitted to the different requirements of our variant population. The progress of a people depends largely upon the upper 1 per cent. Dr. Cox has shown that the leaders of the world, the geniuses of various types who have made civilization, have been exceptionally intelligent as children. Intelligence tests have been sufficiently perfected to enable us to select such a group. Psychologists cannot guarantee that they will all be leaders; they can guarantee that the leaders will come from among them. What greater service to humanity could a government perform than to select and train everyone who shows promise of outstanding ability, no matter from what walk of life he comes?—Edward M. East, *Biology in Human Affairs*, pp. 189-90

Our opinions may be of very particular things—a toothpaste, a book, a house, a person—but we also carry about with us opinions of more complex matters, and we must use them daily, in college classes, in conversation, in making decisions. Here are two statements, one on the position of labor unions in relation to social organization, and another that may seem simpler but that actually treats in homely terms a question of basic human values.

My guess is that the help which unions are likely to give the community in solving its problems will be more important than the new problems which unions create. The most important fact about the world today is the conflict between the philosophy of life represented by Russia and the philosophy which Western Europe and the United States have inherited from the Greeks and the Anglo-Saxons. The Russian philosophy asserts that the community has interests which are independent of and superior to those of its members. Indeed, it recognizes no rights of the individual against the Government. The philosophy of Western Europe asserts that the supreme values are found in the interests of individuals and that institutions exist in order to serve individuals.

In this great conflict between two philosophies the trade unions are an important ally of the West. In the first place, they are an effective champion of the idea of the dignity of the individual. They have introduced the equivalent of civil rights into industry and have given workers protection against arbitrary treatment by management. Thus they have made a major contribution toward implementing the philosophy of the West.

In the second place, the rise of trade unions and the gradual development of a laboristic community opens up to employes great opportunities to participate in policy-making both in the plant and in the community. Russia is gradually creating a community in which individuals are vassals of the state—a new form of serfdom. Such an economy has little chance of holding its own in competition with a laboristic economy in which responsibility for decisions is widely dispersed and in which millions of employes have a chance to feel that they have a stake in the community.—SUMNER H. SCHLICHTER, "Are We Becoming a 'Laboristic' State?" *New York Times Magazine*, May 16, 1948, pp. 65-66

Too many smart advertisements have suggested that there are no woes which cannot be cured by buying the right soap, or the right scent, or the right girdle. The reader may be sane enough to remember that a salt which will pour evenly in any weather is not an adequate cure for a broken heart, and that the cynicism of our world will not be lessened even if all the young women of America smell sweet. But the repeated suggestion of a million displays—in print, on the radio, written against the night sky—is that there must always be an answer to every problem, and that the answer is something you can buy. If it isn't soap, it may be cigarettes, or perhaps a mouthwash, or a new vitamin. If white bread doesn't make you happy, why not try black? All those hilarious faces in the magazines, those happy bodies, reproach us for remembering that life has problems which cannot be cured at any counter.—HERBERT AGAR, *A Time for Greatness*, p. 155

Obviously this sort of "material" offers problems, since it is more difficult to be accurate when summarizing large numbers of facts or giving our opinions perhaps of complex situations, and since many of our generalizations reflect our prejudices or are simply repeated without actual thought on our part from what we have heard or read.

The best safeguard is to refer our generalizations as far as we can to the particulars to which they apply and to try to be as responsible as circumstances and our temperaments allow. We cannot avoid general ideas, either in living or in writing.

1c. Comparisons and contrasts. We define and sharpen our ideas naturally by comparing and contrasting two or more things, the qualities of one making clearer the qualities of the other. A large part of our thought, especially as we approach making a decision or as we attempt to clarify an opinion, is carried on by comparison. Consequently one of the most useful ways of making our ideas clear to other people is by showing them how these ideas are like or unlike other ideas. The basic methods are comparisons and contrasts between things in the same general field and comparisons and contrasts between things in quite different fields but still having something in common.

In Chapter 9 of *The Horse and Buggy Doctor*, Dr. Hertzler compares and contrasts the work of a surgeon under the primitive conditions of "kitchen surgery" with his work in the operating room of a modern hospital, a comparison within the same field of work. Instead of giving an account of first one and then the other, perhaps following these with his opinion, he keeps both working conditions constantly before the reader, giving first some details of one and then of the other, with his opinion clearly stated or implied all along, as in this sample paragraph:

> I have interpolated the preceding in order to show that kitchen surgery had many advantages. Even the modest, intelligent, well meaning assistant can make himself a nuisance. Only one person can work at a time and while an assistant is doing something the operator is idle—that is his hands are, but his mind is thinking horrible thoughts. On the other hand if one operates alone in a kitchen his instruments are just where he placed them. One kept the instruments in the dishpan, took them out when needed, and put them back in again when he had finished with their use. They were always to be found in an area of a foot and a half, the diameter of the dishpan. There was no nurse to grab them, rub off real or imaginary blood and then place them somewhere else.—ARTHUR E. HERTZLER, *The Horse and Buggy Doctor*, pp. 221-22

Sometimes an unusual comparison both clarifies and fixes in mind an idea, as in this likening of some characteristics of a dog on a walk and the ways of a political liberal:

> The liberal holds that he is true to the republic when he is true to himself. (It may not be as cozy an attitude as it sounds.) He greets with enthusiasm the fact of the journey, as a dog greets a man's invitation to take

a walk. And he acts in the dog's way, too, swinging wide, racing ahead, doubling back, covering many miles of territory that the man never traverses, all in the spirit of inquiry and the zest for truth. He leaves a crazy trail, but he ranges far beyond the genteel old party he walks with and he is usually in a better position to discover a skunk. The dog often influences the course the man takes, on his long walk; for sometimes a dog runs into something in nature so arresting that not even a man can quite ignore it, and the man deviates—a clear victim of the liberal intent in his dumb companion. When the two of them get home and flop down, it is the liberal—the wide-ranging dog—who is covered with burdocks and with information of a special sort on out-of-the-way places. Often ineffective in direct political action, he is the opposite of the professional revolutionary, for, unlike the latter, he never feels he knows where the truth lies, but is full of rich memories of places he has glimpsed it in. He is, on the whole, more optimistic than the revolutionary, or even than the Republican in a good year.—*The New Yorker,* Jan. 17, 1948. Reprinted by permission. Copr. 1948. The New Yorker Magazine, Inc.

1d. Qualifying statements. Our ordinary thought tends to be in broad terms and not examined for accuracy, but under pressure of need to be exact or as a result of training we can make ourselves relatively exact within the limits of our knowledge. Perhaps this is more of an attitude than a "kind of material," but the signs are in added details and statements that qualify, set limits, define the topic. Sometimes the qualification consists only of a word, like *sometimes, generally,* or of saying *some* instead of *all,* of dropping *only* or *nothing but.* Usually it is in a slight elaboration of detail, as in this paragraph:

> In seeking to improve our political life we must be careful not to expect too much, and not to rest our democratic faith on assumptions which cannot be supported. If we say that the common man is infallible, or that the voice of the people is infallible, we are talking nonsense and inviting the disappointments which must ensue. But if we say that the opinions of the common man, when he is given a fair chance to form opinions, tend to show good sense and to be the best basis for the decisions of government, we are saying what can be proved both from the record of the past and from the experience of the present. On this unboastful statement we can build a politics consonant with man's dignity, and we may even hope in time to unite the world in the name of that dignity.—HERBERT AGAR, *A Time for Greatness,* p. 79

In definitions a writer sets the limits and gives the essential characteristics of the thing or situation he is telling about, as in this definition of *cartels:*

> A cartel, simply stated, is a small ring of producers or distributors that acquires control of domestic or foreign markets and uses that control to crush competition and new enterprise, prevent maximum production and establish rigid high prices in a scarcity economy which brings huge profits to the few through exploitation of the consumer. There are many different

kinds of cartel, but generally they comprise a group of industrialists who gain monopolistic control of a raw material, such as tin, or of a commercial product, such as synthetic rubber. These industrialists agree among themselves on a theoretical price having little relation to cost, and divide up domestic and foreign markets so that one firm or group has a monopoly in each area. In order to prevent other firms from entering this monopoly the cartels depend upon patent laws which they manipulate skillfully so that their processes, their established technology and their absolute control cannot be menaced by any independent firms which have not subscribed to their quota.

In addition to monopolizing and dividing markets (where any arbitrary price can be established because there is no competition), the cartels establish quotas on production. With restricted production, scarcity can be maintained and high prices determined with little difficulty. Obviously, competition (the very essence of traditional capitalism) which would encourage competitive prices, high production and technological progress, and new inventions which would enable other firms to enter the fields dominated by cartelists through patents, are incompatible with the cartel system.— ROBERT REUBEN, "The Menace of the Cartels," *The New Republic*, Oct. 11, 1943, 109:476

An important element in a definition may be making clear what the term does *not* mean, as John Dewey does in running over various senses of the word *thinking* to define the particular sense (reflective thought) in which he is interested:

In its loosest sense, thinking signifies everything that, as we say, is "in our heads" or that "goes through our minds." He who offers "a penny for your thoughts" does not expect to drive any great bargain. In calling the objects of his demand *thoughts*, he does not intend to ascribe to them dignity, consecutiveness, or truth. Any idle fancy, trivial recollection, or flitting impression will satisfy his demand. Day-dreaming, building of castles in the air, that loose flux of casual and disconnected material that floats through our minds in relaxed moments are, in this random sense, *thinking*. More of our waking life than we should care to admit, even to ourselves, is likely to be whiled away in this inconsequential trifling with idle fancy and unsubstantial hope.

In this sense, silly folk and dullards *think*. The story is told of a man in slight repute for his intelligence, who, desiring to be chosen selectman in his New England town, addressed a knot of neighbors in this wise: "I hear you don't believe I know enough to hold office. I wish you to understand that I am thinking about something or other most of the time." Now reflective thought is like this random coursing of things through the mind in that it consists of a succession of things thought of; but it is unlike, in that the mere chance occurrence of any chance "something or other" in an irregular sequence does not suffice. Reflection involves not simply a sequence of ideas, but a *con*sequence—a consecutive ordering in such a way that each determines the next as its proper outcome, while each in turn leans back on its predecessors. The successive portions of the reflective thought grow out of one another and support one another; they do not come and go in a medley. Each phase is a step from something to something—technically speaking, it is a term of thought. Each term leaves a deposit which is utilized in the next term. The stream or flow becomes a train, chain, or thread.—JOHN DEWEY, *How We Think*, pp. 2-3

It is possible to make a definition—or any other statement—readable as well as clear and accurate. Responsible writing depends on qualifying statements, making the statements mean only as much as they reasonably should.

1e. Relationships between facts. One of our characteristics as human beings is that we are forever seeing and noting relations between our facts: one comes after another, one is the cause of another, or the reason for a belief, or an example of a class, and so on. The examples here only suggest the presence of this sort of thinking.

In this paragraph from a protest against mismanagement in the first world war, Mr. Montague puts first the effect, then the cause, and then returns to the effect (*And so . . .*).

> The winter after the battle of Loos a sentry on guard at one part of our line could always see the frustrate skeletons of many English dead. They lay outside our wire, picked clean by the rats, so that the khaki fell in on them loosely—little heaps of bone and cloth half hidden now by nettles and grass. If the sentry had been a year in the army he knew well enough that they had gone foredoomed into a battle lost before a shot was fired. After the Boer War, you remember, England, under the first shock of its blunders, had tried to find out why the Staff work was so bad. What it found, in the words of a famous Report, was that the fashion in sentiment in our Regular Army was to think hard work "bad form"; a subaltern was felt to be a bit of a scrub if he worried too much about discovering how to support an attack when he might be more spiritedly employed playing polo; "The nobleness of life," as Antony said, when he kissed Cleopatra, was to go racing or hunting, not to sit learning how to forecast the course of great battles and how to provide for answering their calls. And so swathes of little brown bundles, with bones showing through, lay in the nettles and grass.—C. E. MONTAGUE, *Disenchantment*, p. 196

Here Mr. Fadiman sketches his reasons for believing that "the trash of my generation was superior to the trash of today."

> I say trash. Actually such books are "trash" only by standards which should not be applied to children's reading. They have the incalculable value that listening to perfectly inane, adult conversation holds for children: they increase the child's general awareness. They provide admittedly rough paradigms of character, motivation, life experiences. That is why it seems to me that the trash of my generation was superior to the trash of today. I submit that *The Rover Boys in the Everglades* and *Frank on a Gunboat* are preferable to Superman and his kind on two counts: they were cleanly and clearly written, and their characters were credible and not entirely unrelated to the child's experience. When I was nine I could learn something interesting about life from even such highly colored affairs as the Frank Merriwell series, but I know that my son can learn nothing whatsoever of

genuine interest (that is, which he can check against the expanding universe within himself) from the comics. I believe firmly that the current juvenile literature of the impossible is meretricious compared with the honest hackwork my own generation enjoyed. I also think that the kids are about ready to kick over this thriller fare in favor of something saner and more natural.—CLIFTON FADIMAN, *Reading I've Liked*, Preface, p. xvi

Without labeling explicitly the relation between his statements, Professor Barzun is giving reasons for passing examinations:

Examinations are not things that happen in school. They are a recurring feature of life, whether in the form of decisive interviews to pass, of important letters to write, or life-and-death diagnoses to make, or meetings to address, or girls to propose to. In most of these crises, you cannot bring your notes with you and must not leave your wits behind. The habit of passing examinations is therefore one to acquire early and to keep exercising even when there is a possibility of getting around it.—JACQUES BARZUN, *Teacher in America*, p. 215

Although we usually associate these relationships with earnestness and "logic," they may be quite individual, as in the statements that lead up to the *consequently* of Mr. Saroyan's last sentence:

Under the foregoing circumstances, how may the playwright do his work, maintain his integrity, and manage to survive economically? I have already remarked that I sometimes bet on the horses. I should like to enlarge a little on this. Horse betters as such are generally regarded as fools, and it is proper to accept this view without embarrassment. They are especially foolish if they lose, and more often than not they do. But the virtue to the playwright of seeking to exempt himself from the urgent need of money by studying the races and occasionally making a bet is this: that it establishes more swiftly than any other activity the essential irrelevance and worthlessness of money, whether the sums involved are enormous or insignificant. This, in turn, re-establishes emphatically the profound relevance and worth of art, of integrity, of pride, of indifference toward material success or failure. In short, it permits the playwright to work hard, as hard as he is able to work, on a play *for its own sake.* For he knows that while it is not easy, it is nevertheless true that money as such, as money, *may* be abundantly obtained by so simple a process as believing one horse among eight or nine will run faster than the others, and backing up his belief with a bet. By the same token, he knows that much needed money may disappear that easily, too. Consequently, money by itself is seen to be so nearly meaningless as to be unworthy of any broader identification.—WILLIAM SAROYAN, "Confessions of a Playwright," *Tomorrow*, Feb. 1949, p. 19

1f. Development of paragraphs. Sometimes conscientious students feel that developing an idea fully, building out a statement into a paragraph, is "just padding." There are two chief reasons why a bare statement is insufficient: First, it does not really represent the consecutiveness or fullness of the writer's thought and often gives such a small sample that he does not seem to know his subject or at least does not seem to be thinking about it at the time of writing. Second, it cannot convey to a reader, who may know nothing about the subject, enough to let him see the subject as the writer sees it. To make an impression on the reader, it is necessary to control his mind for a brief time; it is necessary not just to mention the subject but to present it, develop it, lead him to think about it and to see it as the writer sees it.

Actually developing paragraphs by full use of the appropriate materials also removes a frequent worry of student writers, "getting the required length." Most writing in the world is planned for a fairly definite length (a page of a typed letter, an article for a specific magazine) so that specified length for compositions is natural. "About 600 words" means that the student is to take a subject and select from his thinking about it what can be conveyed in about that number of words. The bulk of the actual space in most papers will be taken up with specific details, but all pertinent material should be used. A final test question for a paper is "Have I put in enough of what I know and believe about this subject to lead a reader to see it as I do?"

2. Paragraphs in the making

When a person sets about putting on paper the material he has in mind on a subject that he wishes or has to write about, he is consciously or unconsciously concerned with paragraphs. Writers differ greatly in the amount of preliminary planning they do. The material for a short paper on a relatively simple or familiar subject groups itself; that is, the small stages in the thought become paragraphs without much conscious attention. More complex material may require considerable planning, including the making of outlines and indicating of specific paragraphs. At any rate some of the elementary questions about writing can be considered and understood as aspects of making paragraphs.

2a. Visualizing paragraphs. Except in letters and other personal sorts of writing, the physical features, the looks, of paragraphs are determined by the practices of periodical and book editors. Because of the usually simple narratives of news stories and the narrow columns, which make long, unbroken stretches of type forbidding, and because they are intended for hasty reading, paragraphs in newspapers run distinctly short, the great majority of them being under

75 words, 20 to 50 words being typical. Paragraphs in magazines of restricted circulation approach book paragraphs in length, but in fairly popular magazines the paragraphs would rarely be 200 words long and typically run from 100 to 150 words. Books show great variety, but as a rule paragraphs of less than 125 words would be short and paragraphs of over 250 rather long except in books intended for a rather limited audience. Fiction shows considerable variety in paragraph length, approximating periodical length. In any given article, of course, the paragraphs will vary considerably, because subordinate points will be of differing importance, some deserving fuller and others shorter treatment.

Here are some figures from typical pieces of writing that illustrate characteristic paragraph lengths in factual writing. The first two are from news stories, the next two from magazine articles, and the remaining from books. They are based on a count of 16 consecutive paragraphs, except the Santayana essay, which contains only eight.

Length of paragraphs in order	Longest	Shortest	Average
Two news stories:			
93, 29, 75, 57, 23, 43, 40, 51, 26, 22, 43, 18, 18, 29, 24, 20	93	18	38
30, 38, 18, 53, 50, 29, 57, 56, 55, 71, 44, 30, 49, 23, 23, 36	71	18	41
Article in the *Atlantic Monthly:*			
66, 96, 113, 65, 85, 101, 83, 85, 86, 112, 69, 100, 100, 90, 136, 141	141	65	95
A *New Yorker* profile:			
192, 111, 99, 163, 13, 306, 137, 174, 110, 16, 274, 232, 245, 208, 95, 11	306	11	149
Vannevar Bush, *Modern Arms and Free Men:*			
29, 87, 147, 91, 163, 178, 125, 74, 96, 165, 244, 151, 378, 116, 97, 149	378	29	143
Margaret Leach, *Reveille in Washington:*			
136, 211, 53, 118, 207, 135, 216, 83, 182, 129, 109, 302, 171, 55, 143, 100	302	53	147
From Chapter 1, sections 1 to 3 of *Writer's Guide and Index to English:*			
166, 80, 141, 99, 97, 142, 225, 149, 115, 93, 31, 105, 102, 106, 94, 41	225	31	112
George Santayana, "Skylarks":			
290, 180, 294, 333, 435, 159, 513, 438	513	159	330

There are some standard exceptions to these conventions of paragraphing. Each speech in a dialog is set off in a separate paragraph. Occasionally, in complex subject matter, a single sentence that shows the transition in thought between two paragraphs or sections will stand as a separate paragraph, and sometimes an important or emphatic sentence will deserve a paragraph by itself. In advertising and a good deal of business writing, single sentences are indented as paragraphs for display purposes, the real paragraphs often being indicated by extra spacing between groups of these sentences. Editorials in some newspapers are printed in this way, with gain in legibility as compared with the forbidding editorial pages of the more conservative papers, but writers usually find it harder to show relationship between their ideas in this form. It is more appropriate for short, suggestive statements than for presenting a "chain of reasoning." A successful combination of one sentence paragraphs and more fully developed ones can be worked out, as in this editorial:

> More and more people these days are shouting the word "loyalty." Not just publishers and politicians, but even educators are speaking of it. And the more oratorical they become in talking of it, the more confusing it is to some students to discover what all the fuss is about.
> What do they mean by "loyalty"?
> Do they mean unquestioning obedience to authority of either one's state or one's family or one's university?
> Or do they mean personal sympathy with the aims of the group of which one is a member?
> Or do they mean by "loyalty" a devotion to what is best within any group or institution?
> How can one be just loyal? It doesn't make very much sense. . . . Maybe those who are speaking so emphatically about "loyalty" do not mean that it should make sense.
> Maybe "loyalty" is for them an instrument by which minds may be molded to suitable patterns. Maybe those to whom "loyalty" is the highest form of state and university patriotism are more concerned with enlisting emotions in support of their projects than they are in objective values. Maybe they really do not know what they mean and are merely repeating, because of ignorance or expediency, what has become a public cry.—*The California Daily Bruin*

The quoted paragraphs in section 1 of this chapter show a typical range of developed paragraphs: the shortest is 69 words, the longest 362, and the average 168 words. (The complete range in length is: 362, 319, 255, 254, 234, 226, 214, 209, 195, 174, 167, 166, 145, 142, 138, 124, 121, 121, 110, 102, 98, 89, 80, 69.)

All this discussion of length does not mean that a writer should stop to count the words in his paragraphs, but he should be able to visualize the length of his paragraphs as they would stand in typical magazine and book form. Most writers get about 200 words of longhand on a page and about 300 in double spaced typing. It is obvious that a writer should look closely at any page of his manuscript that shows more than two paragraph breaks—not that they are necessarily wrong, but he should be sure that they represent actual stages of his material, that they are appropriate to the subject, to the reader, and to the emphasis he intends. Conspicuously short paragraphs are likely to be symptoms that he is not developing his material sufficiently, is not putting in enough details, is not building enough small ideas together, or else that he is dividing his subject into units too small to guide his reader to an understanding of the relationships between points.

Similarly, he should look closely at paragraphs that run over a manuscript page, to see if they are actually unified or if perhaps they shouldn't be broken for emphasis or for the reader's convenience. Paragraphs are likely to be longer than average when the thought is consecutive, emphasizing relationships between facts or ideas. In works of criticism, in philosophy and science, the paragraphs are rightly longer than in pictures of the life around us. Length is a symptom of other qualities of paragraphs, and is to be considered in the light of subject matter and purpose, and should be a sign of adequate and appropriate development. At the beginning of a composition course paragraphs are likely to be conspicuously short, sometimes averaging under 75 words.

2b. Focusing statements. Although our natural flow of thought has its little tensions and climaxes, it usually lacks form, so that preparing it for someone else to follow requires giving it some shape and putting in some guideposts. Giving his material an occasional point of focus is natural for a writer and very convenient for a reader. In factual writing a sentence that states in general terms the subject of a paragraph and perhaps summarizes some of its content is called a *topic sentence.*

If the topic sentence stands first, it leads the reader to expect further development. When Professor Schlichter begins a paragraph "A fourth way in which our economic order creates friction between workers and business owners is by its selling and advertising activities," we expect details of these selling activities and their bearing on unrest. When Lincoln Steffens starts a paragraph "One of the wrongs suffered by boys is that of being loved before loving," we expect a discussion of the idea or specific instances. Often it seems more natural to put the particulars first, pointing toward the general statement at the end, as in the paragraph by Saroyan on page 181, which he concludes with the statement "Consequently, money by itself is seen to be so nearly meaningless as to be unworthy of any broader identification."

In the following paragraph there are two contenders for the title of topic sentence, the last and the one in the middle beginning "A sense of the public psychology." Perhaps neither entirely focuses the material of the paragraph, but considering the subjects of nearby paragraphs, the former would be taken because it is more in line with the idea of the whole and indicates the contribution of this particular paragraph to the whole. Frequently the context or general purpose of an article will help select the topic sentence in this way.

Large automobile companies, in elaborate advertisements, present their skilled mechanics as "craftsmen," making a title of the term. A certain absurdity, yet almost a pathetic intensity, of this tendency is revealed in the yearning for the myth of individual handicraft betrayed by such phrases as "Tomato Soup . . . . by Campbell." General Motors still clings to the lost carriage maker in the insignia and motto, "Body by Fisher." *Personal* names for *mass* products are at a premium. There is commercial value in "Fanny Farmer" candies, or "Mrs. Wagner's Pie." A sense of the public psychology is revealed in these oblique apologies by manufacturers for the industrial standardization of their products. This is not to imply that there are not many commodities which industry produces with better results than could the individual. But it's worth noting that when the sewing machine was first invented especially high prices were charged for clothing made on it. "Untouched by human hands" was once the miraculous advertising appeal for other milled or machined commodities. Yet today, the label "hand made" is worth an illogical amount in the retail value of many products.—Scott Graham Williamson, *The American Craftsman*, p. 9

Practiced writers are not usually conscious of their topic sentences, in fact have more trouble in finding them than someone less familiar with the subject. But if their minds are working well, the material is focused. Occasionally it is useful for a beginner to concentrate on these focal statements. It may help to write a topic sentence, or a series of them for the various paragraphs of a paper, and then develop the ideas as stated. If you are having trouble developing your subject fully, becoming aware in this way of just what a given paragraph is to do may make the development easier. Or if your paragraphs are disjointed, focusing your material in advance can lead to more consistent and continuous development.

The writer of the following first paragraph was simply setting down one statement after another:

I have chosen cancer for my subject because medicine is one of the things upon which I am deciding to make my life's work, and because cancer is one of the most dreaded and baffling diseases known to the medical profession. Several of my family have died of cancer and I didn't know whether it was hereditary so I decided to find out. A positive cure has not been found as yet nor has a positive cause. Thousands are cured of this affliction each year by early treatment, and yet, 150,000 people in the United States alone die of cancer every year. This death rate is second to only heart failure. To stem this steadily increasing number of deaths by cancer, the United States Government has founded the United States Public Health Service National Cancer Institute at Bethesda, Maryland. An appropriation of $570,000 a year for this institute helps it to support itself and others like it and to bring together cancer researchers the country over to collaborate on this immense problem.

He could have developed the idea of the first sentence, the appeal of the subject to him, or the social importance of cancer, or steps being taken to discover a cure—but hardly all three. Framing a topic sentence might have helped him.

The important point, however, is not the topic sentence—that is only a sign—but actually bringing to a focus the material that is sufficiently related to form a natural paragraph.

2c. Actual writing. People's habits of writing differ so much that it is hardly safe to generalize on what they do in the actual process of composition. But it seems safe to say that if they have thought over their subject matter they will write several sentences without stopping (much), and that it would be well if they could get the habit of writing at least a whole paragraph at a time. Certainly you shouldn't let your attention wander after a statement that is intended to lead into another statement. Try to write a full paragraph before you let your attention shift to something else, or before you go to look for more material, or before you get up to walk around the room or chat with your roommate. Of course efficiency demands that you keep your attention fixed as much as possible on your writing, but if you do pause, try to pause between paragraphs or between the larger stages of your paper. Make the writing of a paragraph continuous, so that it can keep as close as possible to your actual thinking.

If you are writing from a good outline it is easy to see the stages in the material and so concentrate on one stage at a time. The outline is roughly related to the paragraphs, but as a rule they do not correspond exactly to outline heads. A main head may be one paragraph in a short paper or several paragraphs in a fuller treatment of the subject. In a very full outline several subheads might be covered in a single paragraph. The outline is a guide to the order of material and to the scale of treatment but the number of divisions does not always represent the number of actual paragraphs.

In general, make your first drafts as full as you can. One of the fundamental knacks in writing is packing in details, using particular facts and particular pictures as contrasted with general statements. The details may be few but striking and representative, or they may be numerous, carrying force in part by their number. Vague statement and lack of detail usually make for unsuccessful writing. Instead of reading "The hat had a peculiar feather," the reader wants specific details so that he can see in what way the feather was "peculiar"; instead of "The people in the bleachers were of all shapes and sizes" he needs three or four details that would give a glimpse of the people—and at the same time let him feel that the writer had really seen the crowd he was talking about.

Successful detail does not have to be unusual but simply accurate enough to let the reader see and believe:

> His light blue eyes are watery, and deep wrinkles show in the corners as if they were used to squinting into the sunlight. His long narrow nose has a twist, as if it had had some exciting contacts and had lost to its opponents. His cheeks are thin and the skin is stretched tight over a determined jaw. His neck is encircled by a once brilliant black neckerchief which has now turned a powdery gray from the dust kicked up by the pushing cattle.

Most students (and other writers) who have trouble meeting the expected length of assigned papers would find their work easier if they would get the habit of developing details, first by seeing more small facts and bits of picture that their subject needs, and second by putting these details down on paper. Their manuscripts then would not only say more and be more convincing, but they would be much more interesting. Writing which is alive with concrete detail is also easier and more satisfying, because it has not been padded out with irrelevant matter but built by proper means. It is much easier to draw a line through details that in revision seem unnecessary or out of place than it is to open up a paragraph and put more matter in. Consequently put in too much rather than too little in the first draft.

Since the first draft shows you for the first time your ideas definitely expressed in words, you will expect to rework it. Make this revision easy by giving the first draft plenty of space on the paper. Don't crowd the copy to the margins or let the lines stand so close together that you can't write new words between them. Some writers put only one paragraph on a page or use only the upper half of the sheet in the first writing, so that they have plenty of room for additions and alterations of all sorts. Work out some scheme of physical arrangement on paper so that your writing can be carried on with as little inconvenience as possible.

2d. Revising. How much revision your paragraphs need depends of course on how well they appear in the first writing. You write them, more or less following your thinking as you have decided it should go, and then read them carefully to see if they will do. The purpose of revision is to remove the faults and increase the virtues of the first draft, and in particular to examine so far as a writer ever can the fitness of his presentation for his intended readers. In paragraphs the good old principles of *unity* (singleness of idea or of impression), *coherence* (continuity, relation between statements), and *emphasis* (exactness with which the writer's view is interpreted for the reader) are useful checks.

To check for these matters in revision of paragraphs, it may be most convenient to ask yourself these questions:

1. Does each paragraph develop a clearcut stage of the subject?

One of the danger spots is at the end of the paragraph because we are likely to have afterthoughts and tack on a minor or somewhat unrelated statement. Often this statement can be thrown away, or put with the following paragraph, or tucked in inconspicuously at an earlier point in the same paragraph. Sometimes two really unrelated matters are put together, though more often the fault is neglecting to show the connection that really exists between the statements. If the subject actually changes, turns a sharp corner within a paragraph, the paragraph should be divided at that point or completely rewritten.

2. Are any paragraphs conspicuously over- or underdeveloped?

This is partly a matter of physical length, as was described in § 2a. More important, it is a matter of content. Are there too many details or illustrations or repetitions of idea? Are there too few? Readers who are unfamiliar with the subject or are hostile to it, or who are supposed to think slowly, need more elaboration; those more or less informed and sympathetic need less elaboration, unless it is used to arouse immediate interest.

3. Do the paragraphs end strongly and on the point that I want my readers to get especially?

This emphasis is not so important for accounts of personal experience, and perhaps not for other narrative, as it is for developing a line of reasoning. You want to be sure that your emphasis is clear to the reader. You should note that the beginnings and ends of paragraphs offer the emphatic position.

4. Are the statements within a paragraph so related that my readers can follow naturally from one to the next?

Will the relation that is clear to me be clear to them? This continuity is the crux of writing good paragraphs and is elaborated in section 3 of this chapter.

2e. Manuscript form. The specific conventions of spacing for paragraphs can be quickly stated. In print a paragraph is usually indented by one em (that is, by a unit as wide as the type is high). In longhand manuscript the indention should be enough to be clearly seen, about an inch in typical handwriting, perhaps a little less for smaller than average writing. In typescript a paragraph is indented from five to eight spaces. A stop on the tabulator bar can be set so that it will make uniform indentions with one pressure of the tabulator key when the carriage is pulled back to the left margin.

In some business letters or mimeographed matter which is written single spaced, a block form is used in which the paragraph is not indented and the only sign is the line left between paragraphs. This form is not used for general manuscript.

Some students make their copy confusing by indenting the first line of each page, even when it is not the beginning of a paragraph, or by leaving part of the last line on a page blank so that it looks like the end of a paragraph. If you have formed either of these habits, you should break it. If you want to indicate the beginning of a paragraph in copy that you have written solid, put the paragraph symbol in the left margin and draw an angle before the first word of the new paragraph, like this:

```
   If you have formed either of these habits, you
   should break it. ⌐If you want to indicate the
 ¶ beginning of a paragraph in copy that you have
   written solid, put the paragraph symbol in the
```

If you want to indicate that what you have written as two paragraphs should be joined as one, write No ¶ in the left margin and draw if possible a line from the end of the preceding to the beginning of the following paragraph.

In typewritten manuscript it is better to start a new page than to allow the first line of a paragraph to stand alone at the bottom of a page, and it is better to avoid starting a new page with the last line of a paragraph.

3. Connection within paragraphs

A writer's purpose in each paragraph is to advance his subject, to leave his reader more informed or interested at the end than he was at the beginning. Whether or not even a meaningful paragraph makes its full point depends largely on the way the reader is led from one statement to the next. It is not enough that the relation between the statements is obvious to the writer; it should be obvious also to the reader for whom it is intended. To make sure of this, the writer usually needs only to check his paragraphs in revision, taking a reader's point of view so far as he can. If a sentence sounds as though the paragraph was beginning again, it probably needs attention. If it is difficult to pass from one statement to the next, the reader is thrown off the track. If the statements can be firmly tied together, they will probably compose a satisfactory paragraph and embody a consistent chain of thought. The connection must first exist in the ideas and then be shown.

The second sentence of the following paragraph does not follow from the first; it seems to make a new start. The whole paragraph needs to be rewritten from a definite point of view (either of the player trying to find a good polo pony or of the attempts that have been made to furnish good ponies) and the relation between the statements made clear:

> For many years men have been breeding, raising, and schooling different types and breeds of horses in an effort to produce the ideal polo mount. When a player wishes to purchase a high-type pony, he looks for four things —quickness, speed, stamina, and ability to stop easily. A combination of these four essentials is difficult to find in one animal. Several have two or three of the qualifications, but very seldom do you find a pony with all four.

Fortunately the means of showing the connection between statements are natural and simple. The common ones are:

1) Continuing the same subject from sentence to sentence, in the same words, in synonyms, or by means of pronouns

2) Some words of the first sentence, perhaps the object, used as the subject of the second or at the beginning of the second

3) A pronoun referring to a word in the preceding sentence

4) A thought relationship (cause or effect, reason, illustration ...) shown directly by a conjunction or adverb (*however, but, and* ...) or only suggested

5) Parallel structure of the sentences

The following paragraph shows the most common of these signs of continuity.

(1) Critics have not been lacking, *of course*, who pointed out what a hash democracy was making of its pretensions to government. (2) *These critics* have seen that the important decisions were taken by individuals, and that public opinion was uninformed, irrelevant and meddlesome. (3) *They* have usually concluded that there was a congenital difference between the masterful few and the ignorant many. (4) *They* are the victims of a superficial analysis of the evils they see so clearly. (5) The *fundamental difference* which matters is that between insiders and outsiders. (6) *Their* relations to a problem are radically different. (7) Only the *insider* can make decisions, not because he is inherently a better man but because he is so placed that he can understand and can act. (8) The *outsider* is necessarily ignorant, usually irrelevant and often meddlesome, because he is trying to navigate the ship from dry land. (9) *That* is why excellent automobile manufacturers, literary critics and scientists often talk such nonsense about politics. (10) *Their* congenital excellence, if it exists, reveals itself only in their own activity. (11) The *aristocratic theorists* work from the fallacy of supposing that a sufficiently excellent square peg will also fit a round hole. (12) *In short*, like the democratic theorists, *they* miss the essence of the matter, which is, that competence exists only in relation to function; that men are not good, but good for something; that men cannot be educated, but only educated for something.—WALTER LIPP-MANN, *The Phantom Public*, pp. 149-50

Suggests continuation from a preceding paragraph

Subject of 1 repeated

Pronoun, referring to *critics*, subject of 1 and 2

Pronoun, as in 3

Fundamental contrasts with *superficial* of 4; *difference* repeated from 3
Pronoun *Their* refers to *insiders and outsiders*
Insider repeated

Outsider repeated from 5, contrasting with *insider* in 7

Pronoun *That*, summarizing idea of 8

Pronoun *Their*, referring to the subjects of *talk* in 9

Aristocratic theorists echoes *critics* of first sentences; *excellent* echoes *excellence* of 10

In short connective
Pronoun *they*, referring to *theorists* of 11; *democratic theorists* contrasting with *aristocratic*
A firm, emphatic final sentence, topic sentence and goal of the preceding statements

It would be impossible to begin reading this paragraph at any sentence without feeling that something had gone before, something needed to get its full meaning. Even at the spots where the connection is least close (sentences 5, 7, 11), the sentences definitely mean more because of what has preceded.

One of the most important things to work on in practicing writing paragraphs is this connection between statements, trying to find natural ways of showing that the thought is continuous.

4. Transitions between paragraphs

This continuity of ideas needs also to be shown from one paragraph to another. The connection between the parts of the subject, the words that lead the reader from one thought to another, are called *transitions*.

One of the most common weaknesses of amateur writing is beginning a later paragraph as though nothing had been said already, instead of building on what has gone before. The two following paragraphs could have been linked by some expression like "The principal advantage that I found in the prep school is that every student gets individual attention."

> I think that a preparatory school education is better than a high school education. During the last four years I went to prep school. Many times my friends would tell me that it was just a waste of time. They'd say, "Gosh! but you're missing a lot of fun" or "Don't be a sucker and spend the best four years of your life in prep school."
>
> Individual attention is the main objective of prep schools. Classes are limited to ten or twenty students. We never had to study in a room where another class was reciting. The work is not entirely left to the pupil, as regular study halls are held. If one is low in a subject the prof will find time to tutor him. Tests are corrected and recorrected until every mistake is cleared. Most fellows coming to college from a prep school know how to study. This does not mean that they are smarter than anyone else but that they have been taught to budget their time.

There are two parts to indicating transitions: one is connecting with the topic of the whole paper, the other connecting with the topic of the preceding paragraph. If it can be done naturally, it is emphatic to name or allude to the topic of the article, or at least of a subdivision of the article, in the first sentence of each paragraph. In a run of six paragraphs dealing with the city of Buffalo in the following excerpt from Carl Carmer's *Listen for a Lonesome Drum*, the city is named near the beginning of each:

> Buffalo is a place of contrasts—of big and distinctly different communities bound together into a huge blustery city beside the tossing waters of Erie, stormiest of the Great Lakes. . . .
>
> And the people in those depths are equally indifferent to the lake shore. To thousands of its people Buffalo means the golden glow and desperate drudgery of a steel furnace, the stuffy interior of a flour mill, . . .
>
> The casual wanderer through Buffalo's residential streets will not walk far without coming upon a corner redolent with the smell of beer and sauerkraut, cheese and apple dumplings. . . .
>
> Last and most powerful of the groups that make up Buffalo are the rich old families living in heavy elegance behind the respectable excesses of the scroll saw. . . .
>
> The four chief streams of Buffalo's population become aware of each other only at City Hall and in the downtown business section. . . .
>
> The Irish, the Germans, and the rich old families have kept Buffalo on the conservative side politically through most of its later history. . . .
>
> CARL CARMER, *Listen for a Lonesome Drum*, pp. 43-46

And of ten paragraphs by Mr. Carmer on the city of Rochester, all but one name Rochester in the first sentence.

The connection with the paragraph immediately preceding is easier and perhaps more important. The purpose is to show the reader that the subject is being continued. When paragraphs are short, the signs of continuity may not differ essentially from those used between sentences. There are transitional words and phrases like *this* or *that* or other words that refer directly to a word or idea at the end of the preceding paragraph and transitional expressions like *on the contrary, another reason, in the second place, besides this,* and other indications of thought relationship. Such genuine connectives are more essential than the flabby *then too* or mechanical expressions like *Now let us turn to* . . . or *It is interesting to note* . . . which are symptoms that the writer has not sensed the actual relationship between the points he is making.

The sign of transition between paragraphs appears usually at the beginning of the following rather than at the end of the preceding paragraph. Often it is enough to carry over only an essential word or two or an idea expressed in slightly different words from the end of the preceding paragraphs, as in the passage by Professor Schlichter on page 176:

> . . . The philosophy of Western Europe asserts that the supreme values are found in the interests of individuals and that institutions exist in order to serve individuals.
>
> In this great conflict between two *philosophies* the trade unions are an important ally of the West. . . . Thus they [the trade unions] have made a major contribution toward implementing the philosophy of the West.

In the second place, the rise of *trade unions* and the gradual development of a laboristic community opens up to employes great opportunities to participate in policy-making both in the plant and in the community. . . .

A little attention to transitions in revision of a paper will make it easier for a reader to follow the line of thought.

5. Beginning paragraphs

The first few sentences of a paper have a double function: they must get the subject under way, or at least get definitely started toward it, and they should interest the reader enough to make him want to read on. Herbert Read summarizes their qualities: "the first words should be either familiar or arresting, and the last should be emphatic."

Regard for the reader is particularly important in beginnings. Amateur writers are often tempted to concoct an elaborate "introduction" and so postpone the real matter of the paper, or to begin routinely ("It is the purpose of this paper to show how to select vacation work"), or even to open with an apology. They frequently begin with a large generalization. "On the banks of the great St. Lawrence waterway are many towns and settlements, some on the American side, and some on the Canadian" is so obviously true that it does not need saying. And the following sentence, so general in its application that it might begin a paper on almost any social topic, actually began one on sharecroppers: "All men are endowed by their Creator with certain inalienable rights, among which are life, liberty and the pursuit of happiness."

Of course when writing the first draft the important thing usually is to get started and it is unwise to wait until a perfect beginning arrives. A formalized opening will let the writer get under way, but he should realize that one of the chief points of revision is to look at his first sentences to see if they really meet the reader. It is the experience of many writers that their beginning paragraphs are their worst and should be simply discarded and the paper begun, as it often can be, with the second or third paragraph, or sometimes that a new opening must be written.

The reader's attention can be picked up by putting first the part of the subject that is nearest his concern or by beginning with details that have definite human interest. Perhaps the writer can dramatize some fact by putting it in action, having people say or do something. In the more routine sorts of writing, as in reference articles or scientific and scholarly articles, the writer may begin with an exposition of background or with a set quotation or with some general statement:

> The psychiatrist's interest in matters of child training and child rearing has come to equal the interest of the professional educator in these matters as an inevitable consequence of more available knowledge concerning the causes of the various disorders of personality.

That may be a good beginning for an audience that is interested in the subject, familiar with its vocabulary, and disposed to listen or read—though they too would probably not object to something more interesting. But such a remote beginning would never win the attention of a more general or more critical group. For these readers some specific details, an anecdote, an opinion dramatized—anything with human interest—would be more appropriate.

Of the nine informational articles in one issue of *The Atlantic Monthly* (June 1949), four begin with specific narrative. Two of these are historical and begin with details that place the events to be recorded rather than with a generalized summary:

> In the middle of May, 1941, Britain's fortunes were low. For practically a year she had been standing all by herself in face of the powerful and victorious Axis Powers; Hitler's forces had conquered Norway, Denmark, Holland, Belgium, and France in 1940. Early in 1941 they had overrun Yugoslavia and had passed on to the invasion of Greece.—CAPTAIN RUSSELL GRENFELL, R.N., "The 'Hood' and the 'Bismarck': The Sinking of the 'Hood' "

> The winter months of 1820-1821 were spent by Teresa in her father's house in Ravenna—and by Byron in the Palazzo Guiccioli, visiting her every day. It was a very different winter from the previous one. Then the love affair was in its most stormy phase: although they were living in the same house, their meetings had been uncertain and perilous, their lovemaking frustrated by quarrels and mutual reproaches, and their future completely uncertain. In public they had still maintained the semi-formal relationship of a lady and her *cavaliere servente,* driving together in Teresa's coach-and-six, and attending the theater and the carnival balls.—IRIS ORIGO, " 'My Only and Last Love': Byron's Unpublished Letters to Countess Teresa Guiccioli"

The other two narrative openings show the writers' relations to their subjects. The first discusses the question of segregation in college fraternities and the second a legal matter, book contracts:

> During the year just past I have found myself deeply concerned with the affairs of a group of fine youngsters who, acting from high motives, were

unexpectedly embroiled in a major social problem. Under vicious attack, for a time they were dismayed and confused; but they came through and, I think, won their final trial.—ALFRED S. ROMER, "The Color Line in Fraternities"

Some years ago, I was negotiating for the publication rights of a book originally owned and published by the Commonwealth of Massachusetts. The negotiations were tedious, since state property cannot legally be sold or leased to an organization operating for private profit. At last a way was found. The governor's legal adviser turned to me with a patient sigh. "Well," he said wearily, "we lawyers are used to this sort of thing." I wasn't particularly flattered. He assumed that I was a lawyer, since he knew no more than I about the legal aspects of a book contract. No wonder. It is a very unusual sort of document.—PAUL BROOKS, "What Is a Book Contract?"

Of the other five, one begins with a quotation, with the actual quoted words built into the writer's sentence rather than coming first, and though it does not get specifically to the man who is the subject of the article, it prepares for him, and he is named in the very next sentence:

The fame of classical authors, said Arnold Bennett, "is originally made, and maintained, by a passionate few. . . . The one reassuring aspect of the literary affair is that the passionate few are passionate about the same things." It was the passionate few who in 1946, twelve years after his death, brought into book form, under title of *The Little World Waddies*, a collection of stray stories and verses by Eugene Manlove Rhodes.—J. FRANK DOBIE, "Gene Rhodes: Cowboy Novelist"

An article on an aspect of income tax law starts with a light allusion:

The Federal statutes, rather sober documents, have recently had in them something approaching sex appeal. The Revenue Act of 1948, enacted over the President's veto by the much maligned Eightieth Congress, devotes over 70 per cent of its ponderous phraseology to enumerating new privileges and relationships between husband and wife. Strangely enough, the inducements there set out for a husband to do nice things for his wife by way of gifts, either during his lifetime or at his death, not only are inexpensive, but may *save* rather than cost money.—LYNN LLOYD, "The Marital Deduction"

One, on tidelands, opens with a definition, not the type of definition found in a dictionary but one that directs attention into the article's subject:

A new frontier, one-tenth the size of the United States, and rich in petroleum and other natural resources, extends seaward from our shores. This frontier, often called the tidelands, is that part of the continental shelf covered by the comparatively shallow waters of the Gulf of Mexico and the Atlantic and Pacific oceans.—ROBERT E. HARDWICKE, "The Tidelands and Oil"

Two others are in terms of people, the first enumerating the topics to be treated, a little like a newspaper lead, and the second giving a summary statement that has the effect of drawing the readers into the article by the repeated phrase "like adults."

> As the pressure on Eastern trout streams grows heavier year by year, more and more fishermen are discovering the Rocky Mountains. They are learning that in the Rockies they can find a vastly greater number and variety of streams than they can find at home, less brush and fewer insect pests, a longer fishing season with more and larger trout, less pollution, fewer posted and privately leased waters, more exciting scenery and pleasant weather.—JOHN HODGDON BRADLEY, "Fishing in the Rockies"

> It is very seldom that a child before the court comes from a good home where the parents are living happily together in a district devoid of slums and with adequate open space for play. There always has been juvenile delinquency and there probably always will be, for there are children who, like adults, are weak-willed and have not enough strength to resist temptation, and there are children who, like adults, are unhappy.—BASIL HENRIQUES, "Britain's Young Offenders"

The openings of these articles suggest that it is possible and effective to begin directly with some part of the material that is to be presented and that instead of leading up to the subject it should be started at once, and started as interestingly as possible. The reader who finds himself in the very first sentence in a definite time and place very often will be led to read on. Considering the prospective audience in beginning to write is as important when writing a theme as when writing an article, and paying attention to the opening sentences will help remove the impression that so many themes give of being written in a void.

6. Concluding paragraphs

The last paragraph of a paper, like the beginning paragraph, has a double function: It rounds out the subject that has been discussed, and it represents a final emphasis. If it is rightly done it will leave the reader with exactly the impression the writer wishes him to carry away. It should also sound like a last paragraph, that is, by its subject matter and its style it should satisfy a reader's sense of having reached the end. The style should be distinctive to leave a good impression.

There are no rules for making a satisfying conclusion, but some typical problems and practices follow:

6a. Unemphatic conclusions. There are two types of ending that are usually unsatisfactory: (1) A concluding paragraph made up of *minor details* or references to other matters that could be but are not discussed in this particular paper is usually unemphatic. It sends the reader's mind off in other directions instead of concentrating it on what has been said, as does this ending of a theme on pitching when it suddenly turns to a generalization about the other members of a baseball team:

> Baseball is one of America's favorite sports, and to spend an afternoon at the Yankee Stadium or Polo Grounds, watching two great pitchers battling for a victory, attracts thousands of fans. What I have said about pitching gives you an idea as to what a pitcher must keep in his mind while out there on the mound, or as a substitute on the bench. There are eight other players on the team besides the pitcher and the same can be written about each individual player and his position.

It is true that every subject suggests others and is in some way related to others, and sometimes this relation should be indicated. But if it is, or if incidental matters are referred to, they should be thrown in earlier in the paper, not allowed to blur the final emphasis. (2) An *apology* as a conclusion also weakens the effect, or attempted cuteness may let a paper die away when it should end strongly:

> All in all, Mike was not an unusual character. Just a plain citizen who had had more than his share of bad luck. After two beers we left the inn. Today is the first time I've thought of old Mike. I don't know why he should have been recalled to my memory now. Maybe it's spring, weather, or something else. I really don't know.

Often a writer feels quite properly that his subject needs a better treatment than he can give it; sometimes he needs to explain why the treatment is limited in some way. But the place for such qualifications is early in the paper (though not at the beginning, because there it would make a weak start). If such explanations are made early and briefly, the ending can then represent the best the writer is capable of and form a vigorous conclusion.

6b. Typical endings. (1) SUMMARY. A mechanical summary of what has been said is rarely needed in a short paper, and such bald statements as "In this paper I have shown that . . . " are inappropriate to an informal paper. If the material has been very complex or in some way difficult to follow, a summary is sometimes necessary. A summary is more in keeping with a formal paper, especially if the stages by which the ideas have been presented have not been closely related. Even a summary should end with the particular emphasis the writer intends.

This last paragraph from an article on Thoreau's reputation summarizes points already made and then ends strongly on the idea of chief concern to the writer:

> I have been trying to account for Thoreau's growing fame in the modern world and have brought forward four suggestions: that the modern emphasis upon efficient writing has resulted in a new appreciation of his "vigorous and pithy" prose; that the compensatory need of nature in a nation of city-dwellers has led to the discovery of his matchless colloquies with nature; that many readers, pinched by economic depression, have found wholesome lessons in his philosophy of economy; and that those who oppose the authoritarian state have been fortified by his insistence upon the rights and responsibilities of the individual citizen. But whatever the reasons—whether these or some others—the increasing prestige of Thoreau in recent years is a fact, which, according to my way of thinking, is a hopeful sign, for his doctrines, if sufficiently rooted in the America he loved, will help us to preserve the integrity of our own minds."—RANDALL STEWART, "The Growth of Thoreau's Reputation," *College English,* Jan. 1946, 7:214

2) SUGGESTIONS FOR ACTION. If the article has been a criticism of some thing or situation and is especially intended to lead to some action by the reader, the last paragraph should suggest what the action is and in so far as possible how it is to be carried out. "Something ought to be done about it" is too weak to be worth saying.

Often the effect aimed for is in thought rather than in action. For this, questions that suggest genuine answers may be useful, or a suggestion for action, as in this chapter ending in a book on relations between races:

> To avoid crippling disillusionments, steps taken to improve race relations have to be made in the full knowledge that some Negro Americans and some white Americans are not ready for them. At the same time that we open jobs to Negroes that have not been held by Negroes before, and neighborhoods to Negroes where they have not lived before, we will have to be providing the education which will make them equal to their new responsibilities. Simultaneously, we will have to educate white people the way the canteen educated them—by laboratory demonstrations that interracial projects will not only work, but will free the white people who participate in them of a very considerable burden of guilt.
>
> We will, to sum up, have to do many things at once. This is neither so novel nor so frightening a prospect as may at first be imagined. Any woman who keeps house can testify that the moment the doorbell rings is almost always the precise, identical segment of time when the rice boils over and the baby falls downstairs. There is nothing especially new to human experience in having to take care of everything at once. Wives and mothers and Henry J. Kaiser do it all the time. It is often, as a matter of fact, referred to

with pride as The American Tradition. "The difficult we do right away. The impossible takes a little bit longer."—MARGARET HALSEY, *Color Blind*, pp. 147-48

3) ROUNDING OUT THE IDEA. In planning a paper a writer usually puts as his last topic the most important or most revealing of his various points. If this last topic has been rightly chosen, a direct statement of it will make a satisfying ending.

Articles that are primarily series of facts or incidents can be concluded by a distinctive incident, as in this informal account of hockey as a sport:

> Not all the spirit is taken out in "fierce fun" of this sort. The game is spotted with almost legendary feats of play in emergencies. Perhaps the most famous of these occurred during the Stanley Cup series of 1928. This is a three-out-of-five-game play-off between the leaders at a season's close— the world series of hockey. The New York Rangers had lost the first game and were battling to save the second. Suddenly, in the opening period, their goalie was struck down by a puck over the eye. He couldn't continue. Good goalies are so rare no team can afford to carry spares. There was a long delay. The Rangers, apparently, were through.
>
> Then a gray-haired man appeared on the ice with the huge goal pads and gloves on. The galleries were silent a moment, then burst into spontaneous applause at the gallant gesture. Les Patrick, out of the game since 1921 and even in his playing days not a goalie, was skating into the Ranger nets. He was the Rangers' manager. But he was going in. The crowd applauded the spirit and sat back to await the massacre. It never came. Playing with a cold frenzy, Patrick turned back the attack of one of the greatest teams in the game and the Rangers won 2 to 1. For the third game they got another goalie and went on to win the series. That stand of the gray-haired Patrick is one of the game's legends now.—ROBERT F. KELLEY, "For a Fierce Game, There's Hockey," *The New York Times Magazine,* Feb. 27, 1938

The writer of this conclusion of a book states in a more formal style the idea that he wishes the reader to carry away and carefully focuses attention on what are to him the two most important words— "courage and magnanimity":

> Before the vast magnitude of the tasks ahead, man's spirit has for the moment faltered and his vision contracted. The public mood is apprehensive where it should be bold, and defensive where broad and generous policy is most required. Everywhere men fly to new tariffs and restrictions, to nationalist policies, domestic currencies, parochial purchasing and personal hoarding—like frightened rabbits each scurrying to his own burrow. Surely it is for the moment only. Which country of us has not, but a few years since, shown the resources we now require of courage, of personal devotion, of industrial and financial leadership, of public direction, in a need no greater and in a cause less worthy? We are, if we could but grapple with our fate, the most fortunate of the generations of men. In a single lifetime science

has given us more power over nature, and extended further the range of vision of the exploring mind, than in all recorded history. Now, and now only, our material resources, technical knowledge, and industrial skill, are enough to afford to every man of the world's teeming population physical comfort, adequate leisure, and access to everything in our rich heritage of civilization that he has the personal quality to enjoy. We need but the regulative wisdom to control our specialized activities and the thrusting energy of sectional and selfish interests. To face the troubles that beset us, this apprehensive and defensive world needs now above all the qualities it seems for the moment to have abandoned—courage and magnanimity.— SIR ARTHUR SALTER, *Recovery—The Second Effort.* Copyright, 1932, by the Century Co. By permission of Appleton-Century-Crofts, Inc.

This comment on political attitudes is informal but comes to an emphatic last statement that represents the writer's main point:

It is no fun to be a political anemic. We believe in technocratic doctrine— feel that it is sound and that steps will have to be taken. We deplore a system which tends to elevate a few persons and degrade many. Yet, so fickle is the human animal, we find ourselves deriving an unwonted pleasure from signs of better times; that's how we know we are useless to reform movements. A reformer of any stamina hates recovery—he is happiest during a depression, knowing that only when great numbers of people are miserable is there any possibility of Change. We know it, too; but when we walk out in the cool of the afternoon and see shopkeepers sprucing up and stores looking busy and people sitting in cafés and having a good time, believe us it takes all our strength not to feel good about it, for we have very little capacity for sustained dismality. We're not defending our temperament, merely pointing out a paradox: that Utopia's best friends are its worst enemies.—"Utopia's Friends," *The New Yorker,* May 25, 1935

6c. Style. The style of the final paragraph, as these examples have shown, is of special importance because it contributes conspicuously to the tone, whether it is a tone of humor, simple directness, encouragement, impressiveness, or some other. This means that the last paragraph should be especially scrutinized in revision to take out empty phrases, false phrases, and anything that might detract from the intended effect. It means also that the phrasing may need to be intensified slightly, that the words should be meaningful and, when possible, suggestive. In short, the ending should be as well expressed as you can make it, and the last sentence, the last phrase, should if possible be both exact and happy.

Suggested study and writing

The exercises in this chapter emphasize the material and the writing of paragraphs. The first two exercises may be used for individual discussion with the instructor; exercises 3, 4, and 5 for class-room discussion; and 6, 7, and 8 for written assignments.

1. Make a study of the material and the paragraph structure of your recent papers. Take notes on the following points:

a) With what kind of material do you feel that you do your best writing?

b) To what extent does the material seem to be chiefly general-izations and opinions, or facts and illustrative details?

c) What comments have been made on your papers about your use of specific details?

d) Count the number of words in each paragraph and the number of paragraphs in each paper. Compare the length of your paragraphs with the length of those listed in the table on page 183. How do your paragraphs compare in length and number with the average in your classroom?

e) See § 2d, "Revising," page 189. To which of the four points in revision do you feel that you need to pay particular attention?

2. Prepare an outline for your next paper, framing a topic sen-tence for each paragraph you intend to use. Fill in as completely as possible the details for each general idea. When you have written the final draft, compare its organization with your outline and com-ment briefly on any significant changes you have found necessary to make.

3. With what kind of material does each of the following para-graphs chiefly deal? Point out by means of the line numbers the topic sentence or sentences of each paragraph, and trace the movement of the writer's thought, dividing it where you can into steps. What specific words or phrases in each paragraph are used for transition or to express the relationship between ideas? Is the last sentence of each paragraph clearly related to the topic sentence or to the paragraph as a whole?

1 1. Our heroes are not the Carnegies or the Morgans but the intellectuals—
2 the atomic scientists, the cultural historians, the writers, the commentators,
3 the thinkers of global thoughts who, we assume for lack of another faith,
4 know better than anyone else how we should cope with what we call with
5 new resonance our national destiny. What we want are oracles, and the
6 best substitutes we can find are the intellectuals. Einstein makes headlines as
7 Millikan never did. Toynbee's popularity is to be reckoned with as Spengler's
8 never was. Even Calvert whiskey has selected as Men of Distinction more
9 artists, architects, writers and commentators than it has industrialists or
10 financiers. What we are headed for is a sort of social structure in which the
11 highbrows are the élite, the middlebrows are the bourgeoisie, and the low-

¹² brows are *hoi polloi.*—RUSSELL LYNES, "Highbrow, Lowbrow, Middlebrow," *Harper's Magazine*, Feb. 1949

2. The defects of the present content and outlook of humanistic education as a preparation for leadership in a democratic society may all be summed up in the single statement that knowledge is encouraged as a means to more knowledge instead of being a means to action. The only part of the educational curriculum which makes demands on *ability to do* in contra-distinction to *facility of expression* is experimental science. So individuals with conspicuous executive capacity, *i.e.*, ability to do as opposed to ability to dispute, are attracted to the natural sciences. Since neither natural science nor any form of manual craftsmanship are obligatory, nothing is done to de-velop general competence in those who elect a course of social studies because they lack constructive aptitude. The machinery of educational selection there-fore operates to recruit the nation's statesmen from those who can talk glibly, write elegantly and argue forcibly without the capacity to act competently. When the need for action is urgent, they can only continue to talk glibly, write elegantly and argue forcibly. If democracy can produce only leaders who can talk it is doomed, and we can only hope to preserve it by a policy of educational selection which favors competence more than fluency.—LANCELOT HOGBEN, *Retreat From Reason*, p. 11

3. The standard portrayal in fiction of the truck driver as a stupid fel-low, a roughneck, or a homely philosopher is perhaps as inaccurate a job of type casting as has occurred in American letters. It is no less so than the literary stencils that represent all cabdrivers as witty and observant, all bus drivers as surly, all bartenders as patient, all barbers as talkative, and all paperhangers as drunk. In reality, these characters, stock on the national scene, often don't shake out that way. I got to thinking the other night about the false impression the term "truck driver" has come to give while I was sitting in Lafie Heishman's truck stop, outside Harrisburg, a few miles off the Pennsylvania Turnpike, which is the main truck route between the East Coast and the Middle West. At that time, I had just completed about two-thirds of a fairly sleepless forty-four hour journey by truck, and I was of the opinion that over-the-road drivers, as the fellows who pilot the big loads from city to city are called, are, by and large, as competent and intelligent a group of skilled workers as one could find anywhere, and, too, that they are the most courteous drivers on the road. I still feel that way about them.—MARK MURPHY, "Over the Road, Legal," *The New Yorker*, Nov. 19, 1949

4. The main street was by now empty: today nothing more would happen. Before noon the housewives had swarmed, so completely, whitely, stripping the shops that one might ask oneself why these remained open. A scale or two adhered to the fishmonger's marble slab; the pastrycook's glass shelves showed a range of interesting crumbs; the fruiterer filled a long-standing void with fans of cardboard bananas and a "Dig for Victory" placard; the greengrocer's crates had been emptied of all but earth by those who had somehow failed to dig hard enough. The butcher flaunted unknown joints of purplish meat in the confidence that these could not now be bought; the dairy restricted itself to a china cow; the grocer, with costless courage, kept intact his stocks of dummy cartons and tins. In the confectioner's windows

¹²the ribbons bleached on dummy boxes of chocolate among flyblown cut-outs ¹³of pre-war blondes. Newsagents without newspapers gave out in angry red ¹⁴chalk that they had no matches, either. Pasted inside a telephone booth, a ¹⁵notice asked one to telephone much less.—ELIZABETH BOWEN, *The Heat of the Day*, p. 78

¹ 5. We are inclined to look upon ourselves as the products of a growth ²from within, upon the unfolding of our personality as something that would ³have been the same upon Crusoe's manless island as it has been in the par-⁴ticular social environment of which we are a part. No belief could be more ⁵erroneous. The ideas that guide our lives and make us what we are have ⁶all been thrust upon us from without. Whether our outlook and attitudes, ⁷our manners and beliefs and prejudices shall be those of Australian abo-⁸rigines, of ancient Romans or of twentieth century Americans depends not ⁹on ourselves but on the social environment into which we happen to have ¹⁰been born. Had there been no social environment, had we been shut off from ¹¹earliest infancy from all human intercourse, we would have had neither ¹²outlook and manners, nor beliefs and prejudices, but would instead have ¹³been just a part of the animal creation around us, set off solely by the greater ¹⁴cunning of our brain. It is through society that we became what we are; ¹⁵through society that we became human.—JOHN A. UDMARK, *The Road We Have Covered*, p. 43

4. The following passage was written in eight paragraphs. After you have read it, write down the numbers of the sentences that seem to you to begin new paragraphs. You may have more or less than eight paragraphs, but be prepared to give reasons for the divisions you have made.

(1) As I walked out of the building two women ran up to me. (2) "Oh, Mrs. Lindbergh," said one, "the women of America are so anxious to know about your clothes." (3) "And I," said the other, "want to write a little article about your housekeeping in the ship. (4) Where do you put the lunch boxes?" (5) I felt depressed, as I generally do when women reporters ask me conventionally feminine questions. (6) I feel as they must feel when they are given those questions to ask. (7) I feel slightly insulted. (8) Over in the corner my husband is being asked vital masculine questions, clean-cut steely technicalities or broad abstractions. (9) But I am asked about clothes and lunch boxes. . . . (10) I turned to look at the plane. (11) Perched on top of the big pontoons, it seemed small and dainty. (12) They were rolling it down the pier. (13) I thought of all the emergency equipment for North and South, land and water, all parts of the world, packed into that little space. (14) I thought of the two of us, ready to go in it anywhere, and I had a sense of our self-contained insularity. (15) Islands feel like this, I am sure, and walled cities, and sometimes men. (16) It was ready now; we could get in. (17) "No, thank you, I don't need a ladder to climb up." (18) A mechanic was just clambering out of my cockpit. (19) I had a moment to wait and watch the crowd. (20) A radio announcer was speaking into his microphone. (21) "Mrs. Lindbergh," he started smoothly, with a glance at me, "is wearing a leather flying helmet and a leather coat, and high leather flying boots." (22) "Why!" I thought blankly, looking down

at a costume which did not correspond at all to his description. (23) What nonsense! (24) It was much too hot to wear leather. (25) The sun beat down on my bare head and sticky cotton blouse; the hot planks of the pier burned through my thin rubber sneakers. (26) What had made him say that, I wondered. (27) Oh, of course, it isn't the conventional flying costume. (28) They have to say that I am dressed in leather. (29) I see, you needn't bother to tell me again, I thought, looking at the announcer. (30) I know, "The Great Radio Public must not be disappointed!" (31) The spray sluiced over the windshield as we started to take off—faster now—we were up on the step—we were trying to get off the water. (32) I held my breath after each pounding spank as the pontoons skipped along from wave to wave. (33) Weighed down with its heavy test load of fuel, the plane felt clumsy, like a duck with clipped wings. (34) It met the coming wave quivering with each effort to rise. (35) Now the spanks were closer together—quick, sharp jolts. (36) I put my hand on the receiving set. (37) It was shaking violently. (38) Suddenly all vibration smoothed out. (39) Effortlessly we rose; we were off; a long curve upward.—ANNE MORROW LINDBERGH, *North to the Orient*, pp. 38-41

5. Each of the following paragraphs or groups of paragraphs from student papers is unsatisfactory in one or more ways: interrupted movement, poor transition, change of direction, lack of focus, unemphatic beginning, weak ending, or failure to group separate ideas together (over-paragraphing). Be ready to discuss in class the flaws in the organization of each paragraph, and to give your suggestions for improving the paragraphs.

1. *The Psychological Effect of Movies on the Personality of Youth*

The motion picture has a definite effect upon the attitudes, behavior, and prejudices of children and young people. The movies that children and youths see give them new patterns for methods of committing crimes. However, that movies cause delinquency has not been proven, or that they are even a contributing factor cannot be truthfully stated. Nevertheless, young men and boys have been found on occasions to use ideas and techniques seen in movies. These boys were susceptible to crime and in their own criminal actions idealized themselves imaginatively as possessing the attractiveness of the gangster movie hero.

Several tests have been made to see the effect the movies have upon the prejudices of youth by measuring the attitudes they have toward Jews after seeing "Gentleman's Agreement."

We are all familiar with the arguments that some give against movies, stating that young people who see undesirable actions on the screen will do the same things in their own lives. Some parents blame the movies for causing changes in the behavior of their children. In many cases children doubtlessly do follow the examples set by movies, but we cannot explain all child problems in such a simple manner.

The cinema does strongly effect child behavior but it is unwarranted to describe such entertainment as completely negative. Even though the motion picture's influence is not always great, there are certain circumstances in which movies contribute tremendously to conduct.

2. Education for Traffic Safety

Safety is one of the biggest community projects under way at the present time. Education has taken upon itself to teach the youth of America to be careful and, in some cities, how to handle cars. Town meetings bring in speakers to talk on the subject and cultivate the true meaning of care on the highway. Safety posters are tacked to every other tree in town with the captions "Drive Carefully," "Not Over 50," "Obey Traffic Signals," and so on. One week a year is set aside as Safety Week, and drives are put on by the schools and town officials to create safety in the home and on the street. In the other 51 weeks we make up for the damage we didn't do during that "sacred" week. Automobile manufacturers come out with the new safety devices and convince the public they are put on the car for the safety of the passengers. Yet they make cars that will travel 65, 75, and 80 miles an hour. With all these safety precautions there still remains the fact that over 40,000 lives are snuffed out each year through automobile accidents, and the injured figure climbs up into the millions.

3. Pro Football in College

The subject I have chosen to write on is professionalism in college sports. There has been a good deal said about the methods employed by colleges to acquire good football material. Every fan knows that collegiate sports are supposed to be amateur sports and that the players are participating because they love the sport and not for the love of money.

According to national collegiate football rules, a college cannot pay a student solely for his athletic ability. The breaking of this rule results in the suspension of the college's amateur status. As you know, the college is then considered professional and is not allowed to compete with other schools. Also, once a person has turned professional, he can never regain his amateur status.

If a college could pay its football players, the team with the most money would be the best. In my opinion, this is defeating the purpose of school spirit and the idea of playing "for the fun of it." The larger institutions have found a way around the rule and are causing quite a controversy among the public and the sportswriters. Some colleges are finding small part-time jobs for the football players. The jobs are located on the campus and pay unusually large salaries. Many institutions offer free room and board to their football players. Naturally, the player chooses the school offering him the most and he becomes a "pro" football player. The only way to stop this is to banish all ways of paying the athlete. Many attempts have been made to do this, the best being the method of fining the guilty schools. This has not proved too satisfactory, for the school with the most money would still have the best team.

"Pro college football" is a delicate subject and it is going to take drastic action to abolish it. Let us hope action will be taken soon.

4. Adjustments in College Life

The average freshman upon entering college is faced with many personal adjustments. Probably for the first time in his life he finds that he has responsibilities. I know that I, for one, had to make these adjustments and face these responsibilities. Also I think that a large number of the upper class students have to face the problem, to a lesser extent, of organizing themselves again for the new college year.

My personal feeling about this change is the ease with which it is accomplished.

After three months of golf, sleeping, traveling and complete freedom I find it practically no hardship whatsoever to step back into the simple routine of college life. I no longer have that restless feeling that accompanies aimless living. I have found in these first few days that it is just this simple routine that I missed so much during the vacation.

Eating and sleeping somewhat regularly as compared with summer living is certainly a happy and healthful adjustment.

Classes and outside preparation do have their disadvantages but the satisfaction of getting something accomplished and the prospect of a few extra qualifications is ample reward.

Looking now into the future is also equally pleasant as it was this summer. Overlooking classes, a golf game next Sunday afternoon is more anxiously awaited than an ordinary golf game. In the same way that date at Skidmore will be worth two at home, and an occasional bull-session with friends in somebody's room can't be topped.

6. Read the opening paragraphs of the nonfiction articles in one issue of *The Atlantic Monthly, Harper's Magazine, The Saturday Evening Post*, or any other periodicals suggested by your instructor. Copy the paragraph you consider to be the most effective introduction and give specific reasons for your choice. Describe the kind of material used (see the classification on pages 196-198) and tell why the paragraph would be likely to capture a reader's interest.

7. Prepare a report on the length of paragraphs in three different types of reading material: in the textbooks used in your various courses; in fiction and factual articles in popular magazines or magazines of restricted circulation; and in the different sections of your local newspaper. What conclusions can you draw about the relation of paragraph length to material, type of audience, and ease of comprehension?

8. Write three or four paragraphs comparing or contrasting any one of the following ideas, or similar ones suggested by your instructor. Use as many details and illustrations as you can to support your generalizations or conclusions.

The radio and the newspaper as sources of news
Speech courses and composition courses as required subjects
Sportsmanship in tennis and sportsmanship in baseball
Campus politics and national politics
The attitude of children and the attitude of adults toward the comics
Misspelling words and mispronouncing words
Women's hats and men's neckties
Writing papers in class and writing papers at home
The working girl in the movies and the working girl in actual life

Kinds and qualities
of paragraphs

*A paragraph is to a sentence what a sentence is to
a word.*—Barrett Wendell

*But the first thing to remember is that the division
[into paragraphs] is for the benefit of the reader
or hearer. It is a device for making the whole
clear to someone else. This does not in the least
make the process less valuable to the writer; it
merely forces upon him the right point of view.
A division is good in proportion as it helps a
hearer or reader to follow.*—Charles Sears Baldwin

*Is it possible that writers are forgetting what to
ask of their paragraphs? ... We must get sturdi-
ness from somewhere—must seek some kind of
physical muscle and its mental counterpart.*—
Kenneth Burke

SUGGESTIONS FOR USING THE CHAPTER: *This chapter develops other points about paragraphs and could follow Chapter 7 immediately, or might better be postponed, perhaps to a second term, to avoid prolonging a single subject unduly. Analysis is likely to be most useful as a means to further progress after some degree of skill has been acquired.*

———————————————

THERE is an old saying that anyone who can write a good paragraph can write a good paper. There is a good deal of truth in this because the kinds of movement found in paragraphs are also found in whole stories, articles, and books, and the qualities of a piece of writing can be seen in its component parts. A study of paragraphs is almost a study of composition.

Of course when a person is writing, he is thinking of what he is saying rather than of the form in which he is saying it. He is not interested then in describing the kinds of sentences or paragraphs he is putting on paper. But for purposes of study it is useful once in a while to analyze what he has done and see if there are some ways in which he can improve or see what his desirable traits are that he can intensify. The analysis is somewhat arbitrary, since continuous communication is the important thing, but without analysis we cannot describe or discuss our writing in any detail.

1. Kinds of paragraph development

Paragraphs can be classified in various ways, but perhaps the most useful is according to the movement of the thought, the general relationship that exists between the statements. The kinds of paragraphs are often found in combination, though one kind is usually dominant.

1a. Narrative paragraphs. Probably the most common, and certainly the easiest, movement in speaking and writing is chronological, the time movement of narratives of **real or** imagined events. In conversation we give accounts of what I did, what we did, what they did; and we write accounts of personal experiences, autobiographies, biographies, explanations of how things are done, processes, and so on; or we may write fiction—short stories and novels.

1) THE TIME RELATION. The connection between statements in a narrative paragraph is usually simple. Time controls. One detail appears after another as they happened in time or as they are imagined to have happened. The verbs usually carry this movement, and the continuity is made stronger by the continuation of the same subject from one sentence to another. The time may be emphasized and made more obvious by adverbs—*then, after this, before, soon, when, in a few days*—or by adverbial clauses: *When he got to the corner . . . . After the last dance . . . .*

Indicating the verbs and adverbs of time in this opening paragraph of a short story shows how large a part time and action play in narrative:

> Elizabeth Montgomery *woke up in the morning* wondering whether or not she *was* engaged. She *had been out* with Bob McEwen *the night before* and *at the end* there *had been* some spontaneous and apparently serious love-making. That is, she *knew* she *must have felt* pretty serious about it because *this morning* she *couldn't remember* where she *had put* her gloves. And *now* he *had left* for Chicago *for a few days* and he *had promised to write.*—SALLY BENSON, *People Are Fascinating*, p. 27

Since narrative is usually of events that have happened or of a story that is told as though it had happened, it is usually written in the past tense. Occasionally for liveliness, especially when the passage records vivid feelings or vivid sense impressions, the present tense is used. This "historical present" is used by D. H. Lawrence in describing the bustle (note the verbs) and the sensations of his leaving Palermo:

> Our ship is hooting for all she's worth. An important last-minuter comes surging up. The rope hawsers are being wound clankily in. Seagulls—they are never very many in the Mediterranean—seagulls whirl like a few flakes of snow in the upper chill air. Clouds spin. And without knowing it we are evaporating away from the shore, from our mooring, between the

great *City of Trieste* and another big black steamer that lies like a wall. . . .
Slowly, slowly we turn round: and as the ship turns, our hearts turn.
Palermo fades from our consciousness; the Naples boat, the disembarking
crowds, the rattling carriages to the land, all fades from our heart. We see
only the open gap of the harbour entrance, and the level, pale-grey void of
the sea beyond. There are wisps of gleamy light—out there.—D. H.
LAWRENCE, *Sea and Sardinia*, p. 41

As a rule the past tense should be used unless there is some definite
reason for using the present; and meaningless changes in tense should
be avoided.

Narrative paragraphs, whether of fact or fiction, are the easiest of
the main types. The chief difficulties are lack of detail, unnecessary
intrusion of general statements or interpretations that interrupt the
narrative, or a change in point of view.

Lack of detail is fatal, because it is only by means of the small
particular actions that we see what is going on. A boy who had told
elaborately of preparations for a particular baseball game ended his
paper with this paragraph, which gives a reader no clue at all to
what really happened:

> The game itself did not prove to be an exceptional one. I know that I,
> for one, played in better games that summer and I might add I also played
> better games as an individual. Even so, it will be a very long time before I
> forget this great experience.

The reader wonders why the game will be so hard to forget.

As a rule the narrative should run continuously without being
interrupted by comment or interpretation. If the comment is unavoidable it should be kept brief and so far as possible be done in terms
of the narrative. (For example, in the Hemingway passage, quoted
on pages 214-215, the sentence of explanation "Animals on a plain
can see so far that they have confidence and feed very differently
from animals in the woods" is closely related to the scene being described.) The following paragraph has a crude interruption, here
set inside brackets:

> It was the seventh of August, 1940. My friend and I were hitching from
> one of the towns in the northern part of the state. Unlike most adventurers I
> did not notice the sky nor did I feel the impending danger. [I guess I
> don't make a very good hero. Now I must get back to my story.] After
> waiting a few minutes we were picked up by two men in an old Chevvie.

Change in point of view is generally unconvincing and distract-
ing. Usually a paragraph of narrative should keep the same point
of view, not shift from one actor or group of actors to another, as
the following paragraph does:

The four of us went in, laughing and pushing each other around. We sat in a booth in the back corner and noisily ordered our drinks. [Shift:] The bartender thought that he would be in for some trouble before long. He began to be very busy but kept throwing an eye in our direction. [Return to original point of view:] We kept up our racket and arranged for Eppie and Lew to stage a friendly little scrap.

2) TYPES OF NARRATIVE. There are three sorts of narrative movement, classified according to how close the reader is brought to the events being presented.

The least common is *generalized* narrative, repeated or typical actions sometimes used to give a notion of typical events or to characterize people or their sort of life by telling what they usually did. The verbs are often formed with *used to* or *would*:

"Bluebells, cockleshells, evie, ivy, over," the children's voices would begin in the morning on the path, which ran the length of the block and back. These were the skipping-rope jumpers, and "Your mother, my mother, live across the way!" they would sing, skipping out the rhythm of it as they came. They and the M.P.s and the Indians would pass through the I. G. Farben official's living room and mount the stairs to where Fife's mother sat, and they would lean their tanned arms and place their skipping ropes and their handcuffs on the papers scattered on the table by the bed, and her fingers would come to a halt on the typewriter keys. "Why is half of the ribbon black and the other half red?" Rosemary, or Linda, or Joan, might ask, and Fife would know the answer.

"The red is to write the exciting things with," he would say, "and the black is to write the ordinary things, like—you know, 'Once upon a time' or 'So the next day.' "

"Go to the end of the line, so we can hear the bell ring," the M.P.s or the Indians might plead, or they might ask for the carbon paper that was too worn to use any more.—KAY BOYLE, "Fife's House," *The New Yorker*, Oct. 15, 1949. Reprinted by permission. Copr. 1949, The New Yorker Magazine, Inc.

Summarized narrative gives a condensed account of specific acts or events. The reader does not "see" the action going on but is told what happened. This is the characteristic movement of biography and history and of personal narrative. In his autobiography, Lincoln Steffens tells that he had promised Israel W. Durham, one time political boss of Philadelphia, to tell him just before his death what his "real sin" had been. In his last illness Durham had wired, "Come; you promised to," and Steffens tells the story of their meeting:

That interview—Durham's story pieced out with pertinent parts of other bosses' stories, the boyhood of Charlie Murphy, the Tammany boss, and President Roosevelt's description of Senator Matt Quay on his death-bed—I wrote all this as fiction under the title *The Dying Boss*. The plain facts are that Durham, weak and stricken, told me that he was ready, at last, to hear what his "real sin" was, and I said that it was disloyalty. He was shocked and incredulous. Since he held that loyalty was his chief and perhaps his one virtue, since he had never gone back on his friends, and—whatever else he had done, which was a-plenty—since he had been always a true, square friend, my charge was totally unexpected and hardly believable. And my argument, as it gradually convinced him, was devastating. He was a born leader of the common people, I reasoned; he had taught them to like and to trust him, even with their votes; he had gathered up and organized the power which lay in their ballots, their trust and their loyalty to him; and he, the good fellow, had taken his neighbors' faith and sovereignty and turned it into franchises and other grants of the common wealth, which he and his gang had sold to rich business men and other enemies of the people. He was a traitor to his own. He had asked for it straight, I gave it him—straight, and he got it. Not one word of evasion or excuse. He took it lying down, and all he said after a long, wan silence was: "Say, I sure ought to go to hell for that, and what'll they do to me? Do you think they'll set me on fire for—for what you said—disloyalty?"

I had to repair the damage I had done. I had to say something to reassure him; he looked as if he would faint. So I asked him what he did to fellows in his gang that went back on him. He said that he didn't do much; he let 'em go. Well, I answered, as brutally as I could put it, didn't he believe that his God was as merciful and forgiving as he, "Iz" Durham, was? He got that, too. He looked better, and he lingered longer than the doctors had predicted.—LINCOLN STEFFENS, *Autobiography*, pp. 418-19

The bulk of that narrative is summarized, though it does include a couple of specific quotations from the actual conversation.

The following account is more detailed, but still summarizes in a single paragraph the actions of perhaps a couple of hours:

In the morning Karl and his outfit started for the salt-lick and Garrick, Abdullah, M'Cola and I crossed the road, angled behind the village up a dry watercourse and started climbing the mountains in a mist. We headed up a pebbly, boulder-filled, dry stream bed overgrown with vines and brush so that, climbing, you walked, stooping, in a steep tunnel of vines and foliage. I sweated so that I was soaked through my shirt and undergarments and when we came out on the shoulder of the mountain and stood, looking down at the bank of clouds quilting over the entire valley below us, the morning breeze chilled me and I had to put on my raincoat while we glassed the country. I was too wet with sweat to sit down and I signed Garrick to keep on going. We went around one side of the mountain, doubled back on a higher grade and crossed over, out of the sun that was drying my wet shirt and along the top of a series of grassy valleys, stopping to search each one thoroughly with the field glasses. Finally we came to a sort of amphitheatre, a bowl-like valley of very green grass with a small stream down the middle and timber along the far side and all the lower edge. We sat in the shadow against some rocks, out of any breeze, watching with the glasses as the sun rose and lighted the opposite slopes, seeing two kudu cows and a calf feed out from the timber, moving with the quickly browsing, then head lifted, long staring vigilance of all browsing animals in a forest. Animals on a plain can see so far that they have confidence and feed very differently from animals in the woods. We could see the vertical white stripes on their gray flanks and it was very satisfying to watch them and to be high in the mountain that early in the morning. Then, while we watched, there was a boom, like a rockslide. I thought at first it was a boulder falling, but M'Cola whispered.—ERNEST HEMINGWAY, *Green Hills of Africa*, pp. 170-72

In fiction, action may be similarly summarized, usually to prepare for a scene that is presented directly, or to show what has gone on since the preceding scene, or to run over quickly action that does not deserve more detailed or vivid telling. In this passage from a short story, a period of action is summarized, leading into a scene (or dramatic narrative) in which the conversation is given directly:

They roamed the decks again after lunch, and sat for a while in the sun-parlor at the back, in wicker chairs, watching the stern of the ship swoop up and down in quarter-circles against the sea, which seemed to be coming right up over the ship but never did; and for a while the old deckhand, a sailor with a nice white beard, stood with his pail in his hand and talked to them about the "old country." He also told them about a hawk that had been blown on to the ship. It was exhausted, he said. It had probably been chasing some other bird and followed it out to sea, and then didn't know how to get back. It stayed on one of the masts for a while, and they put out food for it, and then the next day they found it on the bow, huddled up against an iron thwart. It fought when they came near it, and it wouldn't eat, so they decided they'd better kill it. Finally, one of the sailors threw his hat over it and jumped on it, and killed it.

"Oh, what a shame!" said Margaret. "I think that's a shame."

The old sailor grinned, half-embarrassed.—CONRAD AIKEN, "Farewell! Farewell! Farewell!" *Costumes by Eros*, p. 95. Copyright, 1928, by Conrad Aiken.

The most detailed narrative is in direct scene, and may be called *dramatic*. As a rule this includes conversation, or at least details that give a relatively full picture of what is going on, so that the reader feels he is directly observing it. The following are typical story paragraphs from a scene.

There were a lot of people at the Shepherdsons' and the Shepherdsons' dog, Juniper, had crawled under the couch the way he always did when there was a lot of noise. The blond girl in the white satin dress was trying to coax him out. "Come Juniper," she called. "Come get the rats! Rats, Juniper!" But he only crawled farther under the couch, where he lay with his head on his paws and trembled.

Mrs. Shepherdson came across the room with a strange man in tow. She walked across the room looking very determined, the way hostesses do when they have a lot of people on their hands. "Elise," she said, "I'd like you to meet Mr. Martin. He's from Minneapolis and he doesn't know anybody. So get up off the floor and take him under your wing, like a darling."

Elise got up from the floor and brushed herself off a little. "Dog hairs," she explained. "He's shedding. Are you really from Minneapolis, Mr. Martin? Imagine!"

Mr. Martin said that he was, and they sat down on the couch together.

"I was engaged once to a man from Minneapolis," she told him. "Maybe you know him. His name was Sidney something. Let's see, it was Sidney Hitchcock or Babcock or something. Did you ever know anyone named Sidney Babcock?"

Mr. Martin thought a minute and then said he didn't believe he had.— SALLY BENSON, "Hotel Child," *People Are Fascinating*, p. 226

A considerable part of the art of fiction (and of other narrative too) consists in knowing what action can well be summarized and what should be presented dramatically.[1]

Since a narrative is usually continuous, breaking it into paragraphs is somewhat arbitrary. In most fiction the paragraphs are rather short. A new paragraph represents a new emphasis, a new focus of attention in the action, or a change in time, or movements of a different person (the real reason for paragraphing the speeches in a conversation). The purpose of narrative paragraphs is to represent to the reader the small stages of the action that the writer wishes to mark off, to emphasize.

1b. Descriptive paragraphs. Although a good deal has been written about a science or art of descriptive writing, the key to successful pictures in words seems to lie in the mind of the writer. So long as he puts down details that he recalls, or imagines, more or less in the order that they impress him, he is probably safe. Systematic description, going, for instance, from top to bottom or from left to right in a scene, may be necessary in certain types of expository writing, as in reference works and handbooks; but for more general writing the task is to focus the reader's attention first on what would strike an actual observer's attention and then to fill in the rest of the picture with details more or less in the order in which they would be observed.

This means that conspicuous and keenly suggestive details or those that focus the impression will stand out and that others will be subordinated. The scene will be bounded in space; that is, it will be limited by the area to which the observer is directing his attention, but the relation between the details is not only spatial. It depends on the senses, attention, and associations of the writer. To show this, simply ask two or more people to describe a scene. They may men-

---

[1] See Percy Lubbock, *The Craft of Fiction* (London, 1921).

tion the same conspicuous details, but they will almost certainly put them in a different order, and they will choose and arrange differently the less conspicuous details. The selection and order depend on the interests and past associations of the writer, and it is these that make the paragraph a unit and not a mere enumeration of separate details. Without the unity that comes from an observer's mind we have merely a chaotic series of details that do not fuse into a picture, as in this bit from a story:

"Come on, kids, let's go out on the porch and make plans," suggested Jeanne. She was a tall blonde of seventeen, a couple of years younger than her five guests. Good teeth were prominent in the smile that was almost constantly on her small, round face. She grabbed Don Mumford's hand and half-pulled him along with her. Her actions and her slim figure were like her mother's.

In the following descriptive paragraph, the individual statements are linked in part by pronouns and other typical machinery of paragraph continuity and in part by words for space (*here and there, beyond*). In spite of some literary embroidery, the immediate sense impressions of Mr. Franck are the basis for the blending of sight and sound in the description of Cuzco, and its essential unity comes from the pattern the scene made in his mind.

But more striking even than prehistoric ruins is the view of Cuzco from the foot of the inevitable wooden cross at the summit of Sacsahuama. So steep is the hill on this side, and so close to the town, that it seems almost to bulge out over it, and all the Imperial city lies spread out beneath, as from an aeroplane, its every plaza and patio in full view to its very depths, the activities of every family as plainly visible as if some magic wand had lifted away the concealing roofs. Here and there, even on a Sunday, an Indian in crude-colored garments and his pancake hat crawls along the fortress hill behind his oxen and wooden plow, with the Imperial city of his forefathers as a background. Beyond, the greenish valley of the Huatenay stretches away southward between velvety-brown, wrinkled hills, the four royal highways diverging from the main plaza as principal streets and sallying forth to the "Four Corners of the Earth" as directly as the configurations of the Andes permit. But always the eye drifts back to the city below, spread out in every slightest detail. Under the Incas it may have been "bright and shining with gold and gay with color, its long and narrow streets, crossing each other at right angles with perfect regularity, adorned with beautiful palaces and temples"; even to-day, under the rays of the unclouded Andean sun, it is a scene no mere words can bring to him who has not looked down upon it in person. The soft red of its aged tile roofs and the rich brown of its bulking churches leaves no need for golden adornment. The Sunday-morning noises come up distinctly—school-boys playing in the patios of monasteries, fighting-cocks haughtily challenging the world to combat, a weary bell booming a belated summons, the half-barbarous, half-inspiring screech of trumpets rising as a regiment of the garrison that keeps Cuzco loyal to "those degenerate negroes of Lima" sets out on a march; yet all blending together into a sort of pagan music that carries the imagination back to the pre-Conquest days of long ago.—HARRY A. FRANCK, *Vagabonding Down the Andes*. Copyright, 1917, by the Century Co. By permission of Appleton-Century-Crofts, Inc.

The details may be chosen and held together by some mood or purpose of the writer, as for mild satire:

> The north transept of Westminster Abbey, by which you go in, is tall and shadowy, like a church, and has a churchly smell, but it is so stuffed with monuments and plaques that the traveler automatically begins to look around for price tags.—MARGARET HALSEY, *With Malice Toward Some*, pp. 47-48

Or they may be chosen and unified by some particular sense impression, as by color in this:

> The brown earth turned dark and the trees glistened. The cut ends of the stubble turned black with mildew; the haystacks grayed from exposure to the damp, and on the roofs the moss, which had been all summer as gray as lizards, turned a brilliant yellow-green.—JOHN STEINBECK, *The Long Valley*, p. 222

In writing today the descriptions of people are less like posed studio photographs and more like candid camera shots. The details seem to be casually presented, and usually the character is doing something, so that the picture is relieved by bits of action and especially by his thoughts and feelings. In this way the reader meets the character more naturally.

The first of the two following paragraphs, from a short story, shows a small but revealing handful of impressions; the second, from a novel, a fuller portrait with more action. Note that both women are "described" in a definite time and place, and that the settings become quite "real."

> Snow fell softly and the sidewalks were wet but Mrs. Rose Carey had on her galoshes and enjoyed feeling thick snow crunching underfoot. She walked slowly, big flakes falling on her lamb coat and clinging to hair over her ears, the lazily falling snow giving her, in her thick warm coat, a fine feeling of self-indulgence. She stood on the corner of Bloor and Yonge, an impressive build of a woman, tall, stout, good-looking for forty-two, and watched the traffic signal.—MORLEY CALLAGHAN, "An Escapade," *A Native Argosy*, p. 135

> The man sitting beside Jenny continued to puff steadfastly at his pipe, lost in the news, holding mechanically in his further hand the return ticket which would presently be snatched by the hurrying tram-conductor. He was a shabby middle-aged clerk with a thin beard, and so he had not the

least interest for Jenny, whose eye was caught by other beauties than those of assiduous labour. She had not even to look at him to be quite sure that he did not matter to her. Almost, Jenny did not care whether he had glanced sideways at herself or not. She presently gave a quiet sigh of relief as at length the river was left behind and the curious nervous tension—no more lasting than she might have felt at seeing a man balancing upon a high window-sill—was relaxed. She breathed more deeply, perhaps, for a few instants; and then, quite naturally, she looked at her reflection in the sliding glass. That hat, as she could see in the first sure speedless survey, had got the droops. "See about you!" she said silently and threateningly, jerking her head. The hat trembled at the motion, and was thereafter ignored. Stealthily Jenny went back to her own reflection in the window, catching the clearly-chiseled profile of her face, bereft in the dark mirror of all its colour. She could see her nose and chin quite white, and her lips as part of the general colourless gloom. A little white brooch at her neck stood boldly out; and that was all that could be seen with any clearness, as the light was not directly overhead. Her eyes were quite lost, apparently, in deep shadows. Yet she could not resist the delight of continuing narrowly to examine herself. The face she saw was hardly recognizable as her own; but it was bewitchingly pale, a study in black and white, the kind of face which, in a man, would at once have drawn her attention and stimulated her curiosity. She had longed to be pale, but the pallor she was achieving by millinery work in a stuffy room was not the marble whiteness which she had desired. Only in the sliding window could she see her face ideally transfigured. There it had the brooding dimness of strange poetic romance. You couldn't know about that girl, she thought. You'd want to know about her. You'd wonder all the time about her, as though she had a secret. . . . The reflection became curiously distorted. Jenny was smiling to herself.—Frank Swinnerton, *Nocturne*, pp. 14-15

The chief danger in descriptive movement, as in chronological, is that it will be interrupted by a different kind of material, by comment or by a general statement of fact, which will take the reader away from the picture that is being shown. To avoid this and any change in point of view, simply imagine as you are writing that you are actually facing the scene and put down what you "see with your mind's eye." Everyday writing offers so many opportunities for practice that a little attention should soon develop a sure handling of details. Putting a little more actual picture and scene into your letters, making the account a little fuller than a careless writing would make them, is a good way to start.

1c. Association paragraphs. Many paragraphs of facts or fancy are not built on a logical plan but represent some more informal associations in the writer's mind. The paragraph may be an enumeration of details that are held together by some feeling or attitude, by the recollection of some experience. The reader is led from one bit to another, surrendering himself to the train of association or to the succession of images, and if the writer's mind is interesting or orig-inal, the reader is pleasantly rewarded. This extract shows a rather elementary example of this type of movement:

> I believe that the most efficient people are seldom the most charming. For a journey of any length I believe a companion to be essential. I am dead against the current system of trial by jury. I do not like men who talk business during dinner or children who ask unanswerable questions. I find it increasingly difficult to lie successfully over the telephone.
>
> I prefer the soft, blue haze of twilight to the cold harsh glare of dawn, and a night splashed with stars to both. I know of few people who are able to wear sudden wealth with grace. I am unable to subscribe to the modern passion for disguising a transatlantic liner as a combination tea-garden-supper club, and believe there is nothing the least disgraceful about a ship's looking like a ship.—CHARLES G. SHAW, "How I Look at Things in General," *The New Yorker*, April 25, 1931

These seemingly random details suggest a definite point of view. Structurally they are related by the parallel starts of the statements and by the continuance of the subject (*I*) and by the use of a series of verbs naming the writer's attitudes (*believe, am dead against, do not like, prefer* . . .). The paragraphs gain a sort of emphasis from the especially striking details that stand last.

A naturalist trying to give an impression of autumn cannot be logical, nor can he present a single particular scene. He will usually select impressions that have for him a special appeal and that can lead the reader to a similar understanding, as Mr. Peattie has done in this selection (one of three paragraphs on autumn):

> Autumn is the blooming of the goldenrod all through the oak woods and across the fields. Autumn is the cricket's cry, the swarming of the monarch and the storms of the Lisa butterfly. It is the odor of leaf fires, the smell of crushed marigold leaves, of tansy, and the sharp terebinthine scent of walnut husks that look so apple green and leave so brown a stain.—D. C. PEATTIE, *An Almanac for Moderns* (September 15)

Successful association paragraphs obviously depend on the selection of interesting and appropriate details and (especially for holding these together) on some attitude or facet of the writer's mind that can be echoed in the reader's.

1d. Support paragraphs. In the last two kinds of paragraphs the writer has seemed to exercise a good deal of freedom in the selection and arrangement of his material. In the next two kinds, paragraphs of support and of climax, he does also, but since the rela-tionship between statements in these two types is somewhat more obvious and might occur to many minds, it seems to be relatively objective, and in fact the two types are sometimes called "logical" paragraphs. They are comparable to the two sorts of plans for papers discussed on pages 14-15.

In the support paragraph some general statement comes first or at least early and is followed by particulars of some sort that elaborate or support it, stand in some direct relation to it. The first statement may be a topic sentence or a summarizing sentence. As a rule the last statements of the paragraph are details.

The first four sentences of the paragraph below state a generalization that is then developed by a series of specific activities supporting it:

> A fourth way in which our economic order creates friction between workers and business owners is by its selling and advertising activities. It is one of the strangest phenomena of modern industry that business men, who least of all desire unrest, should spend millions upon millions each year in creating it. In comparison with the expenditures of business organizations for the purpose of making people dissatisfied, those of the I. W. W. and other fomenters of discontent are small indeed. Nevertheless, the deliberate and systematic stimulation of dissatisfaction by industrial establishments appears to be an inherent characteristic of free capitalistic enterprise. It is inevitable that business houses should seek to extend their sales. To do this, they endeavor to make people desire things which they do not possess, to render them dissatisfied with their lot, to get them to aspire to a higher—or at least a more expensive—standard of living. Influenced by salesmen and advertising experts and emulative consumption—which in turn is skilfully stimulated by business enterprises—the wage earner's wants increase more rapidly than his earnings. What is more natural than that, feeling intensely the need for greater income, he should regard his income as unfairly low? As long as business spends huge sums on carefully planned efforts to make people discontented, individual enterprises must expect relations with their workers to be strained.—SUMNER H. SCHLICHTER, "The Organization and Control of Economic Activity," *The Trend of Economics*, edited by R. G. TUGWELL. Copyright, 1924, by F. S. Crofts & Co., Inc. By permission of Appleton-Century-Crofts, Inc.

The idea of this paragraph is stated in general terms in the first four sentences, focused in "Writers have the somewhat different social task of speaking for the human imagination," and then made specific in terms of people in the latter part.

> There is a special need for good writers in these times. The part they can play isn't the one sometimes assigned to them, that of inducing men to accept new political doctrines. The political organizers and agitators can play that role more effectively. Writers have the somewhat different social task of speaking for the human imagination, which at present needs all the voices it can find; for the fact is that lack of imagination is the principal malady from which the world is suffering. Most of us have become so torpid emotionally that we are no longer able to picture the joys or sufferings

of other men. If they are citizens of a foreign country, if their skins are black or yellow, if their noses are a quarter-inch too long, or if they simply live on the wrong side of the tracks—if they are factory workers instead of business men, or farmers instead of clerks, or clerks instead of farmers—then most of us cannot believe that they really suffer or really enjoy themselves in the fashion of superior people like ourselves.—MALCOLM COWLEY, "For the Postwar Writers," *The New Republic*, Dec. 3, 1945, p. 752

In these paragraphs of support the connection between the statements is made definite by the continuation of subjects of sentences, the use of pronouns and connectives, and the other devices discussed in Chapter 7, § 3, pages 191-193; but the essential movement of thought is in the relation between the later specific statements and the earlier general ones, which they support.

1e. Climax paragraphs. Paragraphs of climax begin with particular details that increase in meaning and in value, usually moving toward some point the writer wishes to make, a "particular to general" order. *Climax* may be too strong a name for this natural and common pattern, but it emphasizes an actual movement frequently found in writing.

In this a description leads to a generalization about human nature:

We stopped for half an hour the other afternoon in bright sunshine to watch the digging where the Murray Hill Hotel used to be. There were about forty of us kibitzers, every one a male. A huge Diesel shovel named Lorain was hacking the last few tons of dirt and rubble from the hole and dropping them deftly onto trucks. This was a large-scale operation—big, ten-wheel Mack trucks, plenty of mud and noise and movement. The shovel operator was conscious of his audience and played to it. Bathed in sunlight and virtuosity, he allowed his cigarette to drip lazily from his lips while he plucked his levers as cunningly as a chimesmaster. We men in the audience were frozen in admiration, in respect, in wonder. We studied and digested every trick of the intricate operation—the thrust, the hoist, the swing, the release—conscious of the power and the glory. To a man, we felt instructed, elevated, stimulated. To a man, we were at the controls, each one of us, learning the levers, nudging the rocks, checking the swing, clicking the jaws to coax the last dribble. The sun warmed us in our studies. Not a woman, of the many who passed, paused to watch and to absorb. Not one single female. There can be no question but that ninety-five percent of all the miracles in the world (as well as ninety-five percent of all the hell) are directly traceable to the male sex.—*The New Yorker*, Feb. 19, 1949. Reprinted by permission. Copr. 1949, The New Yorker Magazine, Inc.

It would be natural in reading the following paragraph by Bertrand Russell to regard the first sentence as a "topic sentence," but after finishing the paragraph we find that the first sentence merely serves as a guide and that he has really been moving toward the moral questions arising from fear of boredom, not just describing acts to avoid boredom. There is a development in the weight of the details, from avoiding boredom through mere entertainment to avoiding it through murder and war.

> We are less bored than our ancestors were, but we are more afraid of boredom. We have come to know, or rather to believe, that boredom is not part of the natural lot of man, but can be avoided by a sufficiently vigorous pursuit of excitement. Girls nowadays earn their own living, very largely because this enables them to seek excitement in the evening and to escape "the happy family time" that their grandmothers had to endure. Everybody who can lives in a town; those who can not, have a car, or at the least a motor-bicycle, to take them to the movies. And of course they have the radio in their houses. Young men and young women meet each other with much less difficulty than was formerly the case, and every housemaid expects at least once a week as much excitement as would have lasted a Jane Austen heroine throughout a whole novel. As we rise in the social scale the pursuit of excitement becomes more and more intense. Those who can afford it are perpetually moving from place to place, carrying with them as they go gayety, dancing and drinking, but for some reason always expecting to enjoy these more in a new place. Those who have to earn a living get their share of boredom, of necessity, in working hours, but those who have enough money to be freed from the need of work have as their ideal a life completely freed from boredom. It is a noble ideal, and far be it from me to decry it, but I am afraid that like other ideals it is more difficult of achievement than the idealists suppose. After all, the mornings are boring in proportion as the previous evenings were amusing. There will be middle age, possibly even old age. At twenty men think that life will be over at thirty. I, at the age of fifty-eight, can no longer take that view. Perhaps it is as unwise to spend one's vital capital as one's financial capital. Perhaps some element of boredom is a necessary ingredient in life. A wish to escape from boredom is natural; indeed all races of mankind have displayed it as opportunity occurred. When savages have first tasted liquor at the hands of the white men, they have found at last an escape from age-old tedium, and except when the Government has interfered they have drunk themselves into a riotous death. Wars, pogroms, and persecutions have all been part of the flight from boredom; even quarrels with neighbors have been found better than nothing. Boredom is therefore a vital problem for the moralist, since at least half the sins of mankind are caused by the fear of it.—BERTRAND RUSSELL, *The Conquest of Happiness*, pp. 59-60

The following paragraph also begins with a guiding statement, which connects it with what has gone before. Through an informal grouping of details, some involving contrast between the past and present, it builds up in the last three sentences to Mr. Huxley's notion of the effects of our preoccupation with comfort. It shows that often style is a factor in climax, the distinctiveness of the expression at the end giving an added emphasis to the climax of thought.

Having now briefly traced the spiritual origins of modern comfort, I must say a few words about its effects. One can never have something for nothing, and the achievement of comfort has been accompanied by a compensating loss of other equally, or perhaps more, valuable things. A man of means who builds a house today is in general concerned primarily with the comfort of his future residence. He will spend a great deal of money (for comfort is very expensive; in America they talk of giving away the house with the plumbing) on bathrooms, heating apparatus, padded furnishings, and the like; and having spent it, he will regard his house as perfect. His counterpart in an earlier age would have been primarily concerned with the impressiveness and magnificence of his dwelling—with beauty, in a word, rather than comfort. The money our contemporary would spend on baths and central heating would have been spent in the past on marble staircases, a grand façade, frescoes, huge suites of gilded rooms, pictures, statues. Sixteenth-century popes lived in a discomfort that a modern bank manager would consider unbearable; but they had Raphael's frescoes, they had the Sistine chapel, they had their galleries of ancient sculpture. Must we pity them for the absence from the Vatican of bathrooms, central heating and smoking-room chairs? I am inclined to think that our present passion for comfort is a little exaggerated. Though I personally enjoy comfort, I have lived very happily in houses devoid of almost everything that Anglo-Saxons deem indispensable. Orientals and even South Europeans, who know not comfort and live very much as our ancestors lived centuries ago, seem to get on very well without our elaborate and costly apparatus of padded luxury. I am old-fashioned enough to believe in higher and lower things, and can see no point in material progress except in so far as it subserves thought. I like labour-saving devices, because they economize time and energy which may be devoted to mental labour. (But then I enjoy mental labour; there are plenty of people who detest it, and who feel as much enthusiasm for thought-saving devices as for automatic dishwashers and sewing-machines.) I like rapid and easy transport, because by enlarging the world in which men can live it enlarges their minds. Comfort for me has a similar justification; it facilitates mental life. Discomfort handicaps thought; it is difficult when the body is cold and aching to use the mind. Comfort is a means to an end. The modern world seems to regard it as an end in itself, an absolute good. One day, perhaps, the earth will have been turned into one vast feather-bed, with man's body dozing on top of it and his mind underneath, like Desdemona, smothered.—ALDOUS HUXLEY, *Proper Studies*, pp. 296-99

Most paragraphs can be found to belong to one of these five kinds. The various kinds of movement are all natural, made necessary by different sorts of material and fitting into existing habits of mental action, both of writers and readers. Revising paragraphs with a notion of these kinds in mind may sometimes help make them more consistent, more effective in transferring ideas from one person to another. Their real use is not in classifying existing paragraphs but in improving the natural ways of setting down a writer's own material in paragraphs that have not yet been written.

2. Qualities of paragraphs

Various lists of qualities of paragraphs can be made up. There was the triad of nineteenth-century rhetoric: unity, coherence, emphasis; Scott and Denney varied these to unity, selection, proportion, sequence, variety; more recently Herbert Read discussed unity, liveliness, dignity, rhythm, configuration. Some of these are general qualities of composition, some perhaps of style. In this treatment we will summarize some of the desirable characteristics of paragraphs under four heads: development, movement, continuity, emphasis.

2a. Development. The basic quality is the presentation, the development of an "idea," a small topic. The material should be as complete as the situation of the writing demands. That is, it should represent the writer's knowledge and attitude fully enough to lead a reader to reconstruct that knowledge and attitude in his own mind. The repeated emphasis in these paragraph chapters on "putting in detail" is intended to show the typical means of development. It is important to select the materials that really do further the aims of the particular piece of writing and to omit the irrelevant and the obvious. But the practice in writing paragraphs in a composition course can get students in the habit of an appropriately full development of their material in book type paragraphs.

2b. Movement. Obviously the thought of a paragraph moves: the reader is better off, more informed at the end than he was at the beginning. The various kinds of paragraphs in the preceding section show typical movements: narrative, descriptive, associational, support, climax. Sometimes some specific guidance is necessary, as in the paragraphs that announce their topic at the beginning but do not state it completely till the end.

Paragraphs differ greatly in their speed or tempo, some very compact, others more relaxed. There should be variety in the material—some details, some generalizations—and in the statements—longer or shorter, emphatic or relaxed, and so on—from which often a reader senses a variety in the movement that may deserve to be called rhythm. But the essential is that the reader should be aware of the progression, the movement of the material itself.

2c. Continuity. Long paragraphs frequently show subordinate stages within them (as in the one on boredom on page 223), but if they have been written with some care, there is an obvious continuity between statements. It is impossible to jump into the middle of the paragraph without some lessening of the meaning of a statement. There should be no sudden breaks, no unexplained shifts in point of view. The signs of continuity discussed in Chapter 7 (pages 191-192) are simply signs of a continuity in the thinking being recorded. Since the writer is usually quite at home with his material, it is often necessary for him to look carefully at the coherence, the continuity of his statements, while revising a paper to make sure that a reader can follow from one to another as easily and surely as the writer can. If a genuine continuity exists between the statements of a paragraph it will have unity.

2d. Emphasis. Emphasis might be regarded as a summary of the various qualities, since its purpose (or effect) is to convey to the reader the precise notion of the writer's view of his subject. It depends on the full statement of the material and on proper qualifying of the statements so that they will not seem to mean more than he intends. The positions of beginning and end are especially important for emphasis, since the eye falls on these spots and the mind is accustomed to look at and to note what is said there. Mass or proportion help, the fuller statement naturally implying greater importance. Repetition, in the same or other words, fixes a point in the reader's attention. And distinctiveness of expression—in the words, figures of speech, novelty, dignity, or force of statement—contributes to emphasis. By these means a writer can make the statements of a paragraph mean what he intends, no more and no less.

3. Analyzing paragraphs

It is useful to examine paragraphs occasionally in some detail as background for examining and improving one's own. Analysis shouldn't be carried further than is useful in finding the sources of the impression the writing makes on us. (It can help sharpen attention in reading as well as serve as a background for writing.)

In the two passages that follow some points are made in the left-hand margin about the *material*, the content, and at the right about the signs of *continuity*. Although this discussion is not here organized according to the four qualities described in the preceding section (Development, Movement, Continuity, Emphasis), they will all be touched on.

The first passage is from an advanced textbook in psychology, the opening paragraphs of a chapter on *canalization*. This introduction to the subject is not technical, though much of the treatment that follows is. The paragraphs are conspicuously close knit; the generalizations and details tied closely together.

Material		Continuity
Topic sentence (generalization)	(1) Needs tend to become more specific in consequence of being satisfied in specific ways.	(Starts a new unit)
Example (and evidence)	(2) Children all over the world are hungry; their hunger may be	Relation obvious
Details	satisfied by bread, by ice cream, by peanuts, by raw eggs, by rice,	Repetition of *satisfied* from 1
General idea repeated in less general terms	or by whale blubber. (3) Eventually they develop, when hungry, not a demand for food in general, but a demand for what they are used to; in one part of	*they* refers to *children* of 2; *hungry* repeated from 2
Repeated in details	the world peanuts are good food, whale blubber disgusting, and	
Another example	vice versa. (4) So, too, over the face of the earth, children enjoy rhythms; the need is satisfied by	*So, too*, connective; *children* repeated as subject
Made more specific	different kinds of rhythms, different games, different types of	
Part of general idea restated	music. (5) Soon they find the ones which they are "used to" natural and satisfying; others seem awkward, difficult, unsatisfying.	*Soon* suggests continuity, *they* referring to *children*
Idea repeated	(6) If a person is hungry, oriented toward food in general, he may nevertheless be more hungry for bread than for corn, for	*hungry* echoes preceding paragraph
with two examples	beef than for mutton. (7) Attitude toward food is general, the	*Attitude* translates *oriented toward; food* and *general* repeated;
Idea progressively refined and limited	valuation of absent food is general; but specific attitudes are defined within the general, and within the specific there are some still more specific, so that	*specific* repeated from preceding paragraph
Illustration	one wants not only currant buns but the one with the darkest	
Compact restatement of general idea	crust. (8) Tastes have become specific. — GARDNER MURPHY, *Personality*, p. 161	*Tastes* echoes *attitudes* and *needs; specific* repeated

The first paragraph is of the support type, beginning with the general statement that is developed in more specific terms; the second is of the climax type, beginning with particulars and ending on a strong general statement. A conspicuous trait is the repetition of the key words of the first sentence: in the two paragraphs *specific* occurs six times (and contrasting with it, *general* four times), *satisfied* and *satisfying* four times, and *needs* and its equivalents (*demand, attitude, wants, taste*) eight times. Since the words represent the core of the idea, their repetition is not troublesome but seems to keep us in continual awareness of the general idea: "Needs tend to become more specific in consequence of being satisfied in specific ways." The last forceful sentence, "Tastes have become specific," is the final source of emphasis.

The second passage, from a book for general readers, is not quite so compact. It gives reasons for moving from the opinion of the first sentence to the opposite opinion in the last. The words that continue the thought are less exactly equivalent than in the preceding example but they still carry on the general theme unmistakably.

Material		*Continuity*
The topic (but not a topic sentence)	(1) Public opinion polls contrive to give the impression that as a nation we are in a constant state of agitation over all sorts of domestic and foreign problems.	
Restatement in more specific terms	(2) Eighty or ninety or sometimes ninety-nine per cent of the people interviewed are able to say that they are for or against a particular man or a particular measure, and that is what the investigators want.	*people interviewed* connects with *polls* in 1
An objection or qualification	(3) Some experts, however, have begun to admit that people often have opinions on subjects about which they are less than adequately informed.	*however,* connective
Specific instance	(4) The man in the street, they confess, may strongly support or bitterly oppose a bill that is before Congress without being able to describe one of its provisions.	*they,* referring to *some experts* in 3
Writer's opinion of 3-4	(5) This admission is healthy, but the experts need to take another step.	*This admission* refers to idea of 3-4; *experts* repeated from 3
Writer's point Topic sentence	(6) A man may turn up an opinion on demand, and yet have only the slightest interest in the subject about which he is being interviewed.	
Restated in specific questions	(7) How much does the individual in question think about the subject? (8) Does he feel that it has any	Restatement of *another step; individual* refers to *man* in 6; *he* and *his* refer to *individual*

real relevance to his own life? (9) How do his thoughts and emotions on this subject compare with his thoughts and emotions on other subjects?

Roughly parallel question form, 7-9

General point restated

(10) The problem that I wish the experts would investigate is not what people think about this or that but what they think about.

the experts, what people think carried over

Made more specific

(11) Both psychologists and novelists suggest that people think mostly about themselves.

people think repeated

(12) The stream of ideas—call it interior monologue or what you will—that passes through

stream of ideas equals what people think

Details

the average human mind is concerned with *me:* my health, my state of mind, what people think about me and what I think about them, my problems, my children, my job, what I said to Joe and what he said to me,

concerned with me equals about themselves of 11

Concluding generalization, directly contrary to that in 1

mostly what I said to him. (13) Even the most public-minded citizen, I suspect, devotes only a fraction of his attention to the affairs of city, state, and nation, and any conception of democracy that postulates the constant and alert interest of the citizenry is purely romantic.—GRANVILLE HICKS, *Small Town*, pp. 100-101

Even has connecting force; public-minded citizen contrasts with average human mind of 12

Both of these paragraphs are of the climax type (showing that the label "climax" does not demand intensity) since in each the writer is moving *toward* his important point. The first is in three stages (sentences 1-2, 3-5, 6-9), of which the third carries the main point. The thought proceeds easily, but each paragraph ends with a direct and forceful phrasing.

Analysis can prepare for evaluation of paragraphs by pointing out the specific qualities of their development. The final evaluation of paragraphs, as of other aspects of writing, depends on their appropriateness—appropriateness to the writer, to the subject and situation, and to the readers. Examining in some detail varied sorts of paragraphs can, by developing judgment, prepare for writing varied and effective papers.

The study of composition suggests that paragraphs are the most important aspect of writing that can be isolated for attention, certainly more important than sentences and rivaled only by the types of phrases into which individual words are grouped. After some conscious consideration of paragraphs, the way to effective control of them lies in practice, putting together interesting and important material in papers for possible readers.

Suggested study and writing

These exercises are for practice in analyzing qualities of paragraphs and in writing different kinds of paragraphs. The first two exercises may be used for classroom discussion; exercises 3, 4, 5, and 6 for written assignments; and the last exercise for individual discussion with the instructor.

1. Study the following paragraphs carefully. Classify the development of each as predominantly narrative (generalized, summarized, dramatic), descriptive, association, support, or climax. Prepare a brief analysis of each paragraph, commenting on the movement, use of detail, emphasis, methods used to achieve continuity and transition.

1. On the morning of July 4, 1927, the routine of Sing Sing Prison was disturbed by a tragic accident. The inmates were taking their exercise in the prison yard overlooking the Hudson River, when a canoe bearing three young men with supplies and equipment for a picnic came unsteadily down the river, the surface of which was roughened by a fresh wind. When near the prison pier the canoe capsized. Convicts who saw the incident moved, as if by impulse, toward the three figures who were struggling in the water. Apparently unable to swim, the youths were clinging to the sides of the overturned craft and calling for help. Six of the prisoners volunteered, even begged with tears in their eyes, for permission to swim out to the rescue; but the keepers, who carried rifles in their hands, would not allow it. According to the warden himself, the guards had to threaten to shoot the prisoners in order to keep them back. One by one the victims, their strength ebbing and their cries dying away, sank into the river and disappeared. It was reported that the incident produced a profound depression throughout the prison, dampening the holiday spirit which might otherwise have prevailed.— FLOYD H. ALLPORT, *Institutional Behavior*, p. 49

2. The film industry had its inauspicious birth as a peep-show attraction in penny arcades. Edison, one of its inventors, thought so little of it that he never bothered to spend the few hundred dollars necessary to protect the European rights to his invention. The public, however, greeted the infant industry with explosive enthusiasm. The clink of pennies, foreshadowing the more musical ring of dimes and quarters, attracted numerous promoters, investors and entrepreneurs. The motion picture moved from penny arcades and dime museums to empty shops and lofts, then to unused theaters. Before the infant industry was out of swaddling clothes, it was subject to the first of the many forms of domination that were to characterize the course of its spectacular development.—MORRIS L. ERNST, *The First Freedom*, p. 185

1   3. In Alabama, the streets were sleepy and remote and a calliope on parade
2 gasped out the tunes of our youth. There was sickness in the family and
3 the house was full of nurses so we stayed at the big new elaborate Jefferson
4 Davis. The old houses near the business section were falling to pieces at
5 last. New bungalows lined the cedar drives on the outskirts; four o'clock
6 bloomed beneath the old iron deer and arbor-vitae boxed the prim brick
7 walls while vigorous weeds uprooted the pavements. Nothing had happened
8 there since the Civil War. Everybody had forgotten why the hotel had been
9 erected, and the clerk gave us three rooms and four baths for nine dollars
10 a day. We used one for a sitting room so the bell-boys would have some
11 place to sleep when we rang for them.—F. SCOTT FITZGERALD, *The Crack-up*,
p. 54

1   4. When you are engaging in silent reading, you do not look at each
2 letter separately, and very often not even at each word. Many ideas are ex-
3 pressed not by any single word but by a series of words which together make
4 what is called a phrase. Thus, the idea expressed in the phrase "in a day
5 or two" is not contained in any one of the words, but in the entire phrase.
6 If you read each word separately you do not get as well or as rapidly the
7 meaning that the author intended you to get. Look at the sentence: "We
8 shall reach Yellowstone Park in another two days if we drive 200 miles
9 each day." There are really five ideas in this sentence, although there are
10 sixteen words: "We shall reach" is one idea; "Yellowstone Park" is an-
11 other; "in another two days" is the third; "if we drive" is the fourth idea;
12 and "200 miles each day" is the last. When you read this sentence you
13 should read not sixteen words, but five ideas—or five phrases.—C. GILBERT
WRENN and LUELLA COLE, *How to Read Rapidly and Well*, p. 3

1   5. The turning point of Hook's career came that autumn, when the brush
2 in the canyons rustled dryly, and the hills, mowed close by the cattle, smoked
3 under the wind as if burning. One mid-afternoon, when the black clouds
4 were torn on the rim of the sea and the surf flowered white and high on
5 the rocks, raining in over the low cliffs, Hook rode the wind diagonally
6 across the river mouth. His great eyes, focused for small things stirring in
7 the dust and leaves, overlooked so large and slow a movement as that of the
8 Japanese farmer rising from the brush and lifting the two black eyes of his
9 shotgun. Too late Hook saw, and startled, swerved, but wrongly. The surf
10 muffled the reports and nearly without sound Hook felt the minute whips
11 of the first shot, and the astounding, breath-taking blow of the second.
12 Beating his good wing, tasting the blood that quickly swelled into his
13 beak, he tumbled off with the wind and struck into the thickets on the far
14 side of the river mouth. The branches tore him. Wild with rage, he thrust
15 up, clattered his beak, challenging, but, when he had twice fallen over,
16 knew that the trailing wing would not carry, and then heard the boots of
17 the hunter among the stones in the river bed, and, seeing him loom at the
18 edge of the bushes, crept back amid the thickest brush and was still. When
19 he saw the boots stand before him, he reared back, lifting his good wing
20 and cocking his head for the serpentlike blow, his beak open but soundless,
21 his great eyes hard and very shining. The boots passed on. The Japanese
22 farmer, who believed that he had lost chickens, and who had cunningly
23 observed Hook's flight for many afternoons until he could plot it, did not
24 greatly want a dead hawk.—WALTER VAN TILBURG CLARK, "Hook," *The
Atlantic Monthly*, August 1940

1 6. A college practice field, except for occasional bursts of noise from the
2 normal young men engaged in working out, has very much the atmosphere
3 of a classroom. The squad, for a good part of the time, will be broken up
4 into smaller groups. One will be linemen, another backs, another passers
5 and receivers. They will go over and over certain plays, with the assistant
6 in charge of the particular group breaking in every now and then and, in
7 classroom voice, explaining mistakes, asking questions and once in a while
8 demonstrating.—ROBERT F. KELLEY, *The New York Times*, Oct. 14, 1941

1 7. It is difficult to find adequate comparisons for a topsy-turvy creature
2 like a sloth, but if I had already had a synthetic experience with a
3 Golem, I would take for a formula the general appearance of an English
4 sheep dog, giving it a face with barely distinguishable features and no ex-
5 pression, an inexhaustible appetite for a single kind of coarse leaf, a gamut
6 of emotions well below the animal kingdom, and an enthusiasm for life
7 excelled by a healthy sunflower. Suspend this from a jungle limb by a
8 dozen strong hooks, and—you would still have to see a live sloth to ap-
9 preciate its appearance.
10 At rest, curled up into an arboreal ball, a sloth is indistinguishable from
11 a cluster of leaves; in action, the second hand of a watch often covers more
12 distance. At first sight of the helpless ball of hay, moving with hopeless in-
13 adequacy, astonishment shifts to pity, then to impatience, and finally, as we
14 sense a life of years spent thus, we feel almost disgust. At which moment
15 the sloth reaches blindly in our direction, thinking us a barren, leafless, but
16 perhaps climbable tree, and our emotions change again, this time to sheer
17 delight as a tiny infant sloth raises its indescribably funny face from its
18 mother's breast and sends forth the single tone, the high, whistling squeak,
19 which in sloth intercourse is song, shout, converse, whisper, argument, and
20 chant. Separating him from his mother is like plucking a bur from one's
21 hair, but when freed, he contentedly hooks his small self to our clothing
22 and creeps slowly about.—WILLIAM BEEBE, *Jungle Days*, pp. 97-98

1 8. This simplicity is best illustrated from pidgin, which is English meat
2 with Chinese bones, as we say in China. There is no reason why a sentence
3 like "He come, you no come; you come, he no come" should not be consid-
4 ered as clear as the more roundabout "You needn't come, if he comes, and
5 he needn't come if you come." In fact, this simplicity makes for clarity of
6 expression. Moon, in *Dean's English*, quotes an English Somerset farmer as
7 testifying before the judge: "He'd a stick, and he'd a stick, and he licked he,
8 and he licked he; if he licked he as hard as he licked he, he'd a killed he,
9 and not he he," and this seems to me a much more sensible way of talking
10 than one with the Germanic case-distinctions. For according to the Chinese,
11 the difference between "I lick he" and "he lick I" is perfectly clear without
12 the subjective-accusative complex, and the adding of the third person singular
13 ending "*s*" is as superfluous as it is already proved to be in the past tense
14 (I had, he had; I went, he went). Actually lots of people are saying "us
15 girls" and "them things" without ever being misunderstood or losing any-
16 thing except a meaningless "class" which has nothing to do with beauty of
17 expression. I have great hope that English and American professors will
18 one day bravely and respectably pronounce a "he don't" in the classrooms,
19 and that the English language may one day become as sensible and clear as
20 the Chinese, through the influence of pidgin.—LIN YUTANG, *My Country and
My People*, pp. 81-82

1   9. What, precisely, is "thinking"? When at the reception of sense-im-
2 pressions, memory-pictures emerge, this is not yet "thinking." And when such
3 pictures form series, each member of which calls forth another, this, too, is
4 not yet "thinking." When, however, a certain picture turns up in many such
5 series, then—precisely through such return—it becomes an ordering element
6 for such series, in that it connects series which in themselves are unconnected.
7 Such an element becomes an instrument, a concept. I think that the transi-
8 tion from free association or "dreaming" to thinking is characterized by
9 the more or less dominating role which the "concept" plays in it. It is by
10 no means necessary that a concept must be connected with a sensorily cog-
11 nizable and reproducible sign (word); but when this is the case thinking
12 becomes by means of that fact communicable.—ALBERT EINSTEIN, "Notes for
an Autobiography," *Saturday Review of Literature*, Nov. 26, 1949

1   10. Dan Furlong, every morning until the children were grown, would
2 wake up around five o'clock and wonder what time it was. The entire
3 household was quite incapable of maintaining a clock in good punctuality.
4 Within a week every clock that they had ever obtained would become a
5 liar, so that Dan would miss a shift of work as a result, or the children
6 would be late for school, or Monsignor Phelan would have to talk back to
7 himself at Mass, because his altar boy, Jerry Furlong, had trusted a clock
8 and so was not at the side altar to serve him. Right and left and fore and
9 aft of the Furlongs there were clocks and watches ticking away with mo-
10 notonous regularity, but somehow they all broke step when the Furlongs
11 got a hold of any of them, so it was to hell with timepieces in that house-
12 hold. Not one of the family would have trusted the sundial in the Vatican
13 gardens, and small blame to them.
14   Every morning, then, around five o'clock, Dan Furlong would lie awake
15 blinking at the dim ceiling wondering whether he was early or late or just
16 right. The few warm waking minutes were a great delight to Dan, as they
17 are to most men, and he used to ponder in them. Since the last St. Patrick's
18 Day, when he had worn his herringbone coat, and his companion the Usher
19 had worn his Irish frieze, their sartorial splendor had often been the
20 subject for his pleasant contemplation. For years the two of them had
21 been shabby leaders of the parish contingent for the procession, but now they
22 both possessed coats that would outwear them both. It was a warm, secure
23 feeling.—W. B. READY, "A Coat for St. Patrick's Day," *The Atlantic Monthly*,
March 1950

1   11. Tall and thin, his white hair pushed straight back from his forehead,
2 his long face reamed with wrinkles, his eyes sharp and commanding, Jackson
3 was a noble and impressive figure. On foot, with firm, military step, com-
4 pressed lips and resolute expression, or on horseback, where his seat was
5 excellent, his hand light and his carriage easy, he had a natural grandeur
6 which few could resist. Many in this bitter day shared the emotions of the
7 conservative Boston merchant who watched out of his window to catch a
8 glimpse of the old General, "regarding him very much as he might have
9 done some dangerous monster which was being led captive past his house."
10 When Jackson finally appeared, his hatred abruptly collapsed. Exclaiming,
11 "Do some one come here and salute the old man!" he thrust his small daughter
12 forward to wave her handkerchief. Jackson, as Josiah Quincey said, "wrought
13 a mysterious charm upon old and young."—ARTHUR M. SCHLESINGER, JR.,
The Age of Jackson, pp. 38-40

2. How would you evaluate the following paragraphs, written by students who were trying to develop as fully as possible in one paragraph the topics they had selected? Analyze the material and continuity of each passage, using the method shown on pages 227-229. Which paragraph seems to you the most effective, and why? What specific changes would you make in material, development, and wording of these paragraphs?

1. *Pep Rallies*

I believe that pep rallies are the most important gatherings that colleges have to arouse pep and spirit and to stir up the hearts of all the students. The reason why I believe this is because I have never seen a pep rally fail. Every rally I have attended always accomplishes what it is striving for. This aim is to inspire the members of the team by rooting and cheering. Whether it is a football team or a golf team, the members always become impressed when someone is rooting for them, and this undoubtedly makes them fight harder for their alma mater. Besides inspiring the team, the pep rally makes the team fight harder. Also it brings the students closer together, since they are all stirring up their emotions toward the same goal. The result is cooperation and friendship, and these are very essential factors in college life. In conclusion, I believe that when a college graduate is looking back over his past college career, that these pep rallies which he attended will stand out in his mind more than anything else.

2. *An Impression of Niagara Falls*

My first impression of Niagara Falls was one of grandeur. I thought that nothing else on earth could equal it. The great surge of white water swept over the brink plunging a hundred feet into the gorge. When I first saw the Falls from afar, I was quite disappointed, as I had expected a cataract fully three times that height. Later, however, upon standing in the small, pipe-coiled cubicles made for the express purpose of allowing tourists to come to the edge of the spray, I felt terribly small, insignificant, and virtually worthless for any purpose on this earth. That sheet of roaring water was an incredible depth of six or seven feet at the brink. Farther down, near the bottom of the gorge, the thickness was even greater. The terrific force falling on huge jumbled brown rocks at the bottom sent out a rain-like spray covering a large area all around. A few hardy folks feeling their way precariously along the single-file wooden traverse of the "Cave of the Winds" were soundly drenched. This tiny walk, perched on the jagged rocks, gave one a happy feeling that man could at least do something in the face of this avalanche of water. There were other symbols, too, of man's conquest of the Falls. For fifty years men have been sailing the waters of the gorge in the "Maid o' the Mist," in the thick of the mighty whirlpools, ever ready to grasp any stray floating object. And there were power houses, built by men, located snugly in the walls of the gorge. Upon leaving, I experienced a feeling of regret, that when necessity demanded more power, more and more water would be diverted to the power houses, and Niagara Falls would dwindle to a mere trickle.

3. *Stamp Collecting*

Stamps are not only valuable for collection purposes, but are also valuable for the learning which they impart. A person may start to collect a few stamps for the purpose of making some money for himself in a few years. This person will probably be disappointed in time, since money cannot be made on stamps unless a person has experience. There is also the other type of person who starts collecting just for the fun of it. If this person does not derive any pleasure from stamps in a few years, he will soon lose all his former interest, and will either sell them for what he is able to get, or give the collection to a friend. But once a person becomes interested, he usually keeps on building his collection. An important advantage of this hobby is that you make some of your best contacts in the stamp world. You will be surprised how much your knowledge of history and geography have increased in the short time you have collected stamps.

4. *Spectators at a Football Game*

Did you ever remain calm enough at a football game to notice the rooters play the game with the team? Watching them is as interesting as watching the football players. As the whistle shrills the signal for the kick off, every eye is glued on the ball, watching it arc through the air turning end over end and finally being caught by a player who immediately races back up the field. The crowd roars and comes to their feet as the tackle is made. Then they settle in their places and tensely wait the next play to be put into action. As the ball is whipped back and the quarterback, with arm outstretched, head low, ball tucked in the pit of his stomach, his legs working like pistons, bucks through the line, the spectators snap their bodies taut and lunge with him. It is just as if they themselves were playing the game, fighting hard to advance that ball a little farther down the field. Have you ever felt the rooter next to you, who has entered into the spirit of the game, lean against you as the play was being carried out? Have you noticed, for instance, when a player was making a wide, sweeping end run, how the rooter twists, squirms and strains to elude the player who is about to tackle him? Perhaps you have done the same thing yourself, for you and the rest of the spectators go through many of the same contortions that the players do. Thus through the whole game the rooters push and strive in their own manner to help their team win.

3. Write a descriptive paragraph on one of the following topics or on a similar one:

    The building in which the class meets
    The student union building at lunch time, or at any other specified hour
    The opening kickoff of a football game
    An R.O.T.C. review
    The confusion of registration day
    A classroom two minutes before a final examination
    A specified campus figure (anyone from the football coach to a well-known janitor)
    The main entrance to the campus
    The campus as a whole

After the class has been divided into groups of four or five, students in each group can work on the same topic. This exercise has a double point: to give practice in writing descriptive paragraphs and to bring out the difference between details observed and selected by different people with the same opportunity for observation.

4. Select a general statement for development in three or four paragraphs using the method of support. The statement may be one that you have read, or heard on the radio, in classroom discussion, or in everyday conversation. These examples may suggest others to you: "The real purpose of radio programs is to get people to listen to the commercials"; "The study of algebra trains a person to think logically"; "Despite what they may say to the contrary, most girls come to college to find a husband"; "Fat people are generally more jolly than thin people"; "Those who can, do; those who can't, teach" (G. B. Shaw); "Work consists of whatever a body is obliged to do, and play consists of whatever a body is not obliged to do" (Mark Twain). When you have found a suitable statement, use as many details or illustrations as you can in developing your viewpoint. If possible, make the last paragraph one of climax.

5. In not more than one page give a clear synopsis of a play or movie you have seen or a book you have read. Work it out in direct time sequence. (Books and movies frequently begin part way through the story and later cut back to give earlier events.) Be particularly careful to keep the sequence of tenses consistent.

6. Compare a condensation of an article in *The Reader's Digest*, or a similar "digest" magazine, with the article as it was originally printed. How do the paragraphs compare in length and in number in both versions? What type of material has been omitted in the condensation—generalizations, details, introductory matter? Is the transition between paragraphs the same in both versions? Do you notice any change in emphasis? Summarize your conclusions on the relative effectiveness of both articles, pointing out any qualities that have been lost in condensation.

7. Make a detailed analysis of the paragraph structure of one of your longer papers. Use the method shown on pages 227-229 of this chapter. For each paragraph copy the topic sentence (if you have one) and list the number of supporting details you have used. Mark transitional words and phrases and also any sections that need better transition, both within and between paragraphs. Prepare a brief statement on both the strong and weak features of the paragraphs as you wrote them.

Sentence form

A sentence is a symbol for a state of affairs, and pictures its character.—Susanne K. Langer

Words and sentences are subjects of revision; paragraphs and whole compositions are subjects of prevision.—Barrett Wendell

SUGGESTIONS FOR USING THE CHAPTER: *This chapter, with some sections of Chapter 4, covers the elementary matters of form in sentences but regards them as means to an end, conveying meaning. It would be best taken after students have done some writing, because elementary problems in sentences tend to disappear rapidly under attentive practice. The general point of view of the chapter should be emphasized, with only as much stress on its detail as a class actually needs.*

W E USE SENTENCES so naturally and so continually that any effort to study them seems artificial and perhaps even discouraging. But they can be studied, and from a number of points of view: for their relation to "thought," psychologically; for their meaning, according to logic or semantics or just common sense; for their structure, grammatically; for the impression they make, rhetorically. This chapter takes up a selection of topics on sentences, those that seem most important for review and emphasis at the college level and those that are of most immediate concern in the activity of writing. These topics serve also as a background for considering in Chapter 10 various qualities of sentences that give greater effectiveness and interest to writing.[1]

1. Spoken and written sentences

Our use of language begins in our thought, the mixture of images and words that is such a large part of our behavior but that we know so little about. It is possible that it consists chiefly of key words and is not cast in very exact patterns or grammatical forms. (Do we use conjunctions, for instance, in our thinking?) We are a little more aware of the flow of our speech in rapid conversation, but we are not

---

[1] REFERENCES: Ballard, Chapters 4, 5; Bloomfield, Chapter 11; Schlauch, Chapter 6; L. A. Sherman, *Analytics of Literature* (Boston, 1893), Chapters 19-24; Summey, Chapters 3 and 4 and index references.

conscious of its form, certainly not of its sentences, unless they become so confused that they are not carrying out our purposes.

But there are sentences in this continued speech: a stenographer has little trouble in distinguishing them. They are marked by various sorts of stress, pause, and intonation that we make and understand automatically. *This is mine,* for example, can be said quietly, with a falling voice, so that it could be written with a period; or more intensely so that an exclamation point would be appropriate; or with a rising inflection making it a question; or it could be said as part of a sentence, as in "This is mine, I think." *Yes* can be said so that it will mean to a listener anything from "You are absolutely right" to "I don't really believe what you are saying." In spoken sentences the qualities of voice are an important contribution to the meaning of the words and to the way we would interpret them as a sentence form.

In writing, the sentences are clearer, because the writer checks and revises them in the light of his intention and according to the conventions of form and punctuation that now prevail in published material. It is fair enough to say that a written sentence is what a person with some experience in the language intentionally puts between end stops. Professor Ballard says, "It is as much of my full purpose as I care to reveal at the very moment—as much of my meaning as I wish to deliver in one handful." Miss Rickert uses more learned words for the same idea: A sentence is ". . . a deliberately separated phase of the thought continuum; to the ear set off by a longer pause than obtains at any point within it; to the eye by an end punctuation mark."

These attempted definitions suggest that sentences are to a considerable extent a matter of judgment, certainly of choice among a great variety of possibilities. In fact they are so individual that sometimes a writer does not see why someone else objects to a particular one he has written. But the more we know about the typical sentence forms, the easier it is to describe and examine our specific sentences and come to an agreement about them.

Because of the lack of qualities of voice, and of gesture and facial expression, written sentences have to be more exact, especially in word order and use of words. And because the written sentence can be looked at more closely than the spoken, some matters of form, as in pronouns, are more carefully followed. Although the similarities and differences between spoken and written sentences have not been sufficiently studied, a few general comparisons can be made.

In length spoken sentences seem to be shorter than written, perhaps averaging—except for people accustomed to talking a good deal in public—below twelve words; the written average these days is close to twenty. Except for the chance in speaking to back up and start a sentence over, spoken sentences tend to be more direct than written, to make a full statement and then limit or qualify it by additions. ("Everybody was there, everybody but Jim" would be more likely written "Everybody but Jim was there.") Shifts in construction are less noticed, less damaging in speech than in writing. Some constructions, such as *that* clauses or infinitives as subjects (That he might be blamed didn't occur to him; To get home before the rain came was his aim) are rarely used in speech. Short constructions, without connectives or without subjects, are common. And the ease with which we can hold two clauses together without a connective in speaking (They must have heard my shout, why didn't they answer?) is a factor in the "run-on" sentences that occur in writing, as discussed on pages 253-257. The emphasis that in speech comes so much from voice stress, in writing has to be provided by changes in word order and by using more exact or more vigorous words.

Formal writing is patterned more on the formal speech of oratory and sermons and prepared lectures than on conversational speech. Today good informal writing, like so much of the best prose of the past, is close to natural speech—not to sloppy or careless speech but to good conversation—in words and constructions and movement. In fact one of the best tests of writing is reading it aloud in a natural tone of voice. If it "sounds good" it is probably "good." The days of approaching writing as though it was a different language from our speech are happily over. A corollary of this is that the better—the more expressive—our speech is, the better basis it is for our writing. Skill and improvement in speech and in writing go along together.

2. Meaning and purpose in sentences

Sentences occur in situations: they are acts. We are telling someone something, or asking for information, or trying to get something done, or often just trying to find out "what I think" about something by talking our ideas out or writing them down. Their most important feature then is how well they serve their purpose. They are to be judged not singly but in their context and according to how well they represent what seems to be the writer's purpose and especially how well they convey this purpose to the intended reader.

2a. Purpose in sentences. The conventional classification of sentences into declarative, interrogative, imperative, and exclamatory represents the general purposes of sentences well enough. Of these the first is by all odds the most common and the most important—Professor Summey found that 96.5% of the sentences in the expository materials he studied were declarative statements, and most discussions of sentences in grammars and books of rhetoric are about them. They may be more or less specific; they may be intended to inform or to prove or to startle or to deceive; but they all make assertions. They fall into various types but they, as well as the questions and exclamations, are responses to particular situations and contribute to them.

Students have usually been told to "vary their sentences" by using occasionally questions and exclamations instead of statements. It is true that a question can focus attention, but used *just* for variety it is likely to be artificial, like the questions in sales letters. They should be genuine questions, capable of answer or at least of leading to a line of thought. The writer should genuinely *think* the question, not just translate a statement into a different form. There is variety enough possible in the form of statements to make a pleasing style without making mechanical shifts in form.

One of the chief signs of development in the use of language is in the control of sentences. It is so intimately bound up with processes of thought that formal instruction, except in very elementary matters, is difficult; it is a matter of growth. Youngsters and people without much feeling for their language use sentences in a rather random way: their sentences are likely to be "choppy" or else to "run on and on." More mature thinkers develop, unconsciously for the most part, a sense of the sentence as a unit and succeed in holding together the small phrases of their thought so that a reader feels that he is following an actual train of thought and sees not only *what* the writer thought but *how* these thoughts are related to one another. The best way to grow in sentence skill is to write as much as possible in purposeful situations, from letters (and perhaps even a diary) to statements of as complex facts and ideas as you can muster. Any successful fashioning into consecutive statements of actual thought is a small victory—and helps to make further writing easier.

2b. Advancing the thought. Although the writer's intention is the controlling factor in what goes into a sentence, a number of matters can be considered from the reader's point of view. These are the most elementary aspects of sentences, and even they are matters of judgment, judgment of effectiveness and appropriateness. The most important of them have to do with the meaning of the statement.

The complete "meaning" of a sentence usually depends on what has gone before and what comes after, one reason why the definition "a group of words expressing a complete thought" is impossible. There may be pronouns referring to something in the preceding sentence, or there may be words clear or at least more fully meaningful in the context in which they occur, or other links with surrounding statements. The point is that the individual sentences should contribute something to the meaning in some essential way, contribute something to the reader's sense of the advancing thought.

Perhaps all the points that can be made about sentences fall under this heading. But three types of statement that definitely interfere with the advance of thought are:

1) Two STATEMENTS FOR ONE. Amateur writers frequently say in two statements what could be more effectively said in one, so that a reader has to do more rearranging of the thought than he should.

Two statements	*One statement*
It was three or four miles to the nearest village and these people used to walk it at least once a day.	These people used to walk the three or four miles to the nearest village at least once a day.
This is only a typical example; the author has many of them.	This is typical of the author's many examples.

| By being in the fresh air most of the time, as a hunter is, it tends to keep a person healthy and to develop his body. | Being in the fresh air most of the time, as a hunter is, tends to keep a person healthy and to develop his body. |

2) INCONGRUOUS STATEMENTS. A sentence may put together details that do not seem to belong together, which may raise a question in the reader's mind or even confuse him.

> As Byron is the poet of youth, it is appropriate that we should publish on March 1 the new and completely reset edition of his *Poems*.

Presumably *youth* and *March 1* are to be related in some way, but the association seems pretty far-fetched.

> Lady Beaconsfield affectionately called him "Dizzy" and she did everything in her power to make him the success he was.

Combining a nickname and a wife's help in building a statesman's career can only make a reader smile. He cannot make the leap between the ideas thus presented, and the writer shouldn't ask him to.

> He has a nervous habit of toying with the last two buttons on his vest when thinking and uses his deep voice to the best advantage when excited or angry.

Perhaps these two characteristics could be put together as signs of nervousness, but certainly they are too different to be connected simply by *and*. Two sentences would be easier to grasp.

3) STATEMENTS THAT CANCEL OUT. A surprising number of sentences contain two parts, one of which cancels the other. They come sometimes from an effort to put in a fact that doesn't quite belong, as in the first two examples, and sometimes from a clumsy attempt at qualifying a statement, as in the third:

> Her marriage to another writer, who teaches at Harvard, may have some influence upon her style; *however there is no evidence to support this.*
> *To do Sicily, one might start in at Taormina and end up at Palermo,* but father and I determined on doing it in the opposite direction, probably because it is convenient to take the overnight boat from Naples to Palermo.
> The next day we visited the ancient mosques, where we tried to walk in sandals which fitted—*or rather refused to fit*—over our shoes.

In revising the sentences of a paper it is well to see that the individual sentence and its various parts really advance the thought.

2c. Amount of meaning. Length of sentence is primarily a matter of style: a writer has a choice between relatively short and relatively long statements. (See Chapter 10, § 1.) Here the more elementary matter of making the individual sentence worth while is the point, since amateur writers sometimes let sentences stand that say little or nothing, that do not give the reader his money's worth. Here are three examples:

> Now what business does need is some good, sound supervision. Many laws have been passed. The Sherman Anti-trust Act forbade monopolies.

Of course "Many laws have been passed." Perhaps the writer meant "Among the laws passed attempting to regulate business, the Sherman Anti-trust Act. . . ."

> There were also several groups which were campaigning for the Senator in this election. These groups in the election of 1948 were for the most part unheard of.

Of course there were several groups campaigning; the first sentence has not advanced the idea at all. Perhaps the writer meant "Several groups that campaigned for the Senator were almost unheard of in 1948."

> My first course in math was taken at Riverside High School in Milwaukee. This was first-year or elementary algebra.

The reader feels that he is not getting his money's worth from the individual sentences. It might go: My first course in math, elementary algebra, was taken . . .

Some of the more useful but commonly overlooked ways of packing more into a single sentence are:

1) SERIES. Two or three details instead of one give more meaning per sentence:

> It is not newspapers, radio scripts, and movies that spoil our tongue so much as textbooks, official documents, commencement speeches, and learned works.—JACQUES BARZUN, *Teacher in America*, p. 55
> Oxford men are no more brilliant, no better looking, no more cultured and possessed of no greater inherent ability than countless undergraduates of American universities; but they think they are.—KENNETH ROBERTS, *For Authors Only*, p. 350

2) COMPOUND PREDICATES. Using more than one verb for a single subject often makes it unnecessary to have several short sentences of little meaning:

> Under the foregoing circumstances, how may the playwright do his work, maintain his integrity, and manage to survive economically?—WILLIAM SAROYAN, "Confessions of a Playwright," *Tomorrow*, Feb. 1949, p. 19

3) MODIFIERS. The most common way of making sentences mean more, and the one most neglected by amateur writers, is a greater use

of full modifiers, phrases and clauses that make particular words or the whole statement more exact:

> As we passed swiftly, the natives rushed out on the shaky board-and-log bridges, staring in wonder, the women with babies astride of their hips, the copper-skinned children now and then tumbling into the water in their excitement.—WILLIAM BEEBE, *Jungle Peace*, p. 85
>
> This nation embraces an increasing number of middle-sized cities, large enough to make metropolitan gestures and to entertain metropolitan pretensions, yet small enough to become infuriated over the same neighborhood matters which stirred the passions of the ancestral Four Corners settlement.—DUNCAN AIKMAN, *Harper's Magazine*, 150:513

At first a student may have to revise his sentences, consciously combining small statements into more complete ones, or adding informing details, but after a little practice he will automatically put more into his statements and so make them sound more mature.

2d. Exactness of meaning. Conveying exact meaning is largely a matter of using words accurately, but it is also a matter of careful control of sentences.

One annoying and confusing characteristic of some writing is a general fuzziness in the statement, coming perhaps from lack of practice in exact phrasing.

Fuzzy	*Clearer*
My own outlook on the subject of whether I gained or lost in my first semester is more inclined to be on the loss side of the argument.	I am afraid [or some such qualifying expression] that in my first semester I lost more than I gained.
Several of my family have died of cancer and I didn't know whether it was hereditary so I decided to find out.	I decided to find out whether cancer was hereditary, because several of my family had died from the disease.

Sometimes well meant sentiment that might pass in conversation seems nonsensical when it is stated in writing:

> When both the team and the student body are in there fighting and cheering till the final whistle, they really cannot be beaten, no matter what the score.
>
> He has made mistakes, yes, but who hasn't; we must never criticize too severely a man who tries.

The elements of sentence structure that contribute most specifically to exact meaning are probably connectives, showing the relationship that actually exists between parts of the statement. Consider the use of connectives to improve the following loose or inexact sentences:

Loose or inexact	*More exact relationship*
The spectators were keyed up and in very good spirits by two o'clock when the jumping event began, but nothing happened which was out of the ordinary, which seemed a terrible disappointment to them.	The spectators were keyed up and in very good spirits by two o'clock when the jumping event began, but *when* nothing out of the ordinary happened they were terribly disappointed.
The college graduate has been confronted with a great many more problems than one who hasn't been to college and thus in my estimation knows more about things in general.	*Since* a college graduate has been confronted with a great many more problems than one who hasn't been to college, in my estimation he knows more about things in general.
Some of the racers are forced out of the race because of motor trouble or lack of gasoline and when the winner finally skims over the finish line he is at least a half lap ahead of his nearest competitor, although occasionally a close race is seen.	Some of the racers are forced out of the race because of motor trouble or lack of gasoline, *so that as a rule* a race is not too close and when the winner finally skims over the finish line he is at least a half lap ahead of his nearest competitor.

Sometimes connectives are omitted entirely:

> He has a very strong will, once his mind is made up no one on earth can change it, he is rather stubborn at times, still for the most part he tries to see the other fellow's point of view.

The main trouble with this is not that four grammatically complete statements are run together with nothing stronger than commas between them, but that the conflicting statements have not been built together so that a reader can understand the relationship between the stubbornness of the person described and the sympathy with which the last clause credits him.

Because of the difficulty in tying parts of statements together, students tend to write shorter sentences than they need to. Practice in writing material with which they are familiar and some study of good current prose can do much to show the variety possible and to suggest how natural, meaningful sentences are put together. In the following passage, taken at random from a biography, each sentence advances its subject and leads a reader easily from one point to another:

> A man who accepts a religion without being religious lets himself in for more hardships than one would suppose. My father persisted most manfully in going to church; and he usually entered its portals at peace with the world and settled himself down contentedly in his end seat: but somehow before very long his expression would darken, as his hopes of hearing a sensible service little by little were dashed; and he came out in an inflamed state of mind that could not have been good for him.

The Episcopal service in general he didn't criticize; it was stately and quiet; but the sermon, being different every Sunday, was a very bad gamble. And once in awhile there would be an impromptu prayer that he would take great offense at. Sometimes he disliked its subject or sentiments—if he chanced to be listening. Sometimes he decided it was too long, or its tone too lugubrious. I remember seeing him so restive during a prayer of that kind, that—although the entire congregation was kneeling in reverence— he suddenly gave a loud snort, sat up straight in his pew, and glared at the minister's back as though planning to kick it.—CLARENCE DAY, *God and My Father*, pp. 17-18

3. The favorite English sentence

Meaning and intention are the basis of sentences, and the most necessary aspects to consider in writing. But our meaning is expressed in patterns that have become standardized in the centuries that English has been a language. The pattern most commonly used ("the favorite English sentence," as Jespersen has called it) is the one centered grammatically on a subject and verb, the basic relationship in the simple sentence and in the clauses that make up compound and complex sentences. Fortunately we learn the various patterns for sentences by imitation as we grow up. Since the written language is more exact than the spoken, it is necessary to become conscious of some of the patterns, especially those that are debatable or that we are inclined to neglect. To talk about our sentences, it is necessary to be able to distinguish the principal elements of which they are made up and to be able to name them.

3a. Elements of the sentence. The relation between the words in a sentence may be shown by several grammatical means. In "Jimmie's shoes" and "They saw him" the relation is shown by *form*, by the case ending *'s* and the case form *him*. English does not use this means very much, since its nouns and verbs have so few forms, compared, say, with German. In "He looked around cautiously" we know that *cautiously* modifies the verb *looked around* partly because of its *-ly* ending (though a number of our adverbs do not have the *-ly*). Words are also held together by *word order*, by being in the usual position we have come to expect and to understand. In "The eagle was attacking the fishhawk" our experience has taught us that *eagle* is the subject of *was attacking* because it precedes the verb, and that *fishhawk* is the object because it follows the verb. Our adjectives usually come before the nouns to which they refer: we say "a hot summer" and we know that in "That summer hot weather came in July" *hot* relates to *weather*.

A word may be related to the rest of the sentence by being in a subordinate construction, in a phrase or in a clause. In each of these the word group is an element of the sentence, connected to the other elements by a function word. In "The beginning of the term" *term* is related to *beginning* by the preposition *of*. In "The first day after the term began, she lost her book," the clause *after the term began* modifies *day* as if it was a single word, obviously related through the conjunction *after*, and *term* takes its place in the sentence through its place in the clause.

For convenience in labeling the parts of sentences, we can indicate the elements by letters and indicate three main levels of relation and two others, apposition and connection.

1) MAIN ELEMENTS. The typical English sentence is composed of a *subject* (s), the starting point of the statement, and a *verb* (v) or *linking verb* (LV), sometimes called "copula" (*be, become, feel, seem*). The meaning of the verb may be completed by an *object* (o) or an *indirect object* (IO) or both, and the meaning of a linking verb is completed by a *complement* (c), which may be either a noun or an adjective.

The subject, verb, and object form the frame of the typical sentence, to which other elements stand in some definite relationship that can be described in grammatical terms.

These examples show the main elements in ordinary patterns:

```
       s              v            o
Mrs. Pennoyer  |  bought  |  a dozen eggs.
    s       LV     c
Harold  |  felt  |  tired.
              s                   LV          c
The highest ranking student  |  becomes  |  valedictorian.
                       s
That the others might have some trick plays  |
        v              IO
had never occurred  |  to them.
 s      v          o
He  |  said  |  that they ought to know better.
```

(Note that in the last two sentences the subject of one, *That the others might have some trick plays,* and the object of the other, *that they ought to know better,* are clauses with subjects and verbs of their own, but that they serve the same purpose as a single word or phrase might serve.)

2) SECONDARY ELEMENTS. Words, phrases, and clauses that are not one of these main elements may be related to the sentence by modify-

ing one of the main elements (The *highest ranking* student becomes valedictorian). These secondary elements, modifiers, may be indicated by м: adjective elements modifying the subject (мs), or modifying the object (мo), or the complement (мc); adverbial elements modifying the verb (мv).

```
           MS              S       V          O          MV
 Coming into the open, |  he  | could see | the tracks | plainly.
    MS              S                       MS
 The high school | orchestra, | which was directed by Mr. Appley, |
    V       MO       O              MV
 played |  two  | numbers | between each act.
```

The sentence as a whole is often modified by a word or group of words, a *sentence modifier* (мS):

```
   мS        S      V      O
 Certainly, | he | knew | it. (This differs from "He certainly knew
   it," in which *certainly* modifies *knew*.)
                    мS                 S        V
 When he came into the open, |  he  | could see |
        O           MV
   the tracks | more plainly.
                 мS                      S           LV
 If we take motive into account, | the crime | does not seem |
   C
 so serious.
```

3) THIRD ELEMENTS. Other words may be related to the pattern of the sentence by modifying these secondary elements (The *local* high school orchestra, *more* plainly). Since their relationship to the secondary elements is like that of secondary elements to the main, there is no need for a separate symbol for them, but if it is necessary to indicate the relationship, another м (ммs for *modifier of modifier of subject*, and so on) can be used:

```
   MMS      MS      S          V       MMV    MV
 The local high school orchestra | played | unusually well.
```

There may be further degrees of modification (An almost / completely / accurate / description), but since the fundamental relationship is the same, it is rarely worth while regarding them as a separate rank in describing the movement of the sentence.

4) APPOSITIVES. Some words repeat the content and function of other words, are in *apposition* (a) to other words:

```
    S        SA       V             C
 The word *company* | may be | either singular or plural.
```

5) CONNECTIVES. Prepositions that introduce phrases, and conjunctions that introduce clauses are not elements of the whole sentence but of the constructions in which they occur. The phrase or clause as a whole is an element of the sentence.

> Phrase: *between* each act
> Clause: *when* the party broke up

If a conjunction relates a sentence to the one before, it is an element of the sentence and can be indicated as a *sentence connective* (SCON).

<pre>
                    MS   s   SCON   LV   c
Sentence connective: This plan, | however, | seemed | useless.
</pre>

6) ORDER OF SENTENCE ELEMENTS. The effect of a sentence depends in part on the order in which its elements stand. The more elaborate the sentence is, the more important is the way it is built up.

The typical order of the main sentence elements is: subject—verb—object or complement.

<pre>
           s   v   o
Sixty students | got | permission to leave early.
           s   LV   c
Ash Wednesday | is | the first day of Lent.
</pre>

No matter how many modifiers may be in the sentence, its basic pattern will ordinarily be s—v—o.

The typical order of sentence elements is so much a part of English grammar that we really identify subjects and objects by their position before or after the verb respectively (Jim [s] beat Frank [o]). This sense of position is responsible also for such informal usage as *who* instead of *whom* when as an object it precedes the verb or preposition controlling it. (*Who* [in writing usually *Whom*] was he with?)

One standard departure from this typical s-v-o order is *inversion*, in which the complement or an emphatic modifier of the verb stands first, followed by the verb and the subject standing last (c-v-s). Or the object or complement may precede the subject and verb in their usual order (o-s-v).

<pre>
          o   s   v   MV
This book | he | was now reading | for the third time.
       c   s   v   CA
Foolish | he | was, | just plain foolish.
</pre>

Inversion of subject and verb is the usual order in questions:

<pre>
   v s   v   o   MS   v   s   v o
Does he think he can fool us?   Where did you get it?
</pre>

v   s   o
Have you a few minutes?

An emphatic modifier often is the reason for inversion:

MS   v   s   v   o
Only then did he realize what he had done.

The English habit of placing modifiers close to the words they modify is another important part of grammatical word order. Subordinate elements should clearly refer to the words they modify.

Faulty order	*Conventional order*
But the principal disapproved of the petition and enforced the law which he had made *with the aid of the hall squad.*	But the principal disapproved of the petition and *with the aid of the hall squad* enforced the law which he had made.
The jury convicted the defendant of assault and battery *after deliberating two hours.*	*After deliberating two hours* the jury convicted the defendant of assault and battery.

These matters of order are a matter of grammar because they affect the meaning of a sentence. Order of elements is also a matter of style, giving variety and emphasis. These uses are discussed in Chapter 10, §§ 2 and 4.

3b. Compound sentences. Since the majority of sentences contain more than one clause, the means by which relation between clauses is shown is an important part of grammar. The relation should be clear to the reader and it should represent the writer's intention. In traditional English grammar there are two types of relation between clauses: in compound sentences the clauses are of equal importance, that is, *coordinate;* in complex sentences one clause is less important than the other, that is, *subordinate* to it. We usually identify the kind of clause by the connective which introduces it.

1) COMPOUND SENTENCES WITH CONNECTIVES. The majority of clauses in compound sentences are joined by one of three kinds of connectives: *Coordinating conjunctions*—and, but, for, nor, or, yet; *Correlative conjunctions*—both . . . and, either . . . or, neither . . . nor, so . . . as, not only . . . but [but also], whether . . . or; *Conjunctive adverbs*—accordingly, also, besides, consequently, hence, however, indeed, namely, nevertheless, so, and some others.

The first type is by all odds the most common:

We had expected to get there by noon, *but* the radiator delayed us.

The chief danger is an overuse of *and* when some other connective would be more exact, especially a subordinating conjunction.

Correlative conjunctions are not very much used in speaking or informal writing, except *either . . . or:*

> *Either* the postman hasn't come *or* there isn't any mail for us today.

Conjunctive adverbs are formal words, out of place in short sentences—usually *but* is better than *however*—and in current writing more likely to connect two separate sentences than two parts of the same sentence:

> There is a growing body of evidence that no significant growth in personality is brought about by such education. *Indeed,* there is some good evidence that the contrary often occurs, and that the prolongation of formal education results in a deterioration of personality.—Henry C. Link, *The Return to Religion,* p. 145

Their connecting force is so weak that when used within a sentence the clauses are usually punctuated with a semicolon:

> In aristocratic societies—and all of our societies are aristocratic to a degree—some of these places, being hereditary, require no special ability on the part of the incumbents; *yet* in order to establish them ability was once necessary, and some sort of service to the group is required in order to maintain them.—D. H. Parker, *Human Values,* p. 162

2) Without connectives. When there is no connective between the clauses of a compound sentence, the individual clauses are called *contact clauses;* the conventional punctuation between the clauses is a semicolon:

> In American sports, especially in baseball, the umpire is not respected; he is frequently challenged, and occasionally threatened by the players, and most frequently insulted by the partisan spectators. Nevertheless, it is the "umpire" aspect of the American government which meets with the least suspicion and contempt; the Supreme Court and its members are seldom suspected of improper attempts to increase its or their authority.—Geoffrey Gorer, *The American People,* p. 36

The two parts of these sentences are loosely related and in many styles would stand as separate sentences; but the writer wished to hold the ideas together and so made them compound sentences. Professor Summey found that one fourth (102 out of 400) of the compound sentences in his materials had no connective. Of these 75 were punctuated with a semicolon, 13 with a colon, and 5 with a dash. These all indicate a break almost as great as the break between two sentences.

3) RUN-ON SENTENCES. There is more of a problem when two or more main clauses are written with only a comma between them (or even, in very careless writing, with no mark at all). A sentence of this kind is called "run-on." Judged by their grammatical form the two statements could be separate sentences. Whether or not they should be written as two sentences or revised in some other way depends in part on current practices in punctuation and sentence form, but more on the relations between the statements themselves.

a) *Contact clauses.* In books and articles by writers of high standing we find run-on sentences—and they have been passed, furthermore, by editorial copy readers. Here are a few:

> Men are said to be partial judges of themselves. Young men may be, I doubt if old men are.—T. H. HUXLEY, *Autobiography*

> She loved Marise, nobody had a nicer little girl, nor a prettier.—DOROTHY CANFIELD, *Rough-Hewn*, p. 135

> The theatre was dark, the second show was over.—THOMAS WOLFE, *Look Homeward, Angel*, p. 275

> This is to be our vision of them—an imperfect vision, but it is suited to our powers, it will preserve us from a serious danger, the danger of pseudo-scholarship. . . . They are gateways to employment, they have power to ban and bless. . . .—E. M. FORSTER, *Aspects of the Novel*, pp. 22, 24

Such sentences have always been common in speech ("Hurry up, we'll be late"—spoken without dropping the voice after *up*) and recently, with the increasing colloquialness of written style, they have become more common in writing. (Nine of Professor Summey's 102 contact clauses were separated only by commas.) One of the best ways to test such a run-on sentence is to speak it aloud in a natural tone. If your voice drops as it does at the end of a sentence, it is a comma fault and should be written as two sentences or revised to some other form. If your voice does not drop ("They had to take him out finally, he was crying so loud") and if the two clauses read naturally with no more pause than ordinarily stands between two clauses of the same sentence, it may be a good sentence.

In addition to using this oral test, you should consider the closeness of the relation between the ideas of the two clauses. The punctuation between two contact clauses should represent the writer's intention. A period marks the greatest degree of separation, two statements that the writer wishes to keep separate. A semicolon between them means that to the writer the statements are not closely related, but still the relation between them is closer than that between either of them and the statement preceding or following. A comma should mean that they are very closely related and that they can be spoken as one genuine sentence.

Besides the relation between the thought of the two clauses, you should consider their appropriateness to other features of your writing. You should remember the widespread prejudice against run-on sentences, and that editors do not often let them stand in matter they are to publish. Run-on sentences are almost always inappropriate in formal English, which usually avoids colloquial constructions. Two contact clauses in the midst of a rather fully and formally developed passage will ordinarily seem a let-down, a bit of carelessness. They are rare, too, in discussions of ideas, even when the discussions are rather informally written, because exposition primarily shows the relationships between statements, and that means, ordinarily, linking them by specific connectives. Occasionally the relationship is obvious, or some other trait of style, especially parallel construction, makes running together natural:

> That is why, in the rather ramshackly course that lies ahead of us, we cannot consider fiction by periods, we must not contemplate the stream of time.—E. M. FORSTER, *Aspects of the Novel*, p. 28

Contact clauses are most useful in easy, rapid narrative (factual or imaginative), in which the clauses are relatively short, approaching the short turns of actual speech, and in which relationships can be rapidly grasped without connectives. In fact connectives would ordinarily bring an unneeded note of formality into such narrative.

These principles can usually help a writer decide in revising his manuscript whether he should let a run-on sentence stand or should rewrite it. A sentence like "After stepping back to survey his work, he finds that the steps are not even, another brick must be put under the bottom one" would not be noticeably bettered if it was made more conventional by adding a second *that:* "After stepping back to survey his work, he finds that the steps are not even, that another brick must be put under the bottom one." Nor, in a definitely informal context, would a more elaborate version of this sentence be an improvement: "Gosh, I thought, if anything more can happen to us, bring it on, I can stand anything now."

b) *Comma faults.* A carelessly run-on sentence is variously referred to as a "comma blunder," a "comma fault," or a "comma splice." In the following "sentence" three locutions with a subject and complete verb (and so capable of standing as separate sentences) are run together:

> Their future looked pitifully black, they were working and getting nowhere, instead of profiting by their labors they were losing.

Since in reading these aloud your voice drops at the end of each, they should be written as three sentences or rewritten in another form:

> Their future looked pitifully black. They were working and getting nowhere. Instead of profiting by their labors they were losing.

After their years of school English, college students should have no difficulty in knowing when they have a grammatically complete sentence or when they have joined two of them. The students who turned in these were probably not paying attention to their work:

> We burned wood then and he always made a great deal of noise with the lids, you could hear him all over the house.
> In the autumn of 1930, forty-eight persons were shot by an order of the Gay-Pay-oo, among this group were many distinguished professors.

Probably most of the comma faults in student writing occur because the writer has made two sentences grammatically complete in form for what should have been made a main and a subordinate statement with the relationship between them clearly indicated.

One of the commonest types of comma fault has a personal or demonstrative pronoun (*he, it, they, this, that*) used instead of a relative pronoun (*who, which*):

Unsuccessful	*Improved*
The Ranger's crew is made up of 26 professional sailors, most of them are of Scandinavian ancestry.	The Ranger's crew is made up of 26 professional sailors, most of whom are of [*or:* most of them of] Scandinavian ancestry.
While a boy lives at home he is dependent on others, they help him out of his difficulties and provide at least for his necessities.	While a boy lives at home, he is dependent on others who help him out of his difficulties and provide at least for his necessities.

Many comma faults are due simply to separating ideas that should be fused into one statement:

Unsuccessful	*Improved*
This last piece of work was very difficult, the hack-saw blades grew hot and broke.	This last piece of work was so difficult that the hack-saw blades grew hot and broke.

Unsuccessful	Improved
One part receives the stimulus from outside and transmits the impulse to the cell, this is known as the dendrite.	One part, known as the dendrite, receives the stimulus from outside and transmits the impulse to the cell.
The pressmen were a good natured bunch who seldom complained about their conditions, instead they usually joked about them.	The pressmen were a good natured bunch who usually joked rather than complained about their conditions.

Another common type of comma fault is one in which a second verb is used in a construction that does not require it as in the sentence below:

Unsuccessful	Improved
Then came the speeches, some of them were very amusing while others were very serious.	Then came the speeches, some of them very amusing, others very serious.

In each of the comma fault examples the thought seems to be single and rightly put in one sentence but the connection between parts of the thought was not made close enough. Of course very often sentences profit from more drastic revision than is shown in these examples.

Sometimes a conjunction can be inserted in a comma fault sentence that will make the sentence conventionally compound or complex:

Unsuccessful	Improved
I think it would do a lot of Americans good to read this book, they would get a background on which to form a more exact knowledge of the English people.	I think it would do a lot of Americans good to read this book because they would get a background on which to form a more exact knowledge of the English people.

Only once in a while will the easiest (laziest) change, repunctuating with a period or semicolon, make the sentence really any better. A semicolon between the two clauses is often suggested, but it would not have helped materially any of the sentences given above and usually should not be used unless there is a connective.

The vigilantes did not bother with courts, which might cause a wait of six months for satisfaction, [; better here] instead they hung their men as close to the scene of the crime as possible and left the body there as an example.

The long days of Front and Market streets were a thing of the past, [probably better as two sentences] the store now opened for business at eight in the morning and closed at six-thirty, including Saturdays.

Business today does not wait for a young fellow to learn, [; or . depending on emphasis desired] if the new employee does not seem fitted for the job, another is found to take his place.

In reading all of these you drop your voice at the comma, which shows that the clauses have the form and value of two separate sentences. The point to consider is whether the ideas are closely enough related to stand properly in a single sentence, and then whether the relationship has been shown. The purpose in examining run-on sentences is to carry out the writer's intention, seriously considered, and to meet a reasonable expectation of a reader.

To guard against carelessly run-on sentences (comma faults), some teachers ask students to mark contact clauses they wish to leave by a star or the word *intentional* in the margin.

3c. Complex sentences. Nearly half the sentences in current writing are complex, having one main clause and one or more subordinate clauses. (Professor Summey reports 44.5% complex sentences and only 5.95% compound sentences in his passages.) They are less stiff than compound sentences, more varied, and—most important— more exact because the connectives are more numerous and more special in meaning than the coordinating conjunctions.

Subordinate clauses are related to the main clause by the relative pronouns (*who, which, that, what*) and by subordinating conjunctions, of which the most common are:

after	because	since	when
although	before	so that	where
as	how	though	while
as if	if	till	why
as long as	in order that	unless	

1) RELATION BETWEEN CLAUSES. The most important fact is that connectives represent the relationship between *ideas;* the exact meaning of the connective (cause, time, contrast, condition, and so on) is more important than subordination or coordination.

The general principle is that the more important, the principal statements should be in independent clauses, and the less important should be in subordinate clauses or in phrases. When a main idea is made subordinate or a less important one made into a main clause, we have "upside-down subordination."

The following inexact sentences, with possible revised forms, will illustrate how careful subordination can make statements more accurate.

Inexact	*Revised*
Illustrations were given in every case *and* the plan was easily understood, which made it all the more interesting.	Illustrations were given in every case *so that* the plan was easily understood and all the more interesting.
The Stanley Steamer looked like one of those cars of the nineties in every way except its wheels, *and* they were changed so as to use pneumatic tires.	The Stanley Steamer looked in every way like one of those cars of the nineties except for its wheels, *which* were changed so as to use pneumatic tires.
Often a grave will contain no burial goods. Others might contain a few tools or beads. The latter is the more usual.	*Although* often a grave will contain no burial goods, usually they will have a few tools or beads.
He may have attended both of the preceding classes, *and* by chapel time he begins to feel the desire for a respite from mental work.	*If* he has attended both of the preceding classes, by chapel time he begins to feel the desire for a respite from mental work.

2) SUBORDINATION AND SENTENCE MOVEMENT. The use of subordinate clauses is one of the marks of an accurate and mature style. Children are said to subordinate about fifteen percent of their statements, while mature writers subordinate about half of theirs. Sentences with subordinate elements are not only more accurate, they give greater variety and more exact emphasis than a series of coordinate statements.

The following brief quotation contains six subordinate clauses. The loss from translating them into simple declarative sentences shows something of the advantages of subordination.

Statements subordinated	*Without subordination*
The contention that democracy is *per se* identical with mediocrity is a wanton assumption considering the fact that democracy, until it is realized economically as it has not yet been in capitalistic countries, has not been tried at all. Until it is tried economically it is too early to tell what the common man may contribute to uncommon achievement in literature and art and thought.—IRWIN EDMAN, *Four Ways of Philosophy*, p. 155	It is contended that democracy is *per se* identical with mediocrity. This is a wanton assumption. Democracy not realized economically is not democracy. In capitalistic countries this has not been tried at all. [The statements of Mr. Edman's second sentence are so closely interrelated that they cannot be broken down into separate statements in this fashion.]

Subordination is the principal means of avoiding or overcoming choppy sentences. Notice how the following paragraph was improved by subordinating some of the elements.

Original paragraph	Student's revision
We made our second stop at a hotel on the top of the mountain. This hotel, six thousand feet above the sea, was equipped with modern conveniences. We were grateful for the limeade at twenty cents and the rhum at twenty-five cents. The lack of ice wasn't noticeable. Any drink would seem cool at 102°. The flower garden around the hotel was a welcome relief after the barren road we had traveled. The hotel had a banana plantation of about twenty-five trees. Our drinks were served on a terrace over the garden.	At the crest of the mountain, 6000 feet above sea level, with the temperature at 102°, we welcomed drinks of limeade (20c) and rhum (25c), which were cooling even though they lacked ice. These drinks were served on the terrace of a modern hotel that overlooked a flower garden and a banana plantation of twenty-five trees, a scene that offered a pleasant relief from the barren road we had traveled.

The final adjustment between main and subordinate statements is one of the concerns of revision.

3d. Compound-complex sentences. A rather small number of sentences have two or more main clauses and one or more subordinate clauses:

> [First main clause:] The teacher is a kind of medical man [adjective clause:] whose purpose is to cure the patient of childishness, [second main clause] but he is not allowed to decide for himself on the basis of experience [noun clause:] what methods are most suitable to this end.—BERTRAND RUSSELL, "The Function of a Teacher," *Harper's Magazine*, June 1940

Such compound-complex sentences are not peculiar or difficult in any way but are the least common of the four grammatical sentence types in current writing.

4. Minor sentence types

The great majority of English sentences belong to the "favorite" type, centered on a subject and verb. But enough good sentences without one or the other or both of these elements occur so that the definition "A sentence is a group of words having a subject and predicate" is not quite accurate, and a realistic grammar must take account of the sentences without these elements. Nothing is omitted from these sentences and no words should be "understood" in analyzing them. They are natural forms of expression to be taken just as they are.

4a. Subjectless sentences. Sentences without subjects are much less common than sentences without verbs. There are a few of a raditional pattern like *No sooner said than done* and commands and requests (imperative sentences):

> Don't let me ever hear you say that again. Please try.

Other subjectless sentences are confined almost entirely to narrative in which the subject is easily carried over from the context, or to very informal and familiar writing. The most commonly omitted subject is *I*, which receives very little stress in speaking. This type of sentence is most appropriate in representing dialog in stories or in informal sketches of people:

> "Guess I can live on the town if I've a mind to. Been paying taxes for thirty years and more."—ERSKINE CALDWELL, *We Are the Living*, p. 219

> They took no interest in civilized ways. Hadn't heard of them, probably.—CLARENCE DAY, *Life With Father*, p. 30

> You needn't be alarmed about the water's having fish in it. Means it's on the alkaline side.—*The New Yorker*, Oct. 30, 1937

4b. Verbless sentences. There are several types of sentence without a main verb that are common and in good if rather limited use in all levels of speaking and writing. The verbs are not "left out"; they are not thought, spoken, or written. The statements are complete and independent without them.

1) EXCLAMATIONS, from *Ouch!* and other monosyllables to *What a mess!* and on to complicated phrasing of feeling.

2) ANSWERS TO QUESTIONS, from *Yes* and *No* and *Not if I know it,* to specific answers to definite questions:

> And what was the philosophy behind the Sherman Act and the Clayton Act? *Individualism, pure and undefiled.* "*The New Freedom*" *as President Wilson phrased it in literary language.* "Break up the trusts and let each tub stand on its own bottom." That was the cry among little business men.—C. A. BEARD, *The Myth of Rugged American Individualism*, p. 14

3) DESCRIPTIVE DETAILS, ADDED MODIFIERS. Often in passages that are chiefly descriptive, especially if the details are given as impressions, the only verb possible would be a colorless *is* or *are* or *has* or *have*. Without a verb there is no loss of meaning and there is a gain in economy and sharpness.

> And after all the weather was ideal. They could not have had a more perfect day for a garden-party if they had ordered it. *Windless, warm, the sky without a cloud.* Only the blue was veiled with a haze of light gold, as it is sometimes in early summer.—KATHERINE MANSFIELD, *The Garden Party*, p. 59

There was one in particular of Mother looking very roguish and chic in her voluminous dress, sitting way up on top of a tall and insolent camel, with two big black men in white turbans standing off at one side. *No other member of the party around. Not a soul in sight but the black men and Mother.* Father looked at that photograph often and groaned about it at night, and kept shouting things to himself about "the ends of the earth."—CLARENCE DAY, *Life With Father*, p. 116

The fat old porter knocks. Ah, me, once more it is dark. Get up again before dawn. *A dark sky outside, cloudy. The thrilling tinkle of innumerable goat-bells as the first flock enters the city, such a rippling sound.* Well, it must be morning, even if one shivers at it. And at least it does not rain.—D. H. LAWRENCE, *Sea and Sardinia*, p. 35

Often in passages portraying a character's thought there are no verbs, increasing the speed and naturalness of movement:

Principles—he mused—*au fond* were pocket; and he wished the deuce people wouldn't pretend they weren't! *Pocket, in the deep sense of that word, of course, self-interest as members of a definite community.* And how the devil was this definite community, the English nation, to exist, . . . JOHN GALSWORTHY, *The White Monkey*, p. 3

4) APPOSITIONAL SENTENCE. The sentence in which an adjective or other modifier is set beside its noun without a verb is very common.

An understatement, this.—S. E. MORISON, *Harvard College in the Seventeenth Century*, p. 320

No verb no predication.—P. B. BALLARD, *Thought and Language*, p. 83

Easy enough to argue that the increased estate taxes are devoted to governmental social programs in the public interest.
Hard to drive out the fear of politics in the administration of public philanthropy.—*Nation's Business*, Dec. 1936

Appositional sentences often serve as transitions:

So much for the proviso "English." Now for a more important proviso, that of "period or periods."—E. M. FORSTER, *Aspects of the Novel*, p. 21

5) CLAUSES AND PHRASES. Occasionally an expression in the form of a phrase or subordinate clause stands alone as a sentence. These are usually light (*Which is another story. Not that it matters.*) or almost formulas; or sometimes a *because* or a *which* clause is set off by itself for emphasis:

There we are; now let us classify them. *Which he does.*—E. M. FORSTER, *Aspects of the Novel*, p. 27

Marks! Your marks had to be up to a certain standard. You had to get good marks to get promoted. *Into the next grade. Into high school. Into college.* Marks counted.—JOHN R. TUNIS, *Ladies' Home Journal*, Sept. 1938

Such sentences are rare, for usually participial phrases and subordinate clauses suggest by their very form that they are dependent upon what precedes or follows and should rarely be left standing as sentences.

4c. Fragmentary sentences. Most other types of incomplete sentences are unsuccessful and to be avoided. A sentence part that is carelessly or ineffectively punctuated as a whole sentence is called a *fragmentary sentence*. It is usually the result of the writer's carelessness, or of his not being sufficiently conscious of the relation between parts of his statements, or, very often, merely of lack of practice in writing. Prepositional phrases, participial phrases, and subordinate clauses show by their form as well as by their incomplete meaning that they are parts of other constructions and are not meant to stand alone. Because readers rightly expect the form of statements to represent the actual relation between their parts, editors and teachers expect most sentences to fall into the typical s-v-o pattern.

Here are specimens of three common types of fragmentary sentences with suggested remedies. All of them show by their form that they are dependent elements, not stable enough to stand alone.

1) PARTICIPIAL PHRASES

Faulty	*Improved*
Looking carefully through his water glass he finds a liner deep in the quicksand, lying on her side. *The nearest porthole being twelve feet down.* He dives down to the porthole and tries to break it.	Looking carefully through his water glass he finds a liner deep in the quicksand, lying on her side, her nearest porthole twelve feet down. He dives down to the porthole and tries to break it.
National elections and student elections in my high school may be compared as closely as an object and its own photograph. *The only difference being in size.*	National elections and student elections in my high school may be compared as closely as an object and its own photograph; the only difference was in size.
At the end of each reporting period each subject was marked numerically, on the basis of one hundred. *The Deportment column covering the behavior of the child.*	At the end of each reporting period each subject was marked numerically, on the basis of one hundred. The Deportment column covered the behavior of the child.

2) SUBORDINATE CLAUSES

Faulty	*Improved*
At the time my old rowboat with its three horsepower motor seemed to be a high speed job to me. *Although it only attained a speed of about twelve miles an hour.*	At the time my old rowboat with its three horsepower motor seemed to be a high speed job to me, although it only attained a speed of about twelve miles an hour.

Leather-Stocking was first drawn as an old man and his youth described last of all. *While the other periods of his life were filled in in a very erratic order.* Yet he is the same character from beginning to end.

Green Mansions is a weird, wandering story, the main part of which is taken up with description of the South American jungles. *While the characters, who provide a beautiful romance of the tropical forests, seem incidental.*

Although Leather-Stocking was drawn first as an old man and the other periods of his life were filled in in a very erratic order, his youth the last of all, he is the same character from beginning to end.

Green Mansions is a weird, wandering story, the main part of which is taken up with description of the South American jungles. The characters, who provide a beautiful romance of the tropical forests, seem incidental.

Contrast the two *because* clauses in the following examples, the first of which seems stable because it is in direct answer to a question, the second not stable because it directly explains the preceding statement and should be related to that statement:

Why? Because service and ethics are service and ethics, and the business of business is business.

Finally another season came to an end but this had been a more happy one for me. Because I now had my own boat and I thought I was on my way to bigger and better outfits.

3) BRIEF EXPLANATORY ENUMERATIONS, especially when introduced by a phrase like *"such as"*:

After these cards have been run through, the firm knows what volume of business has been done during the week in each of the departments. Such as tobaccos, candies, canned fruits, fresh produce. [Simply join to the preceding sentence, using a comma after *departments.*]

Weak fragment

When I first arrived all was quiet, but soon men began to gather with their dinner pails. Some on foot, others in wagons, and the higher class in Model T Fords.

Improved

When I first arrived all was quiet, but soon men began to gather with their dinner pails, on foot, in wagons, and the higher class in Model T Fords.

Most fragmentary sentences like these are careless, and a writer revising his paper with attention and care would not let them stand.

In deciding whether or not to let a minor sentence form stand in your writing, apply the principle of appropriateness and consider the types of reputable ones described in sections 4a and 4b. Certainly remove those that are careless and that suggest by their form that they should be built on to neighboring sentences. In rather formal writing, an incomplete sentence that is not of a generally recognized pattern like an answer to a question or an exclamation is usually out of place. In informal writing there is more leeway, but still you should remember that most readers are more or less offended by departures from the typical English sentence patterns.

Teachers and students will not always agree on whether a particular minor sentence is legitimate or a fragment, any more than professional writers and editors of publishing houses agree on such matters. But the classifications we have suggested should make it possible to agree on grounds of effectiveness and appropriateness.

To guard against careless incomplete sentences, some teachers ask students to indicate that one is intentional by putting a star or the word *intentional* in the margin.

5. Writing and revising sentences

It is much easier to describe sentences than it is to make suggestions for writing them effectively. One reason is that we are not conscious of individual sentences in speaking—and shouldn't be in writing. We can figure out the plan of a paper before writing, and we can see the general form of a paragraph in our mind before putting it on paper. But sentences are best written without too much conscious attention—*and then revised*.

The points that have been made in this chapter should be applied in revision, when you read over what you have written and can consider matters of form without interfering with your thinking. Some analysis of sentences may be necessary, to show how they are put together. One method of analysis is shown in section 3a: dividing a sentence into its word groups, the elements of which it is made up, and then seeing the relation between these, the subject-verb-object relationship and the words to which the modifiers are related.

Some conscious practice, as in exercises, may be useful to focus attention on different phases of sentences and to give practice in remaking them. Then you can do the same to your own sentences, if they need it. Gradually your first draft sentences will improve and less revision will be necessary.

If you have got as far as college without picking up the fundamental patterns of English sentences, you should make up for lost time in a hurry. College students and college teachers shouldn't waste their time on sixth-grade work. But no matter how correct your sentences may be, there is still chance for further growth in other qualities.

Various Classifications of Sentences

1. BY TYPE OF STATEMENT (Chapter 9, § 2a):

   Declarative (statements)
   Interrogative (questions)
   Exclamatory (exclamations)
   Imperative (commands, requests)

2. BY NUMBER AND KINDS OF CLAUSES (Chapter 9, § 3):

   Simple: A single independent clause
   Compound: Two or more coordinate clauses
   Complex: One independent clause and one or more subordinate clauses
   Compound-complex: Two or more independent clauses and one or more subordinate clauses

3. BY ORDER OF ELEMENTS (Chapter 9, § 3a; Chapter 10, §§ 2a, 2b, 2c):

   Direct: (M) S V O (M)
   Inverted: V S O
   Interrupted: S (M) V (M) O

4. BY STOPPING POINT (Chapter 10, § 2d):

   Loose: Meaning and construction complete before end
   Periodic: Meaning and construction complete at end

5. BY AMOUNT OF MEANING (Chapter 10, § 1):

   Segregating: Relatively short
   Aggregating: Relatively long; statements combined

6. BY GRAMMATICAL FORM (Chapter 9, §§ 3, 4):

   "Favorite" English sentence: Subject and verb nexus
   Subjectless sentence: Lacking stated grammatical subject
   Verbless sentence: Without a conventional main verb
   Fragmentary sentence: Unsuccessful without main verb
   Comma fault: Clauses unsuccessfully combined without connective

7. BY BACKGROUND (Chapter 9, § 1):

   Informal: Conversational; background in ordinary educated speech
   Formal: Background in formal, public speech
   Bookish: Literary or unusually formal writing

Practice in writing will show real effect in increased skill in composing mature, meaningful sentences. Letters, papers in other courses as well as in the composition course, even short impromptu bits jotted down and thrown away will help. One of the surest ways to grow in these details would be to write something every day, even if it wasn't more than half a page, and glance it over for sentence form. Any practice in writing you can give yourself will show in increased control of sentences. If you remember that the reason for examining and discussing sentences is to make it easier for you to convey your meaning to readers in language forms that are appropriate and effective, the work will be rewarding and can even be interesting.

Suggested study and writing

These exercises are to acquaint students with different kinds of sentences and to give practice in analyzing the function of elements within sentences. Additional practice on other aspects of sentences may be found in the exercises for Chapters 4 and 10.

1. The following paragraph has been revised so that both important and unimportant ideas are given approximately equal emphasis. Recast and combine the sentences, adding connectives where desirable, to stress important ideas and subordinate less important ideas.

> Now I don't believe in the factory's producing happiness. I have said this before. I am, nevertheless, willing to believe in it. You do believe in happiness resulting from steam power. Show me one or two examples of it. Show me your own happiness from it. I can show *you* examples of happiness without it. I can show you millions of happy people. These people are made happy by their own industry. I can show you farms in Bavaria, Switzerland, the Tyrol, and similar places. These men and women are happy. They have no mechanical power. Show me one happier English family. It has the products of the steam engine. I can be convinced by any sort of evidence. Bring me the testimony of one or two English families. Perhaps you can't do that. Can you convince them? Perhaps actually they are happy. They may not realize it. They claim not to be.—Adapted from JOHN RUSKIN, "Fors Clavigera"

2. Various types of errors in sentence form are illustrated in these sentences from student papers: comma splices, ineffective fragments, upside-down subordination, shifted constructions, inexact connectives, ambiguity or contradiction in meaning. Point out the specific kind of error in each sentence group and indicate how the passage might be revised.

1. There are many types of soil in the United States, thus making conservation a difficult problem.

2. If a fellow has been fortunate enough to attend prep school and been made to study, college studying comes much more easily to him if he wants an education, but there are many things much more interesting to him than studying but now there is no one going to tell him that he had better get his homework in.

3. There are various forms of eczema. In infancy this disorder occurs on foreheads, Or often in the folds of the elbows and knees. Food protein causes this.

4. John is really a fine boy and a sophomore at the local high school.

5. The tendency in recent years has been toward urban living, Chiefly because there is a greater variety of employment in the larger metropolitan areas, such as New York, Chicago, and Los Angeles.

6. At night the snow falls like a shower of featherweight diamonds seen in artificial illumination, each flake has its own particular mission, however devious its path. That is to reach the earth.

7. Should children take music lessons against their wills? This is a big question. There is both a pro and a con for an answer. I myself do not think that a child should be forced to take music lessons.

8. A very close friend of mine was forced to learn to play the clarinet. He stayed with it only three months. From then on he used the clarinet to scare the pigs, as he lived on a farm. An investment of about $80 thrown away. As they say, you can lead a horse to water, but you can't make him drink.

9. College professors are better teachers than high school teachers. The reason for this, college professors are more up to date on their subjects at all times, generally.

10. One thing that the author used throughout the article that made it easy to read was his use of examples familiar to every reader.

11. The social life in the sororities and fraternities helps the student to get acquainted with many new people. They have their exchanges, among different organized houses, dates are arranged for fellows and girls who would not otherwise meet.

12. The system employed by our journalism advisor facilitated the use of everyone. Each week a new person would have his name opposite "Editor-in-Chief"; therefore, a new type of front page would be produced, instead of one specific type of front page for the whole semester.

13. Observing the passengers on the bus as I ride to and from school each day, I have learned that a man's occupation cannot be determined from his appearance, but even more revealing would be to discover more about each person's character and interests.

14. We were so weary when we returned from that mountain trip. We found it difficult to keep our eyes open while eating dinner.

15. Some crops need certain minerals which are found in limited quantities in the soil, thus the same crop planted year after year would eventually consume all the minerals in the soil, causing the soil to lose its fertility.

16. Am writing on this subject because I have been interested in it for many years. Have studied it in high school and read about it whenever I had time.

17. When approximately a freshman in high school, one of my elective subjects was the Oral Expression class, believing such a class might possibly be an aid in speech, helping to overcome my self-consciousness.

18. Being in a hospital bed all day for seven days the scene outside my window was different every day.

19. I kneeled on my right knee and brought the rifle to my right shoulder and about fifty feet away was a buck deer running for safety. I fired one shot at him while running and missed, causing him to stop and look at me.

3. Copy the following sentences from a student theme and analyze the main elements in each. See pages 248-251 for illustrations of this method. First indicate by symbols the subject (s), verb (v) or linking verb (lv), and the object (o), indirect object (io), or complement (c). Then show the modifiers of these elements by symbols (ms, mv, mo, mio, mc, and mS [sentence modifier]). Use vertical lines to mark off main elements. State whether the sentences are simple, complex, compound, or compound-complex.

1. Perhaps no one is better aware of the weaknesses which characterize mankind than is the modern advertiser.

2. He knows that through careful appeal to these shortcomings he can compose advertisements that will get results.

3. We are easily confused by the names of things, and in this fact lies unlimited opportunity.

4. Clever advertising can lead us to confuse brand names with the categories to which these brands belong.

5. Such trademarks as Coca Cola, Spam, Simonize, and Frigidaire are examples of the success of this "organized confusion"; many people, for instance, think all electric refrigerators are Frigidaires, and all canned meat is Spam.

6. The one weakness most widely cultivated by the advertisers, however, is our susceptibility to flattery.

7. When a woman is told that the only way in which she differs from some current film beauty is in a quality that a certain face cream will provide her, she wants to believe this is true.

8. And we are also continually being told that the world will recognize our intelligence and discrimination if we use a particular brand of cigarettes.

9. So popular is this advertising device that whole volumes could be filled with examples of its use.

10. But why repeat what everyone in this country already knows?

4. Make a similar analysis of the sentences in these paragraphs:

1. (1) The great adventure of modern American education has just begun. (2) During recent decades many of the schools have been built, the colleges expanded, the teaching staffs assembled. (3) The students have come to the schools. (4) In 1920 only 32 per cent of adolescents of high-school age attended school; in 1940, 73 per cent. (5) This year about two and one-half million students are enrolled in American colleges and universities. (6) In the past generation we have had, as it were, a shakedown cruise. (7) Now we must settle down to the serious enterprise of trying really to educate all American youth to the extent of their capacities.— THOMAS CLARK POLLOCK, "English for Maturity," *College English*, Feb. 1949

2. (1) Patton labored under continual anxiety. (2) Cautious, hard-working, and terribly ambitious, he was the kind of competitor who, in the old Greek phrase, always smelled of the oil of the gymnasium rubbing room. (3) At West Point he never missed football practice but could never make the team. (4) At polo he developed slowly, by dint of enormous concentration and heavy expenditure for mounts. (5) His highest handicap, 4, was attained in 1932, when he was forty-seven years old. (6) He built up his professional skills in the same way, by internal sweat, but he had them ready by the time of the war. (7) The clownish, swashbuckling façade was as spontaneous as the lobby display at Radio City Hall.—A. J. Liebling, *The Wayward Pressman*, p. 144

3. (1) Sometimes we talk simply for the sake of hearing ourselves talk; that is, for the same reason that we play golf or dance. (2) The activity gives us a pleasant sense of being alive. (3) Children prattling, adults singing in the bathtub, are alike enjoying the sound of their voices. (4) Sometimes large groups make noises together, as in group singing, group recitation, or group chanting, for similar presymbolic reasons. (5) In all this, the significance of the words used is almost completely irrelevant. (6) We may, for example, chant the most lugubrious words about a desire to be carried back to a childhood home in old Virginny, when in actuality we have never been there and haven't the slightest intention of going.—S. I. Hayakawa, *Language in Thought and Action*, p. 71

5. Make a similar analysis of the sentences in one of your recent papers. Are the relationships between different parts of your sentences clear and reasonably exact, or do some of the statements seem merely to be tacked on? Do you tend to use one type of sentence structure more than another? On the basis of your analysis, what particular points in sentence structure should you bear in mind when revising future papers?

6. In your reading of expository material, look for examples of writing (not dialog or direct discourse) that seem to you to approach good conversational speech. When you have found an example, copy the passage, with the name of the author, title, and date of the publication, and a statement about the kind of material with which the article is concerned. Be prepared to comment on specific features of the writing that led to your choice—sentence length, movement, omission of connectives, choice of words or idiom. Is the style appropriate to the audience for whom it is intended?

7. Study the sentence structure in full page advertisements of popular magazines—*The Saturday Evening Post, Collier's, Good Housekeeping, Ladies' Home Journal, Time, Newsweek, Life*. Which of these sentence types predominate: declarative, interrogatory, imperative, exclamatory? What generalizations can you make about the sentence length in these advertisements and their use of "minor sentence types"? What specific devices are used in the writing to capture and hold the reader's attention?

8. Here are six definitions of sentences, some written many years ago, others of recent date. Read them carefully, and then answer the questions that follow.

1. A sentence is a group of words that expresses a complete thought.— GEORGE LYMAN KITTREDGE and FRANK EDGAR FARLEY, *An Advanced English Grammar* (1913)

2. A sentence generally is defined as *one thought completely expressed* in words.—CHARLES HARVEY RAYMOND, *Essentials of English Composition* (1923)

3. The sentence is a complete communication in words, containing a verb of independent rank, with its subject.—JANET R. AIKEN, *A New Plan of English Grammar* (1933)

4. It seems wiser for the grammarian not to attempt any scientific definition of the sentence, but to rest content with some approximate description, such as the statement, for example, that sentences are the separate structural units into which thought is broken as it proceeds step by step in a sequence of expression.—GEORGE P. KRAPP, *The Knowledge of English* (1927)

5. A verbal expression of an idea the structure of which accords with requirements of formal unity in communication; typically, an associating of a person, thing, or quality, expressed in the *subject*, with an action, state, or condition expressed in the *predicate*.—By permission. From Webster's *New Collegiate Dictionary*, copyright, 1949, by G. & C. Merriam Co.

6. A linguistic form (a word or a sequence of words arranged in a grammatical construction) which is not part of any larger construction, typically expressing an independent statement, inquiry, command, or the like, e.g., *Fire!* or *Summer is here* or *Who's there?*—From *The American College Dictionary*, copyright, 1947, 1949, by Random House; Text Edition, copyright, 1948 by Harper & Brothers.

a) What points of agreement and disagreement can you find among these definitions? Would you expect all dictionary definitions to agree?

b) What exceptions can you think of to any or all of these definitions?

c) Why is a sentence difficult to define?

d) Can you make a satisfactory definition? If not, do you think you have, nevertheless, a fairly good working idea of what a sentence is?

CHAPTER **10**

Qualities of sentences

Composicion . . . is an apte joyning together of wordes in suche order, that neither the eere shal espie any jerre, nor yet any man shalbe dulled with overlong drawing out of a sentence.—Thomas Wilson (1553)

Literature maintains an endless quarrel with idle sentences.—Robert Lynd

For of uttering them alone, there are three ways of trying to make them attractive when uttered. You may state them about twice as big as they are, or about half as big as they are, or, if you have skill and complete confidence in your skill, you may state them only just as big as they are.—C. E. Montague

C HAPTER NINE discusses chiefly grammatical points, matters of fundamental form that are to be considered in nearly all sentences. It is necessary, for instance, for the subject and object to be clear and the modifiers rightly placed. The form of a sentence should appear stable and intentional to the reader and lead him to a direct understanding of its meaning. But there are a number of more variable qualities of sentences in which a writer has more leeway, more freedom for personal choice. He may make his sentences long or short, direct or involved, emphatic, rhythmical—he may or may not use many facilities of the language, as his habits or taste or purpose suggest. These are not matters of grammar but of style. They raise questions of appropriateness and effectiveness rather than of correctness. It is in these qualities that one writer's sentences differ from another's. An examination of these will show many possibilities for growth in effectiveness and individuality of writing.

1. Sentence length

The most obvious of these characteristics is length, because a conspicuous and basic difference between sentences is in the amount of substance they contain. Some writers tend to give a detail or two in each sentence; others build several details together into longer, more complicated sentences. The shorter type, which isolate details, are *segregating* sentences; the longer type are *aggregating* sentences.[1] A writer naturally uses a variety of sentence patterns, but usually he

---

[1] See Rudolph Flesch, *The Art of Readable Writing* (New York, 1949), Chapter 11; E. H. Lewis, *The History of the English Paragraph* (Chicago, 1894), especially p. 56; Rickert, Chapter 4.

---

is inclined, intentionally or not intentionally, toward one or the other of these types.

1a. Segregating sentences. The shorter type of sentence is characteristic of most newspaper writing, of much business writing and advertising, of familiar writing, as in diaries and letters, of most stories today, and of many discussions of ideas in both books and magazines. At the worst, these sentences become choppy and jerky, breaking the ideas into too small units for a reader to follow conveniently; or they become unemphatic and monotonous, tiring a reader if they occur in long sequences. At the best, the ideas come directly, follow each other naturally, as they were thought, or at least as they would be spoken. Shorter sentences can be taken in more rapidly in silent reading, but this probably is more a consequence of their necessarily rather direct movement than of the length alone.

Here are two examples of segregating sentences. The first is from a journal. The 8 sentences range from 1 to 17 words in length, averaging just under 10. The clauses are short and uninterrupted, one statement following another as in conversation:

> Oct. 7th, Monday—Morning. Overcast and bleak. The sea looks icy. It is the coldest it has been. We are expecting the Piercys to lunch, but I doubt if they will come. Stephen thinks *Yes* so we are keeping big fires going in the dining room and sitting room. I cut and arranged all fresh flowers, but my hands almost froze while I was outside. Ellison's ears and nose are scarlet, and his eyes watering, but he keeps saying, "*This* isn't cold."—ELIZABETH ETNIER, *On Gilbert Head*, p. 115

In the following paragraph, a discussion of an idea, the sentences range from 5 words to 69 in length, but over half of them are between 8 and 17 words, and they average 16. Except in the two longer sentences, the ideas are analyzed, almost presented singly: "The word dresses the stage. The word brings on the actors. The word supplies their look, their clothes, their gestures." In a different style these might be fused into one sentence, but here they appropriately stand as three. The paragraph is a well connected chain of reasoning.

> The first fact which everyone knows is that radio is a mechanism which carries to an audience sounds and nothing but sounds. A radio play consists of words and word equivalents and nothing else. There is no visible actor disguised to assume a part. There is no stage-set contrived to resemble a place. There is only the spoken word—an implement which poets have always claimed to use with a special authority. There is only the word-excited imagination—a theater in which poets have always claimed peculiar rights to play. Nothing exists save as the word creates it. The word dresses the stage. The word brings on the actors. The word supplies their look, their clothes, their gestures. The more packed and allusive the word, the more illuminating its rhythms, the more perfectly is the scene prepared, the more convincingly is the play enacted. On the stage, verse is often an obstacle because the artifice of the verse and the physical reality of the scene do not harmonize: it is for this reason that verse is easily accepted on the stage only where the scene is made remote in time and therefore artificial to begin with, or where the verse is blurred out and made to sound as much as possible like prose. But over the radio verse is not an obstacle. Over the radio verse has no visual presence to compete with. Only the ear is engaged and the ear is already half poet. It believes at once: creates and believes. It is the eye which is the realist. It is the eye which must fit everything together, must see everything before and behind. It is the eye and not the ear which refuses to believe in the lovely girlhood of the middle-aged soprano who sings Isolde, or the delicate, water-troubling slenderness of the three fat Rhine maidens ridiculously paddling at the ends of three steel ropes. With the eye closed or staring at nothing verse has every power over the ear. The ear accepts, accepts and believes, accepts and creates. The ear is the poet's perfect audience, his only true audience. And it is radio and only radio which can give him public access to that perfect friend.—ARCHIBALD MACLEISH, *The Fall of the City*, Preface

Since the sentences of most students tend to run rather short, the point of this section is not so much to encourage the use of short sentences as to suggest that even when they predominate they can be purposeful and so related to each other that they advance the thought closely and evenly. A run of sentences from any part of the MacLeish paragraph will illustrate this.

1b. Aggregating sentences. Longer sentences, in which several contributing details are presented as a unit, are characteristic of formal styles, especially of discussions of ideas; they are also fairly common in fiction, especially in descriptive passages, and in newspaper leads, where an attempt is made to summarize the most important information of a news item in the first sentence or two. The following examples show how naturally several details may be fused into a unit if they appear to the writer to be closely related. The first example has 87 words.

> And so far, the reconversion to peacetime movies seems to have produced even fewer outstanding films than during the war years, when at least we had *Sahara, Gung Ho, Action in the North Atlantic, Guadalcanal Diary, Bataan,* and a few more, to leaven the hundreds and hundreds of meretricious, formula-bound "war pictures" which brought the war down to a B-movie level and thus insulted millions of men and women joined in a serious effort that deserved either artistic interpretation or silent approval, but surely nothing in between.—BUDD SCHULBERG, *Dartmouth Alumni Magazine,* April 1947

The second example, of 90 words, is more simply constructed, since its length comes in part from enumeration:

> In general it may be stated, without further attempt at proof, that the basic feature of the new economic system that must be built is the provision in ample quantities to all the populace of the basic material needs, food, clothing, shelter and other present-day necessities and reasonable luxuries, as a community responsibility similar to the provision of a postal service, water, police and fire protection, education, parks and national defense; and that this involves public ownership of the basic means of production and distribution, and a controlled monetary mechanism.—ALFRED M. BINGHAM, *Insurgent America,* pp. 4-5

Both of these sentences are considerably longer than their authors' averages. They show how a rather long segment of thought can be presented as a unit. Each has one main clause and three subordinate clauses but a characteristic of each is a number of full phrases, often with several modifiers ("millions of men and women joined in a serious effort"—"the basic material needs, food, clothing, shelter and other present-day necessities and reasonable luxuries"). We certainly would not want our reading to consist entirely of such sentences, but an occasional well filled statement can give firmness to a passage and is likely to be a sign that the writer is presenting his subject fully, with plenty of details, and binding these together into meaningful units.

1c. Length of sentences today. In current writing the sentences are notably shorter and more direct than they were two or three generations ago.[1] A passage from *The New Yorker* "Talk of the Town" averaged 29.1 words to the sentence; one from a short story by Katherine Mansfield averaged 18. Typically the sentences in newspapers

---

[1] For comparison see L. A. Sherman, *Analytics of Literature* (Boston, 1893), Chapter 19, "Literary Sentence-Length in English Prose," and following chapters.

and popular magazines average from 10 to 20 words; the sentences in more restricted periodicals and serious books average around 25 or 30 words. (The first 21 sentences of this chapter range from 6 to 40 words and average 19.9.) Longer sentences are found in discussions of ideas and in formal styles; shorter ones in rapid narrative and informal writing. Children begin writing short sentences and gradually increase their length and complexity until as college students they approximate those of professional writers, as shown in the following table:

Average number of words to the sentence

4th grade	11.1 words		High school freshmen	17.3
6th grade	12.		sophomores	17.8
7th grade	13.5		juniors	18.
8th grade	15.2		seniors	19.8

University freshmen	19.9
upperclassmen	21.5
Professional writers	20.9

M. J. Stormzand and M. V. O'Shea, *How Much English Grammar?* p. 19

The sentence averages of a student whose sentences were growing in maturity would show a rough correspondence with these figures, though the figures given for university upperclassmen and certainly those given for professional writers may be a little lower than is really typical.

These figures are *averages*, and to give an average of 20 there are usually sentences in the forties to balance the very short ones. The graphs on page 277 of the sentence lengths in two passages show a characteristic range and variation. Commonly there is a run of two or three rather short and then two or three longer, rather than a massing of either or an alternation of both. Although a writer usually has a definite tendency to one or the other type of sentence, he will vary considerably: In the volume of short stories *Winner Take Nothing*, on pages 12 and 13, Mr. Hemingway's sentences run from 1 to 21 words, with an average of about 8½, but in a different story (pages 63-65), they range from 16 to 133 words with an average of 49. There is more variety in the length of sentences today than the averages indicate, though the typical length is distinctly lower than in the nineteenth century.

You should know whether in general you tend to build your material into aggregating sentences or tend to present it in smaller units, in segregating sentences. Then in revising a particular paper you should see whether your sentences present your material in the units in which you see it and wish the reader to see it.

Sentence Lengths

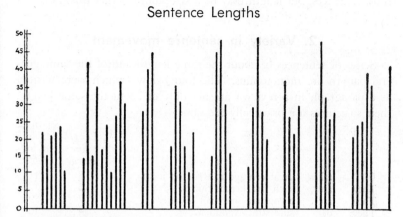

The first fifty sentences from *Paths to the Present* by Arthur M. Schlesinger range from 10 to 49 words, averaging 27.3.

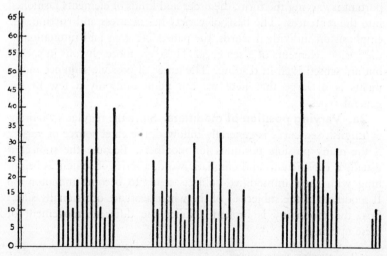

The first fifty sentences from "In Memoriam, W. J. B.," *Prejudices, Fifth Series,* by H. L. Mencken range from 5 to 63 words, averaging 19.7.

If your sentences in an expository paper average less than 18 or 20 words or more than 30, you should look at them to make sure, if the figure is low, that you are building your details together into mature sentences or, if the figure is high, that the sentences are clear and appropriate to the material. There is no special virtue in long or short sentences, but length may be a symptom of other qualities.

2. Variety in sentence movement

Series of sentences of about the same length and of the same general pattern are monotonous. The four below (which were written as a paragraph in a review) are not only of about the same length, their structures are practically the same.

s	v	o or c	Length in words	Length in syl- lables
It	takes	great courage to write on ideas.	8	11
They	are	such treacherous things.	5	7
They	are	a constant source of dispute.	7	9
They	defy	successful exposition.	4	10

Varying the length helps avoid such monotony, but even more important is varying the form, the order and kinds of elements fashioned into the sentences. The basis of variety lies in stress and rhythm, the emphasis on individual words, the pauses between and intonation of the various elements of a sentence. These are more obvious in speech but are sensed even in reading. The range of possible sentence movements is so large that here we can point out only a few of the general types.

2a. Varying position of modifiers. Since the regular s-v-o order of English sentences is generally followed, the chief source of variety is the many possible positions for modifiers. Because the subject is usually a conspicuous and emphatic word, a series of sentences beginning with their unmodified subjects tends to become monotonous. If modifiers of the subject or of the whole sentence occasionally stand first, the monotony is broken. Notice the different movement of these openings:

> The attempts were failures.
> The first serious attempts were failures.
> In spite of their seriousness, the first attempts were failures.
> Although he worked with great seriousness, his first attempts were failures.

An occasional sentence beginning with a long phrase or with a subordinate clause takes the stress away from the subject and makes for variety. Professor Summey found (page 241) that about half his sentences began with the subject (often with an adjective modifier) and over a quarter began with adverbial modifiers, ranging from connectives like *however* and sentence adverbs like *certainly* to long phrases and *when, if, although* clauses. Similarly the sentence may end with the object, or with a modifier of the object, and phrases and clauses can fall between the elements.

In a textbook passage with six similar facts to state, half the sentences begin with the subject and half with modifiers that vary the sentence opening:

> [Subject:] The *theoretical type* seeks to grasp the nature of things. [Adverbial modifier of sentence:] When the reality sought is not local and temporary but cosmic, we have the *religious type*. [Adverbial modifier of sentence:] When not the abstract relations but the persons about one are valued, we have the *social type*. [Adverbial phrase:] In the person for whom individuals are significant not for themselves but as pawns in a game for power, we have the *political type*. [Subject:] The *economic type* finds value in the relations of gain and loss. [Subject:] The *esthetic type* values the relations between sensory objects that are directly and immediately satisfying.—GARDNER MURPHY, *Personality*, pp. 283-84

2b. Inverted movement. A less common means of varying the sentence pattern is *inversion*, in which the order of the main elements departs from the usual s-v-o. Some inversions are purely grammatical, as in questions (Can you come tomorrow? How could you say that?), but in other constructions a writer has a choice of inverting or not. A complement or an emphatic modifier of the verb may stand first, followed by the verb and then the subject (c-v-s, mv-v-s); or a complement or object may precede the subject and verb (o-s-v).

MV	V	S	MS
Then	came	the greatest treat	of all.

O	S	V	MV
This job	he	kept	six years.

C	S	LV	SM
A bargain	it	was,	at that price.

Inversion is not very common and ordinarily is not used unless the words put first really deserve special emphasis. It has been a mannerism of *Time* magazine ("Singular was the U.S. attitude in one respect"), which *The New Yorker* critically parodied, "Backward ran the sentences until reeled the mind."

2c. Interrupted movement. As a rule we do not put words between the major elements of a sentence unless they are short modifiers closely related to one of the main elements (as in "He does *not* *always* pay his bills promptly"). If the modifiers are long or not very closely related to the main elements, the movement of the sentence is sufficiently interrupted to affect the impression:

> This background of crusades and crimes, *with imaginary castles and gallows in the distance,* shed a kind of glamour on the lives of these mild Quakers, who, *in spite of the Quaker ban on worldly fiction,* must, *it appears,* have been reading *Waverley Novels* on the sly. And was it not for them all perfectly authentic? Had not one of them crossed the Atlantic and made a special pilgrimage to Scotland, and there, *on the spot, when visiting the estate of this family,* been overcome by a profound conviction of its truth? . . . What genealogist could demand, *what documents, the family felt, could provide,* more convincing evidence than that?—LOGAN PEARSALL SMITH, *Unforgotten Years,* pp. 6-7

Such interruptions give variety to sentences, but they also make ‚lower and sometimes even difficult reading. They are more characteristic of conspicuously formal style than of current informal style, in which such modifiers are likely to precede or to follow the main sentence elements. Usually it is better to allow only very short modifiers to come between the main sentence elements. The following sentences show how awkward interruption usually is in ordinary writing.

Interrupted	*Direct*
During the summer of 1942, I, as did so many others, found the draft board casting a significant eye in my direction.	Like so many others in the summer of 1942, I found the draft board casting a significant eye in my direction.
Ski trails down the sides of the biggest mountains in New England were cleared.	Ski trails were cleared down the sides of the biggest mountains in New England.
Then he impresses on the freshman the fact that he is getting the pictures practically at the price the materials on which they are printed cost.	Then he impresses on the freshman the fact that he is getting pictures practically at the cost of the material they are printed on.

2d. Loose and periodic sentences. A sentence in which the meaning is not completed until the end is called *periodic;* a sentence which continues after the main statement is complete is called *loose.*

> [Periodic] He who starts on a ride of two or three thousand miles may experience, at the moment of departure, a variety of emotions. [Loose] He may feel excited, sentimental, anxious, carefree, heroic, roistering, picaresque, introspective, or practically anything else; but above all he must and will feel a fool. [Loose] It is like sitting down to read the Faërie Queen right through, only worse. [Periodic] Not yet broken in to the stately un-

hurrying tempo of the caravans, not yet absorbed in the life of the road, he finds, in the contrast between the slowness of the first short stage and the hugeness of the distances before him, something keenly ridiculous. [Periodic] His imagination and his sense of drama reject so little a beginning to so great an enterprise. [Loose] His mind is full of the immensity of his ambitions; his body, sitting on a horse, makes the first move towards their fulfillment at a pace which is often exceeded by old ladies in bath chairs. He feels a fool.—PETER FLEMING, *News from Tartary*, p. 107

Loose sentences are characteristic of our conversation, in which we typically add subordinate statements after the main statement. Periodic sentences are somewhat more formal. The reader's or listener's attention is suspended until the end; he has to hold the complete sentence in mind rather than let later elements modify the earlier parts. The danger of periodic sentences is that they may seem unnatural; the danger of loose sentences is that they may be unemphatic. We could wish that the last clause of the following sentence was omitted or tucked away somewhere in the unemphatic middle:

It is becoming a commonplace to say that in thought and feeling, or at least in the language in which they are expressed, we are living in some bygone century, anywhere from the thirteenth to the eighteenth, although physically we belong to the twentieth century.—JOHN DEWEY, *Individualism Old and New*, p. 13

The two following sentences are loose and would be as natural to conversation as to writing.

One rather felicitous definition runs as follows—"Culture is what is left over after you have forgotten all you have definitely set out to learn"— and in this sally you get at least a useful warning against associating culture too closely with the academic paraphernalia of education.—JOHN COWPER POWYS, *The Meaning of Culture*, Preface

For Pope was merely repeating St. Thomas, who had written twenty volumes to reassure a world on the verge of doubt—twenty volumes to say that it was really right that things should be wrong, God only knows why.—CARL L. BECKER, *The Heavenly City of the Eighteenth-Century Philosophers*, p. 67

This last sentence above could be stopped comfortably at three different points (after *St. Thomas, verge of doubt, should be wrong*), and yet it is a complete and satisfying unit.

The following sentence is periodic:

An intelligent and experienced observer of affairs at Washington has said that all political questions which he has heard discussed in Washington come back ultimately to problems connected with the distribution of *income.*—JOHN DEWEY, *Individualism Old and New*, p. 97

This periodic sentence is perfectly natural, yet by postponing the crucial phrase till the end it holds attention all the way and gives an intensified emphasis to *the distribution of income.*

There is no reason to strive for either loose or periodic movement, especially in a generally informal style made up largely of segregating sentences. By far the larger number of sentences are loose. For this reason an occasional sentence in which the meaning is not completed until its end contributes not only suspense but variety.

2e. Parallelism and balance. (1) PARALLEL MOVEMENT. In Chapter 4, § 6 we learned that putting parts of the sentence that are of equal value in the same (parallel) construction was one way of making the sentence a unit. More elaborate parallel movement becomes an element of style and stands out sufficiently among the more casually constructed sentences to give a note of variety. It is more characteristic of formal than of informal writing.

The first of the following examples of parallelism is natural and simple; several of the later ones are elaborate and rather conscious examples of parallelism controlling the movement and rhythm of their passages, but still the parallel locutions are sufficiently varied in length and form so that they do not seem monotonous:

She walked slowly, big flakes ‖ falling on her lamb coat and
                          ‖ clinging to hair over her ears . . .
          MORLEY CALLAGHAN, *A Native Argosy,* p. 155

The good life is one ‖ inspired by love and
              ‖ guided by knowledge.
          BERTRAND RUSSELL, *What I Believe,* p. 28

‖ Although some were shouting,
      ‖ like the men and women on the pier,
‖ although some were hysterical,
      ‖ like the men and women crowding around the plank,
‖ although some were dazed,

                    there was a difference between them and the
                    persons who awaited them.
     LEANE ZUGSMITH, *Home Is Where You Hang Your Childhood,* p. 65

The teacher must realize
           ‖ that usage varies from the grossly illiterate to the most precise
              of literary distinctions,
           ‖ that the line between permissible and nonpermissible uses is
              by no means fixed, and
           ‖ that the correction of expressions accepted by a high per-
              centage of linguistic experts is a sheer waste of time.
           An Experience Curriculum in English, p. 241

Don Andrés de Ribera, the Viceroy of Peru, was the remnant of a delightful man, broken by ‖ the table,
‖ the alcove,
‖ a grandeeship and
‖ ten years of exile.

As a youth ‖ he had accompanied embassies to Versailles and Rome;
‖ he had fought in the wars in Austria;
‖ he had been in Jerusalem.

He was a widower and childless of an ‖ enormous and
‖ wealthy
‖ woman;

he had collected ‖ coins a little,
‖ wines,
‖ actresses,
‖ orders and
‖ maps.

‖ From the table he had received the gout;
‖ from the alcove a tendency to convulsions;

‖ from the grandeeship a pride so ‖ vast and
‖ puerile

that he seldom ‖ heard anything that was said to him and
‖ talked to the ceiling in a perpetual
‖ monologue;

‖ from the exile, oceans of boredom,
a boredom that was so pervasive that it was like pain—

he ‖ woke up with it and
‖ spent the day with it,

and it sat by his bed all night watching his sleep.
THORNTON WILDER, *The Bridge of San Luis Rey*, p. 170

2) BALANCED SENTENCES. When the parallel locutions, especially clauses, of a sentence are noticeably equal in length and similar in movement, the sentence is called *balanced*. Even in a plain style, balanced sentences are fairly common for emphatic statements and especially for comparisons and contrasts:

They have been educated to achieve success; few of them have been educated to exercise power.—WALTER LIPPMANN, *A Preface to Morals*, p. 66

The busy years hastened away; the traces of Time's unimaginable touch grew manifest; and old age, approaching, laid a gentle hand upon Victoria. The grey hair whitened; the mature features mellowed; the short firm figure amplified and moved more slowly, supported by a stick.—LYTTON STRACHEY, *Queen Victoria*, p. 374

3. Sentence economy

Economy in writing means leading a reader to your exact meaning without unnecessary handicaps to understanding. Few, simple, exact words are its basis, but the pattern in which the words stand has a good deal to do with it. The fewest words and simplest constructions are not always the most economical, for they may oversimplify the message, or they may limit its readers to those who are practiced in following a compact style. But *unnecessary* words and *needlessly* complicated expressions cannot be economical. For amateur writers the chief way to economical expression is to remove offending expressions in revision until after a while they fail to appear even in the first draft. If you train yourself to be sensitive to waste in expression, you will soon learn to avoid being wasteful.

3a. Removing deadwood. *Deadwood* is a convenient label for a lazy word or phrase that adds nothing to the meaning of a sentence. A bit of deadwood can be omitted with no loss at all in meaning and with positive gain in neatness. Note the bracketed phrases here:

> Every thinking person these days seems inclined to agree [with the conception] that the world has gone mad.
> Anyone acquainted with violin construction knows that the better the wood is seasoned, the better [the result will be as far as] the tone of the instrument [is concerned].
> An efficient high school system [of today] should include adequate provision for manual training.
> To my surprise the damage was not as bad as I had expected [it to be].
> [It was] during this time [that] the greatest number of cases came down.
> [There is] only one excuse [that] is acceptable, [and that is] "I have a class this hour."
> It was the first time [in my life] I had seen Niagara Falls.
> The part played by tradition in the civilization and culture of a people is nowhere more fully exemplified than in [the matter of] student influence in China and Latin America.
> At the end of an hour and a half we arrived at [the spot where] the red flag [was situated].
> The following statistics [serve to] give a good idea of the effects of tobacco.
> When the stain is dried, the entire surface of the desk is steelwooled to take off any excess stain [that may be present].
> He kept things moving at breakneck speed throughout [the entirety of] the performance.

A common type of dead phrase is the addition of *color* to a word that can mean only color ("green color"), *number* to a number ("nine in number"), *shape* to a definite form ("rectangular in shape"), or locutions like the following:

The architecture [of the houses] and the landscaping [of the grounds] whisper a word of town pride to the passers-by.

A few words are particularly common—and doubly bad in that they not only add useless weight but often take the emphasis from more important words:

> *nature:* He was never popular because he was awkward [by nature].
> *variety:* During the past spring and summer there has been a noticeable dearth of A pictures and not many more pictures of [the] class B [variety].
> *character:* The second was quite different [in character].
> These things, though [of a] useful [character], were not what he wanted.
> *happen:* [It happened that] we were exactly the same age.
> *case:* While this probably would be true in some cases, I do not think it would be true of the average case. ["While this might sometimes be true, I do not think it would be typical"—or something like that.]
> Many of them have been put to death in individual cases [Many individuals have been put to death], and the whole race has been disfranchised and expelled from their professions.
> *line:* He had always thought he would do something along agricultural lines [in agriculture].

This particular nuisance in writing is one of the easiest to correct and prevent. Elimination of deadwood is one of the easiest ways to begin the attack on fuzzy writing.

3b. Direct phrasing. Besides avoiding words that contribute nothing to the meaning of a sentence a writer needs to watch for expressions that use too many words for conveying a single notion, that is, he should avoid circumlocution. The fewest words are not always the best form, but a conspicuous number of roundabout expressions result in flabbiness. They make the writing seem immature, and tire a reader.

Wordy	*Revised*
During the time that she was in Los Angeles, she had at least six different jobs.	While she was in Los Angeles, she had at least six different jobs.
We must realize the fact that the producer's hand is felt at every stage of producing a picture.	We must realize that the producer's hand is felt at every stage of producing a picture.
The way psychologists measure ability is by tests.	Psychologists measure ability by tests.
It has some of the best ski trails in the country and as far as the other cold weather sports are concerned, they have them too, along with one of the most fashionable hotels in the country.	They have a very fashionable hotel, all the cold weather sports, and some of the best ski trails in the country.

Here are some typical examples of circumlocution:

destroyed by fire means *burned*
come in contact with usually means *meet* or *know*
the necessary funds usually means no more than *the money*
in this day and age means *today*
the sort of metal they use for plating the shiny parts of automobiles might mean *chromium*

Because in speaking we often use more words than are necessary, we need to be especially careful in our writing, where circumlocution is more conspicuous.

3c. Long and short constructions. English offers a choice between a long and short way of expressing a number of relationships. Relative clauses frequently do not show a relative pronoun: "the professor I *saw*" is as good as "the professor *whom I saw*." Not all clauses have verbs: "*If possible*, come a little early" or "*If it is possible*." The conjunction *that* may or may not be used: "We like to think *that* our scholarship standards are higher than yours" or "We like to think [ ] our scholarship standards are higher than yours."

The choice between these forms is a matter of style, to be determined by appropriateness. Formal English uses relatively few of the short expressions, tends to fill out all constructions. Informal English uses them more freely, very much more in speaking than in writing. In revising a paper a writer can usually tell from the movement of the passage whether or not he should make his constructions more complete. In ordinary informal writing a fairly frequent use of the short forms makes for naturalness.

3d. Reducing predication. An "idea"—a small part of our meaning—may be expressed in one of four grammatical units: in a word, a phrase, a subordinate clause, or a full sentence. The form ought to be roughly proportional to the value of the idea, important ones in the longer and more weighty forms, less important ones in the more economical forms. In the following example of the scale of expressions, we would probably all agree that the first was the most appropriate, the most economical for an adequate expression of the notion:

Word: The snow *blanketed* the countryside.
Phrase: The snow, *like a blanket*, covered the countryside.
Clause: The snow, *which lay like a blanket*, covered the countryside.
Sentence: *The snow lay like a blanket.* It covered the countryside.

Obviously the chief difference is between the first two, which contain one verb, and the last two, which contain two predications.

Modern style tends to use fewer predications, fewer clauses, than English style of a century ago. One mark of amateur writing is the use of a predication for an idea that a more practiced writer would reduce to a phrase or a single word.

Amateur

Labor was quick to realize the advantages of this new form of passive resistance, and *before the succeeding year rolled around*, no less than two hundred sit-down strikes had been reported.

A few of the fellows *who were less serious* would go to a bar *where they would have a steak dinner and a few glasses of beer.*

I am a native of Florida and am very glad to write on this subject.

We taxied back and forth in front of the starting line, waiting impatiently for the sound of the gun *which would mean that the race was started.*

More economical

Labor was quick to realize the advantages of this new form of passive resistance, and *within a year* no less than two hundred sit-down strikes had been reported.

A few of the *less serious* fellows would go to a bar *for a steak dinner and a few glasses of beer.*

As a native of Florida, I am very glad to write on this subject. Or: *Since I am a native of Florida*, I am very glad to write on this subject.

We taxied back and forth in front of the starting line, waiting impatiently for the sound of the *starting* gun.

Of course as we write, we can't always be stopping to ask ourselves, "How much is this idea worth?" But in revising papers, especially in the early stages of our writing experience, we will occasionally find it worth while to see if we have made the expressions longer than necessary to express our complete meaning. Writing can be made so compact that it is bare and hard to follow, but few beginning writers need to worry about that. They need to be encouraged to use a more tidy, more economical style. Length in a paper does not come from piling up *words* but from piling up *material*, ideas, and especially details of observation that convey meaning. Proper economy comes from trying to say more in a given number of words.

4. Sentence emphasis

The emphasis in a piece of writing comes principally from the use of strong and distinctive words and from a progressive arrangement of statements in paragraphs and of the paragraphs in the whole. But sentences contribute to this general impression, and the general methods of order, proportion, and mass also apply to them. Economy is an important factor, for wordiness buries the meaning. In this section we shall look at some specific means to sentence emphasis.

4a. Mechanical devices. Writing and printing have various mechanical means—underlining (italics), capitals, emphatic punctuation—for stressing words and passages. These devices are used by amateur writers often in an attempt to make up for deficiencies in style or content and usually result in the "forcible-feeble," as in this speech, a crucial one in the novel from which it is taken:

> "*I go on through!*" he repeated earnestly. "I have suffered—but I know that I am Destiny's darling! . . . *You* have suffered but *you, too, can carry on through!* . . . Take it from me! I know! In spite of all the little detainments, disappointments, disillusionments—*I get the lucky breaks! I get the signal to go forward!* I have been delayed—long—long—long—but—at length—*I get the* GREEN LIGHT!"

With increased skill in writing, a person relies less and less on these mechanical devices. He depends more and more on distinctiveness of expression, position, and other rhetorical means of showing that one statement is more important than another.

4b. Intensives. There are several ways of emphasizing meaning by the use of special words, particularly in colloquial language. A speaker can stress a *too* or *very* or *much* so that it will have a good deal of force (and the activity of the stress gives him a certain physical satisfaction). On paper these intensives are less convincing, in part because the tone of voice is lacking and, at least in careful prose, in part because written style is likely to use words more accurately than oral.

A number of adjectives and adverbs are primarily intensives: *much, very, such, too, highly, certainly, extremely, tremendously.* They may be used for a just emphasis, but they usually suggest an oral stress and are often out of place in writing. Too many of them suggest the schoolgirl style. Most small profanity belongs in this category, the words allowing a satisfying stress and bite and not contributing otherwise to meaning.

In writing, quite often a statement would actually be stronger if the intensive was omitted or if the oral type of sentence was changed to a written form:

> We had [such] a lovely time at your party.
> Everybody was [so] tired after the holiday round of parties.

In pushing the product the slogan has [surely] been [unquestionably] of paramount importance.

The colloquial superlative, used to indicate a considerable degree of a quality instead of the greatest, is a typical intensive in conversation, but not so appropriate to writing:

> She had the nicest manners [for *nice* or some more exact adjective].
> He is a most important figure in the book [an important figure].

The pronouns in -*self* are idiomatic intensives in all levels of usage:

> He picked the flowers himself.
> I must see Catherine herself.

Lately *personally* and *in person* have been used as substitutes for *himself*, *herself*, and so on, especially in business English and in slang or familiar conversation.

> It turned out to be Jimmy in person.
> He picks the necessary vegetables for dinner out of his small personal garden [out of his own garden].

There are scores of words of rather intense meaning—*thrill, intriguing, devastating, passion*—all of which have their necessary and legitimate uses and all of which are likely to be abused when applied to some feeling that does not really deserve such a vigorous word. The use of such intensives should be a matter of appropriateness, especially of appropriateness to the subject. But often, particularly in speech, their appropriateness to the person who is using them is more important. At their best they may represent a vigorous and emphatic personality; at their worst they show insensitiveness to the values of words. If they are overused, they are sure to result in a weakening of statements.

4c. Repetition. (1) UNHAPPY REPETITION. Using the same word several times in a short space is often unavoidable, but repetition of words is unpleasant when the writer has a wide possible choice. Such repetition may be the result of small vocabulary, but most of it is due to plain laziness or inattention to writing—certainly to a lack of revision. Both small vocabulary and carelessness are back of the five *beautiful*'s (not to mention one *beauty*) in this:

> The landscape is beautiful. There are myriads of beautiful, stately trees, which contribute greatly to the beauty of the place in every season of the year. There are also many beautiful wild flowers and other pretty forms of undergrowth. The climate and the absence of smoke and dust of the city makes it very easy to cultivate a beautiful lawn, with flowers and shrubs.

The lake is a wonderful part of the landscape. There are many beautiful views in different times of the day and season.

More typical of careless repetition are such sentences as these:

This dam was without doubt going to be the largest [dam] in the world.
[The problem of] feeding her ever increasing population is one of Japan's most acute problems.

Repetition of whole phrases is likely to be more objectionable, because naturally a group of words attracts more attention than a single word:

The next morning we noticed the river had risen considerably and was flowing at a very fast pace. We decided to resume our journey immediately, and soon we were once more traveling downstream, but this time at a much faster pace [better: even faster].

The writer of that passage either has an insensitive ear or else he did not read his paper over. We feel sure it was carelessness when we find this a little later:

Twice I thought our canoe would surely upset, and I could see the fellow sitting in the middle [of our canoe] was scared to death.

Especially to be watched is repetition of the same word in two different senses, easy to do in English because of the number of meanings many words carry:

My marks showed a marked improvement.
No President in time of war has dared to fight the powerful financial interests of this country who have interests in the belligerent countries.

A slightly different form of careless repetition is doubling the meaning of a word unnecessarily. We write *continue on* when *continue* is enough, *repeat again* when we mean merely *repeat*.

The modern college student [of today]
In this modern melting pot, I found people [there] who were unacquainted with the English language.
I believe that colleges should offer scholarships but they should not offer only athletic scholarships [alone].
the [resultant] effect
He told us that if everyone was free Thursday evening [that] we would meet then.
Dams have been built with [about] four or five sluices in them. [*Four or five* is indefinite enough without the *about*.]
I know many officers who try to give you any *possible* assistance that they *can*.
First we should understand what *equipment* and *paraphernalia* are necessary for this sport.

The remedy for all this loose, careless repetition is the same: careful revision. Reading a paper aloud is perhaps the surest way to catch such lapses, since our ears will sense more than our eyes.

2) SUCCESSFUL REPETITION. Repetition of words and repetition of ideas in other words are useful stylistic devices. Repetition may help hold a passage together, it may emphasize ideas, and it may suggest emotion.

A controlled repeating of key words is useful in keeping the reader's attention focused on the subject, and it is especially helpful in binding sentences together. Writing of the Supreme Court, you will have to mention the Supreme Court frequently and it is often better to say *Supreme Court* than to hunt for trite synonyms (like *the highest tribunal*). Simply see that the sentences are economically constructed to avoid *unnecessary* repetition and that pronouns are used where they can be.

The repetition of *name* and *choose* and *select* binds together the thought of this paragraph and emphasizes its meaning:

> Therefore, in every fresh application of a name we can discern two acts: first, the choice of a detail in the thing named, and second, comparison in that detail of the thing named with other things. These two acts are always in a certain sense one, for it is the memory that makes the choice. Naming things is like cutting doughnuts: here is an undifferentiated mass of dough, upon which the cutter, which remembers the character of other doughnuts, descends and makes after that character a definite excerpt. Exactly thus a word descends into a general impression and selects out a clear experience. It selects an experience similar to the ones which it remembers. But since in this process sometimes the act of selecting, and sometimes the act of remembering, is emphasized, we can divide names accordingly into two classes. There are names which predominantly choose, and names which predominantly compare. The words *shaggy* and *lazy*, for example, *choose* a feature of the horse, but they leave those memories with which it is to be compared, undefined. *Pot-bellied* and *strawberry roan*, on the other hand, not only choose the part and the color, but they also declare the comparison to a remembered pot and a remembered strawberry. All names are of one or the other of these two types.—MAX EASTMAN, *Enjoyment of Poetry*, p. 40

Repetition of phrases and constructions is often a matter of emotion and feeling, and may contribute to rhythm. In the following passage the repeated sentence (which occurs frequently in the course of the story) becomes a refrain:

> Night after night Tom watched the sheep upon the downs with empty hollow sockets, till his dead hair grew and covered his poor dead face, and hid the shame of it from the sheep. And the wind blew and blew.

> Sometimes on gusts of wind came some one's tears, and beat and beat against the iron chains, but could not rust them through. And the wind blew and blew.—LORD DUNSANY, *A Dreamer's Tales*, p. 160

Such repetition is rare, of course, and confined to imaginative or emotional writing. Mr. Eastman's repetition is more typical of factual writing. No writer needs to fear repeating the key words of his subject, and rightly used their repetition will add emphasis.

4d. Separating elements. In speaking, one of the most used and most effective means of emphasis is a pause. It allows what has just been said to sink in, or if the voice is suspended, it throws emphasis on what is to follow. It is difficult to transfer this effect to the written page, but something of its value can be had by keeping constructions separate.

The most emphatic separation, of course, is into individual sentences:

> You do not revise dogmas. You smash them.—RANDOLPH BOURNE, "What Is Opinion?" *The New Republic*, August 18, 1915

Internal punctuation, commas and especially semicolons, keep statements separate and tend to force a pause even in quick eye reading:

> One remembers the old stories of invisible kingdoms where princes lived with ladies and dragons for company; and the more modern fairy-tales in which heroes drift in and out of dimensions more complex than the original three.—JOHN STEINBECK and EDWARD F. RICKETTS, *Sea of Cortez*, p. 80

> There are three ways of seeing animals: dead and preserved; in their own habitats for the short time of a low tide; and for long periods in an aquarium.—*Ibid.*, p. 189

(Commas could have been used, instead of semicolons, in those two sentences.)

In a series of parallel words or constructions, repeating the conjunctions or prepositions may add emphasis to the individual elements. Contrast the movement of the two versions of these sentences:

The collecting buckets and tubes and jars were very full of specimens—so full that we had constantly to change the water to keep the animals alive.—*Ibid.*, p. 78	The collecting buckets, tubes, and jars were so full of specimens that we had constantly to change the water to keep the animals alive.
In the course of a lifetime of voyaging he went to China, to India, to all parts of Africa, and even to the Arctic.	In the course of a lifetime of voyaging he went to China, India, all parts of Africa, and even the Arctic.

An abrupt break in the direction of the thought movement may make for sharp emphasis, especially in informal writing:

A hardness about this technicolor epic makes it difficult to enjoy all the way through—the eventual hardness of the theater seat.

Just when you were beginning to get adjusted to Olsen and Johnson's out-patient clinic of the psychiatric ward, *bang*, you had fifty pounds of ice in your lap.

4e. Position. An important means of emphasis is *position*, ordering the words and parts of the statement so that the stress falls unmistakably on the exact words you want it to. The most emphatic position is ordinarily the end of a sentence, and the next most emphatic is the beginning.

Since the subject of a sentence is usually an important element, it properly has the initial emphasis, although often some other element deserves first position. The frequent use of "anticipatory subjects" (*there* is, *there* were, *it* is) is consequently weakening:

Anticipatory subjects	*More emphatic*
There are many people who read history to raise their self-esteem.	Many people read history to raise their self-esteem.
There is some evidence pointing to the gradual disappearance of hazing in our colleges.	Some evidence points to the gradual disappearance of hazing in our colleges.

Departures from the normal word order, as described in §2 of this chapter, are usually for emphasis on the words put first:

Charles he had beaten twice, but never his brother.
And last of all came the man they had expected would be first.
This we have; this you cannot give us; but this you may so easily take away.—G. LOWES DICKINSON, *Letters from a Chinese Official*, p. 38

The ends of sentences deserve more attention. As Barrett Wendell put it, sentences should "end with words that deserve distinction." Since we cannot foresee the ends of our sentences in speaking, we are likely to add various unemphatic elements and in general let them run downhill. In writing we have the opportunity to revise our sentences and give them more definite form:

Unemphatic	*Revised: More emphatic*
In regard to hedging, we had a hard time trying to understand its complexity.	We had a hard time trying to understand the complexities of hedging.
This is nobody's fault but their own with few exceptions.	With few exceptions, this is nobody's fault but their own.

It is easy to avoid such lapses from firm expression, and it is easy and natural, with a little practice, to end sentences strongly. This often means putting elements in an order of *climax*, that is, arranging words, phrases, clauses, or sentences in an order of increasing value. The increase may be in mere physical length, for usually in a series of phrases or clauses the longest is put last. The increase may be in force of sound or distinction of phrasing. Or the increase may be in complexity of meaning or of emotional or ideal value. The scale of value of course is the speaker's or writer's; it is his sense of the importance of the various bits of his idea represented by the climax.

Here is a conventional climax pattern, with the last of the three parallel phrases the fullest in expression and the most important for the writer's purpose at the moment:

> They come from an intellectual level where conformity seems the highest of goods, and so they lack the primary requisite of the imaginative author: the capacity to see the human comedy afresh, to discover new relations between things, to discover new significances in man's eternal struggle with his fate.—H. L. MENCKEN, *Prejudices, Fifth Series*, p. 177

The climax in the following sentence represents the writer's emphasis, since she is most interested in the word *confusing:*

> To be young is always a difficult, dangerous, and confusing business— but it can seldom have been so difficult, so dangerous, and above all so confusing, as in England during the first ten years of the twentieth century.—ANN BRIDGE, *Enchanter's Nightshade*, p. 38

Climax is the natural order for arranging the items of a series unless there is some necessary or logical reason for another order. Failing to use a climactic order results in a weak sentence or, if the last member of the series is conspicuously less important than the preceding, in definite anticlimax:

> It spoiled the rest of the summer for the boys and disappointed them terrifically.
> No degree will be conferred or certificate given unless the applicant shall have sustained a good moral character, settled all college bills, and returned all books and paid all fines to the library.

Intentional use of anticlimax is one of the sources of humor:

> "Because Luxembourg is divine," he said, his eyes lighting. "I spent a most wonderful vacation there a year or two ago. It is a cameo, a miniature. It is a little country and everything in it is little: the inns, the mountains, the waiters, the people, the prices [anticlimax]. It is divine!"—IRWIN EDMAN, *Philosopher's Holiday*, p. 65

Emphasis, like most sentence qualities, is to be tested in revision, when a writer takes the role of reader and tries to make his words represent to someone else his own view of his subject. Finding ways of making this emphasis is one of the most challenging parts of writing.

5. Sound and rhythm

Although prose is not expected to appeal to the ear in the same way that poetry does, unpleasant sounds or combinations of sounds are a slight handicap in reading, even in silent reading, and more pleasing sounds often add a positive pleasure. Sound is not such a conspicuous trait of prose as it was when reading aloud was more in vogue. The average news story, planned for eye reading only, is a form of punishment when read aloud, and so is much writing of other kinds. But a pleasing sound is a characteristic of most satisfying prose. Reading aloud is one test of good prose and should add something to the reader's enjoyment.

5a. Qualities of sound. A pleasing sound depends in part on avoiding unnecessary harsh sounds (too many *g*'s, *dg*'s, and so on), groups of consonants that are hard to pronounce (as in "propelled by the repeated and seemingly needlessly brutal remarks and jabs of the detectives"), and combinations of easily confused sounds (like *s* and *sh*: "This seething mass of shiny sea shells began to wrestle and box"). Such sounds are awkward, and so also are too many conspicuous unstressed syllables ("seemingly needlessly").

The repetition of the same or similar sounds is a factor in binding words together, as well as of giving immediate pleasure in reading. Rime, which is so important in unifying verse, is out of place in prose, where a noticeable rime sound is usually offensive. But an occasional and natural use of some of the other figures of sound may serve to bind together words and phrases.

One of the commonest of these is *alliteration*, the same sound at the beginning of words or of stressed syllables within words:

> the shadow and *h*ush of the *h*aunted past
> the *w*ear and *w*aste of *w*estern life

Alliteration runs riot in much light writing and in advertising slogans ("a wispy, waspy waistline"), but, used more sparingly, it is characteristic of a good deal of other writing.

Assonance, similar vowel sounds in syllables that have different consonant sounds, is quite common in prose:

> a perfume escaped on the gale

5b. Rhythm. We do not need to go into an elaborate study to realize that prose has a definite if varied rhythm, that stresses differ in intensity and in number and in combination.

A conscious concern for rhythm is dangerous unless you want to write patterned prose. But you can at least avoid long series of unstressed syllables that will give a weak or flabby effect; you can avoid tacking on a phrase after a movement has reached an effective stable point; and you can make sure that the stresses do not become monotonously regular.

Probably the fundamental difference is between a simple movement that suggests the rather casual rhythm of conversation and the more elaborate and varied rhythm that suggests formal or "literary" prose.

Some of the general differences between these two movements will be felt in reading aloud two such sharply contrasting passages as the following:

> Walter had just turned the corner of Charles Street into Seventh when he saw her. She was standing a little way up the block talking to a fellow in a black overcoat and a black felt hat, and just the way they were standing—the fellow leaning back against the wall of the building there and she crowded close against him, looking up at him—was enough to let Walter know the kind of talk they were having. Almost without thinking, he stopped and stepped back a pace down Charles, out of sight around the corner.—ROBERT M. COATES, "The Net," *Short Stories from the New Yorker*

> In the stillness of the air every tree, every leaf, every bough, every tendril of creeper and every petal of minute blossoms seemed to have been bewitched into an immobility perfect and final. Nothing moved on the river but the eight paddles that rose flashing regularly, dipped together with a single splash; while the steersman swept right and left with a periodic and sudden flourish of his blade describing a glinting semi-circle above his head. The churned-up water frothed alongside with a confused murmur. And the white man's canoe, advancing upstream in the short-lived disturbance of its own making, seemed to enter the portals of a land from which the very memory of motion had forever departed.—JOSEPH CONRAD, "The Lagoon," *Tales of Unrest*, p. 187

Most modern writing is closer to the plain style of the first of these, but its range and possibilities are great. If you feel that your writing is in a rut, read aloud passages that appeal to you—and that you can read in a natural tone of voice. This may help you realize more fully the potentialities of your writing and suggest to you how you can add to its other qualities some of the pleasure that comes from a fitting rhythm.

6. Good sentences

Talking about qualities of sentences one by one and in such detail makes writing seem much more complicated and more artificial than it really is. All of our discussion has been intended to show some (it has by no means covered all) of the possibilities of this simple and unavoidable unit of speech and writing. Granted some experience in talking and writing, the surest way to good sentences is familiarity with what you intend to say and confidence that you can say it so that someone else will be glad to read it. This will let you write rapidly, so that the ideas will really move and will seem to follow each other naturally.

If for some reason you have not had much practice in purposeful writing, you can profit by study of the points in these two chapters, by attentive reading of good prose, and by some conscious experimentation and certainly by careful revision of the sentences that come haphazardly. Gradually—sometimes rapidly—the general texture of your sentences will change for the better. The aim is not any one pattern but a varied and pleasing style that not only will convey your meaning but will be appropriate to it and to your hoped-for readers and to yourself. Write naturally and merely tidy up your first efforts in the light of what experienced writers have found to be the effective qualities of good sentences.

Suggested study and writing

The exercises in this chapter offer further practice in analyzing sentence structure and opportunity to judge the effectiveness and appropriateness of different kinds of sentences.

1. Make a close study of at least twenty consecutive sentences in one of your recent papers. Take notes on the following points:

a) The length of the sentences in words: the shortest, the longest, the average number of words per sentence. Compare your figures with those in the table on page 276.

b) The types of sentences you have used: aggregating and segregating, loose and periodic. Compare the number of sentences that follow the subject-verb-object order with the number that vary this pattern.

c) The manner in which your ideas are expressed: by long or short constructions, through circumlocutions or direct phrasing. Put brackets around each word or phrase that adds nothing to the meaning, and around any sentence that does not seem to advance the thought. Estimate the amount of material that could have been omitted without changing either the meaning or the effectiveness of your paper.

2. On the basis of this analysis, write a report telling what you have discovered about your sentences. Discuss any ideas in this chapter or in other chapters that may be helpful in solving your problems. Point out the good features of your sentences as well as those that may need improving.

3. The following passages from student papers contain many words and phrases that add nothing to the meaning. Revise each passage by removing the deadwood and subordinating wherever possible to achieve greater economy of expression.

1. There are two reasons for my preference in wanting to write on a subject that is related to a course which will be part of my major: the first reason is influenced by the fact that I have a large amount of material on hand to write about; and in the second place, the time limit for writing this theme makes it important that one have a good grasp of his subject matter so that he won't have to waste time on its organization.

2. Many people have the belief that ignorance is an inborn trait, but in this they are quite wrong, for if they will investigate the facts pertaining to this situation, they will be quite surprised by what they find concerning the actual facts of the case.

3. I have tried to correlate these situations together and to show how little most modern people of today really know about the subject of education of children.

4. The thrill of riding a galloping horse over the hills was only one of the many thrills I experienced during the summer months I spent on a ranch in the summer of 1949.

5. Students who wish to enter the University are mailed cards with certain dates marked on them. These dates are arranged with the advisors so that the students can come and have a conference with the advisor and also obtain first-hand information about the facts of registration.

6. Among the many numerous magazines on the newsstand today are two magazines that I consider to be magazines for the so-called "upper-middle brow" class of people. These magazines are *The Atlantic Monthly* and *Harper's*.

7. For thorough enjoyment of these magazines one must have a rather good background of knowledge in history, geography, economics, and literature, for they deal extensively and exclusively with matters concerning the fields of social sciences, world politics, and literature.

8. I do not object to radio announcers who have the type of voice that is pleasant to listen to. It is to the announcers' voices that wrack the nerves of the listeners that objections are raised to. It seems to me that it would be common sense to realize that the latter type of voice distracts attention from what is in the commercial.

9. Our instructor made a statement to the effect that if the city officials and the county officials combined some of their duties together, the expense in terms of taxes would be much less.

10. There are many students who have trouble handing in their compositions punctually on time. It is not that the work is too hard. In the case of the ordinary paper, the average student can write it in about an hour to an hour and a half. Every student can give this long a quantity of time to his work. The trouble, in respect to most students, is due to the fact that they postpone doing the work too long until it is too late to write the paper and still have it ready on time.

4. Recast the following sentences, removing shifted constructions and putting related elements in parallel form.

1. Making a preliminary outline has improved my speaking ability, but my problems in writing haven't been solved by the same practice.

2. People living in the city must pay relatively high prices for dairy products, whereas if you live in a rural community, you can get the same products for much less.

3. My landlady was one of those women who spend most of their time gossiping with the neighbors, puttering around the garden, or else she fusses over a hot stove.

4. I believe that the important thing I learned in Writing Laboratory was not that anyone can write or that everyone has something to say, but it is how we say it and if we are sincere or not that makes a composition good or bad.

5. First take a good look around you and then you should decide what section you want to aim for.

6. We decided to take Highway 99 because it was the shortest route and with most to offer in the way of scenery.

7. I would much rather make an attempt, no matter how feeble, at playing baseball myself than watching Joe DiMaggio hit a home run.

8. There is nothing more satisfactory to me than fulfilling an obligation satisfactorily or an assigned task that has been accomplished successfully.

9. Other questions asked in the 1950 census concerned incomes, type of work, how many days people had been sick, did they own their own homes, and many other items.

10. To become a good swimmer, a person has to learn to coordinate arm and leg movements and the proper method of breathing must be mastered.

Additional exercises on parallelism and shifted constructions may be found in exercise 6, Chapter 4.

5. For practice in constructing longer sentences, rewrite the paragraph by Archibald MacLeish on page 274, changing segregating sentences to aggregating. Leave out none of the ideas. You will have to add connectives and make small changes in wording. At present there are twenty three sentences averaging 16.08 words. Aggregating sentences should reduce the number of sentences to 7 or 10, and raise the average number of words to more than 40.

6. In your reading of books, magazines, or newspapers, look for examples of (a) the dullest and flattest sentences you can find, and (b) the best sentences of several different types. Comment on the reasons for the effectiveness or ineffectiveness of each example.

7. Study the sentences in the following student paragraphs. In which of the paragraphs do the sentence length and movement seem most appropriate to the material? Which paragraphs are least successful? What specific changes would you suggest in sentence structure for better movement, variety, and emphasis?

1. In 1944 we had approximately thirteen million people in the services and twenty million more engaged solely in war work. Yet in that year, with all these people missing from our consumer-goods production set-up, we produced more consumer goods than ever before. Astounding? I don't think so. People know we have a wonderful productive capacity. They have grown to expect great things of this country. They should. It is the richest country on earth—in machines, trained men, resources. But there is one question people don't stop to think about. That question is: What are we going to do with the workers displaced by machines during the war? Maybe someone knows the answer. I don't.

2. It was my senior year in high school. Our basketball team had won the championship trophy the year before. This year the team was considered even stronger. Nearly every member of the pep club was seated. It was the final game. We had come all the way through the tournament without a defeat. This game would determine which team would be the champion. I looked toward the end of the gymnasium. The referees were talking. They, too, were excited. Would that starting gun never go off! My hands were clammy. My cheeks burned.

3. The big alarm came on December 10th. A large flight of planes was reported coming toward the Manila area. They came in in several waves from the direction of Formosa, twenty-six planes to a wave. Their objective was Cavite. They had no opposition from our airforce. Our anti-aircraft shells were bursting about five thousand feet below their formations. They proceeded to level the naval base. When their bombs were exhausted, they started strafing the harbor shipping. It was then that Torpedo Boat 35 destroyed one plane, and Boat 31 got two.

4. Just about two years ago a family moved into the house next door to us, a family consisting of just two middle-aged women. They had no servants in their employ and did all the work connected with a house by themselves. Both of these women got along quite successfully in their work and then one day late in summer an old couple, a man and his wife, came along and moved in with them. The man was about seventy years of age, while the woman was slightly under sixty-five, and after the arrival of this old couple all the work was shifted to their shoulders while the two women who owned the house had a life of comparative ease. It turned out that one woman and the old man's wife were sisters. The cause of the arrival of this old couple at the sister's house is quite interesting.

8. Compare the qualities of the sentences in the paragraph by George Santayana with those in the revision which follows it. Do the shorter sentences in the second paragraph represent a gain or a loss in sentence economy? Point out specific differences in sentence variety and sentence movement, in rhythm, clarity, and emphasis. Try reading both versions aloud.

(1) Very different was dapper Mr. Groce, our teacher of English composition and literature, a little plump man, with a keen, dry, cheerful, yet irritable disposition, a sparkling bird-like eye, and a little black mustache and diminutive chin-beard. (2) I suspect that he was too intelligent to put up patiently with all the conventions. (3) Had he not been a public-school teacher, dependent on the democratic hypocrisies of a government committee, he might have said unconventional things. (4) This inner rebellion kept him from being sentimental, moralistic, or religious in respect to poetry; yet he *understood* perfectly the penumbra of emotion that good and bad poetry alike may drag after them in an untrained mind. (5) He knew how to rescue the structural and rational beauties of a poem from that bog of private feeling. (6) To me this was a timely lesson, for it was precisely sadness and religiosity and grandiloquence that first attracted me in poetry; and perhaps I owe to Mr. Groce the beginnings of a capacity to distinguish the musical and expressive charm of poetry from its moral appeal. (7) At any rate, at sixteen, I composed my first longish poem, in Spenser's measure, after *Childe Harold* and *Adonais*, full of pessimistic, languid, Byronic sentiments, describing the various kinds of superiority that Night has over Day. (8) It got the prize.—GEORGE SANTAYANA, *Persons and Places*, p. 157

(1) Mr. Groce was our dapper teacher of English composition and literature and he was very different. (2) He was a little plump man, who had a cheerful, dry, keen disposition, which was irritable, nevertheless. (3) Also he had a sparkling, bird-like eye. (4) Mr. Groce wore a little black mustache and a diminutive chin-beard. (5) He was too intelligent to put up with all the conventions patiently, I suspect. (6) He might have said things that were unconventional if he had not been a public-school teacher who was dependent on a government committee's democratic hypocrisies. (7) This inner rebellion kept him, where poetry was concerned, from being sentimental, moralistic, or religious. (8) However, he *understood* perfectly the penumbra of emotion that both good poetry and bad poetry may drag after them in a mind that is untrained; consequently, he knew how to rescue from that bog of private feeling the structural and rational beauties that a poem has. (9) This to me was a timely lesson, as what first attracted me in poetry was precisely religiosity, sadness, grandiloquence. (10) I perhaps owe the beginnings of a capacity to distinguish poetry's musical and expressive charm from its moral appeal to Mr. Groce. (11) I composed my first longish poem at the age of sixteen, at any rate. (12) This poem was written in the same kind of measure that Spenser had used, and it resembled *Childe Harold* and *Adonais*, being full of pessimistic and languid Byronic sentiments. (13) It described the various kinds of superiority of Night over Day; nevertheless, the poem was awarded the prize.

9. Before submitting your next paper (or any other paper), read it aloud, or if possible, have someone read it to you. Examine any passage that needs to be reread for its meaning or that fails to convey the emphasis you intended. Revise all repetitious and awkward constructions, and any sections that need more variety or better movement. Although you may not be writing your papers to be read aloud, this practice will frequently reveal grammatical errors and ineffectual phrasing that might otherwise escape your attention.

The meaning of words

Any man's available speech material is a complete record of his conscious experience as far as he remembers it. . . . The words and phrases that he has at his disposal, if they could be collected, would serve as an index to his life, his reading, and what he has been told.—E. H. Sturtevant

In other words "meaning" is a property of the mutually relevant people, things, events, in the situation. Some of the events are the noises made by the speakers. But it is important to realize that "meaning" is just as much a property of the people, their "sets," their specific behaviour, the things and events of the situation as of the noises made.—J. R. Firth

SUGGESTIONS FOR USING THE CHAPTER: *Sections one to three of this chapter give background for some consideration of the students' stock of words, for increasing vocabulary, and for use of dictionaries. (A vocabulary test would be a useful supplement.) The last three sections form a unit on the meaning of words that can be applied to reading selections as well as to student writing.*

A NYONE WHO is even casually concerned with his speaking and writing becomes interested in words and their ways. His curiosity naturally turns to their meaning and to the various ways in which they are used; he becomes conscious of some words that he lacks but really needs and of some that he only partially knows. This book might have begun with a discussion of words, since they are the fundamental elements of speech and writing. But if our purpose is communication, we are first aware of ideas expressed consecutively, of words as they stand in individual statements (sentences) and in groups of statements (paragraphs). In fact, words do not properly exist by themselves but only as they are put to some use. It seems more natural to consider first those wholes and later to look more closely at the qualities of the single words of which they are composed. This and the following chapter discuss various points about the meaning and use of words, about what they do and do not accomplish for us in our attempts to tell others something or to understand what others say.

1. The supply of words

1a. The English vocabulary. The exact number of English words is not known and cannot be exactly known. The unabridged dictionaries now contain about 500,000 entries, the Second Edition (1934) of *Webster's International* advertising 600,000. Many of these are compound words (*livery stable*) or different derivatives of the same word (*rare—rarely*). The *Oxford English Dictionary* breaks down its entries into these categories (Of course most of the "main words" are given with more than one "meaning" and some with dozens of different meanings.[1]):

| Main words | 240,165 | Special combinations | 47,800 |
| Subordinate words | 67,105 | Obvious combinations | 59,755 |

Total   424,825

The dictionaries contain thousands of obsolete words to help us read the older literature. But on the other hand they do not attempt to cover completely many groups of words that can be drawn upon, especially slang, localisms, trade names, the colloquial technical words of the various trades and occupations, and words used only occasionally by scientists and specialists in many fields. Besides these there are the foreign words that may be borrowed (*raison d'être, Weltanschauung*). Some are made up for special occasions (like *unparlorable*) but are not used enough to become a part of the regular language. Spencer Armstrong says (*How Words Get into the Dictionary*, p. 29):

> However, it is no flight of fancy to state that there are between 1,000,000 and 1,250,000 words in our language today. At least two-fifths of these are ultrascientific terms used only in the recesses of the laboratory; they are not to be found in standard dictionaries and figure in special glossaries of the sciences to which they belong.

New words are being constantly added to the vocabulary, Mr. Armstrong estimates, at the rate of about 3000 a year or as many as 5000 in years of special activity such as war. Radio broadcasting alone, he says, has put 5000 words into the large dictionaries.

[1] References: Spencer Armstrong, *How Words Get into the Dictionary* (New York, 1933); Kennedy, Ch. 10, "The Modern English Vocabulary"; *Oxford English Dictionary*, Prefaces to Vols. 1 and 10; Robert L. Ramsay, "Taking the Census of English Words," *American Speech*, 1933, 8:36-41.

The words of the well defined center of our language, perhaps 200,000 of them, we may meet in our reading, especially if it is broad enough to include both older and modern literature and some scientific fields. And these same words make the reservoir from which as speakers and writers we draw the raw materials of our expression.

1b. The individual's vocabulary. It is hard to tell what portion of this store of words an individual uses. It used to be fashionable to say that a grown person of average social standing used only a few hundred words, but actual counts have shown that children soon pass the mark that was set for adults. More recent studies put the figure much higher. Professor Seashore calculates the average college student's recognition vocabulary at about 62,000 words with 96,000 derivative words. Methods of estimation are not very sure, but we certainly all have a large number of words—think how many objects with names (and names for their qualities and for what they can do) there are in any store or factory or even in a kitchen or a barn and how many a student learns in a college course in a new field! The number of words in general use is steadily increasing. New machines and new products increase the number used in practical affairs as the increase of general and theoretical knowledge adds to the vocabulary of the educated person.[1]

However many words a person may "know," he will know them in different ways. The figures of the preceding paragraph refer to his *recognition* vocabulary, the words that he will understand more or less accurately in reading or listening but that he may or may not use. This recognition vocabulary is usually regarded as roughly three times as large as his *active* vocabulary, the words he will use easily in speaking and writing. Very little is known about the relation between these two active vocabularies, the spoken and the written. They may be about the same in size but include different words: A good many words of conversation would not appear in writing, and many, used in writing, a person might not use in his conversation.

In the following paragraph of academic prose some of the words illustrate possible distinctions between a recognition and an active vocabulary. They are italicized for later discussion.

> Two sorts of experience are recognized as having *worth,* or as capable of having it, an *active* and a *passive;* one is *creation* or control, and the other *appreciation.* These are not strictly separate experiences, but rather *"aspects"*

---

[1] References: Kennedy, § 84 and the sources there referred to; Robert H. Seashore, *Elementary English*, 1948, 25:137-52.

of experience, yet they are practically *separable* to a large degree. The worth of active creation or control is a kind of appreciation; usually the worth of the experience of activity depends more or less upon a feeling of worth toward or appreciation of some "result" brought about. But though the two things are usually more or less associated and overlapping, we are all familiar with extreme cases in which on the one hand the feeling of worth is nearly or quite purely passive and on the other the worth of an activity is nearly or quite independent of the character of the result. The literature of *value*, like that of science, shows a *bias* for *monism*, so there is a tendency to reduce all value to "*contemplation*" or to the "joy of being a cause," according to the *temperamental predilections* of the particular writer, but a *candid* observer must accept both, and all sorts of mixtures of the two.—FRANK H. KNIGHT, "Scientific Method in Economics," *The Trend of Economics*, edited by R. G. Tugwell. Copyright, 1924, by F. S. Crofts & Co., Inc. Used by permission of Appleton-Century-Crofts, Inc.

Probably most college students would recognize and understand more or less accurately every word in this passage, except perhaps *monism*, though some would have trouble defining *predilections*. A good many would recognize but would not ordinarily use *aspects*, *separable*, *bias* (though they would use *biased*), *contemplation*, and perhaps *temperamental*. *Passive*, *creation*, and *appreciation* they might use in writing but ordinarily would not use in their conversation unless they were trying to "make an impression." The words *worth* and *value* are common enough, but not in the senses in which they appear here: *worth* is here a noun instead of, as more commonly, an adjective ("worth so much"), and *value* is used in a philosophical sense. Probably most students would not use *candid* outside the phrase *candid camera*. It is quite proper that many of these words remain in the average person's recognition vocabulary; it would be for the individual to decide whether he could conveniently use *bias* or *candid* or *monism* or any of the others. But it is important to recognize that there are different strata in everyone's vocabulary.

2. Increasing your vocabulary

"But my vocabulary is so small" is one of the commonest excuses of students in composition courses and of older people who have some intention of speaking or writing. They seem to think that if they had more words they could write, and they often sound as though having a small vocabulary was an affliction like myopia or hay fever, to be got over by wearing glasses or by some miracle of medicine. If their vocabularies really are small, that is only the symptom and not the real disease, for words cannot be considered apart from their meaning and usefulness. A small vocabulary means either that a person does not have the information he thinks he has or, if he does, that he does not talk about it and perhaps even does not think about it. People may have moods and feelings (or "affective states" as psychologists say) without the words to tell of them, but they do not have facts or ideas without the words to tell of them because these do not exist in their minds apart from the words. The only exception would perhaps be sense impressions, a particular shade or tint, an odor, something seen or heard or sensed, for which they lack an accurate name; though if the image is clear enough in their memories, they can usually find some way of describing it at least roughly.

Not everyone needs the same words. The ones it is necessary to be concerned about are those that you need for understanding and discussing subjects that you are actually dealing with or thinking about or that you might reasonably expect to use in talking or writing.[1] One trouble with learning "a word a day" is that very often the additions are not particularly useful. A published word-a-day scheme suggested learning these words:

| obdurate | contiguous | esoteric | implacable | turgid | lucent |
| amenable | corporeal | sedulous | lassitude | tortuous | exemplary |

These are all good English words that will occasionally crop up in the more highbrow books and magazines. But they are hard to work into ordinary conversation because they belong to the formal level of the language, and they really are not needed anyway, even in writing, because everyone already has perfectly good words for the same ideas: *obdurate* is *hard, harsh, hard-hearted, stiff-necked, stubborn* . . . and *amenable* may mean either *liable* or *yielding, submissive* . . . and so on.

There are more natural and more effective ways of adding to your stock of words.

2a. Transferring words to active vocabulary. Your recognition vocabulary grows chiefly through reading, to a less extent through listening and observation. Some of these words that you recognize but do not use would be convenient in your active vocabulary. Little is gained by adding words that exactly translate what you can already say. It is more important to practice using words that let you say something you couldn't say without them or that let

---

[1] The correlation between size of vocabulary and practical success is discussed in Johnson O'Connor, "Vocabulary and Success," *The Atlantic Monthly*, Feb. 1934 (reprinted as the Introduction to his *English Vocabulary Builder* and elsewhere).

you say something more exactly than you now can. The way to get words you recognize in reading into your active vocabulary is to use them, perhaps by taking some special pains, by talking and writing more, and by talking or writing more exactly.

Occasionally in your reading, pay particular attention to these words, especially when the reading is about a subject that you might well write or talk about. Underline or make a list of words you find in reading that you feel a need of and look up the less familiar ones in a good dictionary. And then before very long make it a point to use some of them in speaking or writing. After you have used a word two or three times, it will be yours always.

2b. Learning new subjects. The most natural way to learn new words is by learning something new, whether it is from observation or conversation or from a magazine article or a college textbook. You can't take facts or ideas away with you unless they are in verbal form. The easiest way to increase your vocabulary is by acquiring groups of words from new experience. You will learn several in visiting a printing plant for the first time; a person who learns to drive a car will pick up a number of new words. There are words from every experience, from every job, every sport, every art, every book (most authors have vocabularies of their own), from every field of thought and study. Consider the words that would be added to a person's vocabulary from a newly acquired interest in radio, in printing, in sailing, in music, in the poems of Dylan Thomas, in astronomy, in biology.

To make these new words your own, tell someone about what you have just learned, talk the subject over with someone who is also interested in it, or try to teach it to someone who knows nothing of it, or write about it.

In college a student's vocabulary increases enormously and at all levels. He comes to use the words of the college organization (*registrar, curriculum, honors courses, schedule, conflict*); he picks up the colloquial and slang vocabulary of the campus (*dorm, poly sci, home ec, pan hell*, and perhaps some not so widely used, like *prelim* or *tunk*); he may take up a new sport or some other activity and so acquire more words; and the courses he takes will add several times as many words as the other pursuits of college life, some of them technical and of restricted use, many of them of more general application. Acquiring the vocabularies of biology or sociology or history is a very important part of the respective courses; certainly you can't go far without the names of the facts and ideas taken up. The words should be accurately learned *the first time they are met:* scrutinized for their spelling, pronounced as they are in class or as a dictionary specifies, and studied for their exact meaning. Probably a good deal of trouble in courses comes from only partly understanding the specialized words when they are first met. Once they are understood, they should be used. Many of them will be called out in recitation or examination or term papers, but using them casually in conversation, even humorously if they can be made to carry a joke, or using them in talking over the course work with another will help impress them on your mind and make them come more easily. In this way you will acquire those thousands of words which the statistics on vocabulary credit a college graduate with.

2c. Adding individual words. Besides these two most common processes for adding words to your vocabulary, it is possible to acquire individual words that appeal to you. The typical process is seen in picking up slang: you hear the word, and it appeals to you, and you use it, perhaps for its own sake. The same holds for more serious words. Playing with them is a good way to make them your own, unless your attempt at humor is going to seem strained.

Conversation and casual reading will give a good many useful words, perhaps most of them fitting in general situations rather than in special fields of study. They may be words a little off the beaten track but accurate and expressive—*livid, echelon, prink, eupeptic*—the language is full of such words that can make your writing more exact or more vivid. They are the ones to salvage from the vast number that pass through or near your consciousness in the course of a day.

The essential point is that you are not merely "increasing your vocabulary." You are acquiring more meaningful and useful words, increasing your powers of understanding, extending your range of interests, as well as adding to your command of the enormous supply of English words in order to think, speak, and write in the manner of educated people.

3. The use of dictionaries

The most useful tool for a writer, in or out of a composition course, is a good dictionary. Nowhere else can he find so much information about words and their use, and nowhere else, if he is really interested in his language, can he find so much curious, incidental, and even amusing information about words.

But dictionaries are primarily for reference. They answer questions about the meaning of words so that the student can read with more understanding. They settle doubts (or arguments) about single words. And they help a writer decide on the most accurate and effective word or phrase to use. A writer will use his dictionary most in revision and should get the habit of turning to it frequently while revising a paper and preparing the final copy.

3a. Evaluating dictionaries. There is no such thing as "the dictionary," which can be quoted to settle any question about words. There are a number of dictionaries, all (except the scholarly historical dictionaries) commercial ventures—that is, the editors compile the best book they are capable of and able to prepare with the money allowed by the publisher. Dictionaries consequently vary, and choosing one to satisfy a person's needs is sometimes difficult. Dictionaries obviously vary in three fundamental respects (as well as in minor matters like typography and arrangement of entries), in *date*, *size*, and responsibility of *editing*.

1) DATE. An up-to-date dictionary is necessary because words are continually being added to the general stock of the English language, other words are used in new senses, words drop out of use, spellings and pronunciations change. Although some alterations are made between printings, the date of compilation—not of printing—is important. To find this date look at the copyright statement on the back of the title page. Many dictionaries offered at low prices or given as premiums are new printings of old dictionaries and are of less use because of their age. It is probably more profitable in the long run to buy a recently revised dictionary of the "college" size, with about 140,000 entries, than one with three times the number but perhaps twenty years old. In consulting dictionaries in libraries you should look for one recently revised.

2) SIZE. For specialized reading and serious work with words it is necessary to go to a recent "unabridged" dictionary, which will have upwards of half a million entries. For everyday work, the smaller size, costing usually from $5 up, according to binding, is more generally useful. The less common words are left out in the abridgment, but those needed for most reading and writing are included. Still smaller dictionaries, down to the pocket size, may be handy for checking spelling, but they are not sufficient for college work.

3) EDITING. Date and size of a dictionary are easily determined, but it is very difficult to judge the editing of such a complex work. Responsible editing makes the dictionary really useful, gives it what "authority" it may possess. That is, it should be a compilation from a vast accumulation of actual recorded uses of words, not a compilation from existing word books. It should be based on an enormous file of recent quotations from all sorts of writers from all over the English-speaking world. This raw material then should be worked over by specialists in various subjects and by trained editors who digest the evidence of use into the dictionary's brief articles.

Since it is difficult to judge a dictionary, most people have to rely on reviews or the advice of someone who has made a study of dictionaries. The two generally considered to be the best edited at this writing are the *American College Dictionary* (1947) and Webster's *New Collegiate Dictionary* (1949). The reproductions of dictionary entries later in this chapter are from them.

Other general dictionaries will be found listed, with critical notes, in I. G. Mudge, *Guide to Reference Books* (6th edition; Chicago, 1936, and supplements), on pages 51-85, and dictionaries of special subjects on page 86 ff.

3b. Uses of a general dictionary. Obviously, to get the most out of a dictionary, its owner needs to know what various matters it includes. He should look through its table of contents to see what units of material there are besides the main alphabetical list of words. He should see if it contains a supplement of new words. He should read a page or two consecutively to see how words and phrases are handled, and he should try pronouncing some familiar words to see how the pronunciation key works. Pains taken learning to use a particular dictionary will be more than repaid by its increased usefulness.

1) SPELLING. A word is entered in a dictionary under its usual spelling. As a rule a writer can come close enough to this so that he can find a word he is in doubt about, but sometimes he has to keep in mind other common spellings of a sound—so that if he fails to find *gibe* he will look under *jibe*. When usage in spelling is divided, two spellings are given for the word. The one the editors believe is more common is put first: *hemoglobin, haemoglobin; although, altho.* Ordinarily a writer will take the first of the two forms unless the second for some reason is more appropriate to other traits of his writing. The spelling entries in a dictionary give the division of a word into syllables and so show where it should be divided at the

end of lines, as in *mor ti fi ca tion, dis par ag ing ly*. They also give the spelling of compound words, showing whether the editors have found them most often as two words, as one word, or with hyphen. Most dictionaries recommend the use of more hyphens than are necessary, certainly for informal writing. The introductions to most dictionaries contain general discussions of English spelling.

2) PRONUNCIATION. Dictionaries respell words in specially marked letters to show their pronunciation. The exact sounds represented by the symbols are usually shown at the bottom of the page and are further explained in a discussion of pronunciation in the preface.

ac·cli′mate (ă·klī′mĭt; ăk′lĭ·māt), *v. t. & i.* [F. *acclimater*, fr. *à* to + *climat* climate.] To habituate, or become habituated, to a climate not native; to acclimatize. — **Syn.** Inure, season, harden. — **ac·cli′mat-a·ble** (ă·klī′mĭt·à·b′l), *adj.* — **ac′cli·ma′tion** (ăk′lĭ·mā′shŭn; ăk′lĭ-), *n.*

cer′ti·o·ra′ri (sûr′shĭ·ô·rā′rī; -râr′ī), *n.* [From *certiorari* to be certified; — a term in the Latin form of the writ.] *Law.* A writ from a superior court to call up for review the records of an inferior court or a body acting in a quasi-judicial capacity.

phi·lat′e·ly (fĭ·lăt′ĕ·lĭ), *n.* [F. *philatélie*, fr. Gr. *philos* loving + *ateleia* exemption from tax (*telos*).] The collection and study of postage stamps, stamped envelopes, etc., of various issues; stamp collecting. — **phil′a·tel′ic** (fĭl′à·tĕl′ĭk), **phil′a·tel′i·cal** (-ĭ·kăl), *adj.* — **phil′a·tel′i·cal·ly**, *adv.* — **phi·lat′e·list** (fĭ·lăt′ĕ·lĭst), *n.*

quay (kē; kwā), *n.* [OF. *kai, cay* (F. *quai*).] A stretch of paved bank or a solid artificial landing place beside navigable water, for convenience in loading and unloading ships.

By permission. From *Webster's New Collegiate Dictionary*, copyright 1949, by G. & C. Merriam Co.

Dictionaries are somewhat imperfect guides to pronunciation because their prime source of material is published books and articles, and actual speech is harder to record, especially in a large country. Usually full or "platform" pronunciation is given, which if followed completely would give a person's speech a slow and somewhat stilted sound. Ordinary speech results in less distinct vowels than the dictionaries indicate, and stress varies with the position of a word in a phrase. Furthermore our dictionaries do not recognize sufficiently the variations in American pronunciation, usually giving New England or Eastern pronunciations most weight. But people learn the common words from hearing them and can rely on dictionaries for pronunciation of the unusual ones.

Dictionaries show divided usage in the pronunciation of many words, as in the Webster examples of *acclimate* shown above. As a rule a person should use the pronunciation most common among the educated people of his community.

The most authoritative guide to pronunciation is Kenyon and Knott, *A Pronouncing Dictionary of American English* (1944), published by the makers of Webster's dictionaries but more discriminating than the dictionaries.

3) DEFINITION. The definitions of words of course take up the bulk of the space in a dictionary. The definitions of unusual words help the reader get the full and actual sense of a passage that treats material new to him. Dictionaries carry many dialect, obsolete, and archaic words to help in reading writers such as Burns and Shakespeare. Scientific, technical, slang, and provincial words are generously included, although by no means all words of these classes are given.

For a writer the dictionary definitions are most useful in checking the meaning of words he is almost sure of, but not quite. When he is revising a paper, he needs to make sure that some words mean what he thought they meant when he put them in the first draft, and he wants to make sure that they stand a good chance of meaning to his reader what he intends them to. Very often he will need more information for this purpose than a dictionary can give because of its limited space and must go to an encyclopedia or other work.

It is not so much the meanings of uncommon words, like *hackbut, pyrognostics,* or *zymurgy,* that a writer needs as the meanings of those near but not quite in his active vocabulary. Almost any series of dictionary entries will illustrate these words and the scope and method of dictionary definition:

check·row (chĕk/rō/), *Agric.* —*n.* **1.** one of a number of rows of trees or plants, esp. corn, in which the distance between adjacent trees or plants is equal to that between adjacent rows. —*v.t.* **2.** to plant in checkrows.
check·up (chĕk/ŭp/), *n.* **1.** an examination or close scrutiny for purposes of verification as to accuracy, comparison, etc. **2.** a comprehensive physical examination.
Ched·dar cheese (chĕd/ər), American cheese. Also, ched/dar.
chedd·ite (chĕd/īt, shĕd/īt), *n.* an explosive used for blasting made up of a chlorate or perchlorate mixture with a fatty substance, such as castor oil. [t. F: f. *Chedde* place name (of Savoy) + -*ite* -ITE¹]
cheek (chēk), *n.* **1.** either side of the face below eye level. **2.** the side wall of the mouth between the upper and lower jaws. **3.** something resembling the human cheek in form or position, as either of two parts forming corresponding sides of a thing. **4.** *Colloq.* impudence or effrontery. —*v.t.* **5.** *Brit. Colloq.* to address or confront with impudence or effrontery. [ME *cheke,* OE *cēce,* c. D *kaak*]
cheek·bone (chēk/bōn/), *n.* the bone or bony prominence below the outer angle of the eye.
cheek by jowl, side by side; in close intimacy.
cheek pouch, a bag in the cheek of certain animals, as squirrels, for carrying food.
cheek·y (chē/kĭ), *adj.,* **cheekier, cheekiest.** *Colloq.* impudent; insolent: *a cheeky fellow, cheeky behavior.* —cheek/i·ly, *adv.* —cheek/i·ness, *n.*

The great need for saving space in a dictionary makes some definitions cryptic, requiring anyone but a specialist to look up words used in the definition. Drawings are a help in leading to an understanding of objects, and illustrative phrases or sentences in which the word is used are a help in showing its meaning and construction with other words.

There are three points to remember in using dictionary definitions. (*a*) A dictionary does not *require* or *forbid* a particular meaning of a word but *records* the uses that have been found for it. Now and then a word is in the process of acquiring a new meaning or somewhat altering its usual sense. (*b*) The dictionary definition is for the most part a record of the denotation of a word and often cannot give its connotation. For this reason it is safest not to use a word unless you have heard or read it and so know it in part from experience, at least what suggestion it carries if it is not a simple factual word. (*c*) Finally and most important, the words of the definition are not the meaning of the word, but they, and perhaps an illustration, are to help let you see what in the world of objects or ideas the word refers to.

4) Levels of usage. Words that are unlabeled in a dictionary are supposed to belong to the general vocabulary; other words are labeled *dialectical, obsolete, archaic, foreign, colloquial, slang, British, United States,* or are referred to some field of activity—*medicine, law, astronomy, baseball, manufacturing, electricity, philosophy.*

These labels are rough guides to levels of usage, but a writer should bring his own observation and judgment to bear on individual words. Many that carry no label are rarely used (*curtilage, moot*) and would mar most writing. In general the editors' point of view is rather conservative, and many words marked *Dial.* or *Colloq.* would fit perfectly well into informal writing. It must be clearly understood that these labels are intended to be descriptive terms and are not intended to prohibit or even to discourage the use of the words so labeled. *Colloq.* means that the word is characteristic of cultivated conversation rather than of formal writing; *U.S.,* that the word is in good use in the United States but not in other parts of the English-speaking world.

5) Synonyms. Most dictionaries gather words of similar meanings into a group and show in what ways they are alike and in what ways different, as in the following entries which appear after the words *argue* and *argument* in the *American College Dictionary:*

—Syn. 1. ARGUE, DEBATE, DISCUSS imply using reasons or proofs to support or refute an assertion, proposition, or principle. ARGUE implies reasoning or trying to understand; it does not necessarily imply opposition: *to argue with oneself.* To DISCUSS is to present varied opinions and views: *to discuss ways and means.* To DEBATE is to interchange formal (usually opposing) arguments, esp. on public questions: *to debate a proposed amendment.*

—Syn. 1. ARGUMENT, CONTROVERSY, DISPUTE imply the expression of opinions for and against some idea. An ARGUMENT usually arises from a disagreement between two persons, each of whom advances facts supporting his own point of view. A CONTROVERSY or a DISPUTE may involve two or more persons. A DISPUTE is an oral contention, usually brief, and often of a heated, angry, or undignified character: *a violent dispute over a purchase.* A CONTROVERSY is an oral or written expression of contrary opinions, and may be dignified and of some duration: *a political controversy.*

From *The American College Dictionary*, copyright 1947, 1949, by Random House; Text Edition, copyright 1948, by Harper & Brothers

The discrimination of synonyms is often more helpful in selecting the right word to use than the definition.

6) LINGUISTIC INFORMATION. The dictionary usually indicates the part of speech in which a word is generally used, whether a verb is used transitively or intransitively, the principal parts of verbs, plural of nouns, and any other distinctive form a word may assume. The origin of the word, how it got into English, is usually given. Sometimes this is merely a statement of the language from which the word came into English (Italian, Latin, Japanese), and sometimes it is a more complicated chain of origin and change of form, as in the *Webster Collegiate* statement on *course*, tracing it from Latin, through Italian and French, to English:

course (kōrs; 70), *n.* [From F. *cours* (OF. *cors, curs*), fr. L. *cursus*, and fr. F. *course*, fr. It. *corsa*, fr. *correre* to run; both fr. L. *currere, cursum*, to run.]

By permission. From *Webster's New Collegiate Dictionary*, copyright 1949, by G. & C. Merriam Co.

The Oxford English Dictionary and the *Dictionary of American English* are historical works, tracing through dated quotations the changes in form and meaning of a word. The introductions to many dictionaries contain histories of our language and valuable information on spelling, pronunciation, and other traits of language.

7) MISCELLANEOUS INFORMATION. Most dictionaries contain some reference material not strictly needed in a book of definitions, such as lists of places and prominent historical figures, abbreviations, foreign words and phrases. Formerly these items were run in lists in the back of the volume, but the tendency in recent dictionaries has been to put them in the main alphabet.

3c. Special dictionaries. Dictionary making (lexicography) is a highly specialized art, or applied science. The general dictionaries are supplemented by a considerable number of special word books and several more are now being compiled.[1]

1) HISTORICAL DICTIONARIES. The *Oxford English Dictionary*, in ten large volumes, is the great storehouse of information about English words. It traces the various forms of each word and its various meanings with dates of their first appearance and quotations from writers illustrating each. There is a *Supplement* giving material on new words and evidence on earlier words not found in the original work. Besides being the standard authority on the history of English words and phrases, the *Oxford English Dictionary* is useful in reading older literature to find exactly what a word meant at a particular time in the past. An abridgment, the *Shorter Oxford English Dictionary*, in two volumes, is on the same plan and is very useful for interpreting past literature.

The *Dictionary of American English* (4 vols., 1938-44) is on the same plan as the *Oxford*, giving the histories of words as they have been used in the United States. An entry begins with the first use of the word found in American writers and continues, giving quotations, to the present. In this way it supplements the linguistic information of the *Oxford* and is especially useful in reading American writers.

Besides these there are dictionaries for Old English and for Middle English, and other period dictionaries are being compiled, like the *Dictionary of Early Modern English* (1500-1700).

2) DIALECT DICTIONARIES. Besides Joseph Wright's *English Dialect Dictionary* (6 volumes), giving words in the various dialects of England, there are a number of special word lists from different regions, in books and in periodicals like *Dialect Notes* and *American Speech*. Eric Partridge's *Dictionary of Slang and Unconventional English* is a historical dictionary of English and American slang from early to recent times. Work is being done on the *Linguistic Atlas of the United States and Canada*, which will eventually appear with very thorough accounts of the use and movements of certain words in this country.

3) DICTIONARIES IN SPECIAL SUBJECTS. Because the general dictionaries cannot give the complete vocabulary in specialized fields of

---

[1] *A Survey of English Dictionaries* (New York, 1933) by M. M. Mathews is a history of English dictionaries.

work, they are supplemented by a growing group of dictionaries in special subjects, like the following:

Alsager, C. M., *Dictionary of Business Terms* (1932)
Ballentine, J. A., *Law Dictionary* (1930)
Dorland, W. A. N., *American Illustrated Medical Dictionary* (20th ed., 1944)
English, H. B., *A Student's Dictionary of Psychological Terms* (4th ed., 1934)
Good, C. V., *Dictionary of Education* (1945)
Hackh's Chemical Dictionary (3d ed., 1944)
Henderson, I. F. and W. D., *Dictionary of Scientific Terms* (3d ed., 1939)—Biological sciences
Rice, C. M., *Dictionary of Geological Terms* (1940)
Shipley, J. T., *Dictionary of World Literature* (1943)

4. Denotation: the core of a word's meaning

Strictly speaking, words have "meaning" only as they are used in particular statements; by themselves, or as they stand in a dictionary, they have typical or possible or potential meaning. Their actual meaning is in a situation and is the result of several elements: (1) the speaker's intention and attitude, his past association with the words, his knowledge of or experience with the thing or idea the statement is about; (2) their typical use by people who speak the language, the associations they are likely to arouse; (3) the listener's attitude and his associations with both the words and the subject; (4) the object or situation or idea to which they are referring. For convenience in a brief discussion of meaning we can limit ourselves or at least begin with this last, taking as the core of a word's meaning what it stands for to the speaker or writer, listener or reader, what in their experience or imagination or feeling it refers to.[1]

This object or class of objects, act, situation, quality, idea, or fancy to which a word refers is called its *referent* (ref'ər ənt), and by representing this referent for many users a word gets a core of meaning, its denotation. In dictionaries the ways in which a word is generally used are recorded, stated in other terms, as *Washington pie* is defined

---

[1] Bloomfield, Chapters 9, 24; Goldberg, Chapter 15; Kennedy, Chapter 13; Schlauch, Chapters 5, 9; George H. Mead, *Mind, Self and Society* (Chicago, 1936), especially pp. 75-82. Hugh Walpole, *Semantics* (New York, 1941) is an introduction to I. A. Richards' contribution to the subject and S. I. Hayakawa, *Language in Action* (New York, 1941) and *Language in Thought and Action* (New York, 1949), and Wendell Johnson, *People in Quandaries* (New York, 1946) are introductions to the "general semantics" formulated by Alfred Korzybski. All of these references will lead to further and more specialized sources.

in Webster: "Layer cake with a cream filling or with a fruit-jam filling." But this definition in other *words* is not the meaning of *Washington pie* but an effort to direct the reader to a recollection or imagination of the word's referent.

One way to show that meaning is *not in the word* is to consider some words that are used in various senses. To take common examples: What is a *knot?* a *cut?* a *seal?* a *play?* a *point?* What do you do when you *play* or *strike*, or *fly*, or *fall?* A *knot* may be a tie of some sort in a rope, a group of people, a spot in a board, a tough problem, the measure of a ship's speed. The meaning is not in the word but in what it refers to. What it does refer to is usually clear from the sentence in which it is used, that is, from its *context*. It is so difficult to say how much we understand from a given word and how much from its context (and how much we contribute from our past experience) that it is not very profitable to consider the meaning of isolated words.

The division of linguistics that studies the meaning and changes of meaning of words is called semantics, or semasiology. In recent years much has been added to our knowledge and understanding of words and the ways in which they are used and misused. In this short account we can only suggest some of the more obviously useful facts of semantics.

Definiteness of meaning varies considerably among different words, depending in part on the exactness with which they bring to mind specific referents. The following three classes of words will show this varying definiteness. Other groups could be made according to some trait of their meaning, but these are enough to suggest that the problem of using words exactly is more complex than it might seem at first thought to be.

4a. Concrete words. Proper names, like *Peter the Great, Peru,* and *Susan B. Anthony,* are the most exact words. Next come concrete words whose meaning is established by more or less regular reference to actual objects. *Chair,* for example, has a definite core of meaning because it is used to apply to a kind of seat. Even though people might disagree over a particular untypical chair—one might be called *stool* or another might be called *sofa*—almost always the meaning of *chair* would be definite enough for one's purposes. *Morris chair, rocking chair, ladder back chair* are more definite in their reference. The specific image that a word raises in the minds of different people will vary somewhat: at a given moment *robin* may mean to one person *robin-pulling-at-a-worm*, to another, *robin-on-a-nest*, to another, *robin-crying-rain*, but in each there is a core of meaning for *robin*. A word with which a person has had no experience (perhaps *spandrel*, *tenon*, *farthingale*, *rickrack*, or *tachistoscope*) will have no meaning for him.

A speaker or writer would not as a rule use these concrete words without a fairly definite knowledge of their core of meaning; a reader or listener will either know this meaning, be able to approach it through a dictionary definition or other reading, ask someone who knows, or learn it by observation. It is lucky for all of us that such a large part of our vocabulary consists of these fairly exact words.

4b. Relative words. Words that name qualities have not so much a definite meaning as a *direction* of meaning, but their reference in a given instance depends a good deal on the experience and intention of the user. *Red*, for instance, runs from orange to violet and for a reasonably definite meaning needs to be qualified by another word, *light, dark, orange*. To a person in "the upper brackets," a family with $3000 a year might be *poor*, but to a person on relief that family might be *well off*. Similarly, *warm, heavy, thick, rough, pretty, honest, beautiful, tall* are relative in meaning. Some attempts have been made to make possible an exact or standard sense for some of these words, as in the color scale for exact naming of colors in art or in physics, standardized weights and measures, or in definitions by law of words like *drunk* and *speeding* so that they can be used in courts.

In using these descriptive words, especially those that record our attitudes and judgments, the most important thing is to remember the various degrees, the exact shading that it is possible to express. In ordinary conversation we don't make many distinctions. A person is *all wet* or a *good egg* (or whatever the equivalent slang is this year), a show is a *flop* or a *wow*, a novel is *fascinating* or *disgusting*. Members of our own group are *honest, generous, loyal*, and so on; our rivals are ———? Actually we know, and when we are trying to talk accurately we say, that they fall somewhere between the extremes. We and our acquaintances are neither saints nor double-dyed villains but somewhere between. Can we say just about where? To try is challenging and a step toward civilized living—as well as a triumph in the use of words.

4c. Abstract words. Even more difficult to use accurately are abstract words, which do not have specific referents against which their meaning can be checked. The most definite abstract words refer to acts or relationships or directions: *trading, murder, cost, citizen-*

ship, nation, height. They have definite meaning simply because English-speaking people generally agree in the way they are used. Other abstract words are collective, that is, they stand for a gathering of individuals—*college, swing music, the administration* (of a college or of the United States). They summarize one or more common traits belonging to a number of particular people or things or situations and have a pretty definite core of meaning but may be used with very different values. The real danger in such words is that often as we use them we lose sight of the particular individuals or things for which they stand. *Personnel,* for instance, is a much used word today that pretty well conceals the notion of living people and may let us or lead us to make statements that we never would make if we visualized clearly even a dozen of them. *Capital,* for instance, means employers and investors collectively, and *labor* stands for workmen. But as they are ordinarily used, there is no notion of people suggested; they may be used as words of praise or blame, so that feeling would be more important than reference to any group of living persons.

Many other words do not have referents even as commonly agreed upon as those. The meaning of such words as *beauty, art, the good life, culture, evil, education, Americanism* is a complex of reasoning and feeling that varies from person to person. An adequate definition of any such word would be an essay, and its meaning would depend on the past experience, the emotions, and the general outlook of the person making it. Obviously understanding is difficult here, because the listener may have a different experience from the speaker, a difference increased by differences in feeling and philosophy.

We cannot expect that more or less haphazard people, as we all are, will always use these words exactly, but we should strive to be as exact as possible. One way to do this is to translate our meaning into other terms and by giving two or three versions reach some sort of exactness, hoping through one or the other to meet the reader's expectations. As speakers or writers our intention is to lead a listener or reader not just to words but to consciousness of objects or ideas in a real or imagined world. To do this we can give wherever possible specific, concrete examples of what we mean.

A more general safeguard is to realize the range of meaning that relative and abstract words have and make clear where in this range our immediate intention falls. The word *poetry,* for example, is often a stumbling block to mutual understanding because it ranges through at least three general senses. It may mean no more than composition in verse; it may be used collectively to mean a body of particular poems; or it may mean an idealized form of writing, that is, poems having certain characteristics that we respect or are fond of. (The *Oxford English Dictionary* and the *Century Dictionary* are particularly useful in pointing out such ranges of meaning.) Obviously for exact and reasonable communication it is highly important that a speaker or writer knows where in the range of possible meaning his immediate meaning falls and that he makes this clear to his listeners or readers. Trying to attain fairly exact communication is one reason for the prevailing concreteness of much modern style.

5. Connotation: the suggestion of words

The denotation of a word is more or less informative and factual and is what we ordinarily intend by its "meaning"; it is what a dictionary definition tries to lead us to. But this meaning is somewhat affected by the circumstances in which the word has been generally used and by the particular context in which it occurs. This suggested quality, as distinct from the central core of meaning, is called its *connotation*. It is an essential part of the meaning of words, separated from denotation only in analysis.

5a. From general use. Looking at a few groups of words having substantially the same denotation will bring out this quality and show why one could not be indiscriminately substituted for another.

> *average* (factual); *mediocre* (derogatory)
> *childlike* (approving); *childish* (derogatory)
> *saliva* (factual, slightly formal, with scientific suggestion); *spit* (the usual word but to many people "an ugly word")
> *killed in battle* (factual); *died a hero's death* (honorific); *slain by the enemy* (emphasis shifted to the baseness of the act)
> *antique* (generally approving); *old-fashioned* (factual, though often suggesting disapproval); *passé* (lightly derogatory)
> *drunk* (in general use); *intoxicated* (more polite); *under the influence* (euphemistic—minimizing); *pie-eyed, soused, stinko* (not necessarily derogatory in meaning but suggesting slangy speech)
> *reporter* (factual); *journalist* (slightly pretentious); *newshawk* (usually with slight disapproval note); *legman* (shoptalk)
> *slender* (factual, tending to approval); *thin* (factual, tending to disapproval); *skinny* (disapproving); *sylphlike* (poetic, formal); *svelte* (fashionable)
> *mongrel* (factual); *cur* (derogatory); *feice* (Southern)

The connotations of these words suggest an attitude or a feeling of the person using them and would arouse a similar (or perhaps an antagonistic) attitude or feeling in most readers or listeners. The context in which the word has been generally used, the level of usage it comes from, and the general social attitude toward its referent and toward the people who generally use it (gangsters, politicians, businessmen, teachers, children, seamen) all contribute to the connotation. The value of slang and of much profanity is more in the suggestion of the words than in their denotation. The connotation of these words may change as they or their referents move up or down in social esteem. *Gift* in *giftbooks, giftware* is acquiring a specific and unhappy connotation. *Methodist* started as a word of dispraise but is now simply factual, the name of a church, or often a word of esteem. *Propaganda* only a few years ago meant a means of spreading a truth or a faith, but it now implies spreading falsehood or at least an unfair presentation of information.

5b. From context. Besides these connotations that are more or less permanent characteristics of words, there are more immediate connotations that come from context, from the way they are used at a specific time or from the other words around them. In speaking we can alter or even invert the usual meaning of a word by the tone of voice or facial expression or gesture. We can call a person a liar in such a way that he will know he is being flattered. In writing, the tone is set by the general style and by the tenor of ideas expressed. *War*, for example, may refer simply to a historical event, or it may be used with suggestions of bravery or of suffering or of chicanery. *Democracy, communism, monarchy* are primarily words for types of social organization, but they may carry also suggestions of loyalty or hate. The full possibility of meaning of many words cannot be indicated by a dictionary; consider what would be omitted in a standard definition of such words as *fascism, income tax, ball game, quintessence, the founding fathers* (of the United States), *scab, the forgotten man, horse and buggy era.*

Besides these widespread connotations and those that are clear in the context, there are often special associations a word may have for a particular person, a suggestion that his past experience or his temperament or his ideals or his imagination has given it for him. In impersonal writing such associations are usually suppressed, but in familiar writing and in fiction and especially in poetry they play a prominent part.

Making use of the connotations of words gives writing a quality of style that is called *suggestion*. The reader is carried beyond the literal meanings, senses the feelings of the writer, and comes to believe in him as a real person. Amateur writers tend to rely too much on impersonal denotations and to squeeze out of their writing this personal quality. In the following paragraph from "A Death in the Country," Mr. Benét uses only ordinary words, but he suggests a definite scene and the emotion of a man remembering the funeral of his mother.

Well, he wasn't looking forward to a pleasant time. He felt fagged and on edge already. There was work for the active partner of Norman, Buckstone, and Carroll in his brief-case, but he could not get down to the work. Instead he remembered, from childhood, the smell of dyed cloth and poignant, oppressive flowers, the black wisp tied on the knocker, the people coming to the door. The house was full of a menace—full of a secret—there were incomprehensible phrases, said in a murmur, and a man in black gloves who came, and a strangeness behind a shut door. Run out and play, run out and play; but there was no right way to play any more—even out in the yard you could smell the sweet, overpowering flowers—even out in the street you could see the people coming and coming, making that little pause as they saw the black wisp. Beautiful, they said, she looks beautiful; but the glimpse of the face was not mother, only somebody coldly asleep. Our sister has gone to dear Jesus . . . we shall meet on that beautiful shore . . . but the man spoke words, and the harsh box sank into the hole, and from it nothing arose, not even a white thing, not even silver vapor; the clay at the sides of the hole was too yellow and thick and cold. He's too young to realize, said a great many voices—but for months nothing was right. The world had stopped being solid, and people's smiles were different, and mother was Jesus' sister, and they gave her clothes away. Then, after a long time, the place was green again and looked just like the other graves, and the knife in your pocket was a comfort, going out there Sundays in the street car.—STEPHEN VINCENT BENÉT, *Thirteen O'Clock*, pp. 257-58

5c. Synonyms. A synonym is a word of nearly the same meaning as another. Often the real difference between them is in the connotation. There are very few pairs of interchangeable words. Even names of specific things, like *rhubarb—pieplant, kerosene—coal oil, flicker—yellowhammer*, differ, for though they refer to the same objects, their connotations are not the same, because one of the pair is used in a definite part of the country, or by a specific group of people, or under certain circumstances, so that one cannot be regularly substituted for another. English is especially rich in words of slightly different shades of meaning: *joke—jest; obedient—dutiful—yielding—compliant—obsequious; multitude—throng—crowd—mob*. Because of these differences in connotation, merely trying to escape repetition of a word is not a sufficient motive for using a synonym. It is better to avoid unpleasant repetition by the use of pronouns or by recasting the sentence.

When a writer looks for a "synonym," he is really looking for a word of nearly the same meaning as the one he has in hand but one that can give his meaning in the particular sentence more exactly. The important point, then, in looking at two or more words of similar meaning is to know how they *differ*.

Some synonyms should be found before writing the first draft; others after the first draft is written. If a writer knows that he is going to discuss a subject with which he is not very familiar, he can think over the words (really his material) and can sharpen his sense of the necessary words before he begins to write. If he expects to need words for colors, or for the qualities of poetry, or for the parts of a radio, he can bring them to mind before he sits down to put words on paper.

But as a rule testing the exactness of words is a matter of revision. He can see then the context in which they are to stand and can test them for exactness of meaning, for appropriateness to the subject and to the readers, for their degree of formality or informality. Sometimes he can find a single word to take the place of a long phrase; sometimes he can replace a general or ambiguous word with one of specific meaning, as *funny* might be *amusing, laughable, odd, queer, different, peculiar;* or *walk* might be replaced by a more descriptive word. Sometimes the change is to bring a word in line with the level of usage of the rest of the paper, choosing one either more or less formal: *want—wish—desire; roomy—spacious; fast—rapidly.* Sometimes it is a matter of finding the exact name for something that the writer has seen but has never named in one word, like the small platform on which an orchestra conductor stands (*podium*), or a part of a landscape (perhaps a *mesa*, or a *hogback*, or an *arroyo*).

There are various tools at hand. Dictionaries group words of similar meaning and indicate the general distinctions between them. There are also several books of synonyms: Allen's *Synonyms and Antonyms* (New York, 1921), Fernald's *Synonyms, Antonyms, and Prepositions* (New York, 1947), Soule's *A Dictionary of English Synonyms* (Boston, 1938), and Roget's *International Thesaurus* (rev. ed., 1946). This *Thesaurus* (thi sô'rəs) is probably the most used book of synonyms. It lists words by topics, in parallel columns giving words of opposite meaning, and offers a wide range from slang to formal and even obsolete words. It does not give definitions of the words, so that its chief use is to remind a person of those that he recognizes but does not use readily. In this way it is very useful in bridging the gap between one's recognition vocabulary and one's working vocabulary. It is often helpful in revising a paper.

But the prime source of synonyms, as of other words, is conversation and reading. A person usually has a plentiful and ready supply of words in the fields in which he is really at home. Cultivating a habit of observing and using words in discussion is the best background for making the choice of exact words easy. And usually the chief difference between a pair of closely similar words is in their connotation.

6. The responsible use of words

The preceding sections show that exactness in the use of words is difficult. Words are only roughly accurate in their meanings because human beings are not exact, or at least are exact only as the result of special training or of some immediate necessity. If a person wishes to deceive, language offers him the means; by intentional misuse of words or by an irresponsible manipulation of the emotional suggestion in words a "propagandist" (or anyone else) can distort truth and make error prevail, at least for a time.

But in spite of some selfish and even evil intentions, an honest attempt at communication can be made to succeed. Our semanticists may make us too suspicious of words. The difficulty is not so much in the words as in the intent of the person using them or the lack of a responsible purpose. Honest failure in communication is possible because of careless or unhappy choice of words, and sometimes we fail to make full use of the facilities of our language. But a sincere effort to convey material with which we are really familiar can be successful.

Absolute exactness is not always desirable. A person who in conversation is overexact or overcareful is likely to become a bore, sacrificing immediate appeal to precision. Often in a poem so much depends on the connotation of the words that several "meanings" are possible, and properly enough so long as a reader does not insist that his interpretation is necessarily the one the writer intended. In simple explanation or statements of fact, especially in scientific writing, the words are likely to be used for their central core of meaning. In attempts to persuade and in any sort of emotional speech, the connotation counts for more.

In contexts where exact words are necessary or desirable, as in most factual writing and in college writing, there are three typical faults to be guarded against:

6a. Mistaken words. Sometimes a word is used for a meaning that it has not acquired in its previous history:

> How are the coaches outwitting their *prototypes* [*competitors?*]?
> An educated man seems to have an expression signifying shrewdness, *comprehensibility* [*understanding?*], and originality.

Usually, as in the last sentence (note the *signifying*), such errors occur when a writer is attempting a level of usage in which he is not at home or when he confuses two words of similar sound (*temerity—timidity, flaunt—flout*). Confusion is especially likely to occur between words of opposite meaning (*concave—convex*). Confusions in writing of words that sound alike (homonyms) are a matter of spelling rather than of meaning. Even if the context makes the meaning clear, as it often does, such inaccuracies are a mark of carelessness.

6b. Vague words. Sometimes words are used that are too general to convey an exact meaning. They are more characteristic of conversation than of writing. Counter words like *fine*, *bad*, *good* should usually be replaced in writing by more definite adjectives, and even words like *interesting* or *important* frequently stand for some particular sort of interest or importance that could better be named, so that the reader's thought could be brought nearer to the writer's intention. Many phrases could be replaced by single exact words with a gain in economy and sometimes in definiteness:

> The men with axes would then trim off the branches, while the men with crosscut saws cut the *large part of the tree* [*trunk*] into ten-foot lengths.
> Last year in a nearby city an *occupant* [*prisoner*] in the county jail escaped.
> The other thing that *I have in mind* [*My other intention—hope—plan?*] is to go to France.

Another type of lack of meaning is the use of traditionally eloquent words that have lost touch with reality:

> Pure democracy is inherently a spiritual quality which voluntarily must spring from the determined will of the people.

6c. Unfair or unintended connotation. Exaggeration is a legitimate form of expression, but often words are too intense for a writer's meaning. Perhaps a *most* should be *many*, or a superlative should be reduced to a less extreme statement, or an *only* or *nothing but* should allow for other possibilities. Or extreme words like *unique, intriguing, thrill* should be replaced by words that are more accurately descriptive.

Epithets that are emotional rather than descriptive (*notorious, ignorant, communist*) should be used with special care, and usually an expansive emotional patch, like the following description of the content of a volume of poems, should be avoided entirely:

> There will be a vivid color and vibrant pulse of life about it. And the pen of each contributor will touch a chord of desire in the readers' heart of thoughts trooping across its pages, gripping with an inward fire of intensity a vast imaginative tapestry of the beauties of America. By sparkling streams and in green hills there will be found undiscovered places to dream and it will be warm and impressive in human emotion.

The best remedy for such writing is to keep looking at the subject and to resolve to present it as it really is. This will help a writer express himself in words that are relatively exact in meaning.

Attention to the words alone will not make communication accurate and effective. An honest intention to convey information or opinion or attitude that the writer really has to a reader in a moderately attentive frame of mind will result in a responsible use of words.

Suggested study and writing

1. Write out the following information about your dictionary.

(1) Title (2) Publisher (3) Date on title page (4) Date of original copyright (on back of title page) (5) Number of words listed (approximate) (6) Does it have a supplement of new words? (7) Does it have a separate biographical or geographical section? (8) Does it have discussions of spelling, pronunciation, and levels of usage in the front of the book?

2. Look up the following words and copy them with the symbols used in your dictionary to indicate their pronunciation. If more than one pronunciation is given, which is the first or "preferred" form? Which pronunciation do you most frequently hear and use?

abdomen	dachshund	details	interest
address (noun)	data	economics	Los Angeles
adult	debutante	envelope (noun)	oblique
advertisement	decorative	finances	research
chic	depot	harass	strata

3. Classify by number the words in the following list as (1) words you now use in speaking or in writing; (2) words that you understand but do not use; (3) words you feel you have seen before and might understand in context; (4) words totally unfamiliar to you. Look up the words under 4. Which ones might be useful to you?

actuary	flexor	marital	satiate
amortization	fugue	meld	scherzo
antimony	ganglion	meretricious	scutcheon
bathos	gasket	metonomy	semantics
beige	gossamer	moot	seraphim
braise	gradient	mulch	snide
candor	gunwale	myopia	sonar
carrel	gusset	nadir	statism
cartel	hedonist	nutria	stet
claustrophobia	heliotrope	odium	stymie
cliché	histrionic	ossify	suave
collateral	ides	pabulum	surreptitious
Cominform	ineffable	paradox	synthesis
decalcomania	innuendo	peroration	teleran
deciduous	intelligentsia	phonetics	tête-à-tête
demurrage	intransigent	pleistocene	thesaurus
derisive	jabot	proboscis	twain
dialectic	jardiniere	psychosomatic	tycoon
eclectic	jovial	quixotic	tyro
emcee	juxtaposition	quotient	unilateral
entrepreneur	laissez-faire	rheostat	vignette
escrow	lobotomy	riffraff	vinylite
euthanasia	lurid	riparian	virtuoso
featherbedding	magneto	rogue	zealous

4. Study an article of some length in the *Oxford English Dictionary* (full-sized edition). (Suggested words: *can, do, eye, gentle, soldier, treasure.*) Bring in a short history of the word you select, its origin, shifts in spelling, meaning, and function, and any interesting developments which it has undergone.

5. Make a list of a dozen or more words of different kinds that you have added to your vocabulary in the past year. To refresh your memory, consult some of your recent papers, check the indexes of your textbooks, and consider the various activities you have engaged in. Prepare a brief statement about the circumstances in which you acquired these words, and the way you learned their meaning.

6. Reread § 2b, "Learning new subjects," page 309. Learn something that is new to you—by reading or by observing (as by visiting, say, a printing plant or a museum) or by talking with someone. Write a paper reporting what you have learned and at the end make a list of the new words you have used and comment on whether they might be useful in future writing or speaking.

7. Here is a partial list of synonyms for the verb *to flatter* in Roget's *Thesaurus of English Words and Phrases*. Discuss the different connotations of these terms, and indicate in what context some of them might be useful in your writing.

> FLATTER, praise to the skies, puff; wheedle, cajole, glaver [*obs. or dial.*], coax; fawn,—upon; humor, gloze [*now rare*], soothe, pet, coquet, slaver, butter [*colloq.*], jolly [*slang or colloq.*]; bespatter, beslubber, beplaster, beslaver; lay it on thick, overpraise; cog [*obs.*], collogue [*obs. in this sense*]; truckle to, pander *or* pandar to, pay court to; court; creep into the good graces of, curry favor with, hang on the sleeve of; fool to the top of one's bent; lick the dust; lay the flattering unction to one's soul, gild the pill, make things pleasant.—C. O. Sylvester Mawson, ed., *Roget's International Thesaurus of English Words and Phrases,* p. 415

8. Make a list of synonymous terms for each of the following words and indicate in what kind of context each might be used.

automobile	friend	policeman	teacher
food	money	student	work

9. Correct mistakes in the meaning of words in these student sentences. Are the mistakes due to spelling or to confusion in meaning?

1. The scientist has to wage numerous battles to achieve success. These battles may be external or internal: internally he has to bicker with his cohorts who are reluctant to accept his theories; externally, he has to withstand the public pressure for practical results.
2. Because all mental patients need some nursing care during the day, other than that which the untrained workers can give, the present small nursing staffs are trying to do an almost inhuman task.
3. I believe that a brief summary of the primitive years of algebra would be a great help to any student at the beginning of his first math course.
4. If you are regurgitated at the sight of blood, you should not enter the medical profession.
5. The people entering the United States are forced to clan together in their own respective circles of society and settlements.

10. Comment on the meaning and wording of each of these sentences. Do any strike you as ambiguous or misleading?

1. In colleges and universities where football has been de-emphasized, undergraduates have no physical outlet for their imagination and their emotions—as well as for their muscle cells—and turn their activities toward social theories that are a complete antithesis to the principles of free enterprise and opportunity which made us the nation we are today.
2. After the shirt was on you hitched it to the top button of your drawers by an appendage, known as a "tab," at the south end of the bosom.
3. Some people oppose capital punishment on the basis that it is difficult to correct if the victim is found to be innocent after his sentence is served.
4. Canada is not suffering from a shortage of automobiles but rather from a gap between a good supply and an abnormal demand.

11. In your reading look for a passage illustrating irresponsible use of words. When you have found a good example, copy it and prepare to discuss in class the individual words in the passage.

Qualities of words

I think we shall have to say that a word is used accurately (1) when its literal meaning does in fact embrace the objects to which the word is applied, and (2) when its emotional character corresponds to the feelings which those same objects, viewed without prejudice, would generally excite.—Barrows Dunham

I have been leading up—or down, if you like— to an extremely simple and obvious but fundamental remark: that no word can be judged as to whether it is good or bad, correct or incorrect, beautiful or ugly, or anything else that matters to a writer, in isolation.—I. A. Richards

SUGGESTIONS FOR USING THE CHAPTER: *Chapter 12 is not directly dependent on Chapter 11. Section 1, "Words that weaken," which treats some elementary matters, and perhaps Section 2, "Abstract and concrete words," might be taken early in a course. Sections 3 to 5 could appropriately wait until later and be used as a basis for some work on style, to be carried out by observation of various styles in outside reading as well as in the students' papers.*

BESIDES THEIR FUNDAMENTAL work in carrying our meaning, words have qualities that add to or detract from the appeal made by speech or writing, that increase or diminish its readability or its listenability. From the point of view of meaning, these qualities are part of the words' connotation; from the point of view of impression (or artistry), they are a part of style. For this chapter at least Jonathan Swift's statement holds: "Proper Words in proper Places, makes the true Definition of a Style."

"Proper words in proper places" carries us back to the principles of appropriateness developed in our chapter on Good English, appropriateness to the subject, to the reader or listener, and to the writer or speaker. These principles apply to all phases of our use of language but are easiest to demonstrate in a discussion of words. Obviously the words spring primarily from the subject and must fit it. Discussing a machine, we have to name its parts, describe its functions, and so on, either in technical or popular terms; discussing baseball, we naturally have to talk about *bases* and *bats* and *pitchers* and *shortstops;* discussing the influence of newspapers, we would likely mention *editorials* and *headlines* and *leads* and *propaganda* and *Associated Press* and *paid advertising*, and our tone would probably be serious. But there are always a number of words not specifically demanded by the subject, that one writer might use and another not. In these some balance is to be struck between the reader's expectation and the writer's usual habits of expression. This chapter is concerned with some of the problems of this balance, considering first some hindrances to a clear meeting between the writer and the

---

reader in their attempt at communication and then some of the traits of words that can add not only to a reader's understanding but to his pleasure.

1. Words that weaken

Most ideas are not particularly complicated or difficult. Such ideas ought to be presented so that they make a direct appeal to the readers for whom they are intended. But the style in which they are expressed may be something of a handicap and may even make the reading more tiring than is necessary. In Chapter 10 we discussed *deadwood*, expressions that added nothing to the meaning of a statement. Here we look at three sorts of words that may convey meaning but that kill the interest of a reader, at least of one with wide enough experience to have any genuine taste or judgment. These are *trite words*, *euphemisms*, and *big words*.

1a. Trite words. A *trite expression* (or a *cliché* or a *hackneyed word*) is a phrase that is overused.[1] It is obvious that certain necessary functional words—*a*, *the*, the prepositions, the conjunctions—do not wear out. More important, the actual names of things and acts and qualities do not wear out; and formulas like *How do you do* and *Yours truly* may be used over and over without attracting any real attention at all. Expressions that deserve to be called trite are not direct, natural expressions. We can call for *bread* as often as we need to—but *staff of life* is quite a different matter, linguistically. It

---

[1] See Eric Partridge, *A Dictionary of the Cliché* (London, 1940).

is a figure of speech, once bright and perhaps even startling, now threadbare and hardly serving even a weak attempt at humor.

We should not be too severe about triteness in ordinary conversation. The common expressions, even if they are figurative, have their place. (Havelock Ellis says "You cannot avoid using *clichés*, not even in the very act of condemning them.") But when they become a conspicuous trait of a person's writing, he had better watch out. Many trite expressions are a symptom that the writer is in a rut or that he isn't taking care or showing interest in the actual writing. A reader will sense this—and a writer should sense it first and prevent it. "There is nothing improper in such phrases from the point of view of correctness," says Professor Krapp, "but from the point of view of style they are worse than incorrect—they are evidence of an effort and a failure to attain animation and originality in expression . . . the wordy expression makes no special bid for attention, whereas the trite expression is supposedly ingenious and worthy of note."[1]

Most trite expressions will be found to be outworn figures of speech, frayed quotations, attempts at a gentility that is not appropriate to the idea, or phrases that somehow are found intact more often than is pleasing, especially journalistic combinations of adjectives and nouns.

1) WORN OUT FIGURES OF SPEECH:

Father Time	tide of battle	flowing with milk
history tells us	irony of fate	and honey
darkness overtook us	commune with nature	trees like sentinels
better half [wife]	crack of dawn	run like a flash
Mother Nature	bolt from the blue	a watery grave

Make your own list. A good deal of slang that is wearing out also belongs in this category.

Especially in expressions of sentiment and emotion we would do better to remain literal than to fall back on these ancient figures: "An icy chill seized him at the pit of his stomach. What could he do? He was caught like a rat in a trap." How did he really *feel?*

2) FRAYED QUOTATIONS. Shakespeare has so many magnificently quotable lines that a writer who confines himself to the most used (All the world's a stage—Uneasy lies the head—To be or not to be—Not wisely but too well) makes his readers guess that he has never actually read Shakespeare or he could make fresher choices. The Bible

---

[1] *A Comprehensive Guide to Good English,* p. xvi.

is similarly sinned against, though so many of its phrases have passed into the common language that it is not always fair to label them trite.

If you want to illustrate a point by quotation, it is safest to take one from your own reading rather than to rely on these stock expressions.

3) EUPHEMISMS. Many readers now are particularly sensitive to verbal attempts to bring our rather stern and rowdy existence in line with "the finer things of life": *honest toil—marts of trade—keep body and soul together—gentle reader.* (See page 337.)

4) ORTHODOX EPITHETS. Some adjectives are found too often before the same nouns; some adverbs become linked to particular verbs. This is particularly a trait of what is called *journalese*, where phrases seem to become traditional and later to lose touch with actual observation.

This sort of triteness (and other sorts as well) Frank Sullivan recorded in his "Cliché Expert" series in *The New Yorker*. In this extract the Cliché Expert, Magnus Arbuthnot, is discussing his calling:

Q—Mr. Arbuthnot, you are an expert in the use of the cliché, are you not?
A—Yes, sir, I am a certified public cliché expert.
Q—In that case would you be good enough to answer a few questions on the use and application of the cliché in ordinary speech and writing?
A—I should be only too glad to do so.
Q—Thank you. Now, just for the record—you live in New York?
A—I like to visit New York but I wouldn't live here if you gave me the place.
Q—Then where do you live?
A—Any old place I hang my hat is home sweet home to me.
Q—What is your age?
A—I am fat, fair, and forty.
Q—And your occupation?
A—Well, after burning the midnight oil at an institution of higher learning, I was for a time a tiller of the soil. Then I went down to the sea in ships for a while, and later, at various times, I have been a guardian of the law, a gentleman of the Fourth Estate, a poet at heart, a bon vivant and raconteur, a prominent clubman and man about town, an eminent—
Q—Just what is your occupation at the moment, Mr. Arbuthnot?
A—At the moment I am an unidentified man of about forty, shabbily clad.
Q—Now then, Mr. Arbuthnot, what kind of existence do you, as a cliché expert, lead?
A—A precarious existence.
Q—And what do you do to a precarious existence?
A—I eke it out.
Q—How do you cliché experts reveal yourselves, Mr. Arbuthnot?
A—In our true colors, of course.
Q—Now, Mr. Arbuthnot, when you are naked, you are . . .
A—Stark naked.
Q—In what kind of daylight?

A—Broad daylight.

Q—What kind of outsider are you?

A—I'm a rank outsider.

Q—You are as sober as . . .

A—A judge.

Q—And when you are drunk?

A—I have lots of leeway there. I can be as drunk as a coot, or a lord, or an owl, or a fool—

Q—Very good, Mr. Arbuthnot. Now, how brown are you?

A—As brown as a berry.

Q—Ever see a brown berry?

A—Oh, no. Were I to see a brown berry, I should be frightened.

Q—To what extent?

A—Out of my wits.

Q—How about the fate of Europe?

A—It is hanging in the balance, of course.

Q—What happens to landscapes?

A—Landscapes are dotted.

Q—How are you attired in the evening?

A—Faultlessly.

Q—What goes with "pure"?

A—Simple.

Q—What are ranks?

A—Ranks are serried. Structures are imposing. Spectacles are colorful.

Q—Thank you, Mr. Arbuthnot. What kinds of beauties do you like?

A—Raving beauties.

Q—How generous are you?

A—I am generous to a fault.

Q—How is corruption these days?

A—Oh, rife, as usual.

Q—How do you point?

A—I point with pride, I view with alarm, and I yield to no man.

Q—What do you pursue?

A—The even tenor of my way.

Q—Ever pursue the odd tenor of your way?

A—Oh, no. I would lose my standing as a cliché expert if I did that.

Q—As for information, you . . .

A—A mine of information.

Q—What kind of mine?

A—A veritable mine.

Q—What kind of cunning do you affect, Mr. Arbuthnot?

A—Low, animal cunning.

Q—And when you are taken, you are taken . . .

A—Aback.

Q—I see. Well, Mr. Arbuthnot, I think that about covers the ground for the time being. I'm sure we're all very grateful to you for your coöperation and your splendid answers, and I think that everyone who has listened to you today will be a better cliché-user for having heard you. Thank you, very, very much.

A—Thank *you*, Mr. Steurer. It's been a pleasure, I assure you, and I was only too glad to oblige.

—FRANK SULLIVAN, "The Cliché Expert Takes the Stand,"
abridged from *The New Yorker*, Aug. 31, 1935

We should not of course slow up our first writing by stopping to find original phrases, but we should be sensitive enough to triteness to remove it from our copy in revision. The remedy is nearly always the same: look squarely at what we are talking about and present it simply and as exactly as possible.

1b. Euphemisms. A *euphemism* is a pale or comfortable word or phrase used instead of the more common or abrupt name for some discomfort or suffering, or for something presumed to be offensive to delicate ears. The substituted expression may be more vague, less harsh in sound or connotation, than the more exact and literal term it displaces; it is often abstract, semilearned, or a Latin derivative instead of the native English word.[1]

The most excusable euphemisms are those intended to soften the misfortunes of life. Though they remind us of the taboos of primitive languages, at their best they are a sign of fundamental kindness: *pass on* or *pass away* for *die, laid to rest* for *buried.* In intimate human relationships, in letters and in conversation with bereaved people, these are a sign of human sympathy; but their use in impersonal situations, in journalism or literature, makes for weakness. *The Style Book* of *The Detroit News* tells its writers (p. 75): "In writing of vital statistics—death, birth, marriage—be content to state the facts without unnecessary embellishment. Forget about the stork, the grim reaper, Hymen and Cupid."

The largest group of euphemisms has a somewhat moral rather than an emotional origin, for it consists of substitutes for many short abrupt words, the vigorous monosyllabic names of certain physical functions and social unpleasantness. One of the aspects of "Victorianism," as it is generally understood, was this rather remote vocabulary. For years *sweat* was taboo among "the upper classes" as both verb and noun, and was replaced by *perspire* and *perspiration. Spit* became *expectorate; drunk* was *intoxicated,* and even *drink* (the verb) tended to become *imbibe* in all uses. *Story* took the place of *lie,* or in various dialects it was *whopper, fib, misrepresentation.* Both *stink* and *smell* gave way to *odor, belly* to *abdomen,* and so on.

One of the conspicuous traits of modern style has been to discard these euphemisms and return to the short and ugly (to some

---

[1] J. M. Steadman, Jr., "Affected and Effeminate Words," *American Speech,* 1938, 13: 13-18, gives a number of such words from students' lists. See also Edwin R. Hunter and Bernice E. Gaines, "Verbal Taboo in a College Community," *American Speech,* 1938, 13: 97-107.

people) words of the common language. Some realistic novelists seemed motivated as much by naughtiness and a desire to shock as by artistic accuracy, but they have now won almost complete freedom, for themselves and for others. A number of euphemisms survive only in a playful dialect—*avoirdupois* and *embonpoint* for *weight* or *stoutness*, *limbs* for *legs*, though the humor is usually more intended than successful.

Euphemisms show one side of the relation between language and social attitudes. They represent timidity sometimes but more often a conscious seeking for "respectability." People who would never say *damn* could say *P. D. Q.* without qualms. At a more serious level newspaper euphemisms like *companionate marriage, love child, social diseases* allowed virtuous people to talk about matters they would never have mentioned by their more common names. The recent recognition of the seriousness of venereal diseases, for example, has led to consistent campaigning by doctors for more direct discussion, so that most papers have taken *syphilis* from their blacklists.

At present there is a conspicuous group of euphemisms found in the treatment of social situations, especially by conservative writers. *Workers* become *our industrial army*. The *aged* or *old people* are *senior citizens*. What in 1893 was known as *hard times* is now called a *depression* and a slighter falling off of business a *recession*. Those *out of work* or *jobless* are the *unemployed*, perhaps the victims of *technological unemployment* (an accurate but distant noun); and the *poor* are the *underprivileged*. We cannot always avoid using these words, but it is necessary for a writer to keep clearly in mind the specific unhappiness and suffering they name.

A third group of euphemisms has developed in "the business world": *funeral director* for *undertaker, tonsorial artist* (now humorous) for *barber, reconditioned* for *second-hand, public relations counsel* for *press agent, laundress* for *washerwoman, paying guest* for *lodger* or *boarder*—and we are even *guests* on the more luxurious trains. Specific industries have two dialects of their own, their necessary technical vocabulary and a euphemistic one for the customers (or "clients"). *The New Yorker* told the story of a young man just taken on to receive complaints in a firm that dealt in oil burners. His first day he noted down a customer's complaint that his burner had exploded. " 'Young man,' said his superior, breathing fire, 'you won't get very far in this business until you learn that we do *not* have explosions. We have puffbacks.' "

Except for these journalistic and commercial terms, and some taboos of the radio and television networks, the movies, and newspapers, the temper of the times is now against euphemisms in writing; and unless circumstances actually demand a substitute for the ordinary names of things and situations, a writer should call a spade a spade—simply of course and without unnecessary emphasis. Fowler's advice is right: "Euphemism is more demoralizing than coarseness."

1c. Big words. We are using the term *big words* to cover several common faults of writing that come from an unhappy use of words. The words may not be long or uncommon (*deem, doff, dwell* are big words in the sense of this article), but they are big in that they are *too heavy for their place*.[1]

There is little objection to long words when they are called for by the subject and are appropriate to the reader and come naturally to the writer. Long words are the only and necessary names for many ideas and for many things, and they must be used in much technical, scientific, and professional writing—though they may be overused even in the writing of specialists. *Sphygmograph, schizophrenia, Pleistocene* all have their place, though it is a restricted place. (If one of these words becomes needed in ordinary speech, a shorter form or a substitute usually arises, as *TNT* did for *trinitrotoluene*.) Some longer words may be needed, especially in formal writing, for rhythm or connotation: *immemorial, multifarious, provocative, infinitesimal, anticipation*.

Here we are looking at big words that do not fit, that are too heavy or too pretentious for the subject or for the writer. They are often written thoughtlessly or to show off, but they are often written also in a serious attempt to "improve" one's expression. The writer fails to realize that he will improve his writing by more exact and more suggestive words rather than by translating his thought from the ordinary words in which it naturally occurs into more pretentious ones. As Fowler puts it in his article on "Long variants": " 'The better the writer, the shorter his words' would be a statement needing many exceptions for individual persons & particular subjects; but for all that it would, & especially about English writers, be broadly true. Those who run to long words are mainly the unskilful & tasteless; they confuse pomposity with dignity, flaccidity with ease & bulk with force."

[1] See Rudolph Flesch, *The Art of Readable Writing* (New York, 1949), Chapters 12-16.

Gelett Burgess has written an eight-page plea for the use of short words entirely in words of one syllable. He begins:

> This is a plea for the use of more short words in our talk and in what we write. Through the lack of them our speech is apt to grow stale and weak, and, it may be, hold more sham than true thought. For long words at times tend to hide or blur what one says.
>
> What I mean is this: If we use long words too much, we are apt to talk in ruts and use the same old, worn ways of speech. This tends to make what we say dull, with no force or sting. But if we use short words, we have to say real things, things we know; and say them in a fresh way. We find it hard to hint or dodge or hide or half say things.
>
> For short words are bold. They say just what they mean. They do not leave you in doubt. They are clear and sharp, like signs cut in a rock.—GELETT BURGESS, *Short Words Are Words of Might*, Chap Book No. 2 of the College English Association

It is natural for a person to feel that his own speech is not good enough to use in public appearances and in writing. It is true that our day to day language is not good enough—but the remedy lies in improving and extending its best features, not in assuming an unnatural language. The goal of much English teaching has been the development of a formal style, and conscientious students have dutifully translated their material into such passages as this, in which a girl introduces us to a fat man oiling a lawn mower at some historic shrine that she does not bother to name or place:

> As we approached one of the beautiful historic buildings of western New York as yet unscarred by time's relentless talons and having about it an intangible aura of antiquity, we observed a man of over ample proportions kneeling beside a lawn mower to lubricate its creaking wheels. The act lent a jarring and anachronistic note to the peaceful scene.

This sins against Good English on three counts: first, the material is a simple picture which is obscured by such phrases as *time's relentless talons, intangible aura of antiquity, a jarring and anachronistic note*—not to mention the man *of over ample proportions lubricating the lawn-mower.* Second, the writer did not visualize her readers. Ordinary people are bored by such formality and the intelligentsia is not fooled by the affectation. Third, and most important, it is not appropriate to the writer, an alert and intelligent girl—who shortly after began to write more naturally.

Big words are a special curse today in much government writing ("gobbledygook"), in the more pretentious journalism, and in some academic writing, especially, it seems, in the social studies. Try turning into your own words the following (quite true) statement:

Out of the interstimulation of conversation there emerges an interweaving of understanding and purpose leading to co-individual behavior. Of course the conversation may be divisive, as well as integrating. But even these divisions may be regarded as mere differentiations within the general synthesis of human behavior. Thus in conversation is found that mutual understanding and common purpose essential to effective and continuous cooperation.

A continued use of big words not only alienates a reader; it may let a professional writer or a student write without feeling or even without really knowing what he is saying. Some of the commonest big words that occur in student writing are:

advent	domicile	peruse
behold	dwell	reside
congregate	metropolis	stated (for said)
deem	nuptials	termed
doff, don	participate	transpire

The remedy for this type of big words is simple: Read aloud to yourself what you have written and if you find it conspicuously different from the way you would *tell* the same thing to a friend, consider the words carefully and see if you can't use the simpler, informal words that are natural to you—let no others stand in your copy except for very good reason.

2. Abstract and concrete words

The names of persons, animals, objects, materials, places—in general, "things" that can be seen and touched—are concrete: *banker, payee, oak, delphinium, police dog, chromium, water, island.* The names of qualities, conditions, actions, summaries of particular facts, and so on are abstract: *goodness, honesty, pep, oomph, fear, height, culture, beauty, infancy, sophistication, system, singing.*

It is easy to identify such clear cut examples, but there are many words which are abstract or concrete according to their use: *youth— a youth; force—forces* (soldiers); *painting—a painting; sprinkling— a sprinkling* (as of pepper). A number of words cannot be classified either as abstract or as concrete outside of their context: *music, war, word.* The names of actions—*racing, stalking, striding*—are grammatically abstract but since they suggest a picture they may seem as vivid as concrete words; but in general, abstract words do not suggest a picture and are less colorful than concrete. This is especially true of divided and borderline words: *youth* is not so clear cut as *boy, young man, student;* *forces* are not so easily visualized as *army, soldiers,* or *troops.*

2a. Abuses of abstract words. Abstract words are for *ideas,* for opinions, generalizations, summaries of experience. One of the less happy traits of much current writing is the use of abstract words where words that suggest a picture would fit better. A movie company, going about the very practical business of getting people to come to a picture, composes a paragraph without a single concrete word in it except, perhaps, *audiences:*

> We confess to a belief that this is a significant and inspiring event in the history of the American cinema—an extraordinary adventure in entertainment. And therefore we prefer that the first audiences be the dominant cultural group in the community.

This use of abstract words is closely related to the use of scientific and pseudo-scientific words instead of more common ones. Students in the upper college classes, after courses in physics, biology, economics, sociology, education, and so on, sometimes have to struggle to write their native language. Customs have become *mores,* jails and prisons *penal institutions,* various twists of personality are *complexes,* opinions are often *reactions.* These are useful words, and people with literary educations are likely to be unduly suspicious of them; but since they lack suggestion they are best left to their respective fields of study if there are common words for the same ideas.

Using such technical terms and imitations of technical terms is one of the principal temptations of thoughtful and well-educated writers. For this fault Malcolm Cowley criticizes Lewis Mumford in a review of Mumford's *The Culture of Cities:*

> Mumford is entirely too fond of fancy words with Greek or Latin roots. Sordor, geotect, resorption, sessile, vermicular, encystment, plexus, nexus, locus, polynucleated, perduring, depauperated: the effect of words like these is to distract attention from the subject under discussion and to center it on the style. Mumford hates a heavily ornamented facade in architecture; why does he tolerate it in his own prose? But there is more involved than a mere question of ornament. Savages believe in the magical properties of words; they think that enemies can be slain and cattle and wives made fruitful by finding the proper incantations. There is a vestige of this belief in every writer, I suppose, but in Mumford there is more than a vestige. When he dislikes some feature of our civilization—for example, trailer camps—he slays it with epithets hurled like thunderbolts. "Mechanical escapism, as embodied in the trailer and the trailer camp, is one of those ludicrous examples of ideological miscegenation of which the modern world is full: the neurotic offspring of romanticism and mechanics, . . ." But people will go on riding in trailers for all of Mumford. Ideological mis-

cegenation is often good fun.—MALCOLM COWLEY, *The New Republic*
April 20, 1938

The fact that people with ideas often have an aloof style partly ex
plains why ideas do not spread more rapidly. Ideas exist only in
words and if the words are foreign to large numbers of people, those
people can't grasp the ideas, can't "think." Some of the blame lies
with writers who make thinking unnecessarily hard. H. T. Webster,
whose cartoons show that he knows the language people use, sums
this fact up:

> And I doubt if we'll ever get far with currency stabilization or other
> international economic adjustments until economists begin abandoning the
> argot of celestial mechanics.
> The trouble with the Better Minds is that They Don't Speak Our Lan-
> guage.—*The Forum*, Dec. 1933

2b. Appropriate use. The point for writing is that specific
facts, narratives of experience, and applications of ideas to particular
situations should be written in concrete terms; general ideas, summaries of experience, and opinions of all sorts need abstract words—
but even they will reach a wider audience and be more emphatic if
they can be expressed in concrete terms. Often a writer makes his
point in both abstract and concrete terms, gaining in emphasis from
the repetition and appealing to different readers through the different qualities of the two sorts of words.

In the following abstract paragraph there are hardly half a dozen
concrete words: *capitalists, coffee crops, cornerstone* (used figuratively),
consumers, Alice in Wonderland, doctors. The abstractions here are
good English, suited to the author (a professor of philosophy), to
the audience and readers (originally the selection was a lecture in a
college series, and was later published as a book for people interested
in general ideas), and to the subject (an opinion about a whole
social system).

> For quite apart from the questionable morality of the profit system or
> the moot question whether a society without some form of the profit motive
> could become a permanent development, there remains a less debatable
> consideration. The capitalistic economy has as the cornerstone of its logic
> not the profit motive but the profit system. If the capitalist economy does
> not work even in the way of steadily producing profits for capitalists, it
> would seem urgently to call for revision. Even the layman is by this time
> familiar, often through bitter personal experience, with the gruesome tale
> of economic collapse, collapse that recurs in cycles and seems fated at each
> cyclic recurrence to become more serious. Capitalism depends on expand-
> ing markets, which in the nineteenth century were findable, as were raw

materials, in hitherto industrially unexploited regions of the world. A more efficient technology demands more buyers for its products. The pyramided concentration of wealth, the saturation of markets, the inability of consumers to buy, the surpluses which must be sold at panic prices or destroyed—one recalls the destruction of bumper coffee crops in Brazil—the consequent unemployment, the increase in technological unemployment with the development of new machinery; these are all symptoms of a permanent disease of our present economy, a disease which 1929 simply made painfully dramatic, as the World War had made clear the consequence of rivalry for markets and raw materials. A system that repeatedly fails to provide profits for the entrepreneurs, and with its cycles of unemployment and its increasing burden of apparently permanently unemployed fails to insure minimum decency of life or security for the employed—only Alice in Wonderland could quite approve the logic of such an arrangement; only a loose user of words could call it a system or a success. No wonder that doctors and witch-doctors have been called in to cure it! No wonder that the uneasy rich and the impatient poor look hungrily for a Messiah!—IRWIN EDMAN, *Four Ways of Philosophy*, pp. 135-36

The nouns in the following paragraph are almost all concrete. They show a more popular—and here a more intense—criticism of one phase of the same industrial system.

Indeed there is much to be said on both sides. Watching a tractor save the labor of fifty men; a steam shovel dispensing with picks and shovels and aching backs; a pulmotor bringing a dead man back to life; a silver airplane against a blue sky—one can only rejoice in the utility and the beauty which the machine has brought. But when one realizes that a fleet of not over five hundred of those silvery beauties, each with a bomb suspended beneath it, is readily capable of utterly destroying a civilization, such as that of England, in something like two hours' time; when one views the dour and besotted ugliness of the Pittsburgh industrial district; when one reads of little girls scalped by machinery while working on the night shift in Chinese cotton mills—the hymn of thanksgiving somehow sticks in one's throat.—STUART CHASE, "The Good and Evil of the New Industrialism," *Current History*, July 1929

Concrete words seem to be closer to the writer's thoughts and feelings, they are easier for a reader to grasp, and they control the reader's thoughts more exactly than general terms can. College students must read a good deal of abstract writing in their courses, but they should remember that their own writing is often of specific, intimate matters and should be as concrete in style as their subjects allow.

3. Figurative use of words

Although we may not be aware of it, we use words figuratively in our conversation all the time, and practically all writing, except perhaps works of reference and purely scientific or scholarly papers, makes some use of figurative language. It is one way to make our meaning more exact, more complete, more interesting, or more intense. The reason for discussing figures is not to be able to name them but to become aware of resources of our language that we sometimes do not make full use of in our writing.

3a. Use of figures. Words have their usual, fairly exact, literal meanings, but they can also be used figuratively.[1] A *table* may be not only a piece of furniture, but the food that is served. A fraternity is a *house*. *Head* has its original, literal meaning as a part of the body but is applied to the highest or foremost or principal part of a wide variety of things—of a screw, nail, pin, army, the force of a stream of water, bay, news story, stalk of grain, hammer, bed, golf club, beer, boil, barrel—not to mention parts of a number of machines and the leaders of all sorts of institutions and governments and movements. Ordinary speech is full of these figures: we *play ball* when we work with others; we may *chime in* by adding our voice to others'. Figures are the basis of much slang—a person may be (like) a *peach*, a *prune*, a *wet blanket*, a *good egg*, a *five minute egg*, a *mole*.

A figurative use may in time become a new "sense" of a word, as *head* of a pin or nail has—there is no other word for it and it is listed as one of the regular meanings of *head* in dictionaries. These are no longer real figures but ex- or dead figures. For style we are concerned with those that still suggest a more or less fresh borrowing of a term from a different field.

Since figures of speech are likely to be a little conspicuous, they need to be used with care, so that they make a genuine contribution to understanding or to the appeal of the passage. It is better to do the best possible with literal words unless a happy and accurate figure comes to mind. These qualities need to be considered:

1) NATURALNESS. Figures should seem to come naturally from the way the writer sees his subject, to be the sort that he might use in his conversation. They should not be tacked on or used just to be different or "to make an impression"—they should bring the reader closer to the writer's actual sense of his subject. There are many figures, especially comparisons (*tired as a dog, lap of luxury*), which are pretty threadbare, but which still work when we're not too

---

[1] See: S. I. Hayakawa, *Language in Action* (New York, 1941), Chapter 12; Rickert, Chapter 3; McKnight, Chapters 14-17. Fowler has articles on the individual figures of speech, as do other reference works on writing and on literature.

fussy about the effect we are making on our listener. But in writing we should be more careful. "Trees that stand like sentinels" is an example of the lazy, trite, and really useless figure. Trees of course do stand like sentinels sometimes—but it would not occur to most of us to say so if we hadn't heard the phrase before, and our repetition of it doesn't help our subject or do credit to our style. More conspicuous still are tags of literary figures (like *the arms of Morpheus* and *Mother Nature*) which wore themselves out long ago—so long ago that they can hardly be used any more even in fun. Either stock or forced figures keep us from seeing the picture clearly and tend to make a reader doubt a writer's sincerity. Some of the more pretentious and less scrupulous advertising loses its effect because of use of extreme figures: "A joy package of surprise ribboned with rainbow laughter," for instance, is an unhappy advertisement for a movie.

Struggling for freshness usually brings on either these trite figures or strained ones. The figures to use are the ones that come naturally to your mind when you are trying to give an exact account of the subject. They do not need to be unusual, but should fit in their context and sound as though you were actually thinking them.

The figures in this paragraph not only help illuminate Mr. Ferguson's point but sound as though they came naturally from his way of seeing things. Each of the italicized phrases could either be omitted or translated into literal words; but if you try it you will see the loss.

Before the newspapers got hold of it, the term "swing" in its best sense was a musician's *shortcut way* of saying that the music *had come alive*, that its phrases ran beautifully together *like foothills* and *filled the world*. There is no word for this transformation *from the passive to the active voice*—or little conscious appreciation of it either, for the more complex music becomes and the farther we get from its sources, the more dependent we are on "interpreters." Music has *two lives:* first the concept in somebody's *head and heart*, second the expression. In between it is *a mummy*, because for all its intricacies, notation can't do more than tell you *where to dig for the body*. It has a great passive beauty even on the flat page of the score, it is true, and any *ham* [borrowed here from its application to actors] symphony orchestra could hit a couple of clean chords from the "Egmont" overture and *bring your heart up to your shoulders*. But virtuosity becomes too greatly prized (the highest soprano, the fastest cadenza) and *pedestrianism* too easily tolerated in *a field where few can walk at all*. And so we have these versions that make you suspect Bach *shot thirty-second notes into the score with a machine gun*, and that music in general could be added up *like a column of figures*. One thing does not run into another; each note being written down and so fixed, *like a fly on a pin*, they play it that way with triumphant tenacity. Whereas music should always flow *as beautifully as words in the speaking voice*.—OTIS FERGUSON, "Benny and the Budapests," *The New Republic*, Oct. 5, 1938

2) Consistency. If a figure is continued through more than one phrase, sometimes it becomes "mixed"—becomes inconsistent in some way:

> As he passed to greater wealth and newer offices he closed the door forever upon the stepping stones by which he had risen.

The sophomore who wrote "My father is a limb in a chain of the business cycle" couldn't have been thinking either about his father or about his writing.

Mixed figures are often used intentionally as a sort of easy but sometimes effective humor—like those attributed to Samuel Goldwyn ("They're always biting the hand that lays the golden egg") or this from *Jurgen:*

> "Indeed, it is a sad thing, Sylvia, to be murdered by the hand which, so to speak, is sworn to keep an eye on your welfare, and which rightfully should serve you on its knees."—JAMES BRANCH CABELL, *Jurgen*, p. 124

As a rule a figure should not be carried very far, but occasionally, especially in interpretations, one may dominate several sentences or a paragraph, as the "breaking up of the Victorian ice" in this:

> To be young is always a difficult, dangerous and confusing business—but it can seldom have been so difficult, so dangerous, and above all so confusing, as in England during the first ten years of the twentieth century. Those years were witnessing the earlier stages of a change-over from one social order to another, a change which was completed by the War. The Victorian ice was beginning to break up, but a great deal of it was still fairly solid, especially away from the centre of the stream, along the banks and in the backwaters. Even there, however, the movements of the central currents were disturbingly felt. Cracks began to shoot through family life, and the firm Victorian faith in the inevitability of family affection; large chunks of the cruder forms of religious belief broke off and were carried away; ominous shivers ran through the sanctity of marriage, filial obedience, the complacent acceptance of social inequality, and other solid-seeming structures. Above all the moral conventions, those delicate tacit assumptions of what constitutes desirable behavior, on which each generation stands, were in motion—they shifted under your feet; pushed by some unseen force, they tilted sideways, and threatened to plunge you into unknown waters.—ANN BRIDGE, *Enchanter's Nightshade*, pp. 38-39

3) Appropriateness. Since figures are used to make the passage in some way more effective, they should be appropriate. They should be accurate enough to contribute to the meaning and they should be in tone with the subject and style. This is out of key:

> In learning more about him I found that he was just about the kindest man I have ever met. He had the heart of an elephant and the mind of a genius.

And these figures seem much too violent to suggest even voracious reading:

> He sank his teeth into the throat of the book, shook it fiercely until it was subdued, then lapped up its blood, devoured its flesh and crunched its bones. . . .

But the metaphors in this add interest and color to Mrs. Lindbergh's picture:

> But the next morning we were *giants again in seven-league boots.* The engine, *roaring* anew after a few hours' work in calm water, lifted us easily into the air. Once more the harbor *dwarfed to Japanese-garden proportions.* The trees became *moss;* the thatch-roofed house, *a child's toy.* And these tiny *doll-like figures* in a miniature boat, waving *match-stick* arms—who were they? Of course, the singing sailors.—ANNE MORROW LINDBERGH, *North to the Orient,* p. 173

3b. Sources and types of figures. Since figures are not just ornament but a means of conveying meaning, their form is not so important to consider as what they contribute to what is being said. On this basis the more common figures can be discussed in six groups.

1) RESEMBLANCE. The most common figures of speech are the various types of comparisons, and very common they are, in both speaking and writing. Conversation uses many metaphors and similes, old standbys such as *red as a rose, go like a shot, a cold shoulder, tower of strength;* the somewhat newer expressions from slang—*a wet blanket,* people *an inch deep,* get a *load* of this, *pulled his punches;* and fresher, special inventions that are more appropriate in writing. It is easy to borrow words from one field of thought or work and make them fit in another—like *fadeout, close-up,* from the movies; *asset, liability* from business, and so on.

Metaphors and similes are characteristic of all writing except routine exposition. They serve the purpose of all proper figures of speech, making the writing more exact, more concrete, more alive and interesting.

Metaphors and similes and analogies all make comparisons, but the three figures differ in form and in fullness. An analogy is usually a rather full comparison, showing or implying several points of similarity; as in the paragraph by Ann Bridge quoted on page 347. A simile makes a comparison exact, labels it by an introductory word, *like* or *as.* A metaphor is the shortest, most compact of these comparisons; in it the likeness is implied rather than stated explicitly. Typically the writer asserts that one thing *is* another (in some respect), or suggests that it acts like or has some of the qualities of something else, as in the examples below:

> But meaning is an arrow that reaches its mark when least encumbered with feathers.—HERBERT READ, *English Prose Style*, p. 16

> And up we had climbed until we were face to face with those giants, snow-streaked, and the bright fog sitting on their shoulders.—ANNE MORROW LINDBERGH, *North to the Orient*, p. 154 (A simile would be "those mountain peaks, *like giants* . . .")

> . . . the tracks of field mice were *stitched* across its [the snow's] surface in the morning.—JOSEPHINE JOHNSON, *Winter Orchard*, p. 307

> . . . for *the waves* cast by a *pebble of thought* spread until they reach even the nitwits on *the shores* of action.—IRWIN EDMAN, *Four Ways of Philosophy*, p. 100

> Two *well-upholstered* ladies leaving the Broadhurst Theatre. . .—*The New Yorker*, April 9, 1938

The difference between a metaphor and simile is merely one of phrasing: where the metaphor implies the likeness, a simile says specifically that one is like the other, using the words *like* or *as*. A literal statement of similarity is not a simile—"the Congress is like a state legislature" is plain statement of fact. A simile is a comparison in which two objects differ in most respects but still may be strikingly alike in some one respect that is important to the writer's immediate purpose:

> . . . woods *like Persian rugs* where Autumn was commencing.—WILBUR DANIEL STEELE, "Bubbles"

> He knows the unfortunate penchant of black bass of the same size for trying to swallow each other, *like competing labor unions*.—A. J. LIEBLING, *The New Yorker*, Feb. 5, 1938

> What seems to be lacking in the older prose is the sense of the uninterrupted flow of the mind: Bagehot, for example, appears to cut off this continuum, shall we call it, into arbitrary lengths, *as we slice chunks off a cucumber.* —BONAMY DOBRÉE, *Modern Prose Style*, p. 225

> And yet if the new generation were fed exclusively upon the best of scientific writing it is doubtful whether they would be conditioned against war. For such great impulses as the dangerous, competitive life are, of course, emotional and spring from ancestral regions into which the logic of facts penetrates *like a bullet which shoots through the trunk of a tree leaving only a hole which the living tissues quickly close.*—H. S. CANBY, "War or Peace in Literature," *Designed for Reading*, p. 89

An analogy compares one idea or situation with another, ordinarily noting several points of similarity instead of just one as in metaphor and simile. Suggestive analogies often bring home or emphasize an idea:

> By what process of reasoning can a man who is quite conversant with the separate meanings of *put*, of *up*, and of *with* ever infer that *to put up with* means *to endure?* We might as reasonably expect the person who has discovered the several properties of carbon, hydrogen, and oxygen to infer from them the amazing properties of alcohol. In neither case do the elements afford a clue to the nature of the compound.—P. B. BALLARD, *Thought and Language*, p. 168

> Most firearms carry a little higher than they are aimed. But not the pen. With that, aim just above the target; and a little to the left.—CHRISTOPHER MORLEY, *The Saturday Review of Literature*, Sept. 24, 1938

2) RELATIONSHIP. Metonymy and synecdoche are two figures of speech which substitute for the exact name of something the name of something closely associated with it. Strictly, synecdoche gives the name of a part when the whole is meant (so many *mouths* to feed, a *sail* in the offing, plant employing sixty *hands*), or of a whole for a part (*Minnesota* won [the team won], the *army* adopts a policy). But synecdoche is now generally regarded as a type of metonymy, the use of one word for another that it suggests:

> The material for the object made of it: *rubber* for footgear made of rubber, or for automobile tires; *glass* for tableware or a window.
> The maker or source for the thing made: *Shakespeare* for Shakespeare's plays; *England* meets *America* in the Davis Cup matches.
> Any name closely associated with the object: *in the red; capital* and *labor* for employers and workmen; men *in the upper brackets,* for wealthy men; a *dish* for something to eat; *White collar class;* "3 Miles of Boys March on Fifth Av."; play to the *grandstand*

Metonymy is not only a common figure of speech (common in both formal and colloquial usage) but it is one way in which the meanings of words change. Long use of *the crown* for *the king,* the *heart* for *courage* or for *sympathy* and similar use of hundreds of other words have given these words definite secondary meanings in dictionary definitions.

3) DEGREE OF STATEMENT. Exaggeration is a figure of speech (also called hyperbole) when it is not intended to deceive but to emphasize a statement or situation, to intensify its impression. Exaggeration may mean choosing a word of broader or more intense meaning than literal accuracy would call for (like *perfect* for *excellent,* or *mob* for *people, starved* for *hungry,* or *rout* for *retreat*), or it may be a more complex exaggeration of statement, as in the following passages:

But the feelings that Beethoven put into his music were the feelings of a god. There was something olympian in his snarls and rages, and there was a touch of hell-fire in his mirth.—H. L. MENCKEN, "Beethoven," *Prejudices: Fifth Series,* p. 89

These little self-contained flats were convenient; to be sure, she had no light and no air, but she could shut it up whenever she liked and go away.— JOHN GALSWORTHY, *The Man of Property,* p. 224

Exaggeration is one of the most common colloquial figures, crystallized in many phrases: "dead tired," "thrilled to pieces," "I'm all ears," "a thousand thanks." Such standard phrases pass off well enough in ordinary conversation but often seem trite on paper.

A too free use of superlatives or of intense adjectives is weakening and should be avoided:

Within the limits of Colorado, New Mexico, Arizona, and Southern California there are four centers of sublime and unparalleled scenic sublimity which stand alone and unrivalled in the world.

Exaggeration is a frequent source of humor, both literary and popular. A mass of American anecdotes and tall tales hinge on the figure—as in the yarn told of Kit Carson (and probably of others) that in the Valley of Echoes in Jackson County, Wyoming, it took eight hours for an echo to return, so that he would shout "It's time to get up" as he went to bed and the echo would wake him up in the morning. The Paul Bunyan stories make a cycle of popular exaggeration.

The figure is as much a part of more sophisticated humor and satire:

Englishwomen's shoes look as if they had been made by someone who had often heard shoes described, but had never seen any, and the problem of buying shoes in London is almost insoluble—unless you pay a staggering tariff on American ones. What provokes this outburst is that I have just bought a pair of English bedroom slippers and I not only cannot tell the left foot from the right, but it is only after profound deliberation that I am able to distinguish between the front and the back.—MARGARET HALSEY, *With Malice Toward Some,* pp. 99-100

Understatement is the opposite of exaggeration and often a form of irony. It may mean stating an idea in negative terms (litotes) or in less strong words than would be expected: "Dempsey was not a bad fighter."

And as he still came toward her, she darted at his legs and threw him. It had been years, thirty or more anyway, since Dr. Hopkins had been thrown off a raft and he had lost the knack. Being thrown off a raft is not an organized sport.—SALLY BENSON, *People Are Fascinating,* p. 71

Irony is implying something markedly different, sometimes even the opposite, from what is actually said. Light irony is a form of humor, severe irony is usually a form of sarcasm or satire—though exact definition in such matters is impossible and rarely fruitful.

> Life, you see, gradually approaches a sort of homely perfection, all the little inconveniences ironed out, only the large grotesqueries remaining unchanged from year to year—war, poverty, melancholia, and the lethal fumes from internal combustion.—*The New Yorker*, Aug. 14, 1937

> "We made two dollars," Merle told her, "off nineteen steers. The cattle business is very good. Next year we might try twenty and buy a big dish-mop in the fall."—JOSEPHINE JOHNSON, *Now in November*, p. 222

The broadest form of irony is an inversion of the intended meaning, as in the following passage from William Saroyan. Saroyan means exactly the reverse of the advice he seems on the surface to be giving about the use of unessential adjectives:

> But rules without a system are, as every good writer will tell you, utterly inadequate. You can leave out "utterly" and the sentence will mean the same thing, but it is always nicer to throw in an "utterly" whenever possible. All successful writers believe that one word by itself hasn't enough meaning and that it is best to emphasize the meaning of one word with the help of another. Some writers will go so far as to help an innocent word with as many as four and five other words, and at times they will kill an innocent word by charity and it will take years and years for some ignorant writer who doesn't know adjectives at all to resurrect the word that was killed by kindness.—WILLIAM SAROYAN, Preface to *The Daring Young Man on the Flying Trapeze*

4) ORDER AND POSITION. Words get an added quality from their position in relation to other words, as we have seen in the discussion of climax and anticlimax in Chapter 10, page 294. Frequently one of the results of a contrast is to emphasize the key words of the two matters contrasted; this is particularly true if the comparison is expressed in balanced sentences. The combination of incongruous or surprising details (as in Mark Twain's "Always tell the truth; it will please some people and astonish the rest") throws emphasis on the pivotal words. The qualities of the context in which words stand affect their meaning and the impression they give.

5) WORD PLAY. Writers have always used and formed words with a certain freedom—after all, writers are in part the creators and custodians of the language. *Clipped words (*natch, home ec, ex-pug*)* and *blends (like *Time*'s *cinemadolescent*) are likely to be familiar or light, but they show the same language processes as the liberties

taken by the makers of literature. Similarly puns (More trouble is made by in-laws than by outlaws; the hire learning in America) are a source of humor but are obvious and easy examples of the use of words that produces compression and double connotations of words. Occasionally a writer hits on a happy new form, as *luminence*, which is not in the dictionaries but may be a more fitting word in a story than either *luminousness* or *luminosity*, which are.

It is true that the success or failure of this freedom with words is a matter of judgment, of effectiveness and appropriateness. For the most part we use the words our culture provides for us. Straining for novelty, even in light writing, may be disappointing, but some freedom in the use of language is natural, and only its excesses are to be discouraged.

6) Sound. Emphasis may be given to words by their sound, and the tone of a statement may be influenced by the consonants and vowels, by alliteration, and by rhythm. Reading aloud what you have written is one of the principal ways of testing not only its pleasantness but also the exactness of the emphasis and meaning the words will have for a reader. A conscious or conspicuous use of sound is one of the factors of style and frequently influences the choice of words, though it is perhaps best regarded as a trait of sentences.

4. Allusion

Since no one can think of a subject in a mental vacuum, a writer who is trying to convey his sense of a subject will include some incidental matter—to add interest, to explain more clearly, to emphasize what he is saying. Some of this will be *allusions*, brief references to literature, to history, to things, to people and what they do. In part these allusions are added content, contributing to the development of the subject. But since they are voluntary additions of the writer, to a considerable extent their purpose is stylistic—a way of saying something that could have been put differently—and may properly be included as a phase of the choice of words.

4a. To literature, written and oral. Many people who write are widely read, and so interested in what they have read that allusion to it naturally appears in explanation of other matters. (They may use quotations, too, but we are talking of a less formal use of reading.) Speeches from two Shakespearean plays are referred to in the following passage:

> *There is nothing new in heaven or earth not dreamt of* [Hamlet] in our laboratories; and we should be amazed indeed if *tomorrow and tomorrow and tomorrow* [Macbeth] failed to offer us something new to challenge our capacity for readjustment.—CARL L. BECKER, *The Heavenly City of the Eighteenth Century Philosophers*, p. 23

William Beebe refers to a Poe story in describing the life-cycle of a tiny animal:

> Poe wrote a memorable tale of a prison cell which day by day grew smaller, and Opalina goes through much the same adventure.—*Jungle Days*, p. 22

Allusion to written literature is more characteristic of formal English than of informal, which is apt to borrow from proverbs, current phrases, advertising ("that good Gulf weather"), and the great stock of colloquial phrases ("more possibilities than a pig bank has pennies").

Homely, everyday phrases can be used to advantage in any informal discussion:

> The thing for the faculty of the University to do is to *take it easy.* Don't get excited. *Walk, don't run to the nearest exit* and *enjoy life in the open.* In a few months the sun will shine, *water will run down hill,* and *smoke will go up the chimneys* just the same.—WILLIAM ALLEN WHITE, *The Emporia Gazette*

And allusions to familiar formulas can be turned to fresh account, as it is here:

> All of Stratford, in fact, suggests powdered history—add hot water and stir and you have a delicious, nourishing Shakespeare.—MARGARET HALSEY, *With Malice Toward Some*, p. 65

4b. To history. We often allude to outstanding events in the past: to Waterloo, Gettysburg, the election of 1932, and to the lives and characters of important persons:

> The voice of duty speaks differently to Savonarola, to Cromwell, to Calvin, to Kant and to the contemporary communist or fascist.—IRWIN EDMAN, *Four Ways of Philosophy*, p. 292

Detailed historical reference is rather characteristic of formal writing; brief reference to better known events characterizes informal writing.

More characteristic of current writing is allusion to current events, persons in the public eye, immediate affairs. But one difficulty with such casual allusions is that time makes them hard to identify—a reason why Shakespeare's plays and other older literature need explanatory notes. This was written in 1921:

> Suppose a young man, just out of college and returned to his moderate-sized home town in Ohio (*why not Marion?*), honestly tries to make those contacts with the national culture which Mr. Sherman so vigorously urges him to make.—HAROLD STEARNS, *The Bookman*, March 1921

"Why not Marion?" is meaningless to young people today, and many of their elders will have forgotten that it was President Harding's home town, often referred to in 1921. But missing the allusion does not interfere with the point of the passage. As with other such references if a reader does recognize the allusion, he has an added pleasure. Such topical allusions are best for immediate consumption, and since most of us are not writing for the ages, they are quite fit. They help make a piece sound as though it was written in the present and as though its writer was awake to what was going on.

4c. To life. One of the most fertile kinds of allusion, and one that is open to everybody, is to the things that people do, the things around us, bits from our work, our sports, our hobbies. It was natural for Carlo Levi, an M.D., to write "The sky was a mixture of rose, green, and violet, the enchanting colors of malaria country" (*Christ Stopped at Eboli*, p. 63). The directness of modern style encourages such allusions to the life around us, as in this bit from a discussion of teachers' oaths:

> But, it is said, teachers have great influence on the young; and we must be sure that the young are under proper care. Very well. If we are to insure the patriotism of those who have influence over the young, let us do so. Let us begin with parents and have them take an oath to support the Constitution. Let us include newspaper men, and especially the designers of comic supplements. Let us line up all the movie stars. Let us insist on an oath of allegiance from radio performers. If the teachers are to be required to take an oath, Amos and Andy should be required to salute the flag and sing the "Star Spangled Banner" twice a day.—ROBERT MAYNARD HUTCHINS, *No Friendly Voice*, pp. 122-23

Besides their real function of adding something to the meaning, allusions also suggest the personality of the writer, even if he is posing, because the allusions that naturally occur to him come from his past experience and are brought to mind because they are interesting to *him*. One reason that many themes seem so depersonalized is that students often leave out these allusions—even take them out after they have naturally strayed into the first draft. We should expect that a student who likes to read Ernest Hemingway or *Li'l Abner* would occasionally refer to something he had read; or that one interested in dogs or sailing or jazz or classical music or the life of Napoleon would occasionally bring in a bit from one of these interests to point up another subject. If an allusion doesn't fit, it is easily taken out in revision; if it does fit, the paper will have just so much more meaning and life, and the words will have not only meaning but a greater depth of connotation.

5. Range and liveliness

The qualities of words that we have been discussing contribute not only to communicating information and ideas but also to the life and force of writing, in a word to its readability. Completely colorless and impersonal writing sometimes may be desirable and even necessary, as in scholarly papers, but it makes a less deep impression and must limit the readers to those already having a concern for the subject.

The following paragraph is quite accurate but quite colorless—and very few people could read through the fifteen-page pamphlet from which it comes.

> Our way of life is menaced today and we are concerned about its defense. The first step in the defense of democracy (as we realize more readily in times of crisis, though it was just as true in easier days of security) is to ensure an understanding and appreciation of its essential values and of the obligations it entails. So many young people have grown up thinking of the advantages of democracy in terms of their personal liberty to do what they like, and so devoid of any sense of the claims of democracy upon their service, that we are now able to see clearly how seriously our educational institutions have been failing to transmit our ideals and to play their part in developing the attitudes and loyalties on which our free society depends for its very survival.

One of the outstanding traits of modern writing is the range and vigor and suggestiveness of the words used. We do not need to go to works that make primarily a literary appeal to find this. Here are paragraphs from two recent factual discussions that show range and a generally lively style. One is from an article on intelligence tests, the other a survey of recent American painting. The writer's attention in each is firmly centered on his immediate subject, but he has not switched off the rest of his mind. He takes words and instances as he finds them, puts them to work, and conveys not only his ideas but a sense of life. An outstanding trait of each is the *range* of the vocabulary, from casual colloquial words to rather technical.

> Half the ability in this country goes down the drain because of the failure of intelligence tests to measure the real mental ability of the children from the lower socio-economic groups, and because of the failure of the schools to recognize and train this ability. This country cannot survive as the leading

world power unless we learn how to discover, recruit, and train more of the brains in the lower-income groups.—ALLISON DAVIS, "Poor People Have Brains, Too," *The Phi Delta Kappan*, April 1949, 30:294

Another irritant contributing to the drift of the American artist into his present state of forthright nationalism was his old grievance against the European portraitist, usually a third-rate member of the pretty-pretty school of eyelash affixers, who crosses the Atlantic to batten on portrait commissions from the culturally illiterate. These "artists" are merely commercial limners, skillful in surface flashiness and clever masters of the technique of publicity and social flattery. Americans who try to click heels with them usually end up on an elbow. The news and society reporters (not the art critics) give them yards of publicity with photographs dramatizing their records among European royalty. A visit to Washington would produce sittings from Congressmen, a member of the Cabinet or even the President—every American ruler since 1912, except F. D. R., patiently sat to some foreign painter, for "reasons of state." After a year among our dollar aristocrats, the "artist" would carry back across the Atlantic with him as much as $50,000—his departure attended by the futile curses of better but less suave American portraitists. It is a condition that obtains even today. American taste in the upper brackets being what it is, our lords and ladies of breeding and position like to feel that the same brush that painted Duchess Thisque or Countess Thatque can be hired by Mrs. Smith to outshine Mrs. Jones.—PEYTON BOSWELL, JR., *Modern American Painting*, p. 73

A college student, alive and thinking, can aim to express his ideas with similar life, and can draw on his total store of words as well as of ideas.

Suggested study and writing

1. The language in the following student theme is noticeably flat and lifeless. Read the theme carefully and make notes on specific words and phrases that contribute to this effect. Point out each vague, inexact, and trite expression that you find, and indicate how the theme might be revised for greater clarity, emphasis, and brevity.

Broadening for Survival

To know one's field well when stepping forth from an institution of higher learning is invaluable, but specialization that neglects the broader aspects of learning is not desirable. The studying of subjects in a given field cannot be pursued too long or too well, as the speed of modern-day living seems to shorten our lives. Any field is almost inexhaustible in its context for the ordinary span of human life. A person could spend all of his waking hours in search of the ultimate goal—complete knowledge—for the whole of his life, and yet die an unsatisfied seeker. This is common knowledge, and yet each and every one of us tries to crack the wall.

When a man, or a woman, as the case may be, matriculates from college in the school of engineering, for example, and knows his subject very well, his chances for survival in that field are fairly good, depending, of course, on the opportunities available. He may know engineering to the letter, but will he make a good engineer if he doesn't understand his fellow man?

In days gone by, a knowledge of only one field was sufficient, but in our complex modern society, all knowledge is related and if a person doesn't want to live a life of seclusion in a hermitage, he must know something about quite a few things.

This broadening of knowledge should infiltrate into all fields through sociology courses, philosophy courses, and even through the reading of books. Such authors as Emerson, Whitman, and others too numerous to mention, give one a way of life that, when bonded to the concrete knowledge of specialized courses, will give him a basis for a life that surpasses all in value. When man realizes that he must broaden his knowledge toward practical living, he will then create for future generations to come a far better world, for man does not live by bread alone.

2. Reread "Abstract and Concrete Words," page 341, then use each of the following words in a sentence, indicating whether you have used it as a concrete or an abstract word.

artistic	Friday	mercy	suspicion
centimeter	humor	Orientals	taffeta
factor	insult	poetic	triangle

3. Study the quality of the words in the following paragraphs, the first from "Macbeth" in *Tales from Shakespeare*, by Charles and Mary Lamb, the second a translation of this passage into "Basic English" by I. A. Richards and Christine Gibson. Which passage uses more abstract words? In which is the language more figurative? Point out by line number significant differences, omissions, and additions in the two passages.

1 Now was the middle of night, when over half the world nature seems
2 dead, and wicked dreams abuse men's minds asleep, and none but the wolf
3 and the murderer is abroad. This was the time when Lady Macbeth waked
4 to plot the murder of the king. She would not have undertaken a deed so
5 abhorrent to her sex, but that she feared her husband's nature, that it was
6 too full of the milk of human kindness, to do a contrived murder. She
7 knew him to be ambitious, but withal to be scrupulous, and not yet prepared
8 for that height of crime which commonly in the end accompanies inordinate
9 ambition. She had won him to consent to the murder, but she doubted his
10 resolution; and she feared that the natural tenderness of his disposition
11 (more humane than her own) would come between, and defeat the pur-
12 pose. So with her own hands armed with a dagger, she approached the
13 king's bed; having taken care to ply the grooms of his chamber so with
14 wine, that they slept intoxicated, and careless of their charge. There lay
15 Duncan in a sound sleep after the fatigues of his journey, and as she viewed
16 him earnestly, there was something in his face, as he slept, which resembled
17 her own father; and she had not the courage to proceed.

1 Now it was the middle of the night, when half the earth seems dead, and
2 men's minds are troubled in their sleep, and no one is about but the animals

₃of the woods and men with crimes to do. This was the time when Lady
₄Macbeth was designing the death of the King. She would not have under-
₅taken an act so shocking to a woman but for her fear that Macbeth had
₆not a hard enough heart to do such a crime. She was certain that he had
₇a great desire to become King, but he had a strong sense of what was
₈right, and was still not ready to do crimes on the scale which is generally
₉necessary in the end for those who have so strong a desire to be great. He
₁₀had been forced by her to give approval to the violent step, but she had
₁₁doubts about his decision of mind; and she had a fear that his naturally
₁₂kind heart (it was softer than hers) would come between, making the pur-
₁₃pose come to nothing. So with a knife in her hand she came near the
₁₄King's bed; having taken care to let the servants of his room have so much
₁₅wine that they were unconscious in sleep, without a thought for their watch.
₁₆There was Duncan, sleeping well after his long journey, and looking at him
₁₇with great attention, she saw that there was something in his face which was
₁₈like her father; and she was kept from the cruel act.—I. A. RICHARDS and
CHRISTINE GIBSON, *Learning Basic English*, p. 64

4. Collect a list of euphemisms from your reading. Ads and business pages in your newspaper make good sources. Carefully vague statements by leaders of business, labor, and government are also good. Be prepared to translate the euphemisms into matter of fact words.

5. Make a list of euphemistic expressions for the following terms and tell under what circumstances or in what contexts each euphemism might be found.

hairdresser	servant	theft
washwoman	stupid	false teeth
janitor	reform school	bad breath
saloon	insane asylum	wig
lie (noun)	poorhouse	

6. Turn back to the "Cliché Expert" (pages 335-336) and study Mr. Arbuthnot's answers. Think not of the words but of the actual object, condition, or action to which the words refer. Then consider the cliché in relation to it. Does it express what you really think? For example, *daylight*, not the word but the condition. Do you think of it as *broad*? *Farmer*, not the word, the man. Does *tiller of the soil* suggest him vividly? Be prepared to discuss ten or fifteen of the clichés in the passage and to suggest words or phrases which express with some accuracy what you actually think.

7. Study the use of figurative language in the following student sentences. Which figures are unsuccessful and why? Which seem best to you?

1. A warm breeze danced as I sat on a chartreuse carpet of middle-aged fir needles. I thought about how nice our camp was and suddenly I wasn't fed up to the teeth with it any more.

2. To rise up from the shadows of poverty and ignorance in which they have been wallowing for centuries, the Chinese will have to take some large steps.

3. To me a fireroom is a place full of enchantment and excitement. Its intricate fuel lines appear from the bilges like vines creeping up the face of the boiler, putting off branch shoots to each individual boiler assembly.

4. You'll soon see for yourself that entering into activities on the campus is like climbing down a pyramid; your opportunities will grow greater and greater.

5. The manner in which he took the bare facts of the city and wove them into interesting angles was very interesting.

6. The lake was gorgeous that night. An egg-yolk moon was beaming over the lime-jello and whipped cream waters that were spanked by a dancing breeze.

7. It had been snowing since early morning, a steady snow driven by a rigid, biting wind. The earth and sky were fused into a furious swirling mass of white. By late afternoon the streets were covered. Only the steaming man-holes remained untouched, sole survivors of the invasion. Windows lost their transparency and became fuzzy rectangles of light. Parked cars turned into pyramids of snow. Pedestrians plodded along at forty-five degree angles, fighting the wind. The tempo of the city came to a slow drawl.

8. Most of us in America are well on our own feet, able to buy and enjoy the things we need, but when a displaced person who is able to crawl under the iron curtain enters the United States, he doesn't know which way to turn and often falls into the wrong hands.

8. Discuss the following figurative expressions on the basis of their literal meaning and connotation, their effectiveness, and their currency in present-day speech or writing. Which of these expressions do you use? Which would you consider trite?

crocodile tears	yellow streak	play possum
crepehanger	dumbbell	chicken-hearted
bonehead	to wolf one's food	a bull market
road hog	greenhorn	doghouse
lion's share	busy as a bee	

9. Collect from your reading one or two examples each of good use of metaphor, simile, analogy, understatement, and exaggeration. Look for these examples in all kinds of reading matter, from classical literature to the sports page. Be prepared to discuss the reasons for your choice.

10. Read the following passages carefully and prepare to discuss in detail the characteristics of the language in each selection. Notice whether the words are predominantly abstract or concrete; note the connotation as well as the denotation of the words, the use of figures of speech, unfamiliar or technical words, and the general clarity and effectiveness of each passage.

1. Ever wish there was something interesting to do on a date besides ordering up a serving of Farley Granger and hamburgers and colas for two? Farley, of course, is fun—but how about doing something *different* for a change? Here are some ideas for "just us" dates, for you and your best boy only, suggestions that are high in fun, low in folding money, and just right for two who "like to do anything so long as it's together."

For instance, how about a Saturday-afternoon date at the art museum in your town? Whether you're a part-time Picasso or a "just looking, thanks" admirer of good art, you can spend a pleasant hour or two going through the galleries or looking at special exhibits. . . .

If you're a big-town gal, a trip to the planetarium, aquarium or science institute, with your own private Einstein in tow, can add up to a neat afternoon. And to kill two birds with one stone (try the aviary on the left, please), you might make a trip to the North Pole via the planetarium, check on giant snails in the aquarium and watch a demonstration of man-made lightning at the science institute—then turn the whole afternoon into a written report plus extra credit for science class at school. Makes wonderful reading in your diary too!—MAUREEN DALY, "Fun for Two," *Ladies' Home Journal*, May 1950

2. B-BOARD: a board (committee, to you) of officers, appointed to determine the qualifications of another officer and his fitness for remaining in service. When an officer has several unfavorable efficiency reports, he is automatically and tentatively put in "Class B" and is ordered to appear before a board of officers which decides if he shall remain in the service, or be eased into civil life with a mere modicum of his pay. They talk of going up before a B-board, and of being B-boarded. The process is not always fatal by a large margin, for there are many who "beat the board."— ELBRIDGE COLBY, *Army Talk*, p. 17

3. Going out to lift some potatoes I put up a hare which had been lying among the withering haulms. He looked as big as a fox as he went up the bank and across the cherry orchard. The next time I went that way I took a gun: not that I have anything against hares, but the meat ration being what it is, humane considerations fail. My gun did not bring a *civet de lièvre* appreciably nearer, because with very little patience, and more than five diopteres of hypermetropia, I can probably claim to be the worst shot in Britain, at a moving target. —EDWARD HYAMS, *The New Statesman and Nation*, April 1, 1950, 39:366

4. Thus, too, there is the mysticism of war. There are those for whom war is a vocation, to whom the thought of the universal holocaust is soothing, who are torn by internal strife unless, in their profession as killers, they can commune with carnage. The imagery of slaughter is for them the way of mortification. As leaders, they are not mere "careerists," looking for a chance to let their friends in on government contracts at a high figure. They are mystic soldiers, devout—and killing is their calling. What of them?

They find solace in the thought of the great holocaust; and they love the sheer hierarchal pageantry, the Stoicism of the disciplinary drill, the sense of unity in the communal act of all the different military orders marching in step, or the pious contemplation of the parade made static and "eternal," in the design of a military burial grounds, with its motionlessly advancing rank and file of graves.

What of *these* votaries, when their motives are hierarchally amplified, and empowered, with the great new weapons? And what of the fragments of such dedication, among the petty officials and journalistic hacks who know nothing of this quiet, deep-lying terror, but would do their lowly bit towards its unleashing, in daily pronouncements and bureaucratic finaglings that add steadily to the general ill will throughout the world?—KENNETH BURKE, *A Rhetoric of Motives*, p. 332

5. *The Big Wind on Capitol Hill*

(A stenographic report of a discussion in the House Appropriations Committee concerning the President's right to withhold money appropriated for the Air Force.)

. . . MR. SHEPPARD: Please, I feel kindly about this issue. I am just concerned about the modus operandi. If the power is vested in any individual to the extent that he supersedes the expressed will of Congress, and where he himself has signed the law, is there any logical reason why he could not do it to a complete degree if he so determined it was the wise thing to do?

SECRETARY JOHNSON: Absolutely, as long as he is exercising sound judgment and discretion and not vitiating the doing of things which are his duties when he defends the United States. I think it is within his province and authority so to act.

MR. SHEPPARD: I do not want to be unduly insistent, but was your answer that he did have the power to the completeness, or only proportionately?

SECRETARY JOHNSON: Repeating it for the third time, my statement is that there are certain duties and obligations that are those of the President of the United States and the Commander in Chief.

SHEPPARD: I will say this much, that our discussion here this morning on the record has been very indicative, insofar as I am concerned, that it is going to behoove this committee in the future to write language in the appropriation bill with mandatory phraseology, if the committee wants its will to be carried out in its completeness. That, I think, has been demonstrated to a definite degree.—VANCE JOHNSON, Washington Correspondent, San Francisco *Chronicle*, February 5, 1950

The reference paper

> . . . *an honest and industrious manufacturer, who has fairly procured the raw materials, and worked them up with a laudable degree of skill and success.*—Edward Gibbon (of himself as historian)

> *His* [*the teacher's*] *problem is to protect the spirit of inquiry, to keep it from becoming blasé from overexcitement, wooden from routine, fossilized through dogmatic instruction, or dissipated by random exercise upon trivial things.*—John Dewey

---

A COLLEGE LIBRARY is for fun and for work. It furnishes an almost limitless number of books and periodicals for leisure reading and for supplementing the laboratories, lectures, recitations, conferences, and textbooks in the main work of education—furthering the intellectual development of teachers and students.

The college library is not fundamentally different from the school and public libraries you have already been using, though it may well be larger and more complexly organized. It has its staff of specialized librarians, stated hours, rules for the circulation of books, a system of classifying and arranging books to which the key is the card catalog, the stacks full of the books themselves, and various special locations of particular kinds of works. All these a student needs to know, for a self-reliant use of the library is absolutely necessary to carrying on college work. This training is necessary too for later life. A college graduate isn't expected to know everything, but he ought to know how to find out about almost anything.

For your leisure use of the library you need to know its general rules, how to find books through the card catalog, the location of the recent periodicals, the new book shelf, the fiction section, the location of any particular sort of book that specially interests you, the provisions for browsing and casual reading, the most comfortable chairs and the best lighting. You need also to know the difference between rapid

---

reading and careful study, that is, know when to read fifty to a hundred pages an hour, getting the gist of a story or of some light book, and when to read thoroughly, digesting carefully all that the writer says.[1]

This chapter does not deal with leisure reading, but with one phase of library *work*, as it applies to writing a paper for which the material is entirely or largely drawn from reading, called variously a library paper, or term paper, or research paper, or source paper, or investigative paper, or reference paper.

1. Purposes of a reference paper

A reference paper is a record of study in some special field, scientific, social, historical, literary. Genuine or "original" research is the discovery and discussion of material that has not been generally known; undergraduate research is usually based on published information that has been gathered by someone else. Most undergraduate papers are primarily a record of intelligent reading in several sources on a particular subject.

---

[1] For helpful suggestions for the former see C. Gilbert Wrenn and Luella Cole, *How to Read Rapidly and Well* (Stanford University, 1935), and for the latter, Mortimer J. Adler, *How to Read a Book* (New York, 1940), Part 2.

Since a good deal of college work consists of acquiring and discussing the information and ideas of others, a standard method of discovering material, making notes of it, and presenting it has been developed. Preparing a reference paper gives practice in using this method. The paper in composition courses often emphasizes method and form and so prepares a student for later papers in other courses. Advanced work in literature, history, and the social sciences especially depends on this sort of study, and in sciences a laboratory experiment is often supplemented by research in what has been previously done. The same methods, more elaborately developed, are the basis of graduate work in the various professional schools, the means by which theses and dissertations and monographs are manufactured. These methods of research are also the basis of many sorts of reports and industrial studies. A glance at the "learned journals" in a college library will show that in every field of knowledge there are periodicals which contain research articles written by specialists, usually for other specialists. Such articles are produced by these research methods and presented in what is only an extension of the form described in this chapter. A freshman "reference paper" is a start on the road of scholarship that extends through the advanced courses in college to the work of professional people who are steadily adding to the knowledge and understanding of the past and the present. It is also practice for various papers that a college graduate may be expected to do, for a club or some special group, as part of a business project, or to answer questions raised in his day-to-day experience, to find good evidence for an opinion an intelligent person can hold.

Besides offering training in research methods, a paper of this sort shows the various stages of the writing process very clearly. Because of its length and often the complexity of its material, each stage becomes of particular importance. A mistake in choice of subject will make all later work a chore; gathering the material is by far the largest part of the task; selecting material and planning the paper are conspicuous because of the amount there is to be said; and the form of manuscript requires special attention because of the footnotes and formal bibliography. Each stage requires time and judgment and provides an opportunity to observe and practice various methods of composition.

At first thought the writer's contribution to a reference paper seems slight. The material is from sources outside his experience, the style is impersonal and rather formal, and the intention is primarily to inform rather than to entertain or move. But actual work on a paper shows how large a part the individual really plays. He chooses a subject in line with some interest of his own. He not only uncovers the material, often using considerable ingenuity, but he must use his judgment constantly in selecting which of dozens of facts fit his purpose. This purpose he has defined for himself, and he arranges his points in a plan that will accurately emphasize his sense of their relative value. The methods of gathering material have been worked out by thousands of research workers who have preceded him, the form of the manuscript has been standardized, but the actual content represents his interest and judgment at every step.

Furthermore, a reference paper is not necessarily a series of facts alone. Facts must be *interpreted*, for only the most common knowledge can stand without some comment on its meaning. Questions of causes, of results, of importance are not settled by recording information; a mind must work on the data to find the proper relationship between them and to see their meaning in perspective. No one can gather and present intelligently research materials without leaving his mark on them.

The main purpose of a research paper, from the point of view of a composition course at least, is to give training in college writing, in gathering, reflecting on, organizing, and putting in readable form material gained from study. But much of the interest as well as the profit for the writer comes from the material itself, from learning something new and becoming a bit of an authority in a small field.

2. Choosing a subject

You can write a reference paper on almost any subject, but if you let yourself choose "almost any subject" at random, you will be sorry. Such a paper is a long job and will become a bore or at least a waste of time unless you take a subject that interests you, that will add something useful to your stock of knowledge. It is a good idea to consider two or three possible fields so that your final selection will represent a choice based on comparison of their possibilities.

2a. Choosing a field. The natural way to begin choosing a subject for a reference paper is to consider a field in which you are really interested. It may be business or medicine or engines or dress design or anything else. It may be a field that you are studying in another course, chemistry or history or social science or a language; any course touches briefly on subjects that you would like to know more about, raises questions that it does not fully answer.

Your own experience has raised many questions that can be answered with a little study. You may have worked in a chain store, or merely traded at one, and wondered about the organization of chain stores, or how much of the country's business they handle, or the reasons for special taxes on them in some states. You may be interested in some person, living or dead, and want to know more about him. You may have wondered about something referred to in the news—the British Labour Party, the anti-trust laws, the cost of living index, French impressionist painting. You may play a saxophone and want to know something of its development and rise to popularity. You may be interested in some recent development in technology: synthetic rubber, the pseudo-bass circuit in small radios, sulfanilamide and related medicines; or in some organization: the Society of Friends, the Associated Press, government agencies of information and censorship, exactly what the C. I. O. is. The range of possibilities can only be suggested. Books and periodicals can furnish information about any one of them to be used in writing a reference paper.

A good type of paper can be developed by taking an opinion you hold or think you hold and doing some reading to find evidence for it. You may approve or disapprove of some of the proposals for "fair employment practices" legislation, or of hazing in colleges, or of the closed shop, of radio supported by public assessment rather than by advertisers, or of any one of scores of problems, simple and personal or complex and socially important. Although starting with an opinion may lead to selection only of material that fits your case, as in a debate, an honest attempt to find sound factual reasons is a useful project— and may result not only in a better based opinion but in a more thorough understanding of the problem.

Although any topic is possible, there are some that you should be warned against. It is good sense to avoid topics that are too commonly used, that do not represent a genuine individual choice, the kind that students fall back on as a last resort—the history of baseball, the American Indian, swing vs. classical music. Your instructor can tell you what topics he has found students take thoughtlessly or that in his experience have worked out badly. Topics for which the material is uncertain, like treatment of cancer, or for which the material is likely to be biased or emotional are difficult because you need unusual judgment to handle them. Your instructor's advice will be particularly useful in finding a field that will not only promise a good paper within the purpose and limitations of the course assignment but one that is good for *you*.

2b. Final definition of subject. Some of the topics just mentioned are specific enough to be treated in papers of two or three thousand words, but most have been *fields* that contain many specific subjects for particular papers. They need to be limited to something that can be treated adequately in the length of paper to be written, treated with enough detail so that you can really illuminate a reader, so that you do something besides enumerate the commonplace facts that most people already know. After a little general reading in the field you can focus on a particular subject, always bearing in mind the length you are to approximate. Better than taking "the Associated Press" would be to take its origin, or its present organization and services; instead of "airplanes" or "aviation," the safety devices in airplanes or air freight lines. Sometimes the library yields information on some phase more readily than on another. Perhaps you will find a topic just to one side of the one you started on, perhaps not "sources of pigments for oil painting" but "tempera as a medium of painting."

As quickly as possible you should narrow your subject to one that is workable, usually while gathering your working bibliography or at least in the very early stages of note taking. Your instructor can offer suggestions for the final selection of a topic, especially if you have indicated the sort of material you would like to work with. Thoughtful and early attention to the choice of subject will make all later stages of the work easier and more profitable.

3. Sources of references

Almost everyone starts work on a subject with one or two sources in mind, such as a discussion in a textbook, or a magazine article, or the name of a writer or of a book that treats the subject. Very often these first readings give references to other works, and notes on them make a natural starting point for the working bibliography of sources to be used. But a businesslike assembling of possible useful sources for your work depends on intelligent use of the resources of the library. There are several aids planned specifically to lead you to references for your purpose.

3a. The library card catalog. The library card catalog lists books by *author*, by *title*, and by *subjects* treated. If you know the name of a man who has written on your subject, look up his name in the card catalog. Look up also the *subject heading* that you are writing about, remembering that your exact subject may not be given but that there may be one that will include it. You may not find the heading *Skyscraper* but may find under *Architecture* or *Building* books that will touch on skyscrapers. The library subject card below (*Public Welfare* is the subject heading) and the working bibliography card made from it show what should be taken down and what should be omitted. The entry on the bibliography card should resemble that of the final bibliography as closely as possible (see pp. 396-398). Then making the bibliography will be simply a matter of arranging the cards alphabetically and copying the entries.

1. Card catalog subject heading
2. Library call number
3. Author
4. Title
5. Facts of publication
6. Miscellaneous facts about the book
7. Subject index
8. Information for librarians

② 325.342
M286w

① PUBLIC WELFARE – Great Britain – Colonies

③ Mair, Lucy Philip, 1901–
④ Welfare in the British colonies ₍by₎ L. P. Mair. ⑤ London, The Royal institute of international affairs ₍1944₎

⑥ 115 p. 21½ᶜᵐ.

"First published 1944."
Bibliography at end of each chapter except the first.

⑦ 1. Gt. Brit.—Colonies—Soc. condit. I. Royal institute of international affairs. II. Title.

44-9322

⑧ Library of Congress ◯ HN398.A5M3
₍4₎ 325.342

A LIBRARY SUBJECT CARD

1. Subject (for the paper
2. Call number
3. Author
4. Title
5. Facts of publication
6. Pages on the specific subject (added from the book)

① *Control of Malaria*
② 325.342 *Mair, Lucy P.* ③
M286w ④ *Welfare in the British Colonies*
⑤ *London, Royal Institute of International Affairs, 1944*
⑥ *pp. 79-83 on malaria*

BIBLIOGRAPHY CARD made from the subject card, with pages added from the book

3b. Periodical indexes. Next to the card catalog the most important source of references is the *Readers' Guide* and other periodical indexes.

1) THE READERS' GUIDE. This reference source, published since 1906, gives under author entries (1, 2, and 3 in the illustration below) and under subject entries (4 to 8 in the illustration) references to articles in some 200 current magazines. It gives references up to the preceding month and is consequently one of the most valuable sources for topics that are of current importance.

SMITH, William M. jr
So old nobody wants you. J Home Econ 41:
308-10 Je '49
SMITHIES, Arthur
Fiscal aspects of preparedness for war. Am
Econ R 39:Pap & proc 356-65 My '49
SMITTER, Wessel
Red warrior who licked Custer. Coronet 26:
117-20 Ag '49
SMOKE detectors
Smoke detectors likely to return on airline
transports. Aviation W 50:50 Je 6 '49
SMOLLETT, Tobias George
Smollett's Humphrey Clinker. W. H. Graham.
Contemp 176:33-8 Jl '49
SMÖRGÅSBORD. See Cookery, Scandinavian
SMUCKER, David E.
Portrait
Time 54:60 Jl 4 '49
SMUGGLING
Cigarette smugglers. Newsweek 33:26-7 Je 27
'49
Customs of the country. Holiday 6:29-30 Jl
'49
Macao; smugglers of gold. il map Life
27:19-23 Ag 8 '49

TYPICAL ENTRIES IN THE READERS' GUIDE

The *Readers' Guide* uses abbreviations for the titles of magazines indexed, for the months, and for various facts about the articles (as, *il.* means an article has illustrations). These are explained on a page at the beginning of each issue. You should write out all important words on your bibliography card before leaving the *Guide*, to avoid later question and to have the data in correct form for future use. ("J Home Econ" in the first entry stands for *Journal of Home Economics.*) In the references the number before the colon refers to the volume and the numbers after the colon refer to the pages of the article: 41:308-10 means volume 41, pages 308 to 310. Putting quotation marks around the title and caps on the important words will give the entry the proper bibliographical form. A bibliography card for the third entry shown follows:

	① *Custer's Defeat*
1. Subject of paper	② *Smitter, Wessel*
2. Author	③ *"Red Warrior Who Licked Custer"*
3. Title of article	④ *Coronet, August 1949, 26:117–20*
4. Facts of publication	

A BIBLIOGRAPHY CARD made from a Readers' Guide entry

2) OTHER MAGAZINE INDEXES. A number of specialized periodical indexes are very useful for work on a reference paper. Most of them appear annually. The ones marked with a † in this list are the most generally useful and should be known by everyone:

Agricultural Index, 1916– Subject index to a selected list of periodicals, books, bulletins, documents

Annual Magazine Subject Index, 1907– Subject index to a selected list of American and English periodicals and historical society publications

Art Index, 1929– Author and subject index for fine arts periodicals and museum bulletins

Bibliographic Index, 1937– Subject index to bibliographies in books and periodicals

†*Biography Index*, 1946– Subject index to biographical material in books and periodicals

†*Book Review Digest*, 1905– Author, subject, and title index to published book reviews. Gives extracts and exact references to sources

Catholic Periodical Index, 1930– Subject index to a selected list of Catholic periodicals

Dramatic Index, 1909– Index to articles and illustrations concerning the American and English theater

†*Education Index*, 1929– Author and subject index for educational periodicals, books, and pamphlets

Engineering Index, 1906– Subject index to technical periodicals; transactions and journals of engineering and other technical societies; reports of government bureaus, engineering colleges, research laboratories

Index to Legal Periodicals, 1926– Author, subject, and book review index for legal periodicals

†*Industrial Arts Index*, 1913– Subject index to a selected list of engineering, trade, and business periodicals

†*International Index*, 1907– Author and subject index to periodicals from various countries; devoted chiefly to the humanities and science; supplements *Readers' Guide*

Poole's Index to Periodical Literature, 1802–1906 Subject index to American and English periodicals, many of which are no longer published but are still important; precedes coverage of *Readers' Guide*

†*Public Affairs Information Service*, 1915– Subject index to books, periodicals, pamphlets, and other materials in economics, government, and other public affairs

Quarterly Cumulative Index Medicus, 1927– Author and subject index to medical literature in many languages

Subject Index to Periodicals, 1917– An English index which includes some American periodical references

United States Government Publications; Monthly Catalog, 1895– Makes available the various publications of the government in all fields

Ulrich's Periodical Directory (5th ed., 1947) lists periodicals under subjects they treat, answering the question: What periodicals are there in this field? It also tells in what works each is indexed so that it becomes an indirect guide to the contents of all magazines.

3) THE NEW YORK TIMES INDEX. Most libraries have *The New York Times Index*, which appears monthly and runs back to 1913. Though this indexes specifically *The New York Times*, it will serve as an index to other papers on matters of general importance because it gives the dates of events which would presumably be covered in all papers of the same date. Through this index it is possible to find many speeches and important documents as well as the news stories of events.

3c. Special bibliographies. Besides these periodical indexes there are many annual bibliographies in the learned journals in special fields and there are many bibliographies in one or more volumes that survey a complete field. Most of these are more elaborate than a student needs for his practice reference paper but when he begins to work in detail in a particular field, as in a college major subject, he should know the special bibliographies that serve it.

The key to these special lists is Besterman: *World Bibliography of Bibliographies* (2d. ed., 3 vols., 1947-49), a standard and comprehensive work, or the shorter Ireland's *An Index to Indexes* (1942). The following standard bibliographies in the fields of history and literature show the extent of bibliographical aids available in many fields of study:

Bibliographical Guide to English Studies (Cross), 9th ed., 1947
A Concise Bibliography for Students of English (Kennedy), 1945
Bibliography of Writings on the English Language . . . to the end of 1922 (Kennedy), 1927 and supplement
Cambridge Bibliography of English Literature, 1940, 4 vols.
Literary History of the United States (Spiller and others), 1948, 3 vols.

Contemporary British Literature (Manly and Rickert), 1935
Contemporary American Authors (Millett), 1940
Literature of American History (Larned), 1902 and supplement
Bibliographies in American History (Beers), 1942
Guide to Historical Literature (Alison and others), 1931

The following miscellaneous indexes are of frequent use to anyone engaged in reference work:

Vertical File Service Catalog, 1932– An annotated subject catalog of pamphlets, booklets, brochures, leaflets, circulars, folders, maps, posters, charts, mimeographed bulletins, etc.
United States Catalog: Books in Print (1899–1934) The four editions and their supplements constitute a comprehensive record of American book publication from 1898 to 1934
Cumulative Book Index, 1898– Supplement to the *United States Catalog;* since 1930 an author, subject, and title index to books printed in English
Catalog of the Public Documents of Congress and of All Departments of the Government of the United States for the Period 1893–1940 (1895–1945, 25 vols.)
Essay and General Literature Index, 1900– Author and subject index to essays and articles in collections and miscellaneous works
Granger's Index to Poetry and Recitations (1904–44) Author, title, and first line index to poetry in collections
Index to Short Stories (1923–36) Author and title index to short stories in collected editions, separate volumes, anthologies, and periodicals
Song Index (1926–34) Author and title index to more than 19,000 songs in collections
Index to Plays (1927–35) Author and title and subject index to plays in collections or separately published from 1800 to 1935
Portrait Index (1906) Subject index to portraits of persons in books and periodicals; *Readers' Guide* and other periodical indexes now indicate portraits in periodicals

3d. Reference works. The reference department of a library has a large number of general and special works which furnish varied and plentiful information. Often it is a good plan to see what one of these has to say about your subject before you do any extensive searching, because its article can help you find your way around more intelligently. The articles almost always refer you to authoritative specialized works so that they are a good starting point for compiling a bibliography.

The general guide to reference books is I. G. Mudge, *Guide to Reference Books*, 6th ed., 1936, and supplements.

1) GENERAL ENCYCLOPEDIAS. Everyone needs to use these great storehouses of information. They are frequently revised and each publishes an annual supplement bringing its topics up to date. You should make sure that you are using the most recent edition available.

Encyclopedia Americana, 1946 issue
Encyclopaedia Britannica, 1947 issue
New International Encyclopaedia, 2d edition, 1922–30

2) SPECIAL REFERENCE WORKS. Less well known but even more important for college work are the encyclopedias and general reference works that have been compiled in various specific fields. Their articles can usually go into further detail than those in the general encyclopedias, and the approach is more specialized. They give brief, carefully selected bibliographies. These works are usually shelved in the reference department of the library but are sometimes kept with other books in their respective fields. An early acquaintance with those which you expect to use will be valuable. Some of the best known are:

Agriculture: *Cyclopedia of American Agriculture* (Bailey), 1908-09, 4 vols.
Architecture: *A History of Architecture* (Bannister-Fletcher), 14th ed., 1948
Art: *Harper's Encyclopedia of Art*, 1937, 2 vols.
  Bryan's Dictionary of Painters and Engravers, 1903-05, 5 vols.
Biography (American): *Dictionary of American Biography*, 1928-37, 20 vols.
  Who's Who in America, biennially since 1899
  Who Was Who in America, 1897-1942 (*Who's Who* biographees dying
    during those years)
Biography (British): *Dictionary of National Biography*, 1885-1937, 63 vols.
  and supplements
  Who's Who, annually since 1849
Biography (General): *Current Biography*, 1940-
  International Who's Who, 1935-
  World Biography, 1948, 2 vols.
Business: *Encyclopedia of Banking and Finance* (Munn), 5th ed., 1949
Chemistry: *Thorpe's Dictionary of Applied Chemistry*, 4th ed., 1937-49,
  9 vols.
Education: *Cyclopedia of Education* (Monroe), 1911-13, 5 vols.
  Encyclopedia of Educational Research (Monroe), 1941
Government: *Cyclopedia of American Government* (McLaughlin and Hart),
  1914, 3 vols.
History (General): *An Encyclopedia of World History* (Langer), 1940
  Cambridge Ancient History (Bury and others), 2d ed., 1928-39, 12 vols.
    and 5 volumes of plates
  Cambridge Medieval History (Bury and others), 1911-36, 8 vols. and 8
    supplementary volumes of maps and plates
  Cambridge Modern History (Ward and others), 2d ed., 1926, 13 vols.
    and atlas
History (American): *Dictionary of American History* (Adams), 1940, 5
  vols. and index
Literature (General): *Dictionary of World Literature* (Shipley), 1943
  Columbia Dictionary of Modern European Literature (Smith), 1947
Literature (Classical): *Oxford Companion to Classical Literature* (Harvey),
  1937
  Oxford Classical Dictionary (Cary and others), 1949

Literature (English): *Cambridge History of English Literature* (Ward and others), 1907-27, 15 vols.

    Oxford Companion to English Literature (Harvey), 3d ed., 1946

Literature (American): *Cambridge History of American Literature* (Trent and others), 1917-21, 4 vols.

    Oxford Companion to American Literature (Hart), 2d ed., 1948

    Literary History of the United States (Spiller and others), 1948, 3 vols.

Music: *Grove's Dictionary of Music and Musicians*, 3d ed., 1935, 5 vols. and supplements

    International Cyclopedia of Music and Musicians (Thompson), 5th ed., 1949

Philosophy and Psychology: *Dictionary of Philosophy and Psychology* (Baldwin), 1910, 3 vols.

    Encyclopedia of Psychology (Harriman), 1946

Quotations: *Bartlett's Familiar Quotations*, 12th ed., 1948

    The Home Book of Bible Quotations (Stevenson), 1949

    The Home Book of Shakespeare Quotations (Stevenson), 1937

    The Home Book of Quotations, Classical and Modern (Stevenson), 5th ed., 1947

Religion: *Catholic Encyclopedia*, 1907-22, 17 vols.

    Jewish Encyclopedia, 1901-06, 12 vols.

    Encyclopedia of Religion and Ethics (Hastings), 1911-27, 13 vols.

    New Schaff-Herzog Encyclopedia of Religious Knowledge (Jackson), 1908-12, 12 vols. and index

    Dictionary of the Bible (Hastings), 1898-1902, 5 vols.

Science: *Hutchinson's Technical and Scientific Encyclopedia* (Tweney and Shirshov), 1935-36, 4 vols.

    Van Nostrand's Scientific Encyclopedia, 2d ed., 1947

Social Sciences: *Encyclopedia of the Social Sciences* (Seligman and Johnson), 1930-35, 15 vols.

General and special dictionaries are described on pages 310-318.

3) YEARBOOKS, ETC. For facts and figures, there are various annual publications that are valuable for the information they contain or can direct you to:

World Almanac and Book of Facts, 1868– This is the one general reference work that an individual can afford to own and one anyone with a serious interest in affairs can hardly afford to be without.

Information Please Almanac, 1947–

The American Yearbook, 1910– Annual record of events in the United States

The Americana Annual, 1923– Annual supplement to the *Encyclopedia Americana*

The Britannica Book of the Year, 1938– Annual supplement to the *Encyclopaedia Britannica*

The New International Yearbook, 1907– Annual supplement to the *New International Encyclopedia*

Statistical Abstract of the United States, 1878– Summary statistics on the industrial, social, political, and economic organization of the United States

Social Work Yearbook, biennially since 1929 Social work and related fields

Statesman's Yearbook, 1864– Statistical and historical annual of political and industrial events throughout the world

United Nations Yearbook, 1946-47– Activities of the United Nations
Reference Shelf, 1922– Reprints of articles, bibliographies, and debates
on topics of current interest
University Debater's Annual, 1915– Constructive and rebuttal speeches
from college and university debates

Besides these specific sources that must be covered, there will always
be chance references. Almost every article or chapter will mention
something else on the subject or give some clue that can be followed
up. Talking with people who work in the field will produce suggestions. The sources of material spread out like a fan—one source leads
to another and, if you work long enough in a field, friends and sometimes even strangers may give you clues without being asked. Because one reference leads to another, it is usually safe to start work
on a subject if you can first turn up two or three works that have
good material for your subject. Systematic work and ingenuity, following up hunches of where material may be found, will almost always enable you to find enough to finish the job.

Since one reason for the assignment of reference papers is to train
students in research methods, you should do as much as possible without help. The library has reference librarians, but they should not be
bothered until you have exhausted your own resources.

4. The working bibliography

Before you concentrate on gathering material for the topic you
have selected, you need to compile a *working bibliography* of references that you expect to consult. The preceding section has suggested
the more probable sources of references. You should see if any of the
special sources listed in it relate to your topic, consult the appropriate
subject headings in the library card catalog and the periodical indexes
most likely to give you references. To make sure that enough material on the specific subject is available in the library, you would do
well to compile the working bibliography before actually starting to
take notes. This preliminary survey of materials saves time and worry
in going about the actual reading and allows for intelligent selection
of books and articles to be read. Finding several promising references
shows that you will be able to go through with the subject and adds to
your confidence in the work.

4a. Materials. Research workers have adopted standard forms
and materials to use in keeping track of references and notes. Everyone should have a consistent method of taking and keeping the notes

from which he works. For casual work, notebooks and odd sheets may do, but for large and important jobs, such as the typical reference paper, and for training in research methods, the most flexible and easily expandable materials are the standard filing cards or slips, either 3x5 or 4x6 inches. The 4x6 size is probably more convenient, since it can hold more than the 3x5 and allows for more generous spacing and labeling of material. *A separate bibliography card should be prepared for each reference;* later note cards on the content of the reference will be added to your file of material for the paper.

4b. Form of bibliographical entries. The purpose of the bibliography card is to record all the facts about the reference that you will need to identify it, to find it in the library when you are ready to use it, and to make the formal bibliography that will stand at the end of the paper. Each card consequently should carry these facts:

1) *The author's name*, with last name first. If the book is edited, put the editor's name, followed by *ed.*

2) *The title* of the article (in quotation marks) or of the book (underlined to represent italics)

3) *The facts of publication:*
(a) Of a book, the city and date, and the name of publisher if you need to use it; (b) Of a magazine, the name of the magazine (underlined), the date, the volume, the pages covered by the article; (c) Of a newspaper story, the name of the paper (underlined), the date, the page, and the column number if you wish

4) *The library call number* and location—preferably in the upper left corner, as it is in the card catalog

5) *Any other facts* that relate to the reference as a reference, such as the particular pages of a book that treat your specific subject, or a comment on the value of the book

A bibliography card may also carry these items if desired:

The subject of the work listed, that is the particular part of your topic that it relates to, best kept at the top center of card. This label is familiarly known as a *slug.*

A number for the reference, in the upper right corner. This number can then be used on the note cards to identify the work that the note is taken from. In the example given, the Schlesinger book might be numbered 4 in the bibliography to which it belongs, and the notes taken from it could be identified by the number 4. Keeping the author's name as the identifying mark is slightly safer, but when there are not many different sources, the number system may be a convenience.

The arrangement of the necessary facts on each type of bibliography card is shown in the specimens reproduced on page 379.

4c. Keeping bibliography cards. Your bibliography cards should be kept in alphabetical order according to author (or first important word of the title if there is no author given). If there are only a few they can be held together with a paper clip or kept in an envelope or an expanding pocket file that can be bought for either of

1. Subject (slug)
2. Call number
3. Author
4. Title
5. Facts of publication
6. Specific part of book

① *Rating of Presidents*
② 917.3 Sch38p *Schlesinger, Arthur M.* ③
④ *Paths to the Present*
⑤ *New York, Macmillan, 1949*
⑥ *Ch. v, A Yardstick for Presidents*

BIBLIOGRAPHY CARD FOR A BOOK

1. Subject (slug)
2. Call number
3. Author
4. Title
5. Facts of publication

② 420.5 AM ① *Business Vocabulary*
Minton, Arthur ③
④ *"The Muse of Mammon"*
⑤ *American Speech, Oct. 1949, 24: 171–80*

BIBLIOGRAPHY CARD FOR A MAGAZINE ARTICLE

1. Facts of publication
2. Headline
3. Description of content

① *The New York Times, March 4, 1950, p. 1, col. 2; p. 28, col. 2*
② *"Mayor Picks Rain-Making Advisers"*
③ *(Plans for artificial rain to relieve N. Y. water shortage)*

BIBLIOGRAPHY CARD FOR A NEWSPAPER

the standard sizes of cards. For large accumulations there are boxes and filing drawers of various sizes.

Students always ask how many references they should have for a paper. Graduate research is expected to show *all* the pertinent material. Undergraduate papers are supposed to represent a fair covering of the subject. You will probably want to glance at all available sources and select those which are neither too technical nor too general for your purpose. No paper should be written relying on only one or two sources, but of course for a short paper that must be done in a limited time, a student can easily be weighed down by too much material. Papers that run from 2000 to 5000 words have typically from six to fifteen or twenty sources, depending on the nature of the subject and the length and thoroughness of the work.

5. Taking notes

Most research workers take their notes on 3x5 or 4x6 slips or cards because they are flexible—they are easy to handle, sort, and rearrange —and because they can be indefinitely accumulated and can be kept in good order by the use of guide cards that have tabs on which subjects can be written. Even for a relatively small job, such as a course reference paper, they are the most convenient form for notes. Students should accustom themselves to using them.

5a. Form of notes. The three essential parts of the contents of a note card are:

1) The material, the facts and opinions to be recorded
2) The exact source, title and page number, from which they are taken
3) A label or slug for the card, showing what it treats

It is usually a waste of time and effort to take notes in numbered outline form. It is important simply that the material is clearly noted and clearly labeled. A handy form of hanging indention, in which the second and succeeding lines are indented, is shown in the specimen on page 381. This works well for typical material that can be taken in blocks. If the data is made up of a number of small particular facts, some scheme of tabulating should be worked out.

Keeping track of the exact source will tax almost any note taker. Since the final paper will have footnotes referring to the exact page from which the material comes, you should work out some system for keeping track of the title and page. Some note takers put these facts at the bottom of the card, but it is easy to forget to write them down after the card has been written.

It is safer to record the source first. The specimen card below shows a convenient form. In the upper right corner put the author's name and a short form of the title—just enough to make reference to the full bibliography card easy and sure. (If the sources are numbered, the number assigned to the Morison book would be in the upper right corner instead of the name and short title.) In the left margin, opposite the note, put the exact page on which the material was found. Inclusive pages (as 87-92) are not to be used unless the note actually describes or summarizes what those pages say. Later cards from the same source can be numbered like pages 2, 3, 4.

Label	*First Harvard Commencement Morison, Founding of Harvard Coll.*
Notes with page references	257 *1st Harvard Commencement Sept. 23, 1642* *Gov. Winthrop, his guard, the magistrates of the Colony come from Boston by ferry or barge* 258 *By 9 or 10 a.m. audience on benches in the college hall. 9 in graduating class. Splendid formal procession. (Details given)* 259 *Long extemporaneous prayer in Latin; Latin salutatory oration; one of the graduates gives oration in Greek; exercises in Hebrew*

SPECIMEN NOTE CARD

The subject or slug of the card is most conveniently placed in the upper left corner, where it can be instantly seen. It should label the subject of the material on that particular card. This procedure not only identifies the card itself but makes it possible to sort the cards in preparation for outlining and writing the paper.

One of the basic practices is not to put too much on a single slip or card; students tend to crowd their notes and so make them hard to use. A card should contain only one point or a few closely related facts.

Use only one side of the card. Cards written on both sides are difficult to handle, and you will certainly forget to turn some over if you use both sides. Sometimes if only part of a statement remains at the bottom of a card, it can be completed on the back. Then *Over* should be put on the front as a reminder.

Notes need not be taken in full sentences—words, phrases, topics are enough. It is not often worth while to copy notes. They are means to an end (a good paper), not works of art themselves. Take workable notes, in ink, as you do the reading, and don't bother about copying them except for some very good reason.

5b. Suggestions for taking notes. Usually it is best to read the article or chapter through rapidly first to see what it contains for your purposes. Then go over it again, taking down the necessary notes. From the first few references you may need to take a good many notes, but after you have accumulated quite a bit of material, perhaps a long reference will give only a few additional facts.

Rules for what to take cannot be laid down. Your judgment will improve as you go on and the guidance of teachers is almost necessary at the start. Here are three general points that will apply to all topics:

1) *Distinguish between the author's facts and his opinions.* Label the opinions "So-and-so thinks. . ." In general pay most attention to the *facts* presented (unless of course your topic is about opinions, as for instance in a paper on "What reviewers said of Hemingway's short stories"). You will need the facts as the basis of your own opinions, and you will need them in writing your paper as material and as evidence for your own opinions.

2) *Distinguish carefully between direct quotation and summary of your writer's material—and take as little quotation as possible.* Quotations should be carefully indicated by quotation marks. They should be taken only for good reason: unusually important material, crucial for your paper; a striking statement you may want to quote in your paper; controversial or difficult material that you need to think about before deciding exactly what it means for your subject. Almost everything else should be digested in your own words and so reduced to the scale of the paper you are writing. The time to do this is when you take the notes.

3) *Distinguish between what you take from your source and any comments you may make of your own* by putting the latter in brackets or by initialing them or drawing a line around them.

Accurate notes are one of the chief tools of scholarship, and early and careful practice in taking them is excellent training that may be useful in all later college courses and in a great many positions after graduation.

6. Evaluating material

Since composing a reference paper is in large part an exercise of judgment, it is important to evaluate the sources being used. "I found a book in the library that said . . ." is a confession of uncritical work; *the point is to find the best books, the most recent authoritative material on the subject.* Most of us cannot evaluate references until after we have done a good deal of work in a field, and we must at first fall back on the opinions of others. In reading several sources you are likely to find remarks about other sources—that one is the recognized authority or that another has misused certain figures, and so on. These criticisms should be noted and if they seem reasonable should be taken into account.

For recent books it is often possible to find a review that will be some indication of the book's value. Many reviews in newspapers and general periodicals deal with the interest rather than the accuracy of a book, though they sometimes discuss this too. The best sources for reviews of serious works are the learned journals of the appropriate fields: the *American Historical Review* for historical works, and so on. The *Book Review Digest* will lead to reviews of the less specialized works.

After you have worked awhile on a subject, you are in a position to evaluate a good deal of the material yourself, and your carefully considered opinion should influence your choice of materials.

Notes of criticism of sources are part of the bibliographical division of the work and should be entered either on the bibliographical card or on a separate card to be kept with it.

Sources are often classed as *primary* (or *original*) and *secondary*. A primary source is a first record of certain facts or the closest that a person writing now can come to the subject he is discussing; a secondary source is something written by someone else using the original sources. In a paper on a literary subject, for instance, the primary sources are the works written by the man you are discussing, or letters, diaries, and so on that he wrote or that were written by others who knew him; secondary sources are what a critic or historian has written about the man and his work. In a science, primary sources are records of observation or experiments; secondary sources are based on these records. In history, primary sources are records of all sorts or responsible reproductions of them: letters, diaries, documents, and remains, such as coins, tools, buildings; secondary sources are a "historian's" account based on these evidences. Textbooks and reference works are all secondary sources.

Graduate research relies chiefly on primary sources. Undergraduate papers are drawn principally from secondary sources, but a student who is trying to do a thorough job should try to use some original sources. He certainly should come as close as he can to the first record of the facts he is to use. In choosing material to present he should try to find the closest and most reliable material he can.

The material needs careful sifting for its usefulness for the particular paper you are going to write as well as for its accuracy. It is a good idea to read through all the notes you have taken, to see what there is, how the information shapes up, and whether there are some spots for which you need more material. This overall view of your material should lead to an exact formulation of the subject that you can and want to develop. If you haven't done it already, you should state the scope of the paper definitely in a full sentence that will show its actual emphasis. For a paper on the evacuation of Japanese-Americans during the war the sentence might be: "The evacuation of 110,000 persons of Japanese ancestry in the heat of the war resulted in unnecessary suffering and humiliation for these people, but at the same time it had some constructive results."

With some such statement it is easy to select the particular parts of your material that you will use. For if you have done a good job of reference work, you will have considerably more than you can use. As you survey your notes and make your outline, you will be sorting your facts out into those that must be used, those that will probably be used, those of incidental importance or interest that may be used, and some that clearly do not belong. It is a good idea to mark in the margins of your note cards the most important points, by a # sign or some other. Of course the final selection of material takes place during the actual writing, but the clearer notion you have before you begin to write, the easier the paper will move and the more satisfactory it is likely to be.

7. Planning the paper

After the material has been pretty well gathered, the work of planning and writing is not essentially different from that of any other type of paper. Since the material is gathered from study instead of from memory or observation, it seems more objective; you can

The Story of the Japanese Evacuation

The evacuation of 110,000 persons of Japanese ancestry at the heat of the war resulted in unnecessary suffering and humiliation for these people, but at the same time it had some constructive results.

I. Military and social forces made evacuation necessary.
   A. From the military standpoint, evacuation was necessary for national security.
   B. A traditional anti-Oriental feeling on the west coast was partially responsible for the move.
II. Camp life, although tolerable, was far from normal life.
   A. The assembly centers were temporary home for evacuees while relocation camps were under construction.
   B. Life in the relocation camps was a little more organized.
   C. Camp life had a demoralizing effect on the evacuees.
III. Conflicting emotions existed among the evacuees towards the government.
   A. The general feeling of the Issei was anti-American.
   B. The Niseis were mostly too young and too stunned by conflicting emotions to form a definite opinion.
   C. The attitude of the Kibei was generally anti-American.
IV. Public sentiment tended to be antagonistic, but this feeling was later changed.
   A. The evacuation increased the anti-Japanese feeling.
   B. At first the public was hostile to returning evacuees.
   C. Certain developments helped to establish healthier attitudes towards the evacuees.
V. The evacuation had some constructive results.
   A. The Japanese population has been more widely dispersed throughout the country.
   B. Japanese-Americans have gained a higher status in the United States.
   C. This experience proved that a group of people cannot be discriminated against merely because of their ancestry.

Sentence Outline for a Reference Paper

review it easily by reading the notes over; you find it easier to think about it as *material* and do things with it.

If you have taken your notes well, with only closely related facts on a single card, you can sort into piles the cards that contain facts belonging together.

Because of the amount of material and the length of the paper to be written, you will have to make some sort of outline before writing. You should try to group the material in from three to six stages—not more unless the paper is unusually long. As in any paper, the main divisions grow out of the material you have to present—it is this material grouped into a few stages. To check the plan, and to make it possible for your instructor to examine it and make suggestions, you should cast it in one of the standard forms of outline. (See *Outline form.)

If you have the time, it is wise to keep the outline around for a day or two and look at it closely to see if it is a real grouping of the facts and ideas you are to present, one that your reader can follow easily and one that represents your understanding of the material and your intended emphasis.

There is a tendency in reference papers to compose an "introduction" that really does not advance the subject. A history of the subject is unnecessary unless it forms an integral part of the paper. Every main head, including the first, should tell the reader something. Pick a natural starting point as close to the main body of the paper as possible and then advance by clear cut stages to the final and most important point.

8. The first draft

By this time you should be thoroughly familiar with your material. Even though you have been reviewing it as a whole and thinking it over in the last two steps, it is a good idea to read your notes through once or twice more to get them fully in mind. Then you can deal with them easily, without just transcribing from note cards to paper.

This review of the material will also help you get it into your own words, to get it away from the form in which you found it and to get it into the proportion in which it belongs in your paper. Digesting the material into your own words is important. If you are inclined to be lazy or hasty, you will tend to follow your sources too closely. It is the intention of the assignment that you are to take information from various sources and work it over into a form of your own. You are supposed to digest it and not just reproduce it. Direct quotation should be kept to a minimum, used only for striking or very important matter, and should always be indicated by quotation marks or, if it is more than a sentence or two, by being indented in the copy. The quotations should be brief; often a part of a sentence will be all that is worth quoting and the rest of the material will be summarized in your own words. The purpose of this advice is not just to "prevent copying" but to encourage the proper method for producing a reference paper, which is to learn something new from reading and then write about it.

Because the finished paper is to give credit in footnotes to the sources from which you have taken your facts, you will have to work out some way of keeping track of the sources in the first draft. One simple way is to put in parentheses after a statement an abbreviated form of reference to the source used. Or the reference may be put in the margin opposite the statement to which it applies. Then when you make your final copy you can present the data in the proper footnote form.

The traditional style of reference papers is formal and impersonal. It is not usually necessary for the writer to refer to himself at all, and if it is made, the reference should be brief. But impersonal writing does not have to be stupid: simply put down your material as compactly and directly as possible. You will often find yourself writing more concretely and more compactly than the sources you are using.

There is a question of the audience to which the paper should be directed. "Term papers" for advanced college courses are usually written for a specialist in the field and in so far as they have a reader audience it is the instructor. In the usual composition course all sorts of material are used. The treatment may vary from that of a specialist, if you are very much at home in the field of your subject, to that of a writer for a general magazine. Your instructor will explain the approach most appropriate for the course and for your particular subject. The most generally appropriate approach is to direct your paper to an intelligent reader with some desire to learn about your subject but with not much background in it, a reader serious enough to prefer accurate information to sensational appeal. Then you can apply all your skill in expression to trying to illuminate him on the subject you have chosen.

9. Footnotes

Any paper that is based on a study of the writings of others should acknowledge the sources used. It is only common courtesy (or decency) to give credit where credit is due; it is a sign of scrupulousness to tell the sources of specific statements, so that a reader can judge for himself the evidence they are based on; and it allows an occasional interested reader to turn to the sources for further information with a minimum of effort. College students are expected to draw their materials from varied sources, and a frank acknowledgment of sources actually used in a paper is not only businesslike—it will raise an instructor's respect for the student who makes it.

In rather informal papers the sources may be given in a note at the beginning or at the end of the paper:

> The material for this paper was taken from Marquis W. Childs, *Sweden— The Middle Way* (New Haven, 1936).

Or the source may be thrown in parentheses following an important statement, or built into a sentence:

> (Marquis W. Childs, *Sweden—The Middle Way*, page 68)
> Marquis W. Childs says in *Sweden—The Middle Way*. . . .

In formal academic papers—reference papers, reports for courses, term papers, theses, dissertations—it is conventional to give exact references to sources of material in footnotes. The forms used at different institutions and in different "learned journals" vary slightly in mechanical details, but the aim of all is the same—*to record in some brief and consistent form the author, title of work, facts of publication, and exact page from which each quotation and each essential fact is taken.* The style suggested in this article covers the ordinary problems of using footnotes in a college reference paper.[1]

9a. Handling footnotes. (1) Footnotes are needed for all direct quotations (except well-known bits from the Bible or other literature that are used for style rather than content) *and for all important statements of facts or opinions that are taken from written sources.* Obviously figures, dates, descriptions of situations, scientific data, opin-

---

[1] This section recommends a slightly simplified form appropriate for undergraduate work. For more complex systems and variations that are found in various fields see: Livia Appel, *Bibliographical Citation in the Social Sciences and Humanities*, 3rd ed. (Madison, University of Wisconsin Press, 1949); S. F. Trelease, *The Scientific Paper* (Baltimore, Williams and Wilkins, 1947); *A Manual of Style*, 11th ed. (Chicago, University of Chicago Press, 1949).

ions, interpretations, and the like that are presented to advance the theme of the paper need a stated source.

Material from conversation, from lectures, from any source that a reader cannot turn to is acknowledged in the text of the paper or in a prefatory note. The source of a diagram, table, or illustration is not given in a footnote but under the title directly beneath the chart (see example on page 61).

If two or more sources contribute to the same information, they may be put in one footnote, separated by semicolons:

> 1 Stuart Robertson, The Development of Modern English (New York, 1938), pp. 516-20; Charles C. Fries, "The Periphrastic Future with Shall and Will in Modern English," PMLA, 1925, 40:963-1024

2) THE REFERENCE FIGURE is placed slightly above the line *at the end* of a quotation or *after the statement* whose source is being given. It follows the end punctuation of the statement to which it applies.

3) THE NOTES ARE NUMBERED from 1 up through a short paper or through a chapter of a book. (They may be numbered from 1 up on each page but this practice is now rare except for articles with a very large number of notes.)

Although the number of sources referred to in a paper must vary with the type of subject and the kind of sources used, typically a student reference paper will show from two to five footnotes to a page of typewritten manuscript.

4) THE FOOTNOTES ARE PLACED at the bottom of the page on which they belong. With a little practice enough space can be saved to contain the needed notes. Occasionally an informational note may be continued to the footnote space at the bottom of the following page, but this should be avoided as far as possible. (Sometimes the footnotes are placed on a separate sheet following the body of the paper. This is a convenience for copy that is to be printed, since the notes can then be set in type together and later distributed to the pages on which they belong. But it is a nuisance when the manuscript is the final state because a reader has to refer continually to the separate page of notes.)

In print each footnote is indented like a paragraph, but in manuscript there is no objection to beginning each one flush with the left margin. The reference number may be slightly raised above the line as in the text, but this is not necessary. If elevated, the number is not followed by a period; if not, use of the period is a matter of choice.

The Story of the Japanese Evacuation

In 1942 a mass migration unprecedented in the history of the United States took place. Most Americans, involved in a world war at that time, were too busy to notice the involuntary movement of 110,000 persons of Japanese ancestry from the west coast.[1] This movement, known as the Japanese evacuation, caused unnecessary suffering and humiliation to the people involved, but at the same time it had its constructive results. The experience proved that although democracy in America is not dead, it is in a precarious position unless it is extended to all inhabitants of the country.

The military historians will say that evacuation was necessary for national security. According to General DeWitt, head of the Western Defense Command and the man most responsible for the evacuation, the Japanese were removed from the coast because they were a "tight-knit and unassimilated group" which had close connections with Japan, and because they tended to settle in the vicinity of "vital defense installations and facilities."[2]

The traditional anti-Oriental feeling on the west coast was the second factor which caused the evacuation. For twenty years preceding the war, certain pressure groups had been working to make life uncomfortable for the Japanese. They passed anti-Oriental laws which deprived the Japanese immigrant of the right to own land and the right of citizenship. They put the Japanese in an unfavorable light by spreading false propaganda about them. Therefore, when war came, these people, along with others, saw a chance to get rid of the "Japs" by sending them into "concentration camps."[3]

----

1 Dillon S. Myer, "Democracy in Relocation," Common Ground, 1943, 3:43
2 General DeWitt's final report of the evacuation, quoted in U. S. War Relocation Authority, WRA, A Story of Human Conservation (Washington, 1946), pp. 177-80
3 G. M. Fisher, "Japanese Evacuation from the Pacific Coast," Far Eastern Survey, 1942, 11:149

First page of a Reference Paper (continued on page 392)

A period is common but not necessary at the end of a footnote unless it forms a complete sentence. It is usual to put a short line (or sometimes a line clear across the page) between the text and the footnotes.

9b. Form of footnotes. The aim of a reference footnote is to tell the reader the exact source from which the important statements in a paper have been taken. Uniformity of reference is a convenience, and one reason for assigning a reference paper is to give students practice in a systematic form of footnote reference. This section gives a pattern for use in undergraduate papers and aims to answer in advance the majority of questions that will arise. Other practices are in use, some of which are given after the recommended form, but the differences are slight, chiefly variants in punctuation marks. The purpose is always the same: to give the author, title, facts of publication, and specific page of the source used.

1) REFERENCES TO BOOKS. *The first time* a book is referred to in a paper give the author's name with initials or first name first, the title underlined to represent italics, the place and date of publication in parentheses, the number of the page with the abbreviation *p.* for *page* or *pp.* for *pages*. Note the punctuation and capitalization of the examples given.

    1 Lyon G. Tyler, Williamsburg, the Old Colonial Capital (Richmond, 1907), p. 224

If the reference includes both volume and page, the abbreviation for page is not used:

    2 Oliver Elton, A Survey of English Literature 1780–1880 (New York, 1920), 3:109–12

Roman numerals are frequently used for the volume number (III, 109-12), but the practice is declining because of their cumbersomeness. Either a comma or a colon may be used to separate the volume and the page, though the colon is preferable when the volume is in Arabic numerals (3:109-12). The publisher's name can be given between the place and year if desired: (New York, Macmillan, 1920).

For *later references* to the same book, use a short form, enough to identify the particular work in the bibliography: Author's last name alone if not more than one work by the same man is being used:

    3 Tyler, p. 239

Author's last name and one or two key words from the title if more than one source by the same man is used:

    4 Tyler, Williamsburg, p. 256

Pamphlets are referred to in the same form as books.

Within three months following the orders to evacuate, seventeen temporary camps to house the Japanese were set up along the coast.[4] These camps, called "assembly centers," were built on race tracks and fair grounds, and they met only the minimum requirements of a home. In the Tanforan Assembly Center in California, twenty-by-nine-foot stalls were cut into two rooms to house one family. Stale odors of horses, hay, and manure permeated the so-called rooms, and according to one evacuee "Spider webs, horsehair, and hay had been whitewashed with the walls."[5]

During the same period the Los Angeles Times printed the following item: "Multimillion-dollar Santa Anita's track--the world's most beautiful and luxurious racing plant yesterday opened its gates as an assembly center for Japanese evacuees."[6] Medical and sanitary facilities were pitifully inadequate in the camps. Recreation and education were unprovided for. Time hung heavy for the evacuees.

After several months of this type of life, the evacuees were sent en masse to more permanent camps known as "relocation centers." There were ten relocation centers situated on government-owned or leased land in California, Arizona, Arkansas, Colorado, Wyoming, Utah, and Idaho. These groups were placed under the supervision of a newly organized group known as the War Relocation Authority.

Life in the relocation centers, although an improvement over that in the assembly centers, was still far from normal. Basic rights were maintained by the evacuees: the right to vote in areas of former residence, the right of uncensored mail, the right to worship, and the right to a small degree of self-government.[7]

----
4 Ibid., p. 145
5 Miné Okubo, Citizen 13660 (New York, 1946), p. 35
6 Los Angeles Times, no date given, quoted in Alexander H. Leighton, The Governing of Men (Princeton, 1945), p. 42
7 Carey McWilliams, What About Our Japanese-Americans? (New York, 1944), p. 14

Second page of a Reference Paper (continued from page 390)

2) MAGAZINE ARTICLES. The first time a magazine article is referred to, give the author's name, title of the article in quotation marks, name of the magazine underlined, year, volume, page:

```
5 Lawrence E. Bowling, "What Is the Stream of Consciousness
Technique?," PMLA, 1950, 65:335
```

In some styles the year is given in parentheses between the volume and page:

```
5 Lawrence E. Bowling, "What Is the Stream of Consciousness
Technique?," PMLA, 65 (1950):335
```

For magazines that page each issue separately instead of consecutively through a volume, the best solution is to give the exact date of the issue used and the page:

```
6 "Mr. Eliot," Time, Mar. 6, 1950, p. 22
```

Later references to a magazine article may be shortened to the author's last name, the name of the magazine in which the article appeared, and the page:

```
7 Bowling, PMLA, p. 345
```

3) NEWSPAPERS. The reference to a news story is to the paper's name underlined, the date, the page. The column number may be given. If there are sections paged separately, the section should be given. Headlines are not ordinarily given, because they are often changed from edition to edition of a paper.

```
8 The New York Times, Mar. 4, 1950, p. 1, col. 8
9 The New York Times, Mar. 12, 1950, sec. 4, p. 5
```

4) IBID. (an abbreviation for the Latin *ibidem*) means "in the same place" and in a footnote means "in the same book or article as the preceding footnote." It is used, underlined, only to refer to the work cited in the immediately preceding footnote:

```
10 Robert S. and Helen M. Lynd, Middletown (New York, 1929), p. 44
11 Ibid., p. 162
```

Ditto marks are not used in footnotes.

5) AUTHOR NOT KNOWN. When the author is not known, the title becomes the first item of the note. "Anonymous" and such substitutes for a name are not used.

```
12 "What Will Follow ECA?" The New Republic, Mar. 13, 1950, p. 6
13 Modern Cartography, Lake Success, United Nations, 1949, p. 18
```

Unsigned encyclopedia articles may be given by title of the article or by the encyclopedia:

    14 "Rhetoric," Encyclopaedia Britannica (Chicago, 1945), 19:248
    15 Encyclopaedia Britannica (Chicago, 1945), 19:248

Unsigned publications of organizations are best listed by title:

    16 American Education and International Tension (Washington,
    National Education Association, 1949), p. 32

6) MATERIAL AT SECOND HAND. When the material used is taken at second hand from a work, both the original source and the source from which it is taken should be given:

    17 William Caxton, Preface to Eneydos (1490), quoted in Albert C.
    Baugh, A History of the English Language (New York, 1935), p. 241

This applies to the citation of an article that has been read in a collected volume:

    18 Wendell L. Willkie, One World, in Prefaces to Peace (New York,
    1943), p. 120
    19 Frank Luther Mott, "Trends in Newspaper Content," in Wilbur
    Schramm, ed., Mass Communications (Urbana, 1949), p. 339

7) PART OF REFERENCE IN TEXT. If part of the reference is given in the text of the paper, it need not be repeated in the footnote. That is, if the author's name is in the text, the footnote may begin with the title; if the author's name and the title are in the text, only the page is necessary in the footnote.

8) EXPANDED FOOTNOTE. Occasionally other matter—an added fact, a statement of a different opinion, a quotation—is included in footnotes, but this sort of thing should be kept to a minimum. In college students' work it is well to confine footnotes to references to sources. If something is worth including, it probably belongs in the text.

9) LAW CASES are cited according to the following form: The plaintiff's last name, v. (versus, meaning "against"), the defendant's last name, the volume number of the reports in which the case is given, the abbreviation for the report series, the page on which the case begins, and the year in which the decision was rendered:

    20 Lochner v. New York, 198 U. S. 539 (1905)

10) BOOKS OF THE BIBLE are not italicized. The reference form is:

    21 Genesis 4:16 (or: Genesis 4, 16)

11) GOVERNMENT DOCUMENTS with an author given are cited like a book:

22 Ella B. Ratcliffe, <u>Accredited Higher Institutions 1944</u>, U. S. Office of Education Bulletin 1944, No. 3 (Washington, 1945), pp. 87-8

When no author is given, they are usually cited by title:

23 <u>Higher Education for American Democracy</u>, Report of the President's Commission on Higher Education (Washington, 1947), 1:26

12) COMMON FOOTNOTE ABBREVIATIONS. The following abbreviations are commonly used in footnotes. Those that come from Latin (like *ibid.*) are underlined to represent italics.

art.—article
c.—copyright
c. or *ca.* (*circa*)—about a given date (*c.* 1480)
ch. or chap.—chapter; chs. or chaps.—chapters
col.—column; cols.—columns
ed.—edited by; edition (2d ed.)
f.—following (one following page); ff. (more than one following page: p. 286 ff.)
ibid. (*ibidem*)—in the same work, as explained in § 4
l.—line; ll.—lines
MS.—manuscript
n. d.—no date (used when the date of publication of a work cannot be found)
n. p.—no place (when place of publication cannot be found)
n. s.—new series (of a periodical: *Science*, 1925, n. s. 42: 418)
p.—page; pp.—pages (p. 162; pp. 162-68)
tr.—translated by
vol.—volume; vols.—volumes. (*vol.* and *p.* are not used when figures for both are given: vol. 3; p. 176; but—3: 682)

The following abbreviations were formerly in general use but are less common now:

cf. (*confer*)—compare (now usually replaced by the English: see*)*
et al. (*et alii*)—and others (used instead of giving all the names when a work has several authors; now *and others:* C. W. Young and others)
infra—below (referring to something discussed later in the article)
loc. cit. (*loco citato*)—in the place cited (referring to a previous indication of source)
op. cit. (*opere citato*)—the work cited (sometimes used instead of repeating the title of a work: Tyler, *op. cit.*, p. 256; but now a shortened form of the title is more usual: Tyler, *Williamsburg*, p. 256, as explained in § 1)
passim—in various passages (indicating that a matter is discussed in several places in a given book or article)
q. v. (*quod vide*)—which see (sometimes used to suggest consulting a work, now more generally replaced by *see*)
seq. (*sequentes*)—following (replaced by f. and ff.)
supra—above (referring to something already discussed in the article)
vide—see (now replaced by the English word)

Any description of the form of footnotes makes their use seem harder than it really is. If you have good notes that have the exact sources of their facts clearly recorded, it is relatively simple to keep track of the necessary sources in the first draft and then to place them in the final manuscript in the proper form.

10. The final bibliography

A finished reference paper has a bibliography of the sources actually used in its writing—which does not mean that all the items consulted will be listed but only those which have given material. This is partly a record of work done, but principally it is to help a reader identify exactly the works used and cited in the footnotes.

The form of bibliographies has been pretty well standardized so that author, title, and facts of publication can be given economically and systematically:

    Abelson, Paul, The Seven Liberal Arts, New York, 1906

A period may be used at the end of the line.

Sometimes the name of the publisher is given between the place of publication and the date:

    Kennedy, Arthur G., Current English, Boston, Ginn and Company,
    1935

The three main parts of the entry may be separated by periods instead of commas:

    Abelson, Paul. The Seven Liberal Arts. New York, 1906.
    Kennedy, Arthur G. Current English. Boston: Ginn and Company,
    1935.

In short bibliographies all the items are run in one list, alphabetically by author. When there is no author given, the first important word of the title (overlooking *a* or *the*) is used as the key word for alphabetizing as *Records* comes between *Quinn* and *Tyler* in the specimen on page 397. Very long bibliographies are sometimes grouped by type of material: Primary Sources, Secondary Sources; Works of an author, Works about him; and so on. They should not be grouped according to type of publication, as books or periodicals.

This short bibliography shows a simple and workable form. The first item is a group of periodical articles, the second an article, the third and fifth are books, and the fourth an unpublished manuscript.

                    BIBLIOGRAPHY

    Ames, Nathaniel, "Diary," Dedham Historical Register, 1890, 1:9-16,
    49-52, 111-119
    Matthews, Albert, "Early Plays at Harvard," Nation, Mar. 19, 1914,
    98:295 (Or: XCVIII, 295)

Quinn, A. H., *A History of the American Drama from the Beginning to the Civil War*, New York, 1923

Records of the Linonian Society 1768-1790, MS in Yale University Library

Tyler, L. G.,*Williamsburg, the Old Colonial Capital*, Richmond, 1907

Specimen bibliographies are at the ends of some articles in the *Index* (*Colloquial and written English) and there is a general bibliography with brief notes on pages xi-xiii. See also page 398.

A student should look at the form of bibliographies in the books and articles he reads and make careful note of the changes from the form presented in this article that are suggested by his teachers.

11. The completed paper

Typically the completed paper would comprise these units (those in brackets are optional):

Title page, giving the title of the paper, writer's name, the date submitted, and any other information asked for, such as course and section number.

[*Preface:* In a preface the writer talks about his work. Usually you will not need a preface, but if you wish to thank someone for special help, or to call attention to some unusual material, or to note some point that you wanted to but were unable to present, state the points briefly in a preface. A preface stands on a page by itself.]

Outline: Make the type of outline directed. Be sure that it is brought in line with any changes in your original plan made in the actual writing of the paper. Check its form by reference to the article *Outline form. The outline can serve as a table of contents if you give at the right the page on which the treatment of each main topic begins.

Text of the paper: This is the final copy of your paper, complete with footnotes, with any diagrams or other illustrative material. Put the title at the top of the first page and follow the manuscript form usually expected of you. Before making this final copy, go through § 9 of this chapter once more to make sure that your footnotes follow the form suggested there.

Bibliography: On a separate page give in the form suggested in § 10 your final bibliography, the list of books and articles actually used in writing your paper. If you want to, make brief comments on the sources, at least indicating the most useful ones.

[*Appendix:* Occasionally a paper needs some rather long table of statistics, too long to work into the body of the paper, or a long quotation, as from a treaty or other document that much of the paper is based on. Such matter can be placed in an appendix.]

A reference paper is usually the largest single job in a composition course. Done carefully, with due attention to each of the stages outlined in this chapter, it may be a satisfying activity and good training for later college work.

Bibliography

Fisher, G. M., "Japanese Evacuation from the Pacific Coast,"
Far Eastern Survey, 1942, 11:145-50

Freed, A. O., "Our Racial Refugees," Survey Midmonthly, April
1944, 80:117-19

Leighton, Alexander H., The Governing of Men, Princeton,
Princeton University Press, 1945

McWilliams, Carey, What About Our Japanese-Americans? New
York, Public Affairs Committee, 1944

Myer, Dillon S., "Democracy in Relocation," Common Ground,
Winter 1943, 3:43-48

Myer, Dillon S., "Japanese-American Relocation," Final
Chapter, Common Ground, Autumn 1945, 6:61-66

Okubo, Miné, Citizen 13660, New York, Columbia University
Press, 1946

Shimano, Eddie, "Blue Print for a Slum: Evacuation Camps for
Japanese," Common Ground, Summer 1943, 3:78-85

U. S. War Relocation Authority, WRA, A Story of Human Conservation, Washington, Government Printing Office, 1946

Bibliography of the Reference Paper

Suggested study and writing

1. The subjects in the following list are too broad or too general for successful treatment in a reference paper of moderate length. Select two that interest you or that you are curious about, and make up for each at least four topics which you believe could be treated adequately in reference papers of the length assigned for your course.

American magazines
Artificial languages
Arthurian legends
Blood bank
Books for children
Cancer
Cartels
Censorship of movies
Chautauquas
Cubism
Detective stories
Diamonds
Eskimos
Etiquette
Euthanasia
Frozen foods
Game laws
Golden Gate Bridge
Gypsies
Hitler
Hydroelectric plants
Hygiene
Indians in America
Israeli
Libel laws

Lewis and Clark
Map making
Metal working
Metropolitan Opera Company
Modern productions of *Hamlet*
Music in industry
Oregon Trail
Parent Teachers Association
Perfumes
Plastics
Postage stamps
Prison conditions
Primitive peoples
Public libraries
Radar
Simplified spelling
Shakespearean theater
Slums
Teaching of poetry
Television
UNESCO
Volcanoes
West Point
Witchcraft
Zoos

2. Choose a subject either from Exercise 1 or of your own invention on which you would like to write a reference paper, and prepare brief answers on the following points:

1. Your reason for choosing this subject.
2. Your present knowledge about the subject and the gaps you would have to fill in.
3. The audience you have in mind and the information you assume this audience already has about the topic.
4. The bibliographies, indexes, and other reference works that would be most useful for the topic you have selected.
5. The method and the particular kinds of material—books, periodicals, pamphlets—most useful for developing your paper.

3. Read at least two articles in general encyclopedias on your topic and one in a special encyclopedia. (See the list on pages 375-376.)

Contrast these articles as to (1) date of publication; (2) completeness of treatment; (3) emphasis, or possible bias; (4) approach, whether popular or technical; (5) interest and general value of the articles for your purpose.

4. Draw a floor plan of the reference library, or that part of the library where you will be gathering material, and show the location of the following reference works, and any others assigned, using the numbers as listed below. If you are unable to locate some of the references, consult the card catalog to see whether your library has them.

1. *Readers' Guide*
2. *International Index*
3. *Encyclopaedia Britannica*
4. *Encyclopedia Americana*
5. *New York Times Index*
6. *Oxford English Dictionary*
7. *Current Biography*
8. *Dictionary of National Biography*
9. *Britannica Book of the Year*
10. *Dictionary of American Biography*

5. Write out in full, using the form recommended by your instructor, these entries from the *Readers' Guide* and the *International Index*. Consult recent volumes of the indexes for the meaning of any unfamiliar abbreviations. What information in these entries would you omit in your footnotes and bibliography? What additional information might you need?

a)

DENTITION
Those teeth will come. A. Usher, il Bet Hom & Gard 25:66+ Je '47

PINKERTON national detective agency
Brothers in crime; train robbery. D. Dressler. Collier's 121:30+ Ap 3 '48
Pinkerton story. R. Jarmen. il Sat Eve Post 220:26-7+ My 15; 34-5+ My 22; 28+ My 29; 28+ Je 5 '48

SHAKESPEARE
Hamlet

Olivier as Hamlet. il (p 11) Good H 127:117 S '48
Olivier's Hamlet. il N Y Times Mag p 20-1 Ag 15 '48
Olivier's Hamlet. il por Time 51:54-6+ Je 28 '48

b)

DICKINSON, Leon T.
Mark Twain's revisions in writing The innocents abroad. bibliog f Am Lit 19:139-57 My '47

MOVING picture laws and regulations
Films and quotes; how far should the new Bill differ from the old Act? N. Mackenzie. New Statesm & Nation 33:451-2 Je 21 '47; Discussion. 33:475; 34:92 Je 28, Ag 2 '47

6. Put the following references to source material in consistent footnote form as they would appear in a reference paper. Keep them in the present numerical order.

1. To page 225 of this book.
2. To an editorial in the Boston Traveler on December 2, 1940, entitled The Responsibility of the Press.
3. To pages 139 and 140 in the second volume of a book by George Philip Krapp called The English Language in America. The book was published by the Century Company of New York and the date on the title page reads MCMXXV.
4. To pages 228 to 231 inclusive of the book mentioned in 1.
5. To an unsigned article called Baby Bombs in volume LV of Time for May 22, 1950, page 69.
6. To page xvii in the Introduction of a book called Burke's Politics. The book has a subtitle Selected writings and speeches of Edmund Burke on Reform, revolution and war. It was edited by Ross J. S. Hoffman and Paul Levack, and was published in 1949 by Alfred Knopf in New York.
7. To an article entitled Letters to the Editor as a Means of Measuring the Effectiveness of Propaganda, written by two men, H. Schuyler Foster, Jr., and Carl J. Friedrich and printed in The American Political Science Review for February 1937, pages 71 to 79. This issue was part of volume 31.
8. To the same pages of the article mentioned in 7.
9. To a quotation by Dr. Raymond B. Nixon in the June 1945 issue of Journalism Quarterly, quoted on pages 78 to 79 of The First Freedom, a book by Morris L. Ernst published in 1946 in New York by the Macmillan Company.
10. To an unsigned article called Isle of Man in the 1941 edition of the Encyclopedia Americana, a thirty volume work published in New York and Chicago by the Americana Corporation. This article appeared on page 414 of volume XV.

7. Put the items in the preceding exercise in proper form and order for a bibliography.

8. Study the use of footnotes in the reference paper, "The Story of the Japanese Evacuation," (pp. 390, 392). Why was a footnote not used at the end of the introductory paragraph? Can you find any passages that might have been footnoted and were not? Or any passage that contains more footnotes than necessary?

9. Below is the preliminary outline for the same reference paper. Compare it with the final form of the outline on page 385, noting which parts have been combined, omitted, or expanded. Which sections of this first outline overlap? Have any changes been made in emphasis?

The Japanese Evacuation

    I. Events leading up to it
       A. Persons affected by the move

B. Attitude toward Orientals on the West Coast
C. Growing war sentiment in the U. S., 1939-41

II. Attack on Pearl Harbor
   A. Japanese excuse for war
   B. Military reasons for evacuating Japanese in America
   C. First assembly centers

III. Camp life
   A. Where relocation camps were situated
   B. Number of camps
   C. How they were run

IV. Sentiment of the Japanese toward evacuation
   A. Lack of educational facilities and political freedom
   B. Increase in juvenile delinquency
   C. Typical incidents in camp

V. Contributions of Japanese toward war effort
   A. Desire of young men to enlist
   B. Record of the 442nd combat team
   C. Awards and decorations won

VI. Public sentiment toward the evacuation
   A. Feeling of Americans toward Orientals before the war
   B. Hostility toward returning evacuees

VII. Treatment of the returning evacuees
   A. Anti-Japanese demonstrations
   B. Difficulty of finding work
   C. Loss of business establishments and farms

VIII. Good and bad results of the evacuation
   A. Japanese no longer segregated in big cities
   B. New realization of the value of citizenship
   C. Dangers of anti-racial feeling in U. S.

IX. Conclusion

10. Prepare to write a brief report in class on one of the following or similar topics. Bring your bibliography and note cards with you for reference.

1. A summary or précis of your paper, giving the essential ideas and the emphasis of the original.
2. Different methods by which you could have developed your paper, and why you chose the one you did.
3. The sources you found most useful and why.
4. Some problems you encountered in organizing your paper and how you solved them.
5. The material you omitted from your rough draft, and your reasons for eliminating it.
6. Some interesting by-products of your research—information you have gained about finding material, about the subject itself, or about further areas for investigation.

Part Two

Index to English

a Entries on particular words
and constructions

b Entries for correction
and revision of papers

c Page references to subjects treated
in the chapters

d Articles on English grammar

e Articles on various facts of language

Suggestions
for using the Index articles

This *Index* contains entries in alphabetical arrangement that fall roughly into five categories:

a. ENTRIES ON PARTICULAR WORDS AND CONSTRUCTIONS, such as *continual, continuous; *fiancé, fiancée; *get, got; *like—as; *route; *shall—will; *so . . . that; *very. Their standing in actual usage today is given. Since the discussions are in terms of "levels of usage," you should read Chapter 2, Varieties of English, in order to make intelligent use of recommendations that place a word or construction as General, Colloquial, Formal, and so on.

b. ENTRIES FOR CORRECTION AND REVISION OF PAPERS, indicated by longhand abbreviations before the entry word. A list of these entries is given at the end of the book. These subjects are so important that they are likely to be studied in class and so are usually treated most fully in the chapters of the *Guide;* but for convenience in revising papers the basic points are given in the *Index* entry, with a page reference to the fuller treatment in the chapter.

c. PAGE REFERENCES TO SUBJECTS TREATED IN THE CHAPTERS (like Incomplete sentences, Topic sentences, Vocabulary), when there seemed no need for repeating the material in the *Index*. There are also cross references to other articles in the *Index*. A reference to the *Guide* is indicated by chapter, section title, and page number (ch. 2, "Informal English," p. 39) and to other *Index* articles by an asterisk plus the entry word (*due to). The main treatment of an item has been put under the entry that most people would be likely to look for, with cross references from other possible approaches.

d. ARTICLES ON ENGLISH GRAMMAR giving definitions and examples of such matters as *Case, *Conjunctions, *Plurals, *Principal parts of verbs. These are necessary for a full description of the language but are not of immediate use at the time of writing.

e. ARTICLES ON VARIOUS FACTS OF LANGUAGE (such as *American and British usage, *Foreign words in English) that are more for general information than for immediate application.

To make the maximum use of this *Index*, it would be well to read first Chapters 2 and 3 of the *Guide* to get the general principles involved, and then to read a few consecutive pages of the *Index* articles (or a selection of them, such as those referred to on page 405) to see those principles applied, to get the feel of the articles, and to see how they fit with your present usage and present attitude. With this preparation the articles should prove of immediate and convenient use in your actual speaking and writing.

References to the sources most used in gathering the material for this book are usually made to author's name only. The exact titles of these sources will be found on pages xi-xiii.

A full discussion of the symbols by which pronunciation is represented appears in the article *Pronunciation § 3.

A   The letter *a* represents several different sounds in English, and these sounds are also spelled in a number of other ways. It represents three principal sounds, described in sections 1 to 3 below, and several that are less common:

1. 'Long *a*' (ā), as in *ale, fable, hate*. This sound is also commonly spelled *ei* or *ey* (*neighbor, veil, obey*), and *ea* (*break*), and *ai* or *ay* (*maid, pay*). In unstressed syllables long *a* loses some of its *a* quality (contrast the first *a* with the second in *vacation*) and is sometimes called "half long *a*." Since its changed value comes naturally from the reduced stress, no separate mark is needed for this sound (vā kā'shən).

2. 'Short *a*' (a) as in *fat, ladder, detach*. This is a very common English sound, especially common in American pronunciation. Short *a* in unstressed syllables, like other unstressed vowels, tends to lose its distinct sound and to become a neutral vowel represented by ə: *against* (ə genst').

3. 'Broad *a*' (ä), as in *far, larger, father*, and in *hearth* and the first syllable of *sergeant*.

4. 'Intermediate *a*' in a troublesome group of words called the "ask words" because the sound is sometimes referred to as "*a* as in *ask*." The fact about *ask, aunt, bath, can't, grass*, and a number of other words is that their pronunciation varies with different people of very good standing all the way from short *a* to broad *a* with many intermediate stages. In certain parts of New England, especially around Boston, and in a few other American cities, and among people who have been influenced by the pronunciation of these places or that of southern England, broad *a* (chäns, fäst, päth) is used, but most Americans use short *a* (chans, fast, path), or a sound very close to short *a*. Usage is divided on the pronunciation of these words, and a person should use whichever sound is native to him or is used by the circle in which he lives and not try to use a different one which he assumes to be more correct but which he is almost certain not to use consistently. In this *Index* these sounds are marked as short *a* (a) with a reference to this paragraph (*A § 4).

5. **'Open o' sound.** *A* frequently spells the "open *o*" sound, especially before *l* plus a consonant, and after *w: all, ball, tall, Walter, warm.* In our pronunciation key this sound is represented by ô (ôl, bôl, wôrm).

(Reference: *Webster's New International,* "A Guide to Pronunciation," §§ 76-96.)

a- *A-* as a prefix from Greek meaning *not* is used in forming many words in the formal and scientific vocabularies:

| amoral | asexual | asymmetrical | atypical | achromatic |

It is usually pronounced ā (ā si met′ri kəl) though "short *a*" is heard, especially in *amoral* and *achromatic.*

A prefix *a-* from various Old English origins is found in many words (*abed, aloud, asleep*) and survives in vulgate English in phrases like *going a fishing, a hunting.* See dictionaries for details of origin and use.

a, an 1. **The choice between 'a' or 'an'** depends on the initial sound of the word that follows:

A is used before all words beginning with *a consonant sound,* that is, before all words spelled with initial consonants except silent *h,* as in *hour,* and before words spelled with initial vowels that combine consonant and vowel sounds, as in *eulogy, unit* (yōōl′ə ji, yōō′nit):

| a business | a European trip | a *D* | a usage |

An is used before all words beginning with *a vowel sound,* including words spelled with initial silent *h* (see *H):

| an apple | an *F* | an hour apart | an honor |

Questions sometimes arise over words beginning with *h* but not accented on the first syllable, as in *histo′rian, hotel′.* Formerly this *h* was not pronounced, so that *an* was used. Now that the *h* is pronounced, some people continue to say *an hotel′, an histor′ical event* (but *a his'tory*). *A hotel', a histor'ical event,* and so on are more common and generally preferred pronunciations.

2. Repeating 'a' or 'an' before each noun of a series tends to keep the various words distinct and make the expression emphatic: *a pen, a sheet of paper, and an envelope* (*a pen, sheet of paper, and envelope* would be less emphatic).

3. Awhile, a while. The adverb *awhile* (He came *awhile* ago) is written as one word, but not the noun (he came for *a while*), or *a lot, a bit, a little.*

(SEE *half for *a half hour, half an hour,* etc. For *kind of a, sort of a* see *kind of [a], sort of [a].)

a, b, and c See *Series.

Ab **Abbreviations** Correction: Write in full the abbreviation marked.

1. Appropriateness. Abbreviations belong most appropriately to manuals, books of reference, business and legal documents, scholarly footnotes, and other works in which saving space is important. They also fit in familiar writing—notes for our own use, letters to friends. In literature and most formal writing, abbreviations are held to a minimum, though modern informal style is much less strict in this than older style.

Shoptalk, familiar conversation, and slang use many abbreviations for the names of things frequently mentioned: *t.b.* (*tuberculosis*), *d.t.'s* (*delirium tremens*), *b.o.m.* (newspaper: *business office must*), *b.f.* (*boyfriend*), *g.f.* (*girlfriend*).

2. Standard abbreviations. *Dr., *Mr., *Mrs., Messrs.* are always abbreviated when used with a name. A number of abbreviations, such as *St.* (*Saint*), **a.m.* and *p.m., S.E.C., T.V.A.,* and abbreviations for other government agencies are generally used. In formal writing, titles like *Reverend, *Professor, President, and Senator would not be abbreviated at all, but in most writing they are found abbreviated *when initials or given names are used:* not *Prof. Hylander,* but *Professor Hylander* or *Prof. G. W. Hylander.*

English still has many abbreviations of Latin words:

A.D.	*Anno Domini*—in the year of our Lord (*Centuries)
cf.	*confer*—compare (for which *see* may be used)
*e.g.	*exempli gratia*—for example
*etc.	*et cetera*—and so forth
*ibid.	*ibidem*—the same (used in footnotes)
*i.e.	*id est*—that is

Such abbreviations are not italicized, unless there is a special reason for italics (as when *ibid.* represents the title of a book), since they are regarded as English words. Less commonly used abbreviations from Latin (*c.* or *ca.* [*circa*, about, used in uncertain dates], *seq.* [*sequentes*, following]) are usually italicized.

Dictionaries give frequently used abbreviations in the main alphabetical list of words or in a special list.

(SEE ch. 13, "Common footnote abbreviations," p. 395, for abbreviations used in footnotes of reference papers.)

3. Period with abbreviations. Naturally a writer intends to use a period after an abbreviation and omitting it is a careless slip, but a pretty common slip.

Some publishers do not use a period after an abbreviation that is to be followed by a colon (as *i.e:*) and only one period is used when an abbreviation falls at the end of a sentence.

There is a growing tendency today not to use a period after an abbreviation that ends with the last letter of the word abbreviated: *Dr, Mr, Mrs, vs, Wm.* This is more common in British than in American usage.

Periods are frequently not used with the abbreviations of names of government agencies (*SEC, TVA, FBI, UNESCO*), and of other terms if the abbreviation is generally used instead of the name (*OGPU, PMLA*), and of phrases like *mph, hp, kwh, rpm* in scientific contexts or when used with figures (*780 rpm*).

Abbreviations that are pronounced as words (*Wac, snafu, Nazi*) are called *acronyms*.

(COMPARE *Contractions, *Origin of words § 3c.)

ability (to)   The idiom with *ability* is *to* and an infinitive (*ability to do*, not *of doing*):

He has the ability to design beautiful buildings.

The idea is often better expressed by an adjective or verb:

He is able to [He can] design beautiful buildings.

Or the notion of ability can be implied in direct statement of accomplishment:

He designs [is designing] beautiful buildings.

Ablative case   The functions of the ablative case of Latin are performed in English by prepositional phrases: *from home, at the bay.*

(SEE *Case.)

able to   *Able to* is sometimes crudely used instead of *can:*

Crude: This is not able to be done because of lack of time.
Good English: This cannot be done because of lack of time.
Or: They are not able to do this because of lack of time.

-able, -ible

-able, -ible The common and useful suffix *-able*, meaning "able to," "liable to," and so on, is hard to spell because in a number of words *-ible* is found. The point to remember is that *-able* is by far the more common form and that it should be used also in *coining occasional words like *jumpable* or *come-at-able*.

1. -able. This list contains a few of the many words in *-able*:

abominable	hospitable	laughable	sizable
admirable	imaginable	lovable	suitable
advisable	improbable	movable	teachable
applicable	incurable	noticeable	tolerable
changeable	indefatigable	peaceable	unbearable
comfortable	indispensable	perishable	unbelievable
comparable	inevitable	preferable	undefendable
desirable	inseparable	presentable	unmistakable
detestable	intolerable	profitable	unpronounceable
eatable	justifiable	receivable	unspeakable
excusable	knowable	serviceable	usable

2. -ible. The following rather common words have *-ible*:

accessible	discernible	indefensible	reducible
admissible	divisible	indelible	repressible
audible	edible	inexhaustible	responsible
combustible	eligible	intelligible	reversible
compatible	fallible	invisible	seducible
comprehensible	feasible	irresistible	sensible
contemptible	flexible	legible	submersible
convertible	forcible	negligible	suggestible
corruptible	gullible	perceptible	suppressible
credible	horrible	perfectible	susceptible
destructible	impassible	permissible	tangible
digestible	impossible	plausible	terrible
dirigible	incredible	possible	visible

3. -able or -ible. Several words are found with either *-able* or *-ible*. The more common form is put first:

collapsible—collapsable   collectable—collectible
preventable—preventible

(See Fowler, "-able, -ible.")

about (at about) *At about* is a common colloquial and informal doubling of prepositions: "I got there at about three o'clock." In formal writing ordinarily choose the more accurate of the two: "I got there *at* three o'clock," or "I got there *about* three o'clock." *About* is usually the one intended.

The same applies to the colloquial *at around*.

(Reference: Edward G. Fletcher, "At About," *American Speech*, 1947, 22:192-5.)

410

above *Above* is primarily used as a preposition (*above* the clouds) or adverb (the statements made *above* [*above* modifying the verb *made*]). Its common use as an adverb, as in "The story told above" (that is, on the same page or on a preceding page), would be avoided by many writers in favor of "The story I have told . . ." or some such expression.

Above is in general use as an adjective (the above statements) or noun (The above is confirmed), although formal writers tend to avoid it.

(REFERENCE: Pooley, pp. 128-30.)

Absolute phrases Absolute phrases are usually *verbid constructions modifying the sentence as a whole or adding details to the statement. They are not actually "absolute" or independent but "contact constructions," without connectives defining their relationship to other sentence elements.

When they precede the main clause, they often seem unidiomatic: "*The narrows passed*, we went along at a fairly good speed." (Contrast "When we had passed the narrows, we went along at a fairly good speed.")

When they follow the main clause, they are a convenient way of adding details, as in the following sentence where everything except the main clause, *She walked slowly*, is in what are usually known as absolute phrases:

> She walked slowly, big flakes falling on her lamb coat and clinging to hair over her ears, the lazily falling snow giving her, in her thick warm coat, a fine feeling of self-indulgence.—MORLEY CALLAGHAN, *A Native Argosy*, p. 135

(SEE ch. 4, "Verbid phrases," p. 112; *Participles § 4, *Infinitives § 4. REFERENCE: Francis Christensen, *College English*, 1950, 11:401-3.)

absolutely In speech *absolutely* has become generalized to mean "very" or "quite": "He is absolutely the finest fellow I know"—and in slang means simply "yes." It is sometimes a useful word to put force into dialog but would be out of place in most writing, except in its original meaning of "completely, unconditionally."

Abstract and concrete words Correction: **Try to change the** *Abst* **abstract expressions marked to concrete ones.**

Nouns that name qualities, conditions, actions, summaries of particular facts are abstract: *love, civilization, danger, age, flying*. They contrast with concrete nouns, which name persons and things that can be seen and touched: *girl, schoolhouse, tree*.

411

Abstract nouns are necessary in discussing ideas, but are often used where specific, concrete words would be more exact and forceful, as in this sentence:

> Cleanliness of apparatus, particularly glassware, is of utmost importance to insure against the entry of any substance other than that for which the search is being conducted.

(SEE ch. 12, "Abstract and concrete words," p. 341, for discussion of the use of abstract words. For discussion of their meaning, see ch. 11, "Concrete words" and "Abstract words," pp. 319, 320.)

Academic writing One conspicuous trait of academic writing— that is, the publications of teachers and scholars and others engaged in research and in originating ideas—is its documentation, the devices of bibliography and footnote reference that give the sources of material used in preparing the paper. Scrupulousness in giving exact references to those materials sets scholarly writing off from popular books and articles.

(SEE for form ch. 13, "Footnotes," p. 388 and ch. 13, "The final bibliography," p. 396.)

When scholarly articles and monographs deal with particular points of research—the results of experiments, of historical research, of special investigation in any field—they naturally show the specialized vocabulary, compactness, and impersonality of *scientific and technical writing. Less specialized academic writing is dignified and almost necessarily in a formal style.

Partly because many works by professors and research workers are written more impersonally than they need be, "academic" is often used to describe writing that is unpleasantly abstract, distant, and dry, and to describe the style of many books supposedly for general reading that do not show sufficient adaptation to the desired readers. But such failures in communication should not hide the importance of much academic writing. Very often the men engaged in discovering new facts, in originating interpretations of facts, are not particularly interested in popularizing them and leave that task to others.

This passage presents an idea clearly and exactly for a limited group and suggests some of the typical traits of academic writing of the better sort:

> An expert is a person who, in some special field of knowledge, has a technical competence not possessed by ordinary persons. He has the knowledge that is necessary to adjust means to ends. He can diagnose changes or predict results if certain postulates are made. An engineer can calculate the strength of materials required if a bridge is to bear some given load. A

specialist in maternity welfare can indicate the steps it is desirable to take in order to reduce the death-rate in childbirth. An expert in naval armaments can state the thickness of armour-plate required to resist the entrance of projectiles hurled against it. A motoring engineer can devise a car most likely to avoid danger of skidding on a greasy road-surface. In the great society, we could not for a day preserve its scale of living unless there were countless men and women applying their knowledge to the solution of these problems.

But the fundamental issues of society are not the kind of problem the expert is accustomed to handle. They require not specialisation so much as the power to coordinate. They involve judgments of value, predictions about psychological impact, which are the product not of expert technique, but of a certain divine common sense which has no necessary connection with it. It is, of course, true that common sense, even when divine, is helpless without the results of expert knowledge; but the converse proposition is even more important. For the vices of specialisation are of an ultimate quality. There is always the danger that the specialist will over-emphasise the proportionate importance of his results to the total which has to be attained. Sailors can never be safely left in control of a naval department. Doctors have a dangerous tendency to see the population not as normal human beings, but as potential patients. Efficiency engineers very largely forget the psychological factor in their equations. Mr. F. W. Taylor's famous comparison[1] of a certain type of man with the unresisting ox omitted the unfortunate refusal of that type to remain permanently oxlike in character. The problems which the statesman has to decide are not, in the last analysis, problems upon which the specialism of the expert has any peculiar relevance.—HAROLD J. LASKI, *Democracy in Crisis*, pp. 171-72

---

[1] *Principles of Scientific Management*, p. 359.
(SEE ch. 2, "Formal English," p. 48.)

Accent   Accent is the increased force given to certain syllables in speaking. In this *Guide-Index*, stress is used rather than *accent*.

(SEE *Pronunciation § 4, b and c, *Rhythm, *Noun and verb stress.)

Accent marks   French words in English sometimes keep the accent marks with which they are spelled in their original language:

Acute: café   outré   attaché   fiancée
Circumflex: crêpe   tête
Grave: frère   suède

The accent marks are regularly used in formal writing and formal publications. In informal writing those marks that are not needed to indicate pronunciation (as the mark for *café* is) are dropped. Both *fete* and *fête*, *role* and *rôle* are found, for instance. Most newspapers do not use accent marks.

(SEE *Foreign words in English, and for particular words consult a recent dictionary.)

accept   See *except.

accidental, accidentally Watch the spelling (and pronunciation) of *accidentally*, which is an *-ally word.

Accusative case The personal pronouns, except *you* and *it*, have separate forms for the accusative: *me, her, him, us, them; whom* is the accusative of the relative and interrogative *who* (but see *who —whom). Nouns do not have a special form for the accusative; noun objects of verbs and prepositions are in the common case form.

(SEE *Case; *Objects; *Infinitives § 4; *Gerund § 2; *It's me; *Who, whom.)

act In the sense "to behave, bear oneself as being or as if being" (Webster), *act* is a *linking verb, so that its meaning can be completed by an adjective: He acts older than he is. He acts wise.

Active voice A verb is said to be in the active voice when its subject is the doer of the action: "Jimmy's father *gave* him a car" as contrasted with the passive verb in "Jimmy *was given* a car by his father."

(SEE *Voice and *Passive verbs.)

ad *Ad* is the clipped form of *advertisement*, has only one *d*, and should not be followed by a period. Like other *clipped words it belongs to informal and familiar speech and writing.

address Verb stressed on second syllable: ə dres′; noun's stress divided: a dres′ [ə dres′] or ad′res; ad′res is most used in the word's commonest sense, the address of a letter, package, etc.:

> Mr. Thorpe was to address [ə dres′] the meeting.
> Mr. Thorpe then addressed [ə drest′] the meeting.
> Mr. Thorpe's address [ə dres′ or ad′res] was almost an hour long.
> The letter's address [ad′res or ə dres′] was illegible.

Addresses When the various parts of a person's address are written on the same line, they are separated by commas:

> Miss Louise Finney, 48 Adirondack View, Middlebury, Vermont
> Mr. Davis was a native of Carroll County, Va., and a graduate of the College of William and Mary.

(SEE *Letters § 1, b and c for addresses in and on letters.)

Adjective clauses An adjective clause is a subject-and-verb construction that modifies a noun or pronoun. Many such clauses are introduced by relative pronouns, *who, which, that:*

> The man *who lived at the head of the street* has moved away. (Clause modifies *man*.)
> People *who live in glass houses* shouldn't throw stones. (Clause modifies *people*.)

The belief, *which he had held from boyhood*, gradually slipped away. (Clause modifies *belief*.)

Animals *that live in caves* lose their powers of sight. (Clause modifies *animals*.)

The house *where I was born* had just been sold. (Clause modifies *house*.)

One of the oldest, most economical, and neatest constructions, particularly characteristic of English, is the adjective clause without an introductory word (see Chapter 10, "Long and short constructions," p. 286):

The one *I caught yesterday* weighed three pounds. (Clause modifies *one*.)

The girl *he had intended to marry* ran away with his brother. (Modifies *girl*.)

Adjective clauses perform the functions of adjectives.

(See ch. 4, "Adjective clauses," p. 114; *Adjectives, types and forms; *Restrictive and nonrestrictive. REFERENCE: Curme, *Syntax*, chs. 13, 14.)

Adjectives in use Adjectives should add something to the exactness of a writer's statement or to the definiteness of his picture. As Herbert Read puts it, "appropriate epithets may be either exact or happy." In *briny* ocean, the *briny* does not add, because all oceans are briny; *stark* does not add much to the meaning of *tragedy*, or of *madness* either. Very general adjectives like *good* or *bad* or *beautiful* or *wonderful* do not as a rule add; the reader wants a more specific detail, a particular sort of *good* (*generous, affable, efficient*). Many adjectives that are exact enough have been used too often with certain nouns (*fond* farewell, *beady black* eyes) and are merely trite. Because most people do not use exact adjectives in conversation, they often fall back on these flat and stale modifiers in writing —and professional writers sometimes fall back on them too (see *Newspaper English § 2; Chapter 12, "Trite words," page 333).

A writer may try too hard to make a picture exact. Most of the adjectives in the following paragraph are exact; that is, they add clearly to the meaning. But there are too many of them; the writer has been too conscientious. The passage would be more readable if those in brackets, and perhaps others, were taken out.

In a hotel dining room there is not the [*clamorous*,] *raucous* bedlam of its *immediate* surroundings, but a *refined, subdued* atmosphere, pervaded by *distinct*, faintly *audible* sounds. The orchestra, with a barely *perceptible* diminuendo, concludes the [*melodic*,] *slow-tempo* arrangement, climaxed by the [*beautiful*] strains of the "Merry Widow" waltz—*rising, falling, fading* with *plaintive* supplication. Then later, while a *modern, rhythmic* melody is being played, the *hushed* clash of cymbals, the [*musical*] tinkle of the chimes, and the *softened* blare of brass blend harmoniously with the

415

[*pulsing,*] *vibrant* voice of the *featured* soloist, only to be anticlimaxed by the *perfunctory* applause of the diners. The [*constant,*] *relentless* shuffle, shuffle, shuffle of *dancing* feet becomes *monotonous* with its [*endless*] repetition and *imperceptible* variation, while *trite* conversation is often interrupted by the *affected* voice of the *solicitous* waiter. The whispers and [*gay*] laughter, the *discordant* clatter of dishes upon trays, and the [*careless*] scraping of chairs blend into the room's *distinctive* personality.

Such a passage is treated with irony by William Saroyan in the preface to *The Daring Young Man on the Flying Trapeze:*

> All successful writers believe that one word by itself hasn't enough meaning and that it is best to emphasize the meaning of one word with the help of another. Some writers will go so far as to help an innocent word with as many as four and five other words, and at times they will kill an innocent word by charity and it will take years and years for some ignorant writer who doesn't know adjectives at all to resurrect the word that was killed by kindness.

But a sensible and sensitive use of adjectives is necessary. In most exposition the first requirement of adjectives is exactness; they must answer the needs of the material, like the italicized words in the next two paragraphs:

> *Many* counselors on *public* relations had *one* foot in commerce and the other in politics—even *international* politics. The most *eminent* figure in *this* class was the *late* Ivy Lee. It seems a pity that he died silently, leaving behind, so far as anyone knows, no *real* record of *his* activities. The *candid* reminiscences of Ivy Lee would be as *useful* to a *future* historian as Pepys' Diary— and perhaps as *interesting* to the student of *human* souls. He began *his larger* career as counselor for *certain Rockefeller* interests. He was *careful,* nevertheless, not to identify himself with the Rockefellers or *any other* group, so leaving himself *free* to serve *all* clients. He had a hand in an agitation for recognition of Russia as a means of increasing our *export* market. Indeed, he may have directed *this* campaign. So, too, when an element among the bankers decided that cancellation of *European war* debts would benefit *American* finance, they used Lee's talent for sweetening *unpopular* causes. And in the *last* year of his life he was advising the *new German* government on ways and means for making *Nazi* principles and methods less *hateful* to the *average American* citizen.—WILL IRWIN, *Propaganda and the News*, pp. 267-68

In writing that makes a definite attempt to capture the feelings and sensations of the reader, the adjectives must be exact (as they are in the following paragraph) but they must also deserve the epithet "happy"; that is, they must seem to fit and at the same time to contribute an accent, to lead the reader to the writer's feeling; perhaps they may make an imaginative appeal. In describing an actual experience Ernest Hemingway presents a picture rather than a series of facts:

In the *five* days I saw a *dozen* or *more kudu* cows and *one young* bull with a string of cows. The cows were *big, gray, striped-flanked* antelope with ridiculously *small* heads, *big* ears, and a *soft, fast-rushing* gait that moved them in *big-bellied* panic through the trees. The *young* bull had the start of a spiral on *his* horns but they were *short* and *dumpy* and as he ran past us at the end of a glade in the dusk, *third* in a string of *six* cows, he was no more like a *real* bull than a *spike* elk is like a *big, old, thick-necked, dark-maned, wonder-horned, tawny-hided, beer-horse-built* bugler of a bull-elk.—*Green Hills of Africa*, p. 138

Notice that the relatively insignificant *glade, dusk,* and *trees* are not modified but that the *gait* is *soft, fast-rushing.* The gait needed to be described; the dusk and the trees are merely part of the background.

Adjectives sometimes tend to make a slow movement in writing partly because many of them have a falling rhythm; that is, the stressed syllable is followed by one or more unstressed syllables. They may contribute to a leisurely, relaxed effect:

The sheltering trees only emphasized the ashen deadness of the wrinkled clapboards.

Too many of them may result in an excessively slow movement.

Carl Sandburg has been credited with advising a writer, "Think twice before you use an adjective." This is probably sound advice for anyone who is writing a good deal and tends to let thoughtless adjectives slip in. But it is also important for a writer to fix his eye on his subject and write about it as he really sees it. Without stuffing in adjectives he should fill in the qualities that are needed for the reader to re-create the picture or idea for himself. The adjectives then should be at least exact, and some of them may be happy.

(COMPARE ch. 4, "Adjectives and adverbs," p. 99; *Adverbs in use. REFERENCE: Aiken, ch. 10.)

Adjectives, types and forms

1. Types. 2. Forms. 3. Position. 4. Comparison. 5. Phrases and clauses. 6. Other parts of speech. 7. As nouns.

An adjective modifies a noun or pronoun, that is, in some way makes its meaning more exact: a *black* spider, *those* men, *certain blind* interests, *lucky* me, He is *silly.*

1. Types. Adjectives are of three general types: (a) DESCRIPTIVE ADJECTIVES, the most common type, modify the noun by naming a quality or condition of the object it names: a *gray* shutter, *vivid* colors, *difficult* words, a *laughing* girl, the *wrecked* car.

b) LIMITING ADJECTIVES point out in some way the object named or indicate quantity or number: *this* vase, *his former* address, *several* books, *their* ambitions, *seventy five* seats, the *nineteenth* day.

417

c) PROPER ADJECTIVES, derived from proper nouns, originally are limiting adjectives: *French* possessions, the *Puritan* colonies—but often become descriptive: *French* culture, *Puritan* manners. Sometimes they mingle both functions, as *Elizabethan* in *the Elizabethan drama* both limits drama to a period and brings to mind qualities of a group of plays.

Often a proper adjective is used so frequently in a merely descriptive sense that it loses its relation to the proper noun from which it came and becomes a simple descriptive adjective, written without a capital: *bacchanalian, pasteurized, diesel, india* ink, *paris* green.

2. Forms of adjectives. Many adjectives have come down from an early period of the language (*high, handsome, civil*) and many have been made and are still being made by adding a suffix to a noun or verb. Some *suffixes that are still active are:

-able (*ible*)—translatable, dirigible	*-ish*—darkish, womanish
-al—critical, hypothetical	*-less*—harmless, fearless
-ed—sugared, four-footed	*-like*—birdlike
-ese—Burmese, journalese	*-ous*—callous, ferrous
-ful—playful, soulful	*-y*—cranky, dreamy, squiffy, corny

3. Position of adjectives. According to its position in a sentence, an adjective is either attributive or predicate:

a) ATTRIBUTIVE ADJECTIVES are placed next to their nouns, usually preceding, as in *tiny* brook, *horseless* carriages. Sometimes there is good reason for placing an adjective after its noun:

a woman *sweet, simple, home-loving* (Two or more adjectives in formal usage often follow.)

the outfit *complete* (For emphasis)

court *martial*, attorney *general* (Following French patterns)

a good plan *gone* wrong (Participle modified by adverb)

a plan so *complicated* no one could follow it (The adjective modified by other words)

a *white* cap, *small* and beautifully *made* (Avoiding an awkward piling up of adjectives before the noun)

b) PREDICATE ADJECTIVES come after some form of the verb *be* or some other linking verb (*taste, feel, turn*), except in inverted sentence order (*Silent* was the night).

The day is *warm.*   That pie smells *good.*
The train was *crowded.*   For a while I felt *bad.*

(SEE *Linking verbs.)

4. Comparison of adjectives. A greater degree of the quality named by an adjective is shown by adding *-er* or *-est* to the adjective or by placing *more* or *most* before it·

Positive	Comparative	Superlative
learned	more learned	most learned
warm	warmer or more warm	warmest or most warm

(SEE ch. 4, "Adjectives and adverbs," p. 100; *Comparison of adjectives and adverbs for further examples and discussion of use.)

5. Adjective phrases and clauses. Phrases and clauses are used as adjectives:

The man *with his hat on* is Harry.
I like the one *on the end* best.
a bird *with a long bill* (=a *long-billed* bird, a descriptive adjective)
a bird *in the hand* (a limiting adjective)
Everyone *who approves of this* will please raise his right hand.
That was the summer *we went to Yellowstone.*
He asked the first man *he met.*

(SEE *Adjective clauses, *Clauses § 1, *Restrictive and nonrestrictive for further examples and discussion.)

6. Other parts of speech as adjectives. One of the outstanding traits of English is the use of nouns in the adjective function: a *glass* jar, the *Attlee* government, a *hurry* call, *store* bread, *ski* pants, the *high school* course, a *stretcher* case, the *horse and buggy* days. (See *Parts of speech.)

Participles are the adjectival parts of verbs: a *coming* man, a *deserved* tribute.

7. Adjectives used as nouns. Prefaced by an article, words ordinarily used as adjectives function as nouns: *the just, the rich, the unemployed, a high* (of weather), *an* all-time *high, a* new *low.*

(REFERENCES: Kennedy, §§ 52, 105; Curme, *Parts of Speech*, chs. 3, 11; *Syntax*, chs. 5, 13, 14, 25.)

Adjunct An adjunct is a modifier (as adjective of noun, adverb of verb), or a word or group of words that completes the meaning of some sentence element, as the object of a verb, or a predicate adjective. (See *Modifiers.)

adult Pronunciation divided: ə dult'—ad'ult.

Adverbial clauses Subject-and-verb constructions may serve as adverbial modifiers:

After the ball was over . . . He came *because he had to.*
When we got up we found it raining.
He anchored *where the fish was supposed to be.*

(SEE ch. 4, "Adverbial clauses," p. 114; *Adverbs, types and forms; *Adverbs in use; *Clauses.)

Adverbs in use What has been said about the use of adjectives (*Adjectives in use) can be said again about the use of adverbs: Adverbs, too, should be either exact or happy or both. When an amateur writer wants to portray rapid or violent action, he is quite likely to make too free a use of adverbs and kill the whole effect. In this paragraph we would be relieved—and see the picture more clearly—if the writer had abandoned his adverbs:

> Shrill horns scream *threateningly*. Automobiles careen *wildly*. Giant buses lumber *dominantly* along. Policemen shout *warningly* and then *desperately*. Pedestrians scurry across the broad avenue. And then more squeaky, impatient cars, more terrifying trucks, and more lumbering buses.

Some writers tend to qualify their writing too much, to make a statement and then draw part of it back with such words as *probably, apparently:*

> I shall [probably] try to read your paper tonight.

It is better to choose the most accurate word available and use that.

Many of the longer adverbs are unemphatic because they are unstressed toward the end, and when two or more of them come close together they make a clumsy or unpleasant sounding phrase. The repetition of the *-ly* is especially enfeebling:

> . . . she sang *resonantly*, if *slightly nasally*, between the towering walls of the adjacent buildings.
> They each respond to recurrent temperamental differences, and to analogous though *chronologically distantly* separated social conditions.

Because of the colloquial tendency to use superfluous adverbs, a writer needs to watch out for adverbs that add nothing to his meaning:

> We found [out] that what had looked like snow was a mound of quartz.
> The college student meets [up with] a different type of instructor in English than he had in high school.

Sometimes writers use an adverb plus an adjective or a verb when an accurate adjective or exact verb would be neater and just as expressive.

> Scholarships should be kept for those who are *studiously inclined* [that is, for those who are *studious*].
> When no one was looking I took the goggles and *swiftly made my way* out of the store. (Even *hurried* would say as much and a verb like *scurried* might say more.)

(SEE ch. 4, "Adjectives and adverbs," p. 99; *Prepositions § 3b; *very. REFERENCE: Aiken, ch. 11.)

420

Adverbs, types and forms   Correction: Make the adjective marked *Adv*
an adverb by adding '-ly'. (See § 3.)
> 1. Classed by function. 2. Classed by meaning. 3. Forms.
> 4. Comparison. 5. Other constructions as adverbs.

An adverb modifies a verb (He came *fast*, He loved not *wisely*
but too *well*), an adjective (*thoroughly* bored), an adverb (*too* well,
quite rightly), or a whole clause or sentence (*Possibly* you are right.
When they got to the corner, they saw the road start straight up a
hill.). Adverbs may be classed by meaning and by function:

1. Classed by function: (a) SIMPLE ADVERBS, modifying a single
word or sentence element:

> He will come *today*. (Modifying verb *come*)
> She was *rather* shy. (Modifying adjective *shy*)
> *Almost* immediately we saw them. (Modifying adverb *immediately*)

b) SENTENCE ADVERBS, modifying whole sentences:

> *Perhaps* he will come today. *Unfortunately* there were no more left. *Later*
> I was sorry. *That evening* I was sorry. *As soon as I said it*, I was sorry.

c) CONJUNCTIVE ADVERBS, which connect clauses and also modify
their meaning:

> *Consequently* we agreed to call the matter closed. They were, *however*,
> by no means convinced.

(SEE *Conjunctive adverbs.)

d) INTERROGATIVE ADVERBS, introducing questions:

> *When* did you begin to feel this way?
> *Where* was the car when you first saw it?

2. Classed by meaning. Adverbs have a wide variety of meanings and can be variously grouped. A convenient grouping follows:
a) How? (Adverbs of manner)

> alike   so   well   worse   keenly   openly   painstakingly

b) WHEN? IN WHAT ORDER? (Adverbs of time and succession)

> afterwards   when   finally   late   lately   never   soon

c) WHERE? (Adverbs of place and direction)

> below   far   north   there   upstairs

d) HOW MUCH? To WHAT EXTENT? (Adverbs of degree and
measure)

> all   almost   less   little   much   quite   completely   equally

421

e) WHY? (Adverbs of cause and purpose)

consequently   therefore

f) YES OR NO. (Adverbs of assertion, condition, and concession)

yes no certainly doubtless not perhaps possibly surely truly
Slang, colloquial: O.K. nix absolutely

3. Forms. Most adverbs are adjectives or participles plus the ending *-ly:* "He rowed *badly*"; "She was *deservedly* popular"; "*Surely* you heard that." Some have forms that have developed from Old English forms without a special adverbial sign: *now, quite, since, then, there, where.*

There are a number of adverbs with the same forms as adjectives. Some of these are:

bad	doubtless	hard	much	slow
better	early	high	near	smooth
bright	even	late	right	straight
cheap	fair	loose	rough	tight
close	fast	loud	second	well
deep	first	low	sharp	wrong

Most of these also have forms in *-ly* too, so that we can write "He sang loud" or "He sang loudly." The *-ly* forms are likely to be preferred in formal English and the shorter forms in informal and familiar writing. The shorter forms are often more vigorous than the longer:

Go *slow*. Don't talk so *loud*. It was so windy that I had to hold on *tight* to the iron stand to keep from being blown off the summit.

In speech and informal writing some other short forms of adverbs are used:

Informal: Take it *easy*.   It came *easy*.   He talked *big*.

In vulgate and careless usage there is a tendency to drop the *-ly* from commonly used adverbs, such as *real, special, considerable* for *really, specially, considerably*. This should be avoided in writing and ordinarily in speech.

4. Comparison of adverbs. A greater degree of the quality named by the adverb is shown by adding *-er* or *-est* or by placing *more* or *most* before it:

Positive	Comparative	Superlative
hard	harder	hardest
slow	slower	slowest
slowly	more slowly	most slowly

Most adverbs of more than one syllable are compared with *more* and *most*. See *Comparison of adjectives and adverbs.

5. Other constructions as adverbs. Nouns may be used as adverbs (see *Genitive case § 2):

> He came *mornings*. He plans to stay a *month*.

Phrases may have the functions of adverbs (*Phrases § 1):

> He came *in the morning*.
> *After the examination* he had stopped studying.

Clauses may act as adverbs (*Adverbial clauses):

> *When it came time to go*, he didn't know what to do.
> He stayed on and on *because he didn't know how to leave*.

(References: Kennedy, § 54; Curme, *Parts of Speech*, pp. 73-86.)

advertisement   Ad vûr′tiz mənt is winning out over ad′vər tīz′mənt and is now the more common pronunciation, though both are still heard.

adviser, advisor   Advis*er* has been the more common spelling, but the *-or* form (from analogy with advis*ory*) is being increasingly used. Either is correct.

-ae-, -oe-   Words from Greek and Latin that contain the digraphs *-ae-* and *-oe-* have been for a long time variously spelled in English. (Most printers do not now use the ligatures—the two letters made together, *æ, œ*—except in works dealing with the ancient languages.) Both *-ae-* and *-oe-* are pronounced as though written *e* (either long or short). Many words have been simplified in the past: *economics, pedagogy, penal* were formerly *oeconomics, paedagogy, poenal*.

The present trend is to hasten this simplification. Medicine, for instance, has adopted many of the simpler forms, like *anesthetic* (for *anaesthetic*). The long series of words beginning with *haem-* (meaning "blood") now preferably begin with *hem-* (*hematic, hemoglobin, hemorrhage* and so on). The American Historical Association long ago adopted *medieval*. Dictionaries now give such words as *ameba, cesura, dieresis, esthetic, subpena* either as preferred or alternate spellings. For a particular word consult a recent authoritative dictionary. More formal styles tend to keep the older form with the two letters, more informal styles to use the simple *e*.

Latin plurals in *ae* of course still keep the two letters: *alumnae, antennae, formulae*. (See *Plurals § 4.)

423

In Greek and Latin proper names the two letters are kept: *Boeotia, Caesar, Oedipus*.

affect, effect Since most people make no distinction in pronouncing the first vowel of these words (ə fekt′), the spelling is likely to be confused.

Affect is always a verb, meaning to "influence" or "put on" (compare *affectation*):

> This will *affect* the lives of thousands.
> He *affected* a stern manner.

Effect is most commonly a noun, meaning "result":

> The *effects* of this will be felt by thousands.
> What would be the *effect* of doubling the amount?

Effect is also a verb in formal English, meaning to "bring about":

> The change was *effected* peaceably.

Affectation We pick up our language as children by imitating the speech of people around us, and we change our language later in life by imitating what we hear others say or what we find in reading. So long as these changes furnish us with more varied and more exact ways of saying things, they are proper and necessary, and represent a healthy growth. But sometimes we are led to adopt different pronunciations or different words or different constructions not so much to make our speech more effective as to make it more elegant, or even for the effect of the language itself rather than the effect of what it is conveying. Such changes are affectation and are unpleasant. Writing is more precise than speech, but writing in a style quite different from one's speech is affectation.

Affectation is most easily spotted in pronunciations. In some parts of the United States bēn (for *been*), rä′thər, and ī′thər are common pronunciations, but consciously adopting them is affectation in regions where bin, ra′thər, or ē′thər are usual. For many people expressions like the following are affectations: *aren't I—one should, shouldn't one;* Briticisms like *no end; that which* for *what*. Using slang except for humorous effect is an affectation for a person who knows little slang and seldom uses it in natural speech.

The line between natural and affected speech is hard to draw, since it depends chiefly on motive. In general, picking up expressions not commonly heard from the educated people of a community is dangerous. Increasing the expressiveness of one's speech is praiseworthy, but just trying to be "different" will usually result in bad English. The way to avoid affectation is to consider the appropriateness and expressiveness of language and to shun "big words." (SEE ch. 3, Good English; *Pronunciation § 2.)

again, against   General American pronunciation is ə gen′, ə genst′; ə gān′, ə gānst′ are in general British use but uncommon in the United States.

aggravate   In familiar usage *aggravate* means to "annoy" or "irritate": "I was never so aggravated in my life." In formal English *aggravate* means "to intensify or increase something unpleasant," as to *aggravate suffering* or *a wound* or *a crime*. The same distinction is made with the noun, *aggravation*.

Aggregating sentences   See Chapter 10, "Aggregating sentences," page 274.

Agreement   Correction: **Make the pronoun or verb marked agree grammatically with the word to which it is related: its antecedent if it is a pronoun, its subject if it is a verb.**

Certain parts of speech which vary in form for gender, person, or number should agree when they stand in relationship to each other:

1. Subject and verb agree in number (The *man is* old—The *men are* old) and person (*I go* tomorrow—*He goes* tomorrow). (SEE ch. 4, "Subject—verb—object," p. 104; *Subject and verb, *Collective nouns.)

2. A pronoun agrees with its antecedent in gender (The *man* found *his* keys—The *girl* found *her* keys), in number (The *boy* had lost *his* way—The *hikers* had lost *their* way), and in person. (SEE ch. 4, "Pronouns," p. 108; *Reference of pronouns, *each, *every.)

3. A demonstrative adjective usually agrees in number with the noun it modifies. (*That kind* is inexpensive—*These shoes* cost more than the old ones.) (SEE *Demonstrative adjectives, *this, *kind, sort.)

The chief cause of failure in agreement is that we do not hold our grammatical patterns in mind very well. If several words intervene between the two that should be in agreement, we seem to forget the way we started out. This is especially true if the subject is a collective noun or pronoun, or if several words, some of them plural, come between the singular subject and the verb, so that we are tempted to use a plural verb. (For other problems of agreement see *Apposition and *Tenses § 3.)

agree to, agree with   One agrees *to* a plan and agrees *with* a person. One thing agrees *with* another.

425

ain't   *Ain't* is one of the commonest and most easily identifiable vulgate words, and prejudice against it among educated people has been almost unanimous for the last century or so though it is directly descended from formerly accepted contractions. In actual conversation it is inconspicuously pronounced (ant or nt rather than ānt) and could be an economical single form for *am not, is not, are not, has not, have not* if the social objection could be relaxed. Instead, it is being gradually eliminated by education.

Used in the first person, especially in question form (*ain't I*) where there is no easy natural contraction—*amn't* is hard to pronounce—*ain't* is fairly common among educated speakers and was marked "disputable" and "almost established" in the Leonard study of 1932. *Aren't* is often used in this construction, especially in England: "I'm making real progress, aren't I?" In the first person, both *ain't* and *aren't* should be regarded as colloquial, other uses of *ain't* as vulgate.

(REFERENCES: Curme, *Parts of Speech*, p. 248; Marckwardt and Walcott, pp. 48, 95-6.)

airplane—aeroplane   For several years these two words competed for general usage, but in the United States at least, *airplane* is now both the official and the popular form. *Aeroplane* (pronounced er'ə plān) is more commonly used in England.

a la   *A la* is regarded as an English preposition, meaning "in the manner of": a la Whistler, a la *The New Yorker*. In formal writing and modish advertising (as of cosmetics and fashionable clothes), the accent mark is usually kept (*à la*); elsewhere it is written *a la*. We do not use the other French forms, *à l'* and *au*, except in borrowed phrases (*au gratin*).

alamode   (whether meaning "in the fashion" or referring to ice cream on pie) is usually written as one word without the accent mark. The French form (*à la mode*) is found less often.

alibi   In formal English *alibi* means "a defense on the ground of having been in another place"; in familiar and colloquial English, *alibi* refers to any excuse.

all and its compounds   The following words and phrases need watching:

> *all ready* (adjective phrase): At last they were *all ready* to begin.
> *already* (adverb of time): They had *already* begun.
> *all right* (adjective phrase): The seats seemed *all right* to me.

426

all together (adjective phrase): We found them *all together* in an old trunk. There were six *all together*.

altogether (adverb, equivalent to *wholly*): That's *altogether* another matter.

Alliteration Alliteration is the repetition of the same sound at the beginnings of several words in a series or at the beginnings of stressed syllables within several words close together. Besides contributing to the pleasure that a reader may find in the similar sounds, alliteration serves to bind the phrase, sometimes a series of phrases, into a unit:

> the *c*rowded, *cl*oistered *c*olleges of Oxford.—PAUL ELMER MORE . . . ran over the *s*tarry *s*moothness of the lagoon, and the water between the piles lapped the *s*limy timber once with a *s*udden *s*plash.—JOSEPH CONRAD, "The Lagoon," *Tales of Unrest*, p. 199

Alliteration is one of the figures of sound that contribute to the musical effect of poetry, though not one of the most important:

> Here I am, an old *m*an in a dry *m*onth,
> Being *r*ead to by a boy, waiting for *r*ain.
> > T. S. ELIOT, "Gerontion"

In ordinary expository prose conspicuous alliteration is usually out of place because it tends to attract attention to the expression at the expense of the idea. Its use in formal and elevated prose, especially in prose with an oratorical or poetic background, is more appropriate.

At present, alliteration is one of the chief weapons of advertising sloganeers and makers of flashy titles, who simply push to a conspicuous point the natural binding power of the figure:

> If you *s*ee it in the *S*un it's *s*o.
> *C*orinthian *C*arpet *C*leaners

> *P*otatoes *P*romote *P*rosperity
> *M*ealtime *M*agic with *M*ilk

Alliteration is also characteristic of humorous verse and prose and of any mannered writing on the light side:

> Tell me, what is a man to do
> When the *l*ady his *l*ife is based upon
> Likes to be *w*ooed but *w*on't be *w*on?
> > OGDEN NASH, *Hard Lines*, p. 58

(COMPARE ch. 10, "Qualities of sound," p. 295.)

all (of) *All* is followed by *of* in many constructions where the *of* is not necessary and might not be used in formal writing:

> All *of* the milk was spilled.   They passed all *of* the candidates.
> You can't fool all *of* the people all *of* the time.

All of is usual with a pronoun:

All of them went home.   They wanted *all of it* but got only half.

all right—alright   *All right* is the spelling of both the adjective phrase (He is all right) and the sentence adverb, meaning "yes, certainly" (All right, I'll come).

Alright is a natural analogy with *altogether* and *already*, but at present is found only in advertising, comic strips, familiar writing, and, rarely, in fiction. It will be worth watching to see if *alright* makes its way into typical informal English. Meanwhile, be on your guard.

all-round   Hyphened (or sometimes as two words), an informal adjective: an all-round athlete, an all-round education.

Allusion   See Chapter 12, "Allusion," page 353.

allusion—illusion   See *illusion.

-al ly   English has a number of adjectives with the (Latin) endings *-al* and *-ical: fatal, final, medical, historical, political*. Usually an adverb is made by adding *-ly* to this ending. This should be remembered in spelling these words.

accident*al*	accident*ally*	incident*al*	incident*ally*
politic*al*	politic*ally*	practic*al*	practic*ally*

Several adjectives ending in *-ical* show a tendency to drop the *-al: alphabetic, biographic, geographic, grammatic, philosophic* are becoming more common, following the course of *academic, frantic, emphatic, poetic*, and others that have already shed the final syllable. Although *frantic* and *public* and a few others have adverbs without the *-al-* (*franticly, publicly*), most of these words reinstate that ending before the *-ly:*

academic*ally*	dramatic*ally*	prolific*ally*
athletic*ally*	heroic*ally*	specific*ally*
automatic*ally*	idiotic*ally*	terrific*ally*

almost   See **most* for use of *most* for *almost*.

also   is a weak connective; ordinarily *and* will do its work better:

He came with tents, cooking things, *and* [better than *also*] about fifty pounds of photographic equipment.

(SEE *Conjunctive adverbs.)

alternative   comes from the Latin *alter*, "the second of two"; some

428

formal writers, in deference to the word's origin, confine its mean
ing to "one of two possibilities," but it is commonly used to mean
one of several possibilities, and is so defined in dictionaries.

although   *Although* and *though* connect with the main clause an
adverbial clause of concession, that is, a statement in opposition to
the main statement but one that does not contradict it. *Although*
is more likely to introduce a clause that precedes the main clause,
though one that follows:

> Although [Though] the rain kept up for almost three weeks, we managed
> to have a pretty good time.
> We managed to have a pretty good time, though [although] the rain kept
> up for almost three weeks.

There is no distinction in meaning between *though* and *although*.
Often one of two clauses connected by *but* can be thrown into
an *although* clause with greater accuracy of meaning and with
greater variety in the sentence pattern:

> We had rehearsed that act time and time again, but we all missed our cues
> the first night.
> Although we had rehearsed that act time and time again, we all missed
> our cues the first night.

The spelling *altho* has made more headway than *tho* and *thru*,
and is quite appropriate in familiar and informal writing but would
not be used in formal writing.

(SEE *but. REFERENCE: Curme, *Syntax*, pp. 332-40.)

altogether   See *all and its compounds.

alumnus   In spite of their clumsiness four Latin forms of this word
are kept in English:

One male graduate is an	*alumnus* (ə lum′nəs)
Two or more male graduates are	*alumni* (ə lum′nī)
One female graduate is an	*alumna* (ə lum′nə)
Two or more female graduates are	*alumnae* (ə lum′nē)

By common practice *alumnus* and *alumni* are used for graduates
of coeducational institutions. Because of this complication of
forms, *graduate* and *graduates* are increasingly used. *Alum′* is used
colloquially in some institutions.

a.m. and p.m.   These abbreviations (for *ante meridiem*, "before
noon," and *post meridiem*, "after noon") are now usually written in
small letters except in headlines and tables. They are most useful
in tables and lists of times. In consecutive writing they are used

only with figures for specific hours: "from 2 to 4 p.m." The periods are sometimes omitted in reference style.

M. is the abbreviation for noon: "12 m." There is no corresponding abbreviation for midnight.

Amb **Ambiguity** Correction: Make the meaning you intend unmistakable. **1.** Inexact reference of pronouns. **2.** Modifiers. **3.** Incomplete idioms. **4.** 'Yes' or 'no' after negatives. **5.** Intentional ambiguity. Although inexact writing is common enough, actually ambiguous writing, in which there is possibility of confusing two meanings, is relatively rare. The context usually shows which of two possible meanings must be taken. The most common sources of actual ambiguity are:

1. Inexact reference of pronoun, especially in *indirect discourse:

> He told his father he had been talking too much.

Such a sentence usually needs re-forming, perhaps as:

> "I've been talking too much," he told his father.
> "You've been talking too much," he said to his father.

(SEE *Reference of pronouns.)

2. Modifiers. (a) SQUINTING MODIFIERS that may refer to either of two words or constructions:

> I said *when the game was over* that I would go. (When the game was over I said that I would go. Or: I said that I would go when the game was over.)
> Some people *I know* would go there anyway. (Some people whom I know . . . Or: Some people would go there anyway, I know.)

b) MODIFIERS TEMPORARILY MISLEADING, as in headlines:

> Police repair man killed by car
> Horse bites off ear of owner—Man says he will keep biting mare despite attack

3. Incomplete idioms, especially in comparisons:

> "I like Alice as well as Will" might mean "I like Alice as well as Will does," "I like Alice as well as I do Will," or "I like both Alice and Will."

(SEE *Comparison of adjectives and adverbs.)

4. 'Yes' or 'no' after negatives. *Yes* or *no*, in response to a negative question or in commenting on a negative statement, often needs a clause to make the meaning clear.

> You haven't any more red ink, have you? (Answer, "Yes, I have" or "No, I haven't.")

Let's not use such a long quotation. (No, let's not.)

5. Intentional ambiguity. Incomplete or ambiguous statements are sometimes intentional, like President Coolidge's "I do not choose to run for President in 1928" or the sign in an airport limousine, "Tipping for this service not required," which drew tips from most passengers.

American Since it is inconvenient to form an adjective or a compound in *-man* from *the United States, American* is ordinarily used. It is obviously inexact, since Canadians and Mexicans are as American as we are. But it is no more inexact than many other words and is generally used in this sense. Perhaps we can take an Englishman's judgment:

> The use of *America* for *the United States* & *American* for (*citizen*) *of the U. S.* is open to as much & as little objection as that of *England* & *English*(*man*) for *Great Britain* (& *Ireland*), *British*, & *Briton*. It will continue to be protested against by purists & patriots, & will doubtless survive the protests.—H. W. FOWLER, *Modern English Usage*, p. 18

Use *the United States* rather than *America* as the name of our country but use *American* as the adjective and the name of an inhabitant.

(REFERENCE: H. L. Mencken, "Names for American," *American Speech*, 1947, 22:241-56.)

American and British usage There are several reasons why the English spoken and written in the United States differs from the English spoken and written in England. The English language was brought to North America in the seventeenth and eighteenth centuries, and since that time the language used on both sides of the Atlantic has changed noticeably, and naturally in somewhat different ways. For the past few generations the first hand contacts between Americans and Englishmen have been confined to a handful of the upper classes of both nations (in contrast to the rather frequent movement back and forth among the citizens of the British Empire), so that there has been little chance for the pronunciation of one to affect the other. Even the stationing of American troops in England during the war has not had very widespread effect. The people live under different governments, are brought up under differing educational systems. Social stratification, affecting the ideals and habits of large classes of people, is considerably different. In spite of the mutual circulation of books and periodicals, visits of lecturers, professors, and ministers, and interchange by way of the movies and the radio, many of the factors that tend to keep a language unified and to keep the speech of the British possessions close to that of England cannot operate very effectively between England and the United States.

The differences have led to interesting emotional attitudes on both sides. There has been considerable arrogance. Britishers scorn "vulgar Americanisms," partly from dislike of different language customs, partly from a feeling of superiority in customs and manners: The maker of the glossary to the London edition of Sinclair Lewis' *Babbitt* went beyond simple definition when he wrote for *ice cream soda* "Ice cream in soda water. A ghastly American summer time drink." Fowler says that the realization that Americans had dropped the *u* from words in *-our* stopped the British from making the same change. Many Americans look upon British accent and vocabulary as ludicrous or at best snobbish. The average American's dislike for Briticisms has been intensified by affectation of British pronunciations and British words by some Americans.

As to written style, in recent years the vigor of our literature has done much to give American English standing abroad, and the movies are carrying their version. Forty years ago the Fowler brothers wrote in *The King's English*, "Americanisms are foreign words, and should be so treated"—and they treated them so with gusto. Twenty years ago Ernest Weekley wrote "The foreign language which has most affected English in our own time is contemporary American." In 1938 Eric Partridge put as a subtitle to *The World of Words* "An Introduction to Language in General and to English and American in particular." H. W. Horwill's *Dictionary of Modern American Usage* (Oxford, 1935) is further evidence of a serious regard for our language, attempting to describe the American vocabulary for the English people without belittling it and incidentally telling us a good deal about British usage.

In the written language some spelling differences stand out. The British tend still to prefer *-re* to *-er* in words like *center* and *theater, though they use both forms; they still keep *-our* in a number of words, though they are gradually simplifying; they use *x* in a few words like *inflexion;* they tend to double more consonants, as in *traveller, waggon;* and there are various individual words that differ, such as *tyre* (automobile *tire*). But these distinctions do not affect a large number of words, and actually usage on most of them is divided in both countries. They are just enough to show that a book is of British or American origin but they do not interfere with reading except among patriotic fanatics of one country or the other. They really are one of the better arguments for allowing more individual freedom in spelling, but offer a problem to a publisher who wishes to circulate a book in both countries.

In the United States for a number of years students have been at work discovering and describing our speech. The magazine *American Speech* (founded in 1925) has published specific observations of usage and more general articles. Professor George Philip Krapp's *The English Language in America* (New York, 1925) and John S. Kenyon's *American Pronunciation* (Ann Arbor, 1935) are scholarly works. The four editions of H. L. Mencken's *The American Language* (New York, 1919—) have given a sturdy defense of American as against British usage. Mencken is not quite fair in that he usually pits the American vulgate against formal British, but his main point, the existence of a distinct popular speech in the United States, is well proved. The *Dictionary of American English* presents the record of many words as they have been used in the United States.

There are of course several varieties of English in use on both sides of the Atlantic, and Great Britain presents a greater variety than the United States, in part because of sturdy remains of older dialects in the various counties, in Scotland, and in Wales, and in part because of mannerisms, as "the Oxford accent," of various social groups. Among Englishmen and Americans of about the same degree of education and similar social position, differences in pronunciation are likely to be particularly striking. There are different intonations, different values for the vowels, differences in particular words like the British trā (*trait*), prō cess, con tents′, lef ten′ənt (*lieutenant*), ral′i for the American rô′li (*Raleigh*), and in general a more rapid speech and tendency to slur syllables (such as *-ar* in *dictionary*). The slower, fuller pronunciation by Americans seems wasteful and provincial to a Britisher.

Everyone knows some of the differences in vocabulary in certain common words: In England an *elevator* is a *lift*, *radio* is *wireless*, *crackers* are *biscuits* (*cakes* and *muffins* are also different from those in America), *dessert* is fruit after the sweets, a *sit-down strike* is a *stay-in strike*, a *run* in a stocking is a *ladder*, *daylight saving time* is *summer time*, *installment buying* is the *hire-purchase system*, *white-collar* workers are *black-coat* workers. From the group word *tin can* the British have taken *tin*, Americans *can*. A *truck* is a *lorry*, an *automobile* is a *motor car* (though both are compromising on *car*), *gasoline* is *petrol*, sold in a *gallon* of five quarts. A *billion* is a thousand million in America (and France) and a million million in England (and Germany).

433

There is a vulgate speech in both England and America, a vast array of slang that baffles readers on the opposite side of the Atlantic, and many colloquialisms that belong to each. In a book or play *no end* and rä thûr' are supposed to identify an Englishman as clearly as *guess* or *reckon* is supposed to identify an American. One reason for careful study of the differences between the two speeches was the increased vogue of realistic fiction, which necessarily made use of more colloquial English and more colloquial American. In fact, the increased informality and colloquialness of modern prose in both England and the United States tended to emphasize the distinctions between the two, and probably went a long way toward general recognition of differences.

The grammar of the popular levels of English and of American differs somewhat—contrast the speech of ordinary people in novels of the two countries. But in the formal writing of the two there is less difference in grammar than in vocabulary. Collective nouns are more likely to be plural in British usage (*the government intend*); British writers differ in small matters like the position of *only, the proper preposition with *different*, and distinguishing *like and *as*. (See Stuart Robertson, "British-American Differentiations in Syntax and Idiom," *American Speech*, 1939, 14:243-54.)

A fairly long catalog of such minor differences between these two branches of English could be drawn up, but their importance should not be exaggerated or allowed to obscure the fundamental fact that the resemblances far outnumber the differences and that the speech of the two countries represents two different strands of the English language. With patience a citizen of one country can understand the speech of the other, and with tolerance for small differences one can read the other's books and periodicals without trouble. An Englishman should write for Englishmen and an American for Americans. Too much concern for an "American language" may be mistaken patriotism. It is better to regard our speech as one of several branches of the great English language.

For an American there is no virtue in consciously cultivating British pronunciations or adopting British words and idioms. If he uses generally accepted American English he will reach his proper public, and if what he writes is interesting or important enough he can reach British readers too.

(Many particular entries in this *Index* note differences between British and American usage. Anyone who wishes to look further into the matter can refer to the books mentioned in this article, or he can begin with the shorter discussions in Kennedy or McKnight or other books on English. The *American College Dictionary* discriminates British and American usage more carefully than other dictionaries.)

among See *between.

amount, number *Amount* is used of things viewed in bulk, weight, or sums; *number* is used of things that can be counted in individual units:

> an *amount* of milk (but a *number* of cans of milk)
> an *amount* of beets, corn, oats, wheat (but a *number* of bushels or carloads of any of these)
> a *number* of seats, a *number* of people, a *number* of mistakes
> an *amount* of money, an *amount* of humor

ampersand is the name for the **&** sign (originally a linking of the letters of *et*), called also *short and*. Its primary use, obviously, is to save space. It is used chiefly in business writing and in reference works. In addressing firms, use the form they habitually use (. . . and Company or . . . & Company), and in quoting, follow your original carefully.

Analogy (Figure of speech) See Chapter 12, "Resemblance," page 348.

Analogy in language *Analogy* is the name for the natural tendency in users of a language to make their speech more regular by forming new words like some existing ones, bringing old words closer together in form, or bringing constructions in line with familiar patterns. It is easiest to watch analogy in the attempts of children to master their language. Before they learn the forms conventionally used by grown-ups, they manufacture forms like those they are familiar with: Most children for a time say *mans* before they learn to say *men;* they experiment with verb forms, usually making verbs regular, *singed* for *sang* or *sung*, *digged* for *dug*, or they may say *dag* instead of *dug*.

Analogy is the force that has disposed of many irregularities in the main body of the language. Out of various plural forms used in Old English, *-s* has won in all but a few words and analogy is still bringing more words to that form, like *formulas. Words occasionally are changed in spelling by analogy, as the *-b* was rather recently added to *crumb* and *thumb* from analogy with *comb, dumb*, and so on. *Cole slaw* is often replaced by *cold slaw*. *Adviser* is now changing to *advisor* from analogy with *advisory* and words like *inspector, distributor. Alright* is slowly making its way from analogy with *already*. (See *all right.) New words are formed on analogy with old ones, like *avigation, aerobatics*. Since *who* is the form that usually stands before a verb, as its subject, people ordinarily say *who* instead of *whom* when the object precedes the verb (*Who* were you with?).

(SEE *Change in language, *due to, the words starred in this article, and various other examples of analogy treated in particular *Index* entries. REFERENCE: E. H. Sturtevant, *Linguistic Change* (Chicago, 1917), p. 38 ff., ch. 6. See also the indexes of most works on language for their treatment of analogy.)

-ance, -ence (-ant, -ent) Two of the most troublesome groups of words in English spelling are those ending in *-ance* (*-ant*) and *-ence* (*-ent*). Most of them are nouns and adjectives descended from verbs of different Latin conjugations whose vowel signs are generally represented in these endings. There is no difference in our pronunciation of the endings—both get the neutral vowel ə (di-fen'dənt). There is a slight tendency to level the two in the direction of the ending with *e*, but for the present all we can do is learn the individual forms by memory or frequently consult a dictionary, either of which is an unconscionable waste of time.

Here are some of the commoner words of these types:

-ANCE, -ANT

Noun	Adjective
ascendance, ascendancy ascendant, (or ascendency ascendent)	ascendant (or ascendent)
attendance, attendant	attendant
balance	[balanced, balancing]
defendant	defendant [defending]
descendant	descendant (or descendent)
expectance, expectancy	expectant
extravagance	extravagant
incessancy	incessant
intolerance	intolerant
perseverance	perseverant
preponderance	preponderant
reluctance	reluctant
repentance	repentant
resemblance	[resembling]
resistance	resistant
significance	significant
tenant, tenancy	tenant
tolerance	tolerant
vigilance	vigilant
warrant	[warranting]

-ENCE, -ENT

Noun	Adjective
antecedence, antecedent	antecedent
competence	competent

confidence	confident
consistency	consistent
dependence (-ance)	dependent (also dependant)
eminence	eminent
existence	existent
independence	independent
innocence	innocent
insistence	insistent
obedience	obedient
persistence	persistent
presence	present
prevalence	prevalent
prominence	prominent
reverence	reverent
turbulence	turbulent

A group of similar nouns end in *-ense:*

defense	dispense	expense	offense	pretense	suspense

and 1. Use of 'and.' *And* is the most used connective, joining two elements of equal value. In its typical use, the elements are of equal grammatical rank:

> **Adjectives:** a *pink* and *white* apron; a *blue, green,* and *white* flag
> **Adverbs:** He drove *fast* and a little *carelessly.*
> **Nouns:** *trees* and *shrubs; trees, shrubs,* and *plants*
> **Verbs:** I *found* the book and *opened* it at the exact place.
> **Phrases:** *in one ear* and *out the other*
> Subordinate clauses: *While the boys were swimming* and [*while*] *the older folks were resting,* I was reading.
> Coordinate clauses: *The first generation makes the money* and *the second spends it.*

In careless writing, elements of unequal grammatical value are sometimes connected by an unnecessary *and:*

> Main verbs and participles: Three or four men *sat* on the edge of the lake with their backs to the road, [and] apparently *watching* the ducks.
> Main and subordinate clauses (*which § 4): *A contract has been let to install new copper work on the Post Office* [and] *which will require 4500 pounds of lead coated copper.*

2. **Overuse of 'and.'** *And* is often used in amateur writing where no connective is needed or where some other connective would be more accurate:

> All the passages inside the muskrats' house tended to head upward and we pushed the traps far enough in to reach dry ground. (Since all the passages . . . , we pushed . . .)
> At prep school we had certain hours for study and during that time [during which time] the dormitories were quiet.

The freshmen have a number of required courses and [but] the upper-classmen almost none.

3. At beginning of sentence. In current writing, especially informal writing with rather short sentences, *and* often stands at the beginning of sentences:

> You cannot permit investment bankers to manage trusts without permitting all of them to do it. And you cannot open it to the good ones without opening it to all. And in practice, the least trustworthy will be the first to rush in to employ this facile instrument of money control.—JOHN T. FLYNN, *Scribner's Magazine*, July 1937

If this usage becomes conspicuous, some of the *and*'s should be dropped or two sentences put together as a compound sentence.

4. Omission of 'and.' In some compact writing *and* is omitted between series of items. Judiciously used, this omission makes for economy, but used very frequently it is a mark of a "telegraphic" style, which is usually inappropriate for general writing. Three *and*'s would be possible in this sentence:

> An expert at making points of dogma crystal clear, Father LaBuffe had a blackboard handy, [and] covered it with white, red, green, [and] yellow chalk marks demonstrating the meaning of the Trinity, Original Sin, Transubstantiation, [and] Incarnation.—*Time*, Sept. 27, 1937

(These *Index* articles involve *and:* *Compound predicate, *Compound sentences, *Compound subject, *Conjunctive adverbs, *Coordinating conjunctions; *between you and me, *which (*and which*); *Series.)

and etc. is a careless redundancy, since *etc.* (*et cetera*) already contains *and* (in the Latin *et*). See *etc., et cetera.

and/or is primarily a business and legal locution. It is useful when three alternatives exist (*both* circumstances mentioned or *either one* of the two): *fruit and/or vegetables* means "fruit" *or* "vegetables" *or* "fruit and vegetables."

The use of *and/or* in general writing is objected to by many people because of its business connotation, but it is increasingly seen:

> There is something in the power of "great" personalities, but to found a theory of history on it is to deny the demonstrated existence of surrounding circumstances which condition and/or determine the conduct of leaders, heroes, and dictators.—C. A. BEARD, *The Discussion of Human Affairs*, p. 107

and which See *which § 4.

angle *Angle* is often *deadwood and suggests a colloquial or business phrase that is out of place in general writing:

> In a preparatory school the masters go at the matter from a different angle [that is, *differently*] and make the same kind of literature more enjoyable.

Anglicizing The process of making foreign words into English words. See *Foreign words in English.

Antecedent An antecedent is the word or statement to which a pronoun or pronominal adjective refers. It may stand before or after the pronoun:

> We did not hear their call again and when we found the Thompsons they were almost exhausted. (*The Thompsons* is the antecedent of the pronominal adjective *their* and the pronoun *they*.)

(For relations between antecedents and their pronouns see *Reference of pronouns.)

antenna In zoology the Latin plural *antennae* is usually kept, but this is too foreign a form for most of us in talking about radios, so that the customary plural form of the radio antenna is *antennas*.

anti-, anti The prefix *anti-*, meaning "against" in its various senses, is hyphened only before root words beginning with *i* and before proper nouns:

anticlimax	antifreeze	antimonarchic	antisocial
anti-imperialistic	anti-intellectual	anti-British	anti-Semitic

Anti- is pronounced an'ti or often, more emphatically, an'tī.

Anti is a colloquial and informal noun, meaning "a person opposed to something"; plural *antis*.

> The supporters of the plan spoke amid boos from the antis.

Anticipatory subject See *there is, there are, *it § 2.

Anticlimax Arrangement of a series in order of descending importance of the elements. It may be intentional, as a form of humor (as in Pope's "Men, monkeys, lap-dogs, parrots, perish all"), or unintentional because of a lapse of judgment that should be corrected.

(SEE the discussion of climax and anticlimax in ch. 10, "Position," p. 294.)

Antonym An antonym is a word that means the opposite of another word: *hot, stingy, boring* are antonyms of *cold, generous, entertaining*. Most books of synonyms also give antonyms, as do the synonym entries in dictionaries.

any, and compounds with any 1. *Any* is used primarily as an adjective (*any* member of the family; *Any* dog is a good dog), but also as a pronoun (*Any* will do).

In comparisons of things of the same class, *idiom calls for *any
other:* "This book is better than *any other* on the subject"; but: "I
think a movie is more entertaining than *any* book" (not the same
class of things).

2. Compounds with 'any': *Anybody, anyhow, anything,* and *anywhere* are always written as single words. *Any rate* is always two
words: "At *any rate.*" *Anyone* is written as one word when the stress
is on the *any,* and as two when the stress is on the *one:*

> *Anyone* (en'i wun) would know that.
> I'd like *any one* (en'i wun') of them.

Anyway is one word when the *any* is stressed (I can't do it *anyway*
[en'i wā]) and two when the stress is about equal (*Any way*
[en'i wā'] I try, it comes out wrong).

3. Pronouns referring to 'anybody,' 'anyone.' *Anybody* and *anyone* are singular and take singular verbs (Anybody [Anyone] feels
bad at times). They are referred to by *one* or more often by *he,
his, him* (Anybody knows what he deserves).

Informally *anyone* and *anybody* often are treated as collectives
and are referred to by a plural pronoun:

> . . . and a top that goes up and down without anybody losing their
> temper.—THORNTON WILDER (letter), *Theatre Arts,* Nov. 1940

(COMPARE *every and its compounds; Fries, p. 50.)

4. Colloquial forms. *Any place* is colloquial for *anywhere* (He
wasn't *any place* I looked). *Anyways* is colloquial for the generally
used *anyway,* and *anywheres* vulgate for *anywhere.*

Aphorism See *Epigrams.

Apos **Apostrophe** (') Correction: **Insert an apostrophe where it belongs
in the word marked; or take out a wrongly used apostrophe.**

1. In genitives. The most common use of the apostrophe is in
spelling the *genitive (possessive) case of nouns and of the indefinite
pronouns (*anyone, nobody, someone*—See *Pronouns § 8):

> Dorothy's first picture
> The companies' original charters
> Everybody's business is nobody's business.

It should be kept in singular genitives of time even though they
carry no idea of possession: a day's hike, this month's quota.

It is frequently omitted from plurals that can be regarded as
nouns used as adjectives: teachers college, a girls school.

(SEE *Genitive case for discussion of special examples of possessive form.)

2. In contractions. The apostrophe is also used to show the omission of one or more letters in contractions: *can't, I'm, I'll, it's* [*it is*]. (See *Contractions.)

3. In plurals. An apostrophe is used in plurals of figures, letters of the alphabet, and words being discussed as words:

three *e*'s   the 1920's   The first of the two *that*'s

There is a growing tendency to omit this apostrophe:

> The legendary Miss Millay, the feminine Byron of the 1920s . . .—Louis UNTERMEYER, *Modern American Poetry*, p. 485

4. In representing colloquial speech, an apostrophe is used to show that certain sounds represented in the usual spelling were not spoken:

Good mornin'   He was goin' to see fer himself.
"An' one o' them is the new schoolmaster," he shouted.

This is a legitimate use, but too many apostrophes make a spotted page and confuse the reader. It is better to suggest occasional colloquial pronunciations than to try to represent them conscientiously. (SEE *Conversation.)

5. Personal pronouns. Apostrophes are not used in the genitive of the personal pronouns (*his, hers, ours, theirs, yours*) or to apologize for a commonly used simplified spelling form (*altho*, not *altho'*; *thru* rather than *thro'*).

appearing   Inflated (or unnecessarily formal) for *looking:*

a comfortable looking [better than *appearing*] street
a fine looking [better than *appearing*] house

appendix   The English plural *appendixes* has overtaken the Latin *appendices* and is the better form except in quite formal usage.

Apposition, Appositives   Apposition is a method of modifying a noun or other expression by placing immediately after it an equivalent expression that repeats its meaning:

Alexander [appositive:] *the Great*
The word [appositive:] *apposition* means "putting beside."

Appositives are either close (restrictive) and not set off by commas, or loose (nonrestrictive) and usually set off by commas. (SEE *Restrictive and nonrestrictive.)

Close: Washington *the Capital* is a symbol of democracy and America. Washington *the city* is a symbol of almost everything that sincere and

thoughtful men know is wrong with democracy and America.—Alden
Stevens, "Washington: Blight on Democracy," *Harper's Magazine*, Dec. 1941

Loose: Literary critics have repeatedly called attention to the pathetic
fallacy, *the reading of emotion in emotionless things*, the angry thunder,
the benign sunshine.—Irwin Edman, *Four Ways of Philosophy*, p. 29

Close (*restrictive, limiting*)	Loose (*nonrestrictive, descriptive*)
Coach Bradley	Our coach, Bradley,
My aunts Mary and Agnes (He had more aunts.)	My aunts, Mary and Agnes, . . . (He had only two.)
Fletcher the grocer	Fletcher, our grocer, . . .
William the Conqueror	William I, conqueror of England, . . .
	Wisdom, the property of few, . . .
The fact *that he had been over the road before* gave him an advantage.	This fact, *that he had been over the road before*, gave him an advantage.

An appositive pronoun agrees with its headword in number and
case:

He called the two of us, *John and me* [object].
The two of us, *John and I* [subject], were going together.

(Reference: Curme, *Syntax*, pp. 88-92.)

Appropriateness The doctrine of this book is that Good English
is based on appropriateness in the language to the subject and situation, to the reader or listener, and to the writer or speaker. For
discussion, see Chapter 3, §§ 3-5, pages 76-86.

apt See *likely.

Arabic numerals Our ordinary numbers, 1, 2, 647. See *Numbers.

Archaic Words and constructions formerly common in the language but now going out of use (*methinks, goodly, aye, thou*).
See Chapter 2, "Archaic English," page 56.

Areas of usage See Chapter 2, "Variations due to use," page 37.

arise Situations may *arise*, but not people, except in poetry. See
*rise. Compare *wake.

around See *round—around.

Articles See *a, an; *the.

as *As* is one of the most versatile words in English and one of the
most frequently used. Some of its more common uses at present are:

442

1. Adverb:

Of degree: I came *as* soon as I could.
Introducing appositives: There were several kinds of shellfish, *as* scallops, oysters, crabs, lobsters. (This use is informal.)

2. Pronoun: In formal English usually with *same* or *such* as antecedent: "It was such a day *as* one rarely sees."

It also, as a common vulgate relative pronoun, takes the place of *who* and *that:* "Everyone *as* has his ticket can go in."

3. Preposition: "in the position of," "in the role of":

She had a job *as* stenographer.   He was in the cast *as* Mercutio.

In the colloquial construction "I don't like him as well *as her*," (meaning "I don't like him *as well as I like her*") *as her* may be construed as a prepositional phrase: "Who would want to go with such a poor skater *as* me?" (Formal usage would often have ". . . with such a poor skater as I [am].")

There is a growing tendency to use *as* instead of *like* as a preposition (see *like):

Some writers, as Faulkner, take their material from a particular region.

4. Conjunction: *As* occurs most commonly as a conjunction, introducing several kinds of clauses.

Degree or manner: . . . as far *as* I could.
Time=while: *As* I was coming in he was going out.
Cause: *As* it was getting dark, we made for home.

Such a handy word is of course much used in speech, which often prefers *counter words to more exact ones. But the very variety of possible uses makes *as* a problem in written English. It is necessary in comparisons (We went as far *as* he did) and for attendant circumstance (*As* we walked along he told us stories) though *while* is preferable if the emphasis is on the time or the action (*While* we were walking along he told us stories).

As is weak in the sense of *because*. Usually *since* or *because* would be better in writing and certainly better in formal English:

Colloquial: *As* it was almost time to go, we were getting more and more exasperated.
More exact and emphatic: *Since* it was almost time to go, we were getting more and more exasperated.
Because it was almost time to go, we were getting more and more exasperated.

(REFERENCES: Curme, *Syntax*, pp. 269-71; *Parts of Speech*, pp. 78-82, and index references in both books. Kennedy, p. 541.)

as . . . as **1. In double comparisons** we sometimes fail to complete the first construction with a second *as:*

> He is fully as tall if not taller than his older brother.

This reads more accurately if completed:

> He is fully as tall *as,* if not taller than, his older brother.

But since the interrupted sentence movement is undesirable in informal English, it is usually better to complete the first comparison and then add the second:

> He is fully as tall as his older brother, if not taller.

2. In negative comparisons formal English sometimes prefers *not so . . . as:*

> The winters are *not so* long or so cold *as* they used to be.
> The winters are *neither so* cold *nor so* long *as* they used to be.

Informal English does not as a rule make this distinction:

> The winters are *not as* long or as cold *as* they used to be.

Which idiom is to be used depends on the formality of the context.

as if (as though) In formal English the subjunctive is used after *as if* or *as though:*

> He acted *as if* [*as though*] *he were* losing his temper.

In informal English the subjunctive would not usually be used:

> He acted *as if* [*as though*] *he was* losing his temper.

(SEE *Subjunctives.)

as or like For the conflict between *as* and *like* (I can't swim *as* I used to—I can't swim *like* I used to), see *like—as.

asset Currently a *counter word, overused for *advantage, aid, benefit, property,* and so on.

Association paragraphs See Chapter 8, page 219.

Assonance Rhyme is the correspondence in two syllables of the vowel sounds and the consonants (if any) following them (*leaf— sheaf, lake—wake*); assonance is the like sound of vowels in syllables having different consonants (*brave—vain, lone—show*). Assonance is a common and effective sound element in verse and is also common in prose, especially in an emotional or *heightened style:

"that ideal country, of green, deep lanes and high green banks."—Osbert Sitwell, *Trio*, p. 89

Asterisk (*) Except in reference works, the asterisk or star is not used so much now as formerly, because it is a conspicuous mark and attracts more attention than is necessary.

1. In works which have very few footnotes, an asterisk may be used as a reference mark, placed after the statement calling for the note and again at the beginning of the footnote.

2. Asterisks are sometimes used to indicate a rather long omission in a quotation, as of a stanza or more from a poem, or a paragraph or more from prose, though now spaced periods are more in favor. (See *Ellipsis.)

3. In fiction a group of asterisks has been used to suggest that action is not given or to indicate passage of time between movements of a story, but here again a line of spaced periods or extra space between the movements is more common. (See *Ellipsis.)

4. In this book, where frequent cross references are helpful, the asterisk is used to refer to *Index* articles.

as to *As to* is often a clumsy substitute for a single preposition, usually *of* or *about*:

Practice proves the best teacher as to [in, for, of] the use of organ stops. If the question contains words as to the exact meaning of which [of whose exact meaning] you are uncertain, by all means get out your dictionary.

athlete, athletic, athletics Watch your spelling of these, and help your spelling by pronouncing them in clear cut syllables: ath′lete, ath let′ic, ath let′ics.

When *athletics* refers to sports and games it usually takes a plural verb and pronoun:

Our athletics *include* football, basketball, and baseball.

When *athletics* refers to skill or activity it usually takes a singular verb and pronoun:

Athletics *is* recommended for every student.

Attributive An adjective that stands next to its noun is attributive (a *blue* shirt; a shirt, *blue* and *clean*), as contrasted with a predicate adjective that is related to its noun by a *linking verb (The shirt is *blue*). A noun modifying another noun (*horse* race, *football* field) is used *attributively*.

Author card, Authorities See Chapter 13, "Sources of reference," and "The working bibliography," pages 369, 377.

autobiography See *biography.

Auxiliary verb A verb used with another verb to form a phrasal tense, voice, or mood is called an *auxiliary verb:*

> I *am* going.   He *will* go.   They *were* lost.   He *should* watch out.

Be, do, have are the commonest auxiliaries; *can, may, shall, will, must, ought, should, would, might* are frequently used as auxiliaries; *get, let, need,* and *used* sometimes function as auxiliaries. See *Index* entries on these verbs, the general article *Verbs, and Chapter 4, "Shall—will and other auxiliary verbs," page 101.

awful In formal English *awful* means "inspiring with awe." In familiar and colloquial English it is a general utility word of disapproval—"ugly, shocking, ludicrous" (*awful* manners, an *awful* run in my stocking). As a result of this contamination the word is seldom used in careful writing; *awe-inspiring* has taken its place. *Awfully* is an example of *schoolgirl style.

awhile, a while *Awhile* is an adverb (They talked *awhile*). Strictly, a prepositional phrase, in which *while* is a noun, should be in three words (*for a while, in a while*), but *awhile* is sometimes found.

Awk **Awkward** Correction: Rewrite the passage marked.

A rather general word of disapproval conveniently used in correcting themes. It may refer to clumsy phrases, unnatural word order, unnecessary repetition of a word or phrase, or other phrasing that attracts unpleasant attention or handicaps a reader. The remedy is to recast the sentence.

aye Used for *yes* in voting; pronounced ī.

B The letter *b* is chiefly conspicuous in English for its frequent appearance as a *silent letter and therefore a possible snare in spelling and sometimes in pronunciation. Many silent *b*'s, especially after *m*, represent *b*'s that were pronounced in Old English but perhaps have not been generally sounded for hundreds of years: *climb* (klīm), *comb* (kōm), *dumb* (dum). The *b* is pronounced in the formal or archaic *clamber* and in *limber*. A *b* has rather recently been added in *crumb* and *thumb*. Other silent *b*'s represent sounds that had been in the Latin ancestor words but that were dropped as the words passed through Old French: *debt* (from *debitum*), *doubt* (from *dubitare*), *subtle* (from *subtilis*). Some of these *b*'s were inserted by Renaissance scholars because they wished to tie English closer to Latin: Chaucer wrote *det* but we cannot.

When *b* comes next to *p* the two sounds sometimes are assimilated to one: *cupboard* (kŭb'ərd), *subpoena* (sə pē'nə).

Back formations   See *Origin of words § 3d.

bad, badly   *Bad* is an adjective of varied application:

a bad man	a bad night	bad weather	a bad light
a bad cold	a bad accident	bad news	a bad taste

In "I feel bad about it," "She looks bad," *bad* is a predicate adjective. *Badly* also is an adjective in the predicate position: I feel badly. (See *Linking verbs.)

Both *badly* and *bad* are also used as adverbs, the latter more often colloquially:

He draws badly [colloquial: bad]. The starter has always worked badly [bad].

(REFERENCE: Lillian M. Feinsilver, "How Bad(ly) Do You Feel?" *American Speech*, 1949, 24:161-70.)

Worse, worst, the comparative and superlative of *bad*, of course come from a quite different root. They were earlier used in comparing *evil* and *ill*, and when *bad* acquired the meaning of those words, *worse* and *worst* were used for it too.

Bad grammar   *Bad grammar* is used as a term of reproach and is applied to all sorts of locutions from "I ain't got none" to supposed confusions in the use of "shall" and "will." Our attitude toward such locutions may be less severe if we recognize their sources. Some people feel that these expressions are sins against good English, that they are lapses from a standard. Generally they are expressions from a different dialect, often from colloquial or vulgate speech, that occur in the midst of more formal English. The objection to them is not that they are sins against "grammar," for most of them are perfectly conventional ways of expression in their appropriate dialect, but that when they appear in a different setting, they are *inappropriate*, and consequently to be avoided. Other instances of inappropriate grammar are due to imperfect mastery of a construction usual in a given level, as in various *shifted constructions. See Chapter 3, Good English, page 69.

447

Balanced sentences   Sentences in which two parts are of conspicuously similar length and form. See Chapter 10, "Balanced sentences,"
page 283.

Barbarism   is a term used to describe a word that is irregularly
formed or that is not in good use, like *irregardless* and *preventative*.
See *Long variants, *Origin of words § 3.

be   1. Forms.   The English verb *be* has forms from three originally
separate verbs (as in *are, was, been*) but we use the verb so much
that the various forms give little trouble:

> Present: I am, you are, he is; we, you, they are
> Present subjunctive: I, you, he, we, you, they be
> Past: I was, you were, he was; we, you, they were
> Past subjunctive: I, you, he, we, you, they were
> Infinitive: be; Present participle: being; Past participle: been

Some old forms survive in stock phrases ("the powers that *be*")
and in the vulgate, as in "You ain't [sometimes *be'n't*] going, *be*
you?" The vulgate also continues to use *was* in the plural ("*Was*
the Adamses there?"), which would have been good informal usage
two hundred years ago. This levels the past tense to one form (*was*),
like the past of other English verbs.

   2. As a linking verb: *Be* is the most common *linking verb,
linking, without adding specifically a meaning of its own, a subject
and a predicate nominative or adjective:

> Jerome was the secretary. (Predicate nominative)
> She is sick. (Predicate adjective)

With the finite parts of *be* the predicate noun or pronoun is in
the nominative case in written English:

> It was *he*. (Colloquial: It was *him*.)

"*It's I*" is formal for colloquial and familiar "*It's me*." (See
*It's me.)
   When the infinitive has a subject and complement, both are in
the objective form:

> I wanted *him* to be *me*.

When the infinitive has no subject, formal usage has a nominative as the complement (I wanted to be *he*) but informal usage
would more often have an accusative (I wanted to be *him*).
   3. As auxiliary verb. Forms of *be* are used with the present
participles of other verbs to form the progressive tense form:

I am asking   he was asking   you will be asking

Forms of *be* with past participles form the passive voice:

I am asked   you will be asked   he was asked

In colloquial English, a form of *be* is often used in two different functions, as linking verb and as auxiliary:

Colloquial: They were ready and getting into the car.

In formal English the form of *be* would be repeated:

Formal: They were [linking verb] ready and were [auxiliary] getting into the car.

4. As verb of complete predication. *Be* is a verb of complete predication when indicating states or positions:

He *was* at home anywhere.   The fire *was* just across the street.

In the sense of "exist," "live" (Hamlet's "To be, or not to be," "Can such things be?") *be* is now rather rare but can be used sometimes with strong effect:

You have heard nothing of your wife and your children. They do not know if you are dead or alive or blinded. You do not know where they are, or if they are.—DOROTHY PARKER, *The New Yorker*, Feb. 5, 1938

(SEE *Subjunctives; *Subject and verb; *ain't, *It's me.)

beau   Plural *beaus*, or formally, *beaux;* pronounced bōz.

because   introduces a subordinate clause giving the reason for the independent statement:

Because we were getting hungry, we began to look for a convenient restaurant.

Since and *as* can be used in such clauses, but they are less definite, more casual, and more characteristic of easy speech than of writing:

In a small rural school these young children have to stay for the rest of the day's session, because [more definite than *as* or *since*] there is no one to take them home.

For, which also introduces reasons, is a more formal word, rather rare in conversation and informal writing. It also often has the sense of giving evidence for the statement, for the writer's knowledge of the fact stated, rather than for its cause:

Informal: I know he is reliable, because I have traded with him for years.

449

More formal: I know he is reliable, for I have traded with him for years. ("He is reliable because [or *for*] I have traded with him for years" would not be exact.)

(SEE *reason is because, *for, *as.)

become   See *Linking verbs.

been   Pronounced bin; rarely bēn in the United States but more commonly in England.

Beg   **Beginning paragraphs**   Correction: Revise the opening paragraph to make it lead more directly into your subject and if possible to arouse your reader's interest.

For discussion of qualities of beginning paragraphs and examples, see Chapter 7, "Beginning paragraphs," page 195.

beside—besides   *Beside* is a preposition referring to place, "by the side of," as in "beside the road," "beside her," and is used figuratively in a few rather formal idioms like "beside the point," "beside himself with rage." (*Beside* is less commonly used as an adverb, with the meaning of *besides*.)

Besides is an adverb or preposition meaning "in addition to" or "except":

We tried two other ways besides. (adverb)
Besides our own members, . . . (preposition)
He said that his wife was a regular farm wife who helped him milk the cows besides raising five fine healthy children. (preposition)

It is used as a conjunctive adverb:

He didn't think that he ought to get into the quarrel; besides, he had come to enjoy himself.

between, among   *Among* implies more than two objects:

They distributed the provisions among the survivors.

Between is used of only two:

It's somewhere between 40th and 43d streets.
They divided the prize between Kincaid and Thomas.

But the attempt to limit *between* to use only with two items has failed. (The *Oxford English Dictionary* says that from the first it has been used of several.) So used, *between* tends to suggest the individuals involved more than the situation:

The family of seven hadn't a pair of shoes between them.

(REFERENCE: Pooley, pp. 135-37.)

between you and me Since the object of a preposition is grammatically in the accusative case, the correct form is *between you and me, for you and me, to you and me* (or when the pronouns are objects of a verb, "He will take *you and me*").

Between you and I is frequently heard—reversing the usual colloquial tendency to use *me* (as in *It's me), perhaps because the speakers remember the prejudice against *It's me* and carry over the taboo to a different construction.

Bible, bible *Bible*, referring to the Christian Scriptures, is capitalized but not italicized: "You will find all that in the Bible, and more too." *Bible* in the sense of an authoritative book or (informally) a book much consulted or quoted, is not capitalized: "Gray's *Manual*, the botanist's bible, . . ."

The usual form of particular references to parts of the Bible is:

the Old Testament   the New Testament (capitalized but not italicized)
The Ten Commandments are in Exodus xx (or: in Exodus 20).
The Ten Commandments are in Exodus 20:3-17.
I Corinthians 4:6

The adjective *biblical* ordinarily is not capitalized.

Bibliography A bibliography is a list of books and other published material consulted in writing a paper (a final bibliography), or to be consulted in gathering material for a paper (a working bibliography).

Details of form and method of both bibliographies are given in Chapter 13, The Reference Paper: "Sources of reference," page 369; "The working bibliography," page 377; "The final bibliography," page 396.

Big words Correction: Use a simpler, more natural word instead of the formal or heavy one marked.   *Big W*

Modern writing uses direct and ordinary words instead of "bigger" ones—*home* rather than *domicile, think* or *believe* rather than *deem, happen* rather than *transpire,* and so on. For full discussion of big words and suggestions for avoiding them see Chapter 12, "Big words," page 339.

biography Pronounced bī og'rə fi (or bi-, not bē-). A biography is the life of a person written by someone else; an autobiography is the life of a person written by himself.

Blanks for names and dates have gone out of fashion. The present style is all for specificness. Don't write "In 18—" but, if the exact date isn't to be given, "About sixty years ago."

Similarly, "Mr. ———" or "Mr. X" or "A man whom I shall call Mr. Wheeler, though that is not his name" would be avoided. Real names are used wherever possible, or if they cannot be used, the avoidance is made as inconspicuous as possible by "A man," "Someone," or some such expression.

Blend A word made by fusing two words, often with a syllable in common: *paratroops, cinemactress, imagineering, smog, motel, beautility, snoopervise.* (See *Origin of words § 3b.)

Until a blend has made its way in the language, as *electrocute* (from *electric* and *execute*) has, it is usually more appropriate to informal than formal writing.

blond, blonde As a noun, *blond* is used of a man, *blonde* of a woman:

He is a blond.   She is a blonde.   a peroxide blonde (or blond)

In its adjective use, the *-e* is gradually disappearing and in informal writing, at least, *blond* can always be written. Some write *blonde* when it refers specifically to a woman (a blonde Helen) and *blond* elsewhere, including *blond hair.*

Brunet, brunette are in the same situation: masculine noun *brunet*, feminine noun *brunette*, with perhaps a tendency to use *brunette* as the adjective (to help represent the accent on the second syllable).

Boners Confusion of two similar words, mistaken constructions, combinations of ideas that don't belong together have always been a source of fun for everyone except the persons who made them. Volumes of these boners have been gathered and several periodicals run specimens that they find in other publications. Here are a few that have cropped up in themes:

My papers have a decided tendency toward longevity.
He is descended from one of the most virulent [really *poisonous?* or merely *virile?*] families in the U.S.A.
Jean is no plastic saint.
For the lowly freshmen are moved by sediment rather than by intellect in their voting.
The arduous loves of movie stars are not always convincing.
Many times I started for the library to do some research on Gestalt's psychology.
[Of the cross country team, running on back roads:] Not even the sharp stones can dampen their spirits.

Keep your eye out for boners in manuscript and in print and get what fun you can from them—but most of all scan your own writing to catch them before they come to anybody else's attention.

book refers especially to the contents, *volume* to the physical appearance. A *book* may be in two or more *volumes.*

book These compounds with *book* are spelled as one word:

bookbinder	bookmaker	bookshop (book shop)
bookbindery	bookmark	bookstack
bookcase	bookplate	bookstore
bookkeeper	bookseller	bookworm

As two words:

book club	book end	book learning	book review

born, borne 1. The past participle of *bear* in most of its senses is *borne:*

> They had *borne* this poverty without complaining.
> The ship was *borne* along by a fast breeze.
> The ship, *borne* along by the breeze, was soon out of sight.

Bear in most of these senses is somewhat formal; *carry* or *endure* would be more common.

In the sense of "give birth to," the past participle of *bear* is spelled *borne* except in the (very common) passive when not followed by *by:*

> She had *borne* five children.
> Of the four children *borne* by his first wife . . .
> He was *born* in 1891.   A *born* liar.
> The children, *born* in Chicago . . .

2. In autobiographical papers, writers often become self-conscious or humorous in giving the facts of their birth: "I saw the light of day first on June 28, 1934"; "No planets blazed on the night of June 28, 1934, when a squally infant appeared in the home of Mr. and Mrs. . . ." None of these is any improvement over the simple and natural statement "I was born June 28, 1934."

Borrowed words See *Foreign words in English; *Origin of words § 2.

both *Both* is a favorite way of emphasizing two-ness:

> The twins were both there. They are both alike. Both Harry and his brother went.

Strictly speaking, all these *both*'s are redundant but they give legitimate emphasis. A sentence like "The both women got along well enough together" is a localism for "The two women got along well enough together."

both . . . and See *Correlative conjunctions.

Brace { } is the mark used to group two or more lines of writing. Its use is chiefly in technical writing, especially in tables and formulas. Examples of braces will be found in *English language and the Levels of Usage table on page 40.

Brackets [ ] Brackets are rarely used in general writing and are not in the standard typewriter keyboard, but in much academic and professional writing they have specific and convenient uses.

Brackets are primarily editorial marks, used to show where some explanation or comment has been added to the text, especially to quoted matter:

> The preposition *due to* is not more incorrect than the preposition *owing to*, which is approved by the same dictionary [the *Concise Oxford Dictionary*], but it is not yet so thoroughly established in the language.—G. O. Curme, *Syntax*, p. 561
>
> and by the Accounts thereof, made up by Mr. Peirce, Master of the said ship, and [*torn*] Agent for Mr. Craddocke, one of the Owners; being al [*torn*] by Mr. Peters . . .'—S. E. Morison, *The Founding of Harvard College*

If the torn word had been filled in by the editor, the conjectured letters would be in brackets: being al[lowed] by Mr. Peters . . .

In quoting material, *sic* in brackets is sometimes used to indicate that an error was in the original: "New Haven, Conneticut [sic] . . ."; or a correction may be inserted in brackets: "When he was thirty-eight [Actually he was forty-three] he published his first novel."

Brackets are used, though now rarely, as parentheses within parentheses. They are likely to be found particularly in legal documents or in footnotes to theses, etc.

In this *Index*, brackets are used in examples of faulty writing to inclose words that might better be left out, or to suggest an improved expression:

> Throughout [the course of] the year I read such books as *Oliver Twist* and *Boots and Saddles*.
>
> The continuously moving belt makes a noise *similar to* [*like*] a cement mixer.

Brevity See discussion of economy, Chapter 10, "Sentence economy," page 284, and *Wordiness.

British usage See *American and British usage.

broadcast The past tense and past participle of *broadcast* are both *broadcast* (or *broadcasted*).

Broad reference A pronoun referring to a preceding idea rather than to a particular antecedent is said to have a broad reference. See *Reference of pronouns § 1.

bunch In formal English *bunch* is limited to objects that grow together or can be fastened together (a bunch of carrots, roses, keys) and to expressions like "a bunch of cattle." Colloquial and informal English holds to the older usage of *bunch*, applying it to a small collection of anything—including people.

burst, bust The principal parts of *burst* are *burst, burst, burst:*

> One *bursts* almost every day. Two tanks *burst* yesterday. One tank had *burst*.

> *Bust* is vulgate in the sense of "smashing" or "exploding" or "breaking out." It is slang in the sense of "being broke" but good English in *"busting* a bronco" or *"busting* a trust."

> It was the idea of busting the trusts and imprisoning their officers that roused the crowd.—N. A. CRAWFORD, *The Ethics of Journalism*, p. 65

bus has plural *buses* or *busses*, the first more common American usage.

Business English The writing of business English has attained a very high standard of mechanical form. The layout, spacing, and mechanics of most business letters and reports are excellent, reflecting the skill of professional typists; and the skill of layout men and printers is available for printed matter.

But the usage and style of these business communications vary considerably. Most firms at present pay a good deal of attention to the style of their written and printed matter. The old clichés— *in re, the above, Yrs. of 23d inst. rec'd and contents noted, and oblige*—have practically disappeared. Naturally all degrees of formality and informality are found. The prime virtues of good business writing are *directness* and *adaptation to reader*. Adapting the style to the reader is especially difficult in writing advertising and business letters, since usually the writer is not acquainted with his reader and in spite of elaborate market analyses may not visualize him right. If the letter is sent broadcast, there is the difficulty of making it *seem* personal when it really cannot be personal. But for most purposes "business English" is merely good English applied to the specific needs of industry and trade. The only necessary difference from general English is in the vocabulary, the words needed for business situations.

At present a good deal of business writing is informal—not only in the attempts to get the back-slapping approach on paper, but also in its naturalness, or even colloquialness. Like our realistic novelists, business people have adopted a simple style and have handled English with the freedom a living language deserves. They have pioneered in the much needed shortening of our spelling. Business writers have used all the native resources of the language in making new names and in brightening style—outright coinages like *kodak, vaseline, fabrikoid*, blends like *servicenter, unisteel, sunoco*, compounds and respellings like *cutex, denticuring* (preventive dentistry), *tudor* (cars), *lubritory*. Though many such words are ludicrous or overcute or in poor taste, some are expressive and are normal language developments. They are much better than attempts at false dignity (*client* for *customer, favor* for *letter, the business world* for *business, cheque* for *check*) and the exaggeration of a good deal of advertising—seen most clearly in movie ads.

The question of fitness arises when certain words with obvious business connotation are used in other contexts. Some are frequently borrowed and are useful: *deal, asset, feature, bank on*, and *take stock in* are common colloquial usage. But many people, who perhaps do not like to be reminded that they live in a society primarily commercial, are offended by *advise, *angle, *and/or, *contact, *realtor, receptionist, selling point*. Such words may be out of place in formal writing and in discussions of ideal rather than practical affairs; but in informal writing business locutions are often useful. H. S. Canby used ordinary business terms to point up a comment on current literature:

> No; public taste, ease of publication, variety of interest, even editorial capability, have all risen with the intellectual development of the country; only the professional writers, as a class, have not progressed. They have become astonishingly clever, as clever as the mechanism of a Ford; but as a class they have not moved ten feet towards literature. *They have standardized their product without improving the model.*—Saturday Papers, p. 56

(SEE *Letters; *Reports; ch. 12, "Euphemisms," p. 337; ch. 2, "Shoptalk," p. 45.)

Business letters See *Letters.

business world Inflated for *business* or *businessmen*: I expect to enter the business world [I expect to go into business].

but
1. Connects equals. 2. Connects statements in opposition. 3. 'But' with 'however.' 4. At beginnings of sentences. 5. Punctuation. 6. Minor uses of 'but.'

But is the natural coordinating conjunction to connect two contrasted statements of equal grammatical rank. It is more natural
than the heavy and formal *however* or *yet*, but more emphatic
than *although.

1. Connects equals. The locutions connected by *but* should be
of equal grammatical weight:

> Adjectives: not blue but green.
> Adverbs: He worked fast but accurately.
> Phrases: He didn't come in the forenoon but in the early evening.
> Clauses: We just rested the first day, but the second we got down to real
> work.
> Sentences: Enigma of the semitropics, the Rio Grande defied the best
> engineering minds of two countries for a century. But $10,000,000 in flood
> control work has harnessed the treacherous stream.

(See *which § 4 for comments on *but which*.)

2. Connects statements in opposition. The statements connected
by *but* should be actually in opposition; contrast the first example
with the second and third:

> He knows vaguely that the nation is not much good any more; he has
> read that the crust of the earth is shrinking alarmingly and that the universe
> is growing steadily colder; but he does not believe that any of the three is in
> half as bad shape as he is.—James Thurber, *My Life and Hard Times*,
> Preface
> He supported a wife and three children on this pittance *and* [not *but*]
> he seemed very proud that he wasn't on relief.
> Our view was limited to about twenty yards down Tuckerman Ravine;
> [not *but*] beyond that everything was in clouds.

3. 'But' with 'however.' *But* should be used efficiently, carrying
its real meaning. It should not be doubled by a *however* which can
add nothing:

> The students wanted to extend the Christmas vacation a day beyond
> New Year's, but [*however* not needed] the Administration couldn't see their
> point of view.

A *double negative with *but* is found in colloquial usage:

> Formal: There are but three eggs left.
> Informal: There are only three eggs left.
> Colloquial: There aren't but three eggs left.

4. At beginnings of sentences. *But*, like *and*, often stands at the
beginning of sentences, especially if the sentences are short.

5. Punctuation. Two clauses connected by *but* should ordinarily
be separated by a comma. The contrast in idea suggests the use of
punctuation even when the clauses are relatively short.

I couldn't get the whole license number, but it began with A30.

But is part of the clause in which it stands and should not be separated from it by a comma. A parenthetical phrase following the *but* may of course be set off by commas:

His speech was supposed to be extemporaneous, but he had really been practicing it for a week.
His speech was supposed to be extemporaneous, but, to be quite truthful, we must add that he had practiced it for a week.

6. Minor uses of 'but.' (a) As SUBORDINATING CONJUNCTION, after *no doubt*, in questions with *know*, and in a few other constructions:

There is no doubt but [or *but that*, or more formally, *that*] he had tried his best.
Who knows but everything will come out right?
Nothing would do but I must spend the night with them.

b) As A PREPOSITION, equivalent to *except:*

We didn't get anything but a couple of shad.
No one could have done it but me.

c) As A RATHER FORMAL ADVERB, equivalent to *only:*

If he but stops to think, he can bring together these reactions to form an image of himself.

(REFERENCES: Fowler, article "but"; Kennedy, p. 539; Curme, *Parts of Speech*, index references.)

but that—but what *But that* is the usual conjunction in written English:

He didn't know but that [colloquial: *but what*] the other car could still turn out.
Formal: I do not doubt that he will come.
Informal: I don't doubt but that he will come.
Colloquial: I don't doubt but what he'll come.

C In Old English *c* represented two sounds: Usually it was *k—cruma*, "crumb," *cempa*, "warrior," *cyning*, "king"; but before *e* or *i* it often represented *ch* (*ceosan, ciepan, cild*). This second sound is spelled *ch* in Modern English: *choose, cheap, child*. It was the Norman Conquest that really complicated *c*, for it brought in many French words in which *c* was sounded *s*. Today *c* is an unnecessary letter, doing work that could more certainly be done by *k* and *s*. Many words spelled with *c* must be respelled with *k* or *s* to show pronunciation: sit'i (*city*), sel (*cell*), fōrs (*force*), kōld (*cold*), kum (*come*), ärk (*arc*).

Before *e, i,* or *y, c* is regularly pronounced *s: cent, civil, cynic;* before *a, o, u,* and any consonant but *h, c* is regularly *k: can't, coffee, cute, fact.* Marked with a cedilla, as in *façade, c* has the *s* sound before *a, o,* or *u.*

C may represent *sh: ocean* (ō'shən); *conscience* (kon'shəns); *special* (spesh'əl).

C is silent in *czar, indict, muscle,* and a few other words.

Before *e* or *i, cc* spells *ks: accident, occident, success, vaccine;* otherwise it is *k: acclaim, accommodate.*
(SEE *ch.)

-cal, -cial Words ending in *-cal* (*critical, historical, musical, political*) are sometimes confused by careless writers with those ending in *-cial* (*artificial, beneficial, judicial*). (See *-al ly.)

calculate, guess, reckon *Calculate* (cut in vulgate to kalk'lāt or even to kal'āt), *guess, reckon* are localisms for the *think, suppose, expect* of good English. (Which is the word in your region?)

can—may (could—might) **1. In general English.** In general usage *may* occurs rather rarely except in the sense of possibility:

It may be all right for her, but not for me.

Can is generally used for both permission and ability:

Can I go now? You can if you want to.
I can do 80 miles an hour with mine.

This is in such general usage that it should be regarded as good English in speaking and in writing.

Can't almost universally takes the place of the awkward *mayn't:*

Can't I go now? We can't have lights after twelve o'clock.

2. In formal English. In formal English some distinction is made between the auxiliary *can* when it has the meaning of ability, "being able to," and *may,* with the meaning of permission.

You may go now. He can walk with crutches. You may if you can.

The distinction makes possible the classic dialog at many tables:

"Can I have some more meat and potato?"
"You *may* [with a withering accent] have some more meat and potato."

May also indicates possibility: He may have the right one.

3. Might and could. *Might,* originally the past of *may,* and *could,* the past of *can,* are now used chiefly to convey a shade of doubt, or a smaller degree of possibility.

> It might be all right for her, but it isn't for me.
> It might have been all right for her, but not for me.

Adverbs are likely to be used instead of *may* or *might* in such constructions, especially for the past tense:

> *Perhaps* it was all right for her, but not for me.

Could also suggests doubt or qualified possibility:

> Perhaps I could write a poem, but I doubt it.
> I could do 80 miles an hour in mine, too.

Be able to tends to replace *can* and *could* when the idea of ability needs emphasis:

> I am able to live on my income.

(REFERENCE: Gladys D. Haase, *College English,* 1950, 11:215-6.)

cannot, can not   Usage is divided with *cannot* the more common.

can't help but   There are three possible idioms:

> Formal: I *cannot but feel* sorry for him.
> General: I *can't help feeling* sorry for him.
> Colloquial: I *can't help but feel* sorry for him.

The last is an established idiom, though avoided by many writers.

(REFERENCE: Marckwardt and Walcott, pp. 98-9; Russell Thomas, *College English,* 1948, 10:38-9.)

Cap   **Capital letters**   Correction: Capitalize the word marked, for one of the reasons shown in this article; or, if the word marked is written with a capital, make it a small letter.
1. Sentences. 2. Proper names. 3. Lines of verse. 4. Titles. 5. 'I,' 'O.' 6. Names of relatives. 7. Deity. 8. Street, etc. 9. Abstract nouns. 10. Stylistic capitals.
*Proofreading marks can be used for correcting themes. Three lines under a small letter means: make this a capital. A slanting line drawn through a capital means: make this a small letter.

> march 15   He came from West of Buffalo.

Certain uses of capitals, as at the beginning of sentences or for proper names, are conventions followed by everyone; certain others show divided usage or are matters of taste. In general, formal English tends to use more capitals than informal English, and newspaper usage tends to cut them to a minimum.

This article summarizes the principal uses of capitals in current writing. Further discussion and examples will be found in the articles marked by asterisks.

1. Sentence capitals. The first word of a sentence is capitalized. In quotations, the first word of a quoted sentence or part of sentence is capitalized, but when the quotation is broken, the second part is not capitalized unless it is a complete sentence:

> He said, "The first time I came this way almost none of the roads were hard surfaced."
> He said, "Perhaps," and went on.
> "The first time I came this way," he said, "almost none of the roads were hard surfaced."
> "That was your last chance," she said. "Don't ever ask again."

Complete sentences that stand in *parentheses are capitalized always if they stand between other sentences, but if they stand within sentences they usually are not.

> The men were very stiff and self-conscious in their swallowtail coats (the dinner jacket had not been invented), bulging shirt fronts, white kid gloves (which often smelled of naphtha), and the enormously high "poke" or "Piccadilly" collars. . . .—E. Alexander Powell, *Gone Are the Days*, p. 138

A complete sentence standing after a *colon would not be capitalized if it was short and closely connected to the preceding words, but usually would be if it was long or if for some reason the writer wanted to emphasize it or keep it distinct:

> Charles Sumner wanted to know his opinion on European law journals: what should he say?—H. S. Commager, *Theodore Parker*, p. 109
> Possible explanation: The nestlings were struck by an eastern Arctic storm which only the older birds were able to escape.—*Time*, Nov. 7, 1938

2. Proper names. Proper names and abbreviations of proper names are capitalized: names of people, places, races (Indian, Negro, Caucasian), languages (French, Latin), days of the week, months, companies, *ships, institutions, fraternities, religious bodies, historical events (the Revolutionary War), documents (the Constitution), *course names.

The names of the *seasons (*summer, fall, midwinter*) are not capitalized except for emphasis or stylistic reasons.

The points of the compass (*north, southwest*) are not capitalized when they indicate direction, but are usually capitalized when they denote a region (though this practice is now declining):

His grandfather had come west in 1849.
He was much more popular in the West than in the East.

Army, Navy, and so on, are not capitalized unless they refer to
the organized forces of a particular nation: United States *Army,* the
British *Navy.*

Proper nouns that have become common nouns (*tweed, sandwich, burnsides, plaster of paris*) are not capitalized, nor are proper
adjectives in senses that no longer suggest their origin: *Paris fashions*
(fashions originating in Paris), but *paris green.*

3. Lines of verse. The first letter of a line of verse is capitalized
unless it was originally written without a capital, as in the second
example below:

> These lovely groves of fountain-trees that shake
> A burning spray against autumnal cool,
> Descend again in molten drops to make
> The rutted path a river and a pool.
>> ELINOR WYLIE, "Golden Bough"

> Ecstatic bird songs pound
> the hollow vastness of the sky
> with metallic clinkings—
> beating color up into it
> at a far edge,—
>> WILLIAM CARLOS WILLIAMS, "Dawn"

4. *Titles of articles, books, etc. The usual convention is to capitalize the first word, all nouns, pronouns, verbs, adjectives, and
adverbs as well as prepositions that stand last or contain more than
five letters:

With Malice Toward Some   *The Book of a Naturalist*
You Can't Take It with You   *Pity Is Not Enough*

5. 'I,' 'O.' The pronoun *I* is capitalized (not from any sort of
egotism, but simply because a small *i* in manuscript is likely to be
lost or to become attached to other words). The exclamation *O* is
capitalized, but not *oh* unless it begins a sentence or is to be especially emphasized.

6. Names of relatives, individuals. In letters and familiar writing,
names for members of one's family are often capitalized as a mark
of courtesy (Father, my Brother Wren) but not in general writing.
President referring to the President of the United States is always
capitalized, and ordinarily titles of people in high office when referring to an individual (the Senator). Other titles may be capitalized
when referring to a particular person (The Colonel was there).

7. References to Deity. *God, Jesus,* nouns such as *Savior,* and pronouns referring directly to a sacred figure are capitalized—though practice is divided on the pronouns:

> Webster for the first time in an English Bible rendered Jesus's saying as He said it.—HARRY R. WARFEL, *Noah Webster,* p. 411
> As we think of him [God], do we think of what he has done or what he can do for us? Do we love him so much that we would keep him for ourselves?—S. K. YEAPLE, *Your Money and Your Life,* p. 30

Pronouns referring to pagan deities (Zeus, Jove, Venus) are not capitalized.

8. Street, river, park, etc. Usage is divided over capitalizing such words as *street, river, park, hotel, church* when they follow a proper name. Typically, books and conservative magazines would use capitals; more informal writing, in many magazines and most newspapers, would not:

Formal:	the Mississippi River	Thirty-second Street
Informal:	the Mississippi river	Thirty-second street

An organization is likely to capitalize more words pertaining to its functions than an outsider would, as the Government Printing Office capitalizes many words having to do with government.

9. Abstract nouns. Abstract nouns are likely to be capitalized, more often in formal writing than in informal, when they are personified or when they refer to ideals or institutions: "The State has nothing to do with the Church, nor the Church with the State."

10. Stylistic capitals. Some writers, usually in a rather formal style, use capitals as a form of emphasis, to lead the reader to stress certain words a little or give them more attention:

> *My Mission*
> But when in modern books, reviews, and thoughtful magazines I read about the Needs of the Age, its Complex Questions, its Dismays, Doubts, and Spiritual Agonies, I feel an impulse to go out and comfort it, to still its cries, and speak earnest words of Consolation to it.—LOGAN PEARSALL SMITH, *Trivia,* p. 34
> And a woman is only a woman, but a good Cigar is a Smoke.—RUDYARD KIPLING, "The Betrothed"

(For more details of general practice, consult the stylebooks of periodicals and publishers.)

car is a satisfactory and economical solution of the contest between *automobile, auto, motor car,* and other terms for "a gasoline propelled pleasure vehicle."

Card catalog See Chapter 13, "The library card catalog," page 370.

Cardinal numbers The numbers used in counting—*one, two, three* . . . *sixty eight*—are called *cardinal numbers. Ordinal numbers* indicate order or succession: *first, second, third . . . sixty eighth.*

Cardinal and ordinal numbers are grammatically construed as adjectives or pronouns.

For their use and representation in writing see *Numbers.

C **Carelessness** Correction: **Correct the obvious and apparently careless mistake marked.**

Conferences with students on their themes show that well over half the mistakes and slips that an instructor has to mark are due not to ignorance but to carelessness. Everyone is liable to careless lapses in hasty work. But a course paper is not supposed to be hasty work; it should represent the best you are capable of. Slips like *it's* for *its* (or the other way around), *detract* for *distract,* most comma faults and fragmentary sentences, and scores of others are due to lack of attention in the final stages of preparing a paper. An instructor can sympathize with lack of knowledge but not with lack of care; in fact, he should refuse to read an obviously careless paper.

One of the best investments is a careful reading of your final manuscript. It will make the paper more presentable (and worth a better grade), as well as give you the satisfaction that comes from seeing a job through to the best of your ability.

Caret (∧) An inverted v-shaped mark put in a line of manuscript to show that something between the lines or in the margin should be inserted at that point:

```
    Yes, they were smart, but there wasn't any reason why they
                because
    shouldn't be, all they did was study.
              ∧
```

This is a respectable way to revise papers and should be used to improve a paper to be handed in or to make a correction suggested by an instructor, though too frequent use shows lack of care in the preliminary writing and revision.

A caret may be used by an instructor as a correction mark to show where something should be inserted.

In reading proof the matter to be inserted is put in the margin. (See *Proofreading.)

Case One of the ways in which the relation may be shown between a noun or pronoun and another element in a sentence is by case. In languages like Latin and German, whose nouns and pronouns (and adjectives too) are fully declined, the case endings of the nominative, genitive, dative, and accusative (and ablative in Latin) are important clues to meaning. In English, case is a much less useful factor in grammar. Our adjectives do not take any endings; nouns are reduced to two forms, a genitive and a common form that serves for all other relationships (*soldier's—soldier*), and the personal pronouns are reduced to three, a nominative, genitive, and accusative (*I—my—me*).

We express the relation of nouns and pronouns to other sentence elements through *word order* (an accusative object following its verb or preposition, for example) and by means of *prepositions* (*to Fred* instead of a dative). The few problems in case that we have come chiefly from the surviving accusative form of pronouns (*It's me, *who—whom*).

This *Index* has articles on four cases to call attention to the few functions in which the case forms are significant, to note problems in usage that are due to case forms, and to make possible some comparison between English and the languages which rely more definitely on case to express relationship between words:

*Nominative (or subjective)—the subject of a verb, complement of a linking verb

*Genitive (or possessive)—indicating not only possession but various adjectival and adverbial relations

*Dative—principally notions of interest or location or "indirect objects"

*Accusative (or objective)—the object of a verb or preposition

Fuller accounts of the grammatical points involved will be found in the articles on the various functions indicated: *Subject and verb, *Objects, *Infinitives § 4, *Linking verbs, *Gerund § 2; and *Genitive case, *Nouns, *Pronouns, *Word order.

(For more complex treatments of problems of English cases, see Kennedy, pp. 465-67; Jespersen, ch. 14 [the two-case system]; Curme, *Parts of Speech*, pp. 127-36 [the four-case system].)

case Some of the commonest bits of *deadwood in writing are various locutions with the word *case*. They are wordy and keep the real person or situation or thing (whatever the "case" stands for) one construction away from the reader.

These quotations, some from student papers, some from published articles, show how easy it is to let an unneeded *case* slip into careless writing.

> Drinking went on very moderately except in a few scattered cases. (Written of a convention. The "cases" would be delegates?)

> Perhaps it is because I like fiction to have happy or at least satisfactory endings that I disliked these books. In not one [case] was I satisfied with the ending.
>
> . . . but that does not happen to be the case [but that isn't true].
>
> In many cases a corporation may wish to carry on only one type of business and in such a case it is necessary for such a charter to be obtained in a state where this particular line of work is to be carried on. (If a corporation is to carry on only one type of business, it must secure a charter in the state in which it will operate.)

catalog—catalogue Spelling divided, with the shorter form gaining. Over half the colleges now use *catalog* as the name of their annual bulletin of announcements.

Cause Statements of cause are usually found in clauses introduced by *as, *because, *for, since*. See the articles on these connectives.

Cause and effect For discussion and example of paragraphs developed by showing the relationships of cause or effect between statements, see Chapter 7, "Relationships between facts," page 180.

-ce, -ge A few special spelling problems arise from the use of *c* for the sound of *s*, and of *g* for the sound of *j*.

A word ending in -*ce* (pronounced *s*) or -*ge* (pronounced *j*) keeps the final *e* before suffixes beginning with *a, o,* or *u* to indicate the pronunciation: *courageous, noticeable, peaceable, vengeance.* Before a suffix beginning with *e* or *i* the final *e* is dropped: *diced, noticing, encouraging.*

Usually a word ending in *c* (pronounced *k*) adds a *k* before an ending beginning with *e* or *i* or *y* so that it will still be pronounced *k*: *colic, colicky; picnic, picnicked, picnicking.*

(See also *-ei-, -ie-.)

Cedilla A mark under the letter *c* (ç) to show that it has the sound of *s* before *a, o,* or *u*. *Façade* is the most common English word spelled with a cedilla. Other words with cedillas are *Provençal, garçon, aperçu, soupçon*.

center around (or about) *Center around* (The story *centers around* the theft of a necklace) is the informal idiom. The formal idiom is *center on* or *upon*.

Centuries Remember that the fifth century A. D. ran from the beginning of the year 401 to the end of the year 500, the nineteenth century from January 1, 1801, through December 31, 1900. That is, to name the century correctly, add one to the number of its hundred. It will help to remember that you live in the *twentieth* century.

466

Popularly the distinction is not closely kept, since people feel that the century changes when the figure for the hundreds changes: there were celebrations for the beginning of the twentieth century on January 1 of both 1900 and 1901. (Compare the debate over whether the second half of our century begins with 1950 or 1951.)

Partly because of the frequent errors made in this scheme of indicating centuries, the informal practice of naming the hundred is becoming more and more used, even in formal writing: the seventeen hundreds, the nineteen hundreds . . . .

Dates before Christ are figured like those after: The first century B.C. runs back from the birth of Christ through 100, the second century from 101 through 200, the fifth century from 401 through 500, and so on.

The abbreviation A.D. (*anno Domini*, in the year of our Lord) is written before the year: A.D. 1950. Strictly it should not be used with centuries, since it means "in the year . . . ," but actually it is by historians (the fifth century A.D.). B.C. (before Christ) follows the year: 431 B.C.; the fifth century B.C.

certain Deadwood in "this *certain* person," "just one *certain* thing" . . .

cf. For Latin *confer;* sometimes used in footnotes for *compare, see* a given reference for other or further facts. *See* is increasingly used instead.

ch *Ch* spells the sound *tsh* (pronunciation symbol *ch*); as in *arch, bachelor, chatter, check, cheese, child, church.* When the sound is not at the beginning of a word, it is often spelled *tch* (*batch, watch*) and *ti* in such words as *question, Sebastian.* Compare also *righteous* (rī'chǝs) and *literature.*

In some words rather recently taken in from French, *ch* has the French sound of *sh: champagne, chagrin, mustache, machine.*

In a number of words from Greek, *ch* is sounded *k: chemist, chimera, chorus, echo.*

Change in construction See Chapter 4, "Consistent constructions," page 116, and *Shifted constructions.

Change in language (oral and written) Since language exists only as it is used, and since it is used by people as a tool rather than as an end in itself, it is subject to change. Occasionally changes are relatively sudden and far reaching, as after an invasion by a nation with a different language, but ordinarily they are slow and casual, the accumulation of slightly different pronunciations, casual or designed changes in the meanings of words, gradual changes in grammatical forms and constructions. English shows many changes during the hundreds of years that we are able to study it. (See *English language.) When we think of the millions of varied people using our language and of the wide territory over which they are spread, the wonder is that change is not more rapid. The spread of school systems, the wide circulation of books and periodicals, and the radio all tend to slow up change somewhat, but the English language is still changing. One of the fundamental principles of linguistics is recognizing that this change is natural and unavoidable in language.

Attempts to direct the course of English have not been very successful. The development of formal grammar in the eighteenth century affected the speech, or at least the writing, of a small and influential group but left untouched the great majority of users of the language. The simplified spelling movement has had much less effect than we should expect from such a sensible and needed effort. Today advertising is the chief source of spelling change, although some teachers and nearly all linguists believe that our spelling should be modified. In general, schools and publishing houses have taken a pretty firm stand against change, some of them even now presenting usage of the middle nineteenth century. It is possible that this will not always be true. As Professor Sturtevant stated it:

> In the past such efforts [of teachers] have usually been directed against a usage that was supposed to be an innovation, but there seems to be no reason in the nature of the case why the school should not some day be enlisted in an effort to improve the language.—*Linguistic Change*, p. 177

A person interested in writing needs to be aware of the naturalness and necessity of change in his language and should cultivate the habit of watching the small signs of change that he hears and sees in speech and writing. He needs also to decide whether he is going to oppose change, to welcome it in all its forms, or to try to discriminate, adopting in his own work those new words and forms and constructions that seem to be more convenient and more expressive than older forms. Following the direction in which English has already been moving (as the increase in nouns making their *plural with -s) is a good general principle to follow.

Several discussions in this *Guide-Index* treat points of change in current English. Reading them will suggest what to watch: Meaning of words (in Chapter 11), *Origin of words, Spelling (Chapter 6), and specific articles like *all right—alright, *-ally, *due to, *like—as, *shall—will.

The study of the changes that have taken place in English and the reasons for them is fascinating, and ample materials exist for carrying it on. The *Oxford English Dictionary* gives the history of individual words from their first appearance in the language, recording their changes in form and in meaning. Histories of the language, like those by H. C. Wyld, Albert G. Baugh, and Stuart Robertson, tell the story in detail. The general and orderly process of change is described in Otto Jespersen, *Language*, Part iv, and in E. H. Sturtevant, *Linguistic Change* (Chicago, 1917). See also Bloomfield, Chapter 20 ff.; Kennedy, Chapter 14.

chaperon Sometimes found with a final *e* but most commonly *chaperon*. Pronounced shap′ər ōn. The verb is *chaperone*.

Chapters Chapters are numbered in Roman (i, ii, iii) or Arabic (1, 2, 3) numerals, the latter increasingly used. In bibliographies also lower case Roman numerals (i, ii, x) are now more common than capitals (I, II, X), and Arabic more common still.

In formal book style, references to titles of chapters are quoted. In most writing they are simply capitalized.

> Formal: Kennedy, Chapter xiv, "Improvement of the English Language"
> General: Kennedy, Chapter 14, Improvement of the English Language

Charts See *Diagrams, graphs, etc.

check—cheque *Cheque* is the regular British spelling but its use in the United States is formal or pretentious.

Chinese Preferred by natives of China (and others) to *Chinaman, Chinamen*, because of the belittling connotation of those words. Say *a Chinese, the Chinese*. In compounds *Sino-* (sī′nō or sin′ō) is used: *the Sino-Japanese War*.

Choppy sentences See Chapter 10, "Segregating sentences," page 273.

cinema The regular British term for moving pictures. It has made little headway in the United States.

Circumlocution is the use of several words for an idea that might be conveyed by fewer. See Chapter 10, "Sentence economy," page 284, and *Wordiness.

Cities The name of the country or state need not be given with the name of well-known cities: Athens, Berlin, Chicago, Hollywood, London, New York, Rome, San Francisco. Many American cities and towns bearing the same names need identification if used in writing that is to circulate outside their states: Athens, Georgia; Berlin, New Hampshire. See *Proper names; *Comma § 8b.

Clauses 1. Definition. A clause is an element of a compound or complex sentence that ordinarily has a subject and a finite verb. (But see § 3.) By means of a conjunction or of an implied connection the clause construction is related to the rest of the sentence. A simple sentence, like "The bird flew higher and higher in slow easy circles," is not called a clause.

Compound sentences have two or more coordinate clauses of grammatically equal value, connected usually by *and*, *but*, *for*, or another *coordinating conjunction.

> [First clause:] Then Italy, in February, was finally persuaded to sign the Non-Intervention Pact, [Second clause:] and a few days later twenty thousand Italian soldiers landed at Cadiz.—*Kaltenborn Edits the News*, p. 48

Complex sentences have at least one main clause, grammatically capable of standing alone, and one or more subordinate clauses, joined to the main clause or clauses by *as*, *because*, *since*, *when*, or some other *subordinating conjunction, or by a relative pronoun: *that*, *who*, *which*.

> [Main clause:] There are, besides, certain differences in the domestic and foreign policies of the two democratic nations [Subordinate clause:] which influence their behavior in the Spanish situation.—*Kaltenborn Edits the News*, p. 48

2. Function. Subordinate clauses are classified according to the grammatical function they serve in the sentence: **(a)** NOUN CLAUSES are subjects and objects of verbs or objects of prepositions:

> [Subject, usually formal:] *That herons fed at night* was not news to him. No one knew [Object:] *which way they had gone.*

b) ADJECTIVE CLAUSES modify nouns:

> The man *whom they met* [or: The man *they met*] did not return.
> The cement road turned into a macadam road, *which in time turned into a clayey unsurfaced road.*

c) ADVERBIAL CLAUSES add notions of time, place, cause, effect, concession, etc.:

> *When they finally got that straightened out*, it was too late to go on.
> They were discouraged *because they had tried very hard.*

Here is a passage of 19 sentences in which four (6, 7, 9, 18) are simple, one is compound-complex (11), and the others complex.

The subordinate clauses are in italics, and at the end of the passage are the conventional grammatical interpretations of them.

(1) Without question a young man *who is not a radical about something* is a pretty poor risk for education. (2) The relevant question to ask is, *What does this young man's radicalism express?* (3) In general, *if it is doctrinaire,/if he has learned all the answers to the world's problems out of a book or from a wise guy outside*, the worth of his beliefs is slight, both to him and to society. (4) The cut-and-dried patter must first be got out of him *before his mind will give a clear tone.* (5) It is true *that the reasons for the early adoption of ready-made beliefs often deserve sympathy.* (6) Poverty, injustice, a sense of wrong connected with a physical or other defect, are predisposing causes. (7) In other instances it may be great intellectual curiosity coupled with a yearning for absolute truth. (8) This is *why students —though the Trustees do not trust it—can go so easily from the doctrine of Karl Marx to the doctrine of Saint Thomas.* (9) By means of these systems, converts can act out their dissent from the regular way and secure the comforts of a vast intellectual edifice.

(10) But dissent of a different type remains the really fruitful element in undergraduate thought; *though here again quality is important.* (11) Dissent from teacher *because he is an authority* is meaningless, but the defiant conviction *that it is no atrocious crime to be a young man, born later, with a different world impressed on the mind, with the consciousness of untried powers and unlimited courage*—that form of dissent is without doubt the one quality to nurture when found and to shield *if need be* against all literal conformity. (12) For *what it fulfills* is the solitary truth rattling through the empty periods of the Commencement orator *when he says:* "Young man, the future is in your hands."

(13) Imagine a generation of young men *who did not think/they could govern better than their fathers,/who did not want to revolutionize the world with new inventions or make T. S. Eliot's laurels fade.* (14) *If they do not believe / they can do this*, who will tell them? (15) Certainly not the institutions *that rightfully nurse a Tradition.* (16) But a tradition lives by being added to, and it is the young men *who must make the effort of creation.* (17) It is irrelevant to suggest *that this ambition moves thousands of hearts every year and ends in workaday routine and indolence.* (18) That is to look only at the husks. (19) *As long as we cannot prophesy / who will turn out a winner*, we have no right to question initiative and self-dedication.—
Jacques Barzun, *Teacher in America*, pp. 238-39

1. Adjective clause modifying *young man*
2. Noun clause, complement of *is*
3. Two adverbial clauses (condition), modifying the main clause
4. Adverbial clause (time), modifying the main clause
5. Noun clause, postponed subject of *is*. (Obviously here the "main" idea is in the "subordinate" clause.)
8. Noun clause (*why . . .*), complement of *is;* adverbial clause (*though . . .*), modifying the *why* clause
10. Adverbial clause modifying the main clause (though it has the value of a coordinate clause, as is borne out by the punctuation)
11. Adverbial clause of reason (*because . . .*) on the face of it (but what does it "modify"?); noun clause (*that . . .*), in apposition with *conviction;*

adverbial clause of condition (*if* . . .), modifying *to shield. When found* could be regarded as a subjectless clause of time.

12. Noun clause (*what* . . .), subject of *is;* adverbial clause of time (*when* . . .), modifying the main clause, or it could be regarded as modifying the quotation. A quotation is conventionally regarded as a noun clause, object of the verb of saying.

13. Two adjective clauses modifying *young men;* noun clause object of *think*

14. Adverbial clause (condition), modifying the main clause; noun clause, object of *do believe*

15. Adjective clause, modifying *institution*

16. Adjective clause, modifying *young men*

17. Noun clause, object of *to suggest*

19. Adverbial clause of time, modifying main clause; noun clause, object of *prophesy*

(The coordinate-subordinate category is not as important as it was once supposed to be, not as important as the functional classification of subject, object, modifier, for instance, but it is continued here as a convenient familiar classification.)

3. Verbless clauses. The typical clause has a subject and verb, but just as there are verbless sentences (see Chapter 9, "Verbless sentences," page 260), there are clauses without finite verbs. They are of two types:

a) Elliptical clauses, in which the verb can be supplied from another part of the sentence or can be added with certainty because of the frame of the sentence:

I don't believe it any more than you [Supply: *do,* or *believe it*].
When [Supply: *he was*] sixteen, he had gone to work.

b) Genuine "abridged clauses" in which no verb element stands (or ever has stood). These should not be construed as elliptical clauses, since no verb ever enters the speaker's or listener's mind. Two familiar sayings illustrate the abridged clause:

The more, the merrier.
The better the day, the better the deed.

(SEE ch. 9, "The favorite English sentence," p. 247, and *Complex sentences, *Subordination, *Restrictive and nonrestrictive. REFERENCE: Curme, *Syntax,* ch. 10.)

Cl **Clearness** Correction: **Make this statement clear to a reader by fuller statement or by making the words more exact or by straightening out the grammatical construction.**

Clearness is one of the fundamental virtues of writing, perhaps the fundamental virtue, but it is a little hard to discuss. No accumulation of small virtues or banning of particular faults will produce essential clearness. It is true in writing that pronouns should match their antecedents, that verbs and subjects should agree, that constructions should not be wantonly shifted. These are traits which, though often ignored in speech, require care in writing.

But clearness will be gained not so much by attention to these details as by determining to convey to the reader the ideas and feelings you wish him to find in what you say. Clearness is the chief virtue of writing because it enables writing to carry out its fundamental purpose, communication. But writing has other purposes too—influencing people, entertaining them—and expression also has other virtues. Even in exposition, where clearness is the first demand, it is not the only one. Preoccupation with clearness for its own sake will produce writing that is clear—but also cold and dry. Without clearness a paper will certainly be bad, but with clearness it may not be particularly good. There are overtones demanded by certain situations; there are special considerations of the sensibilities of readers; there are small signs of the writer's own sense of the matter, even his sense of himself. All of these elements may detract in some small way from immediate clearness and yet add importantly to a complete understanding of the whole and so be intrinsic to good English.

Many of the articles of this *Index* discuss small contributions to clearness. Give them the attention they deserve but remember that clearness comes really from habits of thought.

Cliché   A worn-out word or phrase. See Chapter 12, "Trite words," page 333.

Climax   Climax is the arrangement of a series of words, phrases, clauses, or sentences in an order of increasing value and usually of increasing length. See Chapter 10, "Loose and periodic sentences," page 280. For "Climax paragraphs" see Chapter 8, page 222; for climactic order in papers, see Chapter 1, page 14.

Clipped words   See *Origin of words § 3c.

Cognate   *Cognate* means "related, of the same family." It is applied to languages that are from the same stock, as Spanish and French are both descended from Latin. *Cognate* is often used of words in different languages which are modern forms of some one word in an older language: German *Wasser,* English *water.*

(REFERENCES: Kennedy, § 80; the origins of words given in dictionaries, especially in the *Oxford English Dictionary*.)

Coh **Coherence** Correction: Make the relation between the parts of this sentence or between these sentences or paragraphs exact and clear to a reader.

Coherence—the traditional name for *relationship, connection, consecutiveness*—is a difficult and necessary virtue in writing. It is necessary because a reader does not have the same mind as the writer, does not see the same relationships, and consequently must be led through a line of thought, guided from one stage, from one sentence, to another. It is difficult because a coherent piece of writing is a triumph over natural human casualness; it represents an editing of a writer's thought so that it can be grasped by others.

Coherence is the name of a quality of finished writing and is to be checked finally in revision. A writer cannot be always worrying about the connection between his statements while he is at work, but careful planning will make coherence more likely. Unless he is mentally ill, there is always some relation between his consecutive "thoughts," but the relation may be entirely personal. Carefully thinking over material before beginning to write should help prepare a coherent paper, especially if some sort of plan, arranging the different stages in a natural and sensible order, is drawn up. But coherence must be tested after writing. The writer must go over his copy as impersonally as he can to see if what he has written not only hangs together for him but will hang together for those he wants to read it. He should ask himself, "Is the relation between these statements clear? Can a reader pass from this sentence or from this paragraph to the next, without feeling a break?"

A natural arrangement of material is not enough for this; there must often be signs of the relationship between sentences and paragraphs. These signs, various suggestions pointing toward coherence, and examples of successful and unsuccessful attempts at coherence are discussed in this *Guide-Index*, especially in *Conjunctions, *Prepositions, *Reference of pronouns, Chapters 7 and 8 (Paragraphs), Chapters 9 and 10 (Sentences), and Chapter 1, "Planning the paper," page 13.

Coining words Making up a word for a particular statement (like *was-ness*) or for general use (like *fabrikoid*) is called *coining*, and the word made is called a *coinage*. For discussion and examples see *Origin of words §§ 1 and 2.

Coll **Collective nouns** Correction: Change, according to the principles of this article, the verb and/or the pronoun to agree with the collective noun marked.

474

1. A collective noun is a noun whose singular form names a group of objects or persons or acts. Some common collective nouns are:

army	contents	herd	*politics
*athletics	*couple	jury	*public
audience	crowd	lot	remainder
band	dozen	majority	rest (= remain-
class	flock	mankind	der)
*committee	gang	*number	row (of trees)
company	group	offspring	team

When a writer means the group as a whole, a collective noun takes a singular verb and singular pronoun; when he means the individuals of the group, the noun takes a plural verb or plural pronoun:

> The *crowd* that *has* been noisily engaged in finding *its* seats *settles* down and the incessant murmur of voices slowly quiets.
> The *crowd* that *have* been noisily engaged in finding *their* seats *settle* down and the incessant murmur of voices slowly quiets. (The first version is preferable.)
> The first *couple* on the floor *was* Tom and Janet.
> One day when we were near where the old *couple were* living, we dropped in to see *them*.

In the United States the singular is generally used with nouns like *the government, the public;* in England the plural.

2. In writing, a collective should not be treated as both singular and plural in the same context:

> The *company was* organized and immediately sent out *its* [not *their*] representatives.
> Mess is over and the guard have [not *has*] a busy morning ahead of them [not *it*].

There is often a temptation to use a collective noun and try to keep it singular when the meaning really calls for a plural construction. Often the writer slips unconsciously from singular to plural in such a passage:

> Into the church troops the entire town, seats itself on the uncomfortable wooden benches and there remains for a good two hours, while an aged curé preaches to *them* [consistency demands *it*] of their [*its*] wicked lives and awful sins. (This might better have started "Into the church troop all the people, seat themselves . . .")

In making inconsistent constructions consistent, the first member is fully as likely to need to be changed as the second, as in the sentence above about the church.

3. In speech (and consequently in some informal—and most unedited writing) our tendency not to continue constructions across intervening words usually operates: The verb, which comes close to the noun, is singular, but a pronoun some words away tends to refer to the individuals, in the plural.

Spoken: The team *was* called together for last minute instructions and sent out to *their* positions.
Written: The team *were* called together for last minute instructions and sent out to *their* positions.
Spoken: The election committee *has* from the beginning misused *their* rights in issuing false instructions for absentee ballots.
Written: The election committee *has* from the beginning misused *its* rights in issuing false instructions for absentee ballots.

4. The plural of a collective noun signifies different groups:

The audiences of New York and Chicago differed in their receptions of the play.

5. In measurements and amounts a plural noun is often followed by a singular verb:

Eighteen inches is half a yard.
About 80 pounds of carbon disulfide is [or *are*] added.

(SEE *Subject and verb § 2; *every and its compounds § 1. REFERENCES: Curme, *Syntax*, pp. 539-540, 50-51; Fries, pp. 48-50, 54, 57-59; Pooley, pp. 85-88.)

Colloq **Colloquial and written English** Correction: The colloquial expression marked is inappropriate to the context in which it stands. Change it to one more formal, in line with the general style.

1. Colloquial English. **2.** Appropriateness of colloquial English in writing. **3.** Some differences between colloquial and written English.

1. Colloquial English. Colloquial means conversational, used in speaking. Since the speech of people varies with their education, work, and social status, there are obviously many different types of colloquial English, from the rather bookish speech of some professors and others through the "cultivated colloquial" of fairly well educated persons, to the "low colloquial" of the majority of everyday people, which makes up the vulgate level of English. The bulk of conversation is informal, and consequently *colloquial* suggests informal rather than formal English. It need not, however, mean the speech of uneducated people, and in this book it applies to the language spoken by people of some education and social standing, to language that can be safely used except on decidedly formal occasions.

Dictionaries mark words *Colloq.* to suggest that in the editors' judgment they are more common in speech than in writing. Many people take this label to mean that the dictionary frowns upon the use of these words, but the Webster definition of *colloquial* shows that this is not true:

> acceptable and appropriate in ordinary conversational context, as in intimate speech among cultivated people, in familiar letters, in informal speeches or writings, but not in formal written discourse (*flabbergast; go slow; harum-scarum*). Colloquial speech may be as correct as formal speech.
>
> By permission. From *Webster's New International Dictionary*, Second Edition, copyright 1934, 1939, 1945, 1950, by G. & C. Merriam Co.

The three colloquial expressions that are given as examples prove that Webster is not using *colloquial* as a word of dispraise or even of suspicion, for though *flabbergast, go slow*, and *harum-scarum* suggest speech rather than formal writing, they are accurate, expressive, useful words, to be used with confidence in most situations.

Speech is of course the basis of a language, and writing is to a large degree a representation of speech. We learn to speak by unconsciously imitating our elders, and somewhat later we learn to write, but consciously and under the direction of teachers, so that the great majority of people never come to be quite at home "on paper." They do much more talking than writing, and for some, speech may be almost their only medium.

Many educated people, especially in the professions, get most of their information from periodicals and books, so that the written language naturally colors their speech. In certain limited areas, especially the upper levels of scientific, scholarly, and philosophical fields, and in some literature, the primary relation between oral and written language is reversed. The topics are rarely spoken of, even by specialists, and almost never are in familiar speech. Here the written forms are the norms, imitated in speech.

The language taught and to a large extent used in schools in the past has been written and formal. Dictionaries are based primarily upon the written language, and the pronunciations they give are those of formal public address. The grammars have also been based chiefly on written literature and, except the more recent reference grammars, have ignored the spoken. With more work in oral composition and an increasing attention to spoken English in language work, there is now less of the attempt to make students talk as their elders write and more of a tendency to give colloquial English its due place. Since a language really lives as it is spoken, it is not healthy when the written language gets out of touch with the colloquial.

2. Appropriateness of colloquial English in writing. The chief problems come in the appropriateness of colloquial locutions in writing.

a) IN FAMILIAR WRITING. Obviously, familiar writing, as in letters to friends or in personal notes for our own use, is and should be close to speech, to the writer's speech. Contractions, clipped words, short cuts in constructions all help bring the writer close to his reader, and their number and use will depend upon the extent to which he uses them in his speech.

b) IN INFORMAL ENGLISH. Informal written English is closely related to colloquial English. It is based upon speech rather than upon traditional written literature. It is not a mere setting down on paper of casual, lazy, careless speech, but it is a refinement of good talk, especially of the words and the movement of good talk. Some people hesitate to let their writing become colloquial because they think it means cheapening it, reducing it to the level of prevailing speech. But the basis of a person's writing is his own speech, not somebody else's. He takes as the starting point for his growth in writing his own way of talking rather than the writing of others.

c) IN FORMAL ENGLISH. More serious questions arise in formal writing, in impersonal discussions of facts and ideas, as in college papers, and in articles and books for special and rather restricted groups of readers. Although formal English now has a wider range than it did, still its background is really the written English of a generation or so ago and in so far as it is influenced by speech it is by the speech of the platform rather than of conversation.

Once in a while a contraction is used for the sake of rhythm, even in formal writing, and in vigorous formal writing there is now a wide range in words that will include some characteristically colloquial. But in general, formal English relies on words that have made their way in writing, and its constructions are usually filled out, not shortened as in speech. In these days it is not necessary to avoid colloquialisms altogether, but they should be appropriate and not attract attention to themselves.

3. Some differences between colloquial and written English. The early stages of preparing a talk for an audience or a paper for readers are pretty much the same. The subject is chosen to fit the situation and to appeal to the intended readers or listeners; material is gathered to carry out the subject; and the plans of a good talk and of a good article do not materially differ. If there are differences in these stages they probably come because it is harder for a writer than for a speaker to keep his future audience in mind; a speaker knows that he will face a definite group of people and finds it easier to work directly for them from the very beginning.

In later stages, and in the actual presentation of the material, there are some unavoidable differences, more or less obvious.

a) Obvious differences. Pronunciation, intonation, the enunciation and stressing of words belong to speech; spelling, only to written language. Handwriting or typing may correspond in a poor way to the bodily presence of a speaker, but in printed articles and books even that touch of individuality is lost. Instead of the pauses and stresses of speech, writing has the feeble substitute of punctuation, italics, and so on, and really the writer relies more on the quality of his words, on repetition and word order, than on these mechanical signs of emphasis. The contractions of the colloquial language may be carried over to informal writing, but abbreviation is primarily the method of shortening written words. For the loss of the oral means of emphasis—gesture, facial expression—the writer must again rely on a resourceful use of words.

b) Pace and rhythm. A speaker can control the pace of his listeners—he can make his words (and his statements) come slow or fast as he wishes. A writer cannot control the speed with which his readers will go over his material. Some readers will read too slowly and make too much of small matters; others will race over the pages and miss much, perhaps even essential points. Of course, listeners cannot be made to take in what they hear, but in so far as they do, they will be going along with the speaker at his pace. The pace of printed prose will be much less evident, though it does vary among writers. Some prose seems written for slow reading, because of "hard" or perhaps merely exact words, because of indirect sentences, unfamiliar turns of expression; other passages suggest rapid reading, because of familiar and simple words, short, direct sentences. Even the printing can help, as in the short lines of newspaper columns.

Similarly the rhythm of a passage may be suggested even in print. The impression a speaker makes depends in part on his rhythm, on the heaviness and frequency with which he stresses his words. This rhythm represents the speaker and guides the listener in understanding what he says. The natural speech rhythms of, for instance, New Englanders, Southerners, Scotsmen, and Londoners differ conspicuously. Even though the rhythm of speech can only be suggested on the printed page, a writer can convey rhythm to the page. Rapid silent reading catches little of it, but slower reading, in which the words may be almost pronounced, will usually sense it. One reason why much stereotyped writing, such as reference books, academic writing, and news writing, is colorless and unpleasant to read—and cannot be read aloud with pleasure—is that the writer has suppressed so completely his natural speech rhythm (See *Rhythm.).

c) VOCABULARY. One characteristic of the spoken vocabulary is usually unsatisfactory on the written or printed page—the rather loose use of words. In talking we often get along with general words (*thing, stuff, like that*), rarely trying to find exact adjectives in describing something or in giving our opinions. We fall back on *good, bad, pleasant*, perhaps even on *nice*, and express the degree of our meaning by tone of voice, gesture, or facial expression. In writing we need exact words to make up for the oral support that we give vague words in speaking. It might be better if we used more exact words in conversation, but searching for words while we are talking is likely to take the life out of our speech and may make it seem formal and aloof. Very often the added exactness of writing does not mean using rare words, but just more exact ones, as in this simple descriptive statement:

> At the top of the pole crouched a shivering gray kitten, mewing faintly and clinging desperately to the wood with her claws.—WILLA CATHER, *O Pioneers*, p. 5

But the typical specific words of spoken English have more useful qualities. They are likely to be shorter and to stand closer to experience. We would usually speak of *words* rather than of *vocabulary, bugs* than of *insects, jobs* than of *positions*. We like expressive words like *harum-scarum* and *flabbergast;* we *sponge* on our relatives; we think someone is *no great shakes*. We are likely to use *verb-adverb combinations instead of specific verbs: *give in* for *surrender, give up* for *sacrifice*. To *pepper and salt* is a good colloquial verb, and so is to *keep an eye out for*. Most people's speech includes some localisms, slang, and vulgate expressions. A good talker is likely to take whatever words fit his meaning and his mood, without ordinarily questioning their ancestry or social status.

d) SENTENCES AND SYNTAX. Spoken sentences are usually shorter than written, or if they are long, it is because one statement is added to another rather than because clauses are carefully built together with subordinating conjunctions and manipulation of word order. In speaking, we must, like Henry Ward Beecher, plunge into a sentence, "trusting to God Almighty to get us through it." We are likely to split constructions, to shift in the middle of a sentence, to let the agreement of verbs follow the meaning rather than grammatical requirements, to use pronouns casually, and so on. Speech goes rapidly by and is not carefully scrutinized for details of expression. In writing, the words lie on the page and can be analyzed. A writer is therefore more careful. Since he has the opportunity to revise, as the speaker does not, he is usually held responsible for a fairly strict following of the conventions of the level of usage in which he is writing.

The closeness of written literary English to the colloquial language of the time has varied from period to period. In the nineteenth century the two were conspicuously far apart—consider Arnold and Ruskin, and even more the rank and file of lesser writers, such as Sir Arthur Helps. The last 75 years in England and the last 40 in the United States have seen a closer approach of written to spoken style. The colloquial vein in modern writing is very strong. It fits in fiction, in intimate narrative, and in much general exposition, as these two brief extracts show:

> I don't know why Father and Mother chose Irvington to go to, that summer. There were lots of other places to go where we boys could have enjoyed ourselves better, but we weren't consulted of course, and we'd have been surprised if we had been.—CLARENCE DAY, *Life With Father*, p. 41

> If you have the sort of money that runs to seagoing yachts or even to shiny mahogany runabouts your opinion of outboard motors—if any—is probably low. Likely you carry an outboard-powered dinghy or tender, and any time you drop anchor in a sporting harbor like Nantucket or Boothbay you are sure to see a couple of fussy little boats with outboards clamped to their sterns, kicking up a great wake and bouncing around like shag dancers. If someone invited you to go out for a ride in an outboard you might go, the same way you might condescend to take a ride in the subway to see how the other 99 per cent lives, or the I'll-have-fun-if-it-kills-me way you might put on torn overalls for one of Elsa Maxwell's parties. But you wouldn't take outboards seriously. If they came up in the course of a conversation you would either look as though you'd never heard of them, or you would guillotine them with a contemptuous "Oh, those."—"The Put-Put," *Fortune*, Aug. 1938

Writing like this is not only highly readable but it can be used to convey a wide range of information, thought, and feeling. Probably the most practical as well as the most honest thing for a beginning writer is to study his own speech and see how far it can serve as the basis for his writing. "One would like to think," says Bonamy Dobrée, "that all of us will come to the stage of refusing to write what we would not, indeed could not, say."

(SEE also *Conversation and Chapter 2, Varieties of English. Anyone wishing to study the relationship between colloquial and written English will find further material (and varying opinions) in these: Lascelles Abercrombie, *Colloquial Language and Literature*, Society for Pure English Tract xxvi (Oxford, 1931); Henry Bradley,

Spoken and Written English (Oxford, 1919); Curme's *Parts of Speech* and *Syntax* pay special attention to colloquial forms and constructions; Dobrée, Part iv; John S. Kenyon, "Levels of Speech and Colloquial English," *English Journal*, 1948, 37:25-31; Thomas A. Knott, "Standard English and Incorrect English," *American Speech*, 1934, 9: 83 ff.; Mencken; L. A. Sherman, *Analytics of Literature* (Boston, 1893), 285-86, 311-12, and index references; C. H. Woolbert, "Speaking and Writing—A Study of Differences," *Quarterly Journal of Speech*, 1922, 8: 271-85; Henry C. Wyld, *A History of Modern Colloquial English* (New York, 1920), and *Historical Study of the Mother Tongue* (New York, 1906)

Colon **Colon** **(:)** Correction: Use a colon here.

> **1. Anticipatory use. 2. Between clauses. 3. In time and references. 4. Stylistic use. 5. Capitals following. 6. After abbreviations.**

The colon is a mark of anticipation, directing attention to what follows. It is a formal mark and usually emphatic. Its use contrasts to that of the semicolon, which is a stop, almost a period. Students do not use as many colons as they should, and often use a semicolon instead:

> Yesterday I received a clipping from home, the essence of which is as follows: [not ;]. . . .

The principal uses of the colon are:

1. Anticipatory use. A colon is used after an introductory expression, as in the second line above, and after the salutation of formal letters:

> Dear Sir: (Contrast the comma in informal letters: Dear Fritz,)

It is generally used to anticipate quotations in factual writing (not in fiction), especially if the quotation is a complete grammatic unit and runs to more than one sentence. Whether or not a colon is appropriate with shorter quotations depends in part upon the formula with which it is introduced. If the quotation is closely built into the sentence, a comma is usual (*says*, in the quotation below); if the introduction is more formal, a colon is usual (below, *was added:*).

> A card made out at 10:45 P.M. on Nov. 4, 1928, says, "Arnold Rothstein, Male, 46 years, 912 Fifth Avenue, gunshot wound in abdomen, found in employee's entrance, Park Central Hotel, 200 West Fifty-sixth Street. Attended by Dr. McGovern, of City Hospital. Removed to Polyclinic Hospital. Reported by Patrolman William M. Davis, Shield 2943, Ninth Precinct." Two days later the word "fatal," in parentheses, was written in after the word "abdomen," and a second report, with more detail, was added: "Rothstein apparently had been engaged in card game with others in Room 349 on third floor of Park Central Hotel when an unknown man shot him and threw revolver out of window to street. Body found by Lawrence Fallon of 3164 Thirty-fourth Street, Astoria, employed as house detective for the hotel."— MEYER BERGER, *The New Yorker*, Nov. 26, 1938

2. Between clauses. A colon is used between clauses when the following one is either an illustration of the first, a restatement in different terms, or an amplification of the first:

> If a gunnery officer can't explain what he wants done, one of two things is going to happen: either the gun won't be fired or he'll have to do it himself.
> Lazy minds give up in despair: "I can't write anyhow," say students to me year after year; they mean that they won't think.—Barrett Wendell, *English Composition*, p. 136
> The supposition that words are used principally to convey thoughts is one of the most elementary of possible errors: they are used mainly to proclaim emotional effects on the hearers or attitudes that will lead to practical results.—H. R. Huse, *The Illiteracy of the Literate*, p. 21

3. In time and reference. There are a few conventional uses of the colon, though they vary among publishers:

a) Between hours and minutes expressed in figures:

> 11:42 a.m.   3:28 p.m.   (or: 11.42 a.m., 3.28 p.m.)

b) In formal bibliographies and formal citations of books:

> Between volume and page—*The Atlantic Monthly*, 160:129-40
> Between author and title—Stuart Chase: *Men and Machines*
> Between place of publication and publisher—New York: Holt, 1930

In the last two of these a comma would often be found.

4. Stylistic use. Some writers prefer colons where most would use commas or semicolons:

> It [a castle] is a shut place that commands by its shutness the open place about it. A castle is builded of the stone of its world: it rises from the stone of its world: it *is* the stone of its world. A castle is austere toward the world which it defends. It is invariable, forbidding: its strength is that of a perpetual shutting-out of all which lies outside it. Sun beats on the castle wall: inside it is dark. Moon melts its bastion and bathes its county blue: it is harsh and rigid. Water and wind make song of the green hills: the castle is silent. It is the lord of its county because it is apart from it. A castle is hot in a cold land: a castle is cold in a hot land: a castle is high in a low land: a castle is full in a land of dearth: a castle is dry in a land of verdure.
> —Waldo Frank, *Virgin Spain*, p. 108

This is a matter of taste rather than of correctness, and usually (as here) formal. The mark usually attracts some slight attention to itself when used this way.

5. Capitals following. After a colon either a capital or a small letter may be used. The capital is more usual when the matter following the colon is in the form of a complete sentence, a small letter when it is a subordinate element. That the deciding factor is largely the closeness of thought relation between the two parts of the sentence is suggested by the following quotations from a single article:

> Thus the task of democracy has always been a twofold one: to prevent political privilege from reëstablishing itself, and to make peaceful settlement of disputes possible in a society without privilege.
>
> Those who believe that fascism is simply a tool which Big Business created as soon as it found democracy dangerous overlook one important fact: the opposition of Big Business to democracy is much older than fascism.
>
> The ways in which the kings settled social disputes were very different, in spirit as well as in technic: The kings of France, after having subdued the rebellious nobles, protected the social privileges of the nobility to the point of subjecting both citizens and peasants to cruel oppression; the kings of Prussia, who occasionally liked to be called "kings of beggars," without fully living up to the implications of that title, tried to restrict exploitation of the masses; so, much earlier, did Elizabeth of England.—CARL LANDAUER, in *The American Way*, by D. C. Coyle and others

6. After abbreviations. When a colon follows an abbreviation the period of the abbreviation is usually omitted: *i.e:* rather than *i.e.:*

column, columnist Usual pronunciation kol′əm, kol′əm ist or kol′əm nist. Vulgate kol′yum, kol′yum ist is often used humorously and increasingly for a newspaper "column" and is sometimes represented in the spellings *colyum, colyumist.*

combine *Combine* (kom′bīn) as a noun came into use either from the verb *combine* (kəm bīn′), with the characteristic change in stress (*Noun and verb stress), or perhaps as a *back formation from *combination*. It is not in good use in the abstract senses of *combination*, but is good colloquial English for a group of people joined together for business or political gain and usually implies either shady or forceful activities. *Combine* (kom′bīn) is the right name for the machine that reaps and threshes in the field.

Comma **Comma** (,) Correction: Insert or remove a comma at the place marked, in accordance with one of the sections in this article.
 1. Between clauses. 2. Lists and series. 3. With nonrestrictive modifiers. 4. With interrupting and parenthetical words and phrases. 5. Commas with main sentence elements. 6. For emphasis and contrast. 7. For clearness. 8. Routine conventional uses. 9. Comma combined with other marks.
 There is a general treatment of the uses of commas in Chapter 5, page 140. The principal uses are reviewed here for convenience in revising or correcting papers.
 1. Between clauses.
 a) Between coordinate clauses. A comma is used when the clauses

Uses of the Comma

The following list of uses of the comma outlines the treatment in this article. The numbers and letters refer to sections and sub-sections. Brackets mean that a comma should be avoided.

1. BETWEEN CLAUSES
   a. Between rather long coordinate clauses, especially those connected by *but, not, for*
   b. After subordinate clause or long phrase preceding the main clause
   c. Before a subordinate clause following the main clause and not closely related to it
2. IN LISTS AND SERIES
   a. Between units of a list or series
   b. Between coordinate adjectives in the same relation to their noun
   c. [Not between two words or phrases joined by *and*]
3. AROUND NONRESTRICTIVE MODIFIERS
4. AROUND INTERRUPTING AND PARENTHETICAL ELEMENTS
   a. Around interrupting constructions
   b. Around conjunctive adverbs not standing first in their constructions
5. WITH MAIN SENTENCE ELEMENTS (S-V-O)
   a. [Not between a short subject and its verb]
   b. Sometimes after a long or heavily modified subject
   c. [Not between verb and its object]
   d. [Rarely between compound predicates]
6. FOR EMPHASIS AND CONTRAST
7. FOR CLEARNESS
   a. Before words of two possible functions (*for, but*)
   b. To prevent a noun being taken as an object
   c. To prevent wrong interpretation
   d. To separate consecutive uses of the same word
8. IN CONVENTIONAL PLACES
   a. In dates   b. In addresses
   c. After salutation of informal letters   d. In figures
   e. With degrees and titles   f. With weak exclamations
   g. [Not to show omission of a word]
9. WITH OTHER MARKS OF PUNCTUATION
   a. [Not with a dash] (*Dash § 6)
   b. With parentheses (*Parentheses § 5)
   c. With quotation marks (*Quotation marks § 4, b and c)

are rather long and when it is desirable to emphasize their distinctness, especially if the clauses have different subjects.

The frozen steel edges shrieked as they bit into the ice-covered turns, and the driving sleet slashed against their goggles and jackets with such force that it was impossible to keep clear vision.

A comma is generally used between two coordinate locutions joined by *but* or *not,* to emphasize the contrast:

I can remember mother telling me that a book was one's best friend, but I couldn't understand how anyone could feel that way.
Those who hold these ideas are to be pitied, not blamed.
(COMPARE § 6.)

A comma is generally used between clauses connected by the conjunction *for,* to avoid confusion with the preposition *for:*

Conjunction: They are obviously mistaken, *for* all intercollegiate sports are competitive.
Preposition: The English teacher had assigned us "Treasure Island" [ ] *for* a book report.
(COMPARE § 7.)

A comma is not used when the clauses are short and closely related in meaning especially in easy narrative:

The elevated rushed into an underground shaft [ ] and in the hollow, re-echoing roar only the high runs of the sax could be heard.

For commas between complete clauses that could stand as separate sentences, see Chapter 9, "Run-on sentences," page 253, and *Comma fault.

b) After a subordinate clause (or long phrase) that precedes the main clause or is not closely connected to it:

If that lake wasn't frowning at something or other that night, I'll drink it down to the last drop.
Although willing to use his athletic ability, he wouldn't study hard enough to become eligible.

When the preceding clause or phrase is short and closely related in thought to the main clause (especially when the subjects of the two clauses are the same), there is usually no comma following it:

In my opinion [ ] these youthful marriages are justifiable in every respect.
When we had all gathered near the fence [ ] we could see that they were bums. (Subjects the same.)
When appropriations are before the House he continually checks the Democrats' expenditures. (A close relationship between the statements)

c) Before a subordinate clause that follows the main clause. A comma usually stands before a subordinate clause (or long phrase) that follows the main clause if it is not closely related in thought.

> Kemal Ataturk's death came as a blow to a nation of 14,000,000 people, although he reformed their social customs, their religion, and their economics with dictatorial zeal and speed.
> They had tried four times to start it, the starter every time giving just a short whine.

2. Lists and series. (a) The comma is the natural mark to use between the units of enumerations, lists, series (unless the units are long or contain commas within them, when semicolons would be used—see *Semicolon § 1).

> There are, among others, an actor out of a job, a murderer, a Mexican dipsomaniac, a man obsessed with a philosophical concept of time, an Indian oil millionaire who prefers waffles to any other food, and assorted females, mostly tough.—*The New Yorker*, Nov. 26, 1938

Commas ordinarily are not used when conjunctions stand between the units of the series:

> A bit of tarnish on the brass work [ ] or untidy life preservers [ ] or matches on the decks seem to be of little concern to him.

Usage is divided on the comma before the last item in a series: *celery, onions, and olives*, or *celery, onions and olives*. (See *Series.)

b) Adjectives in series. In the sentence

> When the long, cold, lonesome evenings came, we would gather about the old wood stove and eat the chestnuts.

there are commas between *long—cold—lonesome* because each stands in the same relation to the noun *evenings*. There is no comma between *old* and *wood* because *old* modifies *wood stove* rather than just *stove*. A comma following *old* would throw more emphasis upon *wood* and might sometimes be wanted. Compare these two versions:

> The room presents a colonial effect with its old-fashioned, cross-beamed ceiling and gray, brick fireplace.
> The room presents a colonial effect with its old-fashioned cross-beamed ceiling and gray brick fireplace.

Either version is correct, but in the first, *cross-beamed* and *brick* stand out as separate modifiers of their nouns.

c) Two items connected by *and* are not usually punctuated:

> In high school the student is paid six dollars a month for helping the teachers in their work [ ] and for doing odd jobs about the school building.

Comma

3. With nonrestrictive modifiers. Modifiers which do not limit the meaning of a noun or verb but add a descriptive detail are nonrestrictive and are set off by a comma or commas. The expressions in italics are nonrestrictive:

> From where I was standing, *almost directly above the treasure,* I could see many articles that had been lost. (The clause *that had been lost* is restrictive and so not set off by a comma.)
> Pigeons breed in the spring and the hen lays two eggs, *one of which usually hatches into a cock and one into a hen.*

A restrictive modifier, one that is essential to a correct understanding of the word it modifies, is not set off by punctuation. The expressions in italics are restrictive:

> Wouldn't it be as just to remove from his suffering a person *who has committed no crime* as to make suffer one *who has committed a crime?*
> Great tracts were left, eaten bare of the grass *which had kept the soil in place.*

Many modifiers may be considered either restrictive or nonrestrictive, and their punctuation should follow the writer's sense of the closeness with which they limit the word they modify. The expressions in italics in these sentences might be set off by commas, depending on the writer's intention:

> A winding road *that seemed to lead nowhere in particular* passed through the village.
> It was quite a satisfaction *after working a difficult logarithm problem* to know that something had been accomplished.

(Further examples of restrictive and nonrestrictive expressions will be found in *Restrictive and nonrestrictive and in Chapter 5, "With close and loose modifiers," p. 144.)

4. With interrupting and parenthetical words and phrases. (a) A phrase or clause that interrupts the direct movement of the sentence should be set off by commas, *two* commas:

> This last semester, *if it has done nothing else,* has given me confidence in myself.
> Over in the corner, *beside the dark and broken window where a newspaper was stuffed to keep out the rain,* sat Verona.
> Did intelligent people, *he asked himself,* do things like that?

Usage is divided over setting off short parenthetical words and phrases like *incidentally, of course.* Setting them off with commas is more characteristic of formal than of informal writing, though there is often a difference in emphasis according to whether or not commas are used:

488

These early attempts, of course, brought no results.
These early attempts of course brought no results.
The famous artist, oddly enough, preferred the company of common laborers to that of his own kind.
The famous artist oddly enough preferred the company of common laborers to that of his own kind.

Adverbs that modify the verb or the statement closely should not be set off by commas when they are in their natural position:

Perhaps [ ] they had never intended to come.
They had never intended to come, perhaps.

b) When a *conjunctive adverb stands after the first phrase of its clause, as it often does, it is usually set off by commas, and often it is set off when it stands first in the clause:

The next morning, however, they all set out as though nothing had happened.
The second plan, therefore, was the one determined upon for the holiday.
However, the next morning they all set out as though nothing had happened.

But and other lighter conjunctions are a part of the clauses in which they appear and should not be set off:

I was positive that if someone would just give me some guidance I could do much better. But [ ] the semester continued the same as before.

5. Commas with main sentence elements. (a) Short subjects. Care should be taken not to separate short subjects from their verbs:

The first family to come [ ] sends word back to those left in the Old Country.
The six boys [ ] all came on the run.

b) Long subjects. When the subject of a sentence is a long phrase or a noun followed by modifiers, that is, when it is a locution of five or six words or more, formal usage often puts a comma between it and the verb, but informal usage does not.

Whether a program is appealing or not [Formal (,)] is quickly reflected in the sale of the sponsor's product.
Everything that I had picked out as a flaw to be pounced upon and criticized [Formal (,)] assumed a different meaning and became a vital part of the work.

c) Verb and object. There is some temptation to put a comma after a verb, separating it from its object or complement. This is especially true after verbs of saying. Such commas should be taken out in revision:

Since they know nothing whatsoever about their future occupation, they must start what might be termed [ ] a second schooling.

We all know [ ] that the person who is hardworking and willing has a good deal put over on him.

d) COMPOUND PREDICATES. Usage is divided over separating the two verbs of a compound predicate. The better and more common usage is not to use a comma between the verbs unless the predicates are long or contrasted:

Thus in fifteen years rabbit raising has ceased to be a hobby [ ] and has taken a definite place among the industries of the world.

Pop could talk himself out of trouble [ ] and also talk himself into a lot of trouble.

6. For emphasis. The pause indicated by a comma tends to keep distinct the constructions it separates and to emphasize slightly the construction that follows the mark:

Temporarily the wine industry was all but ruined, and farmers turned to dairying, and to cooperation to give them a market.

This is especially true when a connective is omitted:

And afterwards I told her how I felt, how I kept feeling about her.

In idioms like *the more . . . the greater*, formal usage tends to have a comma, informal not:

. . . And the more meaning the Grammarian finds crowded into the verb [,] the happier he is.—P. B. BALLARD, *Thought and Language*, p. 87

7. For clearness. Often a comma can guide a reader in interpreting a sentence and make it unnecessary for him to go back over it for meaning. In material that is likely to be read aloud, the writer should give special heed to this device. Two such constructions are especially helped by commas:

a) When a word has two possible functions. *For* or *but* may be either a conjunction or a preposition, and confusion may be avoided by using a comma before either when it is used as a conjunction:

The surgeon's face showed no emotion, but anxiety and a little nervousness must be seething behind that impassive mask. (To avoid reading "no emotion but anxiety")

b) When a noun might be mistaken for the object of a verb.

When the boll weevil struck, the credit system collapsed and ruined a great part of the landowners and tenants. (Not: When the boll weevil struck the credit system . . .)

It is not necessary to have a session like this very often, but when you do, get everything off your mind that is disturbing you. (Not: but when you do get everything off your mind . . .)

c) Sometimes a faulty interpretation of word grouping can be prevented:

The only way that you can develop honestly is to discover how you write now, and then write naturally in everything you hand in. (Not: how you write now and then . . .)

d) Ordinarily when the same word occurs twice consecutively a comma should be used:

What the trouble really is, is of no interest to him.

8. Routine, conventional uses. (a) In dates, to separate the day of the month from the year: *May 26, 1952.* When the day of the month is not given, a comma may or may not be used: *In September 1952* or *In September, 1952.* The neater use is without the comma.

b) In addresses, to separate town from state or country when they are written on the same line:

Washington, D.C., is too hot and humid to be a nation's capital.
Chicago, Illinois   Berne, Switzerland
Hamilton, Madison County, New York

c) After salutations in informal letters: *Dear Dot, Dear Len,*
d) In figures, to separate thousands, millions, etc: 4, 672, 342
e) To separate degrees and titles from names:

Elihu Root, Esq.   Charles Evans Hughes, Jr.
Wallace W. Emmett, A.B.   Wallace W. Emmett, A.B. '36

f) After a weak exclamation like *well, why, oh* when it does not carry much stress

g) A comma is not now commonly used to show the omission of a word that is required to fill out a grammatical construction:

He must have taken the right-hand turn and I [,] the left.

9. Comma combined with other marks. (a) A comma is now rarely used with a dash. (See *Dash § 6.)

b) When a parenthesis comes within a construction that would be followed by a comma, the comma stands after the parenthesis. (See *Parentheses § 5.)

c) For use with quotation marks see *Quotation marks § 4 b, c.

(REFERENCE: Summey, index entries under *Comma.*)

CF   **Comma fault**   Correction: Revise the sentence marked by changing the comma to a semicolon or a period, or by inserting an appropriate conjunction, or by rephrasing to make it a more effective sentence. You should do more than merely remove the comma fault; you should make an effective statement. Your instructor's mark means that in his judgment it is not an effective run-on sentence.

A comma fault (or comma blunder or comma splice) is two or more statements in the form of independent sentences that are punctuated as a single sentence—that is, with a comma between them (or even run together with no mark at all). A few sentences of this sort are effective (see "Run-on sentences," page 253), but here we are considering only those that by their form and by the lack of thought relation between the clauses are not.

There are various remedies for a comma fault:

1) The easiest, that satisfies the minimum requirements of conventional grammar, is to repunctuate, using a semicolon or a period instead of the comma. This often leaves two weak sentences instead of one good one.

2) If the statements really belong together in one sentence, the clauses may be joined by a conjunction that shows the relationship, probably retaining the comma.

3) Often the sentence needs to be rephrased—perhaps a relative pronoun used instead of a *this* or *these*—or to be completely rewritten. Remember that the aim is to make an effective sentence.

The following examples show some common types:

The comma fault	*Suggested revision*
He took a couple of steps, stopped, reached out and turned a valve, as he did that he told us that all the valves were right-hand valves.	He took a couple of steps, stopped, reached out and turned a valve. As he did that he told us that all the valves were right-hand valves.
Two volumes of his great work are now completed, the first will be published next year.	Two volumes of his great work are now completed, the first of which will be published next year.
	Two volumes of his great work are now completed, and the first will be published next year.
	Two volumes of his great work are now completed. The first will be published next year.
Charley then crossed the room and threw a switch which started a motor, returning he wiped the perspiration from his forehead with the back of his hand.	Charley then crossed the room and threw a switch which started a motor. Returning he wiped the perspiration . . .

492

They still produce aluminum tips for broken skis, these are very successful as a device for temporary repair.	They still produce aluminum tips for broken skis, which are very successful as a device for temporary repair.

Carelessly run together sentences are one of the most serious faults in elementary writing and anyone who has not learned to avoid them must take extra pains to eliminate them from his writing.

(For a more complete discussion and more examples of comma faults and of successful run-on sentences, see ch. 9, "Run-on sentences," p. 253. SEE also *Contact clauses, *Conjunctions.)

Commands and requests Direct commands are expressed by the simple (infinitive) form of the verb:

> *Hurry up!*   *Shut* the door, please.
> *Fill out* the coupon and *mail* it today.

In speech the force of the command or request is shown by the stress and tone of voice, which are hard to represent on paper. Emphatic commands are punctuated with an exclamation mark, less emphatic with a period. The form with *do* is often emphatic (*Do* come!). Negative commands are expressed with *not* and the *do* form of the verb: Don't go yet.

Softened or more polite commands and requests depend on phrasing and usually involve auxiliaries or adverbs of courtesy. Often these commands and requests are in the pattern of a question, which would be written either with a period or a question mark, depending on the intonation intended.

> Try and [or *to*] get them in on time.
> You will write at least six pages.
> Please think no more of it.
> Would you be willing to take part in this program?
> Would [or *Will*] you please close the window.
> Let's go around and see what we can do with him.
> Suppose we say nothing more about it.

In indirect discourse a command becomes an infinitive with *to* or a clause with *should:*

> He told us to write a 5000 word paper.
> Or: He said that we should write a 5000 word paper. (Direct form: "Write a 5000 word paper.")
> He wired me to come at once. (Direct: "Come at once.")

(For further discussion of forms of commands see Curme, *Syntax*, pp. 419, 430-36.)

Commercial usage See *Business English.

committee is a *collective noun, to be construed as singular or plural according as the group or the individuals are meant. The singular would usually be the form desired.

> The committee meets today at four.
> The committee get together with difficulty.

Common noun See *Noun § 1.

comparative—comparatively—comparison So spelled in our inconsistent language.

compare—contrast *Compare* is used in two senses: (1) To point out likenesses (used with *to*); (2) To examine two or more objects to find likenesses or differences (used with *with*). *Contrast* always points out *differences*.

> He compared my stories *to* Maupassant's [said they were like his].
> He compared my stories *with* Maupassant's [pointed out like and unlike traits].

When the things compared are of different classes, *to* is used:

> He compared my stories *to* a sack of beans.

In the common construction with the past participle, either *to* or *with* is used:

> Compared *with* [or *to*] Maupassant's, mine are pretty feeble.
> In comparison *with* [not *to*] Maupassant's, mine are pretty feeble.

Idioms with *contrast*:

> He contrasted my work *with* [sometimes *to*] Maupassant's.
> In contrast *to* [rarely *with*] Maupassant's, my stories are pretty feeble.

Stress: the noun *contrast* (kon'trast); the verb *contrast* (kən-trast', kən trast'əd, kən trast'ing).

Comparisons For comparisons as figures of speech see "Resemblance," page 348. For idioms for comparisons, see Chapter 4, page 116. For comparisons and contrasts, as materials that go into paragraphs, see Chapter 7, page 177.

Comp **Comparison of adjectives and adverbs** Correction: Change the form or construction of the adjective or adverb marked, in accordance with the section below that applies.

1. Uses of the comparative. 2. Uses of the superlative. 3. Idioms. 4. Absolutes. 5. Choice of forms.

Adjectives and adverbs change their forms (see § 5) to show a greater degree of the characteristic named in the simple word (*long, longer, longest*). The forms are simple enough but a number of questions arise in using them.

1. Uses of the comparative. The comparative degree expresses a greater degree (It is *warmer* now) or makes specific comparison between two units (He was *kinder* [*more kind*] than his wife).

The two terms of a comparison should be comparable:

Comparable: His salary was lower than a shoe clerk's [Or: than that of a shoe clerk]. Not: His salary was lower than a shoe clerk.
Comparable: His face was round and healthy looking, like a recent college graduate's. Not: His face was round and healthy looking, like a recent college graduate.

With a comparative, idiom calls for *other* when the comparison is with something in the same class of things but not when the comparison is with things of a different class:

She is a better dancer than the other girls.
She is a better dancer than the boys [than any of the boys].

The comparative is frequently used absolutely, with no actual comparison involved (*higher education, the lower depths*), or the reader is left to supply a comparison (*Look younger—Live longer*).

(REFERENCE: Esther K. Sheldon, "The Rise of the Incomplete Comparative," *American Speech*, 1945, 20:161-67.)

2. Uses of the superlative. The superlative is used to indicate the greatest degree of a quality among three or more people or things (He was the *jolliest* of the whole group; This is the *brightest* tie in the showcase). The form with *most* is also used as an intensive to indicate an extreme degree (You are *most kind;* She is *most clever*) in which no specific comparison is intended.

Superlatives are not completed by *other:*

Jerry was the best cook of all the [not *other*] cooks in the surrounding camps.
The Egyptians had obtained the highest degree of cultivation in medicine that had up to that time been obtained by any [not *other*] nation.

In colloquial and familiar English a superlative is often a form of emphasis: "We saw the loveliest flowers when we visited her garden."—"Hasn't she the sweetest voice?" It is also used in comparing two items: "His new novel is the best of the two." Fries says (p. 101): "The use of the superlative rather than the comparative for two, thus ignoring a dual as distinct from a plural, is a fact of Standard English usage and not a characteristic limited to Vulgar English."

(REFERENCE: Russell Thomas, "The Use of the Superlative for the Comparative," *English Journal* (College edition), 1935, 24:821-29.)

3. Idioms with comparatives. (a) *as much as if not more than.*
Colloquially people are likely to say "The styles vary as much if not
more than the colors" but in writing both comparative constructions
should be completed:

> The styles vary as much *as* if not more *than* the colors.
> The lobby is as strong *as* if not stronger *than* it was in 1948.
> Or: The lobby is as strong as it was in 1948, if not stronger.

b) *as . . . as.* Sometimes *than* is carelessly used for the second *as*
in a sentence like this:

> I pay almost ten times as much for it *as* [not *than*] for the bigger bus
ticket.
(SEE *as . . . as.)

4. Comparison of absolutes. In puristic usage such adjectives as
*black, dead, excellent, fatal, final, impossible, *unique* are not compared, since their meaning is thought to be absolute: There are no degrees of *deadness* or *blackness* or *impossibility.* But in common
use the meaning of these words is not absolute so that they are
frequently compared: "This was even *more impossible.*" Many are
used figuratively with less absolute meanings ("This is the *deadest*
town I was ever in"), which naturally admit comparison.

5. Choice of forms. English adjectives and adverbs are compared
in two ways:

a) By adding *-er, -est:*

	Positive	Comparative	Superlative
Adjective:	early	earlier	earliest
	hoarse	hoarser	hoarsest
	hot	hotter	hottest
Adverb:	fast	faster	fastest
	soon	sooner	soonest

b) By using *more, most.* The change in degree may be shown
by prefixing *more* and *most* to the positive form. This form is used
for all adjectives and adverbs of three syllables or more, and for many
of two syllables. It may also be used with those of one syllable, so
that for many comparatives and superlatives there are two forms:

	Positive	Comparative	Superlative
Adjective:	exquisite	more exquisite	most exquisite
	empty	emptier, more empty	emptiest, most empty
	able	abler, more able	ablest, most able
Adverb:	comfortably	more comfortably	most comfortably
	often	oftener, more often	oftenest, most often
	hotly	more hotly	most hotly

496

Words with a short vowel followed by a single consonant double the consonant to indicate the short sound (*thin, thinner, thinnest*). Words ending in *y* change the *y* to *i* before the endings: *dry, drier, driest; shy, shier, shiest* (sometimes *shyer, shyest*).

The meanings of the two forms are the same, so that the one can be used that sounds better. But the form with the ending places the stress on the root part of the word and so tends to emphasize the quality (kind′er), and the *more* or *most* form allows the stress to fall on the sign of the degree (more′ kind; You are most′ kind) so that there is some difference in the suggestion value of the two.

(REFERENCES: Curme, *Parts of Speech*, chs. 11, 13; *Syntax*, ch. 25; Fries, pp. 96-101.)

complement—compliment *Compliment* has to do with politeness and praise:

> He *complimented* them on their progress.
> Their progress deserved his *compliment*.
> "the *complimentary* close" of a letter

Complement means a number or amount that makes a whole, or an allotment (related to *complete*):

> He had his full *complement* of good looks.   *complementary* angles

Complement A complement is the noun or adjective completing the meaning of a linking verb and modifying the subject:

> He was *busy*.   He became *the real head* of the concern.

(SEE ch. 4, "Subject-complement," p. 108, and *Linking verbs, *Predicate adjective, Predicate noun.)

Complex sentences A complex sentence has one main clause (that is, one that could "stand alone" as a sentence) and one or more subordinate clauses. These are subject-verb constructions related to the main clause by a *relative pronoun or a *subordinating conjunction. So many combinations are possible that detailed classification would be tedious. The chief (and perhaps only) advantage of analysis of clauses is seeing the variety of expression possible in sentences and the various means by which ideas are tied together in statements.

(SEE ch. 9, "Complex sentences," p. 257, and *Clauses.)

complexioned (complected) *Complected* in such phrases as "He is a dark-complected man" is colloquial or local for "a dark-complexioned man." *Complected* is a formal word meaning "woven together"; *complexion* and *complexioned* refer to facial coloring.

Compound-complex sentences See *Compound sentences § 4 and Chapter 9, "Compound-complex sentences," page 259.

Compound predicate

Compound predicate Two or more verbs having the same subject are known as a compound predicate: "The youngster *bawled* and *stamped* his feet"; "Ruth *wrote* and *mailed* three letters."

Compound predicates are one of the chief devices of economy in writing. Note how far removed these sentences are from the one-small-idea-to-a-sentence type so often used by immature writers:

> They (1) accepted the quinine and, in their gratitude, often (2) kissed the hygienists' hands. Heeding their advice, they (1) graveled the village roads, (2) began to drain their lands, (3) enlarged the windows of their dwellings, (4) built sidewalks, sanitary backhouses, and concrete platforms for manure, and so on.—Louis Adamic, *The Native's Return*, p. 318

(For further discussion see *Subject and verb.)

Compound sentences contain two or more complete statements (that is, each with a subject and complete verb) of coordinate grammatical value, without a subordinate clause. (See Chapter 9, "Compound sentences," page 251.)

1. With coordinating conjunction. Usually the clauses of a compound sentence are connected by one of the coordinating conjunctions, most commonly by *and, but, for, or,* and the combinations *either . . . or, neither . . . nor:*

> What a fool he was to be thus startled *but* always he had hated cats from childhood.—Walter Duranty, *Babies Without Tails*, p. 11
> *Either* you learned these simple things in high school *or* you will have to learn them in college.

2. Without connective. A compound sentence may stand without a connective (see *Contact clauses). Such sentences are usually punctuated with a semicolon:

> They are generous-minded; they hate shams and enjoy being indignant about them; they are valuable social reformers; they have no notion of confining books to a library shelf.—E. M. Forster, *Aspects of the Novel*, p. 33

(Compare ch. 9, "Run-on sentences," p. 253.)

3. With conjunctive adverb. The clauses of a compound sentence may be connected by a conjunctive adverb (*however, moreover, whereas, consequently, therefore . . .*):

> The F.B.I. had proved themselves expert in publicizing their solution of crimes; consequently some local police gave them only grudging support.

(See *Conjunctive adverbs.)

4. Compound-complex. Since one or more of the coordinate clauses of a sentence can be modified by subordinate clauses, we have the category of *compound-complex sentences:*

498

He was an old man with a long beard, whose clothes were rags; but Mr. Kiddle had all the way wished to tell someone how proud he was of Ada, who did the running, so he was glad to have even a tinker to talk to.—T. F. Powys, *Mr. Weston's Good Wine*, p. 66

This sentence has three main clauses (making it compound): *He was an old man . . . but Mr. Kiddle had all the way wished . . . so he was glad to have . . .*; and three subordinate clauses (making it compound-complex): *whose clothes were rags, how proud he was of Ada, who did the running.*

In current style there are more compound-complex sentences than compound ones.

Compound subject   Two or more elements standing as the subject of a verb are called a *compound subject:*

> *Capitalists, militarists, and ecclesiastics* co-operate in education, because all depend for their power upon the prevalence of emotionalism and the rarity of critical judgment.—Bertrand Russell, *What I Believe*, p. 53

The verb following a compound subject is usually plural:

> Christianity and humanity *have* gone hand in hand throughout history.

Some special cases are described under *Subject and verb § 2b.
(See ch. 4, "Compound subjects," p. 105.)

Compound words   Compound words are combinations of two or more words: *doorknob, notwithstanding, quarter-hour, father-in-law, drugstore.*

Questions about the use of the hyphen in compound words are discussed in *Hyphen, and questions about their plurals in *Plurals § 5. See also *Group words, *book.

Concluding paragraphs   Correction: Revise the very end of your paper so that it rounds out the discussion of your subject and so that the paper ends strongly.   *Concl*

For discussion of concluding paragraphs and examples, see Chapter 7, "Concluding paragraphs," page 198.

Concrete words   Correction: Replace the abstract word or words by concrete ones.   *Concr*

Concrete words name persons and things that can be seen and touched (*bus, waitress, filing case*), in contrast to abstract words for acts, ideas, qualities, relationships (*flowing, theory, cleanliness*).

For discussion see Chapter 11, "Concrete words," page 319, and Chapter 12, "Abstract and concrete words," page 341; see also *Imagery.

Conditions Conditional clauses state a condition or action necessary for the truth or occurrence of the main statement of a sentence. *If* is by far the most common conjunction for conditional clauses, with its negatives *if not* and *unless* (= *if not*), and *whether* (= *if . . . if, if . . . or if*). In formal writing *in case, provided, provided that, on condition that, in the event that,* and other phrases are used.

1. Simple conditions. Simple (or practical) conditions are statements of actual or reasonable conditions under which the main statement will hold. The indicative (ordinary) verb forms are used:

> *If the semaphore arm is horizontal,* you know that a train is in that block of track.
> He will be there *unless something happens to his car.*
> *Whether he comes or not,* I shall go just the same.

An older type of condition survives in some proverbs:

> Spare the rod and spoil the child. (If you spare the rod, you will spoil the child.)

In speech, we often express condition by a compound sentence:

> You just try that and you'll be sorry.

2. Less vivid conditions. Less vivid (theoretical or hypothetical but still possible) conditions are usually made with *should . . . would* or with the past tense:

> *If he should raise his offer another $100,* I would take it.
> Or: *If he raised his offer,* I would take it.
> *If you revised your papers carefully,* your writing would improve and would receive a higher grade.

3. Contrary to fact conditions. Conditions that cannot be met, contrary to fact conditions, formerly were stated with the subjunctive and still are in formal writing (sometimes even with a rather archaic inversion). The indicative is increasingly used in this type of condition:

> General: If I was going to be there, I'd be glad to help.
> Formal: If I were you, I would charge at least that.
> General: If I had known what I do [or know] now, I should [I'd] never have let him go.
> Formal: Had I known what I now know, I should never have let him go.
> General: If he was only here, he . . .
> Formal: If he were only here, he . . .

(SEE also *if, *Subjunctives. REFERENCES: Curme, *Syntax*, pp. 317-32, 421-29; Fries, pp. 104-107; Jespersen, p. 254 ff.)

Conjugation   The inflectional changes and phrasal forms of a verb or a group of verbs of the same type to show person, number, voice, mood, and tense. See *Verbs, *Tenses of verbs, *Principal parts.

Conjunctions   Conjunctions introduce and tie clauses together and join series of words and phrases. In this *Guide-Index* conjunctions are discussed according to their conventional types:

> *Coordinating (*and, but, for,* etc.)
> *Correlative (*either . . . or, not only . . . but,* etc.)
> *Conjunctive adverbs (*however, therefore, consequently,* etc.)
> *Subordinating (*as, because, since, so that, when,* etc.)

There are also articles on many of the particular conjunctions: *although, *and, *as, *because, *but, and so on. The article *Contact clauses discusses joining clauses without connectives; pages 253-257 discuss in detail contact clauses and comma faults.

Obviously the difference between certain coordinating conjunctions and the conjunctive adverbs is slight, and often in use the difference between subordinating and coordinating conjunctions cannot be reasonably seen. The *meaning* of these words is more important than their *type*. Professor Fries says:

> The difficulty of finding a reasonable set of criteria by which to separate coördinate from subordinate clauses and thus coördinating function words from those that are subordinating, argues that, in English, this distinction is really of practically no importance. Each of these function words signals a particular set of relationships between the clauses which it joins and the precise nature of the relationship is vitally important. Whether we further classify that relationship as a "coördinate" or a "subordinate" one makes no difference whatever.—*American English Grammar*. Copyright 1940, Appleton-Century-Crofts, Inc.

But until the studies of conjunctions are more generally accepted, it is perhaps advisable to follow the conventional groupings for purposes of reference.
(REFERENCE: Fries, pp. 206-40; all grammars have discussions.)

Conjunctions, Use   Correction: Make the conjunction marked more accurate (§ 1) or more appropriate to the style of the passage (§ 2).

1. Accurate conjunctions. 2. Weight. 3. Repetition of conjunctions. 4. Coordination vs. subordination.

1.   **Accurate conjunctions.**   The fitting together of clauses marked by an exact use of conjunctions is a sign of mature, practiced writing. In everyday speech we get along with a relatively small

number—*and, as, but, so, when,* and a few others. We don't bother to emphasize shades of meaning and exact relationships, which are suggested by pauses, tones of voice, gestures. In writing, accurate connectives go a long way toward making up for the loss of these oral means of holding ideas together.

Accurate use of conjunctions needs to be stressed. There are some easy temptations, like using *but* when there is no contrast between the statements (see *but § 2). Some conjunctions vary in definiteness of meaning: *As* means *because,* but means it very weakly (*as § 4); *while may mean *although* or *whereas,* but the core of its meaning relates to time. Such niceties in the use of these words are discussed in the articles on the particular conjunctions.

2. Weight. It is important for the conjunctions to be appropriate to other traits of style. Their weight should fit with the weight of other words and with the formality or informality of constructions.

The most common fault in weight of conjunctions has to do with the *conjunctive adverbs (*however, therefore, consequently . . .*) in ordinary, informal writing. These words are heavy and fit best in rather formal style. *But* and *however,* for example, both connect statements in opposition, but one cannot always be substituted for the other. *But* fits in all levels, but *however* is often too formal or too heavy for informal writing:

> The entrance and registration desk didn't strike me as beautiful. From here, however, I went upstairs and then I could see what they meant. (But from here . . .)

The English language has a number of long connecting phrases that will weaken a written style when used in place of shorter, more compact conjunctions:

> At that time football was distinctively a military pastime in Rome *in the same manner in which* [better: *as*] polo is among the soldiers today.
> (SEE *Conjunctive adverbs and *Function words.)

3. Repetition of conjunctions. Repeating a conjunction at the beginning of each element of a series gives distinctness to each element, avoids possible confusion, and gives the advantages of clear cut *parallelism. This is more characteristic of formal writing and often gives a definite rhythm:

> . . . designs of spears and shields and bastions and all the pomp of heraldry.
> —NORMAN DOUGLAS, *Siren Land,* p. 152
> For these five days and nights the Australians lived and ate and slept in that gallery of the mine of death, . . .—JOHN MASEFIELD, *Gallipoli,* p. 165

In opposition to this, omitting *and* before the last member of a short series results in a crisp emphasis:

High vacuums are essential not only to the distillation of vitamins but also in the manufacture of thermos bottles, radio tubes, X-ray apparatus, [ ] electric lamps.—*Time*, Nov. 28, 1938

(See *Series, *Telegraphic style.)

4. Coordination vs. subordination. For discussion of this phase of the use of conjunctions see *Subordination and Chapter 9, "Complex sentences," page 257.

(References: Kennedy, §§ 56 and 110; Curme, *Parts of Speech*, ch. 7, and *Syntax*, §§ 19 and 21, and index references.)

Conjunctive adverbs 1. A number of words primarily adverbs are used also as connectives. They are called *conjunctive adverbs* (or *transitional adverbs*, or *illative conjunctions*). Their adverbial meaning remains rather prominent, so that they are relatively weak connectives and need special discussion. Used between clauses they are regarded as making compound sentences. The most common are:

accordingly	furthermore	*namely
*also	*hence	nevertheless
anyhow	*however	(*so)
anyway (colloquial)	indeed	still
*besides	likewise	*then
consequently	moreover	*therefore

Adverb: No campaign, however violent, could make him vote.
Conjunction: The results were poor; *however* we were not surprised.
Adverb: The lights were not *yet* turned on.
Conjunction: He had been appointed by the governor, *yet* he did not support the party's policies.

2. Weight and use. The important fact about the conjunctive adverbs is that most of them are relatively heavy connectives. With the exception of *so* they are most appropriate in formal writing and in rather routine, stiff exposition, but are not so appropriate in informal writing. They are now more used to connect the thought of separate sentences than the thought of clauses within the same sentence.

One of the duties of theme readers is to remove these stilted connectives from the ordinarily simple and straightforward writing of students. (They probably appear as a result of school exercises in the use of semicolons.) Note these appropriate and inappropriate uses:

It is, *therefore*, unfortunate that at a time like the present, which plainly calls for a Socrates, we should instead have got a Mencken. [Appropriate, as

503

is suggested by the formal sentence structure; connects with thought of preceding sentence]—Irving Babbitt, *On Being Creative*, p. 205

Herr Zweig has gone to quite a bit of trouble to pad out his story, which is hardly rich or complex enough to bear the weight of a full-dress biography. *Also*, he talks a great deal about "Destiny," that convenient item of verbal idiocy by the use of which Teutonic biographers live and have their very being. [*And* would do at least as well as *also*.]—Clifton Fadiman, *The New Yorker*, Dec. 5, 1938

When morning came, *however*, I was still sick, *yet*, when the bugle blew, I got up. *Consequently*, I looked very white at breakfast. (Connectives much too heavy for the material and context.)

3. Position. Conjunctive adverbs are often placed within their clauses instead of at the beginning. This helps take the initial stress from them and gives it to more important words. When they are so placed, they are usually set off by commas as in the sentences in §2 above.

4. Punctuation. The conventional rule of editors is that a clause introduced by a conjunctive adverb is preceded by a semicolon. This is generally true, but with *so* a comma is sufficient:

The whole forenoon had been a complete bore, *so* we wanted to make sure that we had a good time after lunch.

The advice sometimes given to strengthen *so* and *then* by adding *and* ("*and so* we wanted to make sure . . .") is usually wrong, since *and* adds nothing to the meaning of the connective. If the illustrative sentence above was to be really improved, it could be written:

The whole forenoon had been such a complete bore that we wanted to make sure we had a good time after lunch.

connected with, in connection with Wordy locutions, usually for *in* or *with*:

The social life in connection with a fraternity [in a fraternity] will be something you have never experienced before.

Connectives See *Conjunctions and *Prepositions and the articles there referred to. See also Chapter 7, "Connection within paragraphs," page 191.

Connotation The connotation of words—their overtones, the meanings and values that are suggested rather than definitely expressed in their dictionary meanings—is discussed in Chapter 11, "Connotation," page 322, and in Chapter 12.

considerable—considerably In speech there is a tendency not to distinguish the adverb *considerably* from the adjective *considerable*. The following are correct:

The night crew came on and that helped considerably. (Adverb modifying *helped*)

The night crew was of considerable help. (Adjective modifying *help*)

Consistency See Chapter 3, especially "Appropriateness to speaker or writer," page 84; Chapter 4, "Consistent constructions, page 116; Chapter 12, page 347 (consistency in figures of speech).

Consonants In a consonant sound the breath is either restricted or stopped—as contrasted with vowel sounds, which are made with less friction and with fuller resonance. The letters representing consonant sounds are called *consonants: b, c, d, f, g, h, j, k, l, m, n, p, q, r, s, t, v, w, x, z.*

This *Index* has a brief article on each of these letters and on some letter combinations (*sh, th, wh* . . .). See also *Pronunciation, *Doubling final consonants, *Division of words.

Construction Correction: **Revise the obvious fault or inconsistency in grammatical construction.** (For some of the commonest grammatical slips see Chapter 4.) *Const*

Construction means the grammatical setting of a word in a sentence or a group of words in grammatical relationship to each other. In *the black cat, the* is an article, and *black* an adjective, both modifying the noun *cat;* the phrase as a whole is a construction. A grammatical pattern may be spoken of as a construction, as in the phrases *sentence constructions, parallel constructions.*

contact The objections to "Will you contact Mr. Hubble?" and so on, rest on the fact that the use came out of salesmanship—and many people have unpleasant associations with being "contacted" or with brokers' "contact men." Others object to using business terms in non-business contexts. The boy who wrote on an examination that he was "glad to have contacted Dostoievsky in the course" was using a word inappropriately.

Contact clauses Two or more clauses of a sentence that stand together without a specific connective between them are known as *contact clauses.*

Many coordinate sentences are in the form of contact clauses, as in the famous "I came, I saw, I conquered" or in "But in him the pretence is justified: he has enjoyed thinking out his subject, he will delight in his work when it is done" (Max Beerbohm, *Yet Again,* p. 77). Clauses which in meaning seem subordinate may also be set beside the main clause without connective:

. . . and Soames lowered his eyes, he did not want to embarrass the girl.— JOHN GALSWORTHY, *Swan Song,* p. 103

> Give your decision, it will probably be right. But do not give your reasons, they will most certainly be wrong.—BERNARD HART, *The Psychology of Insanity*

This very old type of sentence has been outlawed in the past by prescriptive grammar, though never quite abandoned by writers. In recent years it has re-emerged into literature from speech, where it is and always has been a natural and common form of expression.

Contact clauses have a definite bearing upon one of the perennial problems of writing, the "comma fault," since many clauses put together without expressed connectives are really expressive as they stand and need none. They are especially common and effective in rapid narrative where specific labeling of causes and results would slow up the movement, as in the sentence just quoted from Galsworthy. They are less common in straight exposition but occasionally occur. Many, of course, are the result of carelessness but many also, as these examples suggest, are a symptom of a rapid and natural style. Deciding on the effectiveness of contact clauses is one of the more difficult problems of students and teachers.

(Successful and unsuccessful contact clauses are discussed fully in ch. 9, "Run-on sentences," pp. 252-57. REFERENCES: Curme, *Syntax*, pp. 170-73; Jespersen, pp. 360-61.)

content, contents *Adjectives:* The rather formal *content* (He would be content with less) and the more common *contented* (He would be contented with less) are stressed on the second syllable: kən tent', kən ten'təd.

Nouns: As a noun, *content* is used more as an abstract term (the content of the course) and in amounts (the moisture content); *contents* is rather more concrete (the contents of the box, the contents of the book). The nouns are pronounced kon'tent, kon'tents; kən tent' and kən tents' are British.

Context The context is the discourse that surrounds a word or passage that is being separately discussed: "The word sounds insulting, but in its *context* it could not possibly give offense."

1. The context is tremendously important in giving actual meaning to words. What, for instance, does the word *check* mean? By itself no one can tell even whether it is noun or verb or adjective, much less which of the forty senses of the word is meant. Yet in actual use, in definite contexts, it gives no trouble:

> They were able to *check* the fire at the highway.
> The treasurer's books *check* with the vouchers.
> He drew a *check* for the entire amount.
> The tablecloth had a red and white *check*.

He moved his bishop and proclaimed "*Check!*"
With difficulty he held his temper in *check*.
He had the *check* list on the desk in front of him.

And so on. *Check* has more senses than most English words, but a very large proportion have more than one so that their exact meaning must be gathered from the context—and ordinarily it can be.

2. Statements of ideas depend for full understanding upon the context in which they stand, and in quoting or alluding to a writer's thought we should be careful to take the context into account. Cardinal Newman's definition of a gentleman as a man who never inflicts pain is often referred to as though it represented Newman's ideal—but in its context (*The Idea of a University*, Discourse viii) he was showing that this gentleman is all very well but without religious conviction he falls far short of being an ideal type. Taking care that allusions and quotations are true to the context in which they occur, that they really represent the ideas of their authors, is one mark of a careful writer.

(SEE ch. 11, "Connotation from context," p. 323, and "Unfair or unintended connotation," p. 327.)

continual, continuous *Continual* means "frequently or closely repeated," with little or no time between:

Dancing requires continual practice.
He continually interrupted the lecture with foolish questions.

Continuous means "without interruption," "unbroken":

A continuous procession of cars passed during the hour.
He has been continuously in debt for ten years.
But: He is continually running into debt.

Continuity See Chapter 8, "Continuity" (in paragraphs), page 225.

Contractions Correction: **The contraction marked is inappropriate *Cont*** **to the style. Use the full form.**

Since contractions are words from which an unstressed syllable is dropped in speaking, they obviously belong to spoken English and to familiar and colloquial types of informal written English. Contractions are ordinarily out of place in treatments of dignified subjects and in a formal style, whether in routine exposition (as in academic papers) or in more literary compositions.

In informal English the fitness of a contraction is usually determined in part by the naturalness with which it falls into place, in part by the rhythm:

I didn't always appreciate French cooking myself. It tasted all right, but it was dainty and there wasn't much of it.—CLARENCE DAY, *Life With Father*, p. 11

Did not and *was not* would slow up the movement slightly.

Contractions are absolutely necessary in reporting most *conversation and in writing dialog for plays and stories:

"Your mother has the damnedest number of friends I ever heard of," said Father. "She's everlastingly meeting some old friend or other wherever she goes. I never see people I know when I'm traveling. But there isn't a city in Europe where your mother wouldn't spot a friend in five minutes."—CLARENCE DAY, *Life With Father*, p. 114

The apostrophe ordinarily stands in the place of the omitted letter or letters (*doesn't, can't, shouldn't, he's*), though only one apostrophe is used in *shan't, won't,* and *ain't.* Some experimental writers, like George Bernard Shaw, have dropped the apostrophe from the common contractions. That seems a sensible practice in the contractions of *not* (*shant, doesnt*). But a few contractions would, without the apostrophe, look like other words (*I'll—ill, he'll—hell, we're—were*).

Contrary to fact conditions   See *Conditions § 3, *Subjunctives.

contrast   For the word, see *compare—contrast. For contrast as a paragraph relationship, see Chapter 7, "Comparisons and contrasts," page 177.

Conversation   It is harder to write natural and convincing conversation than most people who haven't tried it will suppose. But conversation is necessary, not only in stories and plays but in many expository articles, to add interest and to keep the material in close touch with actual experience by giving glimpses of people and dramatizing facts. Popular exposition (magazine articles) needs anecdotes or small scenes with people discussing or illustrating the ideas of the article; and in giving a portrait of a person it is almost necessary to let the reader hear him speak.

Most amateurs make conversation sound like their own writing; in fact, they merely put quotation marks around their own words. A little observation of how people really talk will show that this is useless. The speeches should, above all, show the words and constructions of *colloquial English, of the English spoken by the kind of person represented, not the more formal turns of typical written English. It should show the contractions, clipped expressions, and casual grammar of everyday speech. The first step in learning to

508

write good conversation is to observe how you talk yourself, and how others talk.

A speech or two may be worked into a paragraph, as in this anecdote, to give it life as well as to carry the point:

> All the newspapers sent photographers to the Shinnecock reservation near Southampton to get pictures of the recent Indian powwow. One brisk little cameraman took a series of shots of a ceremonial dance, then approached one of the dancers with pad and pencil to get data for the captions. "That dance you was just doing," he said, "what do you call it?" "Do you mean the solo dance?" asked the brave. "Yeah," said the cameraman. "What's that in English?"—*The New Yorker*, Oct. 27, 1938

Though written conversation is based on real speech, it isn't a literal reproduction of it. Not even realistic novelists give all of their lustier characters' profanity and vulgarity. (See *Profanity.) It is not necessary to present completely the grammar of vulgate English if it is clearly suggested, if obvious literary and formal constructions are avoided, and if the general sentence movement is oral. Nor is it necessary to suggest the pronunciation exactly. A few *g*'s dropped, a few local vowel sounds respelled are better than a page speckled with apostrophes and distorted spellings. The latter usually attract more attention to themselves than they deserve and hinder the reading. The point is to *suggest* rather than *reproduce* the effect of speech.

Most writers like to see, occasionally, how close they can come to reproducing speech, but this passage shows the cost in conspicuous spellings:

> "Sure," I says. "It's out in Bensonhoist. Yuh take duh Fourt' Avenoo express, get off at Fifty-nint' Street, change to a Sea Beach local deh, get off at Eighteent' Avenoo an' Sixty-toid, an' den walk down foeh blocks. Dat's all yuh got to do," I says.
>
> "G'wan!" some wise guy dat I neveh seen befoeh pipes up. "Whatcha talkin' about?" he says—oh, he was wise, y'know. "Duh guy is crazy! I tell yuh what yuh do," he says to duh big guy. "Yuh change to duh West End line at Toity-sixt'," he tells him. "Get off at Noo Utrecht an' Sixteent' Avenoo," he says. "Walk two blocks oveh, foeh blocks up," he says, "an you'll be right deh." Oh, a *wise* guy, y'know.
>
> "Oh, yeah?" I says. "Who told *you* so much?" He got me sore because he was so wise about it. "How long you been livin' heah?" I says.
>
> "All my life," he says. "I was bawn in Williamsboig," he says. "An' I can tell you t'ings about dis town you neveh hoid of," he says.
>
> "Yeah?" I says.
>
> "Yeah," he says.
>
> "Well, den, you can tell me t'ings about dis town dat nobody else has eveh hoid of, either. Maybe you make it up yoehself at night," I says, "befoeh you go to sleep—like cuttin' out papeh dolls, or somp'n."

"Oh, yeah?" he says. "You're pretty wise, ain't yuh?"

"Oh, I don't know," I says. "Duh boids ain't usin' my head for Lincoln's statue yet," I says. "But I'm wise enough to know a phoney when I see one."

"Yeah?" he says. "A wise guy, huh? Well, you're so wise dat some one's goin' t'bust yuh one right on duh snoot some day," he says. "Dat's how wise *you* are."—THOMAS WOLFE, *From Death to Morning*, pp. 92-93

Stage directions can help the reader visualize the scene, sometimes catch tones of voice, and feel the emotions of the speakers; but it is not necessary to label the speakers if it is ·clear from the words spoken who says them. This fragment of a scene is self-explanatory:

"I've been thinking, Reuben, about what is best for you."

"You needn't. I'm all right."

"I don't like to leave you here alone."

"I'm not alone. Susan will stay with me. She told my grandmother so."

With a glance at the open door Deborah lowered her voice, but Susan caught the words.

"Are you happy with Susan?"

"Of course. I'm—I'm used to her."

"And you're not used to me. Is that it?"

"I suppose so."

Deborah gathered herself together as one gathers himself for a first daring plunge into deep water.

"You must know that I want to do all I can for you, Reuben. I'm your mother after all. You're always welcome to come to Boston to stay with me. Your stepfather told me to tell you. The schools are better there, and it might be best for you."

Emboldened by his mother's temerity, Reuben found his own voice. Susan, listening, understood the cost of his words. She could hear him drawing himself slowly up on the cane seat and against the back of his grandmother's chair where he sat.

"Thank you, mother, and my stepfather, too. But I'd rather stay here in my own house where I belong."—MARY ELLEN CHASE, *Silas Crockett*, pp. 279-80

The examples given in this article show the conventions of paragraphing and punctuating conversation. There are further details of these mechanics in *Quotation marks. Books on the writing of fiction have discussions of writing conversation.

Conversion The use of a word generally found as one part of speech in the function of a different part of speech is called *conversion:* a *must* book; a *commercial* (adjective as noun in sense of the advertising part of a radio program); in the *know*.

(For discussion see *Parts of speech § 2.)

Coordinating conjunctions 1. The principal coordinating conjunctions are: **and*, **but*, **for*, *nor* (= and not), **or*, **yet*. **Only*

(I'd come, only I have a class) and *while (He's an expert, while I know nothing about the game) and other connectives are used as coordinating conjunctions. The *conjunctive adverbs (*therefore, however*, and so on) are coordinating connectives, as are the *correlative conjunctions (*either . . . or, not only . . . but*, and so on).

2. These conjunctions are used between words, phrases, clauses, or sentences. It is important that the elements they connect should be equal in grammatical rank and substantially equivalent in thought:

> Words: books and papers; books, pamphlets, and magazines; sugar or salt
> Phrases: in one ear and out the other
> Clauses: I would venture to say *that his description is perfect*, but *that there are some who would not agree with that verdict.*—BONAMY DOBRÉE, *Modern Prose Style*, p. 69
> Independent clauses: What they talk of was in the books, but there was the stimulus of personality.—ARTHUR E. HERTZLER, *The Horse and Buggy Doctor*, p. 181

3. For different effects of repeating or omitting conjunctions in a series see *Conjunctions, Use § 3 and *Series.

4. For coordination vs. subordination see Chapter 9, "Compound sentences," page 251, "Complex sentences," page 257, and *Subordination. For various uses of coordinating conjunctions see *Conjunctions, *Clauses § 1, and articles on individual conjunctions.

Coordination The relationship between two or more elements of the same grammatical rank. See *Coordinating conjunctions § 2.

Copula See *Linking verb.

Copy Manuscript before printing is *copy*. For points of form see *Typewritten copy and Chapter 1, "Preparing the manuscript," page 20.

Corrections in copy For suggestions about making corrections in manuscript see Chapter 1, "Corrections in copy," page 22.

Correlative conjunctions 1. Some coordinating conjunctions are used in pairs:

> both . . . and   either . . . or   neither . . . nor   not so . . . as
> not only . . . but [but also]   whether . . . or

2. Except *either . . . or* and *both . . . and*, these correlative conjunctions are slightly formal, showing a more conscious sentence planning than is common in familiar or informal English:

> Not only was the water muddy, but it had tadpoles swimming in it.

3. Since these correlatives are coordinating conjunctions, the elements they connect should be of equal grammatical value:

> Nouns: He said that both *the novel* and *the play* were badly written.
> Adjectives: He must have been either *drunk* or *crazy*.
> Phrases: They can be had not only *in the usual sizes* but also *in the outsizes.*
> Clauses: Whether *the sale was for cash* or *a mortgage was given*, it seemed too much to pay.

(REFERENCE: Lillian Mermin, "On the Placement of Correlatives in Modern English," *American Speech*, 1943, 18:171-91, and 19:66-8. For number of verb in constructions with *or*, see *Subject and verb § 2b, and as a reference, Dorothy J. Hughes, *College English*, 1941, 2:697-99.)

could See *can—may (could—might).

Counter words Words that are used more frequently than their exact meanings warrant have been called *counter words*. They are especially words of general approval or disapproval. Their use is a matter of fashion and is related to slang, except that they are ordinary English words and lack the element of surprise that good slang has. In Elizabethan times *fair* was such a word; recently *keen, delicious, definitely* have had such currency. In ordinary speech *cute, fierce, fine, grand, lousy, lovely, gorgeous, poor* are samples, and in more reputable circles words like *creative, dynamic, vital,* and often epithets like *red, radical, fascist, conservative, reactionary* are used as vague expressions of like or dislike without regard to more exact meaning.

In advertising and other more or less forced writing *super-, -conscious* (we are *air-conscious, flower-conscious, defense-conscious* by turns), *-conditioned,* and at the moment *streamlined, bottleneck, propaganda* are all counter words. They are appropriate in colloquial English (in which *certainly* has the sense of *yes*) but seem out of place in serious writing:

> Today, the halfway spot in the two-week streamlined fair . . .
> Again, their spirit may be irrevocably broken, their lives turned into a streamlined hell.

couple **1.** *Couple* means strictly two persons or things associated in some way, typically as in "a married couple." Colloquially it is equivalent to the numeral *two:* a couple of pencils.

2. This colloquial usage has resulted in frequent omission of the following *of:*

> He'd had a couple drinks.   I'll be gone only a couple days.
> A couple boys were throwing stones at a dog.

This clipped idiom is finding its way into print in informal or adventurous writing:

> At seven the next morning, a couple [ ] members of the cast, which had sat up to get the reviews, broke into his room screaming "It's historic!"— *The New Yorker*, Dec. 30, 1933

Course names In general discussions, only the names of college subjects that are proper adjectives (the languages) are capitalized:

> He studies algebra, history, chemistry, German, English literature, and the rest without seeing that these are really just the pieces in a great picture puzzle which, if assembled, will reveal the image of the whole world.

In writing a list of courses including one or more of these proper adjectives, it is possible to capitalize them all for consistency (and courtesy), though the distinction would usually be kept, as in the first example:

> My program is biology, chemistry, European history, English composition, and French 105.
> My program is Biology, Chemistry, European History, English Composition, and French 105.

In referring to the various departments of an institution, all names would be capitalized:

> the Department of Applied Psychology   the Department of History
> the English Department   the School of Biological Sciences

In newspaper style *department* and *school* would probably not be capitalized when they follow the proper name.

Current English See Chapter 2, "Current English," page 57.

curriculum *Curriculum* still has the Latin plural *curricula*, though *curriculums* is becoming common. The adjective is *curricular*, and the compound with *extra* is ordinarily written without a hyphen: *extracurricular. Curriculum* is coming to be used as an adjective:

> . . . and his extra-curriculum influence on their morals and manners.— R. M. HUTCHINS, *Harper's Magazine*, Oct. 1936

Curves A name for the punctuation marks ( ). See *Parentheses.

D Besides its typical sound as in *die, do, addict, pod, addle, d* represents *t* when it follows the sound of *f, k, p,* or *s* in the same syllable: *asked* (askt), *blessed* (blest, but bles'ed), *kicked* (kikt), *raced* (rāst), *telegraphed* (tel'ə graft).

Before an unstressed *i* or *y* sound, *d* sometimes becomes *j: grandeur* (gran'jər), *soldier* (sōl'jər). This pronunciation is especially common in vulgate English and explains in'jən (*Indian*), i mē'jit (*immediate*—generally so pronounced in British English), and local extensions of the sound to stressed *u* syllables: jōō'ti (*duty*).

D is a strong sound and besides being the opening sound of a number of words of mild profanity begins many words of a negative meaning: *defeated, dejected, dilapidated, disappointed, disaster, distressed.* (Compare *T.)

Dangling modifiers See *Misrelated modifiers and Chapter 4, "Verbid phrases," page 112.

Dash
1. To mark sharp turn in thought. 2. Before added phrase. 3. Between compound clauses. 4. To enclose parenthetical statements. 5. Overuse. 6. With other marks. 7. Double dash. 8. En dash.

Three dashes of varying lengths are used in printing: – (en dash), — (em dash, the usual mark), and —— (2-em dash). On the typewriter use a hyphen for the first, two hyphens not spaced away from the neighboring words for the usual dash, and four hyphens for the long dash.

The em dash, the one we have in mind when we say just *dash*, has aroused more discussion and more violent feeling than punctuation seems to deserve. Some textbooks and some publishers forbid its use generally, while others specify minute shades of meaning which they believe it indicates. Some writers rarely use it. Others, especially in matter not intended for publication, use it at the expense of other marks.

A dash is roughly equivalent to a comma, that is, it separates units within a sentence, but if used sparingly it suggests a definite tone, usually a note of surprise, an emotional emphasis. From a strictly logical point of view some other mark could always be substituted for a dash, but there would be a difference in movement and suggestiveness in the sentence. At its best it is a rather abrupt and emphatic mark. (See Chapter 5, "Dash," page 148.)

1. To mark sharp turn in thought. The most typical use of the dash is to mark a sharp turn in the thought or construction of a sentence:

Of course, there is one place safe from lawyers—in heaven.—ARTHUR E. HERTZLER, *The Horse and Buggy Doctor*, p. 134

The danger of using terms like "romantic" and "classic"—this does not however give us permission to avoid them altogether—does not spring so much from the confusion caused by those who use these terms about their own work, as from inevitable shifts of meaning in context.—T. S. ELIOT, *After Strange Gods*, p. 27

2. Before added phrase. A dash is often used before an inserted or added phrase, usually one that summarizes what has just been said or that gives contrasting or emphasizing details of what has been said, or often a striking apposition. This dash has the force of a vigorous comma.

> The waiting, the watching, the hundreds of small necessary acts about the sickroom—all this was past.
>
> The elements of every story are these five: character, incident, nature, fate, and milieu—the social, historical, vital background.—D. H. PARKER, *Principles of Aesthetics*, p. 236
>
> . . . but they initiated a process that has culminated in the one indisputable achievement of post-War poetry—its catholicity of diction.—F. W. BATESON, *Poetry and Language*, p. 120
>
> He [the Englishman of the 1870's and 80's] was strongly in favor of peace—that is to say, he liked his wars to be fought at a distance and, if possible, in the name of God.—GEORGE DANGERFIELD, *The Death of Liberal England*, p. 7

3. Between compound clauses. A dash is often used between two compound clauses of a sentence, for abrupt separation:

> The "womanly" woman became as obsolete as the buggy. The nurse must tend the children, the cook must order the meals—life must be spectacular, not frittered away in little household dullnesses.—IRENE and ALLEN CLEATON, *Books and Battles*, p. 92

4. To enclose parenthetical statements. A dash is sometimes used to enclose parenthetical statements that are more informal than a parenthesis would indicate, separating the expression from the context more than a comma but less definitely than parentheses would:

> The general effect upon readers—most of them quite uneducated—is quite different from what the serious messiah intends.—T. S. ELIOT, *After Strange Gods*, p. 36
>
> While books were being stricken from the lists with such alarming inclusiveness—so that Mencken was provoked to remark, "It is possible for anyone to have a book suppressed in Boston merely by advancing the idea. I wager I could suppress four books in as many minutes if I should go to Boston and make the effort"—while this deplorable state of affairs existed, the "art" magazines that were being chased out of many less Puritan cities remained unmolested on Boston newsstands.—IRENE and ALLEN CLEATON, *Books and Battles*, p. 77

5. Overuse of dashes detracts from their special quality and proves that they are, as Mr. Dobrée says, "a sandy joint."

515

She [Marlene Dietrich] was turned into a static image of lorelei charm, frozen in a lovely pose—and to bring that image again to life, there seems to be no proposal except to point again to its over-publicized legs, and its—by this time—rubber-stamp "allure."

(SEE also *Schoolgirl style.)

6. With other marks. Formerly a dash was often combined with other marks, especially with a comma or a colon, but recently this use has declined. The dash adds nothing in the salutation of a letter (*Dear Sir:*—means no more than *Dear Sir:*) and adds a displeasing mark to the page. Within sentences the old comma-dash combination has very generally disappeared also, so that now we find either a comma, or if a desire for emphasis makes it useful, a dash alone.

7. Double dash. Besides being used in some arbitrary places prescribed by particular publishing houses, the 2-em dash is used chiefly as an end stop in dialog when a speech is interrupted:

". . . I can't say, of course, whether or not my layman's logic adds lustre to the gladsome light of jurisprudence——"
"Your reasoning is consistent as far as it goes," cut in Markham tartly. "But it is hardly complete enough to have led you directly to the linen-closet this morning."—S. S. VAN DINE, *The Greene Murder Case*, p. 220

"Harvard Club. You——" The sap, the hopeless sap.—SALLY BENSON, *People Are Fascinating*, p. 30

8. En dash. A writer does not need to worry about the en dash, slightly longer than a hyphen, but printers use it between inclusive figures (*1837–1901*) and instead of a hyphen when one or both elements of an expression ordinarily requiring a hyphen are made up of two words: *the New York–Bar Harbor express.*

(REFERENCE: Summey, pp. 101-04.)

data Pronounced dāʹtə or sometimes datʹə or (affecting Latin) däʹtə.

Strictly *data* is a plural, with a little used singular *datum*. Its meaning is actually collective and may sometimes stress a group of facts as a unit and so be used with a singular verb. When it refers to the individual facts, *data* is used with a plural:

Singular idea: The actual data of history *consists* of contemporary facts in the form of remains and documents.—MORRIS R. COHEN, *Reason and Nature*, p. 381
Singular idea: Data concerning measurement of social attitudes *has* been included in the next chapter . . .—LUELLA COLE, *Psychology of Adolescence*, p. 102
Plural idea: When the data *have* been secured the task is to analyze, to sift, to select and to arrange those data which *bear* upon each particular

phase of the object or event examined until at the end the scientist has what one might call a logical construct.—G. D. HIGGINSON, *Fields of Psychology*, p. 10

Either possible: These data are [This data is] unpublished.

The singular verb can be safely used in any but the most formal writing.

date Informal and colloquial for "appointment, engagement" (I had a date for that evening); slang and familiar in the sense of "person with whom one has an engagement" (After all, she was his date). *Blind date* is one of the more useful and economical colloquial expressions, expressing in two syllables something that would take several words to express in formal English.

Dates Unless you have good reason for some other form, write dates in the common method: August 19, 1950. The form *19 August 1950* is increasingly popular (partly as a result of its use by the armed services) and has a small advantage in that it makes a comma unnecessary.

Never write the year out in words except in formal social announcements, invitations, etc. Expressions like "January in the year 1885" are wasteful. *January 1885* is enough.

If saving space is important, or in business or reference writing, months having more than four letters should be abbreviated:

Jan.   Feb.   Mar.   Apr.   Aug.   Sept.   Oct.   Nov.   Dec.

In familiar and informal writing, figures are convenient: 8/19/50, 11/27/52. (In England and other countries the day of the month is usually put first: 27-xi-52.

Better style now usually omits the *st, nd, th* from the day of the month: May 1 rather than May 1st, September 17 rather than September 17th.

In formal style the day of the month may be written in words when the year is not given (September seventeen or September seventeenth).

Roman numerals are rarely used for the year except for decoration, as on the title page of a book.

(SEE *Numbers § 1a; *Letters; *Social correspondence.)

Dative case English has no form for the dative case. A noun in a construction that in another language might have a dative is in the common case form and a pronoun is in the accusative case form. Usually we have a phrase made with *to, for,* or *on.* (See *Objects, § 2.)

Dead **Deadwood** Correction: **Remove the meaningless word or words, revising the sentence if necessary.**

Deadwood is a convenient label for a type of *wordiness in which a word or phrase adds nothing at all to the meaning of the statement.

> In many *cases* students [Many students] have profited by this.
> He was a handsome [looking] man.
> The book is divided into various sections, all dealing with [the matter of] unemployment.

Many phrases of this sort make writing flabby and are a mark of amateur or careless writing.

(For further examples and discussion, see ch. 10, "Sentence economy," p. 284, and *case.)

Declarative sentences A declarative sentence makes a statement:

> The day that war was declared saw a complete overturn in many people's opinions.
> Considerably over nine tenths of the sentences that we speak and write are declarative.

(SEE articles on *Simple, *Compound, and *Complex sentences.)

Declension Change of form of nouns (and in many languages the form of adjectives and participles also) to show number (singular or plural) and case (nominative, genitive, dative, accusative). Declension plays a relatively small part in English grammar.

(SEE *Case, the articles on the various cases, *Plurals, and the articles referred to there.)

Deductive order See Chapter 1, "Planning the paper," page 14, and Chapter 8, "Support paragraphs," page 220.

Definite article See *the.

definitely *Definitely* is one of the most frequently misspelled words. Remember there is no *a* in it and associate def i *ni* tion with def i *ni*te and def i *ni*te ly.

At present *definitely* is overused as a *counter word to give emphasis or in the sense of "certainly, quite" (I will not do it, definitely; He was definitely worse than usual; She definitely disapproves of those methods) instead of in its exact sense of "clear cut, in a definite manner."

Definitions For definition, as paragraph material, see Chapter 7, "Qualifying statements," page 178.

Degree (of adjectives and adverbs) See *Comparison of adjectives and adverbs.

Degrees Ordinarily a person's academic degrees are not given with his name except in college publications, reference works, etc. When used, they are separated from the name by a comma, and in campus publications are often followed by the year of granting:

Harvey J. Preble, A.B.	Harvey J. Preble, A.B. '08
James T. Thomson, M.A.	James T. Thomson, A.B. '21, A.M. '24

William C. Riley, Ph.D., M.D.

As a rule, except in reference lists, only a person's highest degree in each academic or professional field need be mentioned.

If the institution granting the degree is named, the following forms are usual:

George H. Cook, A.B. (Grinnell), A.M. (Indiana), Ph.D. (Chicago)

The common degrees given "in course," that is, at the completion of a required amount of college or university work, are:

A.B. (or B.A.)—Bachelor of Arts	B.E.—Bachelor of Engineering
A.M. (or M.A.)—Master of Arts	LL.B.—Bachelor of Laws
B.S.—Bachelor of Science	B. Mus.—Bachelor of Music
B. Arch.—Bachelor of Architecture	Ph.B.—Bachelor of Philosophy
B.D.—Bachelor of Divinity	M.S.—Master of Science
M.E.—Master of Engineering	Ph.D.—Doctor of Philosophy
M. Ped.—Master of Pedagogy (*or*,	S.T.D.—Doctor of Sacred Theology
Ed. M.—Master of Education)	M.D.—Doctor of Medicine
M.B.A.—Master of Business Admin-	D.D.S.—Doctor of Dental Surgery
istration	

The common honorary degrees, given by institutions as a sign of respect ("pro honoris causa"), are:

D.C.L.—Doctor of Civil Law	D. Lit., Lit.D.—Doctor of Literature
D.D.—Doctor of Divinity	L.H.D.—Doctor of Humanities
D.Sc.—Doctor of Science	LL.D.—Doctor of Laws
D. Litt.—Doctor of Letters	

Delete means "take out, erase, remove." It is a direction to printers made by putting a Greek small *d* (δ—delta) in the margin and drawing a line through the matter to be removed. (See *Proofreading.)

To delete material in your manuscripts, simply draw a line through it (don't use parentheses or black it out completely).

Demonstrative adjectives and pronouns *This, that, these, those* are called demonstrative adjectives or demonstrative pronouns, according to their use in a sentence:

Adjectives: *This* car we bought in May.
Those fellows never think of anyone else.

Pronouns: *This* cost a good bit more than *those*.
That's a good idea.

(SEE *that, *this, *kind, sort.)

Denotation is the exact, literal meaning of a word, contrasted with its *connotation* or *suggestion*. *Fire* denotes the chemical and physical process of combustion, or a particular burning. It suggests uncontrolled power, destruction.

(SEE ch. 11, "Denotation," p. 318.)

Dependent clause A dependent clause modifies or supports in some way a word or sentence element or the whole sentence:

The house *that stood on the other side* was even more dilapidated. (Clause modifies *house*.)
Since Truman had gone to the same school, they got on famously for a time. (Adverbial clause modifying the following statement.)

Ordinarily a dependent clause does not stand by itself but is part of a complex sentence.

(SEE *Clauses and ch. 9, "Fragmentary sentences," p. 262.)

depot An "Americanism," but a perfectly good Americanism, for "railroad station." *Depot* also has a more general meaning of "a place for storing things, especially merchandising or war supplies." Pronounced dē′pō; often (especially British and military) dep′ō.

Derivation of words See *Origin of words.

descendant *Descendant* is used both as adjective and noun; *descendent*, only as adjective. To be on the safe side, use descend*ant*.

Description, Descriptive order See Chapter 8, "Descriptive paragraphs," page 216.

detail Pronunciation divided: di tāl′, dē′tāl, the first older, the second especially common in situations where the word is used a great deal (army life, architecture, composition, etc.).

Det **Details** Correction: Develop this topic more fully by giving pertinent details.

The development of a topic in writing usually comes from the use of details, small bits of observation, particular facts, and so on. They not only make the reader see clearly what you are discussing but are one of the chief sources of interest.

(For discussion and illustration of various uses of details see ch. 7, "Details," p. 172. See also ch. 12, "Abstract and concrete words," p. 341.)

develop   Usual spelling. Rarely found with final -e.

Development of ideas, development of paragraphs   See Chapter 7, "Materials of paragraphs," page 171, and Chapter 8, "Kinds of paragraph development," page 210.

devil   no longer receives the courtesy of a capital except for stylistic emphasis.

Diagramming sentences   See Chapter 9, "Elements of the sentence," page 247.

Diagrams, graphs, etc.   The function of diagrams, charts, graphs, and illustrations is to make a writer's meaning more clear and more concrete than his words alone could. They cannot be a substitute for a discussion in words, but they can make it easier for readers to grasp figures, to understand relationships, and especially to make comparisons between facts that can be graphically portrayed. They have also an incidental value for an article in that diagrams and charts attract attention and interest. It is part of a writer's work to prepare appropriate diagrams to accompany his text where they can be useful.

   1. **Types of graphic devices.**   Some of the commonest and most useful graphic devices (diagrams, charts, graphs, bars, and pictorial statistics) are illustrated on pages 521-523. Some general points in handling diagrams and charts are discussed on page 524.

   a) DIAGRAM.   A schematic representation of the structure of something, a plan showing dimensions, directions for work, etc., as in the following diagram:

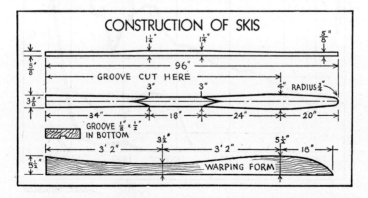

Science and Mechanics, February 1939

b) CHART. Showing organization and relationship:

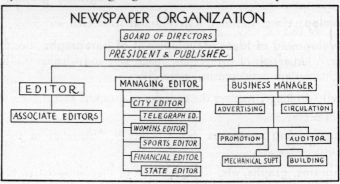

D. J. HORNBERGER AND DOUGLASS W. MILLER,
Newspaper Organization, Appendix B

c) GRAPH. Showing two or more variable facts:

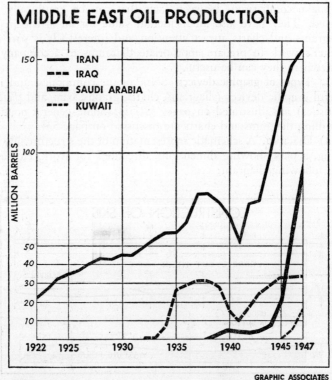

GRAPHIC ASSOCIATES

Headline Series, no. 72, p. 31

d) BARS. To make comparison of amounts, etc.:

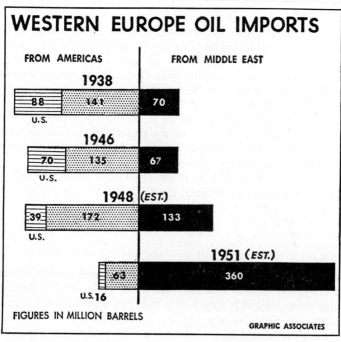

WESTERN EUROPE OIL IMPORTS

FROM AMERICAS   FROM MIDDLE EAST

1938
88   141   70
U.S.

1946
70   135   67
U.S.

1948 (EST.)
39   172   133
U.S.

1951 (EST.)
63   360
U.S. 16

FIGURES IN MILLION BARRELS

GRAPHIC ASSOCIATES

Headline Series, no. 72, p. 28

e) PICTORIAL STATISTICS. Symbols to dramatize the material about which figures are given:

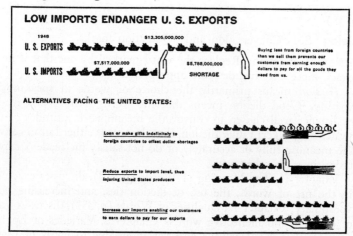

LOW IMPORTS ENDANGER U. S. EXPORTS

1948

U. S. EXPORTS $13,305,000,000

Buying less from foreign countries than we sell them prevents our customers from earning enough dollars to pay for all the goods they need from us.

U. S. IMPORTS $7,517,000,000 $5,788,000,000

SHORTAGE

ALTERNATIVES FACING THE UNITED STATES:

Loan or make gifts indefinitely to foreign countries to offset dollar shortages

Reduce exports to import level, thus injuring United States producers

Increase our imports enabling our customers to earn dollars to pay for our exports

Headline Series, no. 79, p. 43

f) MAPS. A simple map will be found on page 61.

2. General points in handling diagrams and charts. (a) The first step toward a diagram or chart is compiling the data. Guesses, opinions, and so on should not be graphically represented; only definite facts and especially facts that can be measured mathematically. The nature of the material will usually determine which sort of graphic device is appropriate.

b) A graphic device should be accompanied by the exact data it represents, either in the text of the paper or in a table or explanation placed with the graph. A reader needs to know the exact figures upon which the graph is based.

c) The graph should be made intelligible by clearly indicating the years, amounts, per cents, the scale it is drawn on, and so on. This is usually done at the bottom and along the sides.

(COMPARE *Illustration (Pictorial). REFERENCES: Herbert Arkin and Raymond R. Colter, *Graphs—How to Make and Use Them* (New York, 1940); Frederick E. Cuxton and Dudley J. Cowden, *Applied General Statistics* (New York, 1940), chs. 4 and 6; chapters on graphic methods in other introductions to statistics.)

Dialects A dialect is the speech (words, sounds, stress, phrasing, grammatical habits) characteristic of a fairly definite region, or more accurately, it is speech that does not attract attention to itself among the residents of a region.

Localism is used in this book for a dialectical usage. Conspicuous dialectical words are usually out of place in formal writing unless they are used to give a definitely local flavor. They are more effective in speech, in fiction, and in rather informal writing.

(For description of dialects in the United States, see ch. 2, "Variations due to place," p. 58.)

Dialog See *Conversation and *Quotation marks.

D Diction Correction: **Replace the word marked by one that is more exact, more effective, or more appropriate.**

Diction means primarily the choice of words in speaking or writing. Good diction means that the words seem to the reader or listener well chosen to convey the meanings or attitudes of the writer or speaker; faulty diction, that the words either fail to convey the meaning fully or accurately or do not satisfy the reader's expectation in some other way.

Chapter 11, The Meaning of Words (p. 303), discusses exactness in the use of words, the use of dictionaries, and increasing your vocabulary; Chapter 12, Qualities of Words (p. 331), discusses traits of effective and ineffective words. Chapter 2, Varieties of English (p. 33), describes localisms and variations due to levels of usage.

Many specific words have articles of their own (*contact, *drunk, *hope, *however, *notorious, *try and—try to, *ye = the). Very often the solution to a question of diction will be found by referring to a good dictionary.

Dictionaries For description of various dictionaries and suggestions for their use, see Chapter 11, "The use of dictionaries," page 310.

Dieresis (dī er′ə sis) Two dots placed over the second of two consecutive vowels to show they are to be pronounced separately: *reëxamine, coöperation.* A hyphen is often used to indicate that the vowels are to be kept separate, especially in words with *re-* (*re-enlist*). There is a tendency not to use either dieresis or hyphen in the more commonly used words, so that *cooperation, zoology* are now the more usual forms.

different The most common American idiom with *different* is *from:*

His second book was entirely different from his first.
He was so different from his sister that we were all surprised.

In writing, *different from* should ordinarily be used.
Colloquial usage is divided, using *from* occasionally, sometimes *to* (which is common British idiom), and more often *than:*

. . . as smart and vain and sweet a girl as Clyde had ever laid his eyes upon—so different to any he had ever known and so superior.—THEODORE DREISER, *An American Tragedy*, p. 225

Different than is becoming more common when the object is a clause:

The house was a good deal different than he remembered it. (This idiom is neater than "different from what he remembered.")

Different is colloquially used as a synonym for *original, unusual:*

This book is *different* and interesting.

(REFERENCES: D. L. Bolinger, *The English Journal*, 1939, 28:480; Gladys D. Haase, *College English*, 1949, 10:345-47.)

Digraph Two letters used together to spell a single sound are known as a *digraph.* English uses many digraphs:

ea as in *head* or *heat*	*ee* as in *seed*
ei as in *either* or *neighbor*	*oa* as in *coat*
oo as in *book* or *food*	*ph* as in *physics*
sh as in *shall*	*th* as in *then* or *thin*

dining *Dine, dined, dining, dining room* all have to do with eating

—as does *dinner* with two *n*'s and a short *i; dinning* (short *i*) has to do with *din,* "noise."

Dine and *dining* are formal words. *Dinner* is used in all levels.

Diphthong   A diphthong is a vowel sound made up of two identifiable sounds gliding from one to the other. The commonest English diphthongs are:

ī (ä + i)   oi (ô + i)   ou (ä + oo)   ū (i [y] + ōō)

For others and for further details of variations in the pronunciations of these, see Kennedy, pages 186-90, and the pronunciation sections of dictionaries.

Direct address   The name or descriptive term by which persons (or objects) are addressed in speaking, reading, or writing:

My friends, I wish you would forget this night.
That's all right, *Mrs. Shephardson.*
What do you think, *Doctor,* about his going home now?
Rain, rain, go away.

As these examples show, words in direct address are separated from the rest of the sentence by a comma, or if they are in the middle of the sentence, by two commas.

Direct discourse   See *Conversation, *Quotation marks.

Direct object   See *Objects.

Display   Matter that is not written consecutively, that in the written or printed copy is set off by itself instead of being run in with the text, is called display matter. Typical display lines are titles on books and articles, newspaper headlines and subheads, large type lines in advertisements, headings and inside addresses of letters. The type is usually larger and blacker than the body type. Ordinarily no punctuation is needed after display lines.

Ditto marks   (") Ditto marks are used with lists and tabulations in reference works instead of repeating words that fall directly below. In typewritten manuscript, use quotation marks for ditto marks:

```
m, as in man, men, mine, hum, hammer
n, "  " no, man, manner
```

Ditto marks are not used in consecutive writing, nor are they used now in footnotes or bibliographies. In general they are much less used than formerly.

As a word *ditto* (for "I think the same," and so on) is colloquial.

Divided usage Usage is said to be *divided* when two or more forms exist in the language, both in reputable use in the same dialect or level. *Divided usage* is not applied, for example, to *localisms, like *sack—bag—poke*, or to differences like *ain't* and *isn't* which belong to separate levels of the language. It applies to spellings, pronunciations, or constructions on which speakers and writers of similar education might differ.

There are many more of these divided usages than most people are aware of. For instance, both *Webster's* and the *American College* dictionaries record these and hundreds of other instances of divided usage:

In Pronunciation:
ab'domen—abdo'men   lĕ'ver—lev'er
adver'tisement—advertise'ment   i'solate—is'olate
ĕther—īther

In Spelling:
gray—grey   drought—drouth
traveler—traveller   millionaire—millionnaire
catalog—catalogue   although—altho

In Verb Forms:
Past tense—*sing: sang* or *sung; ring: rang* or *rung*
Past participle—*show: shown* or *showed; prove: proved* or *proven*

It is hard for some careful speakers to realize that others may speak somewhat differently from them and still be in good standing. Before calling a person to account, either seriously or playfully, for a usage, we should make sure that his is not a variant that is as reputable as the one we may prefer. Furthermore, we might well give up a desire for uniformity in small matters which make no great difference and in which the experience of the language obviously shows that divergence is possible.

When you have opportunity to choose between variants, choose the one more appropriate to your general tendency or that is more common among the audience you are to reach—or better still, take the one that comes most naturally to your own speech.

Many of the specific entries in this handbook treat questions of divided usage, as *but that—but what, *due to, *either, *gladiolus, *hanged—hung, *proved—proven.

Division of words Correction: Break the word at the end of this *Div* line between syllables.

Whenever it is necessary in manuscript or in print, a word is divided at the end of a line by a hyphen ("division hyphen"). In preparing manuscript if you will leave a reasonable right hand margin, you will not be forced to divide so many words as you will if you crowd to the end of the line. A good habit is to divide words only when the lines will be conspicuously uneven if the last word is completely written or completely carried over to the next line. In manuscript for publication most publishers prefer an uneven right margin to divided words.

When it is necessary to divide a word, break it between syllables. Both the divided parts should be pronounceable; that is, words of one syllable, like *matched, said, thought,* should not be divided at all. English syllables are difficult to determine, but in general they follow pronunciation groups: *autocratic* would be divided into syllables *au to crat ic,* but *autocracy* is *au toc ra cy.*

The following words are divided to show typical syllables:

mar gin	ca ter	hy phen	chil dren	long ing
hi lar i ous	cat ty	ac com plished	ad min is trate	pitch er

Double consonants are usually separable:

ef fi cient	com mit tee	daz zling	bat ted

A single letter is not allowed to stand by itself, that is, do not divide at the end of lines words like *enough* (which would leave a lone *e* at the end of a line) or *many* (which would put a lone *y* at the beginning of a line).

Words spelled with a hyphen (*half-brother, well-disposed*) should be divided only at the point of the hyphen to avoid the awkwardness of two hyphens in the same word.

Division of words is primarily a printing and editing problem and fuller directions than this book gives will be found in the stylebooks of publishing houses (like the *Manual of Style* of the University of Chicago Press). Note the divisions made by the compositors at the ends of lines in this and other books. It will often be necessary to refer to a dictionary to find the syllabication of words.

do Present forms: I, you *do;* he, she, it *does;* we, you, they *do.* Past, *did:* They *did* as well as they could. Past participle, *done:* He knew he had *done* wrong. It was well *done.*

1. 'Do' in verb phrases. *Do* is used to form verb phrases with all verbs except *be* and the auxiliaries (*can, may, shall* . . .):

Present	*Past*
I do wish	I, you, he, she did wish
you do wish	we, you, they did wish
he, she does wish	
we, you, they do wish	

The *do* forms are used:

a) For EMPHASIS:

I do' wish he'd come. (Contrast "I wish he'd come.")
He did' have his lunch, because I saw him go into Carter's.

b) IN QUESTIONS:

Do you think I was right?
Did you like the show as well as you expected to?

c) WITH *not* (Colloquially contracted to *don't, doesn't, didn't*):

He did not feel well enough to go out. I don't expect to go.

2. 'Do' as a pro-verb. *Do* is used to avoid repetition of a simple verb that has just been used:

I like him better than you do. (i.e., than you like him)

3. 'Do' in idioms. *Do* has many idiomatic meanings and is part of many idiomatic phrases: A girl *does* her hair; a steak is well *done;* we *do away* with things; *do for* (which may mean "be enough"—That will do for you—or "put the finishing touches on"— That did for him—or, in some localities, "work for, serve"—She does for Mrs. Lawrence); *done for; do in; do over* (redecorate); *do up* (wrap up, launder, or in past, be used up).
(REFERENCE: Fries, pp. 146-49.)

doff, don   These words, archaic or formal for "take off" and "put on" (especially clothes), are used only by writers who are self-consciously or habitually somewhat affected in their speech.

don't   Contraction of *do not*, universally used in conversation and often in informal writing when *do not* would seem too emphatic or when rhythm seems more comfortable with the shorter form.
    In vulgate usage *don't* equals *doesn't*, and the usage often finds its way into familiar speech and even into casual writing: "He don't look as well as he used to." Educated speakers and writers avoid it. *Current English Usage* (p. 121) marked "It don't make any difference what you think" disputable, because it was approved by 40% of the judges.
(REFERENCE: Karl W. Dykema, "An Example of Prescriptive Linguistic Change: 'Don't' to 'Doesn't,'" *English Journal*, 1947, 36:37-76.)

Double negative   1. In formal and informal English. Two negative words in the same statement are not used in formal and informal English (Not "He could*n't* find it *no*where" but "He could*n't* find it *any*where").

In informal English one negative statement modifying another negative statement often gives a qualified meaning or a meaning with some special emphasis: "He is not sure he won't slip in at the last minute" does not mean "He will slip in at the last minute" but "He may possibly slip in . . ." "And don't you think he isn't clever" stands for something more complex than "He is clever"—for "I've found out he's clever" or "You'd better believe he's clever [though I know you don't yet]."

2. In vulgate English. Although double negatives are probably not so common in vulgate English as comic writers suggest in their cartoons and stories, two negatives are very often used to make an emphatic negative in this level. "I do*n't* have *no*thing to lose" makes negative two parts of the idea and in many speech situations is the vulgate way of emphasizing the negative; if the *nothing* isn't stressed, it is a simple negative in two parts, as French uses *ne . . . pas*. Such a double negative is not a backsliding from the idiom of more formal English but a direct descendant of early English, in which two negatives were used in all levels of the language. Chaucer wrote:

> In al this world *ne* was ther *noon* him lyk.
> A bettre preest, I trowe that *nowher noon* is.

This construction, now lost to written English, survives in vulgate usage. The objection to it is not that "two negatives make an affirmative," for they do not—only a person being perverse would misunderstand a double negative. The objection is simply that the construction is not now in fashion among educated people.

3. Hardly, scarcely. Students sometimes fall into a concealed double negative when using *hardly* or *scarcely*. *Hardly* means "not probably" and *scarcely* means the same a little more emphatically. Consequently in formal and informal English a sentence like "For the most part our college paper contains hardly nothing" should read "For the most part our college paper contains *hardly anything*" and "For a while we couldn't scarcely see a thing" should read "For a while we *could scarcely* see a thing."

(COMPARE *but § 3.)

Double prepositions See *Prepositions § 3b.

Doubling final consonants 1. Words of one syllable ending in a single consonant following a single vowel (*brag, fat, win*) double the consonant before adding a syllable beginning with a vowel (*-able, -ed, -er, -ing, -y*):

brag: bragged, bragging   fat: fatted, fatter, fatting, fatty
win: winner, winning

The consonant is not doubled: In words with two vowel letters before the final consonant (*daub, daubed; seed, seeded*); in words ending with two consonants (*help, helped; hold, holding*).

2. In words of more than one syllable ending in one vowel and one consonant, the final consonant is traditionally doubled if the word is accented on the last syllable (but see § 3 below). A few words so accented are very common:

con trol′: controlled, controller, controlling
re fer′: referred, referring
Also: confer′ equip′ excel′ infer′ occur′ prefer′

If the accent of the lengthened word shifts to an earlier syllable, the consonant is not doubled:

infer′—in′ference prefer′—pref′erence refer′—ref′erence

If the word is not accented on the last syllable, the consonant need not be doubled, and in American usage preferably is not doubled, though usage is divided on many words:

ben′e fit: benefited, benefiting
com′bat (or com bat′): combated or combatted, combating or combatting, but always com′ba tant
o′pen: opened, opening par′allel: paralleled, paralleling

Usage on *bias, diagram, kidnap, quarrel, travel, worship* is divided, but usually one consonant is preferred.

3. The rules given above regarding words of more than one syllable are really unnecessary. *Controled* and *benefitted* spell their respective words as accurately as the traditional *controlled* and *benefited*—really more accurately. In fact, a number of newspapers and periodicals practicing simple spelling regularly use *controled, patroled,* and so on. But writers must realize the weight of tradition and should not use such forms as *controled* and *benefitted* if their readers will be surprised or offended by them.

But the part of the rule for doubling final consonants that applies to words of one syllable is useful, because it keeps distinct a number of pairs of words similar in appearance:

bat: batted, batting—bate: bated, bating
din: dinned, dinning—dine: dined, dining (but dinner)
grip: gripped, gripping—gripe: griped, griping
plan: planned, planning—plane: planed, planing
scrap: scrapped, scrapping—scrape: scraped, scraping
The boy who wrote "The scene in which she almost kills her husband is griping" did not say what he intended.
Outmoded institutions should be scrapped, not scraped.

doct

4. Words already ending in two consonants keep them before suffixes beginning with a vowel but are likely to lose one consonant before suffixes beginning with another consonant:

enroll: enrolled, enrolling, but enrolment (or enrollment)
install: installed, installing, installation, but instalment (or installment)
fulfill   skilful or skillful   welfare   (but) stillness

(SEE ch. 6, "Doubling final consonant," p. 163. REFERENCE: Kennedy, pp. 231, 238-39.)

doubt Idioms with *doubt:*
1. Negative (when there is no real doubt), *doubt that:*

Formal: I do not doubt that he meant well.
Informal: I don't doubt but that [vulgate: but what] he will come.

2. Positive (when doubt exists), *that, whether, if:*

Formal: I doubt whether he meant it that way.
I doubt that he meant it that way (indicating unbelief really more than doubt).
General: I doubt if he meant it that way.

dove—dived The past tense of *dive* is *dived* or *dove.*

draft, draught The spelling of *draught* (from the Old English *dragan,* to draw) has gradually come to represent its pronunciation (draft). *Draft* is always the spelling for a *bank draft,* the *military draft,* a *draft of a composition,* a *draft of air;* usage is divided on the word in the sense of a maker of drawings—*draftsman* or *draughtsman; draught* is more common for a *ship's draught,* a *draught of fish,* and for a *draught of ale* or *beer on draught*—though *draft* is rapidly gaining in both senses.

drought—drouth Both forms are in good use, *drought* probably more common in formal English, *drouth* in informal and colloquial.

It is true the longest drouth will end in rain.—ROBERT FROST

(COMPARE *height—heighth.)

drunk It seems to take courage to use this natural word. We either go formal—*intoxicated;* or grasp at respectability through euphemisms—*under the influence of liquor* or *indulged to excess;* or make a weak attempt at humor with one of the dozens of slang phrases like *get plastered.* But *drunk* is the word.

due to The preposition *due to* is especially interesting as an illustration of the difficulties a locution has in changing from colloquial

532

and familiar usage to the informal and formal levels. *Due to* as it is used in

> The Mediterranean has its share of minority problems and they have become more prominent *due to* Italo-British tension in that area.—*Kaltenborn Edits the News*, p. 99
>
> *Due to* world conditions with which we are all familiar, England will, within ten years, have a protective tariff.—A. EDWARD NEWTON, *The Atlantic Monthly*, Sept. 1924

has long been popular, especially in magazine writing, and occasionally in more formal literature by Galsworthy and others of undisputed respectability. Advocates of strict usage have set themselves sternly against it, forgetting perhaps that *owing to*, which they have usually suggested should be substituted for it, has come from a participle to a preposition in exactly the same way.

Due was originally an adjective and is still most strictly used as one: "The epidemic was *due* to the brown rat," in which *due* modifies *epidemic*. But the prepositional use is convenient and has been increasingly common in print.

Opinion of *due to* as a preposition is then divided. A writer should consider whether or not it is appropriate to his style: if he is rather formal, he should not use *due to* as a preposition; if he is less formal he doesn't need to worry—except perhaps when writing for readers who are known to be formal.

An excellent example of a linguist's approach to a matter of divided and debatable usage is Professor John S. Kenyon's treatment of *due to* in *American Speech* (1930), 6:61-70. He presents an imposing number of quotations from current writers, discusses the history of the phrase, and concludes:

> Strong as is my own prejudice against the prepositional use of *due to*, I greatly fear it has staked its claim and squatted in our midst alongside of and in exact imitation of *owing to*, its aristocratic neighbor and respected fellow citizen.

A person may not care to use *due to* as a preposition, but in view of actual usage today he hardly has the right to deny it to others.

E 1. The "long *e*" sound (ē) is found variously spelled in stressed syllables: s*ee*d, rec*ei*ve, sh*ie*ld, l*ea*d (lēd), p*eo*ple, k*ey*, qu*ay*, *ae*gis, Ph*oe*be, mach*i*ne.

An unstressed or lightly stressed *e* may vary in pronunciation from long *e* in platform delivery (dē send′—*descend*) to a short *i* in ordinary speech (di send′), and *hero* and *zero* may be hi′rō or hē′rō, zi′rō or zē′rō.

2. The "short *e*" sound (e) is also variously spelled, as in fed, leather, bury, many, said, and so on.

Before final *r* or *r* plus a consonant, short *e* represents the sound in *learn, fern, err*, marked û (lûrn, fûrn, ûr).

3. "Unstressed *e*" (as in *kindness, difference*) represents a slight and sometimes indefinite sound in speech. It may represent short *i* (kīnd′nis), or the neutral vowel sound represented in this book by ə (kīnd′nəs).

Before *l, m, n*, and *r* unstressed *e* is really a part of the consonant ("syllabic" *l, m, n, r*). In this book such syllables are represented by ə or by l m n r: set′əl or set′l̩ (*settle*), wood′ən or wood′n̩ (*wooden*).

4. Miscellaneous sounds represented by *e*: *e* may represent *a* before *r*, as in *there* (t̶h̶ar); ä as in *sergeant* and many words in British usage which in the United States have û (*Derby, Berkeley, clerk*).

5. Silent or mute *e*: In general, words spelled with a final silent *e* drop the *-e* before additions beginning with a vowel and keep it before additions beginning with a consonant:

change: changed, changing; changeless (but changeable)
grease: greased, greaser; greasewood
like: likable, liking; likeness
pursue: pursuant, pursued, pursuing
use: usable, used, using; useful, useless
Exceptions: argument, awful, duly, ninth; judgment (or judgement)

A few other exceptions keep *-e* to indicate pronunciation, chiefly after *c* and *g* before suffixes beginning with *a, o*, or *u*:

change: changeable   courage: courageous   notice: noticeable
(See *-ce, -ge.)

In a few words the *-e* is retained to avoid confusion with other words or to keep the connection with the root word obvious:

lineage (lin′ē ij) vs. linage (līn′ij)
singeing (sin′jing), dyeing (dī′ing)

(See ch. 6, "Final e," p. 164. References: Fowler, "Mute-e"; Kennedy, pp. 243-45.)

each 1. As a pronoun, *each* is singular:

Each of the three has a different instructor.
Each ran as fast as his [her] legs could carry him [her].

2. As an adjective, *each* does not affect the number of a verb; when the subject modified by *each* is plural, the verb is also plural:

> Each applicant has to fill out the blank in full.
> Three students, also from this county, each receive a scholarship.
> They each feel keenly about it.

3. Colloquially, and increasingly in writing, *each* is regarded as a collective (compare *every):

> *Each* of these peoples undoubtedly modified Latin in accordance with *their* own speech habits.—BAUGH, p. 35

(REFERENCE: Russell Thomas, "Concord Based on *Meaning* versus Concord Based on *Form*," *College English*, 1939, 1:38-45.)

each other is in good use for more than two, although formal usage frequently has *one another*.

> General: The men from farms on both sides of the river were shouting to each other.
> Formal: The men from farms on both sides of the river were shouting to one another.

eat The principal parts of *eat* are:

> In general usage: eat (ēt), ate, eaten
> In local and vulgate usage: eat, eat (et or ēt), eat (et or ēt).

Eat is more common as the past tense in British than in American writing and is pronounced et.

Echo phrases Sometimes it is convenient to form a phrase on the pattern of one well known, or to echo one less known but apt. This is a type of allusion. It pleases the writer to use it, it should of course convey his idea, and it will be recognized by some readers. The echo phrase may be either serious or light:

> I have seen American textbooks in which lesson after lesson is devoted to the lofty purpose of eliminating *got*. As though the fear of *got* were the beginning of wisdom. ["The fear of God is the beginning of wisdom."]— P. B. BALLARD, *Thought and Language*, p. 205
> . . . and in general she [Kay Boyle] is so determined to be sensitive to scenery and mood at every turn that the god's truth is you can't see the forest for the prose. [He couldn't see the forest for the trees.]—OTIS FERGUSON, *The New Republic*, Oct. 21, 1936
> . . . but democracy means simply the bludgeoning of the people by the people for the people.—OSCAR WILDE, *The Soul of Man Under Socialism*

In informal writing, echoes of common phrases usually fit, and in more formal writing there is certainly no harm in a writer showing that he has read a bit—but a parade of echo phrases may seem pretentious.

economic Pronounced ē′kə nom′ik or ek′ə nom′ik; and so also *economical, economics; economist* is i kon′ə mist.

Economical means "saving, thrifty"; *economic* means "having to do with business or economics."

Economy Economy in writing means leading a reader to the writer's exact meaning without unnecessary handicaps to understanding. Few, simple, exact words are its basis. But the fewest words and the simplest constructions are not always the most economical, for they may oversimplify the message, or they may limit its readers to those who are practiced in following a compact style. Unnecessary words and needlessly complicated expressions are not economical. Exact words in idiomatic constructions, figures of speech that really illuminate the subject, direct development of materials are the means to true economy.

(See ch. 10, "Sentence economy," p. 284; ch. 12, "Words that weaken," p. 333.)

-ed **1. -ed or -t.** In the past tense and past participles of verbs in which the *-ed* is (or may be) pronounced as *t*, simpler spelling has *-t*. A few words have been rather generally adopted with this sound and spelling: *crept, dreamt, leapt, slept. Asked, jumped, shipped, spelled* are more common than *askt, jumpt, shipt, spelt.*

2. -ed or 'd. When *-ed* is added to words that are formed unusually, *'d* is sometimes used instead, as in *un-idea'd, shanghai'd, ok'd.*

3. -ed in adjectives. There is a tendency, especially in informal style, to drop the *-ed* ending from participles commonly used as adjectives, if the form that remains is that of a noun:

bake goods	ice tea	an old fashion manner	a good size town
grade school [now the regular form]		the same color hat

This tendency is characteristic of familiar and informal style and is rare in formal writing.

Editorial standards See Chapter 3, "Editorial standards," page 75; *Stylebooks; *Newspaper English.

Editorial we See *we § 2.

-ee An ending denoting the one who receives or is directly affected by an act or grant of power, the opposite of nouns in *-er* (*payer,* one who pays; *payee,* one who is paid): *employee, draftee, grantee, mortgagee.*

It takes two people to say a thing—a sayee as well as a sayer. The one is as essential to any true saying as the other.—SAMUEL BUTLER, "Thought and Language"

effect See *affect, effect.

e.g. Abbreviation of Latin *exempli gratia*, "for example." *E.g.* is not usually italicized. See *namely, for punctuation and use.

-ei-, -ie- Words with *-ie-* are much more common than words with *-ei-* and on the whole give less spelling trouble. The most common sound represented by *-ie-* is ē.

Some common words with *ie* are:

achieve	cashier	financier	hygiene	priest
belief	chief	frieze	niece	shriek
believe	field	grieve	piece	siege
bier	fiend	grievous	pier	

Plural of nouns ending in *-y:* academies   companies   lotteries
Third person singular present of verbs in *-y:* dies   fortifies   fries
Other words in *-ie-:* mischief   sieve   view

-ie- is not used after *c.*

There are fewer words with *ei* but their spelling needs careful watching.

The most common sound spelled *ei* is ā:

deign	feint	neigh	rein	sleigh
eight	freight	neighbor	seine	veil
feign	heinous	reign	skein	weigh

A number of words spell the sound ē with *ei*, especially after *c:*

ceiling	perceive	either	neither	weir
conceive	receive	leisure	seize	

And a few words spell other sounds with *ei:*

counterfeit	forfeit	height	heir	their

In some words *i* and *e* stand together but are parts of different syllables:

fi ery   headi er   si esta

(SEE ch. 6, "ei and ie," p. 164. REFERENCE: Donald W. Lee, *College English*, 1944, 6:156-59.)

either 1. *Either* means primarily "one or the other of two," as adjective (either way you look at it), or pronoun (bring me either). For emphasis the pronoun is usually supported by *one* (bring me

either one). Used of three or more objects (either of the corners),
it is loose and rare; "any one of the corners" is the more usual
idiom.

Either is usually construed as singular, though its use as a plural
is increasing (Fries, p. 56):

> Either is good enough for me.
> Either Grace or Phyllis is [or: are] expected.

2. *Either* with the meaning "each" is rare in present English
and definitely formal: "broil the fish on either side, with one turning"—"on either side of the river." *Each* or *both* would be more
common in such expressions.

3. The pronunciation ī′thər has not made so much progress in
the United States as in England, and outside some communities
in New England and a few families or circles that radiate from
New England it is usually an affectation. Say ē′thər, unless your
family or social group generally says ī′thər. Similarly, *neither*
is usually nē′thər, occasionally nī′thər. The use of ī′thər and
nī′thər by a public speaker affects an audience unfavorably in a
large part of the country.

either . . . or   See *Correlative conjunctions.

elder, eldest   These archaic forms of *old* survive in formal English
and they are used only for members of the same family: "the elder
brother," "our eldest daughter," and in some phrases like "the elder
statesmen."

Ellipsis (. . .)   1. A punctuation mark of three or sometimes four
spaced periods is called an ellipsis (plural *ellipses*). Formerly
asterisks (* * *) were used but they have been generally discon-
tinued because they are too conspicuous. When an ellipsis comes
at the end of a statement marked with a period, that period is
added, as in the first and third instances in this passage:

> As Beret drank in these words the tenseness all left her; the weapon she
> had seized dropped from her hand; her body straightened up; she looked
> about in wide-eyed wonder. . . . Were those church bells she heard? . . .
> But the voices were beginning again on the other side of the wall. . . .
> Hush! Hush!—O. E. Rölvaag, *Giants in the Earth*, p. 416

2. (a) The ellipsis is an editorial mark showing where a word
or more, which is not needed for the purpose of a writer making
the quotation, has been left out. In the following quotation the
ellipsis marks the omission of two lines not essential for the meaning of the statement:

After long delays caused by the presentation of a list of Italian and German provisos which constitutional governments could not accept . . . , a diplomatic conference assembled in London to map a program for maintaining neutrality.—H. F. ARMSTRONG, *We or They*, p. 32

Any such omission in quoted matter should be indicated by an ellipsis.

b) An ellipsis is also used to show that a series of enumeration continues beyond the units named; it is equivalent to *et cetera:*

the coordinating conjunctions (and, but, for . . .)

3. In narrative an ellipsis is used to mark hesitation in the action, suggesting passage of time, as in the quotation on page 538 from *Giants in the Earth*, and in the one from Conrad Aiken below:

"Well—I can see this much. You *are* in love with her. Or you couldn't possibly be such a fool. But it's precisely when you're in love that you need to keep your wits about you. Or the wits of your friends. . . . You *mustn't* marry her, Harry."
"Well—I don't know."
"No! . . . It would be ruinous."—CONRAD AIKEN, "Spider! Spider!"

It is also used to mark a statement that is unfinished or is let die away:

I go away to a town, a big strange town, and try to hammer out a good book. The days come, the days go, and big ships sail into the harbor. . . .
—ALBERT HALPER, "Young Writer Remembering Chicago"

Elliptical constructions *Ellipsis* and *elliptical* refer to a construction in which a word or words can be supplied from a neighboring construction:

I work a good deal harder than you [Supply: *work*].

The notion of ellipsis has often been misused to apply to the shorter way of expressing a notion. A person may write either:

We went through the same experience that you did [or]
We went through the same experience you did.

The second form is not actually elliptical but a shorter idiom; a *that* is not "omitted," it just isn't thought or spoken or written. The choice between the longer and shorter constructions is a matter of style rather than grammar. Formal English uses the longer ones, tends to fill out all constructions. Informal and colloquial English use the shorter constructions freely.

(SEE ch. 10, "Long and short constructions," p. 286. REFERENCES: Curme, *Syntax*, p. 2 and index references; Jespersen, *The Philosophy of Grammar*, p. 306 and index references; for a more traditional treatment of ellipsis, see Kennedy, pp. 508-12.)

else **1.** Because *else* follows the word (usually a pronoun) it modifies, it takes the sign of the possessive (an *idiom):

> I hated wearing somebody else's clothes.
> At first he thought the book was his, but finally decided it was somebody else's.

2. *Else* is used as a colloquial *intensive and sometimes appears in writing where it is deadwood and should be removed:

> Finally I started talking, just to hear something [else] besides the roar of the motor.

3. *Nothing else but* is a vulgate phrase, not used in written English:

> Written English: There was nothing but wheat as far as you could see.
> Vulgate: There was nothing else but wheat as far as you could see.

emigrate—immigrate *Emigrate* means to move out of a country or region, *immigrate* to move into a country. An *emigrant* from Norway would be an *immigrant* to the United States.

Emph **Emphasis** Correction: **Strengthen the emphasis of this passage by one or more of the methods suggested below.**

1. Position. 2. Mass or proportion. 3. Distinction of expression. 4. Separation, distinctness. 5. Repetition. 6. Intensives. 7. Mechanical devices.

The ideal of emphasis is to lead your reader to see your ideas in the same relative importance in which you regard them—the most important as most important, the less important as less important, the incidental as incidental. Emphasis does not necessarily mean force, but rather the accurate conveying of your view of your subject.

There are several ways in which emphasis can be conveyed, one or more of which will help you in controlling the reader's mind. Most of these are discussed more fully in other articles of the *Guide-Index*, referred to in this summary.

1. Position. In most types of writing, except news stories and reference works, the most emphatic position is the last, and the second most emphatic position is the first. Sentences should "end with words that deserve distinction," and not many should begin with locutions that postpone meaning, "There was," "It is."

(SEE ch. 7, "Beginning paragraphs," p. 195; ch. 7, "Concluding paragraphs," p. 198; ch. 10, "Position," p. 293.)

2. Mass or proportion. Position is supported by the amount of space given to a particular point. It is necessary to watch the last topics in a paper, which are likely to be hurried over and so under-developed that they do not seem as important as their writer intends.

3. Distinction of expression. In general, big words and long *function phrases weaken a statement, as do general and indefinite words. Fresh, concrete, simple words in direct and economical constructions make for a clear cut emphasis. (See Chapter 12, Qualities of Words, page 331.)

4. Separation, distinctness. Marking the stages of thought in a paper by extra spacing or by numbers makes separate ideas stand out more strongly. Careful paragraphing makes units that help clarify the relationship between topics. Putting ideas in separate sentences keeps them distinct, and making the important statements main clauses and the contributing statements subordinate elements shows their relative importance.

(SEE ch. 9, "Complex sentences," p. 257; ch. 7, Writing paragraphs, p. 169; ch. 10, "Separating elements," p. 292.)

5. Repetition. Repetition of valuable words drives them home, and repetition of statements either in similar words or in different, perhaps figurative expressions, is a useful form of emphasis if it is not overdone.

(SEE ch. 10, "Repetition," p. 289.)

6. Intensives. Words added to intensify meaning are generally used in speaking, but they are less useful in writing. See *very; Chapter 10, "Intensives," page 288. *Exaggeration is a legitimate form of intensifying.

Labeling a statement "It is interesting to note," "This is an important phase of the subject" is not usually convincing. Such phrases can be done away with in revision by making the fact or opinion stand out in other ways.

7. Mechanical devices. Writing and printing have various mechanical means—*underlining (italics), *capitals, emphatic punctuation—for stressing words and passages. These devices are often used by amateur writers in an attempt to make up for deficiencies in style or content.

(SEE *Schoolgirl style; ch. 10, "Mechanical devices," p. 288.)

Emphasis is to be tested in revision, when the writer takes the role of reader and tries to see if his paper really represents his view of the subject.

employee This spelling is much more common than *employé.*

en-, in- *In-* is either a native English prefix or a prefix of Latin origin; *en-* is the same Latin prefix modified in French. (*Em-* and *im-* are variant forms.) In several common words, usage is divided, though usually one form is more common. This is a type of problem for which Fowler and other British dictionaries are not safe guides to American usage, for Americans tend to use *in-* more than the English do. The safest way is to consult a recent American dictionary and to be fairly consistent in the form you use from then on.

Here are a few samples with Webster preferences put first when there is a choice:

embark	encourage
embed—imbed	endorse—indorse
embellish	endure
enable	endeavor
enchant	enforce
incase—encase	inquire—enquire
enclose—inclose (gaining)	
ensure—insure (*insure* in the financial sense, *insurance*, etc.)	

The *en-* forms often suggest a slightly more formal style than the *in-* forms.

Endorsing papers   See Chapter 1, "Endorsing manuscript," page 21.

End-stop   A mark of punctuation used at the end of a sentence, usually a period, exclamation mark, or question mark. The double or two-em dash (——— *Dash § 7) is used as an end-stop in conversation when a speech is interrupted. The *ellipsis (. . .) is often used as an end-stop for a sentence that is intentionally left unfinished or that is let die away.

When two end-stops would fall together at the end of a sentence, as when a question stands within a sentence, only one mark, the more emphatic or more necessary for meaning, is used:

> When we say, for example, that Miss A. *plays* well, only an irredeemable outsider would reply "Plays what?" So, too, . . .—C. ALPHONSO SMITH, *Studies in English Syntax*, p. 8

(For further comment on end-stops see the articles on the individual marks.)

English language

1. Old English, 450-1050. 2. Middle English, 1050-1450. 3. Early Modern English, 1450-1700. 4. Modern English, 1700-

English is a member of the Indo-European family of languages, which includes most of the languages of Europe, a large number of the languages of India, the languages of Persia and of certain adjoining regions. The Indo-European family is divided into eight branches. One of these, the Germanic, to which English belongs, comprises the following:

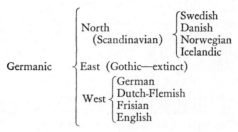

A brief selection of facts about the different periods of our language will show some of the roots of the richness—and confusion—of modern English.

1. Old English, 450-1050. The Angles, Saxons, and Jutes brought to England from their old homes in northeastern Europe somewhat differing Germanic dialects. They pushed back the native Celts from the parts of the island they conquered, so that Celtic speech contributed almost nothing to English, but survived in Welsh, Cornish, and Highland Scotch. The conquerors' languages developed into several main dialects—Northumbrian, Mercian, Kentish, West Saxon—which together are known as Old English (or Anglo-Saxon). These dialects still leave their marks in the vulgate speech of various parts of England. They had many points in common, and were gradually brought together, each making some contribution, but East Midland, a descendant of Mercian, made the largest contribution to what now after seven or eight hundred years we know as English.

Somewhat less than a quarter of the present English vocabulary goes back to the words of Old English. The modern descendants of Old English words are often changed in meaning and almost always in pronunciation—according to regular processes: Old English *stan* becomes Modern English *stone, ban* becomes *bone*, etc. Our common verbs (*go, sit, eat, fight, whistle*), many of our most common nouns (*meat, house, breakfast, land, water*), and adjectives like *fast, slow, high* go back to Old English words, so that though less than a fourth of the dictionary words are of this "native" origin, they play a part in our speech out of proportion to their number.

Furthermore, most of the machinery of our language is from Old English: the articles *a, an, the;* most of the connecting words— *around, at, by, for, from, in, into, out, under . . . as, like, since, when;* most of the pronouns (*I, we, us, . . .*); the inflectional endings of nouns (*house—houses, boy—boys—boy's*) and of adjectives and adverbs: *merry—merrier—merriest* or *more merry—most merry;* harsh*ly*, kind*ly;* the forms of verbs: pass, pass*es*, pass*ed*, pass*ing*. These endings are applied to words borrowed from other languages (*indict-ed, political-ly*), so that although three quarters of the vocabulary may come from Romance or other languages the borrowed words are built into an English pattern. And when we consider word order we see that the texture of English is Germanic and it must be regarded as a Germanic language.

Within the Old English period the practice of absorbing words from other languages was already strong. A number of Latin words, some of them originally Greek, were taken in, most of them pertaining to the church (*abbot, priest, school*), though there was still a tendency to translate the elements of the Latin words into Old English elements, so that we have *gospel* from *god spell*, "good news," which is a translation of the Greek-Latin *evangelium*.

In the ninth century the east and north of England was conquered by the Danes, whose language left a large number of words and forms, partly because it was a closely related language, partly because of the intimacy between the two peoples. The *sk* words are likely to date from this mixture—*sky, skin, scream, skirt* (a cousin of the Old English *shirt*, both related to *short*), place names ending in *-by* and *-thorp*, and a number of common words like *odd, anger, egg*. Nearly five per cent of our words are Scandinavian.

A number of the most conspicuous irregularities of Modern English existed already in Old English: *be, is, are, was, were, been* as forms of the verb "to be"; *may, might, shall, should, ought*, and the other "auxiliaries"; our pronouns—*I, my, me, we, our, us, he, she, it. . . .* These words are in such common use that they show patterns of inflection which have otherwise disappeared. Here and there we have remnants of Old English forms that lost out in the development of the language, like the plurals *children, oxen, men, geese*, instead of the regular plural in *-s*.

There is a considerable body of writing from the Old English period. It includes poems, sermons, riddles, history, translations from Latin, and most conspicuously the *Anglo-Saxon Chronicles, Beowulf*, and the large group of writings and translations in West Saxon made by or at the court of Alfred the Great, King of the West Saxons 871-901. Some 30,000 different words are found in this literature.

2. Middle English, 1050-1450. The conquest of England by the Norman-French in 1066 coincided with the beginning of Early

Middle English. The speakers of Old English in the main became serfs, servants, everything but leaders in affairs. Their language was seldom used in official proceedings and rarely written. One result was the loss of the more elevated Old English words that had been used in poetry and that would correspond to the rather archaic vocabulary of our formal literature.

A far-reaching development of this period was the decline and in some instances complete loss of the inflectional endings that Old English had used. The definite article was no longer declined (our *the* is the sole descendant of eight forms in Old English); *-n* disappeared from the infinitive of most verbs, and other endings, since they were in unstressed syllables and did not receive full pronunciation, dropped away. This process went far to make English one of the least inflected languages.

On the other hand the language of the invaders was making its way. The words for the acts of the ruling class—war, government, law, social activity—were Norman French and they have generally come down to modern English: *siege, soldier, judge, jury, suit, dinner, servant, obey*. The majority of the Norman French words were ultimately from Latin, though considerably changed in form. For many notions Modern English has two roughly synonymous words, one Latin or French, one Old English: *dress—clothes, aid—help, cottage—hut, solitary—lonely*. Some French spellings made their way into English, like *gu* for hard *g—guest, guess; qu* for *cw—queen* for Old English *cwen*.

In 1362 English was restored as the language of the law courts, an official recognition that it was asserting itself once more in higher circles. The speech of the region around London was now the basis for future development, not only of a spoken language but of a literary language. How far the fusion of Old English and French resources had gone can be seen from a few lines by Chaucer, written in the 1380's. The French words are in italics:

> "What folk ben ye, that at myn hoomcominge
> Perturben so my feste with *cryinge?*"
> Quod Theseus, "have ye so greet *envye*
> Of myn *honour,* that thus *compleyne* and *crye?*
> Or who hath yow misboden, or *offended?*
> And telleth me if it may been *amended;*
> And why that ye ben clothed thus in blak?"
> —GEOFFREY CHAUCER, "The Knightes Tale"

Except for the Old English *misboden* ("insulted"), all of these words, both native and French, are in use today, though *quod* (quoth) is archaic, and in spite of some differences in spelling, the passage can be read by anyone. Many of the words show inflectional endings that have since been dropped or changed: *ben* for *are* or *be*, perturb*en*, tell*eth*, and the final *e* of nouns.

3. Early Modern English, 1450-1700. In this period we have the beginnings of conscious concern for the language and actual or attempted "improvement" by manipulation of words and constructions, "schoolmastering the speech." The early printers, from 1476 on, felt the need for uniformity, especially in spelling and choice of word forms, and began the domination of these traits that ever since in the written language has been exercised by publishers. Translators and writers believed the language was rough, unpolished, incapable of doing what Latin and Greek had done and what Italian could do. They set about enlarging the vocabulary, chiefly by transliterating words from Greek and Latin. More than twenty-five per cent of modern English words are pretty directly from classical languages and very often we have two words that go back to the same Latin original, one brought in by the Norman French and one taken in directly later: *paint—picture, certainty—certitude*. Latin was the language of the Church at the beginning of this period, though after the Reformation the Book of Common Prayer and the King James translation of the Bible became tremendous forces for elevated English. Most books of the learned world were in Latin—and college classes were conducted in Latin, even in America, until a century and a half ago.

The spoken language was vigorous and was written down in some popular literature, but most literature that has survived was from the hands of university men and conscious stylists. Shakespeare shows the complete range, from formal, Latinized lines to rough and tumble lines, often combining the elevated and the simple in a single speech:

> No, this my hand will rather
> The multitudinous seas incarnadine
> Making the green one red.

Prose style lagged behind poetic, especially in sentence sense, producing "sentence heaps" running to hundreds of words. In the sixteen hundreds the wealth of experiment of the preceding century was analyzed and many words and phrases were disposed of. The less useful and more ponderous of the Latin importations were dropped, and interest in native words increased the proportion of native words in use. Prose style especially developed in directness and sureness until in Dryden modern English prose is usually said to be established. In spite of small differences in idiom and word order, this paragraph does not seem nearly 300 years old:

> To begin, then, with Shakespeare. He was the man who of all modern, and perhaps ancient poets, had the largest and most comprehensive soul. All the images of nature were still present to him, and he drew them, not laboriously, but luckily; when he describes anything, you more than see it, you feel it too. Those who accuse him to have wanted learning, give him the greater commendation: he was naturally learned; he needed not the spectacles of books to read nature; he looked inwards, and found her there. I cannot say he is everywhere alike; were he so, I should do him injury to compare him with the greatest of mankind. He is many times flat, insipid; his comic wit degenerating into clenches, his serious swelling into bombast. But he is always great, when some great occasion is presented to him; no man can say he ever had a fit subject for his wit, and did not then raise himself as high above the rest of the poets,
>
> _Quantum lenta solent inter viburna cupressi._
>
> The consideration of this made Mr. Hales of Eaton say, that there was no subject of which any poet ever writ, but he would produce it much better done in Shakespeare; and however others are now generally preferred before him, yet the age wherein he lived, which had contemporaries with him Fletcher and Jonson, never equalled them to him in their esteem: and in the last king's court, when Ben's reputation was at highest, set our Shakespeare far above him.—JOHN DRYDEN, _An Essay of Dramatic Poesy_ (1668)

4. Modern English 1700- This _Index_ gives a partial picture of current English and suggests in some of its specific articles changes that have taken place in the last few generations. Such articles may be taken as continuations of this brief historical sketch, for by 1700 English had become substantially the language we now know and use. The vocabulary has been enlarged in the last two centuries chiefly from two sources: borrowings from India and America and from all peoples touched by British and American traders; and through scientific coinages, chiefly from Greek and Latin roots. There has been, especially in recent years, a tendency toward shorter and more direct sentences. The paragraph has become a more distinct unit in written expression. The most important point for study in this period has probably been the different levels of usage, and different traditions of style, especially formal and informal style and the relations between them.

Today the language of England and the British Empire and of the United States is spoken by considerably over 200,000,000 people—perhaps the largest group of people who can easily understand each other.

The result of this varied history is a language full of anomalies, but of unusual range, combining something of the rapidity and smoothness of the Romance languages with the strength of the Germanic.

(REFERENCES: Baugh, Robertson, McKnight; Kennedy, chs. 4, 5. Otto Jespersen, *Growth and Structure of the English Language* (various editions), describes the accumulation of the English vocabulary, and his *Language* (New York, 1923), Part iv, discusses language change especially apropos of English.)

en route Pronounced on rōōt'; formally än rōōt'. *On the way* often fits a sentence more naturally:

> They were en route [on the way] to Philadelphia.

enthuse A back formation (*Origin of words §3d) from *enthusiasm*. Many people object to it, and the dictionaries label it "colloquial." But *enthuse* seems to be an improvement over the only locution we have for the idea, the clumsy *be enthusiastic over* or *about*. It is now in fairly general use.

envelop, envelope The verb *envelop* is pronounced in vel'ǝp; the noun *envelope*, en'vǝ lōp; less commonly—reflecting the word's French origin—on'vǝ lōp; and locally en vel'up.

Envelope See *Letters §1.

Epigrams An epigram is a short, pithy statement, usually with a touch of wit, in either verse or prose. In prose this means really a detached or detachable and "quotable" sentence. In consecutive prose, epigrams sometimes become too prominent, attract too much attention to themselves, or suggest straining for effect. But they can focus attention or put a fact or opinion so that a reader can remember (and perhaps repeat) it:

> One test of musical comedy, we have always felt, is whether it breaks out into song or breaks down into it.—FRANK S. NUGENT, *The New York Times*, Dec. 3, 1937
> It's no disgrace to be poor, but it might as well be.
> Bees are not as busy as we think they are. They jest can't buzz any slower.—KIN HUBBARD, *The Sayings of Abe Martin*

Closely related to epigrams are *aphorisms*—pithy statements but more likely to be abstract and not necessarily witty. The essays of Francis Bacon are packed with aphorisms, and some modern essayists use them too:

> To spend too much time in studies is sloth; to use them too much for ornament, is affectation; to make judgment wholly by their rules, is the humour of a scholar. . . . Read not to contradict and confute; nor to believe and take for granted; not to find talk and discourse; but to weigh and consider. . . . Reading maketh a full man; conference a ready man; and writing an exact man.—FRANCIS BACON, "Of Studies"

Proverbs are the often quoted, concrete expressions of popular wisdom. They are likely to make observations on character or conduct. As a rule their authors are unknown.

> It never rains but it pours.
> Still waters run deep.
> It's hard for an empty sack to stand upright.
> Alcohol and gasoline don't mix.

A special type of epigram is the *paradox*, which makes a statement that as it stands contradicts fact or common sense or itself, and yet suggests a truth or at least a half truth:

> All generalizations are false, including this one.
> Dr. Richards is no mystic; he is a behaviourist, a behaviourist being a psychologist who does not believe in psychology.—P. B. BALLARD, *Thought and Language*, p. 265

(REFERENCE: *The Oxford Dictionary of Proverbs*, compiled by William G. Smith (Oxford, 1936)

-er, -or Names of persons or things performing an act (nouns of agent) and some other nouns are formed in English by adding *-er* to a verb (*doer, killer, painter, thinker*), but many end in *-or*, chiefly nouns taken in from Latin or French (*assessor, prevaricator*).

Since the two endings are pronounced the same (ər), it is hard to tell whether *-er* or *-or* should be written. Here are a few as samples; a dictionary will have to settle most questions.

With -er:

advertiser	consumer	mixer
*advisor (shifted	debater	peddler (pedlar)
from adviser)	engraver	propeller
better (bettor)	manufacturer	subscriber
condenser		

With -or:

accelerator	detector	proprietor
administrator	distributor	protector
ancestor	editor	rotor
bachelor	governor	spectator
benefactor	inventor	sponsor
carburetor	(or inventer)	supervisor
competitor	legislator	transgressor
conductor	motor	ventilator
conqueror	objector	warrior

There are a few nouns of agent ending in *-ar:* beggar, burglar, liar.

-er, -re Many words formerly ending in *-re* are now spelled *-er* in American usage. This group includes the following:

caliber	maneuver	niter	sepulcher
center	meager	ocher	somber
fiber	meter	saber	specter
luster	miter	scepter	theater

British usage tends to *-re* in most of these words, though Fowler says they are being changed to *-er* one by one, because "we prefer in England to break with our illogicalities slowly."

An American writer who wishes a slightly archaic flavor will tend to use the *-re* forms; most will naturally use the *-er* forms.

Theater is divided in spelling, partly because it is found in a good many proper names of buildings and companies which were set up when *theatre* was the more common spelling, partly because of the leisure class associations of the word. Keep the form actually used in proper names and ordinarily use *theater* elsewhere.

Acre, lucre, mediocre keep the *-re* to represent a *c* pronounced *k* (contrast *soccer*), and *ogre* is the current form, though some words with *g*, like *meager*, have changed.

err Usually pronounced ûr; but there is some, and perhaps a growing tendency to pronounce it er, from *analogy with *error* (er′ər).

Esq., Esquire Written following a man's name in the inside and outside address of a letter, *Esq.* or *Esquire* is formal, with archaic or British suggestion, and in the United States is not often used except to professional men, chiefly to lawyers. No other title (such as *Mr., Dr., Hon.*) should be used with the word: Harry A. Kinne, Esq.

Essential modifier See *Restrictive and nonrestrictive, and Chapter 5, "Commas with close and loose modifiers," page 144.

etc., et cetera *Etc.*, usually read *and so forth*, is sometimes a convenient way to end a series that samples rather than completes an enumeration, but it belongs primarily to reference and business usage:

> The case is suitable for prints, maps, blueprints, etc.

Its inappropriateness can be seen in a sentence like this:

> A student's professors can be of immense aid to him because of their knowledge of boys and their habits, customs, needs, ideals, etc.

Writing out *et cetera* now seems an affectation. In consecutive writing most people prefer the English "and so forth." It is better to avoid these end tags (which really take away from emphasis by putting a catchall at the end of a clause or sentence) by rephrasing the list, preceding it by *such as* or some other warning that the list you are giving is not exhaustive:

> The case is suitable for such large sheets as prints, maps, and blueprints.

And etc. shows the writer doesn't realize that the *et* of *etc.* means *and*, so that he is writing *and and so forth*.

Etymology See *Origin of words.

Euphemisms A euphemism is a softened word used in place of one that names more vigorously some suffering, or something unpleasant, or something regarded as not quite nice: *pass away* for *die*, *natural son* for *illegitimate son* or *bastard*, *expectorate* for *spit*, *separate from the college* for *expel* or *fire* or *flunk out*.

Occasionally euphemisms are warranted to avoid hurting someone's feelings. But in general it is safer—and better style—to call things by their right names, even if they are somewhat unpleasant.

For further discussion and examples see Chapter 12, "Euphemisms," page 337.

Euphony means harmonious or pleasing sounds. (See Chapter 10, "Qualities of sound," page 295.)

Evaluating For evaluating material in themes, see Chapter 1, page 12; for reference papers, Chapter 13, page 383.

every and its compounds 1. *Every, everybody, everyone* are grammatically singular:

> Every man on the team did his best.
> Everybody likes the new minister.
> Everyone took his purchases home with him.

Colloquially these words are treated as collectives. A verb immediately following *everyone* or *everybody* is usually singular, but a pronoun referring back to it from a little distance is likely to be plural:

> Everybody is taking off their hats.

This is reasonable, since the reference is to a number of people. To make these expressions conform to formal written usage, it is often better to change the *everybody* to a more accurate plural or collective than to change the later pronoun:

> They all did their best. The crowd are taking off their hats.

(REFERENCE: Fries, p. 50.)

2. *Everybody* is always written as one word; *everyone* is usually written as one word, but when the *one* is stressed, as two:

Everybody knew what the end would be.
Everyone knew what the end would be.
Every one of the family knew what the end would be.

3. *Every so often*, *every bit as* (*happy*, etc.) are useful informal idioms:

Every so often someone in the crowd would give a terrific shout.
They are every bit as happy as they expected to be.

4. *Every place* is a colloquial adverbial phrase, somewhat more reputable than *any place* (*any, § 4):

Every place I looked the people said the same thing.

Exact connective See *Conjunctions § 1 and articles on particular connectives, *as, *but, *so, *while.

Exact use of words See Chapter 11, "The responsible use of words," page 326.

Exactness of meaning See Chapter 9, page 243.

Exaggeration The figure of speech (hyperbole) in which a statement is enlarged or overstated. See Chapter 12, "Degree of statement," page 350.

Examples See Chapter 7, "Details," page 172.

except, accept *Except*, as a verb, means to "leave out, exclude": "He excepted those who had done the assignment from the extra reading." It is decidedly formal, and *excused* or even *exempted* would be more natural in the sentence given.

Accept means to "get" or "receive" and is slightly formal: "I accept with pleasure"—"He accepted the position."

We confuse the two words in writing usually because of carelessness rather than ignorance. Remember that we see and write the preposition *except* ("Everyone except you") much oftener than we do either of the verbs.

exception "And this was no exception" is a colorless and often wordy way of combining a particular statement and a general statement:

Most young actors experience numerous difficulties in their early appearances. I was no exception. (Revised: Like most young actors, I experienced . . .)

Exclamation mark (!) An exclamation mark (or point) is used after an emphatic interjection and after a phrase, clause, or sentence that is genuinely exclamatory, and after forceful commands. Clear cut exclamations offer no problem:

> Oh! Ouch! No, no, no!
> "But," he protested, "it's the chance of a lifetime!"
> A number of children playing on the quay saw him, and with a wild cry of "Squirrel! Squirrel!" went after him.—W. H. HUDSON, *The Book of a Naturalist*, p. 61

But many interjections are weak and deserve no more than a comma:

> Well, well, so you're in college now.

Often sentences cast in exclamatory pattern are really statements put that way for variety (*Exclamations) and the exclamation mark is optional. Its use would depend chiefly on appropriateness and the emphasis intended and on whether the writer tends to close punctuation (which is likely to show a number of exclamation marks) or open (which is more likely to rely on commas).

> The country! [Or, a period] Why anybody ever went to the country. ... He might be in New York with the gang. Playing ball in the streets, dodging the trucks, the cars, the cabs! [Or, a period]

Exclamation marks are more characteristic of imaginative writing, especially of fiction, than of factual writing. In factual writing it is well to remember that in some newspaper offices the exclamation mark is known as a screamer—and that its overuse is a mark of nervousness or of *schoolgirl style.

(SEE ch. 5, "Exclamation mark," p. 140.)

Exclamations are expressions of feeling or emphatic statements of fact or opinion. They range from the simple and often involuntary *Oh!* or *Ouch!* to fully developed sentences.

One word exclamations may be regarded as full sentences if they deserve that much emphasis (*Oh! You nearly upset my plate.*), or as parts of sentences if they seem to belong with other sentence elements: *Oh! you're here at last!* [or] *Oh, you're here at last!*

Many exclamations begin with *what* or *how*: *What a view! How could you! How lucky you are!*

An exclamation expressing an emphatic opinion gives not only emphasis but variety in a passage:

> But the methods chosen for the transition must always bear those human values in mind, for a whole new social order must inevitably result from a new kind of economic system, and in the process of slow nurture and growth

initial trends may be all-important. Compulsion is a bad way to make men free!—ALFRED M. BINGHAM, *Insurgent America*, p. 6

But used just for variety or to give emphasis to what are really commonplaces, exclamations are usually ineffective and give the effect of a strained or schoolgirl style:

> Think how often you have judged a person by the way in which he speaks! Think of a salesman who is a poor talker! It sounds like the height of unreality, but what a situation in this highly competitive world! Think of a college professor who could not intelligently lecture to his classes because he had not learned the art of elocution!

excuse, pardon Small slips are *excused*, more considerable faults (and crimes) are *pardoned*. "Pardon me" is sometimes considered more elegant than "Excuse me" in upper-class social situations. *Excuse* has also the special meaning of "giving permission to leave."

expect means "to look forward to" and also "to look for with confidence." In formal English it is usually kept close to some meaning involving anticipation, but in colloquial usage its meaning is extended and weakened to "suppose"—"I expect you'd better be going."

Experiment in English Language and literary style tend to become stereotyped; the same kinds of words are used over and over in the same kinds of constructions; their effectiveness in conveying individual impressions decreases. The more important writers escape monotony by the force of their message or the individuality of their expression, and most of them more or less consciously either ignore conventions of language or experiment with words or constructions.

Almost anyone with an interest in writing will experiment in his own familiar writing, trying out spelling, unusual words or combinations of words, unorthodox sentence patterns. Some writers in their published work experiment also. We might call any departure from the commonly written and printed English an experiment —if it is not just the result of carelessness or ignorance. Advertisers are active experimenters, using shortened spellings, created words, and free sentence forms. At the other extreme purists may also be regarded as experimenters, trying to limit speaking and writing to the formal vocabulary and formal constructions, as it never has been in all its history.

Writers like Damon Runyon and P. G. Wodehouse are really experimenters, since they create a lingo for their stories by taking ordinary traits of speech and pushing them further than natural usage would. This bit from Mr. Wodehouse shows his potpourri of colloquialisms, slang, literary phrases (and allusions), and created words (*bonhomous*):

> From his earliest years the Biscuit had nourished an unwavering conviction that Providence was saving up something particularly juicy in the way of rewards for him and that it was only a question of time before it came across and delivered the goods. He based this belief on the fact that he had always tried to be a reasonably bonhomous sort of bird and was one who, like Abou Ben Adhem, loved his fellow men. Abou had clicked, and Lord Biskerton expected to click. But not in his most sanguine moments, not even after a Bump Supper at Oxford or the celebration of somebody's birthday at the Drones, had he ever expected to click on this colossal scale. It just showed that, when Providence knew it had got hold of a good man, the sky was the limit.—P. G. WODEHOUSE, *Big Money*, p. 286

Recent writers like James Joyce, Gertrude Stein, and E. E. Cummings have experimented in English prose. One of the chief interests of these writers, aside from freshening the nature of English prose, has been to carry expression closer to thought, creating, especially, sentence patterns that follow or at least suggest the actual thought of a character or of the writer himself.

Gertrude Stein's explanation of why she does not use commas conventionally both describes and illustrates an individual's approach to these problems of language. She holds that because most writers use commas in certain ways is not sufficient reason for her doing it. She asks if commas really convey her sense of her meaning or if they are just lazy props, keeping the reader from a properly active participation in understanding.

> What does a comma do.
>
> I have refused them so often and left them out so much and did without them so continually that I have come finally to be indifferent to them. I do not now care whether you put them in or not but for a long time I felt very definitely about them and would have nothing to do with them.
>
> As I say commas are servile and they have no life of their own, and their use is not a use, it is a way of replacing one's own interest and I do decidedly like to like my own interest my own interest in what I am doing. A comma by helping you along holding your coat for you and putting on your shoes keeps you from living your life as actively as you should lead it and to me for many years and I still do feel that way about it only now I do not pay as much attention to them, the use of them was positively degrading. Let me tell you what I felt and what I meant.
>
> . . . .
>
> When it gets really difficult you want to disentangle rather than to cut the knot, at least so anybody feels who is working with any thread, so anybody feels who is working with any tool so anybody feels who is writing any sentence or reading it after it has been written. And what does a comma do, a comma does nothing but make easy a thing that if you like it enough is easy enough without the comma. A long complicated sentence should

force itself upon you, make you know yourself knowing it and the comma, well at the most a comma is a poor period that it lets you stop and take a breath but if you want to take a breath you ought to know yourself that you want to take a breath. It is not like stopping altogether which is what a period does stopping altogether has something to do with going on, but taking a breath well you are always taking a breath and why emphasize one breath rather than another breath. Anyway that is the way I felt about it and I felt that about it very strongly. And so I almost never used a comma. The longer, the more complicated the sentence the greater the number of the same kind of words I had following one after another, the more the very many more I had of them the more I felt the passionate need of their taking care of themselves by themselves and not helping them, and thereby enfeebling them by putting in a comma.—GERTRUDE STEIN, *Lectures in America*, pp. 219-21.

More recently, in *Finnegans Wake*, James Joyce has gone on to experiment with words, breaking up familiar words, changing sounds slightly, combining elements:

Yet he made leave to many a door beside of Finglas wold for so witness his chambered cairns silent that are at browse up hill and down coombe and on eolithostroton, at Howth or at Coolock or at Enniskerry. Olivers lambs we do call them and they shall be gathered unto him, their herd and paladin, in that day when he skall wake from earthsleep in his valle of briers and o'er dun and dale the Wulverulverlord (protect us!) his mighty horn skall roll, orland, roll.

Liverpool? Sot a bit of it! His braynes coolt parritch, his pelt nassy, his heart's adrone, his bluidstreams acrawl, his puff but a piff, his extremities extremely so. Humph is in his doge. Words weigh no more to him than raindrops to Rethfernhim. Which we all like. Rain. When we sleep. Drops. But wait until our sleeping. Drain. Sdops.

For most readers this is carrying experiment too far. Certainly it is paying little attention to a reader or to demands of communication. A writer of course can write merely to please himself, or for the fun of it (and there is much sheer fun back of most of this experimentation), but he cannot blame readers if they do not feel like bothering to decipher his cryptograms. Joyce was doing this quite voluntarily (or wilfully), for in *The Portrait of the Artist as a Young Man* and in the volume of short stories *Dubliners* he wrote a flexible and effective English. Similarly E. E. Cummings, whose *Eimi* is the story of a visit to Russia written in experimental prose, wrote one of the classics of the first world war in *The Enormous Room*—in a conventional but thoroughly individual prose. These experiments are not the work of writers who can't write English but of talented writers who are trying to make English prose more expressive, to make it come closer to representing their individual view of things.

Though these writers have pushed their experiments to the point of eccentricity, their work is useful. Because of the work of Joyce and Miss Stein, for instance, others, like John Dos Passos, Evelyn Scott, Ernest Hemingway, and a whole younger generation, have written with greater freedom. These, together with the vigorous if more conventional writers like George Bernard Shaw in his *Prefaces* and H. L. Mencken in his *Prejudices*, have gone a long way toward breaking up stereotypes of prose and toward making possible the notable vigor and flexibility of current writing.

These experimenters are worth reading and study—but not direct imitation. They are individualists who have tried to find expression for their individual needs. Imitating the external traits of the style of Damon Runyon or of Gertrude Stein will usually mean failure because the imitator's needs are not the same as those of the pioneers. But reading such writers should give a writer courage to try to find a method of presenting his material as he sees it, even if that means departing from some of the conventions of writing. This is part of the spirit of modern literature.

(REFERENCES: Dobrée, Part iv, § 2, "Experiments"; Gertrude Stein, *Lectures in America* (New York, 1935), "Poetry and Grammar.")

Expletives   See *it, *there is, there are.

Expository writing   Writing that is intended primarily to inform its readers—by presenting facts, giving directions, recording events, interpreting facts, developing opinions—is expository. People do not sit down to write "exposition"; the word is convenient for grouping various articles that convey information.

Expository articles differ in their emphasis from arguments, which are intended to influence the reader's beliefs or to lead him to some action. Imaginative writing is not primarily expository (although novels have been written to explain their author's point of view on something) but aims directly at pleasing or moving a reader. There may be subordinate expository movements, as when in a novel a character's situation or his past is explained.

The bulk of college writing, probably all except imaginative writing done in advanced composition courses, is expository. The articles in this *Guide-Index* are expository.

extracurricular   means "outside the course of study" (extracurricular activities); sometimes hyphened but usually not. *Extracurriculum* is occasionally found as an alternate adjective form.

F

The sound of *f* occurs spelled *f*, *ff*, *ph*, and *gh* (See *-ough). The words with *ph* go back to Greek words with *phi* (Φ): *philosophy, telephone;* a few have been simplified to *f: fantasy, sulfur.*

Nouns ending in *f* usually have the corresponding voiced sound (v) in the plural: *leaf—leaves, loaf—loaves, wife—wives; beef* has either *beeves* or *beefs.*

fact (the fact that) *The fact that* is very often a circumlocution for which *that* alone would do better:

> He was quite conscious [of the fact] that his visitor had some other reason for coming.

(SEE ch. 10, "Deadwood," p. 284.)

Factual and imaginative writing The fundamental distinction underlying types of writing is that in some types the writer's first responsibility is confining himself to facts (in so far as they can be found) or to reasoning based on facts; in others he has the liberty of fabricating any action or picture or idea that may serve his purpose.

The principal types of factual writing are news stories, interviews, characterizations of people, biography, history, informational articles of all kinds; and, involving reasoning upon facts, reviews, editorials, critical articles on all sorts of subjects, personal essays, and discussions of more general ideas such as demonstration of hypotheses, theories, ideals, philosophical concepts. Whatever other qualities these articles may have, whatever their virtues or faults, they are fundamentally good or bad according as they approach the truth and correspond to some strand of human observation or experience.

The imaginative types, in which the writer's conception is the controlling factor, are poems, plays, short stories, novels.

falls, woods Though plural in form these words are really singular (or collective) in meaning. We speak of *a falls* or *a woods* but ordinarily use them with plural verbs (The falls *are* almost dry in August). In proper names they are frequently used with a singular verb: Niagara Falls *is* receding.

famed When *famed* is used for *famous* or *well known*, it usually suggests a journalese style, or a staccato one (as in *Time*):

> famed eating place   famed Nobel prize winner
> At seven thirty we anchored off the famed yachting center.

It is often a sign of amateur writing to label as *famed* (or as *famous*, for that matter) really well known people.

Familiar English Correction: This passage is too familiar to stand in this paper. Make it somewhat more formal.   *Fam*

Familiar English is the way we speak and write for ourselves—as in diaries and notes for future work—and with or for our friends. We know that we are not going to be judged by our language, as in part we are when we speak or write for strangers, and we can use our natural, easy speech—with contractions, clipped words and abbreviated sentences, allusions to our common background that might puzzle an outsider. For others we have to approach the standards set chiefly by editors for the language used in carrying on public affairs, but for our friends we can use what is really a sort of shirtsleeve—but not necessarily slovenly—English, an especially informal informal sort of usage.

(SEE ch. 2, "Familiar English," p. 45.)

farther—further In formal English some people make a distinction between *farther* and *further*, confining the first to expressions of physical distance and the second to abstract relationships of degree or quantity:

> We went on twenty miles *farther*. He went *farther* than I, but neither of us reached the town.
> He carries that sort of thing *further* than I would. He went *further* into his family history. He got *further* and *further* into debt.

In colloquial and informal English the distinction is not kept and there is a definite tendency for *further* to be used in all senses.

Fascism—fascist Pronounced fash′iz m, fash′ist. *Fascism, Fascist* are capitalized when they refer to Italian politics as we capitalize *Republican* and *Democrat* in this country. When the word refers to a movement in another country in which the party has a different name, it need not be capitalized but often is. When it refers to the general idea of fascist politics, or an unorganized tendency, as in the United States, it is not capitalized.

Fascisti (singular, *Fascista*) has also been anglicized in pronunciation: fə shis′ti; Italian pronunciation fä shē′stē. (Compare *Nazi.)

faze A word which has worked its way from dialect (*feeze*, to disturb) to good American colloquial and informal usage. It means "to daunt or disconcert" and is almost always used negatively (The bawling out didn't faze him). Do not confuse this word with *phase*, meaning "aspect."

fellow Colloquial and informal when used to mean "person"; formal in sense of "associate." Most commonly used in writing as adjective: his fellow sufferers, a fellow feeling ("a similar feeling," or "sympathy").

female Usage now restricts *female* to designations of sex, usually in scientific contexts. This leaves English without a single word for female-human-being-regardless-of-age.

fewer See *less, fewer.

fiancé, fiancée About a century ago the English *betrothed* was replaced by the French word (probably by "society" journalists), and now we are cursed not only with accent marks but with separate forms for the man (fiancé) and the woman (fiancée). Pronunciation for both is fē′ɔn sā′, with a tendency to fē än′sā. The plurals are fiancés, fiancées. In newspapers and much informal writing the accent mark is dropped and probably it will soon disappear generally.

Fig **Figures of speech** Correction: This figure of speech is inappropriate, inconsistent, or threadbare. Revise the passage.

Words can be used in their usual meaning or they can be borrowed to apply to other things. We can talk of music in terms of color, or moral problems in terms of a game, and so on. Fresh and appropriate figures can help a reader see and understand what you are talking about, but careless or tasteless figures detract. They may be threadbare, used as often as "a ribbon of concrete" or "old man Winter." This sentence has one trite and one fresh figure:

> The strident shriek of a siren [Trite:] split the silence and [Fresh:] two searching fingers of light swung around the corner as if feeling for the scene of the disturbance.

They may be strained and unnatural, as in this description of dawn:

> Over yonder hill Apollo thrust the blade of his golden sword, severing the filmy mist that blanketed the paths of old Onondaga.

Or they may be inconsistent ("mixed"), as in this mélange:

> The personnel is subject to a further boiling down to the tune that each man should be selected for the qualities that fit him for the special role he has to play.

Such figures stamp a person as an immature writer.

(The effective use of figures of speech is discussed in ch. 12, "Figurative use of words," p. 344. The most commonly used figures (metaphors, similes, metonymy, irony, exaggeration, and understatement) are described in that chapter. Other figures are discussed in *Index* articles: *Alliteration, *Climax, *Epigrams (and proverbs, paradoxes), *Imitative words and phrases, *Incongruous details (oxymoron), *Negatives, *Personification, *Puns.)

Figures (1, 2, 47) See *Numbers.

Final consonants See *Doubling final consonants.

Final e See Chapter 6, page 164, and *E § 5.

finance, financier Pronunciation of these words is divided:

> Verb: fi nans′, fi′nans
> Noun: fi nans′, fi′nans (the latter conforming to the English *noun and verb stress)
> Noun: fin′ən sir′, fi′nən sir′; occasionally (British) fi nan′si ər

fine A *counter word of general approval, slightly more vigorous than *nice*, but of little value in writing and better omitted:

> Spring football practice has one aim, to weld eleven men into a [fine,] coordinated team.

Fine writing "Fine writing" is generally a term of dispraise, applied to writing that is too pretentious to be appropriate. See Chapter 12, "Words that weaken," page 333, and "Use of figures," page 345. For legitimate elevation of style see *Heightened style.

Finite verbs A finite verb form is one that is limited (Latin *finis*, "end, limit"), that is, that can be limited in *person* (by one of the pronouns or by a subject), or in *time* (by a tense form: *goes, went*), or in *number* (singular or plural). These are contrasted with the "infinite" parts, the infinitives (*go, to go, to have gone*), participles (*going, gone*), and verbal nouns (*going*) which are not limited in person or number. They become "finite" in verb phrases in which the variable characteristics are indicated by an "auxiliary" or function word (he *is* going, he *will* go, he *has* gone).

Finite verbs can be main verbs in clauses and sentences (I *had gone* before he *came*); infinite parts are ordinarily in subordinate constructions (*verbids): Before *coming*, *Gone* with the wind. (But see *Infinitives § 4 and *Participles § 4.)

first See *former—first, latter—last.

First draft The preliminary version of a paper. See Chapter 1, "Writing the first draft," page 15; Chapter 7, "Paragraphs in the making," page 182; and Chapter 13, "The first draft," p. 386.

first rate—first-rate Written with or without a hyphen, and sometimes as one word.

fish The plural is also *fish* (We got only six fish in the whole day's fishing), except in speaking definitely of various species of fish, as in "Most of the income of the island is from these fishes: cod, halibut, and sword."

fix   In formal usage *fix* means to "fasten in place"; in informal usage it means to "repair" or to "put in shape." *Fix* as a noun meaning "predicament" (to be in a fix) is colloquial.

flaunt—flout   *Flaunt* (flônt) to "wave, display boastfully," and *flout* (flout), to "insult, treat with contempt," are sometimes confused. See "Mistaken words," page 327.

folk—folks   Formal English and some local speech use *folk* as the plural, as general usage has *folks*, especially in the sense of "members of a family."

Folklore and folkway are written as one word, *folk dance*, *folk music*, *folk tale* usually as two; *folk song* and *folksong* are both used.

Footnotes   For the use of footnotes in reference papers and for their form, see Chapter 13, "Footnotes," page 388.

for   For distinction between *because* and *for*, see *because.

A comma is usually needed between two coordinate clauses joined by *for;* without it the *for* might be read as a preposition:

He was glad to go, for Mrs. Crane had been especially good to him. (Not: He was glad to go for Mrs. Crane . . .)

for example   The conventional abbreviation for *for example* is *e.g.* (Latin *exempli gratia*). For punctuation see *namely.

Foreign words in English
  1. Anglicizing foreign words.   2. Use of borrowed words.
  3. Handling borrowed words.   4. List of borrowed words.

1. Anglicizing foreign words.   English has always borrowed words and roots freely from other languages and is still borrowing, especially from Greek and French. Most borrowed words that have been used for a long time cannot be told from native English words, but those taken in recently often raise questions. They usually cross the threshold of English with their foreign pronunciation and spelling and perhaps with un-English plurals or other forms. The process of anglicizing brings them more or less in line with English usage, but, if they are used commonly, they may keep some of their foreign quality, like the *i* of *machine*, the silent *s* in *debris*, the *t* where English is tempted to put a *d* in *kindergarten*.

Many loan words are in a transition stage, showing two spellings (*maneuver—manoeuvre*, *role—rôle*, *fiancee—fiancée*); with others we are experimenting with pronunciations, the winner not yet clearly seen (*melee:* mā lā′,mā′lā, mel′ā, and even mē′lē; *zwieback:* tsvē′bäk, tswē′bäk, swī′bak, zwī′bak). Some words that have been in English a considerable time are still changing, especially in stress (*debris:* də brē′—deb′rē) and in consonant sounds (*massage:* mə säzh′—mə säj′). These words show how a rough compromise is worked out between English practice and the original form.

The speed and degree of anglicizing depends on the frequency of use of the word, the circumstances in which it is used, and the people who use it. The attitude of linguists is that if a word proves useful it will assume a natural English form. *Hors d'oeuvre* is a useful word and not difficult to say, but its looks are conspicuously un-English. If menu makers would spell it *orderve*, we could all be happy with it.

Formal writers and conservative editors tend to keep the foreign spellings longer than informal writers and popular editors. If the words come in through the spoken language, like those of the automobile vocabulary, they usually become English or near-English sooner than if they come in by way of literature: we have *chassis* (shas′i or shas′is, sometimes chas′is), *chauffeur* (shō′fər—the spelling lagging), *garage* (gə razh′ or gə räj′—in England gar′ij), *detour* (dē′toor). Words that come in through and remain in literary or "polite" circles change more slowly, in both spelling and pronunciation: *tête-à-tête, faux pas, nouveau riche.*

2. Use of borrowed words. The best reason for using an unnaturalized or partly naturalized word is that it supplies a real lack in English, perhaps says in one word what English would have to use a phrase or sentence to express. *Entrepreneur,* "one who undertakes business, especially assumes commercial risk" is useful since the English *undertaker* has a special meaning of its own. *Beige,* "the color of unbleached wool or cotton," *suede, tableau, protégé* are useful. We have also taken in a number of words and phrases of doubtful usefulness: *entre nous,* when we have *between ourselves,* or *in confidence; affaire du coeur* for *love affair, raison d'être* for *reason for being,* and so on. Most of the words given in the list in § 4 are a definite convenience to users of English, but the general use of foreign words needs to be watched.

Sometimes the gain is in force or tone or suggestion, as *ersatz* is stronger than *substitute,* and *liaison* brings with it either a connotation of social unconventionality or of military activity, depending on the context. *Nouveau riche* brings its suggestion of dispraise, replacing an earlier borrowing, *parvenu,* which in turn displaced the more blunt *upstart*. French words are often used for tone, especially in discussing (and more especially in advertising) women's fashions: *chic, svelte, lapin* (*rabbit* in other places)—and even *sacque*, which doesn't exist in French. A couple of generations ago French was used a good deal for polite social euphemisms, to avoid plain English: *demimonde, fille de joie, femme de chambre, enceinte, accouchement, double entendre.* Now these have generally gone out of use except with the falsely modest, their place once more taken by straight English. Parade of foreign words, a temptation to some who are learning a language or have just returned from abroad, is usually in bad taste, and their use even by people wholly at home with the languages is likely to be inappropriate. Fitness to material, to readers, and to the writer himself (at his natural best) will usually decide whether a foreign word should be used.

3. Handling borrowed words in copy. (a) Italics. Words which have not been completely anglicized are printed in italics in magazines and books and should be underlined in copy. Newspapers do not use italics for such purposes, and their practice of course has tended to lessen the use of italics by others. There are always many words on the borderline which will be found sometimes in italics, sometimes not. Formal writers tend to use more italics; informal, fewer. Consult a recent dictionary for doubtful words—remembering that it will represent conservative usage.

b) Accent and other marks. Words recently taken in from French are usually written with accent marks if they were so written in French. Newspapers do not use accent marks except in some departments like the editorial, art, music, and fashion pages. After they have been used for a time in English, the accents are usually dropped unless they are necessary to indicate pronunciation. *Matinee, melee, role* do not need marks; *café* does. Similarly *cañon* is now usually spelled *canyon*, but: *piñon*. A cedilla shows that a *c* before *a* or *o* is pronounced *s: façade, soupçon.*

In German all nouns are capitalized, and recent or infrequent borrowings from German are capitalized in English, usually if they are still printed in italics. *Anschluss, Realpolitik, Weltanschauung*, but *hinterland, kindergarten, blitzkrieg.*

c) Plurals. English usually brings borrowed words into its own system of conjugation and declension, though some words change slowly, especially words used most in formal writing (**formulae—formulas*, and so on). *Beaus* is now more common than *beaux*, and *tableaus* is gaining on *tableaux*. See *Plurals § 4.

A few French adjectives are kept in both masculine and feminine forms: *blond—blonde, debonair—debonaire.*

d) PRONUNCIATION. For pronunciation of borrowed words, see the examples given in the list below or consult a dictionary.

4. List of borrowed words. This list contains a small selection of loan words in fairly common use. Those in italics would ordinarily be italicized in print. When two forms are separated by a dash, they are both common. A form in brackets is less common than the other. Pronunciations are indicated for words which might offer difficulty. A word marked with an asterisk (*) is separately discussed in an article of its own. For words not given here consult a recent dictionary. See *Pronunciation § 3 for key to symbols.

agenda (ə jen′də)
aid-de-camp—aide-de-camp
  (ād′də kamp′)
*a la
à la carte
*alamode
amateur (am′ə choor—am′ə tyoor
  —am′ə tûr′)
*beau; plu. beaus [beaux]
beige (bāzh)
blitzkrieg
*blond (masc.), blonde (fem.)
bourgeois (boor′zhwä—
  boor zhwä′)
brassiere [brassière]
  (brə zir′)
buffet (boo fā′)
bushido (bōō′shē dō′)
cadet (kə det′)
café (ka fā′—kə fā′)
canyon [cañon]
chassis (shas′i, shas′is [chas′is])
chic (shēk—shik; often chik)
cliché (kli shā′—klē shā′)
coiffure (kwä fyoor′)
communiqué (kə mū′nə kā—
  kə mū′nə kā′)
connoisseur (kon′ə sûr′)
corps; plu. corps (kōr; plu. kōrz)
coup; plu. coups (kōō; plu. kōōz)
coup d'état (kōō dā tä′)
crèche [creche] (krāsh—kresh)
crepe—crêpe—crape (krāp)
crescendo (krə shen′dō—
  krə sen′dō)

crochet, crocheting
  (krō shā′, krō shā′ing)
curé (kyoo rā′)
debris (də brē′—dā′brē—deb′rē)
debut (di bū′—dā′bū—dā bū′)
debutante (deb′yoo tänt—
  deb′yə tant)
dirndl
Don Juan (don joo′ən—
  don hwän′)
Don Quixote (don kwik′sət—
  don kē hō′tē)
dramatis personae
  (dram′ə tis pər sō′nē)
éclair—eclair (ā klar′)
*e. g.
ennui (än′wē)
entrepreneur
entree—entrée
ersatz
et al.
faux pas, plu. *faux pas* (fō′pä′—
  fō′pä′)
fete [fête] (fāt)
*fiancé (masc.), fiancée (fem).
  (fē′ən sā′ [fē′ən sā])
garage (gə räzh′—gə räj′)
hari-kari (hä′ri kä′ri)
hors d'oeuvres (ôr dûrv′)
ibid.
*i. e.
kindergarten
liaison (lē′ə zon′—
  lē′ə zən)
lingerie (lan′zhə rē′—lôn′zhə rē′)

565

liqueur (li kûr'—li kyoor')
massage (mə säzh'—mə säj')
matériel—materiel
matinee (mat ə nā'—mat'ə nā)
mayonnaise
melee (mā lā'—mā'lā—mel'ā—
mē'lē)
menu (mā'nŭ—men'ŭ; French
pronunciation not current)
milieu (mē lyû')
monsieur (mə syû'); plu. messieurs—messrs. (mes'ərz—mə-
syû')
moujik—muzhik (moo zhik')
*naive [naïve]—naif sometimes
used
negligee [négligé] (neg'lə zhā'—
neg'lə zhā')
nouveau riche—nouveau riche
(noo vō rēsh') plural: nouveaux
riches (noo vō rēsh')
obbligato—obligato
papier mâché (pā'pər mə shā')
passé (pa sā'—pas'ā)
précis (prā sē'—prā'sē)
première—premiere (pri mir'—
prə myer')
protégé (masc.), protégée (fem.)
(prō'tə zhā)
pronto
quasi (kwā'sī—kwā'zī [kwä'si]
questionnaire [questionary]
(kwes'chən ār')

ragout (ra goo')
rapport (ra pōrt')
en rapport (än rä pōr'—
än rä pōr')
Realpolitik (rā äl'pō li tēk')
rendezvous (rän'də voo),
plural: rendezvous
(rän'də vooz)
repertoire (rep'ər twär
[rep'ər twôr])—repertory
résumé (rez'ū mā—rez'u mā')
revue (ri vū')
ricochet (rik ə shā'—rik ə shet')
*role [rôle]
salon (sə lon')—*salon* (sä lôɴ')
slalom (slä'lōm)
status quo (stā'təs kwō—stat'əs-
kwō)
stein (stīn)
suède—suede (swād)
svelte (svelt)
tableau (tab'lō—tab lō'), plural
tableaux—tableaus (tab lōz')
tête-à-tête (tāt'ə tāt'); accents being dropped in informal usage
via (vī'ə)
viz. (that is)
vs.—vs (vûrsəs)
Weltanschauung
(velt'än'shou'oong)
Weltschmertz (velt'shmerts')
zwieback (tswē'bäk—tsvē'bäk—
[swī'bak—zwī'bak])

(SEE *English language, *Latin and English, *Origin of words, *Plurals § 4. REF-
ERENCES: Kenyon and Knott, § 122; Brander Matthews, "The Englishing of French
Words," Society for Pure English *Tracts*, 1920, v, 3-20; T. R. Palfrey, "The Contribution of Foreign Language Study to Mastery of the Vernacular," *Modern Language Journal*, 1941, pp. 550-57.)

Form of manuscript See Chapter 1, "Preparing the manuscript,"
page 20.

Formal correspondence See *Social correspondence.

Form   **Formal English** Correction: The word or passage marked is too
formal for the subject or for the style of the rest of the paper.
Revise, making it more informal.

Formal English is the level of usage characteristic of people who
work a good deal with books, in general of members of the various
professions. It is appropriate for discussions of ideas, for scientific

and scholarly writing, for addresses to audiences of some education, for literary works that are intended for a somewhat restricted reading public. Formal English is not so appropriate for day to day speaking and writing, for accounts of personal experience, casual comment, and other sorts of writing intended for the general reading public.

(For discussion and examples, see ch. 2, "Formal English," p. 48 and for its appropriateness, see ch. 3, p. 69. See also *Heightened style.)

former—first, latter—last *Former* and *latter* refer to a group of only two units:

> The mountain and the squirrel
> Had a quarrel,
> And the former called the latter, "little prig";
> RALPH WALDO EMERSON, *Fable*

First, last refer to items in a series, usually of more than two:

> The first president had set up a very informal organization.
> His last act was to advise his family on their future.

Latest refers to a series that is still continuing (the latest fashions). *Last* refers either to the final item of a completed series (their last attempt was successful) or to the most recent item of a continuing series (the last election).

Forms of discourse For the last hundred years or so it has been conventional to divide writing into "four forms of discourse"— narration, description, exposition, and argument. This division allows concentration on certain traits of material, organization, and style peculiar to each type. It is now less used than formerly because the types are rarely found in a pure state—description contributes to all, notably to narration, and so on—and a person does not think of himself as writing one of these forms but rather a particular sort of article or type of literature.

This book divides writing into two broad types, factual writing (biography, history, informational and critical articles and books of all sorts) and imaginative writing (poems, plays, short stories, novels).

(SEE *Factual and imaginative writing.)

formula Plural *formulas* or *formulae*, the former the more common.

Formulas Every language has some phrases that have become fixed by long usage in certain situations: *Once upon a time, Ladies and gentlemen, Good morning, How are you? Yours truly.* Occasionally fresh substitutes can be found for these but more often the attempt merely calls attention to itself. Such phrases, though stereotyped, are too useful to be called trite, and they are not, as most trite expressions are, substitutes for some simpler locution. They should be used without apology and without embarrassment whenever they are needed.

Fractions Fractions are written in figures when they are attached to other figures ($72\frac{3}{4}$), or are in a series that is being written in figures ($\frac{1}{2}$, $\frac{2}{3}$, 1, 2, 4), or are in tables or reference matter. Usually in consecutive writing they are written in words. Hyphens may be used between the numerator and denominator if neither part itself contains a hyphen, but they are less used than formerly and are not used at all when the numerator has the value of an adjective (as in "He sold one half and kept the other").

> seven tenths [seven-tenths]   eight twenty-sevenths
> twenty-nine fortieths—twenty nine fortieths

Decimals are increasingly used in place of fractions in expository writing, since they are more flexible and may be more accurate. They are always written in figures: .7   .42   3.14159
(SEE *Numbers.)

Frag **Fragmentary sentence** Correction: **The construction marked is not a complete sentence. Revise by completing its form, by joining to a neighboring sentence, or by rewriting the passage.**

A fragmentary sentence is a sentence part carelessly or ineffectively punctuated as a whole sentence. By their form, phrases and subordinate clauses suggest dependence on another construction and editors usually see to it that they do not stand as sentences. Ordinarily one should be joined to the preceding or following sentence or made into an independent sentence. Since they are almost always careless in college writing, they are one of the most serious errors and should be avoided.

Three common types with suggested revision follow:

Fragmentary sentence	*Revised*
Since 1939 we had been walking slowly in the direction of war. [Phrase:] Step by step until finally there was no other alternative but to declare war.	Since 1939 we had been walking slowly in the direction of war, step by step, until finally there was no other alternative but to declare war.
He talked for fifty minutes without taking his eyes off his notes. [Participial phrase:] Apparently not noticing that half the class was asleep.	He talked for fifty minutes without taking his eyes off his notes. Apparently he did not notice that half the class was asleep.

| The first six books I looked for couldn't be taken out of the library. [Subordinate clause:] Because they were on reserve for an advanced history course. | The first six books I looked for couldn't be taken out of the library because they were on reserve for an advanced history course. |

(For further discussion and other examples of fragmentary sentences, see ch. 9, "Fragmentary sentences," p. 262. See also *Dependent clause, *Phrases.)

French words   See *Foreign words in English.

freshman, freshmen   These words are pronounced alike (fresh′ mən), so that their spelling is often confused, not so often when they are used as nouns (a freshman, forty freshmen) as when *freshman* is used as an adjective (freshman class, freshman spirit). *Freshmen* should never stand before a noun in this construction.

It is not usually necessary to capitalize *freshman* (or *sophomore, junior, senior*) but courtesy or emphasis often makes a capital appropriate, and very often one is used when speaking of the Freshman Class, the Junior Class, as a definite organization.

-ful, full   When the adjective *full* is used as a suffix to nouns of measure (*basketful, spoonful*) or of feeling or quality (*peaceful, sorrowful, soulful*) it has only one *l*.

The plural of nouns ending in *-ful* is usually made with *-s*: *spoonfuls, basketfuls* (or *basketsful*). See *spoonful, spoonfuls.

Function words   **1.** Some words contribute relatively little to the meaning of a statement, serving rather to indicate relationships, to point out grammatical functions. Some such words are:

a) Prepositions, which join nouns to other words in a construction; the *of* in the phrase form of the genitive (of the man) is conspicuously a function word.

b) Conjunctions, which show the relation between clauses.

c) Auxiliary verbs when they indicate time, person, number, of a verb (*is* asking, *has* asked, *did* he ask) without otherwise modifying meaning. Sometimes the various "modal auxiliaries" (*can, may, might, should* . . .) are included, but since they contribute meaning as well as grammatical facts they are not regarded as function words in this book.

d) Relative pronouns, which principally refer from one clause to a preceding.

e) Some adverbs and adjectives, most conspicuously *more* and *most* in comparisons of adjectives and adverbs (more handsome, most handsome).

569

2. Stylistic qualities of function words. Different levels of usage have some characteristic habits in the use of function words. Formal style, for instance, tends to keep relative pronouns, while colloquial and informal style is likely to omit them.

> Informal: Is there such a thing as *modern* prose, with characteristics the older prose does not possess?—BONAMY DOBRÉE, *Modern Prose Style*, p. 210
> Formal: Is there such a thing as *modern* prose, with characteristics [that] the older prose does not possess?

The more elaborate sentences of formal English tend to make appropriate heavier connectives, such as *conjunctive adverbs (however, accordingly . . .)*; informal style tends to rely more on coordinating conjunctions (*but, for, and . . .*) and subordinating conjunctions (*although, because, since . . .*).

Colloquial English shows a good many compound or group prepositions, for many of which formal English would use a single preposition: *in back of (behind); in regard to (about)*. Too many of these long connectives tend to give a rather weak movement to a sentence and a rhythm without many strong stresses. In rapid speech they are passed over easily but they sometimes become conspicuous in writing.

Particular points about the use of function words are made in various articles dealing with specific words or types of words; this article merely suggests that they are worth watching for both linguistic and stylistic reasons.

(REFERENCE: Fries, chs. 7-9.)

Fundamentals The selection of what can be regarded as fundamentals in estimating a piece of writing depends on judgment, and judgments vary. In this book the fundamentals are taken to be the following, the most important first:

1) *The material presented is the most fundamental factor* and deserves most consideration in the process of writing and most weight in criticizing and evaluating a piece of writing. Nothing can take the place of important and interesting material, though its values can be increased or diminished by the treatment.

2) *The method and attitude of the writer* is of next importance. He may use too few details or too many, he may select them according to an intelligent or an unwise or biased principle, he may have an exaggerated idea of the importance of his subject, or approach it with too much or too little sentiment, reverence, humor, realism, he may or may not direct his statements to readers.

3) *The plan* of an article, *the plot* of a story are important, since in part through them the writer guides the reader to see his sense of the matter. Too slow a beginning, too trivial an end are serious faults, as is lack of relation shown between parts.

4) Finally a piece of writing is affected by the *mechanics and style* of the writer, which may either hinder the reader or increase his satisfaction. Poor material presentably written has no future, but worth while material even if poorly written can with sufficient work be made presentable.

We consciously or unconsciously make some such balancing of qualities in deciding what we think of what we read. Realizing the relative worth of these qualities makes it easier for student and teacher to understand each other's judgments.

funny   In formal English *funny* means only "comical," "laughable"; in informal and colloquial English it means also (and almost instead) "odd": "That's funny. I thought he did."

further   See *farther—further.

Future tense, future perfect tense   See *shall—will; *Tenses of verbs.

G, like *c*, spells a "hard" and a "soft" sound. The hard sound is more common than the soft.

1. 'Hard g' (g). G is hard before *a, o,* and *u* (except in the British *gaol* [*jail*]): *garrulous, gong, gutter;* when doubled: *doggerel, noggin, toboggan;* at the ends of words: *beg, dig, fig;* it is hard, exceptionally, in *get,* and frequently before *i: begin, gill* (of a fish), *gig;* and it is hard before another consonant in the same syllable: *togs.*

Gh spells hard g, properly in *ghetto,* uselessly in *aghast* and *ghost.* The g would be hard anyway before the *a* and *o.*

Gu, taken from French, spells hard g: *guard, guess, guide, guernsey.*

2. 'Soft g' (j) is found typically before *e* and *i: gem, gentleman, genus, gill* (the measure), *gibbet, gin.* It is often spelled *ge* or *dge: age* (āj), *edge* (ej), *fudge* (fuj).

3. G is sometimes pronounced *zh,* chiefly in partly anglicized words from French: *garage, massage, mirage.* These words tend to have soft *g* after they have been in English a long time (*carriage, marriage*): *garage* is often gə räj' (in England, gar'ij); *massage* is tending toward mə säj'.

4. 'Silent g.' Initial *g* is silent in *gnaw, gnat, gnome, gnu . . .* and *g* is often silent before *m* or *n: diaphragm, sign*. It becomes sounded in some derivatives of this latter type of word: *signal*.

5. 'Dropping g's.' In formal usage the present participle ends in the consonant sound that is spelled *ng;* in vulgate and in much colloquial English, present participles are ended in *n: singin', laughin'.* This is usually referred to as "dropping *g*'s," though actually there is no *g* sound involved but two different nasal consonants. The form in *n* is the older. Originally the present participle ended in *-and* and later in *-en* or *-in,* and this has always been the form for the majority of speakers of English. In the speech of London and vicinity, which became the basis of written English, the present participle was confused with the verbal noun, ending in *-ung.* Now everyone *writes* the participle with *-ing* but many continue the old pronunciation with *-in.*

(SEE Milton Ellis, *English Journal*, 1937, 26:753. Compare *ng.)

Gathering material   See Chapter 1, "Gathering material," page 11, and for gathering material for a research paper, Chapter 13, pages 369-382.

Gender   Gender is the indication in language of sex or sexlessness. Many languages have special endings for masculine, feminine, and neuter nouns and for adjectives modifying them, but English abandoned this system several hundred years ago. Now, except in pronouns and a few nouns with endings such as *-ess, -us, -a, -or, -ix, -e, -eur, -euse* (*actress, mistress, alumnus, alumna, actor, aviator, aviatrix, administratrix, blonde, comedienne, masseur, masseuse*) gender is indicated only by the meaning of a word: *man—woman, nephew—niece, rooster—hen.* Compounds, partly to show gender, partly for emphasis, are common and expressive: *she-witch, he-bear, boy friend, girl friend.* Nouns referring to inanimate objects are neuter. For most English words gender is identifiable only by the choice of pronoun (*he, she, it*) that would be used to refer to them —and is consequently not a very important grammatical category:

> The speaker hesitated, choosing *his* next words deliberately.
> The novelist has presented *her* chief character effectively.

In formal, literary English there is a weak sort of personification (or animation) in which the sun or moon or a ship or almost any object may be referred to as *he* (The sun sent forth his cheering beams) or more often as *she* (The brig made her way sturdily through the mountainous waves). In colloquial and vulgate usage this plays a still greater part. Pronouns are frequently used, especially if intimacy or affection is involved: a car or a college or a country or any object may be a *she*.

We need a pronoun to represent either-he-or-she. Referring to a baby or an animal of unknown sex, *it* is the usual solution; otherwise *he*. See *he-or-she, *blond, blonde, *naive—naïve.

General English Words, forms, constructions that are found in all levels of usage. See Chapter 2, "General English and varieties of English," page 35.

Generalizations For discussion as kind of paragraph material, see Chapter 7, "Opinions and generalizations," page 174.

Genitive case Correction: Correct the form of the genitive case *Gen* marked. (Usually this means using an apostrophe.)

1. The genitive (or possessive) case in English is formed in three ways:

a) THE *s*-GENITIVE. *'s* is the spelling of the genitive case of all nouns in which the case is pronounced with an added sound (s or z) and the indefinite pronouns (*anyone, everybody* . . .):

boy's	horse's	one's	King of England's
men's	brother-in-law's	somebody's	

An apostrophe alone may be added to words that already end in an *s*, *sh*, or *z* sound, as in regularly made plurals in *s:*

horses'	Moses'	*Jones' (singular)
Joneses' (plural)	coaches'	conscience' (for conscience' sake)

Words of one syllable ending in these sounds seem increasingly to have *'s*, pronounced as an added syllable:

Charles' (chärlz)—Charles's (chärl′zəz)   coach's (kōch′əz)
fish's (fish′əz)   Zeus' (zōos)—Zeus's (zōos′əz)

The *s*-genitive stands before the noun it limits (the doctor's first case), but it may be in the predicate position with no noun expressed (The criticism is Smith's).

When two coordinate nouns are in the genitive, in informal usage the sign of the case is added only to the last one:

Fred and Bert's first attempt. (Formal: Fred's and Bert's)
He had never thought of his wife and children's future.
But: Mary's and Tom's bicycles.

b) THE *of*-GENITIVE: He had never known the love of a child (= a child's love); the plays of Shakespeare.

The *of*-genitive always stands after the noun it limits: the leaves of the tree (vs. the tree's leaves).

The *of*-genitive is rather more common with names of inanimate objects than the *s*-genitive is, but both are used; the *s*-genitive is the more common form with names of people, though both are used:

the car's rattles	the rattles of the car
a stone's throw	the flowers of the field
a day's work	the work of a lifetime
Doctor Clark's house	the house of Doctor Clark

In most instances sound—euphony and rhythm—of the phrase decides whether the *s*- or *of*-genitive is used. The *of*-form is longer, often fits into sonorous and emotional phrases (at the home of Doctor Clark), and allows a more characteristic English rhythm than the compact *s*-genitive.

There is also a possible difference of meaning between the two forms. "Miss Rutherford's picture" would usually mean a picture belonging to Miss R., though it might mean a picture of Miss R. "A picture of Miss Rutherford" can mean only that Miss R. is represented in the picture.

c) DOUBLE GENITIVE. Using both the *s*- and *of*-genitives together is an English idiom of long and respectable standing. It is especially common in locutions beginning with *that* or *this* and usually has a colloquial flavor:

that boy of Henry's, friends of my father's, these hobbies of Miss Filene's

d) GENITIVE OF THE PERSONAL PRONOUNS. The personal and relative pronouns have genitive forms without an apostrophe:

my   your   his   her   its   our   their   whose

It is as important not to put apostrophes in these pronouns (and in the forms used without nouns: *ours, yours, theirs, hers*) as it is to put one in a noun in the genitive. See *Pronouns § 1, *its, *which, *who.

2. Uses of the genitive. The most common function of the genitive is to indicate possession:

the professor's house   my son   Bert's wife

The genitive also indicates a number of other relationships:

Description: a man's job   children's toys   suit of wool
Doer of an act ("Subjective genitive"): the wind's force   the force of

the wind   Sinclair Lewis' second novel   with the dean's permission   with the permission of the dean (The subjective genitive usual with gerunds:) The doctor's coming relieved the strain. (See *Gerund.)

Recipient of an act ("Objective genitive"): the policeman's murderer the murderer of the policeman   the bill's defeat

Adverb: He drops in of an evening.

(SEE ch. 4, "Genitives," p. 97, and "Genitive forms," p. 99. More details of these and other genitive relations will be found in the large grammars. REFERENCES: Curme, *Parts of Speech*, pp. 133-36, *Syntax*, pp. 70-88; Fries, pp. 72-88.)

gentleman See *man, woman.

Gerund Correction: Make the construction with this gerund *Ger* idiomatic.

1. Form and use.   2. Subject of a gerund.   3. Phrases with gerunds.   4. Without 'the.'   5. Idioms with gerunds.

1. Form and use. A *gerund*, or *verbal noun*, is the form of the verb ending in *-ing* when used as a noun. It has the same form as the present participle but differs in use:

Gerund: *Running* a hotel appealed to him.
Participle: *Running* around the corner, he bumped into a cop. (*Running* modifies *he*.)
Broncho Bill Schindler started the ball *rolling* [participle, modifying *ball*] by *crashing* [gerund] into the heavy guard rail.

A gerund may take an object (as in *running a hotel*) or a complement (*being a hero*), and it may serve in any of the functions of a noun:

Subject: *Looking* for an apartment always fascinated her.
Object: He taught *dancing*.
Predicate noun: Seeing is *believing*.
Adjective use: a *fishing* boat (a boat for fishing, not a boat that fishes), *boiling* point, a *living* wage.

When not in one of these constructions a gerund is related to the rest of the sentence by a preposition (§ 3).

Gerunds may be modified by adjectives when the noun function is uppermost, or by adverbs when the verb function is emphasized:

Modified by adjective: *Good boxing* is first rate entertainment.
Modified by adverb: *Playing well* was his great pride.

(SEE ch. 4, "Infinitives, participles, gerunds," p. 102.)

2. Subject of a gerund. The subject of a gerund is sometimes in the genitive and sometimes in the accusative case. In formal writing the genitive is more common, in informal writing, the accusative of a pronoun or the common form of the noun.

a) When the subject is a personal pronoun or a word standing for a person, it is usually in the genitive:

> *His coming* was all that she looked forward to.
> She looked forward to *Bob's coming.*

b) If the subject is a plural noun, it is likely to be in the common form:

> I don't approve of *men drinking.*
> I don't approve of *students coming and going* as they like.
> With a pronoun: I don't approve of *them drinking,* or I don't approve of *their drinking.*

c) If the subject is abstract or the name of an inanimate object, it is usually in the common form:

> It was a case of *imagination getting* out of control.
> The *roof* [or *roof's*] *falling in* was only the first disaster.

d) When the subject is modified by other words, it is the common form:

> In spite of the *plan* of the committee *being voted down* no one could offer a better one.
> The principal's *contract running out* gave them an excuse for letting him go.

e) When the subject is stressed, it is usually in the accusative, even if it is a pronoun:

> Who would have thought of *him* [stressed] *getting* the prize?
> Have you heard about *Gertrude* [stressed] *getting* a job?

(See ch. 4, "Gerunds," p. 108.)

3. Phrases with gerunds. Gerunds are frequently used in phrases that have the value and function of subordinate clauses (see *Verbids):

> *In coming to an agreement,* they had compromised on all points.
> It's the best thing *for coughing at night.*

The gerund phrase should relate to the word it is intended to:

> Misrelated: *In coming to an agreement,* a compromise had to be voted. (The compromise did not come to the agreement, but *they* or some other word meaning the voters.)
> Misrelated: *After reading sixteen books,* the subject is still a blank to me.
> Accurate: *After reading sixteen books,* I am still blank about the subject.

4. Without 'the.' In current style there is a tendency to use gerunds without *the* and with a direct object rather than an *of* phrase. This emphasizes the verbal phase of the word and makes for economy and force.

> His chief amusement is *telling jokes* on the President. (Rather than: His chief amusement is *the telling of jokes* on the President.)
> In *revising the first draft,* a writer can check all the spellings. (Rather than: In *the revising of the first draft.*)

5. Idioms with gerunds. Many words are followed by gerunds, others with infinitives. For example:

Gerunds	Infinitives
cannot help *doing*	compelled *to do*
capable *of painting*	able *to paint*
the habit *of giving*	the tendency *to give*
an idea *of selling*	a wish *to sell*
his object *in doing*	obligation *to pay*

(SEE ch. 4, "Infinitive or gerund," p. 115. COMPARE *Participles, *Infinitives. REFERENCE: Curme, *Syntax,* ch. 24.)

get, got

1. Forms. 2. Have got. 3. 'Get' in idioms. 4. 'Get' as a passive auxiliary.

1. Forms: Principal parts: *get, got, got* or *gotten:*

> I am getting a new racket. I got six inside an hour.
> I had already got [gotten] mine.
> Rebel though I was, I had got the religion of scholarship and science.—
> LINCOLN STEFFENS, *Autobiography,* p. 127

Gotten was brought to America by the colonists of the seventeenth century, when it was the usual English form, and has remained in general American usage ever since, while in England the form has given way to *got.* Today both forms are used by Americans as the past participle, the choice between them depending largely on the emphasis and rhythm of the particular sentence and on the user's speech habits. *Gotten* is probably the more common.

> He could have [*gotten* or *got*] here by now.
> In the past I have [*gotten* or *got*] a good meal here.

2. Have got. *Got* (and not *gotten*) is used as a colloquial way of intensifying *have* in the sense of possess or of being obligated (Have you got a pencil?—I've got to study now). It is true that the *have* alone could carry the meaning, but it is unemphatic, especially when contracted, and anyway is so frequently used as a mere auxiliary of tense that we are not accustomed to feeling it as a verb of full meaning. Consequently the *got* has at least a colloquial advantage. Some formal writers avoid it, but the idiom is in general use and is appropriate in any but the most formal situations.

3. 'Get' in idioms. *Get* is one of the most popular verbs in idiomatic phrases, in most of which it doesn't have its original meaning shown in the sentences under § 1, but is a relatively colorless linking verb. Most of these idioms are colloquial and some are slang:

get cold	get sick	get tired	get scared
get going	get to go	get in touch with	get supper
get left	get on my nerves	get away with	get along with
get me?	get it across	get together	

"But I got to," she cried. "I just have to talk to somebody. I didn't go home. I got worried, awful scared. . . ."—Arthur Somers Roche, *Shadow of Doubt*, p. 93

4. 'Get' as a passive auxiliary. *Get* is increasingly used as an informal emphatic passive auxiliary:

He got thrown out inside of an hour. Our house is getting painted.
We all got punished on Friday.

(See Adelaide C. Bartlett, *College English*, 1949, 10:280-82; Curme, *Parts of Speech*, p. 218; Pooley, pp. 148-51.)

ghost writer A person who writes for another, the latter usually signing the work and taking the credit for it.

Given names Ordinarily either spell out or use the initial of given names (rather than such abbreviations as *Chas.*, *Thos.*, *Wm.*):

F. T. Graves	or	Frederick T. Graves
T. W. Lane	or	Thomas W. Lane

gladiolus A revealing example of *divided usage. The singular is pronounced glad i ō′ləs or glə dī′ə ləs, and, especially among florists, *gladiola*, glad i ō′lə; the plural glad i ō′lī, glə dī′o lī, glad i ō′ləs iz, and (of *gladiola*), glad i ō′ləz. Gla dī′o lus is the closest to the word's Latin origin and is usual with botanists for the name of the genus. The clips *glad* or *glads* are a way out of the confusion.

go 1. *Go* is a useful little word, especially as a *linking verb in a number of idioms, most of them colloquial:

go blind	go on! (= I don't believe you!)
go back on	go in for

2. *Go and* is a colloquial form of emphasis: Go and try it yourself (no actual movement meant); She went and shot the bear herself. These are primarily oral expressions but they would be appropriate in some informal writing.

3. *Going on* in stating ages (seven, going on eight) is a colloquial and familiar idiom—more vigorous than the formal "between seven and eight."

Gobbledygook A suggestive label for an abuse of formal English, characteristic of some government and business communications, marked by over heavy (abstract) words and confusing, pseudo-legal sentences. What relatively simple statement is being made in this sample?

> By encouraging and maintaining a reciprocal interest between the prime contractor and his subcontractors in the business matter of fulfilling the obligations of the prime contract, contractual requirements, particularly inspection, can be greatly assisted in furnishing the consignee with the required information that material has received inspection in accordance with the contract.

good—well *Good* is an adjective; *well* is either an adjective or an adverb: I feel *good* and I feel *well* (adjectives) are both usual but have different connotations (*good* implying actual bodily sensation, *well* referring merely to a state, "not ill").

In vulgate usage *well* is rarely used, *good* taking its place ("He rowed good" for "He rowed well"). Avoid this usage.

good-by—good-bye Both are in use—and the hyphen is dropping out in informal use: *goodbye, goodby.*

Good English Good English is language that is effective for a particular communication, that is appropriate to the subject and situation, to the listener or reader, and to the speaker or writer. (See Chapter 3, Good English.)

government Kenyon and Knott say: "No competent observer can doubt the prevalence of [guv′ər mənt, guv′ə mənt] among the leading statesmen of US and England, even in formal public address." This general pronunciation leads us sometimes to omit the *n* in spelling, but *government* is the only standard written form.

grade school—graded school *Graded school* is the formal word but *grade school* is much more common, and always appropriate.

graduate The idiom *to be graduated from* an institution has generally gone out of use except in formal and somewhat archaic writing, and has been replaced by *graduated from:*

He graduated from Yale in 1902.

Grammar *Grammar* is a word of various applications. It is used to mean the actual form of a language, "the English way of saying things." It is also used to apply to a systematic description of the ways of language or of a language. Sometimes it is used to mean practically the whole of linguistic science; sometimes it includes only a few arbitrarily selected topics. Usually it includes at least the study of *the forms of words, the parts of speech, syntax* (constructions), and frequently *the derivation of words* and *pronunciation.* A particular "grammar" is a selection of the facts of language that suits the writer's purpose. Only the grammars in several volumes, like those of Jespersen and of Curme, approach anything like a complete description of English.

   1. Scientific grammar. There are three types of scientific grammatical study:

   a) DESCRIPTIVE GRAMMAR aims to present the facts of a particular language, gathered from systematic observation of speaking and writing, describing the forms of words, spellings, pronunciations, constructions in actual use, without attempting to guide the language habits of speakers and writers—though obviously serving as the basis for such guidance.

   b) COMPARATIVE GRAMMAR studies the forms and constructions of a set of related languages, as Greek, Latin, German, English, and the other Indo-European languages, to show their earlier history.

   c) HISTORICAL GRAMMAR studies the evolution of the words and syntax of a language, usually explaining present forms and usage in the light of the past.

   Sometimes *philosophical grammar* is spoken of, as in Jespersen's title *The Philosophy of Grammar.* It means a presentation of general principles, equivalent to *linguistic theory.*

   2. Prescriptive grammar. Besides these types of scientific grammar we also speak of *prescriptive* or *normative grammar.* A prescriptive grammar is a body of rules presented as guides to expression, statements of how, in the belief of the writer, people should speak and write. Many English grammars of this type, represented principally by textbooks prepared for the use of students, are now in disrepute because they are far out of touch with scientific grammar and with actual usage. Too many school grammars represent either older usage or traditional rules that are not consistently followed and some that have never been followed by users of English. Typically they present formal English as though it was the only English and definitely discourage informal and colloquial usage, which occupy the center stage in the scientific grammars.

One unfortunate result of prescriptive grammar is that the teaching of formal English has seemed so unreal to students that they, unable to separate the useful from the useless advice, have paid almost no attention at all to their teaching. If they talked as their textbooks said they should, they would be laughed at; consequently they have usually continued their natural colloquial or even vulgate speech.

Although the usage recommended in schools will probably always be a little behind that being practiced by actual writers, school grammar is now gradually getting away from traditional prescriptive grammar and is coming closer in line with the picture of actual usage presented by scientific grammars.

3. Grammatical terms. Many people steadfastly refuse to learn the technical terms of grammar. Students who gaily toss about *schizophrenic, marginal utility, Hanseatic League, dicotyledonous,* or *trinitrotoluene* will not learn the pronunciation and meaning of *parataxis, predicate adjective, subjunctive, metonymy,* or even *apostrophe* or *agreement*—and some teachers of the subject try to work without naming exactly what they are talking about. Many of the words are a bit difficult—Greek or Latin names that have been taken into the language—but they are not nearly so difficult as the vocabulary of psychology or chemistry. It is true that grammatical nomenclature has been in a sorry way and that commissions in both England and the United States have not been able to standardize names for many of the facts of our language, but there is a large and useful vocabulary for discussing language and style, a vocabulary that is absolutely necessary if we are to discuss in any detail our own and others' writing.

This book uses a good many of these terms, without apology, though when there is a choice of name usually the simpler and more suggestive has been taken. It is only good sense to gain control of the words that name common facts of usage and style.

(SEE ch. 3, especially "Personal, editorial, puristic standards," p. 74. *Linguistics; *Latin and English § 3. REFERENCES: The works in the bibliography at the beginning of this *Guide-Index*, specifically Fries and Pooley, discuss many of the particular rules of prescriptive grammar besides offering their own observation of usage; see especially Fries, chs. 1, 2, 11, and Ballard, who shows a similar attack on traditional grammar in England.)

Graphs See *Diagrams, graphs, etc.

gray is much more common spelling than *grey,* but both are used.

Greek alphabet The first college societies, usually for both social and intellectual aims, were formed when Greek was a prominent subject in the course of study. Many of them had Greek names or Greek mottoes and referred to themselves by the abbreviations for these words: Phi Beta Kappa (ΦΒΚ) for Φιλοσοφία Βίου Κυβερνήτης ("Philosophy is the guide of life"). Their descendant societies, although very few of their members know the Greek language, are still "Greek letter societies."

Recent scientists have sometimes used Greek letters to name members of a series, as *alpha-, beta-, gamma-rays.*

Neither the classical nor the English names of these letters are used consistently in fraternity names or other uses of Greek letters in English. Even in the pronunciation of *Phi Beta Kappa* the two systems are mixed: fī (English) bā′tə (classical) kap′ə (English). This worries a few purists, but usage is the guide in language and the prevalent pronunciation should be followed. The accompanying table may be helpful.

The Greek Alphabet

Greek Letters		English	Name	Pronunciation of the Name	
Capital	*Small*			*Classical*	*English*
Α	α	a	alpha	älfa (alfa)	†al′fə
Β	β	b	beta	†bāta²	bē′tə
Γ	γ	g	gamma	gäma (gama)	†gam′ə
Δ	δ	d	delta	delta	del′tə
Ε	ε	e	epsilon	epsilon	ep′sə lon
Ζ	ζ	z (dz)	zeta	†zāta	zē′tə
Η	η	a (ā)	eta	†āta	ē′tə
Θ	θ	th (thin)	theta	†thāta	thē′tə
Ι	ι	ē	iota	ēōta	†ī ō′tə
Κ	κ	k	kappa	käpa	†kap′ə
Λ	λ	l	lambda	lämda	†lam′də
Μ	μ	m	mu	mōō	†mū
Ν	ν	n	nu	nōō	†nū
Ξ	ξ	x (ks)	xi	ksē	†zī, sī
Ο	ο	o	omicron	ōmikron	om′ə kron
Π	π	p	pi	pē	†pī
Ρ	ρ	r	rho	rō	rō
Σ	σ s¹	s	sigma	sigma	sig′mə
Τ	τ	t	tau	tou	†tô
Υ	υ	y (u)	upsilon	ōōpsilon	†ŭp′sə lon, up′sə lon
Φ	φ	f (ph)	phi	fē	†fī
Χ	χ	ch	chi	chē (Ger. ch)	†kī
Ψ	ψ	ps	psi	psē	†sī
Ω	ω	ō	omega	omäga	ō meg′ə, ō mē′gə

¹ *s* is used at the end of a word, elsewhere σ.

² † marks pronunciation more frequently used.

grill—grille The cooking device and the eating place are spelled *grill* (*grille* only in attempts at a fancy name). The decorative iron work is spelled either *grille* or *grill*.

Group words In English many groups of two or more words (that is, phrases) function as though they were single words. *High school* is not the noun *school* modified by the adjective *high* so much as a noun in its own right; it might well be spelled as a single word (and sometimes is). Many of our verbs are made up of a verb plus an adverb: *close up, hold off, look into* (see *Verb-adverb combinations); many prepositions are phrases: *according to, in opposition to, by means of.*

Other typical group words are:

Nouns: hay fever   back door   holding company   home run   safety razor   baby blue   school year   sacrifice hit   express train
Verbs: dig in   back water   back step (military)   flare up   follow through   follow up   show up   blow up
Prepositions: in spite of   in consequence of   previous to   due to

"In such cases," Professor Krapp says, "it is contrary to the idiom of the language to try to analyze the groups into their constituent parts so as to give every word, standing alone, a clearly defined structural value" (*Modern English*, p. 315). Consequently in this book we ignore the superficial difference between a part of speech that is one word and one that is a group of words. "Noun" or "verb" or "preposition" refers both to single words and to *group words* functioning as noun or verb or preposition.

(REFERENCES: Curme, *Syntax*, ch. 30; Krapp, pp. 313-16 [where he calls such phrases "function groups"]).

guess See *calculate, guess, reckon.

gypsy—gipsy Spelling is divided, partly because the odd appearance of the two *y*'s is shifting the spelling to *gipsy*. Capitalize as the name of a specific people and use small letter for the sense merely of "wanderer" (the more common use). Compare *pigmy—pygmy*.

H

1. The *h* (h) sound always occurs at the beginning of syllables: *harsh, heel, high, horrible, ahead.*

2. *H* is likely to be silent at the beginning of unstressed syllables: *forehead* (for'id), *behind* (when spoken rapidly in unstressed part of phrase, bi īnd′), *he, his, her*, etc., when lightly spoken (Give it to *him′* vs. *Give′* it to [h]im).

H is silent in *rh* words—*rhetoric, rhyme, rhythm.*

In many words from French the *h* was formerly not pronounced: *habit, history, hotel* . . . but now is except in *heir, honest, honor, hour.* So long as the *h* was not pronounced, *an* was used before these words and it is still by some people in the forms in which the stress is not on the first syllable: *an historical work, an habitual error,* though *a* is now much more common. See *a, an.

In words like *huge* and *humor* many people drop the *h,* leaving ūj and ū′mər.

(COMPARE *wh.)

Habitual action *Would* is the typical auxiliary for habitual action in the past, especially in formal English:

> He would always go by the longer way.

Habitual action is also expressed by *used to* or by an adverb:

> He used to go by the longer way.
> He usually went by the longer way.

Hackneyed A term describing an overused word or phrase. See Chapter 12, "Trite words," page 333.

had better, had rather *Had better* is the usual idiom for giving advice or making an indirect command:

> You had better take care of that cold.   You'd better go.

Informally a shorter form without *had* is common:

> If he asks you to do it, you better do it.

Had rather and *would rather* are both used to express preference, the latter the more formal:

> He would rather ski than eat. He had rather ski than eat.

Since the *had* or *would* is unstressed in speech (and the contraction *he'd* is frequently used), it is impossible to tell which is being said.

half The more formal idiom is *a half,* the general, *half a:*

> Formal: He ran a half mile; a half hour.
> General: He ran half a mile; half an hour.

A half a (a half an hour) is a redundancy, characteristic of careless colloquial or vulgate usage.

hanged—hung In formal English the principal parts of *hang* when referring to the death penalty are *hang, hanged, hanged*, the archaic forms kept alive by legal phrases such as "hanged by the neck until dead"; in other senses they are *hang, hung, hung*: Murderers are *hanged*, pictures are *hung*.

Informal usage does not keep this distinction, using *hang, hung, hung* in all senses:

> They hung the Turk that invented work
> In the Big Rock Candy Mountain.

In the passive *hang* may mean "to have a picture hung in an exhibition":

> If you frittered your good daylight away chaffing with sparrows, how could you ever get hung anywhere?

hardly See *Double negative § 3.

have **1. Independent meaning.** As a verb of independent meaning *have* means to "own, possess," in a literal (have a car) or transferred sense (have the measles), "to be under obligation" (I have to go home early). There are many idioms with *have*, such as:

> to have a look   the book (or gossip) has it that
> have it your own way   to have it out
> to have the ocean in view
> Informal: He had his arm broken.
> General: He had a broken arm.
> Formal: He suffered a broken arm.

2. Auxiliary. As an auxiliary *have* plus a past participle makes the perfect tense (They have come); *shall* or *will have* plus a past participle makes the future perfect tense (They will have gone by then); *had* plus a past participle makes the past perfect (They had gone to the beach before we arrived). See *Tenses of verbs.

3. Contractions. In speech, *he, she, it has* are contracted to *he's, she's, it's* (He's not tried to in years; It's rained for over a week), and *I, you, we, they have* are contracted to *I've, you've, we've, they've*.

Would have, wouldn't have are sometimes written *would of, wouldn't of*, an erroneous attempt to represent what is spoken as *would've, wouldn't've*.

4. Vulgate idioms. *Had ought* and *hadn't ought* are vulgate idioms, redundant but emphatic:

> Vulgate. He had ought to take better care of himself.
> General: He ought to take better care of himself.

Vulgate: He hadn't ought to lie like that.
General: He shouldn't [or: ought not to] lie like that.

5. Other idioms. For *have got* see *get § 2. Also see *had better, had rather.

healthful, healthy   *Healthful* means "giving health"; *healthy* means "having good health" or "giving health." Places, food are *healthful;* persons, animals are *healthy,* and so are places and food.

height—heighth   Vulgate English usually has *heighth,* like *width* and *breadth* (and the original Old English form had *th*), but *height* is the only form current in formal and informal English. Contrast *drought-drouth.

Heightened style   Typically a heightened style makes conspicuous use of the connotation of words, especially their overtones of sentiment and emotion; it tends to use the more literary and less colloquial parts of the language, it uses figures of speech, sentences with definite patterns, like parallelism, balance, and climax, and it makes considerable use of sound, euphony, and rhythm.

In fiction such a heightening of style is often appropriate for passages of elevated feeling, portraying the emotions of a character, as in Conrad's description of young Marlow's first experience of the East:

"I need not tell you what it is to be knocking about in an open boat. I remember nights and days of calm, when we pulled, we pulled, and the boat seemed to stand still, as if bewitched within the circle of the sea horizon. I remember the heat, the deluge of rain-squalls that kept us bailing for dear life (but filled our water-cask), and I remember sixteen hours on end with a mouth dry as a cinder and a steering-oar over the stern to keep my first command head on to a breaking sea. I did not know how good a man I was till then. I remember the drawn faces, the dejected figures of my two men, and I remember my youth and the feeling that will never come back any more—the feeling that I could last for ever, outlast the sea, the earth, and all men; the deceitful feeling that lures us on to joys, to perils, to love, to vain effort—to death; the triumphant conviction of strength, the heat of life in the handful of dust, the glow in the heart that with every year grows dim, grows cold, grows small, and expires—and expires, too soon, too soon—before life itself.

"And this is how I see the East. I have seen its secret places and have looked into its very soul; but now I see it always from a small boat, a high outline of mountains, blue and afar in the morning; like faint mist at noon; a jagged wall of purple at sunset. I have the feel of the oar in my hand, the vision of a scorching blue sea in my eyes. And I see a bay, a wide bay, smooth as glass and polished like ice, shimmering in the dark. A red light burns far off upon the gloom of the land, and the night is soft and warm. We drag at the oars with aching arms, and suddenly a puff of wind, a puff

586

faint and tepid and laden with strange odours of blossoms, of aromatic wood, comes out of the still night—the first sigh of the East on my face. That I can never forget. It was impalpable and enslaving, like a charm, like a whispered promise of mysterious delight."—JOSEPH CONRAD, *Youth*, pp. 36-37

In factual writing a heightened style is also appropriate in passages with feeling, as when a writer is presenting a course of action or an opinion, especially of full praise or blame, or some ideals about which he feels deeply and about which he wishes his reader not only to think but to feel.

Although this emotional heightening of style is more usual in formal writing, a more informal and "plain" style may show similar traits:

The people came out of their houses and smelled the hot stinging air and covered their noses from it. And the children came out of the houses, but they did not run or shout as they would have done after a rain. Men stood by their fences and looked at the ruined corn, drying fast now, only a little green showing through the film of dust. The men were silent and they did not move often. And the women came out of the houses to stand beside their men—to feel whether this time the men would break. The women studied the men's faces secretly, for the corn could go, as long as something else remained. The children sent exploring senses out to see whether men and women would break. The children peeked at the faces of the men and women, and then drew careful lines in the dust with their toes. Horses came to the watering troughs and nuzzled the water to clear the surface dust. After a while the faces of the watching men lost their bemused perplexity and became hard and angry and resistant. Then the women knew that they were safe and that there was no break. Then they asked, What'll we do? And the men replied, I don't know. But it was all right. The women knew it was all right, and the watching children knew it was all right. Women and children knew deep in themselves that no misfortune was too great to bear if their men were whole. The women went into the houses to their work, and the children began to play, but cautiously at first. As the day went forward the sun became less red. It flared down on the dust-blanketed land. The men sat in the doorways of their houses; their hands were busy with sticks and little rocks. The men sat still—thinking—figuring.—JOHN STEINBECK, *The Grapes of Wrath*, pp. 6-7

There has been a good deal of argument among critics about this heightening of style. Some appear to feel that prose is better the more it has characteristics usually associated with poetry. Those who prefer the plain style seem to feel that any departure from simple direct statement is somehow dishonest. But the question is not of the qualities of poetry and prose. There are several kinds of style, all with long and honorable traditions in English literature. (The heightened style owes much to the Oriental and more poetic passages in the King James Version of the Bible.) All good styles have their uses and the real question is of their appropriateness to the subjects and situations in which they are used. The two special dangers of the heightened style are that it may be used for an ordinary statement that would make its mark better if it was simply told, and that writers believing this style better than others may attempt it even when they have no aptitude for it or when the immediate subject does not call for it.

In a plea for "fine writing," Logan Pearsall Smith tells that seeing a large map of the United States in a consular office abroad suggested to him that American writers are not interested in style—and to most readers his putting of this relatively simple idea will seem decidedly overwritten:

> Youth has its dreams, its longings for distinction; among all the eager young men and women of that vast country, nowhere on those prairies or among those mountains, by the side of no lake or river or of either ocean, in not one of those resounding cities or multitudinous universities, does the thought no longer come to any one, I asked myself, that the instrument of speech which they make use of all day long has resonance sleeping within it of unimaginable beauty? Never to any one of them does it now occur to try to master, as others have mastered, the ironic echoes which are latent in English Prose? The golden sceptre of style gilds everything it touches, and can make immortal those who grasp it: to no one of those aspiring youths does the thought ever suggest itself that it might be an adventure among adventures to try to wield that wand?—LOGAN PEARSALL SMITH, "Fine Writing," *Reperusals and Re-collections*, p. 332

At present a heightened style is out of fashion. Our fiction writers especially seem to avoid it, using instead a plain, and sometimes too plain, telling of their tales. In factual writing it is perhaps more common, because of the interest in and feeling for their ideas that our more earnest writers show. There are various reasons for the vogue of the plain style—the dominance of realistic fiction, the supposedly scientific temper of thought, the journalistic quality of much writing. In fact, heightened style is so out of fashion that some writers with real depth of feeling probably avoid it intentionally. For a writer to repress a genuine tendency to an appropriate heightening of style is as dangerous as forcing it when he does not have sufficient feeling to warrant it.

(REFERENCES: Logan Pearsall Smith, "Fine Writing," *Reperusals and Re-collections* (New York, 1937) and his anthology, *A Treasury of English Prose* (Boston, 1920). The opposite point of view is presented in a review of the *Treasury* by Arthur Clutton-Brock, included in *More Essays on Books* (New York, 1921). Dobrée, Part iii, Emotive Prose.)

hello is the common American greeting. Variants, mostly British, are *hallo, halloo, hollo*. Plural *hello's*.

The verb ("to shout in greeting or to attract attention") is generally given in dictionaries as *hollo* or *hollow*, but this is an archaic form not heard in the United States. We all say *holler* and should write it.

help but See *can't help but.

hence A formal word for the less formal *consequently, therefore,* and the general *so that;* rare in current informal writing. (See *Conjunctive adverbs.)

he-or-she English has no third person pronoun to refer to individuals of either or both sexes. Since we must often refer to nouns that name either or both male and female, the language has developed three ways of making up for the lack of an accurate pronoun:

1. The most usual and most satisfactory way is to use *he* or *his* alone even when some of the persons meant are female, since *he* can be regarded as referring to *person* as much as to *man:*

> There is considerable discussion whether a man or a woman will be appointed to the vacant cabinet post. Whoever receives the appointment will find his task a difficult one.
> Mr. Brown and Miss Trevor led the discussion, each giving his opinion of the poem.

Sometimes when the typical individuals or the majority of the group referred to would be women, use *her* in the same way:

> Each one of the teachers in this school is required to submit her report to the principal in person.

2. Sometimes both *he* and *she* are used:

> A teacher gives his or her own opinions on matters of politics and religion and often influences a pupil to think as he or she does. (Either of the two pronouns would be better in this sentence than both of them.)
> Every student wishes to participate in some activity authorized by his or her college. (*His or her* sounds pedantic here; *his* alone would be better.)

The two pronouns are almost always clumsy and really no more accurate, since the meaning is determined by the antecedent.

3. The third way is to resort to a plural pronoun. This is the usual informal solution, and it is frequently written:

> Neither [a man and a woman] tasted what they ate.—KATHERINE ANNE PORTER, *Flowering Judas,* p. 26

highbrow After a period of slang overuse, *highbrow* has settled down as a useful informal word, and *lowbrow* has too:

The cult of the lowbrow and the technique of showmanship have unquestionably invaded every field of literary and intellectual activity.—*The Saturday Review of Literature*

Middlebrow, a more recent coinage, is making its way.

high school Capitalize only when referring to a particular school (some newspaper styles do not use capitals even then):

I graduated from high school at seventeen.
I graduated from Bismarck High School in 1934.
These two high schools will now play for the championship.
Working on a high school paper is good training.

Some periodicals are now printing the word as a compound: *highschool*.

himself, herself *Himself* and *herself* are used in two ways:
1. As reflexive pronouns, referring to the subject of the sentence:

He took it upon himself to see that it was done.
George has always taken himself pretty seriously.
She looked at herself in the window and gave her hat a little pull.

2. As intensives for emphasis:

He told me himself.
I looked up and there was Mrs. Goodenow herself.

(COMPARE *myself.)

Historical present Using the present tense in a narrative of past events. (See Chapter 8, "The time relation," page 211.)

home, homely, homey 1. **Home** is used as a noun, verb, adjective, and adverb—an example of the English habit of making one form serve several functions (See *Parts of speech § 2):

Noun: His home was now in Cleveland.
Verb: The bird homed in an hour and twenty minutes.
Adverb: He came home unexpectedly. His remark went home.
Adjective: home duties, home manufactures, home run

In "They are home," *home* is a general expression for *at home. To home* in these phrases is vulgate or local.
2. **Home—house.** For a realtor a *home* is any house; in sentimental (and some formal) use a *home* is only the "place of one's domestic affections." But in general use *home* is a lived-in house (or any extension needed for animal, plant, or object).
3. **Homely.** In formal English *homely* means "informal, unassuming, characteristic of home life." In American English *homely* usually means "ugly in appearance."

4. Homey is a good informal word: The lodge had a cheerful, homey atmosphere.

Homonyms Two words of different meanings that are pronounced alike (*bear, bare; plain, plane*) are called *homonyms* (or *homophones*).

English has a great many such pairs of words, most of them in common use. They exist for different reasons. Some Old English words once different have fallen together because of changes in form through the centuries: *bear* (the animal) from *bera, bear* (the verb) from *beran; plain* and *plane* both go back to Latin *planus,* but the spelling of the first was altered in coming through Old French. Many words are from different languages, having fallen into similar forms by accident: *rest* meaning "peace" is from Old English, *rest* meaning "remainder" is from French; and *bark* of a tree is from Scandinavian, *bark* of a dog from Old English, and *bark,* the vessel, a more recent borrowing from French-Italian.

There is very little chance of misunderstanding these words because their context will tell which is which—though their similarity is often capitalized in *puns. But homophones like *plain—plane* make a good deal of trouble in spelling. Much of this confusion is really carelessness, for the words are common. Try to visualize the troublesome ones in phrases that show their meaning, something like these:

priest at the *altar*—Who can *alter* human nature?
Father gave his *assent* to the marriage.—the *ascent* of Mount Everest
bearing pain—*baring* his arm
a lower *berth*—his tenth *birth*day
born in June 1922—*borne* by the wind
the *bridal* party, *bridal* suite—a horse's *bridle*, the *bridle* path
a house-to-house *canvass*—with *canvas* spread
The *capital* of Illinois is Springfield.—The *capitol* has a gilded dome.
A woman despises insincere *compliments*.—the *complement* of the angle
There are five members of the *council*.—*Counsel* is advice.—*counsel* for the defense
a *dual* personality—a pistol *duel*
A *mantle* covered her.—the trophy cups on the *mantel*
a *piece* of paper—*peace* or war
air*plane, plane* geometry—the Great *Plains,* a *plain* statement
He *rode* horseback.—The *road* was macadam.—He *rowed* a dory.
a box of *stationery*—a *stationary* engine, *stationary* desks
tea to drink—*tee* on a golf course

(REFERENCE: Kennedy, § 82.)

Honorable As a title of respect, for persons in political office of some prestige, this word is capitalized and is usually preceded by *the;* it may be abbreviated in addresses when initials or first names are used:

the Honorable Scott Lucas   the Hon. Scott Lucas
the Honorable Member from South Carolina

hope "In hopes of a better day to come" is colloquial and vulgate for *in the hope of.*

> After leaving Montreal, we drove on in the hope [not: in hopes] of reaching Quebec as soon as possible. (or: in hope of reaching)

Or, more usual, with a participle:

> After leaving Montreal, we drove on, hoping to reach Quebec as soon as possible.

Hours In consecutive writing, especially if it is formal, hours are written in words: at four o'clock.

In newspapers and in much informal writing, figures are used, especially if several times are mentioned:

at 4 p.m.   just after 9 a.m.   from 10 to 12   (See *a. m. and p. m.)

however As a connective, *however* is more appropriate to the fully developed sentences of formal style, and is especially useful as a connective between sentences:

> Occasionally the beat man writes his own story in the press room of the public building in which he is stationed, and sends it to the office by messenger. This, however, is unusual as it involves loss of time.—C. D. MACDOUGALL, *Reporting for Beginners,* p. 65

Amateur writers are likely to overuse *however; but* would usually be more appropriate to the simple directness of their statements:

> During the eight weeks I was in the hospital, Al visited me twice, assuring me that as soon as I was able, I could have my old job. But [better than *however*] after four weeks of convalescing at home, it was time for me to go to college.
> Many people think that Model T's are always getting out of order. This is not always the case, however. Ours has . . .
> Better: Many people think that Model T's are always getting out of order, but that is not always true. Ours has . . .

Clauses of one sentence connected by *however* are usually substantial enough to be separated by a semicolon. (See *Conjunctive adverbs, *but.)

human, once a noun in good standing, fell to the level of humorous and undignified usage, and now seems slowly being brought back into good standing:

With all his heart he wants to come close to some other human, touch someone with his hands, be touched by the hand of another.—SHERWOOD ANDERSON, *Winesburg, Ohio*, p. 287

Humor   Humor is primarily a matter of material, rather than of words, coming from shrewd observation of the amusing doings of people, from the ironical contrasts in life, from seeing likenesses or observing incongruous situations that escape the average person, from parodying or farcing ideas, from elaborating the trivial instead of the important strand of a thought, from plain exaggeration or understatement.

A humorous writer is usually an informal writer, using the resources of the language with freedom—old words in new senses, new words, misformed words, colloquial words, words with double connotation (*Puns), and constructions that suit his immediate fancy. An enumeration of the qualities of humor is not very useful, but a few specimens may remind you of some of the possibilities:

> The notion that such persons ["writers of light pieces running from a thousand to two thousand words"] are gay of heart and carefree is curiously untrue. They lead, as a matter of fact, an existence of jumpiness and apprehension. They sit on the edge of the chair of Literature. In the house of Life they have the feeling that they have never taken off their overcoats. Afraid of losing themselves in the larger flight of the two-volume novel, or even of the one-volume novel, they stick to short accounts of their misadventures because they never get so deep into them but that they feel they can get out. This type of writing is not a joyous form of self-expression but the manifestation of a twitchiness at once cosmic and mundane. Authors of such pieces have, nobody knows why, a genius for getting into minor difficulties: they walk into the wrong apartments, they drink furniture polish for stomach bitters, they drive their cars into the prize tulip beds of haughty neighbors, they playfully slap gangsters, mistaking them for old school friends. To call such persons humorous, a loose-fitting and ugly word, is to miss the nature of their dilemma and the dilemma of their nature. The little wheels of their invention are set in motion by the damp hand of melancholy.
>
> Such a writer moves about restlessly wherever he goes, ready to get the hell out at the drop of a pie-pan or the lift of a skirt. His gestures are the ludicrous reflexes of the maladjusted; his repose is the momentary inertia of the nonplussed. He pulls the blinds against the morning and creeps into smokey corners at night. He talks largely about small matters and smally about great affairs. His ears are shut to the ominous rumblings of the dynasties of the world moving toward a cloudier chaos than ever before, but he hears with acute perception the startling sounds that rabbits make twisting in the bushes along a country road at night and a cold chill comes upon him when the comic supplement of a Sunday newspaper blows unexpectedly out of an areaway and envelopes his knees. He can sleep while the commonwealth crumbles but a strange sound in the pantry at three in the morning will strike terror into his stomach. He is not afraid, or much aware, of the menaces of empire but he keeps looking behind him as he

walks along the darkening streets out of the fear that he is being softly followed by little men padding along in single file, about a foot and a half high, large-eyed, and whiskered.—JAMES THURBER, *My Life and Hard Times*, Preface

Always fair game for a humorist are things taken at their face value or things taken more seriously than they really deserve. Applying the judgment of common sense to inflated reputations often results in humor by sheer contrast with the usual opinions. In the following passages two different methods and different styles are shown in this sort of attack, one on a sentimental poem that has been taken too seriously, the other on Shakespeare-worship.

The boy who stood on the burning deck has been played up as an example of youthful heroism for the benefit of the young of our race ever since Mrs. Felicia Dorothea Hemans set him down in black and white. I deny that he was heroic. I insist that he merely was feeble-minded. Let us give this youth the careful once-over: The scene is the Battle of the Nile. The time is August, 1798. When the action of the piece begins the boy stands on the burning deck whence all but him had fled. You see, everyone else on board had had sense enough to beat it, but he stuck because his father had posted him there. There was no good purpose he might serve by sticking, except to furnish added material for the poetess, but like the leather-headed young imbecile that he was he stood there with his feet getting warmer all the time, while the flame that lit the battle's wreck shone round him o'er the dead. After which:

> There came a burst of thunder sound;
>   The boy—oh! where was he?
> Ask of the winds, that far around
>   With fragments strewed the sea—

Ask the waves. Ask the fragments. Ask Mrs. Hemans. Or, to save time, inquire of me.

He has become totally extinct. He is no more and he never was very much. Still we need not worry. Mentally he must have been from the very outset a liability rather than an asset. Had he lived, undoubtedly he would have wound up in a home for the feeble-minded. It is better so, as it is—better that he should be spread about over the surface of the ocean in a broad general way, thus saving all the expense and trouble gathering him up and burying him and putting a tombstone over him. He was one of the incurables.—IRVIN S. COBB, *A Plea for Old Cap Collier*, pp. 40-41

It costs a shilling to cross any doorstep in Stratford, and once inside, the visitor finds himself on the very spot where Shakespeare signed his will or wrote *The Tempest* or did something or other which makes it necessary to charge an additional sixpence for the extra sanctity involved. Through all the shrines surge English and American tourists, either people who have read too much Shakespeare at the expense of good, healthy detective stories or people who have never read him at all and hope to get the same results by bumping their heads on low beams. Both categories try heroically to appear deeply moved, an effort which gives their faces a draped look. Were it not for the countryside round about, I would not stay an hour in Stratford—I keep expecting that somebody all dressed up as the immortal bard will come rushing out with a jingle of bells and a jovial shout, and I will have to confess apologetically that I am a big girl now and too old to believe in Shakespeare.—MARGARET HALSEY, *With Malice Toward Some,* pp. 65-66

Amateurs need to be reminded that a good deal of light writing has already been done and that no amount of word juggling and no number of stale quips emphasized by a question mark (?) can conceal a lack of really humorous insight. A glance at the college comics will show what a groove "humor" runs in—though at the same time it can show the occasional flash of illuminating humor that makes life more genial.

(REFERENCE: Max Eastman, *The Enjoyment of Laughter* (New York, 1936); E. B. and Katherine B. White, *A Subtreasury of American Humor* (New York, 1941), especially the preface.)

Hyperbole See Chapter 12, "Degree of statement," page 350.

Hyphen (-)

> 1. Division of words. 2. Prefixes. 3. With modifiers preceding a noun. 4. Group words. 5. Compound words.

1. Division of words. A hyphen is used to mark the division of a word at the end of a line of manuscript or print. The problem in this use is to divide the word between syllables. This is discussed in *Division of words.

2. Prefixes. In certain types of compounds of a prefix and a root word a hyphen is necessary to avoid confusion, or for emphasis or appearance:

a) Between a prefix ending with a vowel and a root word beginning with the same vowel:

re-elected   re-enter   pre-eminent   pre-existent
(SEE *pre-, *re-.)

Usage is divided on words made with *co-,* the more common ones now generally being written solid:

co-operate or cooperate   co-ordinate or coordinate

b) To avoid confusion with another word:

re-collect—recollect   re-cover—recover

c) Between a prefix and a proper name:

anti-Nazi   ex-President Hoover   pro-Roosevelt

595

d) When the prefix is stressed:

ex-husband   ex-wife   anti-vivisection (or antivivisection)

3. With modifiers preceding a noun:

a) Occasionally some pairs of modifiers might be ambiguous without a hyphen: *a light yellow scarf* might be either a light scarf that was yellow or a scarf that was light yellow, so that *light-yellow* is safest for the latter meaning, and conservative writers would put *light, yellow scarf* for the first. There is a distinction between a *great-grandfather* (indicating relationship only) and a *great grandfather* (indicating quality of a grandfather). When an adverb has the same form as an adjective, many people use a hyphen if the adverb modifies a participle: a *late-flowering iris* (an iris that flowers late), *slow-moving goods*. But ordinarily such expressions would not be mistaken however they were written, except by people perversely analyzing the phrases.

b) Usage is divided on hyphening noun phrases when used as modifiers, as in *seventeenth century philosophy*. Formal writers would usually write *seventeenth-century*, informal *seventeenth century*. This division applies to such expressions as the following:

a Seventh Avenue shop   a college professor attitude
the drugstore clerk manner   summer vacation freedom
two-hundred-pound, six-foot-two halfbacks

c) Other modifying phrases, especially long humorous coinages, are usually hyphened:

Aside from its practical uses, this appeals to what might be termed the "I-know-a-guy-who" streak in human nature.—JACK ALEXANDER, *The New Yorker*, Aug. 1, 1936
That kind of tail-between-the-legs philosophy has no place in America.—*Country Gentleman*, Jan. 1939

Shorter phrases will be found written variously. *Onshore* is usually one word; *first rate* is found as two words or hyphened; *dirt cheap* would usually be two words. A dictionary will give the commoner form of this type of phrase.

d) In formal style a hyphen may be used to carry the force of a modifier over to a later noun ("suspension hyphen"):

The third-, fourth-, and fifth-grade rooms have been redecorated.
In both thirteenth- and fourteenth-century texts

4. Group words. A hyphen is conventionally used in certain group words:

a) In the compound numerals from twenty-one to ninety-nine, and in fractions, though this use is decreasing:

one hundred sixty-two   one thirty-second   three-sixteenths
forty-seven   ninety-ninth

b) In names of family relationships:

Hyphened: father-in-law, daughter-in-law
One word: stepson, stepdaughter, stepmother
Two words: half brother, half sister (sometimes hyphened)

c) In compounds with *self-*, which are usually hyphened in dictionaries but are often found in print as two words:

self-contained   self-government—self government
self-help—self help   self-importance   self-pity—self pity

Selfhood, selfless are written as one word.

If words of this sort raise any question, consult a recent dictionary—but note the comments on the general use of hyphens made in the next section.

5. Compound words. The question of compound and occasionally compounded words is more complex. Many compound words will be found written in three ways: as two words, or hyphened, or as one word. As a rule the form does not affect meaning: *tax payers, tax-payers,* and *taxpayers* all pay taxes; *a red headed roommate, a red-headed roommate,* and a *redheaded roommate* all have red hair. We find *fire escape* and *fire-escape* (but not *fireescape* because of the two *e*'s); *golf links* and *golf-links; sugar beet* and *sugar-beet.*

In the past, words that were becoming fused into compounds were required to pass through a probationary period with hyphens before being admitted as single words. *Baseball,* for instance, was hyphened for a time, and *football* and *basketball* until rather recently. There is less tendency to use hyphens now, except in quite formal writing, and compounds are now made immediately without hyphens if the word is needed. A hyphen is more likely to be used when one of the elements has two or more syllables:

. . . and we have even seen their guilty simulacra in tenement-house and shopfronts.—LEWIS MUMFORD, *Sticks and Stones,* p. 180

Schoolbook is usually written solid, *pocket-book* often hyphened or as two words; *reference book* is almost always two words.

The only consolation is that hyphening is more an editor's worry than a writer's. A publisher may wish for uniformity in principle and may struggle to get it in printing particular words, though absolute consistency is impossible. The University of Chicago Press *Manual of Style*, for instance, devotes nine pages to rules for hyphening, and stylebooks of newspaper and other publications have numerous rules, many of them arbitrary choices of form made simply to insure consistency. In a person's ordinary writing, he does not need to be so particular. For words in common use he can consult a dictionary or do as he finds reputable publications doing.

It is obvious that use of hyphens should be appropriate to other traits of style, especially to punctuation. In general, formal and conservative writers tend to use more hyphens, informal writers tend to use fewer, and those who follow an open punctuation often get along with almost none. The present style is to use rather few, writing the word pairs as two separate words or joined as one.

Contrast these passages from contemporary writers:

> And the face was also surly, hang-dog, petulant, and servile—the face of one of those little men—a door-man at a theater, a janitor in a shabby warehouse, office building, or cheap apartment house, the father-in-law of a policeman, the fifth cousin of a desk sergeant, the uncle of a ward heeler's wife, a pensioned door-opener, office-guard, messenger, or question-evader for some Irish politician . . .—THOMAS WOLFE, "Death the Proud Brother," *From Death to Morning*, p. 43

> At the broker's office there was the usual welldressed elderly crowd in sportsclothes filling up the benches, men with panamahats held on knees of Palm Beach suits and linen plusfours, women in pinks and greens and light tan and white crisp dresses.—JOHN DOS PASSOS, *The Big Money*, p. 382

Thomas Wolfe, consistent with his rather conservative usage, has more hyphens than most people would use; Dos Passos, in keeping with other traits of his venturesome style, runs as single words several which are conventionally hyphenated or written as two words. Such word joinings are a matter of style rather than of correctness, and appropriateness is more important than rules.

The conclusion one comes to after a serious consideration of current habits in the use of hyphens is well put by John Benbow in *Manuscript & Proof*, the stylebook of the Oxford University Press of New York: "If you take hyphens seriously you will surely go mad."

1. **'Long *i*'** (ī). The sound of long *i* is a diphthong, sliding from *a* or *ä* to short *i* or short *e*: *ice, wild, find, guide, night, tiny.* It is variously spelled as in *aisle, aye, height, eye, by, buy, bye, lie.*

In unstressed syllables ī has the same sound but is somewhat shorter: dī am′ə tər.

2. 'Short *i*' (i). As in *bit, city.* Before *r* it spells the sound represented by û: *bird* (bûrd), *third* (thûrd).

3. 'Continental *i*' (ē). In a few words the Continental (European) value of *i* is preserved: *machine* (mə shēn′), *police* (pə lēs′), *visa* (vē′zə), and in recent unanglicized borrowings.

4. As a consonant (y). *I* may represent a *y* sound before a vowel, especially in rapid pronunciation: *opinion* (ə pin′yən).

(For the plural *-ies* see *Plurals § 1b and *Y. See also *-ile.)

I **1. Capital.** The pronoun *I* is written with a capital simply because in the old handwritten manuscripts a small *i* was likely to be lost or to get attached to a neighboring word, and a capital helped keep it a distinct word. There is no conceit implied.

2. As first word. The widely circulated rumor that *I* should not be the first word in a letter (sometimes even that it should not be the first word of a sentence) is unfounded. *I* can be used wherever it is needed. People with only average concern for themselves need not worry; the conceited will give themselves away anyway. Circumlocutions to get around the natural use of *I* are usually awkward and likely to attract attention to themselves:

> There is a feeling in me [I feel] that relief projects are unsound.

The best way to avoid conspicuous use of *I* (or of any other word) is to keep it out of emphatic sentence positions, especially from the stressed beginning of a sentence. A subordinate clause or longish phrase put first will throw the stress off the *I:*

> After a long struggle I decided to go. (Instead of: I decided to go, after a long struggle.)

3. Omission of *I*. In clipped personal writing—diaries, casual and informal letters—*I* is often appropriately omitted if the style is also clipped in other respects:

> A drive to Nahant yesterday afternoon. Stopped at Rice's, and afterwards walked down to the steamboat wharf to see the passengers land.—NATHANIEL HAWTHORNE, *American Note-Books,* Aug. 31, 1835

(SEE *It's me, *myself, *we § 2 ("editorial we"), ch. 3, "Choice between personal and impersonal styles," p. 79.)

ibid. *Ibid.,* the abbreviation of the Latin *ibidem,* "in the same place," is used in a footnote to refer to the work mentioned in the immediately preceding footnote. (See Chapter 13, "Form of footnotes," page 391.)

idea strictly means a "concept," something thought about something. It is frequently used as a substitute for *intention* and similar words in constructions that are usually wordy:

> I got the idea that [I thought] every policeman was my enemy.
> Wordy: We started out with the idea in mind of going to a dance.
> Improved: We started out intending to go to a dance.

Id **Idiom and idioms** Correction: The expression marked is not the idiomatic English construction. Revise it, referring to an article in this Index or to a dictionary if you are not sure what it should be.

The word *idiom* is used in two different, almost opposed, senses:

1. It may mean *the usual forms of expression of a particular language,* as we may compare German idiom with English idiom, meaning the ways in which words are characteristically put together in the two languages. German has been fond of suspended constructions, the separable prefixes (*Wo gehst du hin?*) and participial constructions, but English tends to complete its constructions immediately. In French, adjectives come after the nouns they modify (*une maison blanche*), in English they come before (*a white house*). "Idiomatic English" connotes *natural, meaningful* English rather than *correct* English. It ordinarily is contrasted with stilted or formal English and suggests then not a mastery of academic English but of general usage.

2. The word *idiom* may also mean an *accepted phrase that differs from the usual construction of the language,* either departing from the typical grammar (like *somebody else's,* in which the sign of the possessive is added to the adjective rather than to the noun) or from normal logical meaning (like *to center around,* which is ridiculous when analyzed). These idioms are usually particular phrases which we learn separately—easily in our own language, with difficulty in another—differing from the idioms discussed in the preceding section, which are patterns for large numbers of locutions.

Collecting English idioms is a good sport and trying to analyze them is better. Considering them grammatically and literally, what can you make of these?

to come in handy	be your age
how do you do	strike a bargain
to catch fire	to be taken in (deceived)
catch a cold	look up an old friend
many is the time	getting on in years

The point to remember about these expressions is that though they are exceptional in some way, they are thoroughly respectable members of the language. No one needs to apologize for using them, for they are part of the general stock in trade of the informal language and most of them are appropriate in all levels.

The dictionaries of course give a great many idioms, usually listed under the most important word in the phrase. The *Oxford English Dictionary* is especially rich in idioms. (See Chapter 4, "Idiom and idioms," page 114; *Phrases, *Prepositions.)

-ie- in spelling   See *-ei-, -ie-.

i. e.   is the abbreviation for Latin *id est,* "that is." It is not common now outside rather routine reference exposition, *that is* being ordinarily written. For punctuation with *i. e.,* see *namely, *Colon § 6.

if   1. Subordinating conjunction. *If* is a subordinating conjunction introducing a condition:

> If the weather holds good, we shall stay another week.
> If they had known the beacon was out, they would have come in before sunset.

(SEE *Conditions. REFERENCE: Fries, pp. 224-25.)

2. 'If' and 'whether.' In formal usage, *if* is used for conditions, and *whether*, usually with *or*, is used, though not consistently, in indirect questions, in conditions, and in expressions of doubt:

> Simple condition: If the weather holds, we will come.
> Indirect question: He asked whether the mail had come in. He asked whether they were all going or only some of them.
> Doubt: They had all been wondering whether the doctor would get there in time.
> From the first returns they could not be sure whether the state was Republican or Democratic.

In formal English *if* is not used with *or:*

> No matter whether [Not: *if*] the boy goes to preparatory school or high school, his father has to pay local school taxes.

In informal English *whether* is rarely used:

> He asked if they were all going or only some of them.
> He asked if the mail had come in.
> He was so old, and so shrunken, that it was difficult to tell, at first, if he was a man or woman.—WILLIAM MARCH, *The Little Wife,* p. 101

3. For 'although' or 'but.' Colloquially *if* is used for *although* or *but* in certain expressions:

> She was a good dog, if she did bark at strangers.

(SEE *when, as, and if.)

-ile Usage is divided on the pronunciation of words ending in *-ile*. Some of the more common are:

agile aj′il [aj′īl]	infantile in′fən tīl, in′fən til
fertile fûr′til	juvenile jōō′və nil, jōō′və nīl
futile fū′til	reptile rep′til
gentile jen′tīl	textile teks′til, teks′tīl
hostile hos′til	versatile vûr′sə til

British pronunciation more commonly has -īl: fûr′tīl, hos′tīl, rep′tīl, vûr′sə tīl.

ilk *Ilk* is an archaic Scotch expression which turns up in some English essays or in would-be humorous writing for *sort:* "more of that ilk."

ill See *sick.

illiterate Strictly, *illiterate* means "not able to read or write"; loosely it means "uncultivated." Usage that is often loosely referred to as *illiterate* is called *vulgate* in this *Index.* See Chapter 1, "Vulgate English," page 52.

illusion *Illusion*—"a deceptive appearance," as *an optical illusion, an illusion of wealth*—is sometimes confused with *allusion,* "a reference to something written or to someone or something": He alluded to recent events without describing them.

Illustration (Pictorial) Pictorial illustration greatly helps the interest and understandability of an article—though it cannot (in spite of the great picture magazines) take the place of text. Illustrations for articles and books are often arranged for by the publisher, but the writer can suggest possibilities or he can submit drawings or photographs. Many feature articles are accepted by newspapers and magazines largely because of their illustrations.

A student can often add considerably to the value of a paper by drawings or by snapshots. These can be inserted by tucking the corners into slits cut in the manuscript pages, so that they can be taken off after they have served their purpose. Travel papers, narratives of experience, and explanations of processes profit especially from illustration.

(COMPARE *Diagrams, graphs, etc.)

Imagery An image is a word or group of words that may make an appeal to one of the "senses": sight (*bright, yellow, thick brown hair*), hearing (*rumble, far away shouts, three loud booms*), taste (*sweet, sour, a pickled pear*), smell (*jasmine, a blown out candle*), touch (*smooth, glassy, a tweed coat*), and the muscular tension known as the kinesthetic sense (*squirm, jogging heavily along*). Obviously a word may appeal to more than one sense (*tweed, glassy, jasmine*), though in a specific context one would usually be dominant. Whether a reader's senses are actually "aroused" depends chiefly on his suggestibility. Some people are easily stimulated by words; some are more sensitive to one sense than to another. For the study of imagery in writing, it is enough that words *capable* of suggesting sensory images are present; we cannot be sure of the response of anyone but ourselves. But images—actually sensed or potential—are the foundation of most writing, of all in fact that is not dealing principally with ideas.

Imagery is especially characteristic of poetry, in which ideas, states of mind, and feelings are often represented by images and what they suggest:

> Jack Ellyat felt that turning of the year
> Stir in his blood like drowsy fiddle-music
> And knew he was glad to be Connecticut-born
> And young enough to find Connecticut winter
> Was a black pond to cut with silver skates
> And not a scalping-knife against the throat.
> STEPHEN VINCENT BENÉT, *John Brown's Body*, p. 22

Fiction, too, since it must present pictures of people and places and actions, has much imagery:

> The sun came in warm in long streaks across the floor, and the giant geranium plants made a pattern across its gold. When we touched our glasses, white circles of light would move on the walls and ceiling, and the cut-glass dish with the peaches in it made a rainbow-bar on the cloth.—
> JOSEPHINE JOHNSON, *Now in November*, p. 83

In expository prose, images are the basis of discussions of people, of experience and situations, of things and processes. Even in expressions of opinion and discussions of ideas, most writers keep in close touch with the visible and touchable world. Current writing is conspicuously concrete and imagerial.

Studying the images in a writer's work will usually show what has impressed him in his experience, what appeals to him—colors, lines, odors, what not—and your writing also should show images drawn from your experience. If you are interested in dogs or sailing or fabrics or foods, words from those fields should crop up, not only in papers in which they are the main subject but to add to the interest and detail of other papers, too. Images that come from your own experience and that definitely appeal to you will carry

over clearly to a reader and are infinitely better than the trite
roses and violets of accumulated literature. Don't take out of your
writing an image that really appeals to you, unless it would be inappropriate or would mislead a reader.

(SEE ch. 12, "Abstract and concrete words," p. 341, and "Figurative use of words,"
p. 344. REFERENCES: Rickert, ch. 3, gives a detailed classification of images and suggestions on their use; George G. Williams, *Creative Writing* (New York, 1935),
ch. 7.)

Imaginative writing   See *Factual and imaginative writing.

Imitative words and phrases   A number of words imitate, or suggest in their pronunciation, particular "sounds of nature": *bang,
buzz, clank, swish, splash, whirr, pop, clatter, cuckoo, ping pong.*
These words have become definite members of the English vocabulary and will be found in dictionaries. It is possible to make new
ones to fit specific sounds, and they are often necessary, especially
in fiction. Sometimes it is better to use the conventional forms
even when they are not very exact (*humph, uh huh*) rather than
make new ones, which may puzzle a reader.

When such words are used for special effect in writing they
form a trait of style known as *onomatopoeia* (on'ə mat'ə pē'ə).
Imitative words or sounds in a series that suggest the action or
idea or tone of the subject matter are a useful form of intensification of meaning, as in Pope's famous lines:

> 'Tis not enough no harshness gives offense,
> The sound must seem an Echo to the sense:
> Soft is the strain when Zephyr gently blows,
> And the smooth stream in smoother numbers flows;
> But when the loud surges lash the sounding shore,
> The hoarse, rough verse should like the torrent roar:
> When Ajax strives some rock's vast weight to throw,
> The line too labours, and the words move slow;
> ALEXANDER POPE, *An Essay on Criticism*, lines 364-71

Often a picture or a narrative can be sharpened by using an imitative word instead of a general or colorless word like *said* or
*walked: barked, droned, snarled, whined; clattered, stamped,
strutted.* Conspicuous striving for such words will make a passage
seem melodramatic, but accurate words that come naturally will
add to its effectiveness.

In *The Red Badge of Courage* Stephen Crane frequently uses
imitative words to good effect:

The regiment snorted and blew. . . . The song of the bullets was in the
air and shells snarled among the tree-tops. . . . Near where they stood shells

were flip-flapping and hooting. . . . Occasional bullets buzzed in the air and spanged into tree trunks. . . .

immigrate See *emigrate—immigrate.

Imperative sentences See *Commands and requests.

Impersonal constructions See *there is, there are, *it; Chapter 3, "Choice between personal and impersonal styles," page 79.

Impersonal style See Chapter 3, "Choice between personal and impersonal styles," page 79.

imply—infer Strictly a writer or speaker *implies* something in his words or manner; a reader or listener *infers* something from what he reads or hears.

> The dean implied, by the way he tilted his head and half closed his eyes, that he doubted my story.
> One might infer from his opening words that the speaker was hostile to all social change.

Infer has been used so much with the meaning of "imply" that that is given as a secondary sense of the word in dictionaries.

in **1. Uses:**

> Preposition: in the box   in town   in the rain   in a circle
> in training   in words   in bronze
> Adverb: mix in   They are not in.   Put in the butter.
> Adjective: an in train
> Noun: the ins and the outs
> Verb: (local) to in the beets, to in the car

2. In combinations: *In* is often found in colloquial doubling of prepositions: *in back of, in behind, in between.*

In most writing these would be simply: *back of, behind, between.*
(SEE *Prepositions § 3b.)

in—into—in to *In* generally shows location (literal or figurative); *into* generally shows direction:

> He was in the house.   He came into the house.
> He was in a stupor.   He fell into a deep sleep.
> He walked in the street.   He walked into the street.

Colloquially *in* is often used for *into:* He fell in the brook.

In to is the adverb *in* followed by the preposition *to:*

> They went into the dining room. They went in to dinner.

in-, en- See *en-, in-.

in-, un- *In-* or *un-* (variants *im-*, *il-*) prefixed to many words gives them a negative meaning: *inconsiderate, incapable, uneven, unlovable, unlovely, unloved.* If you are not sure whether a word takes *in-* or *un-*, you will have to consult a dictionary—an American dictionary, since British usage differs in many words. *Un-* is likely to be used with words from Old English and *in-* with words from Latin, but this is not a safe guide (witness *indigestible, undigested, inequality, unequal, inadvisable, unadvised*). A sample list follows:

inadequate	†indecipherable	impractical	unedited
inadvisable	†indistinguishable	unacceptable	unessential
inartistic	inept	unadvised	unnamed
inaudible	†inescapable	unalterable	unnatural
incapable	inexperienced	unbelievable	unnecessary
incapacitate	infallible	uncertain	unnoticeable
incommunicable	†infrequent	uncollected	unrecognizable
incompatible	†insubstantial	uncommu-	unresponsive
incomplete	†insupportable	nicative	unsung
incomprehensible	illiberal	uncompleted	unsustained
inconclusive	illiterate	uncontrollable	unversed
inconsequential	immoderate	uncontrolled	
inconsolable	immoral	undistinguished	

Those marked † also found with *un-*.

incidental, incidentally The adverb should be spelled in full: incident*al ly*. See *-al ly.

Incoherence Writing is incoherent when it lacks connection within itself or when the relationship between parts (of a sentence, of a paragraph, of a whole paper) is not evident. Various examples of incoherence are discussed in *Misrelated modifiers, *Participles, and in Chapters 7 and 9.

Incomplete sentences See Chapter 9, "Fragmentary sentences," page 262.

Incongruous details One minor trait of modern style is the use of contrasting or inconsistent words or details, especially in a series. Used unintentionally, incongruous details may be awkward, but when controlled they have various advantages.

    1. A series of incongruous details is often used instead of an abstract noun, to suggest a variety of objects or experiences. Such a series may be either light or serious:

> The earth, just as she stands, has a lot of qualities which we cherish: we like the climate, we like the food, and we like the view from the porch.—*The New Yorker*, June 30, 1934

In a single-minded attempt of that kind, if one be deserving and fortunate, one may perchance attain to such clearness of sincerity that at last the presented vision *of regret or pity, of terror or mirth,* shall awaken in the hearts of the beholders that feeling of unavoidable solidarity; of the solidarity in *mysterious origin, in toil, in joy, in hope, in uncertain fate,* which binds men to each other and all mankind to the visible world.—JOSEPH CONRAD, *The Nigger of the Narcissus,* Preface

The first group of italicized words in the passage from Conrad is a more exact and more vivid substitute for *emotion* and the second is a colorful and impressive substitute for *human experience* or some such generality.

2. A combination of a concrete and an abstract word is sometimes used as a source of humor, as in Washington Irving's "brimful of wrath and cabbage."

When an abstract and a concrete word are attached to the same construction they need to be watched. "At the expense of democratic people and ideals" would be better if the last phrase was made separate: "At the expense of democratic people and of democratic ideals."

3. A vigorously contrasting detail may heighten the effect of a statement or drive home a point, often with a note of severe irony:

Among those who have much to be thankful for this week are the football players. From now on they do not have to have their faces stepped on and their character molded.—HOWARD BRUBAKER, *The New Yorker,* Nov. 26, 1938

When my generation of country-raised folks were kids, we shure had a lot of hardships to put up with. We had to walk to school, for instance. There were no nice, comfortable school busses for us to ride back and forth and get killed in.—CAL TINNEY, *The Philadelphia Record,* Dec. 6, 1938

incredible—incredulous A story or situation is *incredible* (unbelievable); a person is *incredulous* (unbelieving).

Indefinite article See *a, an.

Indefinite it, they, you See *it, *they, *you.

Indefinite pronouns (*any, some* . . .) See *Pronouns § 8 and the separate articles referred to there, and Chapter 4, "Collective pronouns," page 109.

Indefinite reference of pronouns See *Reference of pronouns § 3, and Chapter 4, "Misleading or vague reference," page 109.

Indention *Indenting* in manuscript or printed copy is beginning a line in from the left-hand margin. In longhand copy, paragraphs are indented about an inch, in typewritten copy from five to eight spaces.

Hanging indention is setting in lines below the first line, as in many newspaper headlines, *outlines, headings, and addresses of *letters. If a line of verse is too long to stand on one line, the part brought over to the second line should be indented:

> Why do they prate of the blessings of Peace? we have
>   made them a curse,
> Pickpockets, each hand lusting for all that is not its
>   own;
>
> ALFRED TENNYSON, "Maud"

(For indenting quotations, see *Quotation marks § 1d; for "Indention and display," see ch. 5, p. 151.)

Independent clause   A clause grammatically complete and capable of "standing alone" but forming part of a compound or complex sentence. This sentence has three independent clauses (which would still be "independent," but in this instance clumsy, if they were connected by *and*):

> In actual life events rarely reach a conclusion as definite and complete as the short story demands; there are always loose threads somewhere; not even death itself ends a career.—DAVID LAMBUTH AND KENNETH A. ROBINSON, *Art and Craft in the Short Story*, p. 3

Indexes   See Chapter 13, "Periodical indexes," page 371.

Indicative mood   The usual form of the verb in sentences and clauses:

> They *sat* on the porch even though it *was* late October.
> *Will* you *come* if you *are invited?*

(SEE *Verbs; compare *Subjunctives.)

Indirect discourse (Indirect quotation)   Quotations that are paraphrased or summarized in the writer's words instead of being quoted exactly as originally spoken or written are in indirect discourse:

> Indirect: He said he wouldn't take it if they gave it to him.
> Direct: He said, "I won't take it if they give it to me."

(SEE *Quotation marks § 2b, *Tenses of verbs § 3.)

Indirect object   See *Objects § 2.

Indirect question   A question restated at second hand:

> Indirect: He asked if everyone was all right.
> Direct: He asked, "Is everyone all right?"

(SEE *Questions § 3.)

Inductive order See Chapter 1, "Planning the paper," page 14; Chapter 8, "Climax paragraphs," page 222.

infer See *imply—infer.

Infinitives

    1. Tenses of infinitive. 2. 'To' and the infinitive. 3. Typical uses of infinitives. 4. Subject of infinitives. 5. Split infinitive.

    1. Tenses of infinitive. The forms of the English infinitive are:

	Active	*Passive*
Present:	(to) ask, (to) be asking	(to) be asked
Perfect:	(to) have asked, (to) have been asking	(to) have been asked

The present infinitive indicates action occurring at the same time as that of the main verb or in a time future to that of the main verb:

    He is here now *to ask* you . . .
    They had come *to ask* you . . .
    He is coming [future] *to ask* you . . .

The perfect infinitive primarily indicates action previous to the time of the main verb:

    I am glad *to have been* one of his boys.

(SEE ch. 4, "Infinitives, participles, gerunds," p. 102, and "Infinitive or gerund," p. 115.)

    2. 'To' and the infinitive. *To* is the "sign of the infinitive" used in most infinitive constructions (Just *to hear* him talk is an inspiration).

    They all tried *to get* in first.   He set out *to get* Phi Beta Kappa.

After some verbs no *to* is used: *can, may, shall, will, do, dare, make, help, need* . . . .

    Do make him *stop*.   It would help us *finish* the job.   We might *be seeing* him.

In short, clear, unemphatic series of infinitives in parallel constructions, the *to* is not repeated:

    To sit and *smoke* and *think* and *dream* was his idea of pleasure.

In more formal series of infinitives, when the actions are not part of one general process, or when the separate verbs deserve emphasis, the *to* is repeated:

    To walk around among these exhibits, *to see* the horse races where runners, trotters, and pacers with Kentucky and Tennessee pedigrees compete on a mile track, and then *to listen* to the political speakers discussing "purr-ins-a-pulls" and "the Const-ti-too-shun"—this made a holiday for the farmers and city people who came.—CARL SANDBURG, *Abraham Lincoln: The Prairie Years*, 2:6

3. Typical uses of infinitives.

Subject: *To err* is human, *to forgive*, divine.
Object: He wanted *to go* fishing. He tries *to do* every one at least twice.
Adjective modifier: wool *to spin*, money *to burn*. They have plenty of fresh fish *to eat*.
Adverbial modifier (to show purpose, result, etc.): He bought *to sell* again. They came *to play*. Reporters are constantly on the move from one place to another *to cover* important happenings.
With auxiliaries: He will *pass* this time. He didn't dare *go* over the top.

4. Subject of infinitives.
The infinitive is coming more and more to serve as a verb in a subordinate construction, so that grammarians now speak of a *to* clause or an infinitive clause. When the subject is a pronoun it is in the accusative case.

Supposing *them to be new men*, we all shouted, "Get off the grass!"
It would be better *for you and me to discuss the matter* before calling in the others.

Often these constructions are absolute:

To judge by the appearances, the party must have been pretty rough. *To make a long story short*, they didn't go.

After the infinitive of a *linking verb that has no expressed subject, formal English would often have a nominative complement, informal an accusative:

Informal: I always wanted to be *him*.
Formal: I always wanted to be *he*.

(COMPARE *Participles §§ 3, 4; *Gerund.)

5. Split infinitive.
See *Split infinitive.

(REFERENCES: Curme, *Syntax*, ch. 23; Jespersen, ch. 32.)

Inflection Inflection is the change of form by which some words indicate certain grammatical relationships, as the plural of nouns or the past tense of verbs. For English inflections see *Case, and the articles referred to there; *Plurals; *Pronouns; *Verbs; *Comparison of adjectives and adverbs.

(REFERENCES: Curme, *Parts of Speech;* Kennedy, ch. 11.)

Inf **Informal English** Correction: The word or passage marked is too informal for the subject or for the style of the rest of the paper. Revise, making it more formal.

Informal English is the typical language of an educated person going about his everyday affairs. It shows more effect of education and social standing than vulgate, but not so much of the more precise usage of formal English. It is appropriate to all the needs of communication except some discussions of ideas and of some elevated subjects intended for a rather restricted audience or for occasions in which a formal style is expected.

(For discussion and examples, see ch. 2, "Informal English," p. 39.)

inquiry Pronunciation divided: in kwīr'i, in'kwə ri.

inside (of) *Inside*, usually with the doubling of the preposition to *inside of*, is colloquially used in expressions of time:

> The snow will all be gone *inside of a week.*

Informal, without distinctly colloquial flavor:

> The snow will be gone *in a week.*

The more formal idiom is *within:*

> The snow will be gone *within a week.*

inst., ult. Abbreviations such as *inst.* (of the current month: "Yours of the 18th inst. duly rec'd and contents noted") and *ult.* (of last month) are not now used by businessmen who pay attention to their correspondence. See *Business English.

institutions of higher learning is a clumsy phrase, and more abstract than *colleges and universities.* It would be convenient if we had one word for the notion, or a group word as economical even as *secondary schools* for "high and preparatory schools." Either *colleges* or *universities* is often used to apply to both.

Intensive pronouns See *Pronouns § 4 (Reflexive pronouns), and *himself, herself, *myself.)

Intensives Adverbs like *very, too, much*, and some constructions, like the superlative of adjectives and adverbs, are used to emphasize meaning. (See Chapter 10, "Intensives," page 288, for discussion, and *very, *Comparison of adjectives and adverbs § 5, *himself, *myself.)

(References: Fries, pp. 200-206; Curme, *Parts of Speech*, pp. 48-50.)

interest, interested, and their opposites The adjective *interested* has two opposites: *uninterested*, which is merely its negative, and *disinterested*, which means "not motivated by personal interest, impartial," though informally the latter is sometimes used in the sense of *uninterested*.

> The students were uninterested in the conflict between science and religion. Osborne was wholly disinterested when he suggested an increase in salary for all county officials.

The noun *interest* has no antonym made from itself (*disinterest* not being a word in general use). It is necessary to resort to specific words like *boredom* or phrases like *lack of interest*.

Interjections See *Exclamations.

Interrogation point See *Question mark.

Interrogative pronouns See *Pronouns § 3.

Interrogative sentence See *Questions.

Interrupted sentence movement See Chapter 10, "Interrupted movement," page 279.

into, in to See *in—into—in to.

intramural No hyphen. It means "within the walls," specifically college activities carried on by groups of the same college; the opposite of *intercollegiate*.

Intransitive verbs See *Transitive and intransitive verbs.

Introductions See Chapter 7, "Beginning paragraphs," page 195, and *Outline form § 2j.

Introductory words For handling words like *namely, that is, for example*, see *namely and other introductory words.

Inversion Placing the verb before its subject—"*Came* the first clap of thunder, and we all struck out for the house." There is a sort of compromise inversion with the auxiliary before the subject, the infinitive or participle after it, which is used grammatically in questions (*Is* he coming? *Will* she go? *Did* he like it?). (See Chapter 10, "Inverted movement," page 279.)

Invitations See *Social correspondence.

invite is ordinarily a verb. Its use as a noun (in′vīt) is colloquial or would-be humorous: "Did you get an invite?"

Irony Irony is implying something markedly different, sometimes even the opposite, from what is actually said. (See Chapter 12, "Degree of statement," page 352.)

irregardless A typical colloquial intensification of meaning (negative prefix *ir-* [*in-*] and negative suffix *-less*); not used in reputable writing.

Irregular verbs See Chapter 4, "Verbs," page 100, and *Principal parts of verbs.

-ise See *-ize, -ise.

isolate Pronunciation divided: ī′sə lāt, is′ə lāt, with the first more common; also ī′sə lā′shən, is′ə lā′shən.

it is the neuter third person singular pronoun, used to refer to an object, a situation, or an idea. *It* is also used to refer to a baby or an animal whose sex is unknown or unimportant for the statement (The dog wagged *its* tail). *It* is used further in certain impersonal statements about the weather, events in general (impersonal *it*):

> It rained all night.   It's the way things go.

It is also used to refer to the idea of a preceding statement:

> We changed two tires in record time. It is not easy to do on a dark and rainy night.

> In general, sentences beginning "It is . . ." or "It was . . ." (anticipatory subject) are wordy and weakening, since they have put a colorless locution in the emphatic beginning of the sentence:

> [It was] then [that] his wife had taken to going with other men.

(SEE *there is, there are, *its, *it's, *it's me.)

Italics In manuscript, both longhand and typewritten, italics are shown by underlining. Specific uses of italics are listed in *Underlining. (See also Chapter 5, "Underlining for italics," page 150, *Foreign words in English, *Titles of articles, books, etc., *Type.)

its The possessive pronoun does not have an apostrophe:

> The dog wagged *its* tail.   A car is judged by *its* performance. But we were deceived about *its* real value.

> Associate *its* with *his* and *hers*.

it's The contraction of *it is* or *it has:*

> *It's* going to rain.   *It's* rained for over a week now.

It's me The argument over "It's me" is a case of theory vs. practice. The theory is that after the verb *be* the nominative form should always be used, but this theory is consistently contradicted by the actual usage of good speakers.

We tend to use the nominative form of a pronoun when it is the subject and stands before a verb and to use the accusative in most other positions, especially when it comes after the verb—"object territory," as Professor Fries calls it. (Compare *who, whom.)

All the large grammars of English regard *it's me* as acceptable colloquial usage—and since the expression is not likely to occur except in speech, that gives it full standing. Fowler approves it, and one of the "judges" in *Current English Usage* (p. 108) wrote:

> *I* sounds quite mad in certain cases; e.g., pointing to a photo: "Which is I?"!!! "Oh, I see, that's I"!!! Absolutely non-English, hang all the grammarians on earth.

Us and *him* after *be* are less common, but usage is divided. *Current English Usage* found "If it had been *us*, we would admit it" uncertainly established and "I'll swear that was *him*" and "I suppose that's *him*" disputable. Very often speakers who try to be correct resort to some circumlocution, saying instead of "It was *she* (or *her*)" "That's who it was."

The upshot of the discussion is that in their natural settings "It's me," "It was him all right," "Something was wrong—was it him or the crowd?" are appropriate.

(REFERENCES: Marckwardt and Walcott, pp. 77-8; Wallace Rice, "Who's there? Me," *American Speech*, 1933, No. 3, 58-63; Robertson, pp. 492-503; Fries, p. 91. SEE *Case.)

-ize, -ise English has many verbs ending in the sound of īz, some of which are spelled *-ise* and some *-ize*, and on many usage is divided. American usage, differing somewhat from British, prefers *-ize*, as in the following common verbs of this class:

anesthetize	dramatize	revolutionize	sympathize
apologize	memorize	sensitize	visualize
characterize	realize	standardize	

In the following *-ise* is the usual spelling:

advise	despise	exercise	surmise
arise	devise	revise	surprise
chastise	disguise	supervise	

Both *-ize* and *-ise* are commonly found in:

advertise—advertize	analyze—analyse
baptize—baptise	criticize—criticise

In general, follow American usage, and when that is divided, use whichever you are accustomed to.

Some readers object to recent extension of the verbs in *-ize*, such as *concertize*, *picturize*, but there seems little reason for the objection except when one duplicates in meaning a verb already in common use.

J is a common spelling for the "soft *g*" sound at the beginning of syllables: *jam*, *jet*, *jibe*, *journey*, *jury*. At the end of syllables the sound is variously spelled, often by *-dge*: *edge* (ej), *judge* (juj).

Some foreign sounds of *j* are kept in particular words: Latin (y), *Hallelujah;* French (zh), *bijou* (bē′zho͞o), *jabot* (zha bō′); Spanish (h), *marijuana* (mä′ri hwä′nə).

Jargon 1. **Applied to style.** Sir Arthur Quiller-Couch popularized *jargon* as the name for verbal fuzziness of various sorts—wordiness, abstract for concrete words, big words, and the use of words that add nothing to the meaning of a statement. (See Chapter 10, "Deadwood," page 284; Chapter 12, "Words that weaken," page 333; and "Abstract and Concrete Words," page 341.)

(REFERENCE: Sir Arthur Quiller-Couch: *On the Art of Writing* (New York, 1916), pp. 100-126.)

2. **Linguistic sense.** *Jargon* is a word used among linguists to mean a dialect composed of the mixture of two or more languages. Jargons involving English are used by non-English-speaking peoples in doing business with the English. The best known of these are the Chinook jargon of the Pacific Northwest, Beach-la-Mar (or Bêche-de-mer) of the Pacific islands, and the Chinese-English jargon, pidgin-English.

(REFERENCES: Kennedy § 17; Otto Jespersen, *Language* (New York, 1922), pp. 216-36; and the sources referred to in these references.)

job Informal and colloquial for the formal *position:* He got a job at an oil refinery. The word *position* has more dignity and is usually thought of as better paid. *Job* is familiar for something made, such as an automobile or refrigerator ("a nice little job there").

Jones—plural and possessive forms The plural of *Jones* and of most nouns ending in an *s* or *z* sound is formed by adding *-es*, pronounced as a separate syllable: *Joneses* (jōn′zəz), *consciences* (kon′shən səz), *Jameses*. When two syllables ending in an *s* or

615

z sound are in the root word, usage is divided: *the Moses* seems more euphonious than *the Moseses*.

In the possessive, usage is divided. We may say and write *Dr. Jones'* (jōnz) *office* or *Dr. Jones's* (jōn′zəz) *office*. Probably the first form is the more common. Also: For *goodness'* sake, *Charles'* collection, though *Charles's* (chärl′zəz) is equally reputable.

The possessive plural is pronounced the same as the plural and is written by adding (') to the plural form: *Joneses'*, *Moses'* or *Moseses'*.

Journalistic, journalese See *Newspaper English.

judgment—judgement *Judgment* is the preferred spelling.

K

The *k* sound is spelled *c* in many words (*call, actual, cute*), *ck* (*back, track*), and also with other letters, as in *queen, chord, cheque*. K before *n* is silent in a number of Germanic words (*knave, kneel, knife*).

Business changes many words spelled with *c* to *k* (*Kwik Kleaners*), either to make the alliteration more obvious or to make a trademark. (See Louise Pound, "The Kraze for 'K,'" *American Speech*, 1925, 1:43-44.)

K is used by many teachers as the theme correction symbol for *awkward*. **Correction: The expression marked is awkward. Revise to make it read more smoothly.**

Keyword A word modified, especially a noun modified by an adjective.

kid *Kid* is colloquial and familiar for *child, youngster*.

kind, sort *Kind* and *sort* are both singular nouns in form:

> This kind of person is a menace at any party.
> This sort of thing shouldn't be allowed.

But *kind* and *sort* are so closely associated with the noun they stand before that they seem like adjectives, and colloquially the demonstrative adjectives used with them usually agree with the principal noun of the construction:

> Those sort of ideas in his head and that sort of life with his wife . . .
> —A. S. M. HUTCHINSON, *If Winter Comes*, p. 324

You next reach the conclusion that, as these kind of marks have not been left by any other animal than man. . . .—T. H. HUXLEY, "The Method of Scientific Investigation"

The *Oxford English Dictionary* has examples of *these kind of* and *these sort of* from the fourteenth century to the present, many of them from the "best authors." Fries found the plural regularly used with *kind* and *sort* by his Group I (Standard English) writers (p. 58). Only the vigilance of editorial copy readers keeps the construction from being as general in writing as in speech. (Jespersen, *Essentials of English Grammar*, page 202, even suggests that *kind* and *sort* be regarded as unchanged plurals and therefore correct.) But the construction still has only colloquial and vulgate standing. (REFERENCE: Curme, pp. 544-46.)

kind of, sort of Colloquially *kind of* and *sort of* are used as adverbs, equivalent to *rather* or *somewhat* in more formal usage:

> I feel kind of logy today.   It was sort of dull, but he said a lot.

In formal and informal English these would be:

> I was rather [somewhat, a little, very, pretty] tired.
> It was pretty [very, rather] dull, but he said a good deal.

kind of [a], sort of [a] Strictly you have a *kind* or *sort* of a class of objects, not of one object: *a kind of story*, not *a kind of a story*. But in informal English *kind of a* and *sort of a* are very common, and they are fairly common among respected writers:

> I want to find someone on the earth so intelligent that he welcomes opinions which he condemns—I want to be this kind of a man and I want to have known this kind of a man.—JOHN JAY CHAPMAN, *Letters*, p. 124

> And now, Catchuman arriving to inquire where he was likely to find a local lawyer of real ability who could be trusted to erect some sort of a defense for Clyde.—THEODORE DREISER, *An American Tragedy*, 2:182

> Now, suppose the battle of Salamis had been fought, not in the full light of Greek history, but in the misty dawn of the Epos, what sort of a story should we have had?—GILBERT MURRAY, *The Rise of the Greek Epic*, p. 200

These two sentences from the same short story show the two idioms in differing degrees of formality, in different tempos:

> . . . he had never once brought her a comical, stuffed animal or any sort of an object with a picture of a Scottie on it.
> Bob McEwen wasn't the sort of man to do a sentimental thing like that unless he meant it.—SALLY BENSON, *People Are Fascinating*, pp. 30, 31

In formal writing *kind of a* and *sort of a* should be avoided.

L   is a "liquid" consonant that varies considerably in the speech of individuals and groups and with its position in a word: *land, leaf, almost, silly, fill.* L is silent in a few common words: *almond* (usually), *folk, half, salmon, talk, walk, would, yolk.* It is often not sounded in other words as in *golf course* (gôf′kors′).

In many syllables no specific vowel is sounded before an *l*, and the pronunciation can be indicated by "syllabic *l*" (l̩): *marble* (mär′bl̩), *tickle* (tik′l̩).

Labeling material   It should usually be unnecessary to label a statement as *interesting, amusing,* or *important,* or to point out a joke or a dig by (?) or (!). A good storyteller doesn't need to begin "You'll laugh at this," and a good writer can usually *show* that what he is saying is interesting or important without labeling it. Instead of beginning "Let me relate an amusing incident," just tell it well and the reader will see that it is amusing.

Labeling an emotion that is clearly suggested in a narrative weakens the effect:

> "What was it, conductor, did we blow a fuse?"
> "No," he said, "we just killed three people back at a crossing."
> [The label:] The effect of this sentence was electrifying. "We just killed three people. . . ." Maybe they were college boys going home for Christmas.

lady   See *man, woman.

laissez faire   The spelling is still French, and the pronunciation (les′ā far′) still near French, but it is not italicized except in conspicuously formal writing.

Language study   See Chapter 2, Varieties of English, page 33, and *Linguistics.

last   See *former—first, latter—last.

last (at long last)   An archaic idiom recently revived. It is slightly more emphatic than *at last*, at least when it is spoken, but usually the phrase has a British or formal connotation, as in this:

> An economic power born of the travail of men at long last asserts its title to political dominance.—HAROLD J. LASKI, *The Rise of Liberalism*, p. 268

last, latest   In formal usage *last* refers to the final item of a series; *latest,* to the most recent in time of a series which may or may not be continued:

His latest (we hope it won't be his last) biography is of Peter Cooper.

This distinction is not strictly kept, so that both words are used as superlatives of *late*.

Latin and English   1. Latin words. Many Latin words came into English in early periods of the language, either direct or through French, and cannot now be told from other English words: *patience, candle, receive* . . . (See *English language). Most borrowings from Latin are subject to the same process of anglicizing as other *foreign words in English, and in general they are pronounced like English words—*agenda* (ə jen′də), *erratum* (i rā′təm or i rä′təm)—instead of according to the system of sounds now taught in Latin classes.

Since no people now speaks Latin, new borrowings come in through written rather than spoken use and belong to the formal dialects, used chiefly in science, law, religion, medicine, and academic work. Since practically all college work was carried on in Latin—by both teachers and students—until about 1750, and a good deal of it later than that, considerable Latin is preserved in college use. Many diplomas are in Latin, and at some institutions the commencement formulas are in Latin. At a more routine level, several Latin words and abbreviations are used in the footnotes of academic research (*ibid., passim, supra, infra, loc. cit.*), though there is a definite tendency to use English words for many of these.

Prefixes of Latin origin (*ante-, ex-, in-, pre-, re-, sub-*) and other compounding elements, such as *uni-* (*unilateral*), *bi-* (*biweekly*), are active in forming new English words. At present scientific words are being formed more from Greek than from Latin elements.

2. Latin forms. English continues to use the Latin forms for some words that are used principally in the formal dialects (*alumnus—alumna, bacillus—bacilli*), but those commonly used have either English plurals or both (*formula, formulas* or *formulae; focus, focuses* or *foci; stadium, stadiums* or *stadia*). (SEE *Plurals § 4, *data.)

3. Latin and English grammar. The first and a number of other English grammars were composed by men thoroughly familiar with Latin, who believed that English was or at any rate should be a language like Latin. As a result, English, which was a Germanic language in structure, was described in terms of Latin grammar, and rules were devised for making the language fit the picture. This may be one reason for the old taboo of the *split infinitive (which would be impossible in Latin because the infinitive is one word, as in *laborare,* where English has *to work*) and of putting a preposition at the end of a sentence (*Prepositions § 3d), which is impossible in Latin but is a characteristic English idiom.

Only recently has English grammar been based squarely on a study of the English language and freed from the categories and some of the rules of Latin grammar.

latter, later *Latter* (lat′ər) and *later* (lā′tər) are often carelessly confused in spelling. The habit of reading your copy aloud to yourself should catch this type of error. (See *former—first, latter—last.)

lay—lie In spoken English the work of these two verbs is generally done by one (*lay, lay* or *laid, laid*). In writing they are kept distinct:

lie ("to recline," intransitive), lay, lain
lay ("to place," transitive), laid, laid

You *lie* down for a rest or *lie* down on the job; a farm *lies* in a valley. You *lay* a floor, *lay* a book on the table, *lay* a bet, *lay* out clothes. Yesterday you *lay* down to rest (colloquially often *laid*), you *laid* a book on the table. Egg laying is *lay, laid, laid.*

-le words A large and interesting group of English verbs ends in *-le—fiddle, giggle, meddle, tickle, waddle, whistle, whittle*—in which the ending usually suggests an action continued or habitually repeated.

Lab*el* (verb and noun), mant*el* (the shelf), mod*el,* and nick*el* give some spelling trouble because they are exceptions to the usual English spelling of this final syllable.

lead, led *Lead* and *led* show the confusion that English suffers because of representing one sound by different symbols. *Lead* (lēd), the present tense of the verb, gives no trouble; but *led,* the past tense, is often incorrectly spelled with *ea* by analogy with *read* (rēd), *read* (red).

Please *lead* the horse away.
The culprit was *led* into the office.

Leaders Leaders, or "period leaders," are a line of spaced periods used to guide the reader's eye across a page. They are often used in statistical tables and the table of contents of a book:

	Page
1. Laying the groundwork	1
a. Defining the problem	2
b. Constructing the preliminary outline	3

In typed copy, hyphens are often used instead of periods.

learn—teach Vulgate English often uses *learn* in the sense of *teach* (He learned me how to tie six kinds of knots). Educated usage keeps the distinction:

> He *taught* me how to tie six kinds of knots.
> I *learned* how to tie knots from him.

leave See *let (leave).

-ledge, -lege Two common words are spelled with the ending *-ledge:*

> acknowledge (acknowledging, acknowledgment)   knowledge

Words spelled with *-lege* should not be confused with them:

> allege (alleged, alleging)   college   sacrilege (sacrilegious)

Legal language Most legal matters are carried on in a jargon bristling with long series of synonyms ("do hereby give, grant, bargain, sell and convey"), archaic or foreign (French, Latin) words for everyday things and situations, abbreviations and stereotyped phrases that puzzle laymen and sometimes lawyers themselves. The need for precision and of certain technical words is of course great, but the reason for much of the jargon is unconsidered tradition. Perhaps this jargon must be tolerated in legal business, but lawyers and others who have much to do with law should realize that it is a trade jargon (shoptalk). When they are off duty they should try to speak and write appropriately to nonprofessional situations.

There are many lawyers and judges whose speeches, briefs, and decisions are written with distinction and with only as many technical terms as the subject demands. The style is properly formal, the allusions must be to cases that give precedents, but room may be found for allusion also to general experience, without any loss of exactness.

A brief dissenting opinion of Mr. Justice Holmes illustrates a compact but readable judicial style. A majority of the Supreme Court had decided that the State of Ohio could tax a membership in the New York Stock Exchange owned by a resident of Ohio, on the ground that it was personal property, not like real estate, which would be taxed by the state in which it lay.

> The question whether a seat in the New York Stock Exchange is taxable in Ohio consistently with the principles established by this Court seems to me more difficult than it does to my brethren. All rights are intangible personal relations between the subject and the object of them created by law. But it is established that it is not enough that the subject, the owner

of the right, is within the power of the taxing State. He cannot be taxed for land situated elsewhere, and the same is true of personal property permanently out of the jurisdiction. It does not matter, I take it, whether the interest is legal or equitable, or what the machinery by which it is reached, but the question is whether the object of the right is so local in its foundation and prime meaning that it should stand like an interest in land. If left to myself I should have thought that the foundation and substance of the plaintiff's right was the right of himself and his associates personally to enter the New York Stock Exchange building and to do business there. I should have thought that all the rest was incidental to that and that that on its face was localized in New York. If so, it does not matter whether it is real or personal property or that it adds to the owner's credit and facilities in Ohio. The same would be true of a great estate in New York land.—*Representative Opinions of Mr. Justice Holmes*, edited by Alfred Lief, pp. 265-66

(REFERENCE: Benjamin N. Cardozo, "Law and Literature" (pp. 3-40 in the volume of the same title—New York, 1931); F. A. Philbrick, *Language and the Law* (New York, 1949)

leisure   Usual American pronunciation, lē′zhər; sometimes lezh′ər.

less, fewer   *Fewer* refers only to number and things that are *counted:*

> Fewer cars were on the road.   There were fewer than sixty present.

In formal usage *less* refers only to amount or quantity and things measured:

> There was a good deal less tardiness in the second term [amount].
> There was even less hay than the summer before.

Fewer seems to be declining in use and *less* commonly takes its place:

> Less hands were required for this work. . . .—KENNETH BURKE, *Attitudes Toward History*, p. 175
> . . . but polled only a sliver of additional votes and won three less seats.—Foreign Policy Association *Bulletin*, Mar. 3, 1950, p. 2

less, lesser   Both are used as comparatives (of *little*), *less* more usually referring to size, or quantity (less time, less food), *lesser* a formal word, referring to value or importance (a lesser writer).

let (leave)   A common vulgate and local idiom is the use of *leave* where formal and informal English use *let*. Both idioms are shown in this sentence by a student who was obviously making a transition between the two levels:

> In high school I was cured of the practice of leaving [local] notebooks go, but I fell into the habit of letting [general] homework slide.

College people should use *let*—*let it go, let it lie where it is.*

let's Contraction of *let us.* Needs an apostrophe.

Letters

1. **General observations on correspondence. 2. Personal letters. 3. Business letters.**

1. **General observations on correspondence. (a)** MATERIALS. The stationery stores are full of novelties, which may appeal to one's taste, but the standard sizes and styles of paper are never outmoded and are usually cheaper and of better quality:

Note paper—A four-page sheet to be folded once across the middle for the envelope.

Club paper—A sheet about 7¼ by 11 inches, with two folds fitting an envelope 3¾ by 7½.

Business letter paper—8½ by 11 inches, to be folded twice across for a long envelope or folded across the middle and then twice more for the ordinary envelope about six inches long.

A fairly good quality of stationery is worth its cost in the good impression it helps make on the reader.

Typewritten copy is of course the norm in business correspondence. In personal letters there is some question, though in the United States so many people do their own typing that among acquaintances typewritten copy is quite good form—and usually welcome. In the earlier stages of a friendship longhand is perhaps preferable, and it should almost always be used for invitations and acknowledgments and in any letters conveying unusual sentiment or feeling. (See *Typewritten copy.)

b) STYLES. The pages should appeal to the reader's eye. This means leaving good margins, centering the body of the letter on the page so that the whole may present a neatly balanced and proportioned appearance, spacing the parts of the letter so that they are distinct but still form a unit, and so on. The paragraphs are usually short, three or four sentences, or less, and spaced distinctly.

Ingenuity can usually find a way of subduing even long addresses that must sometimes be used in headings. Find an arrangement of the lines that looks well in your typing or longhand.

Style in indenting and in punctuation at the end of display lines is divided. In typed letters a straight lining at the left of the heading and inside address is more usual now than a hanging *indention:

Straight form—More common	*Indented form—Less common*
Graham, Sutton and Company	Graham, Sutton and Company
1007 E. Newgate Street	1007 E. Newgate Street
Chicago 3, Illinois	Chicago 3, Illinois

In longhand letters the indented form is more common.

The form used for the address on the envelope should be consistent with that used for the heading and the address on the first page of the letter; that is, either the straight or the indented form should be used throughout. Punctuation marks are not now used at the ends of the lines of address or heading:

Old-fashioned style	Current style
Graham, Sutton and Company,	Graham, Sutton and Company
1007 E. Newgate Street,	1007 E. Newgate Street
Chicago 3, Illinois.	Chicago 3, Illinois

c) ENVELOPES. The first requirements of the address on the envelope are completeness and clearness, for the sake of the post office. "Address your mail to street and number," and in cities include the postal zone.

2. Personal letters. (a) FORM. The form of personal letters varies with the intimacy between the writer and recipient. No heading except the date is needed between regular correspondents, but the writer's address in the heading is often a convenience and a necessity in letters to occasional correspondents. They may not keep address books and aren't likely to remember exact addresses.

The salutation varies:

Dear Bob,   Dear Miss Breckenridge,
Dear Miss Breckenridge: (The colon is more formal.)
Formal: My dear Miss Breckenridge:

Formal personal letters, especially between professional men who are not intimate, may have the salutation "Dear Sir:" and the recipient's name at the bottom, flush with the left margin.

The complimentary close ranges from "Yours" or any other expression of sentiment to "Yours sincerely," "Cordially yours," "Yours very truly," between people little acquainted. When there is any doubt, rely on one of the regular formulas for the close, "Yours truly," "Yours very truly." Sentence conclusions ("Assuring you of our continued interest, I beg to remain, Yours very truly") are now out of fashion.

b) TONE AND STYLE. It would be useless to lay down rules to govern letters to relatives and friends. They should represent your own sense of what the reader will like and what will sound like yourself. They are like conversation, and the style will ordinarily be *familiar or whatever you would use when face to face with the recipient. But, as in so much conversation, we often sink to our laziest in letters to the people we write the oftenest. It is worth while occasionally to read over a letter to see if *we* would enjoy receiving it, to see if we have told enough to make the incidents interesting, to see if we have written with reasonable care, if we are paying our readers the courtesy they deserve in neatness and appropriate expression. Revising an occasional letter will perhaps raise the average of them all.

It is conventional to say that the art of letter writing is dead. Perhaps not so many Contributor's Club essays are sent through the mail as formerly, but an occasional letter we receive and an occasional published volume show that letter writers can still describe events racily, can still hit off the people they meet in apt characterizations, and can occasionally discuss ideas with some insight and gusto. These letters are a challenge to us when we have material that deserves special attention.

(For formal invitations and so on, see *Social correspondence.)

3. Business letters. Since business letters usually pass between people who are not acquainted or who at least are not writing for reasons of friendship at the moment, certain matters of form are important in handling routine information.

The writer's complete address is necessary, either in a printed letterhead or in a written heading, to serve as an address for the reply. An inside address is conventional (and useful when the letter is dictated or when several are being written at the same time or when it is to be filed). In addressing a firm, *Messrs.* is not often used in the United States. The salutations are:

Dear Sir: Gentlemen: Dear Sirs:
Dear Madam: Ladies: (Formal or showy, Mesdames:)

When a letter is intended for a particular member of a firm, this form is sometimes used:

> Graham, Sutton and Company
> 1007 E. Newgate Street
> Chicago 3, Illinois
>
> Gentlemen: Attention Mr. Stephen Lange

A less formal and more direct form of address is perhaps more commonly used:

> Mr. Stephen Lange
> Graham, Sutton and Company
> 1007 E. Newgate Street
> Chicago 3, Illinois
>
> Dear Mr. Lange:

When a man's position is made part of the inside address, arrange it so that no one line becomes conspicuously longer than the others. In general the title should be joined to the individual's rather than to the firm's name:

> Mr. Leonard T. Hosic
> Personnel Director
> Allen, Swift and Company
> 4826 Commercial Street
> Allentown, Ohio

The body of a business letter should be clear, direct, and as brief as is consistent with clearness. A separate paragraph is used for each item or for each subdivision of the message. The tone may be curt

---

TAYLOR BOOKSHOP
80 WINCHESTER STREET
NEW YORK CITY

June 16, 1950

Mr. James T. Foster
2645 Grantham Terrace
Kew Gardens, L.I., N.Y.

Dear Mr. Foster:

Several weeks ago you asked us to let you know when the new Fischer edition of Shakespeare would be on sale. It is obtainable now, and we think you will like it very much. The volumes are three by four inches in size, bound in red and gold.

There are 25 books in the complete set, which costs $15.75, but separate volumes may be bought for 65¢ each. We are enclosing a list of the works included in the Fischer edition.

If you wish to place an order, we shall be glad to take care of it for you.

Yours truly,

Elizabeth Reagan

Elizabeth Reagan

FORM FOR BUSINESS LETTER

in routine matters—amateurs are apt to indulge in unnecessary explanation—or it may be full and persuasive. In all letters, especially those asking questions or outlining plans, all relevant information should be given.

The desire for brevity should not lead to a telegraphic style or shortcuts in expression. The old tags like "Yours received and contents noted," "In reply to your favor of the 12th inst.," and "Would say" have disappeared from the correspondence of careful business houses.

The best way to become informed on business letters is to study the practice of reputable companies. If you are specially interested in business correspondence, start a collection of the best examples that come your way.

The close of a business letter is:

Yours truly,   Yours very truly,   Very truly yours,

or some such formula. Only the first word is capitalized and the phrase is followed by a comma (though some writers are dropping the comma, since it is as unnecessary as those once standing after the display lines).

Although in formal correspondence a woman does not use *Mrs.* or *Miss* with her name in a signature, in informal and business correspondence it is frequently used:

(Mrs.) Dorothy T. Olson   Dorothy T. Olson   (Miss) Dorothy T. Olson
(Mrs. Henry A. Olson)

See *Business English. Recent manuals of business writing will give further details of form and suggestions for content.

Levels of usage   Usage varies according to the education and social class of the writer and reader, speaker and listener, and according to the usual circumstances in which particular words and constructions are found. This is one of the fundamental facts of language, and one that causes many problems in speaking and writing. This *Guide-Index* distinguishes three main levels, Formal, Informal, and Vulgate English, and various subdivisions of these. It is necessary to understand the distinctions between them to be able to apply the specific suggestions made in the various articles. They are described in full in Chapter 2, "Variations due to use," page 37. See especially the table of levels on pages 40-41.

lever   Both lev'ər and lē'vər are in good use.

liable   See *likely—apt—liable.

Library work See Chapter 13, The Reference Paper, page 363.

lie See *lay—lie.

lighted—lit Both forms are in good use as the past tense and past participle of *light. Lighted* is probably more common as the adjective and past participle:

> a lighted lamp   He had lighted a fire.

Lit is perhaps more common as the past tense:

> He lit a cigaret. [or] He lighted a cigaret.

lightning, lightening The flash is *lightning;* making lighter (a load) is *lightening.*

like—as 1. In written English *as* and *as if* are used to introduce clauses of comparison:

> People try to get to college *as* they used to try to get to heaven.
> Habit grips a person *as* an octopus does.
> He dives so that it looks *as if* he would land flat, but he enters the water perfectly.

2. In colloquial English *like* is often used in clauses of comparison. *Like* is less common in the East than in the West and South (where it is standard in formal as well as informal usage), but it is used more or less throughout the United States and in England also:

> He dives so it looks like he would land flat.
> "I get around the country a good bit, gentlemen, and I can tell you as a fact that he's slipping. Like you just said, people are waking up to the fact that somebody's got to pay for all this spending."—GLUYAS WILLIAMS, "Raconteurs," *The New Yorker*, Oct. 8, 1938
> He treated her like a child, joking with her like she was a two year old. (Report of oral testimony in court)

In all regions and in all dialects *like* is used as a preposition introducing a comparison:

> Habit grips a person like an octopus.
> She took to selling like a duck to water.
> That description fits him like a glove.

3. In the last few years the use of *like* as a conjunction has greatly increased. The vogue of fiction, in which it often stands appropriately in the conversation and sometimes in the informal prose surrounding the conversation, and the popular radio programs in colloquial or local English are doubtless in part responsible for

this increased currency. In fact, if editors and publishers did not enforce the use of *as* instead of *like* according to the rules in their stylebooks, it is possible that *like* would become the dominant form, and it increasingly appears in print:

> Eleanor was alone like in her dreams.—JOHN DOS PASSOS, *The 42nd Parallel*, p. 217
> You used to go in there and find Henry not at the middle of his desk, but sitting at one end, nervously, like he was afraid of the job.—CAL TINNEY, *The Philadelphia Record*, Nov. 17, 1938

This use of *like* in public address is quite common. One of our most fastidious radio announcers said:

> You can play Information Please in your home just like the experts do here in the studio.

Historically both forms are good, since both are parts of the older *like as* ("Like as a father pitieth his children . . ."). The speakers of some regions have taken *as*, of others *like*. *Like* is preferable from the standpoint of meaning, because *as* has several different meanings and several functions in the language and so is relatively weak. *Like* is more exact and more emphatic in a comparison than *as* can be.

At the present time so many people object to *like* as a conjunction that it should be used with caution and probably not used in formal writing. But it is obviously on its way to becoming generally accepted and is a good instance of change in usage, one that we can observe as it takes place.

(REFERENCES: Curme, *Syntax*, pp. 281-82; Pooley, pp. 153-55.)

likely—apt—liable   The principal meanings of these words are:

> *likely:* expected, probably
> *liable:* possible (of an unpleasant event); responsible (as for damages)
> *apt:* tending toward, naturally fit

Likely is the most commonly needed of the three, and colloquially both *apt* and (in some localities) *liable* are used in the ordinary sense of *likely:*

> It's *likely* [or, *apt;* or, locally, *liable*] to rain when the wind is southwest.

line   is business English (What's your line?—a line of goods) or slang (He handed her a line). As a *counter word it is usually deadwood and could better be left out:

> My own experience along business lines [that is, *in business*] has been slight.

Another book along the same lines as *Microbe Hunters* [similar to *Microbe Hunters*], but with a fine story, is *Arrowsmith*.

Linguistics **1. The science of linguistics.** The science dealing with language is called *linguistics* (sometimes *philology*, its older name) and a scientific student of language is a *linguist* or *philologist*. Linguistics is a complex science, with numerous subdivisions, each with its technique for observing and considering its material, its hypotheses, laws, and theories, and even forecasts of future trends. The principal subdivisions of linguistics are:

a) PHONETICS AND PHONEMICS, the study of sounds, how they are made by the vocal organs and how they are manipulated in various languages, types of pronunciation, and sound changes. (See *Pronunciation.)

b) MORPHOLOGY, the forms of words, especially their inflections, as in the conjugations of verbs, declensions of nouns and pronouns, comparison of adjectives and adverbs. These forms are discussed under the heads of the various parts of speech: *Adjectives, types and forms, *Nouns § 2, *Verbs, and in other articles like *Accusative case, *Plurals, *Subjunctives.

c) ETYMOLOGY, the derivation of words and the steps by which they have moved from their early to their current forms. See *Origin of words.

d) SEMANTICS (or SEMASIOLOGY), the meanings of words and the ways in which these meanings change. See Chapter 11, The Meaning of Words, page 303.

e) SYNTAX is the study of the use of words in phrases, clauses, sentences. (See Chapter 4, Problems in English grammar, *Grammar, *Idiom and idioms, *Phrases, *Clauses, and many particular entries.)

f) PHILOSOPHICAL GRAMMAR (or LINGUISTIC THEORY), general laws of language and speculations on its possible origins, functions, underlying tendencies.

There are various applications of these sciences, such as *lexicography*, the art of dictionary making, and *orthography*, the study of spelling.

The various types of *Grammar* (a general term for a selection of linguistic facts) are described under that head.

Since language is an activity of people, a phase of conduct, linguists cannot work entirely by themselves but are helped by other scientists, especially psychologists, anthropologists, and sociologists, and in turn give materials to them. And on the other hand, the study of language runs into artistic considerations, contributing to literary criticism and the art of composition, where language is not only described but its effectiveness must be considered, and taste and judgment count as well as scientific principles.

The outstanding trait of a linguist's approach to language is detachment—contrasting with the emotion often shown by nonprofessional users in defending or disapproving matters of speech. A linguist accepts "He ain't got none," "You're all wet" as facts of language—as well as words like *hemolysis* and *sternutation*. This does not mean that he uses all of these locutions himself or recommends them to others, but he notices that certain people use them and he observes and defines their place in the language.

2. Recording examples of usage. If we are going to study our language in college, we should study it scientifically as far as that is possible and so put our effort on a par with other college subjects. This means that first we should observe carefully the spoken and written language of others, especially of those whose language we should like our own to resemble. We should try to get rid of preferences and prejudices that are not supported by evidence of good usage. We should investigate and even experiment with particular usage so far as we can and come to some conclusion as to its fitness for our own expression. In short, we should become amateur linguists—students of our language.

Anyone who is seriously interested in such an approach to his language will do everything possible to sharpen his observation of actual usage, so that he won't have to be completely dependent on dictionaries and handbooks. Especially if he is interested in some particular trend, in sentences, perhaps, or in some idioms, such as the prepositions used with *different*, he might keep track of what he finds in actual listening and reading.

The easiest way to do this is to have a file of observations on 3x5 or 4x6 slips or cards. The 4x6 are probably the more useful, since they have space for recording more than one example and for discussion. The slips should be labeled at the top with the name of the particular point dealt with, under which it will be filed. Exact reference should be made to the source of the quotation, or to the speaker and place and circumstances of speaking.

The first slip reproduced on page 632 shows a quotation taken down to illustrate the use of *verbless sentences. The second slip contains the data that stands back of the entry *drought—drouth in this *Index*.

Keep the slips in alphabetical order, unless you have a great many of them and want to make some topical groupings. You don't need to worry about your file getting unwieldy, for you won't gather

1. EXAMPLE OF USAGE
Sub-class of the topic

Label—the topic illustrated

The example

Exact source— If from speech put down time, place, and identify speaker

> Verbless sentence---Answers to questions
>
> When an editor does the work and you still have to make corrections on the proof because his work was not perfect, can you make him pay for them? Not likely. If the printer does the preparation and you have to make the corrections in the type to get a satisfactory result, will the printer make the corrections gratis? Hardly, unless you have a very clear agreement with him in writing.
>
> John Benbow Manuscript & Proof
> N. Y. Oxford 1937 p. 22

2. TOPIC WITH RECORD OF INVESTIGATION

Label "Authorities"

Special source

Reasoning

Conclusion

> drought--drouth
>
> Web.Coll.5th ed: drought. Also drouth
> Am.Coll.Dict., 1947: drought; Also drouth
> Not in Fowler
>
> Sylvanus Kingsley, editorial writer Portland Oregonian, in Words Sept. 1936: prefers drouth as 'the more practical and popular etymology'-- but 6 of 1 and half dozen of the other
>
> OE drugath. th puts it in group with abstracts width, breadth. See height-highth. Shows influence of events on language, since notable dryness of recent years has given the word currency and brought into prominence the colloquial form
>
> Usage divided. Drought probably more common in formal use, but drouth gaining esp. in newspapers.

many unless you are really interested, and if you are interested they will form a hobby—and will help you make accurate statements about English usage instead of just guessing.

(REFERENCES: The works given in the Bibliography at the beginning of this book. Of these the best for a beginner are probably Kennedy, Krapp, and McKnight, with Bloomfield for a more advanced study.)

Link **Linking verbs** Correction: **The verb marked is used as a linking verb and should be followed by an adjective or noun construction.**

A verb may be used so that it has little or no meaning of its own but functions chiefly in connecting a subject with a predicate adjective or noun. In such a construction it is called a *linking verb* or *copula.*

Be and other linking verbs are followed not by adverbs but by adjectives or nouns in single words or phrases or clauses, known as *predicate adjectives* and *predicate nominatives* respectively.

Be is most commonly used as a linking verb, since in its ordinary use it has little specific meaning and performs chiefly the verb functions of tense, person, number:

> The man *is* a carpenter.   This bottle *was* full.

Many other verbs are used as linking verbs—Curme counts about sixty in current English and says, "Their wide and varied use is the most prominent feature of our language" (*Parts of Speech,* page 67). Instead of having a verb of full meaning like *colden,* English uses the nearly meaningless verb *turn* or *get* and the adjective *cold,* which carries the chief part of the meaning, in such a sentence as *The weather turned cold.* Many verbs are used with full meaning of their own (as *fell* in "The tree *fell* into the water") or as linking verbs (as *fell* in "She *fell* silent" or "He *fell* ill"). Some typical linking verbs are:

> He *became* a doctor. The butter *tastes* rancid. She *felt* sad.
> He *acts* old. The ground *sounds* hollow. He *grew* more and more aloof.
> He *appeared* to be gaining ground. This *looks* first rate. His story *seemed* credible.

> His features *had become* sharper; his eyes, with their black-blue glitter of chilled steel, *had become* harder and more impenetrable. His flaxen hair, still profuse, and his little bi-forked beard, *had turned* darker. His nose *had grown* thinner, reminding one of the beak of a bird of prey.—DMITRI MEREJKOWSKI, *The Romance of Leonardo da Vinci,* p. 403

(SEE *be § 2, *Predicate adjectives. REFERENCES: Kennedy, pp. 476-77; Curme, *Parts of Speech,* pp. 66-69, *Syntax,* pp. 26-28 [list on p. 27].)

Literal use of words   See Chapter 12, "Figurative use of words," page 344.

literary   *Literary,* as applied to style, usually means possessing traits that are characteristic of the more conservative tradition of English literature. Its connotation may be "distinguished" or it may be "bookish." (See Chapter 2, "Formal English," page 48.)

Litotes   (lī′tə tēz, lit′ə tēz)   See *Negatives, *Understatement.

little   *Little* is overused by sentimentalists ("little dear" and so on).

loan as a verb   In spite of attempts to keep *loan* only as a noun and to make *lend* the corresponding verb, *loan* is still properly a verb, at least in American usage:

Verb: I loaned [or lent] him $2. Noun: He got a loan of two dollars.

Loan words Words that have been taken into English from other languages (*khaki, intelligentsia*) and have become English words. (See *Foreign words in English, *Origin of words § 2b.)

Local **Localisms** Correction: **The expression marked is in local use only. Replace it by a word or construction in general American use.**

A *localism*, or *provincialism*, is a word or other expression in regular use in a certain region but not in others in which the same language is used. The southern, western, and northeastern sections of the United States differ somewhat in sounds, in words, and in constructions. Localisms are appropriate to conversation, familiar writing, stories, and to much other informal writing, but are often out of place in impersonal and formal writing. (For discussion see Chapter 2, "Variations due to place," page 58.)

locate is used for *settle* (The family located near the present town of Nashua) and for *find* (I can't locate the letter now). It is dead-wood in defining the location of specific places:

Zermatt is [located] right near the Italian border, just to the west of the Italian Lake District.

Locution is a handy term for referring to a word or a unified group of words; that is, it may be applied to a single word or to a phrase or clause considered as a meaning group. *Phrase, a meaning group, that is* are three locutions.

Long variants Some amateur writers are tempted to add an extra prefix or suffix to a word that already carries the meaning they intend. They write *ir*regardless, though *regardless* already means "without regard to." Some like to add sonorous suffixes that are quite useless, like the *-ation* in *origination*, which means no more than *origin*. Some other tempting long variants to be avoided are:

> *analyzation* for *analysis*
> *confliction* for *conflict*
> *emotionality* when only *emotion* is meant
> *commercialistic* for *commercial*
> *ruination* for *ruin* (*ruination* is a colloquial emphatic form of *ruin*)
> *hotness* for *heat*
> *intermingle* for *mingle*
> *repay* when simple *pay* is meant, as in paying dividends
> *subsidization* for *subsidizing*
> Unnecessary *-al* endings, as *transportation*[al] system, *government*[al] policy
> *utilize* when only *use* is meant

-ly

Some of these words are not in good use at all (*analyzation*) and show lack of observation of language in anyone who uses them. Others are in use but show poor judgment in the writer who chooses them when more compact forms exist. If any number are used they will weigh down a piece of writing and make it flabby.

(SEE *Origin of words § 3 and compare ch. 12, "Big words," p. 339. REFERENCE: Fowler, "Long variants.")

look When used as a verb of complete meaning (to use the eyes, gaze), *look* is modified by an adverb: *look searchingly, look sharp.*

As a linking verb, equivalent to *appear, look* is followed by an adjective which modifies the subject: *He looks well, or healthy, or tired . . . .*

Loose sentences Sentences in which the grammatical form and the essential meaning are complete before the end. (See Chapter 10, "Loose and periodic sentences," page 280.)

lose, loose Associate the spelling of these words with the pronunciation and meaning:

lose   (lo͞oz)—lose a bet, lose sleep, lose money
loose (lo͞os)—loose a knot, a loose screw
loosed (lo͞ost)—untied, freed
lost   (lôst)—a lost road, a lost soul, lost his way

lot, lots of The colloquial uses of these words, appropriate in speech and in some informal writing, are avoided in formal writing:

Colloquial: We tried a lot of different kinds.
Formal: We tried a good many different kinds.
Informal: He has lots of friends . . . a lot of money.
Formal: He has many friends . . . a good deal of money.

Do not join the article *a* to lot: *a lot*, not *alot*.

lousy Except when meaning "infested with lice" *lousy* is a strong slang word of abuse, just now weakened to a counter word of disapproval, expressive if not used too often, but offensive to most ears.

lovely is a colloquial *counter word of approval, useful chiefly because its pronunciation can (by some people) be drawn out indefinitely and practically sung (a lovely time).

lowbrow See *highbrow.

Lower case Correction: Use a lower case ("small") letter instead of a capital in this word. See *Capital Letters, *Type.   *lc*

-ly See *Adverbs, types and forms § 3.

635

M The sound represented by the letter *m* is a nasal consonant made with lips closed: *man, music, diamond, drummer, sum, lamp.*

M may represent a syllable by itself ("syllabic *m*"): *spasm* (spaz′m̩ or spaz′əm), *tell 'em* (tel′m̩ or tel′əm). Some people tend to make *m* syllabic in words like *elm, film* (el′m̩, fil′m̩) instead of pronouncing them as single syllables (elm, film).

madam As a formula of address *Madam* or *Dear Madam* is used for both married and unmarried women.

Magazine indexes See Chapter 13, "Periodical indexes," page 371.

majority, plurality Strictly *majority* means "more than half of" a certain number; *plurality* means "more than the next highest." *Plurality* is not much used now in the United States, the meaning of *majority* being extended to "an excess of votes over all others cast"—and even often used in the exact sense of *plurality*, simply the excess of votes over the next highest. In an election with three candidates and 12,000 votes cast, one received 7000, one 3000, and one 2000; the winner would have a *plurality* of 4000 (in common usage, a majority of 4000); strictly speaking, he would have a *majority* of 1000.

Colloquially *majority* is often used of amounts or quantities as well as of numbers:

Colloquial: We spent the majority of the day there.
Written: We spent most [or: the greater part] of the day there.
Wordy: The majority of students are interested in football.
Better: Most students are interested in football.

Malapropism A malapropism is a confusion of two words somewhat similar in sound but different in meaning, as *arduous* love for *ardent* love. Malapropisms are the cause of many *boners but are often intentionally used for humorous effect, as they were by Sheridan in creating the part of Mrs. Malaprop in *The Rivals*, whose speeches gave the name to these confusions in language:

"I would by no means wish a daughter of mine to be a progeny of learning. . . . Then, sir, she should have a supercilious knowledge in accounts; —and as she grew up, I would have her instructed in geometry, that she might know something of the contagious countries. . . ."—RICHARD BRINSLEY SHERIDAN, *The Rivals*, Act I, Scene ii

Malapropisms are more effective in speech than in writing.

man, woman These are preferred to the more pretentious *gentleman* or *lady*, except when *man* or *woman* would sound conspicuously blunt.

In business English the original social distinctions between *woman—lady*, and *man—gentleman* have been almost reversed. A salesman faced with a customer who wanted to exchange a purchase, turned to his fellow salesmen and said, "Did any of you gentlemen wait on this man?" And a woman looking for work asked, "Are you the woman who wanted a lady to wash for her?"

Ladies and gentlemen is a *formula in addressing an audience. The singular form alone is used as an adjective:

manpower	manholes	woman hater	woman suffrage

(COMPARE *freshman, freshmen.)

Manner Adverbs of manner answer the question *How? Barely, brightly, gracefully, nicely, quick* or *quickly, swimmingly* are adverbs of manner. They are formed now by adding *-ly* to adjectives and participles, though a number of older adverbs of manner do not have the *-ly: sharp* or *sharply, slow* or *slowly*, etc. (See *Adverbs, types and forms § 3.)

As, as if, as though (formal) and *like* (colloquial) are conjunctions introducing adverbial clauses of manner:

He looked as if he'd seen a ghost.   They left as noisily as they came.

Manuscript form Correction: Your manuscript does not have the proper form. Revise or rewrite as directed.   *Ms*

See Chapter 1, "Preparing the manuscript," page 20, for details of good manuscript practice. See also *Typewritten copy.

Material Some suggestions on gathering and handling material will be found in Chapter 1, "Gathering material," page 11; Chapter 13, "Choosing a subject," page 367, and "Sources of reference," page 369; and Chapter 7, "Materials of paragraphs," page 171.

matinee Spelled without an accent mark. Pronounced mat′ ə nā′ (mat′n̬ ā′), but tending toward mat′ə nā′ (as in England).

may See *can—may (could—might).

may be, maybe *Maybe* is a colloquial adverb meaning "perhaps," a cutting down of *it may be; may be* is a verb form:

Maybe you'll have better luck next time. He may be the next mayor.

me See *Pronouns § 1, *between you and me, *It's me.

Mean **Meaning of words** Correction: The word marked is inexactly used. Replace it by one that represents your meaning.

For discussion of meaning of words, see Chapter 11, §§ 4-6, pages 318-327.

Mechanics of writing includes punctuation, spelling, forms of words, word order, and sometimes sentence movement. For discussion of some points of "mechanics" and for exercises, see Chapters 4-6 and numerous *Index* articles.

medieval Some years ago the American Historical Association decided to change the spelling from *mediaeval* to *medieval*, now the usual form. Pronunciation mē′di ē′vl̥, or med′i ē′vl̥.

medium Plural usually *mediums*—always in the spiritualistic sense, practically always in the general sense, and usually now as applied to the different advertising *mediums* (newspapers, magazines, radio, billboards, etc.). *Media* is most used in scientific contexts.

messrs. is the abbreviation of French *messieurs* but pronounced as English, mes′ərz. It is used as the plural of *Mr.* (Messrs. Ives and Johnson) and sometimes, though rarely now in American usage, used in addressing firms (Messrs. Brown, Hubbell and Company).

Metaphor A figure of speech in which a comparison is implied rather than stated: a *finger* of light, a slender *thread* of sense. (See Chapter 12, "Resemblance," page 348.)

meter is now more common spelling than *metre*. The second *e* drops out in derivatives: *metrical, metrics, metric system*. (For a description of English meters see *Verse form.)

Metonymy (me ton′ə mi) A figure of speech in which the name of something closely associated with a thing is substituted for its name: *paper* for financial assets, *in Dickens* for in Dickens' works. (See Chapter 12, "Resemblance," page 348.)

might See *can—may (could—might).

Minimum essentials See Chapter 4, Problems in English Grammar, page 91.

Mis **Misrelated modifiers** Correction: Revise the sentence so that the expression marked is clearly related to the word the meaning requires.

A construction which from its position in a sentence seems to modify a word which it cannot sensibly modify is "misrelated" or "dangles" and should be avoided in writing. See Chapter 4, "Misleading or vague reference," page 109, and "Misrelated modifiers," page 112.

A participle which is used as an adjective should modify accurately either a noun or pronoun:

> Looking further to the left, we saw the spire of a church. (*Looking* clearly modifies *we*.)
> Defined in psychological terms, a fanatic is a man who consciously overcompensates a secret doubt. [*Defined* clearly modifies *fanatic*.]—
> ALDOUS HUXLEY, *Proper Studies*, p. 220

A verbid that precedes the main clause and does not relate to the subject of that clause is misrelated:

> Upon telling my story to the advisor, he stopped and thought. (For: When I told. . . .)
> Motoring down Route 17 toward New York City, numerous signs read "Visit Our Snake Farm." (For: *Motoring* down Route 17 toward New York City, *we* saw numerous signs that read . . .)
> What if, forced to climb over this solid cloud bank, ice should form on the wings and force them down into the wild country? (The ice isn't forced to climb.)
> Born in England in 1853, John MacDowell's seafaring activities began after he had emigrated to this country. (His seafaring activities were not born in England.)

Dangling participles should be avoided simply because educated readers do not expect to find them. As a rule there is no real question of the proper meaning of the sentence, though sometimes the faulty reference of a participle is ludicrous as in Professor Kennedy's gem:

> Having swelled because of the rains, the workman was unable to remove the timber.

Such dangling constructions should not be confused with the *absolute construction, in which the participial phrase is equivalent to a subordinate clause and is properly used, especially for adding details:

> He had worked for four hours, copy piling up quite satisfactorily.

(SEE *Participles for further examples of these constructions. REFERENCES: Curme, *Syntax*, pp. 158-60; Reuben Steinbach, "The Misrelated Constructions," *American Speech*, 1930, 5:181-97.)

Infinitive phrases may be misrelated:

> Faulty: To get the most out of a sport, the equipment must be in perfect condition. (The equipment does not profit from the sport.)
> Improved: To get the most out of a sport, you must have your equipment in perfect condition.

This construction should not be confused with an absolute infinitive phrase which is quite correct:

To judge from his looks, he can't be more than forty-five.

(SEE *Infinitives § 4.)

Phrases are sometimes similarly misrelated:

At eleven, our family moved to Kansas City. (Clearer: When I was eleven, our family moved to Kansas City.)

miss Plural *misses*, sometimes pronounced mis ēz´, distinct from *mis'iz* (*Mrs.*): "the Misses Angel and Joyce." When the misses are from the same family the plural could be, formally, the Misses Smith; informally, the Miss Smiths.

Miss is used only with a person's name—except in humor or sales talk. *Missy* is the diminutive, often disparaging.

Misspelled words See Chapter 6, Spelling, page 155, and *Spelling.

mix, mixer *Mix* is informal and colloquial for *associate with; mixer* for *sociable person* or for the person who develops new acquaintances readily. Though slang in their origin, they seem excusable because of the colorlessness of the more reputable words. The objection often made to *good mixer* is not so much linguistic as that college students seem to overvalue "mixing."

Mixed figures of speech See Chapter 12, "Consistency," page 347.

Mixed usage Many errors in writing spring from the unintentional mixture of different levels of usage. Colloquial or conspicuously informal words or idioms may stray into formal writing; vulgate locutions may appear in informal writing, or so may a word usually confined to law or business. Distinctly formal words and idioms are equally inappropriate in informal writing—and often appear because the writer is trying to avoid some natural expression. The principal way to develop in language is to cultivate feeling for different styles and their fitness for a given job. See Chapters 2 and 3, pages 33-90.

Modal auxiliaries See *Auxiliary verbs and entries on *be, *can —may, *have, *shall—will, and other auxiliaries.

Modifiers Modifiers are words or groups of words that restrict, limit, make more exact the meaning of other words. In these examples the words in italics modify the words in small caps:

a *cold, windy* DAY   He FAILED *miserably.*   a *truly* GREAT—a *truly great* MAN.   *Coming around the corner,* WE met him head on.   *As we came around the corner,* WE SAW HIM BOARDING A TROLLEY.

In general the modifiers of nouns and pronouns are adjectives, participles, adjective phrases, adjective clauses; the modifiers of verbs, adjectives, and adverbs are adverbs, adverbial phrases or clauses.

(SEE ch. 4, "Modifiers," p. 111; *Adjectives in use; *Adverbs in use; *Clauses; *Misrelated modifiers; *Participles; *Phrases; *Restrictive and nonrestrictive.)

Money 1. Exact sums of money are usually written in figures:

72¢ $4.98 $5 $168.75 $42,810

Round sums are more likely to be written in words: two hundred dollars, a million and a half dollars.

In factual books or articles involving frequent references to sums of money, however, figures are often used throughout.

2. In consecutive writing, amounts are usually written out when used adjectively:

A Million Dollar Baby in the Five and Ten Cent Store

Informally, figures are often used: an 85¢ seat.

3. Commas and periods, $ and ¢ signs are used as in the examples in § 1 above. (For an example of writing sums of money in text, see the paragraphs of illustration in *Numbers § 2.)

Monosyllables A monosyllable is a word of one syllable:

asked   bright   feel   fill   longed   word

Monosyllables should not be divided at the end of lines, not even words like *asked, longed.* (See *Division of words.)

A *polysyllable* strictly has three or more syllables, but since we use *dissyllable* (having two syllables) rather rarely, *polysyllable* usually means a word having two or more syllables.

Monotony See *Variety in writing, and the articles there referred to.

Months In reference matter and informal writing, the names of months with more than four letters are abbreviated in dates:

Jan. 21, 1951   Aug. 16, 1950   Dec. 25, 1948
But: May 1, 1949   June 30, 1950   July 4, 1951

When only the month or month and year are given, abbreviation would be rare:

January 1950   Every January he tries again.

In formal writing, the names of the months would not be abbreviated at all.

(SEE *Numbers § 1a; *Dates.)

Mood By the forms of mood, a verb may distinguish the way in which the statement it makes is regarded by the writer:

Indicative: as a fact, a statement
Subjunctive: as a wish, possibility, doubt
Imperative: as a command

(SEE the articles *Indicative mood, *Subjunctives, *Commands and requests, *Verbs.)

moral, morale Although the *e* is not in the French noun we borrowed as mə ral' ("a confident mental state"), it is a convenient and natural English way of showing there is something peculiar in the pronunciation. It also distinguishes this *morale* from *moral* ("concerning right conduct").

Morpheme In linguistic description, the smallest verbal unit conveying meaning, a word (*boy*, *tall*, *go*) or a part of a word (prefixes, suffixes).

(REFERENCE: Bloomfield, pp. 161-68.)

most (almost) *Most* is the common colloquial clip (*Origin of words § 3c) of *almost:* "A drop in prices will appeal to most everybody." It would be used in writing conversation and in informal style, but is ordinarily out of place in written English.

(REFERENCE: Pooley, p. 156.)

Mr. is written out only when it represents colloquial usage and when it is used without a name:

"They're only two for five, mister." (But:) Mr. Schlesser   Mr. John T. Flynn

It is one of the class of abbreviations from which a period is being increasingly omitted. See *Abbreviations, § 3.

Mrs. is written out only in representing colloquial or vulgate usage and is then spelled *missis* (or *missus*):

Mrs. Dorothy M. Adams   Mrs. Adams   "Where's the missis?"

Mrs. is not combined with a husband's title except in small town *journalese. Write *Mrs. Dodd*, not *Mrs. Prof. Dodd*.

A man and wife register at hotels as *Mr. and Mrs. Alex T. Schofield* rather than as *Alex T. Schofield and wife*.

MS. *MS.,* usually in caps, is the conventional abbreviation for *manuscript;* plural MSS. The colloquial and shoptalk word for manuscript intended for publication is *copy.*

must has recently become an (informal) adjective:

> the President's must legislation
> This is a must article for every intelligent American.

It has long been a noun in newspaper shoptalk, a *B. O. M.* being a *Business Office Must,* a story that has to be run because of some advertising tieup. See *Auxiliary verbs.

Mute e See *E § 5.

myself A reflexive or intensive pronoun, referring back to *I* when used as an object or as an intensive:

> Object: I shave myself.
> Intensive: I saw the whole thing myself.

In vulgate and much colloquial English *myself* is used as subject or object as substitute for *me,* but not in good written style:

> Vulgate and colloquial: Another fellow and myself saw the whole thing
> General: Another fellow and I saw the whole thing.
> Colloquial: Sam invited John and *myself* to dinner.
> General: Sam invited John and me to dinner.

(SEE *Pronouns § 4, *self, *himself, herself.)

N (n), as in *now, gnaw, inning, been.* N may be a syllable by itself ("syllabic *n*"), as in *often, listen, garden* (ôf′n, lis′n, gär′dn).

N is generally silent in *kiln* and in a number of words after *m*: *autumn, damn, hymn, solemn.* In derivatives of such words usage is divided on sounding the *n.* It is not sounded in *hymned* (himd) and in *damned* only in archaic or ultra poetic contexts (dam′ned). It is sounded in *autumnal, solemnity,* and in general before a suffix when the suffix begins with a vowel.

An *ñ* (the wavy line called a *tilde*) is found in some words from Spanish. If the word is commonly used, the spelling is usually changed to *ny* (*canyon* instead of *cañon*).

naive—naïve The form without the dieresis (*naive*) is slowly gaining over naïve. It is unnecessary to keep the French masculine form *naif* in English. *Naive* can do all the work. Pronounced nä ēv′.

namely and other introductory words 1. The beginning of wisdom in handling "introductory words" like *namely, that is, for example, such as* is to use them as seldom as possible. *Namely, viz., i.e., e.g.,* and some others belong chiefly in routine expository prose. *For example, for instance, such as* are more adaptable to readable prose. Very often such words can be omitted altogether in compact, informal writing:

> He instructed us in the mysteries of punctuation: [such as] semicolons between clauses of a compound sentence, position of quotation marks with other marks, commas with nonrestrictive clauses.

2. In formal style or in a long, rather complicated sentence, an introductory word would usually be preceded by a semicolon:

> The interview is of value, then, because it aids in discovering certain traits; e. g., emotional and temperamental attitudes—which do not submit so readily to other modes of attack.—G. D. HIGGINSON, *Fields of Psychology*, p. 395

When one of these words introduces a series of short items, it is more often followed by a comma than by a colon:

> The boys in training are thoroughly grounded in the fundamental processes of the work, for example, planning, building, and launching.

No comma should follow *such as:*

> Large animals, such as bears, moose, and elk, are often found here.

Names In factual writing all names used should be complete and accurate. In current writing, handmade names and other dodges are not used much except in humor. In the following they stamp the paper as amateur:

> Across the table sat Cornelius Van Stuck-up between two feminine admirers whose names I will not mention but will call Miss X and Miss Y. Miss X said to Miss Y . . . .

Use the real names of people and places unless there are serious reasons for avoiding them, and if there are, invent convincing names or use pronouns or "a man" or some inconspicuous device. This use of actual names is one trait of the specificness and immediacy of current style.

In imaginative writing judgment and ingenuity are needed to choose satisfactory names for characters. They should suggest real names of people of the right social stratum, but not be the names of actual people (except by accident). They should not be the commonest names nor should they be eccentric ones either; ordinarily they should be somewhere between *John* and *Mary* and *Ichabod* and *Jacquinetta*. Studying names and collecting them and watching those used in stories will furnish raw materials for naming your own creations. (See *Proper names.)

Narrative paragraphs See Chapter 8, "Narrative paragraphs," page 210.

nature For expressions like *of a violent nature* (= *violent*), see *Deadwood, and Chapter 10, "Deadwood," page 284.

Nazi Pronounced nä′tsi, sometimes nat′si, and rarely nä′zi; plural *Nazis* (nä′tsiz). *Nazi* was a political nickname for the National Socialist party of Germany and is capitalized like *Republican* or *Democrat*. The type of party represented by National Socialists is usually referred to as *fascist* or *totalitarian*. (Compare *Fascism, fascist.)

necessary Spelled with one *c* and two *s*'s.
   Very often a verb is more direct and emphatic, less polite than a construction with *necessary:*

   You *must* [or *have to*, rather than *It is necessary that you*] pay your tuition before receiving your class cards.

necessity The idiom is *necessity of* doing something or *for* (not *to* do something):

   I don't see *the necessity of* [or: *for*] *reading* so many pages to get so few facts. (Or, more concise: I don't see *the need of reading* so many pages . . .)

need—needs Both are third person singular of the verb *need*, but used in different idioms. *Needs* is the form in affirmative statements, *need* or *does not need* in negative statements, *need* or *does . . . need* in questions:

	He needs a haircut.
	He needs to have a haircut. (Infinitive with *to*)
	Does he need a haircut?
Formal:	He need not have a haircut. (Infinitive without *to*)
Informal:	He doesn't need a haircut.
Formal:	Need she come?
Informal:	Does she need to come?

Negatives 1. Double negatives. For use of two negatives see *Double negative.
   2. Emphasis. A statement may sometimes be made more emphatic or striking by being put negatively (in a figure of speech known as *litotes* or *understatement*):

He was . . . extremely the antithesis of coarse which "refined" somehow does not imply. . . .—E. E. Cummings, *The Enormous Room*, p. 150

The assimilating power of the English language is not less remarkable than the complexity of its sources.—J. B. Greenough and G. L. Kittredge, *Words and Their Ways in English Speech*, p. 147

Tell us, doctors of philosophy, what are the needs of a man. At least a man needs to be notjailed notafraid nothungry notcold not without love not a worker for a person he has never seen,

that cares nothing for the uses and needs of a man or a woman or a child.—John Dos Passos, *The New Republic*, June 3, 1936

3. Separation from positive. In a specific construction words of positive and of negative meaning usually need to be separated:

I have learned through this practice to overcome stage fright and I have gained in vividness of speech. (Not: I have learned . . . to overcome stage fright and vividness of speech.)

Negro Capitalize, like *Caucasian, Indian.* Plural, *Negroes*

neither For pronunciation and use see *either § 3.

neither . . . nor See *Correlative conjunctions.

Newspaper English
1. Its virtues.   2. Journalese.   3. Headlines and headlinese.

1. Its virtues. Joseph Pulitzer's famous motto for workers on the old *New York World* still stands as the ideal for the material and style of newswriting—*Accuracy, Terseness, Accuracy.* Complete accuracy is not easy for a reporter who has perhaps only a few minutes in which to get the facts of a complicated event, and terseness is not easy either for a man who writes habitually, often of very similar happenings, without any personal interest in his material. The result is that newspapers contain some of our worst writing, but a reporter who tells of events simply, in words that are appropriate to them and to his readers, may produce some of our best writing.

There is of course no special dialect for newswriting. Papers have some conventions for giving ages, names, places of residence, and other routine matters, but good newspaper English is simply informal English applied to the daily recording of affairs. It is a style written to be read rapidly and by the eye—tricks of sound outside the headlines are out of place. The sentences are typically short (except in leads) and have a direct movement, the words concrete and from the general vocabulary.

2. Journalese. The two most common sins of newswriting are inflation (*big words) and *triteness, which we can lump as symptoms of *journalese*. Granting that our "fair city," "ample outlet for her histrionic ability," and scores of such trite phrases belonging to paleo-journalism are not found now outside small town papers, there is still a vast amount of wordy and lazy writing in newspapers. Every *stylebook contains a list of journalese expressions to be avoided. Here are a few collected (and translated) by George Olds, of the Springfield, Mo., *News:*

According to the report issued this morning by City Auditor Ernest Jared	City Auditor Ernest Jared reported today
Shields denied he made a statement he was alleged to have made to police officers admitting he knew—	Shields denied admitting to police he knew
Affirming the assumption that he was resentful of the meeting	Admitting he resented
But Judge Holly dismissed the charges against her. Although he dismissed the charges against Mrs. Coates, Judge Holly commented that her conduct had been "suspicious."	But Judge Holly dismissed the charges against her, although he termed her conduct "suspicious."

Editor and Publisher, Feb. 2, 1935

Such wordiness and ponderous phraseology is likely to be found in newspaper stories of all kinds. Some are italicized in the following quotation:

> Mrs. . . . told the police her husband had been out of work for three years and was despondent. She had just *obtained a position* in a bookbindery. She *arose* at 7:30 a. m. and went into the kitchen to *prepare* breakfast. She *remarked* to her husband she was glad she would not have to *remain* at home *during the day*, because it was getting on her nerves. Then he hit her. . . .

Triteness is the next worst offense in journalese. In *The New Yorker*, Frank Sullivan had his cliché expert, Mr. Arbuthnot, testify to journalistic triteness, including such special topics as these:

> Q—Mr. Arbuthnot, what happens at railroad stations on holidays?
> A—Well, there is what our Society of Cliché Experts likes to refer to as a holiday exodus. I mean to say, fully 1,500,000 pleasure-seekers leave the city, railroad officials estimate. Every means of transportation is taxed to its utmost capacity. . . .
> Q—Mr. Arbuthnot, what kind of hopes do you have?
> A—High hopes, and I don't have them; I entertain them. I express concern. I discard precedent. When I am in earnest, I am in deadly earnest. When I am devoted, I am devoted solely. When a task comes along, it confronts me. When I stop, I stop short. I take but one kind of steps—

those in the right direction. I am a force to be reckoned with. Oh, ask me anything, Mr. Dewey, anything.

Q—All right. How about the weather? Where does weather occur?

A—You think you can stump me with that? Well, you can't. Weather occurs over widespread areas. Winter holds the entire Eastern seaboard in its icy grip. Snow blankets the city, disrupting train schedules and marooning thousands of commuters. Traffic is at a standstill—

Q—Hold on a minute, my friend. You've left out something.

A—I have not. What?

Q—Traffic is virtually at a standstill.

A—Oh, a detail, Mr. Dewey. All right, I concede you that. Ten thousand unemployed are placed at work removing the record fall as cold wave spells suffering to thousands. Old residents declare blizzard worst since '88—.

—FRANK SULLIVAN, "The Cliché Expert Tells All," *The New Yorker*, June 20, 1936

3. Headlines and headlinese. While writers of news stories have to write with an eye on inches of space, headline writers have to watch every letter. A given style of head has a "count" of so many letters, and, as the compositor says, "there ain't no rubber type." This necessity for compression and a desire to "sell the papers" gives rise to the punch of headlines. As the Waterbury, Conn., *Republican* style sheet puts it:

PUT PUNCH IN HEADS
SAYS OLD SLOT MAN

Wants Accurate, Terse, Positive
and Pungent Guides to
News

BEGS FOR ACTIVE VERBS

Bald-Domed Editor Wants Blue
Pencil Novices to Lay Off
Fuzzy Words

This leads to the omission of *function words (*a, an, the*, connectives) and to the use of short words and clipped forms:

Fly ocean; tell fight with gale 3 miles in air—12 Navy planes battered

To save space, short words are used, nouns are used as verbs, verbs as nouns, and any words or even long phrases as adjectives:

Poland Denies *Tie-up* with Reich

Superintendent and Supervisor Refute
Charge of Spying on *Traction Company
Bus Drivers' Union Enrollment* Meeting

Worrying that headline style will ruin our language is useless. Usage in headlines, in spite of abuses, is in line with good informal English—and the requirements of communication will prevent it from becoming too common. Though headlinese style should be kept in its place, the feeble circumlocution of the stories that often stand below the heads is a greater menace to our language than the clipped, emphatic heads.

(REFERENCES: Kennedy, § 14. There are many textbooks on newspaper writing. Two of the most useful are: Curtis D. MacDougall, *Interpretative Reporting* (New York, 1948) and George C. Bastian and Leland D. Case, *Editing the Day's News* (New York, 1943). The stylebooks of newspapers are important. Some, like those of *The Detroit News* and *The New York Times* (1950), are for sale. The magazine *Editor and Publisher* is the best source on current American journalism.)

Newspaper titles   For writing names of newspapers see *Titles § 1.

New words   See *Origin of words, and Chapter 2, "New words and constructions," page 58.

Nexus   Jespersen introduced *junction* and *nexus* as names for two types of word relationship. He called the relationship in which two or more words are joined to form a single name (*a warm day, a first class speech*) *junction*. The relationship in which the two terms are joined by a verb but are kept distinct (*The day is warm. The speech sounded first rate*) he called *nexus*. Under nexus he included locutions that were similar in pattern but did not have a verb, such as He left *the window open* (which obviously is quite different from the junction *the open window*) and *Happy the man* (which is different from *the happy man*), and various others.

The doctrine of nexus is elaborated in Jespersen's *The Philosophy of Grammar*, Chapters 8 and 9, and in *Essentials of English Grammar*, Chapter 9.

ng   is the pronunciation symbol for the base tongue nasal sound most frequently spelled *ng* (*long, bringing*) but also spelled *n:* *anchor* (ang′kər), *angry* (ang′gri), *sink* (singk), *uncle* (ung′kəl). Pronunciation is divided when a syllable ending in *n* is followed by one beginning with *g* or *k:* *congress* (kong′gris) but *congressional* (kən gresh′ən ḷ or kong gresh′ən ḷ).

nice   is a *counter word indicating mild approval, so general in meaning that it is of little use in writing. The word's former meaning of "exact, precise," as in *a nice distinction*, is confined to formal writing. (See Charles C. Fries, *The English Journal*, 1927, 16:602-604).

nickel   Most words with this last syllable (-əl) are spelled -*le*, but *nickel* has not been in the language so long as most of them and keeps the -*el* of its German or Scandinavian origin.

Nicknames Nicknames are rarely appropriate in formal writing. In familiar and informal writing they are appropriate and should be used naturally, without apology. Some writers will put a nickname in quotes the first time it is used, but not when it is repeated.

no For use as a sentence adverb and as a complete sentence see *yes.

No. The abbreviation *No.* for *number* (from the Latin *numero*, "by number") is written with a capital. It is appropriate chiefly in business and technical English. In the United States *No.* is not written with street numbers.

no account, nohow There are a number of colloquial and vulgate phrases made with *no* whose fitness in writing needs to be watched: *a no account cousin* (Formal: a worthless cousin); *we couldn't get there nohow* (Formal, Informal: ... by any means [or] any way we tried).

nobody, nothing, nowhere are written as single words. *Nobody* and *nothing* are *singular*, though *nobody* is informally treated as a collective (See *every and its compounds):

> Nobody thinks that his own dog is a nuisance.
> Informal: Nobody thinks their own dog is a nuisance.
> Nothing is further from the truth.
> The dog could be found nowhere.

Nominative absolute See *Absolute phrases, *Participles § 4.

Nominative case A noun or pronoun that is the subject of a finite verb is sometimes said to be in the nominative (or subjective) case. The form of the nominative singular is the common form of the noun, the form to which, typically, the endings for the genitive and for the plural are added. *I, you, he, she, it, we, you, they* are the nominative forms of the personal pronouns; *who, which,* and *that* are the nominative forms of the relative pronouns. The same form is used in direct address (for which some languages have a separate vocative case): *Polly,* put the kettle on. (See *Subject and verb.)

Nonce word Strictly, a word used but once so far as existing writing shows; a word coined for the occasion and not attaining general use. *Un-black* in this sentence would be called a nonce word:

> She liked black coffee, black cigarettes, black Italian shawls, which was interesting, since she was so distinctly un-black herself, but all creamy and pale gold in the white Capri sun.—WILBUR DANIEL STEELE, "Bubbles," p. 95

(SEE *Origin of words § 2a.)

none, no one *None* is a single word, but *no one* is often used instead of *none,* for emphasis.

None may be either singular or plural, and now is more common with the plural:

> As only ten jurors have been chosen so far, none of the witnesses were called [or: was called].
>
> She tried on ten hats, but none of them were attractive.
>
> I read three books on the subject, no one of which was helpful.

(REFERENCE: Fries, pp. 50, 56.)

No paragraph Correction: Join these two paragraphs, if necessary revising the expression to relate the ideas.   *No P*

No punctuation Correction: Remove the punctuation mark indicated. (See especially Chapter 5, "Commas to avoid," page 146.)   *No Pn*

Nonrestrictive clauses, modifiers See *Restrictive and nonrestrictive.

not hardly, not scarcely See *Double negative § 3.

not to exceed Business and legal; in other contexts *not more than* is usual:

> The undersigned will be liable for property damages, not to exceed $500 for one accident.
>
> The enrollment in the course was to be not more than fifty.
>
> Not more than two people could live on that pay.

Note taking See Chapter 13, "Taking notes," page 380.

notorious means well known for unsavory reasons—"a notorious cheat"; *famous* is well known for accomplishment or excellence—"a famous writer, aviator." *Noted* is journalistic for *famous* or *well known.*

Noun and verb stress A number of nouns and verbs are differentiated in speaking by stressing the first syllable in the noun and the last in the verb although the spelling is identical. Some of these are listed below.

Noun	*Verb*
com′pound	com pound′
com′press	com press′
con′duct	con duct′
con′flict	con flict′ (often con′flict)
con′trast	con trast′ (often con′trast)
con′vict	con vict′

de'crease	de crease'
di'gest	di gest'
es'cort	es cort'
ex'tract	ex tract'
in'cline	in cline'
in'crease	in crease' (often in'crease)
in'sult	in sult'
prod'uce, pro'duce	pro duce'
re'cess (or re cess')	re cess'
rec'ord	re cord'

Several of these that are in common use show the natural English tendency to shift the stress back to the first syllable. The following words are both nouns and verbs with the same stress:

ac'cent   cos'tume   dis'count   im'port

De'tail is both noun and verb where it is commonly used, as in the Army.

Noun clauses A noun clause is a construction having a subject and finite verb, and functioning in a sentence as a noun. Many noun clauses are introduced by *that*, some by *what, who, whoever, whatever, why, when*, and other connectives. They are usually subjects or objects:

Subject: *That anyone could raise his grade by studying* had never occurred to him. *Whether or not he should go* had bothered him for days.
Object: He assured me *that it would never happen again.* Or: He assured me *it would never happen again.*
Predicate noun: His guests were *whomever he met on the way home.*
Object of preposition: Sam is always sure of *what he does.*
Appositive: The doctrine *that we must avoid entangling alliances* was first stated by Washington.

That and *whether* clauses as subjects are, as the examples above show, distinctly formal constructions. (See *Clauses, *reason is because.)

Nouns 1. **Types.** A noun is the name of a person, place, thing, quality, action, or idea: *George Washington, hunter, Washington, D. C., home, automobile, goodness, hunting, immortality.* A noun is further identified by its forms (§ 2) and by its function in sentences (§ 3). Only nouns can take *the, an,* and *a.*

Nouns are conventionally classified as follows:

a) PROPER NOUNS, names of particular people and places, written with capitals and usually without *the* or *a: Anne, George W. Loomis, London, Georgia, France, the Bay of Naples.* (See *Proper names.)

In contrast with these proper nouns, all the other groups are *common nouns.*

b) CONCRETE NOUNS, names of objects: *leaf, leaves, road, panda, manufacturer.* (See Chapter 12, "Abstract and concrete words," page 341.)

c) MASS NOUNS, names of materials in general rather than materials in particular forms: *water, coffee, cement, steel, corn.*

d) COLLECTIVE NOUNS, names of a group of things regarded as a unit: *fleet, army, company, committee, trio, bevy.* (See *Collective nouns.)

e) ABSTRACT NOUNS, names of qualities, actions, ideas: *kindness, hate, manufacture, idealism, fantasy, concept.* Many of these are *gerunds: *fishing, drinking, manufacturing.*

2. Forms. Nouns may be single words or compound words written solid or as two words or hyphened (*Group words): *bathroom, bookcase, log-rolling, high school, hub cap, go getter.*

Nouns change their forms to make the plural, most of them adding *-s: boys, kindnesses, manufacturers.* (See *Plurals.)

Nouns change their form for case only in the genitive, typically by adding *'s: boy's, Harriet's.* (See *Genitive case.)

A very few nouns in English have different forms for masculine and feminine gender: *confidant—confidante, executor—executrix, actor—actress.* (See *Gender.)

3. Functions. The principal functions of nouns in sentences are:

Subject of a sentence: The *wind* blew for three days. (See *Subject and verb.)

Object of a verb: The wind blew the *silo* over. (See *Objects.)

Object of a preposition: in the *night*, behind the *house*, after *breakfast*, of the *president* (See *Prepositions.)

Predicate noun: He became *president* of the firm. (See *Predicate adjective, Predicate noun.)

Possession: The *woman's* first dress for two years (See *Genitive case § 2.)

Apposition: The first settler, *Thomas Sanborn*, came in 1780. (See *Apposition.)

Modifier of other nouns: a *baby* hippopotamus; the best *high school basketball* team in years. (See *Genitive case, *Parts of speech § 2, *Adjectives, types and forms § 6.)

Modifier of verbs or statements: He came two *months* ago. *Mornings* he would work a little. (See *Adverbs, types and forms § 5.)

(SEE ch. 4, "Nouns," p. 96. REFERENCES: Kennedy §§ 50, 103; Curme, *Parts of Speech*, chs. 1, 9, *Syntax*, chs. 2, 4, 26, and other references.)

nowhere near Colloquial and informal:

It was a good score but nowhere near as large as we'd hoped for. (Formal: "not so large as" or "not nearly so large as").

nowheres Vulgate for *nowhere.*

Number *Number* is the singular and plural aspect of nouns and pronouns and verbs. See *Plurals, *Subject and verb, *Reference of pronouns.

number is a collective noun, requiring a singular or plural verb according as the total or the individual units are meant:

> A number of tickets have already been sold.
> The number of tickets sold is astonishing.
> A number of the pages were torn.
> The number of pages assigned for translation was gradually increased to eight.

(SEE also *amount, number.)

Numb **Numbers** Correction: Revise the figure or figures in this passage in the light of the suggestions below.
   1. Uses. 2. Figures or words. 3. Arabic and Roman numerals. 4. Plural of figures. 5. Cardinal and ordinal numbers.

   1. Uses. Figures are used for: **(a)** DATES. Only in formal *social correspondence are dates written out in words. *1st, 2nd* (*2d*), and so on may be used when a date is given without the year, but not ordinarily with the year:

   Oct. 4, 1950   October 4, 1950   October 4   October 4th

Years are always written in figures.
   b) HOURS when a.m. or p.m. is used:

   5 p.m. But: five o'clock

   c) STREET NUMBERS (with no comma between thousands):

   2841 Washington Avenue   Apartment 3C, 781 Grand Street

   d) PAGES AND OTHER REFERENCES:

   page 642   pp. 431-82   chapter 14 (or: chapter xiv)
   Act III, scene iv, line 28

   e) SUMS OF MONEY, except sums in round numbers or, in formal style, sums that can be written in two or three words:

   $4.98   75¢   a million dollars (or, informal: $1,000,000)

   f) STATISTICS and series of more than one or two numbers:

   In the political science class mock election the Republicans gained 50 seats in the House of Representatives, 6 seats in the Senate, and 13 new governorships.

2. **Figures or words.** Usage varies in writing numbers that are parts of consecutive sentences. In general, newspapers and informal writing have figures for numbers over ten, words for smaller numbers; rather conservative magazine and book styles have figures for numbers over 100 except when the numbers can be written in two words:

Informal (newspaper): four, ten, 15, 92, 114
Formal (book): four, ten, fifteen, ninety-two, 114. (But practice is not consistent.)

This passage illustrates a typical book style in use of figures and sums of money:

With a well-integrated, rapidly growing organization, Swedish coöperators were ready to go forward to new triumphs—over galoshes this time. It sounds funny but it is not at all; the victory over the galosh cartel—really the rubber cartel—was a very tangible achievement. Galoshes are a necessity in the Swedish winter, to say nothing of the Swedish spring and the Swedish fall. And four manufacturing firms, formed into an air-tight trust, exploited this necessity for years. Annual profits of 60 per cent, 62 per cent and even, in one exceptional year, 77 per cent were recorded. On a capital of less than a million dollars the four factories realized in fourteen years more than twelve and a half million dollars and voted many stock dividends besides. As in the case of the milling cartel, the public yelled long and loud but with no visible results.

At the annual coöperative congress in 1926 it was decided that K. F. [Kooperativa Förbundet, the Cooperative Union] should declare war on the galosh cartel. This was the unanimous and enthusiastic opinion of the Congress. Within a few weeks, merely on the basis of this announcement, the cartel reduced the price of a pair of men's galoshes more than fifty cents, with corresponding reductions all down the line. K. F. informed the cartel that this was not enough, and when there were no further reductions the war was begun in earnest.

The cartel was obviously not going to sell one of its factories at anything like a reasonable price but when K. F. threatened to build a plant of its own, the enemy heeded the warning, recalling what had happened to other cartels that had remained adamant. In a remarkably short time K. F. had negotiated the purchase of a factory at Gislaved, and by January 1, 1927, after complete modernization, it took over operation of this plant. The result, within a year, was another seventy cents sliced off the price of a pair of galoshes. Having achieved this, K. F. began the manufacture of automobile tires at the Gislaved plant and by 1932 was producing 50,000 tires a year.—Marquis W. Childs, *Sweden—The Middle Way,* pp. 12-13

When most writing was longhand it was conventional to express numbers in words and then repeat them in figures in parenthesis. In clear copy, especially in typewritten copy, this is no longer necessary and is not done except in legal or important business documents.

Except in dates and street numbers, a comma stands between each group of three digits counting from the right:

1952 (the year)   1,952 bushels   4,682,921 $14,672.

Numbers in two words between 21 and 99 are usually hyphened, though the practice is declining: *forty-two* or *forty two*.

In consecutive writing a number at the very beginning of a sentence is written in words rather than in figures:

Two to 3% of loading and up to 10% is common and 20 to 30% in specially surfaced papers. . . . —"Paper Manufacture," *Encyclopaedia Britannica*, p. 234

3. Arabic and Roman numerals. Arabic numerals (*1, 2, 88 . . .*) are used in almost all places where numbers are not expressed in words. Roman numerals (i, ii, cxlvi . . .) are occasionally used to number units in rather short series, as in outlines, chapters of a book, acts of a play, though now less often than formerly. The preliminary pages of books are almost always numbered with Roman numerals. Sometimes they are used on title pages for the date, and on formal inscriptions.

In Roman numerals a small number preceding a larger is to be subtracted from the larger (ix = 9, xc = 90). The following table shows the common Roman numerals (lower case):

1	i	12	xii	40	xl	101	ci
2	ii	13	xiii	41	xli	110	cx
3	iii	14	xiv	49	xlix	199	cxcix
4	iv	15	xv	50	l	200	cc
5	v	19	xix	51	li	400	cd
6	vi	20	xx	60	lx	500	d
7	vii	21	xxi	70	lxx	600	dc
8	viii	25	xxv	80	lxxx	900	cm
9	ix	27	xxvii	90	xc	1000	m
10	x	29	xxix	99	xcix	1500	md
11	xi	30	xxx	100	c	1951	mcmli

4. Plural of figures. The plural of a figure is written either with *s* or *'s:*

Six fives: six 5s, six 5's   By tens: by 10s, by 10's

5. Cardinal and ordinal numbers. The numbers in simple counting, indicating number only, are *cardinal numbers: 1, 2, 3, 68, 129 . . .* The numbers indicating order, *first, second, third . . .* are *ordinal numbers.* Except in numbering items in a rather routine enumeration, ordinals should be spelled out rather than abbreviated to *1st, 2nd, 3rd. . . .*

Since the simple forms *first*, *second*, and so on can be either adjective or adverb, the forms in *-ly* (*firstly*) are unnecessary. (SEE also *Fractions, *Money.)

O Speakers of English vary in their pronunciation of the *o* sounds as they do of the *a* sounds. Pronunciation of particular words, especially with short *o*, can be indicated only roughly because of this widespread variation. Three general types of *o* can be distinguished:

1. **'Long o'** (ō), the sound in *oh, oats, note, soldier, sew, trousseau* (trōō′sō or trōō sō′).

Before an *r* the sound of long *o* is somewhat modified, as in *door* (dōr), and may approach "open *o*" (ô), as in some pronunciations of *horse, born*, and so on.

In unstressed and rapidly spoken words the sound of long *o* is shorter and may differ in quality: *obey* (ō bā′ or ə bā′), *hotel* (hō tel′).

2. **'Short o'** (o). A rounded short *o* is not very frequent and is more characteristic of New England than of other parts of the country. The more common American sound is the unrounded or "open *o*" (ô) or, especially in Western English, broad *a* (ä): *soft* (sôft, säft, soft), *pond* (pônd, pänd, pond). Since there is no single pronunciation of these words throughout the United States, the symbol o is used for them without indicating the regional variants.

3. **'Open o'** (ô), most clearly identified in its spelling *aw* (*law, lawn, spawn*) but also the vowel sound in *lord, all, fault, fought, taught* (lôrd, ôl, fôlt, fôt, tôt).

In slighted syllables *o* may spell the neutral vowel ə: *actor* (ak′tər), *nation* (nā′shən), *button* (but′ən), or it may entirely disappear as in most people's pronunciation of *chocolate* (chôk′lit) or *sophomore* (sof′mōr or at most sof′m̩ ōr).

O represents several other vowel sounds: ōō as in *move*, oo as in *wolf*, and ə as in *son, money;* û as in *work*. (SEE also *ou.)

O, oh *O* is always capitalized, and usually it is so closely related to some other word, often a name in direct address, that it is not followed by a mark of punctuation:

O dear, I suppose so.   O yes.   O God, unseen, but ever near.

Oh is an exclamation, followed by a comma if the force is weak, by an exclamation mark if the stress is strong. It is capitalized at the beginning of a sentence, but not in the middle of a sentence: Oh! Don't do that! Oh, I wish he would.

In informal writing the distinction between *O* and *oh* is not always kept, and *O* is often found where traditional usage would have *oh*.

Objective case See *Accusative case.

Objects 1. **Direct objects.** (a) An *object of a verb* is the noun element (noun, pronoun, noun clause) *following* a verb and directly related to it. In meaning it ordinarily names what is affected or effected by the action of the verb; in certain pronouns the accusative case form (*me, him, her, us, them, whom*) in addition to position identifies the object.

> They made the *boat* themselves. Terry chased the *cat* up a tree.
> He took *her* to the three formals of the year.
> I didn't believe *that he told the truth.*

Occasionally, for emphasis, the object precedes both the subject and the verb:

> This boat [object] the boys [subject] built themselves.

b) It has been conventional to call the object in certain passive constructions a "retained object," but since the position and the relation to the verb are not different from the typical object's, it is simpler to say that a passive verb may take an object:

> He was given a *subscription* to a book club.

2. **Indirect objects.** With verbs of asking, telling, giving, and so on, there is often an indirect object that names the receiver of the message, gift, etc:

> He gave the *church* a memorial window.
> In desperation she showed *him* the snapshot album.

The indirect object comes before the direct object, as in the sentences just given, except when it is a prepositional phrase:

> He gave a memorial window *to the church.*
> In desperation she showed the snapshot album *to him.*

3. **Of prepositions.** The object of a preposition is the noun element whose relation to some other part of the sentence is shown by the preposition, as *some other part of the sentence* is the object of *to* and *the preposition* is the object of *by* in this sentence. The

what clause in "Your grade will depend chiefly on *what you do on the examination*" is the object of *on*. (See *Prepositions.)

4. Of adjectives. A few adjectives take objects:

It was worth *a fortune.*
Are you sure *that she will come?*
He is like *his father.*

Obsolete *Obsolete* describes a word no longer used (like *eft*— "again") or a meaning no longer used (like *can* in the sense of "know," *dole* in the sense of "grief"). See Chapter 2, "Obsolete expressions," page 56.

occasion, occasional, occasionally If you realize that with two *s*'s *occasion* might be misread as ō kash′n (like *passion*) and that *occasion* is pronounced ə kā′zhən, you may not be so likely to misspell these words. Two *c*'s and one *s*.

-oe- See *-ae-, -oe-.

of, off Besides its use as a preposition of numerous meanings, *of* is used to make the phrasal genitive: *of a man* = *man's*, and so on.

Of is frequently used in colloquial doubling of prepositions—*inside of, off of, outside of. Inside of* and *outside of* are also used in informal writing, but not *off of*, which should be reduced to *off:* "He stepped off [of] the sidewalk."

The colloquial contraction *'ve* for *have* is often carelessly written *of:* I ought to have [not *to of*] gone then.

often Pronouncing the *t* is usually a localism, but it is sometimes sounded in singing to make a more emphatic second syllable. *Oft* is archaic, used by amateur poets who have to count their syllables, and *oftentimes* is a colloquial expansion.

oh See *O, oh.

OK, O.K. Business and colloquial English for "correct, all right, approved": "The foreman put his OK on the shipment." Occasionally spelled *okay, okeh*. As a verb the forms are OK, OK'ed or OK'd, OK'ing. *Oke* and *okeydoke* are slang.

one 1. The use of the impersonal pronoun *one* is characteristically formal, especially if it must be repeated:

Formal: One can't be too careful, can one?
Informal: You can't be too careful, can you?

It is difficult, too, I find, to be as frank in talking with women as with men; because I think that women tend more than men to hold a preconceived idea of one's character and tastes; and it is difficult to talk simply and naturally to any one who has formed a mental picture of one, especially if one is aware that it is not correct. But men are slower to form impressions, and thus talk is more experimental; moreover, in talking with men, one encounters more opposition, and opposition puts one more on one's mettle.—A. C. BENSON, *From a College Window*, p. 75

This repetition of *one*, often to avoid *I*, often when *you* would be more natural, is deadly. American usage stands firmly by older English usage in referring back to *one* by pronouns of the third person—*he, his, him* (or *she, her*):

One is warned to be cautious if he would avoid offending his friends and bringing their displeasure down upon his head.

(SEE *they, *you.)

2. *One* may be used to avoid repeating a noun in the second of two compound elements:

Fred took the new copy and I took the old one.

The plural *ones* is often used:

She has two velvet dresses and three silk ones.

3. *One* is very often *deadwood, taking emphasis from the adjective which carries the real meaning:

The plan was certainly [an] original [one].

(REFERENCE: Fries, pp. 245-46.)

-one *One* is written solid with *any-, every-, some-* in making an indefinite pronoun; but when the *one* is stressed it is written as a separate word:

Anyone can do that. Any one of the four will be all right.
Everyone may study late. Every one of us was surprised.
Someone ought to tell her. Some one of the plans will work.

(SEE *any § 2, *every and its compounds, *some and compounds.)

one of those who In written English the clause following *one of those who* and similar locutions is plural:

He is one of those people who believe in the perfectibility of man. [*Who* refers to *people*.]
That's one of the books that make you change your ideas. [*That* refers to *books*.]

Colloquially the singular is often heard:

He is one of those people who believes in the perfectibility of man.

only 1. The importance of the position of *only* has been greatly exaggerated. Logically it should stand immediately before the element modified:

> I need only six more to have a full hundred.

But usage is not always logical, and in this construction it is conspicuously in favor of placing the *only* before the verb of the statement. There is no possible misunderstanding in the meaning of:

> I only need six more to have a full hundred.

There are instances in which the placing of *only* can make a foolish or a funny statement (with only a face that a mother could love). But placing *only* with the verb is a characteristic and reputable English idiom:

> In reality we only have succession and coexistence, and the "force" is something that we imagine.—HAVELOCK ELLIS, *The Dance of Life*, p. 91

> They only opened one bag and took the passports in and looked at them. —ERNEST HEMINGWAY, *The Sun Also Rises*, p. 94

2. The same is true of *even, ever, nearly, just, exactly,* and such limiting adverbs, though they are used much less than *only*, and some of them only in formal English, so that the idiom is not so common. Like *only* they can be placed so that they spoil the emphasis:

> The way I can stand in front of a store window and persuade myself that I need some novel article even surprises me [better: surprises even me].

3. As a coordinating conjunction, meaning *but*, *only* is chiefly colloquial: I'd love to come, only I have to study for an exam.

Onomatopoeia See *Imitative words and phrases.

onto—on to When *on* is an adverb and *to* a preposition in a separate locution, they should of course be written as two words:

> The rest of us drove on to the city.

When the words make a definite preposition, they are usually written solid:

> The team trotted onto the floor.   They looked out onto the park.

Onto is frequently used as a colloquial double preposition when *on* or *to* by itself would be used in writing:

> They finally got on [Colloquial: onto] the bus.
> The crowd got to [Colloquial: onto] James Street.

or is a coordinating conjunction and, like *and*, *but*, or *for*, should connect words or phrases or clauses of equal value. (See *Coordinating conjunctions, *Compound sentences.)

> Words: He must be drunk or crazy.
> Phrases: We could go by car or by train.
> Clauses: We could go by car or we could go by train.

Two subjects joined by *or* take a singular verb if each is singular, a plural verb if both are plural or if the one nearer the verb is plural:

> Cod liver oil or halibut oil is often prescribed.
> Cod liver oil or cod liver oil capsules have the same effect.
> Cod liver oil capsules or cod liver oil has the same effect.

The second construction would usually be used instead of the third.

Or correlates with *either* and sometimes in informal English with *neither:*

> Either ē′thər or i′thər is correct.
> Informal: Neither ā′thər or i′thər is widely used in America.
> Formal: Neither ā′thər nor i′thər is widely used in America.

(See *Correlative conjunctions.)

-or, (-our) American spelling prefers *-or* in such words as *color*, *governor*, *honor*. When referring to Jesus Christ, *Saviour* is frequently spelled with the *u* but in other senses without it. *Glamour* still survives, but the *u* is rapidly being dropped from this word.

British usage is divided on this point, though of course to an American reader the words in *-our* are conspicuous. Fowler said that the American change to *-or* has actually hindered the simplification that was going on in England:

> Those who are willing to put national prejudice aside & examine the facts quickly realize, first, that the British *-our* words are much fewer in proportion to the *-or* words than they supposed, &, secondly, that there seems to be no discoverable line between the two sets so based on principle as to serve any useful purpose. By the side of *favour* there is *horror*, beside *ardour pallor*, beside *odour tremor*, & so forth. Of agent-nouns *saviour* (with its echo *paviour*) is perhaps the only one that now retains *-our*, *governor* being the latest to shed its *-u-*.—H. W. Fowler, *Modern English Usage*, p. 415

In quoting directly from British writings and in referring to British institutions, like the Labour party, their spelling should be exactly followed; otherwise use *-or*.

(References: Fowler, "-our & -or"; *Oxford English Dictionary*, "-or"; John Benbow, *Manuscript & Proof* (New York, 1937), pp. 75-77, discusses spelling in American books that are to be circulated in England.)

oral, verbal Strictly, *oral* means "spoken," and *verbal* means "in words"; but *verbal* has been so long used in the sense of *oral* that the sense is recognized in dictionaries:

He delivered an oral message.   He had only a verbal agreement.

Ordinal numbers See *Numbers § 5.

Organization of papers See *Outline form, and Chapter 1, "Planning the paper," page 13.

Origin of words

1. The study of word origins. 2. New words. 3. Changes in form of words.

1. The study of word origins. The words that we use all have histories. Some, like *chauffeur, mores, television, parapsychology*, are relatively new in English; some have been in the language for centuries, like *home, candle, go, kitchen;* others have recently added new meanings, as *antenna*, a biological term for the "feelers" of insects, probably now means for most people a piece of radio equipment. *Etymology*, the study of word origins, traces the changes in spellings and combinations of word elements (as in *dis/service, wild/ness, bath/room, room/mate*) and pursues the word or its component parts to Old English and beyond or to a foreign language from which it came into English, and so on back to the earliest discoverable forms. Of some words, especially colloquial words like *dude, stooge, rumpus*, the origin is unknown; for others, like *OK* or *blizzard*, it is debated. But the efforts of generations of scholars have discovered pretty full histories for most words. These are given briefly in most dictionaries and more fully in the *Oxford English Dictionary* and in special works.

Most people working with words have some curiosity about where they come from and about how new ones can be made. They find that our everyday words in general come down directly from Old English (*brother, go, house, tell*), or if they are of foreign origin, that they were borrowed many centuries ago (*candle, debt, pay, travel*). The vocabulary of high society has many French words, of both early and recent borrowing (*debutante, gallant, fiancée*). The vocabulary of philosophy and abstract thought has a large Latin element (*concept, fallacy, rational, idealism*), and the vocabulary of science has many Greek words (*atom, hemoglobin, seismograph*).

The sources of words will often reveal something about our history, as the many Norman French and Latin words in law (*fine, tort, certiorari, subpoena*) remind us of the time, following 1066, when the government of England was in the hands of the

Norman French. But it is more important to discover what meanings the words have had, in their earlier career in English and in the foreign languages from which they have come. These early meanings have often left traces in the suggestive value of the words, and often even abstract words, which once had specific, concrete meanings, may become more vivid when their histories are known. *Supercilium* in Latin meant "eyebrow," so that our *supercilious* suggests a scornful lifting of the eyebrow. *Rehearse* is from a French word meaning to "harrow again." *Sarcophagus* is, according to its Greek originals, "a flesh eater," referring to the limestone coffins that hastened the disintegration of bodies. *Profane* (Latin) meant "outside the temple" and gathered the meaning of "against religion, the opposite of sacred." *Alcohol* goes back to an Arabic word for a finely ground powder, used for painting eyelids, and from its fineness the word became applied, in Spanish, to specially distilled spirits, and so to our alcohol.

Following up the biographies of words is interesting—it makes a good hobby—and it very often will sharpen a writer's sense for the exact meaning and for the suggestion carried by a given word. Such results are personal and depend on finding bits about a word's past that appeal to you. This article chiefly presents the various ways in which words have arrived and are still arriving in English. There are two general processes—making new words, either created or borrowed, and compounding or clipping words and parts of words that are already in the language. Then this stock of words is increased in usefulness by changes in meanings of the already established forms.

2. New words. (a) CREATION OF WORDS. Outright creation of words is rare. Even *gas*, first used by Von Helmst, a Belgian scientist, probably had the Greek *chaos* or some Dutch or Flemish word behind it. *Kodak* is probably an actual creation, as are some other trade names. Popular words like *dud*, *burble* were also creations, good sounding words someone made up. *Imitative words like *buzz*, *honk*, *swish*, *whiz* are attempts to translate the sounds of nature into the sounds of language. Various exclamations of surprise, pain, scorn started unconsciously—*ow*, *ouch*, *fie*, *phooey*—but they became regular words, used by anyone. But most words now used by English-speaking people have a background in already existing words or elements of words.

Occasionally a person coins a word for a particular statement, known as a *nonce word* (used but once). One might write that a certain person "was the acme of hasbeenivity" and *hasbeenivity* would be a nonce word, and would probably remain one. As a rule arbitrary coinages do not stick. Of the large group suggested by Gelett Burgess (in *Burgess Unabridged*) not many are used, and only two have made the serious dictionaries (*blurb*, *goop*). Many similar words used in localities or in particular families, perhaps originated by children, never become part of the language.

b) BORROWED WORDS. English has always borrowed words freely, from Latin, German, French, and from less dominant languages with which English-speaking people have come in contact. It has assimilated words of quite un-English form: *khaki* (Hindustani), *seersucker* (Persian, Hindustani), *tycoon* (Japanese), *ski* (Norwegian), *hors d'oeuvres* (French), *intelligentsia* (Russian). The various words for *porch*, itself Norman French but the oldest and most English-seeming of the group, come from various languages: *piazza* (Italian), *portico* (Italian), *stoop* (Dutch), *veranda* (Anglo-Indian).

Dictionaries, histories of English, and books on language detail the story of past English borrowings. The process is still going on, though perhaps more slowly than at some periods. Some words come into English at the formal level and remain formal words: *intelligentsia, bourgeois, chef-d'oeuvre, objet d'art, Zeitgeist, Anschluss,* and many others of political, philosophical, scientific, or literary bearing. *Sphygmograph* and many other scientific words are recent compoundings of Latin and especially of Greek words which are not otherwise in English usage—so that they may be regarded as borrowings as well as compounds. Other words come in at the informal level, especially when large numbers of people go abroad, as during a war (*boche, camouflage, poilu, ersatz*) or when a foreign invention becomes suddenly popular, as in *chauffeur, garage, chassis, tonneau* of the automobile vocabulary. Some words brought by immigrants have stuck: *sauerkraut, kohlrabi, pronto, piñon, kosher, shillalah* (*shillaly*), *goulash.*

Many are dropped before they gain any general currency. The useful words are more or less adapted to English spelling and pronunciation and become true English words: See *English language, and for suggestions about the use of recently borrowed words, *Foreign words in English.

3. **Changes in form of words.** (a) WORD COMPOSITION. Most new words are made by putting together two or more word elements to make a new word of different meaning or function, as *un-* added to *interesting* gives a word of the opposite meaning, *uninteresting,* or *-ize* added to the noun *canal* gives a verb, *canalize.*

The elements may be a prefix placed before the root word (*mis-related*), or a suffix added (*foolish-ness*), or a combining element like *mono-* (*mono-syllable, mono-rail*), or two independent words built together (*book-case, basket-ball, gentle-man*). *Group words like *high school, out of town*, though not written as single words, could be included as a type of word composition.

A list of prefixes and suffixes that are still active in English would take several pages. A few of the more common prefixes are:

> *a- (not): asymmetrical, amoral, atypical
> ante- (before): anteprohibition era
> anti- (against): antiprohibition
> bi- (two): bivalve, biplane, bicycle
> dis- (not): disinterested, dispraise
> in- (in): income, impart, instill
> in- (not): inelegant, impractical
> mis- (wrong): mistake, misnomer
> *pre- (before): preview, prenatal, pre-empt
> *re- (again): revise, redecorate
> up- (up): upend (verb), upswirl (noun)

A few suffixes are:

> -en (to make a verb): heighten, lighten, weaken
> -ful (full): playful, spoonful
> -fy (to make): electrify, horrify
> -ish (to make an adjective): dryish, foolish, smallish
> -ize (to make a verb): circularize

Combining elements include a number of words or roots, many of them Greek:

> -graph- (writing): biography, photograph
> micro- (small): microcosm, micrometer, microphone
> mono- (one): monotone, monorail
> -phil- (loving): philanthropy, philately, Anglophile
> -side-: sidewall, sideswipe, ringside
> -smith: locksmith, silversmith, gunsmith
> -trop (turning): geotropic, heliotropic

For more complete lists of prefixes, suffixes, and compounding elements see Kennedy, pages 335-51.

Sometimes unnecessary and unused elements are added to words, as in [ir]regardless, origin[ation]. For such words see *Long variants.

Several pairs of prefixes and suffixes have the same meaning, so that two words of the same meaning but somewhat different in form exist side by side, especially words with *in-* (not) and *un-* and nouns with *-ness, -ity*, or *-tion*:

aridness, aridity	indistinguishable, undistinguishable
completeness, completion	torridness, torridity
corruption, corruptness	unobliging, disobliging
ferociousness, ferocity	unrobe, disrobe
humbleness, humility	

When such a pair exists, take the one that is more familiar to you or that fits best in the rhythm of the sentence. But try not to make your style conspicuous by coining a form when there is already a similar word in good use. The only sure way to know is to consult a good dictionary.

b) BLENDS. Informal and colloquial English have a number of words that show the liberties that the users of language have always taken with their words and always will take. Some of their experiments have proved useful and have become a part of the main English vocabulary.

One common type is *blends*, or portmanteau words, made by telescoping two words into one, often making a letter or syllable do double duty. *Squish* is probably a blend of *squirt* and *swish; electrocute* of *electro-* and *execute, avigation* of *aviation* and *navigation*. Many *"Time* words" are blends: *cinemactress, socialite, P W Administrator;* and they are common in business: *servicenter, corrasable* (a paper—*correct* plus *erasable*), the names of many firms and products, like *Socony, Nabisco, Richlube.* In colloquial humor they abound: *positutely, absotively, solemncholly, absogoshdarnlutely*, and also in more serious conversation, often presenting two ideas at once: *snoopervize* (*snoop—supervize*), *politricks, happenstance, anecdotage, slanguage.* They are specially useful in a humorous context or in one of suggested disparise.

c) CLIPPED WORDS. One of the commonest types of word change is clipping, dropping one or more syllables to make a shorter and more speakable form: *ad* from *advertisement, bus* from *omnibus, taxi* from *taxicab* (earlier from *taximeter cab*), *quote* from *quotation, mob*—an eighteenth century clip from *mobile vulgus— auto, movie, plane, phone, Frisco*, and so on. *Shoptalk has many clips—*mike* for *microphone* or *micrometer*, and so on. The speech of any closely related group is full of clips; campus vocabulary shows a full line: *ec, home ec, poly sci, grad, prom, dorm, ad building, varsity, lab, exam, gym, prof, pre-med*, and scores more.

Clipped words are written (when they are appropriate to the context) without apostrophe or period, as they stand in the paragraph above.

d) BACK FORMATIONS. A back formation differs from clips like *exam* and *auto* chiefly in that it is formed on analogy with other

Originality

words and is usually needed to serve as a different part of speech. *Beg* was formed from *beggar*, corresponding to *hunt, hunter*. A number of back formations have made their way, like *diagnose* from *diagnosis*, *edit* from *editor;* some, like **enthuse*, are slowly making their way into the common vocabulary; but most are formed in fun, like *burgle*, and are used either in humor or in a derogatory sense, like *orate*. *Donate* seems unnecessary, since we have *give*, but *enthuse* is more justifiable, since it takes the place of the clumsy *be enthusiastic over*.

e) COMMON NOUNS FROM PROPER NAMES. A number of words have come into general use because of some association with a person or place: *boycott*, from the name of an Irish land agent who was "boycotted"; *macadam*, from the name of the inventor of the road surface, John L. MacAdam; *sandwich*, from an Earl of Sandwich; *jersey*, from the island of Jersey; *madras* from Madras, India.

f) PLAYFUL FORMATIONS. Blends and back formations are likely to have a playful note and so do some other word shifts that can't be classified, except that they often represent a popular pronunciation, like *nooz* or *colyumist*. *Colyum* and *colyumist* are making their way, since they make it possible to point out a particular kind of *column*. Some, like *hire education*, are convenient puns. Some become quite generally used: *dingus, doodad, beanery, sockdolager*. *Jalopy* seems a perfect word for its meaning.

Watching these recent and familiar formations may lead to a study of the earlier and less obvious origins of words in the general English vocabulary.

(REFERENCES: The great authority on the origin of English words is the *Oxford English Dictionary*, and now the *Dictionary of American English* is supplementing it for words peculiar to the United States.

Besides general books on English, the following pay special attention to origin of words: Otto Jespersen, *Growth and Structure of the English Language* (various editions); George H. McKnight, *English Words and Their Backgrounds* (New York, 1923); *Picturesque Word Origins* (Springfield, Mass., 1936); H. F. Scott, W. L. Carr, G. T. Wilkinson, *Language and Its Growth* (Chicago, 1935); Kennedy, ch. 9.)

Originality is applied to writing in two somewhat different senses:

1. The first refers to material. Material is "original" when it is gathered by the writer from his experience, from his observation of people, events, or places, or from documents like letters, newspapers, and other sources that have not been worked over. Secondary or secondhand material has been worked over by someone else, as in textbooks, encyclopedias, most magazine articles and books. This material has been organized and given form in words. Original material has to be sorted, selected, and laid out by the writer. Obviously one can learn more and find more profitable

practice in handling original material than in handling secondary material.

Most student papers should contain some original material. The content may come entirely from the writer's experience. At least the central idea, the purpose can come from his present desires, some of the examples, details, or applications can come from his observation, and the opinions and the point of view can represent the way he thinks. Merely rewriting a magazine article is not a profitable exercise in composition. Putting together material from several such secondary sources is more useful, since it requires selection and comparison of material. But the most useful work for growth in writing is in composing papers in which a good deal of the material is original. The writing is a little harder, but it is more fun, and the gain is much greater than in simply working over what others have done. Compare *Plagiarism.

2. Originality in expression, in style, is a different matter. The English language has been used a long time, and absolutely new words and phrases are rare. The most threadbare figures and phrases can be avoided, and an honest attempt to tell exactly what the writer sees and believes will ordinarily result in straightforward, readable writing, which is more valuable than mere novelty. The one sure fact is that striving too hard for originality is almost certain to result in strained writing, uncomfortable to writer and reader alike. When a style deserving the label "original" appears, it is usually the byproduct of an active and independent mind, not the result of trying to be different.

Orthography means spelling. See Chapter 6, Spelling, page 155, and *Spelling.

other in *Comparison of adjectives and adverbs §§ 1, 2.

ou represents the sound of *ou* in *bout, out, house,* of *ow* in *cow* (kou), of *ough* in *bough* (bou).

Words spelled with *ou* are variously pronounced: trouble (trub′l), soul (sōl), soup (sōōp), trousseau (trōō′sō).

-ough (-augh) A handful of words containing *-ough* and *-augh* are one of the minor scandals of English spelling. They are common words, so that children learn most of them well enough—but it is hard to believe they should be asked to do so.

The objection to these forms is not so much that they are cumbersome, as that they "spell" such different sounds—*although, bough, cough, thorough, through, bought, taught.* This can be explained by the history of the pronunciation of the individual words, chiefly by the fact that the pronunciations now generally current have come from different localities of early English speech—but that does not defend them.

At present *altho* and *tho* and to a less extent *thru* and *thoro* are widely used in familiar writing and are commonly used in business writing, especially in advertising. They are used in a number of periodicals and in some books, though most publishers still go by traditional stylebooks. They are given as alternative spellings in the recent dictionaries. In a questionnaire answered by over a hundred college and university English teachers, nearly one half allowed or encouraged the use of these forms in themes. They are still out of place in formal writing, and their use in informal writing should depend chiefly on their appropriateness to other traits of style and to the expectations of readers.

ought See *have § 4 for *had ought* and *hadn't ought*.

-ous, -us *-ous* is an adjective ending: *fictitious, ominous; -us* is a noun ending: *cactus, campus, impetus*. (See Chapter 6, Spelling, page 155.)

Outl **Outline form** Correction: Revise the form of your outline according to the directions given in this article.

    1. Types of outlines. 2. Outline technique. 3. Position of outlines.

An outline is a schematic statement of the material that has been or that is to be presented in an article, showing the order of topics and the general relationship between them. An outline can test the organization of a paper that has been written. But the chief purpose of outlines is to make writing both easier and more effective. Once the material has been laid out, writing is relatively easy. You can focus on one stage at a time. You can see how the whole will shape and won't have to worry whether to put *this* in *here* or wait until later—you can write with confidence. Short, simple papers do not need formal outlines, though often some scratch notes will be handy. But the longer the paper and the more complicated the material, the more important a plan, represented by some sort of outline, becomes.

The way an outline grows out of the material you have decided to present in your paper is described in Chapter 1, "Planning the paper," page 13. This *Index* article takes up questions of forms of outlines.

    1. Types of outlines. (a) SCRATCH OUTLINE. Most writing is done from very casual notes jotted down with due attention to

II. Macomber and Mitty were trying to find a
little happiness.
    A. Mitty couldn't face reality so
      he went to his everyday world of
      make-believe where he was always
      the hero.
    B. Macomber sought happiness by hunting
      big game and the like.
III. They both found some degree of happiness.
    A. Mitty found some happiness from

comparison of

James Thurber's The Secret Life of Walter Mitty and

Ernest Hemingway's The Short Happy Life of Francis Macomber

I. Both Walter Mitty and Francis Macomber were very unhappy men.

  A. Mitty was unhappy because he didn't seem to be able to do anything.

    1. He couldn't even take the chains off his car without getting them wound around the axle.

  B. Macomber was unhappy because his wife did not love him.

    c. Their wives' actions helped to make them more unhappy.

    1. Mitty's wife was domineering and told him "what to do when."

    2. Mrs. Macomber was unfaithful.

meaning but without regard to form of the notations. The points are grouped according to some system of the writer's own devising. This is proper, and more themes should be written from such informal notes. Since this outline is an entirely personal document, not to be shown to anyone else, there is no point in making suggestions for it. Every writer should work out some method by which he can help himself sort out and organize his material and can make it easier for him to write an orderly paper.

b) Topic outline. The most common type of formal outline is the topic outline. The subjects are noted in brief phrases or single words, numbered consistently as they are in the following example:

I Have Learned to Work   [Title]

Learning to work in my early years has given me money for clothes and for my college education and has established habits that have been useful in many ways. [Sentence statement]

I. Early formation of work habits   [Main head]
   A. Parents' warning against the evils of idling [Subhead]
   B. Required chores for all children in my family
   C. A newspaper route for fun and profit
II. Summer vacation work during my high school years
   A. Necessity of earning money
      1. For various school activities
      2. To save for my future college expenses
   B. Ways and means
      1. Selling popcorn and candy at baseball games
      2. Selling magazines and subscriptions
      3. Acting as lifeguard at seashore resort
III. Beneficial results of this work
   A. Practical results
      1. Many additional clothes and social activities
      2. A bank account for my college expenses
      3. Skills and contacts valuable for getting jobs during college vacations
   B. More permanent results
      1. Strengthening of character
         a. Avoiding mischief
         b. Habit of industry
      2. Realization of value of money
      3. Carry-over of work habits into academic life
      4. Development of self-reliance

c) Sentence outline. A sentence outline differs from a topic outline only in that each head and subhead is a complete sentence. It is more formal, requires more effort to draw up. Its chief advantage is that it forces the outliner to think through his ideas more thoroughly in order to give them more complete and elaborate statement. The following outline is for a paper based on Stephen Crane's *The Red Badge of Courage*.

The Transformation of Henry Fleming

Henry Fleming's romantic ideas of war were destroyed in his first battle, from which he ran away but to which he returned and by overcoming his fear regained his confidence and became a man.

I. Henry's boyish idea of war underwent a change on the eve of battle.
  A. He had enlisted because he thought of war romantically and pictured himself performing heroic feats.
  B. A few days before his regiment was to have its first engagement, his idea of the glory of war was modified.
    1. He observed his fellow soldiers, listened to their boastful remarks.
    2. He began to doubt his own courage, feared he might run from danger.

II. He failed in the first test.
  A. As the regiment went into the firing line, he wished he had never enlisted.
  B. For a time he remained in the line and did his duty.
    1. He was bewildered.
    2. Feeling himself to be in a "moving box," he did as the others did about him.
  C. Overcome by fear, he finally turned and ran to the rear.
  D. As a skulker, he had a miserable experience.
    1. Discovering that his regiment had unexpectedly held its ground, he felt cheated.
    2. Joining a column of the wounded, he was shamed when asked about his own wound.

III. He regained his self-confidence.
  A. Dealt a blow on the head by a deserter, Henry rejoined his regiment, expecting to be ridiculed.
  B. When his fellow soldiers assumed that he had been wounded in action, Henry saw that his cowardice had passed unnoticed.
  C. In the next day's battle he acted creditably.
    1. Enraged at the enemy, he fought furiously and desperately.
    2. Praised by his lieutenant, he saw himself in a new light.
    3. He became color bearer and urged his fellows on to the charge.

IV. After this engagement, Henry was no longer his old self.
  A. He had had a chance to see himself in a new perspective.
  B. For a time he was tortured by thoughts of his cowardly conduct of the first day.
  C. Then he rejoiced at having become a man and overcome fear.

d) PARAGRAPH SUMMARIES. It is sometimes helpful to prepare for writing a short paper by jotting down in advance the topic of each paragraph. This method would not work well for long papers, because it does not distinguish subheads. This is the only type of outline in which the entries correspond exactly to the paragraphs of the paper.

2. Outline technique. Most of the conventions of outline form are shown in the examples just given, but they may be worth isolating for comment.

a) THE TITLE. The title of the paper should stand over the outline, but it is not a part of the outline and should not be numbered. The heads should carry their full meaning and not refer back to the title by pronouns.

b) SENTENCE STATEMENT. It is a good idea to put between the title and the first main head a sentence stating the subject and scope of the whole paper. If this is done it should be a full, meaningful sentence, not a mere announcement of the topic.

c) NUMBERING SYSTEMS. The most widely used numbering system alternates letters and figures, as shown in the examples in this article. Avoid intricate or confusing schemes of numbering.

d) INDENTION. Write the main heads flush with the left margin and indent subheads two or three spaces—enough to make them clearly in a different column—from the left, as shown in the examples. Heads that run over a single line should be further indented, as in the sentence outline in § 1c.

e) PUNCTUATION AND CAPITALIZING. No punctuation is needed at the end of lines in a topic outline. In the sentence outline the punctuation should follow regular sentence practice as shown in the example. Only the first word of a head and proper names are capitalized: an outline head is not a title.

f) MEANINGFUL HEADS. Each head should be meaningful, understandable by itself. This outline is useless:

My Vocation

    I. The work I am interested in
   II. Why I prefer this type of work
  III. What my responsibilities would be
  IV. Some of the attractions of this position
   V. The chances for success
  VI. Why I want this particular position

A more exact statement of topics would show that II and IV belong together, and very likely V and VI as well.

Subheads should carry full meaning. General labels like "Causes" or "Results" are useless, as are these from an outline for "The House of Morgan":

    A. Started by Junius Spencer Morgan
      1. What he did

> B. Succeeded by J. P. Morgan I
>   1. What he did
> C. Succeeded by the present J. P. Morgan
>   1. What he is doing

Meaningful heads are especially important in outlines which are to be made part of a finished paper or to be shown to someone for criticism.

g) HEADS OF EQUAL IMPORTANCE. The main heads of an outline, those usually marked by Roman numerals, should be of equal importance to the subject: they show the several main divisions of the material. Similarly, the first line of subdivisions of these heads, those usually marked by capital letters, should designate logical and equally important divisions of one phase of the subject. The same principle applies to further subdivisions under any subhead.

Equal headings:	*Unequal headings:*
Books I Have Enjoyed	Books I Have Enjoyed
I. Adventure stories	I. Adventure stories
II. Historical novels	II. Historical novels
III. Character studies	III. *Treasure Island*
IV. Autobiographies	IV. Autobiographies
V. Books on ethics and religion	V. What I like most

h) HEADINGS IN PARALLEL FORM. Parallel heads or subheads are expressed in parallel grammatical form. A sentence outline should use complete sentences throughout, not lapse into topical heads; a topic outline should use topic heads, not sentences. Topic heads or subheads should use phrasing parallel to that of other heads of the same rank; that is, the heads in a particular series should be all nouns or all adjectives or all phrases, or whatever is the most appropriate form.

Parallel heads:	*Heads not parallel:*
The Art of Putting	The Art of Putting
I. The stance	I. The stance is fundamental
II. The grip	II. The grip
III. The back-swing	III. Importance of the back-swing
IV. The contact with the ball	IV. Stroking the ball
V. The follow-through	V. Follow through with care

i) DIVISION OF TOPICS. Since a topic is not "divided" unless there are at least two parts, an outline should have at least two subheads under any main head. For every heading marked *I* there should be at least a *II*, for every *A* there should be a *B*, and so on.

Proper subdivision:	*Illogical single heads:*
The Tripartite System of Government	The Tripartite System of Government

I. The executive branch
  A. President
  B. Cabinet
	I. The executive branch
	  A. President and Cabinet

II. The legislative branch
  A. The House of Representatives
  B. The Senate
    1. Special functions
    2. Special privileges
	II. The legislative branch
	  A. The House
	  B. The Senate
	    1. Functions

III. The judicial branch
  A. The Supreme Court
  B. Lower courts
	III. The judicial branch
	  A. The Supreme Court

A single detail may be included in the statement of heading, as, for an organization in which the whole executive power lay in the president:

I. The executive branch (The President)

Sometimes an exception is made for an outstanding illustrative example, which may be put in an outline as a single subhead:

B. Injustice of grades in figures
  1. Example: My almost-Phi Bete roommate

j) INTRODUCTIONS AND CONCLUSIONS. Dividing a paper into "I. Introduction—II. Body—III. Conclusion" is bad practice. The introduction and conclusion to a paper are usually too short to need a special heading—the paper is all body. The first and last topics are from the main body of material, chosen with a special view to their fitness for meeting and for leaving a reader. See Chapter 7, "Beginning paragraphs" and "Concluding paragraphs," pages 195, 198.

3. Position of outlines. An outline of less than half a page may stand on the first page of a paper, and the text can begin below it. A fuller outline should stand on a page by itself and be placed before the first page of text.

out of date *Out of date, out of doors, out of town* are hyphened in formal writing when they stand before a noun but not necessarily in informal writing:

Formal:	He has an out-of-date model.
Informal:	He has an out of date model.
General:	His model is out of date. (In predicate)

over- Compounds with *over* are not usually hyphened:

overanxious   overalls   overdraft   overseas

owing to See *due to.

P is characteristically pronounced as in *purr, tip, puppy*. It is silent in a few common words (*raspberry, cupboard, receipt*) and in a number of words from Greek—*pneumonia, psalm, psychology*.

After *m, p* is often silent in such words as empty (em′ti), and a *p* is generally sounded after *m* in words such as *dreamt* (drempt) and *warmth* (wôrmpth). In *pumpkin*, two pronunciations are recognized, pump′kin and pung′kən.

paid (payed) *Paid* is the spelling of the past tense and past participle of *pay* (He *paid* his bills) in all senses except *payed out a line, rope, etc.*, and occasionally in that sense also.

pair In informal usage the plural of *pair* is *pair* when it comes after a number: six pair of socks. In other positions *pairs* is the usual plural.

pants—trousers In formal usage the word for men's breeches is *trousers;* in the other levels the word is *pants*.

Paradox See *Epigrams.

Par **Paragraphs** Correction: This paragraph is unsatisfactory. Revise or rewrite it. The most common faults in paragraphs are:

1. Underdevelopment—Lack of details to establish the picture or statement intended.

2. Lack of connection—Either actually unrelated statements put together, or the existing relation between statements not made clear to a reader.

(Paragraphs are fully discussed in ch. 7, Writing Paragraphs, p. 169, and ch. 8, Kinds and Qualities of Paragraphs, p. 209. These two chapters include the following topics:

Chapter 7: 1. "Materials of paragraphs" (p. 171): Details, Opinions and generalizations, Comparisons and contrasts, Qualifying statements, Relationships between facts, Development of paragraphs. 2. "Paragraphs in the making" (p. 182): Visualizing paragraphs, Focusing statements, Actual writing, Revising, Manuscript form. 3. "Connection within paragraphs" (p. 191). 4. "Transitions between paragraphs" (p. 193). 5. "Beginning paragraphs" (p. 195). 6. "Concluding paragraphs" (p. 198).

Chapter 8: 1. "Kinds of paragraph development" (p. 210): Narrative, Descriptive, Association, Support, Climax. 2. "Qualities of paragraphs" (p. 225): Development, Movement, Continuity, Emphasis. 3. "Analyzing paragraphs" (p. 226).

Parallel constructions Correction: **Make the two or more elements** *Paral*
in this series parallel in form. Typical shifted (unparallel) constructions are these:

Shifted:	*Made parallel:*
To me orientation week seems both [noun:] a necessity and [adjective:] worth while.	To me orientation week seems both [two adjectives:] necessary and worth while.
Jack has received offers from Hollywood not only [phrase:] for his fishing experiences but [clause:] because he resembles the late Will Rogers.	Jack has received offers from Hollywood not only [two phrases:] for his fishing experiences but for his resemblance to the late Will Rogers.

For other examples and suggested remedies see *Shifted constructions; Chapter 4, "Consistent constructions," page 116, and
Chapter 10, "Parallelism and balance," page 282.

Paraphrase A paraphrase is a restatement of a writer's ideas in different words. It is now usually applied to digesting the contents of
a passage in one's own words, as in note taking.

Parataxis *Contact clauses; Chapter 9, "Contact clauses," page 253.

Parentheses ( )
1. For additions. 2. For apologetic asides. 3. To enclose numbers
in an enumeration. 4. For action on different planes. 5. With
other marks.

1. **For additions.** Parentheses (often called *curves* and by printers
called *parens*) are sometimes used in writing, chiefly to inclose
words, phrases, or whole sentences that add to the clearness of a
statement without altering its meaning and that are allowed to stand
outside the construction of the sentence. These additions are likely
to be (1) illustrations, (2) definitions, or (3) added information
thrown in for good measure, as in the first sentence of this paragraph.

This bill, commonly called the Lockport plan, has been the basis of all
later city-manager charters (there are now 438).

Of all such emotions religious earnestness is the most fatal to pure
biography. Not only does it carry with it all the vices of hagiography (the
desire to prove a case, to depict an example—the sheer perversion, for such
purposes, of fact), but it disinterests the biographer in his subject.—HAROLD
NICOLSON, *The Development of English Biography*, p. 111

Sondelius even brought in the negro doctor, Oliver Marchand, not on the
ground he was the most intelligent person in the island (which happened
to be Sondelius's reason) but because he "represented the plantation hands."
—SINCLAIR LEWIS, *Arrowsmith*, p. 376

These uses are slightly stiff and belong most appropriately to rather formal exposition, and should be used sparingly.

2. For apologetic asides. Sometimes parentheses are used to mark an apologetic aside, as much as to say "You know this, but let me remind you"—though this use is less common today than formerly.

James Madison (the fifth President) enunciated the doctrine in 1823.

3. To enclose numbers in an enumeration. Parentheses are often used to inclose the letters or figures used to mark items in an enumeration, as in § 1 of this article, though this tends to make the numbers or letters more conspicuous than they deserve to be.

4. For action on different planes. Recent fiction has developed another convenient use of parentheses. When the action is carried on in two different planes—one in the present, another in the past; one in a character's mind, the other in the action—the one which receives less space, is less emphatic, may be put in parentheses:

> . . . ears are still in outside world, peeping Toms sticking out on both sides of my head, why can't I take them in like snails, but you can't, you can close your eyes but you can't make your ears stop thinking. ("Thirty love! Net ball!" float in from that other world.) Voices outside losing their separateness, merging, sweet distant song, like shell held to ear, going round and round in Natalie's brain, ears going to sleep at last. . . .—TESS SLESINGER, *Time: The Present*, p. 341

5. With other marks. When the parenthetical unit is a complete sentence, the period comes *inside* the curves, though it may be omitted if the expression falls within a sentence. Punctuation marks belonging to the sentence including the parenthesis come *after* the second curve:

> There is a sort of glum morality about the scene in which we are shown what would have happened if the inventor had married for money instead of love (Mr. Anderson's gifted mechanism is equipped not only to recall the past but also to mix it up a little), and in the end, the suggestion that the device might be manufactured in quantity and sold on the installment plan seemed ominous to me.—*The New Yorker*, Oct. 9, 1937

> Misbehaviors which meant disqualification: "babbling" (barking to the extent of interfering with the chase); "loafing" (showing no inclination to hunt); "running cunning" (failing to work fairly on a trail).—*Time*, Nov. 28, 1938

Parse Parsing is describing the grammatical forms and functions of the words in a sentence. The sentence *A hermit lived in the ruined abbey* might be parsed: *Hermit* is a noun, subject of the verb *lived; in the ruined abbey* is an adverbial phrase of place; *abbey* is a noun, object of the preposition *in*, modified by the adjective *ruined*.

part (on the part of) is often a rather clumsy way of saying *by,* *among, for,* and the like:

> In the past ten years there has been a definite move on the part of [*by* or *among*] our religious leaders to unite all Protestants in one church.
> It resulted in less wild driving on the part of [by] young people.

Participles Correction: The participial construction marked is not *Part* good English. Revise it in the light of § 2 (making it modify a particular noun as an adjective) or § 4 (stating the idea in a subordinate clause).

1. Forms of participles. 2. As adjectives. 3. In absolute constructions. 4. Unidiomatic participles.

1. Forms of participles

	Active	*Passive*
Present:	asking	being asked
Past:	having asked	asked, having been asked

The simple participle forms (*asking, asked*) are used in various verb phrases:

> I am asking   I am being asked   I have asked   I have been asked

Although the participles are referred to as present and past, they do not indicate definite time themselves but time in relation to the context in which they are used.

2. As adjectives. When not a part of a phrasal verb form, the participles are most commonly adjectives. They have qualities of adjectives in that they modify nouns and pronouns (the pen *used* in signing the treaty; a *coming* era; the leaves *falling* in the street). They have qualities of verbs in that they may take an object (*Following these clues,* he soon found her) and be modified by adverbs (The car, *rolling crazily* . . .).

Sometimes in analyzing a sentence it is difficult to tell a participle used as an adjective from a passive voice. The decision rests on whether the participle modifies the subject, as a predicate adjective with a linking verb, or whether it describes an action.

> Passive voice: The candidate of the Republican party was defeated.
> Predicate adjective: The candidate was defeated but happy.

When used as an adjective, a participle should refer clearly to some particular noun or pronoun:

> *Opening* his shirt at the neck, he went back to his chopping. (*Opening* modifies *he.*)
> A college education, *looked* at from this point of view, may be a liability. (*Looked* modifies *college education.*)

There should be no reasonable doubt of what is modified. A modifying participle "dangles" or is "misrelated" when it seems to refer to a word the writer does not mean it to refer to:

Misrelated: Walking on the campus, several of my class usually pass by.
Clear: Walking on the campus, I usually meet . . .
Misrelated: Combined with his scientific understanding, Dr. Hertzler is a man who would have made his name for wisdom in any profession.
Clear: Dr. Hertzler's scientific understanding would have made him a name in any profession.

Because the reader expects these participles to refer to the subject of the following clause, he is disappointed. It is not so much a matter of meaning, for the sentence with a dangling participle is rarely ambiguous (though it may be amusing). It is rather a matter of accurate expression: Participles used as adjectives should modify definite words. (See *Misrelated modifiers.)

3. In absolute constructions. The participle-as-adjective should not be confused with the participle in a phrase which relates to the whole sentence (to the situation) rather than to a particular word. Some such phrases are very common, perhaps even *formulas.

Judging from her looks, she isn't under fifty.
Beginning with the class of 1943, the tuition was raised $50.

(See *Verbids.)

4. Unidiomatic participles. The use of participles and verbal nouns in English seems to be increasing, but there is a tendency for amateur writers to use participles in constructions in which they would ordinarily use a subordinate clause when speaking:

Uncle Joe was prompt, *necessitating our hurrying* [so that we had to hurry].
The sea was running heavily, *being boosted* by a strong southeast wind. (Omit the *being*.)

Especially conspicuous are unidiomatic "nominative absolutes," made like Latin ablative absolutes:

He being right there, I let him do the work. (Since he was right there . . .)
Then, *the feature being ended,* everyone began to file out of the theater. (Then, after the feature was over . . . or, perhaps, The feature over, everyone . . .)

(For *very* with participles see *very § 2. Compare *Gerunds. References: Curme, *Syntax*, pp. 158-60; C. A. Smith, *Interpretative Syntax* (Boston, 1906), pp. 55-59; Reuben Steinbach, "The Misrelated Constructions," *American Speech*, 1930, 5:181-97; H. C. Wyld, *A Short History of English*, pp. 237-58.)

Parts of speech Although in our speaking and writing we are not conscious of using nouns or verbs or adjectives, we need to be able

to identify the parts of speech if we are going to describe and discuss
grammatically what we have written. For analysis we have to know
whether we are using nouns or verbs, pronouns, prepositions.

1. Identifying parts of speech. There are three criteria for placing
a word in a certain part of speech: the grammatical function it serves
or generally serves in speech—subject, object, modifier, and so on;
its type of meaning—the name of something, description of a quality,
a connecting relationship, and so on; and the forms it may assume—
like the *'s* of the noun genitive or *-er* of the comparative of an
adjective or adverb. The part of speech to which a word belongs
cannot be decided by looking at the word by itself; we need to know
how it is used. These qualities are all discussed in the articles on each
part of speech. Here the traditional eight parts are identified by their
type of meaning, an imperfect but the simplest criterion.

Nouns—Names of people, places, things, qualities, acts, ideas, relationships:
President Roosevelt, Key West, gearshift, confusion, gambling, relativity.

Pronouns—Words which refer indirectly to people, places, things, etc:
he, it, someone, which.

Adjectives—Words which point out or indicate a quality of people, places,
things, etc: *both, highest, warm, thorough, Hanoverian.*

Verbs—Words that specify actions, states, feelings, existence (of people,
places, things, etc.): *fall, fall into, dislike, become.*

Adverbs—Words which, typically, tell how, where, when, to what degree
acts were performed, or that indicate a degree of quality, etc: *severely, there,
yesterday, much.*

Prepositions—Words that link nouns and pronouns to other words by
showing the relationship between them: *to, about, behind.*

Conjunctions—Words that connect words (the horse *and* carriage), phrases
(in the house *and* in the garden) and clauses (The rain was over *and* we
started again, or *After* the rain was over we started again).

Exclamations—Words that are expressions of strong feeling: *Ouch!*

(REFERENCES: Jespersen, *The Philosophy of Grammar*, chs. 4-6; Curme, *Parts of
Speech*, pp. 1-105; Kennedy, ch. 8.)

2. Conversion of parts of speech. English uses one part of speech
to perform the function of another part of speech with great freedom.
Hurry may be a verb (I'll hurry right over), or a noun (I'm in a
great hurry), or an adjective (a hurry call); *better* is the comparative
of the adjective *good* or of the adverb *well* ("I could have better
[adverb] spared a better [adjective] man"); it is a verb (to better
your condition); or a noun (our elders and betters); *home* is used
as a noun, a verb, an adjective, or an adverb; and so on through a
long list of words. This change of function from one part of speech
to another is called *conversion*. It is a sign of the economy of our
language in forms of words, and is made possible in part because

in English we have so few particular endings belonging specifically to various parts of speech. These shifts are not confusing because the word's position or context in a sentence shows what its function is, actually determines its "part of speech."

This trait of our language is one reason why the parts of speech classification is not very important in English grammar. It is not basic and can be understood only after discussion of the functions of words in sentences.

The use of adjectives as nouns is particularly characteristic of informal English: *wets* and *drys* were the two factions in the prohibition argument, an *empty* may be a bottle or a freight car. Many of the semi-technical words of trade and business are of this type: "The regular driver handles the ordinary orders, but I take the *rushes* [adjective to noun] out in the *pickup* [verb to adjective] truck."

One of the most convenient forms of conversion is the use of a noun in the adjective function: the *art* room; a *baseball* game; the *high school* gymnasium; a *basement* tenement. Most of these do not attain to full conversion, that is they do not become complete adjectives so that they can be compared, yet they serve as adjectives and have to be construed as adjectives. Nouns are especially common as adjectives in newspaper headlines, in which they often replace longer adjectives ("Let *U. S.* Citizens Alone, Italy Told") or replace phrases with *of* ("Madison *Oil Trial* Prosecutor to Head *Medical Trust* Quiz"). (See *Newspaper English § 3.)

The use of a noun or some other part of speech as a verb is likely to increase vividness: She jumped into the roadster and *nosed* her down the street; *Power* your car with reliable gas. "Don't you *she* me!" (as a Russian princess said to an American girl who was not following the courtly locutions in talking about her). The opposite change, from verb to noun, is less spectacular but very convenient: He had five *tries;* a friendly *get together;* I have taken a five room *rent* in Springfield.

Conversion is an outstanding trait of colloquial and informal English, though less used in formal English. Need and appropriateness can be your guides. When an equally expressive verb or noun exists, there is no reason for running the risk of attracting attention to your words by a borrowing from some other part of speech—but freedom in handling the parts of speech is in the best tradition of our language. Convert a noun into an adjective or into a verb whenever it seems the natural form of expression.

(REFERENCE: Kennedy, *Current English* § 58.)

party See *person.

passed, past The past tense and past participle of *pass* are *passed* (He *passed* the first post; He had *passed*), though *past* is fairly common as the participle. *Past* is the adjective (*past* favors), preposition (*past* the crisis), and adverb (*past* due, They went *past*). Pronunciation: past or (Eastern) päst. (See *A § 4.)

passer-by Usually hyphened; plural *passers-by*.

Passive verbs Correction: Change the passive verb or verbs to *Pass* active.

Amateur writers tend to use passive statements ("The music *was enjoyed* by us" instead of "We *enjoyed* the music") when active verbs would be more natural. Awkward passives are sometimes used to avoid *I*:

Passive: The situation *was taken in* by me with great amusement.
Active: I took in the situation with great amusement.

This passage shows both effective and ineffective passives:

1951 is here. With it comes a host of '51 model automobiles. Most of these cars *were heralded in* during the closing months of 1950. They *were awaited* in anxious curiosity by the buying public. In many instances, they *were looked forward to* with too much anticipation.

Were heralded in is a legitimate passive, although an awkward phrase, because the "heralders" need not be named; and *were awaited* throws *the buying public* to the end of the sentence for emphasis and the passive would not be noticeable if it was not followed by *were looked forward to*, which clearly shows that the writer is not paying attention to his work. Those two sentences might better stand:

The buyers awaited them in anxious curiosity, often with too much anticipation.

The use of passive verbs is often objectionable because it involves a thoughtless shift from the active voice and adds to the wordiness of what is usually already wordy and fuzzy writing.

For profitable use of the passive voice see *Voice § 3.

Past tense, Past perfect tense See *Tenses of verbs.

patriot, patriotic Pā′tri ət and pā′tri ot′ik are the dominant American pronunciations. Pat′ri ot′ik is more common than pat′ri ət.

peeve Informal and colloquial for *annoy*. As a noun *peeve* (and *pet peeve*) is probably still slang. *Peeve* is a back formation from *peevish* (*Origin of words § 3d).

per *Per* (Latin, "through, by, by the, among," etc.) is most appropriate when used in phrases that are still close to their Latin originals —*per capita, per cent*—or in a definitely commercial setting—*$18 per week, $2.60 per yard, forty-four hours per week,* or in certain standardized technical phrases—*revolutions per minute.*

Because of its commercial and technical connotation, *per* is less appropriate in general prose, where the English equivalent phrase usually fits more naturally: *$18 a week, 20¢ a quart, four times a year.*

per-, pre- Many English words begin with these two prefixes. Do not spell the *per-* words with *pre-:* write *per*form, *per*spire, *per*fect, and so on.

percent is not followed by a period, and may be written as two words; it is informally used instead of *percentage* or even of *proportion:*

> Only a small percent of the class was [or, *were*—collective agreement] there.

With figures the percent sign (%) is ordinarily used: 97.6%.

Perfect tense See *Tenses of verbs.

Period (.) 1. At the end of statements. The principal function of the period is to mark the end of a statement, that is, the end of every completed sentence not definitely a question or exclamation. This gives us no trouble, though sometimes in hasty writing we carelessly omit the period. (See Chapter 5, "Period," page 139.)

Sometimes sentences in the form of exclamations or questions are really to be regarded as statements. After such a sentence a writer may use the exclamation mark or question mark, but he will usually have a period if the tone is lacking in emotion or if he wishes to minimize the emotion of the sentence form he has chosen. (See *Rhetorical questions.)

2. Miscellaneous conventional uses:

a) After *abbreviations: Oct.   n.b.   Mr. Wm. Fraser

b) In sums of money, between dollars and cents: $5.66. The period is not used unless the dollar sign is used: 66 cents or 66¢; $0.66.

c) Before decimals, or between the whole number and the decimal: .6, 3.14159, 44.6%

d) A period is sometimes used between hours and minutes represented in figures (2.36 p.m.) though a colon is more usual (2:36 p.m.).

e) Three spaced periods (. . .) are used as *ellipses, to mark the omission of words.

3. Period in combination with other marks. Most American publishers place a period coming at the end of a quotation inside the quotation marks: "The longer you put it off," he said, "the harder it's going to be." (See *Quotation marks § 4b.)

Period fault See Chapter 9, "Fragmentary sentences," page 262, and *Fragmentary sentence.

Periodic and loose sentences See Chapter 10, "Loose and periodic sentences," page 280.

Periodical indexes See Chapter 13, "Periodical indexes," page 371.

Person Pronouns are classified in three *persons:*

First person, the one speaking: *I, my, me, we, our, us*
Second person, the one spoken to: *you, your*
Third person, the one spoken of: *he, she, it, one, they, him, his, her, them,* and so on

Nouns are regarded as third person.

Except in the verb *be* (*I am, you are, he is* . . .) English verbs have only one form to distinguish person, the third singular of the present tense: I have, you have, he *has;* we, you, they have.

person is the ordinary word for referring to a human being. *Individual* has the same meaning (though it is applied also to single objects and animals as well) but emphasizes the person's singleness, aloneness, and is slightly heavy or pretentious unless that emphasis is needed. *Party* is legal or vulgate.

In person and *personally* are current intensives in business and colloquial usage (Ronald Colman in person; I personally think). These expressions are usually not appropriate in writing.

Personal pronouns See *Pronouns, types and forms § 1.

Personification Personification is a *figure of speech in which an object or animal or quality or ideal is given some attributes of a human being:

> Deal gently, *Love*, with him and her
> who live together now!
>
> REX WARNER, *Poems*, p. 71

It is less common today than formerly, and less common in prose than in verse. Flat and unessential personification is likely to have an amateur sound: No steam engine can brag of such efficiency.

ph is a *digraph for the *f* sound in words of Greek origin: *phlox, photography, photograph.* . . . In *Stephen, ph* represents *v.*

Most words with *ph* belong to the formal vocabulary, so that the natural and expected simplification to *f* is rather slow. A few, like *fantasy* and *sulfur* are already changed. Advertisers and humorists are experimenting with *telegraf, foto,* and so on.

phenomenon, phenomena The plural of *phenomenon* is *phenomena* (phenomena of the mind).

Since *phenomenon* means "any observable fact or event," care should be taken to see if some more exact word would be more effective.

Phi Beta Kappa See *Greek alphabet.

phone is the usual informal and colloquial clip for *telephone* (on the phone; Phone me later). No apostrophe.

Phoneme A phoneme is the smallest meaningful unit of sound in a language, as *weak* is composed of three phonemes, w, ē, k, and *bought* of b, ô, t.

There are about thirty five phonemes in English, some of them, like r, being far from uniform in actual speech. A phonemic alphabet or any system of recording pronunciation is an effort to indicate the phonemes in use in particular words.

(REFERENCES: *Pronunciation; Bloomfield, ch. 5, and other recent books on linguistics.)

Phonetics is the division of language study that deals with the sounds of language, their formation, changes, and the exact representation of pronunciation by phonetic symbols.

Phrasal verb A verb formed by an auxiliary and an infinitive or past participle: *will go, must go, has gone, had gone.* Even in the tenses which have simple forms (*goes, went*), we get slightly different shades of meaning by using phrasal forms (*am going, did go, was going,* etc.). Called also *periphrastic* verbs.

(SEE *Verbs. REFERENCE: Kennedy, pp. 522-29.)

Phrases 1. Forms and functions. A phrase is a group of two or more words without a subject and finite verb that functions as a grammatical unit in a clause or sentence. Phrases are classified according to the words of which they are composed:

Prepositional: in the morning   before the war   in the room
Participial: coming into the room   pasted on the wall

Gerund: before his learning French
Infinitive: to live peacefully   to catch fish
Phrasal parts of speech: (Verb:) have gone   am going   (Adverb:) fore
and aft   (Preposition:) in regard to   (Noun:) high school

The term *phrase* is somewhat confusing because it covers these various and actually quite different patterns of expression. It would be clearer to keep the word to apply to expressions centered on nouns (up the steep hill) and use another, as *verbid* is used in this book, for those centered on participles, gerunds, and infinitives.

Phrases function as single sentence elements:

Nouns: (Subject) *The first four games* were lost.   (Object) He lost *the first four games.*   (Genitive) the works *of the masters*
Verbs: They *will go* in the morning.
Adjectives: a heart *of gold*   *Crossing the street,* he nearly was hit by a car.
Adverbs: beyond the town   in the morning   He did it *in the Dutch manner.*
Prepositions: in regard to   in order to   alongside of

2. A unit of expression. Most words by themselves, as they stand in a dictionary, cannot fit into sentences until they are set in phrases. They need modifiers to make their meaning more exact; they need connectives to tie them to other words. Out of such phrases, clauses and sentences are built. A good case could be made for regarding phrases as the central feature of writing and speaking, more fundamental than sentences, rivaled only by paragraphs in importance for study and practice.

Phrases are not only units of meaning; they are the physical units of reading, since we read by meaningful groups of words rather than by single words. Most phrases fall within the limits of the typical eye span (what an eye grasps at one fixation)—six words or thirty letters. Phrases that are easy to grasp with the eye and easy to comprehend with the mind are fundamental to good writing.

(For the use of phrases see *Idiom and idioms, *Participles, *Prepositions, and ch. 4, "Noun phrases," "Verbid phrases," p. 112.)

pianist, piano   Pronunciation divided: pi an′ist, pē′ə nist, the first the more common by a great deal. The word applies to both men and women players, so that *pianiste* is unnecessary as a feminine form.

Piano is pronounced pi an′o; rarely pi ä′no. Plural *pianos.*

picnic   Before endings beginning with a vowel, *k* is added to the second *c* to make the *k* sound sure: *picnicker, picnicked, picnicking.*

Place names   See *Proper names; for punctuation, *Comma § 8b.

Plagiarism *Plagiarism* means taking material written by another and offering it as one's own. The copied matter may range from a few sentences to a whole paper copied from another student or from a book or magazine. (We are not considering here the more complicated problem of plots taken from stories or movies, and so on.) There are various reasons for copied papers in a composition course. A very few students are dishonest, trying to get credit without any mental effort. Once in a while one is playing the ancient game of putting-something-over-on-the-instructor, in part at least to see if it can be done. More often, at least in beginning courses, the motives are more complex. A student who plagiarizes may be scared or so befogged in what is for him a difficult or puzzling course that he resorts to the only way he sees of getting a good grade. And sometimes a student doesn't clearly understand what rights he has in using the materials of others or in receiving help.

In English compositions obviously the work should be done independently, not in "collaboration" with another student.

If he copies from dishonest motives, the student must take the consequences if the source of his paper is recognized, or even if the instructor is sure by comparing it with his other papers that it is not his own work. If he copies from fear or ignorance of proper practices, he deserves consideration and help. Whatever the motive, the penalty—failing the paper or perhaps, if it is an important one, failing the course—is not an instance of vengeance, but a sign of failure, failure in the fundamental purpose of a composition course, which is to increase students' skill in communicating their information, ideas, and fictions to others. Copying others' work is the most complete failure possible.

The student who is scared or puzzled should go at once to his instructor and discuss his situation frankly, the reasons for his difficulties, the present faults in his work, and ways to overcome them. Serious effort intelligently directed will always bring improvement. And a student who feels he is moving in the right direction, even if he is moving slowly, is doing something important, and in the long run work is more satisfying and less wearing than worry.

The student who has not learned how to handle material got from reading and study needs guidance in the fundamentals of study and scholarship. A writer expects that what he has published will be read and will be used; but he has a right to expect that his exact words will not be used without his receiving credit and that his facts and ideas will not be used in print without his permission.

Anyone using published material, then, has a twofold responsibility: first, of absorbing the ideas into his own thought, and second of giving credit to important sources. A student—or anyone else—is not *composing* when he is merely copying. He should read and digest the material, get it into his own words (except for brief, important quotations that are shown to be quotations). He should be able to *talk* about the subject before he *writes* about it. Then he should refer to any sources he has used. This is not only courtesy, but a sign of good workmanship, part of the morality of writing. In an informal paper the credit can be given informally, perhaps a note on the cover saying "This paper is based on . . ."; or it may be in the body of the paper: "Professor Keane said in a lecture . . . ," "Walter Lippmann wrote recently . . . ," or "So-and-so said . . ." Or credit may be given more formally in footnotes at the bottom of the page (as described in § 9 of Chapter 13, page 388). Footnotes must be used in a research paper, but one or two would be in order in any paper for which a student has found material in print. The greatest temptation to plagiarize is in a research paper, in which the material is supposed to be based on reading various sources. But a research paper offers also the best opportunity for learning how to gather, digest, and give credit for material from published sources. At any rate it is necessary for college students to learn how to use such material accurately and honestly—by getting it into their own words and giving appropriate credit to sources used.

Planning a paper   See Chapter 1, page 13, Chapter 13, page 384, and *Outline form.

plenty   *Plenty* as an adverb (I was plenty worried—The car is plenty large) is marked colloquial by the dictionaries. It is in good informal use but would rarely be found in formal writing.

The colloquial omission of *of* after *plenty* (plenty of time—plenty time) results in an adjectival use. This idiom is sometimes found in print:

> Out into darkness, out to night,
> My flaming heart gave plenty light, . . .
> JOHN MASEFIELD, *The Everlasting Mercy*

Pleonasm   Pleonasm is repetition, especially using two words for the same grammatical function (My Uncle Fred, *he* said he would give me twenty five cents for every bird I could find and name). It is quite common in children's speech and in colloquial English and occasionally for emphasis in written prose.

Plurals (nouns)

 1. Special groups in '-s' or '-es.' 2. Same form for both singular and plural. 3. Survivals of older English plural forms. 4. Foreign language plurals. 5. Compound and group words. 6. Plurals of figures, words, letters. 7. Plural substitutes.

The plural of the great majority of English nouns is made by adding an s or z sound, spelled -*s*, to the singular form of the noun. This -*s* is pronounced as part of the syllable to which it is added.

  buckets rats days rooms trees
  There are five *Romes* in the United States.

But several groups of words form their plurals in other ways:

 1. Special groups in '-s' or '-es,' chiefly a matter of spelling:

 a) Nouns ending in the *sound* of ch, j (*edge*), s, sh, or z, in which the -*s* could not be pronounced as part of the final syllable, add the sound iz, spelled *es*:

  birches churches bridges ledges *buses (or busses)
  kisses bushes *Joneses axes fixes buzzes quizzes

 b) Nouns ending in -*y* preceded by a consonant change the *y* to *i* and add -*es*:

  beauties bodies caddies cherries cities cries

Drys, standbys are exceptions to this rule (speaking of a prohibitionist as a *dry*).

 Words ending in *y* preceded by a vowel merely add -*s*:

  bays boys moneys [sometimes *monies*] monkeys toys

These plural forms should not be confused in writing with the genitive singular in '*s*: *beauty's, body's, caddy's,* and so on.

 c) Words ending in -*o* preceded by a vowel make a regular plural with -*s*: cameos, folios, studios.

 Words ending in -*o* preceded by a consonant vary and have to be remembered or looked up in a dictionary. Some of the commoner of these are:

  With -*s* only: banjos cantos dynamos Eskimos Filipinos pianos
  silos solos sopranos
  With -*es*: echoes heroes Negroes noes potatoes tomatoes
  torpedoes vetoes

 Several words in -*o* are used with either -*s* or -*es*. The -*es* form is usually the more common, but the increasing number of -*os* forms suggests that English is gradually reducing these irregular words to the regular plural form:

cargoes, cargos   desperadoes, desperados   hoboes, hobos   zeros, zeroes

d) Some words ending in an *f* sound have their plural in *-ves:*

calf, calves   half, halves   knife, knives   leaf, leaves
self, selves   shelf, shelves   thief, thieves   loaf, loaves

Many words ending in *f* sounds are regular:

beliefs   chiefs   dwarfs   fifes   gulfs   proofs   roofs

Some have two forms:

elf, elves—elfs   hoof, hoofs—hooves   scarf, scarfs—scarves
staff, staffs—staves   wharf, wharfs—wharves

2. Same form for both singular and plural:

Names of animals: fowl, sheep, fish [*fishes* for varieties of fish]
All words in *-ics:* athletics, civics, mathematics, politics
Colloquial measurements: foot, pair, ton
A number of words rarely, if ever, used in the singular:

barracks	headquarters	odds [in betting]	smallpox
bellows	means	pains	species
billiards	measles	pants	tactics
gallows	morals	scissors	trousers
goods	mumps	slacks	

3. Survivals of older English plural forms:

In *-en:* child, children   ox, oxen   brother, brethren [Church use]
Change of vowel: foot, feet   goose, geese   louse, lice   man, men
mouse, mice   tooth, teeth   woman, women

4. Foreign language plurals. English keeps the foreign form of many words that have been borrowed from other languages. As they become more commonly used, the plural is usually formed regularly in *-s;* words used chiefly in scientific or formal writing tend to keep the foreign form longer. *Antenna*, for instance, makes *antennae* in biology but *antennas* for the more popular radio and television use. When the word is in transition, both forms will be found.

A few borrowed words that now regularly have plurals in *-s* or *-es* will suggest the extent of the change to English forms:

area	census	encyclopedia	museum
arena	circus	era	panacea
asylum	cupola	forum	panorama
bonus	dilemma	ignoramus	plateau
bureau	diploma	metropolis	quota
campus	dogma	minus	

Some common words that still have the foreign form or sometimes are found with the foreign plural (as in academic, formal, or scientific writing) are:

addendum -da	erratum -ta	neurosis -ses
alumna -nae	focus -ci (scientific),	nucleus -clei, -cleuses
*alumnus -ni	-cuses (general)	oasis oases
ameba -bae, -bas	*formula -las, -lae	opus opera
analysis -ses	fungus -gi, -guses	ovum ova
apparatus -tus,	*gladiolus -luses, -li	parenthesis -ses
-tuses	hiatus -tuses, hiatus	*phenomenon -na,
appendix -dixes,	hypothesis -ses	-nons
-dices	index indexes,	psychosis -ses
automaton -ta,	indices	radius radii, radiuses
-tons	larva -vae	rostrum -trums, -tra
axis axes	libretto -tos, -ti	species species
bacillus -li	locus loci	stadium -diums, -dia
basis bases	madame mesdames	stimulus -li
*beau beaus [beaux]	matrix -trixes,	stratum -ta, -tums
cactus -ti, -tuses	-trices	syllabus -bi, buses
chateau -teaus,	*medium -dia,	synopsis -ses
-teaux	-diums	synthesis -ses
cherub cherubs,	memorandum -da,	tableau -bleaus,
cherubim	-dums	-bleaux
(scriptural)	momentum -tums,	terminus -nuses, -ni
crisis crises	-ta	thesis -ses
criterion -teria	monsieur messieurs	trousseau -seaus,
curriculum	moratorium -iums,	-seaux
-lums, -la	-ia	vertebra -brae, -bras
datum *data	nautilus -luses, -li	vortex -tices, -texes
diagnosis -ses	nebula -las, -lae	

5. Compound and group words. Most compound words and group words add -s to the end of the group, whether written as one word or several:

attorney generals (or attorneys general)   bookcases   high schools
cross examinations   postmaster generals (or postmasters general)

In a few the plural sign is added to the first element:

daughters-in-law   kings of England   mothers-in-law   passers-by
poets laureate (also, poet laureates)   sons-in-law

6. Plurals of figures, words, letters. Usually the plural of a letter of the alphabet, of a word discussed as a word, or of a figure is written with -'s:

There are two *c*'s and two *m*'s in *accommodate*.
Three 2's   six 8's
Don't use several *that*'s in a row.

But usage is divided and the plural of figures and capital letters especially is increasingly made with -*s* alone:

three 2s   six 8s   two Cs and two Fs
And there are few more useful practical suggestions in composition than this: Use no more *ands* or *buts* than you can help.—BARRETT WENDELL, *English Composition*, p. 145

7. Plural substitutes. A plural notion is expressed often by a phrase that remains grammatically singular:

College after college has gone in for intramural sports.
The coach, with the captain and manager, makes up the schedule.
The coach, together with the captain and manager, makes [often *make*] up the schedule.

Singular and plural constructions are treated in *Subject and verb, *Reference of pronouns.

(REFERENCES: Curme, *Parts of Speech*, pp. 112-27, *Syntax*, pp. 539-48; Kennedy, pp. 438-45; Fries, p. 40 ff.)

p.m. See *a.m. and p.m.

Poetry When a full line or more of verse is quoted, it should be lined off as it was written, somewhat indented, enough so that it is nearly centered if the line is short. The first word of each line should be capitalized if it was capitalized in the original. Quotation marks are not needed around lines of verse quoted in prose when so spaced. See *Verse form for English meters.

politics is construed as either a singular or plural word but should not be both in the same passage.

In almost any group, politics is a subject which will arouse controversy.
Republican politics were offensive to the Federalists.

Polysyllables See *Monosyllables.

Positive degree of adjectives and adverbs is the simple adjective form (*poor, high, golden*) or adverb form (*slow, slowly, bitterly*). See *Comparison of adjectives and adverbs.

Possessive adjective *My, your, his, her, its, our, your, their* (the genitive case forms of the personal pronouns) are called possessive adjectives when they modify a noun:

my car   his first lecture   their experiences

Possessive case See *Genitive case. Use of the possessive with verbal nouns in -*ing* is discussed in *Gerunds.

Possessive pronouns See *Pronouns.

practical *Practical* and its derivatives give some trouble in spelling:

> *practical,* adjective: a practical scheme, He has a practical mind.
> *practically,* adverb: They were practically minded. (colloquial in phrases like "practically all there")
> *practicable,* adjective; a practicable method.
> *practicability,* noun: They questioned the practicability of the idea.

pre- The prefix *pre-,* meaning *before* in time (*pre-exist, pre-Victorian*), or in place (*precerebral*), or rank (*pre-eminent*), is separated by a hyphen from the root to which it is joined: (1) when the root begins with *e: pre-election, pre-eminent, pre-empt, pre-engaged, pre-existence;* and (2) when the root is a proper name: *pre-American, pre-Elizabethan.* To other words it is joined directly: *prearrange, preoccupied, preheat, preprint, preview, prewar.*

Précis A *précis* is a concise summary of facts, or, more often, of an article or other written document, giving in a brief space the essential content, the attitudes, and emphasis of the original.

Precious, preciosity Applied to style, *precious* and *preciosity* (or *preciousness*) mean "excessive attention to, fastidiousness in the use of words."

Predicate The predicate of a clause or sentence is the verb with its modifiers, object, complement, etc. The subject and predicate are the two main elements of a sentence. The predicate may be a simple verb of complete meaning (The big bell *tolled*), a verb and adverbial modifier (The sun *went behind the cloud*), a transitive verb and its object (He *finally landed the big fish*), a *linking verb and complement (The oldest member of a family *is usually the first to go*).

Two verbs depending upon one subject are known as a *compound predicate:

> The three of them *washed* and *wiped* the whole lot in fifteen minutes.

(See *Subject and verb, *Compound sentences, *Complex sentences, and ch. 10, "Reducing predication," p. 286.)

Predicate adjective, Predicate noun Adjectives and nouns that follow linking verbs are called predicate adjectives and predicate nouns (or nominatives):

> Predicate adjective: The horse is *fast.* I feel *bad.* It is going to turn *warm.*

Predicate noun: Gibbon was a *historian*.   Jackson became a *doctor*.

(SEE *Linking verbs and ch. 4, "Single word modifiers," p. 111.)

predominant is the adjective: "a predominant sentiment," "a sentiment predominant in the village." *Predominate* is the verb: "This sentiment predominated in the village." These words are heavy for *prevailing, prevail,* or some such word.

prefer The better idiom is with *to:*

> I prefer *Babbitt* to *Main Street.*
> He preferred going by train to going in their car.

*Had (or *would*) *rather . . . than* is less formal and more used:

> He *had* [or *would* or *He'd*] rather go by train than in their car.

Prefix A prefix is an element that can be placed before a word or root to make another word of different meaning or function: *anti-* (*antiprohibition*), *bi-* (*biweekly*), *mis-* (*misfit*). See *Origin of words § 3a.

Prepositional phrase A phrase made up of a preposition and its object: *without hope, in a hurry, toward a more abundant life.*

Prepositional phrases are modifiers, construed as adverbs or adjectives:

> They came *at just the right time.* (Adverb of time)
> He lives *in the white house.* (Adverb of place)
> The woman *in the black dress* has left. (Adjective)

To suggest the importance of prepositional phrases in English, here is a sentence of forty two words in which twenty seven stand in prepositional phrases (in italics), fifteen in other constructions:

> The settings *of the novels* ranged *from the fjords of Norway to the coasts of Tasmania,* and every page betrayed that intimate knowledge *of a foreign country* which can only be acquired *by a thorough study of the chattier sort of guide-books.*—STEPHEN VINCENT BENÉT, *Thirteen O'Clock,* p. 71

Prepositions Correction: Change the preposition, making it more exact or idiomatic (§ 3a), less conspicuous (§ 3b), or making the construction less colloquial (§ 3c, d).   *Prep*

1. Definitions. 2. List of prepositions. 3. Uses of prepositions.

1. Definitions. A preposition is a word which relates a noun or phrase or clause to some other element of the sentence: to a verb (He showed her *to* her room), to a noun (the click *of* flying wheels), or to an adjective (old *in* experience). A noun following a preposition is called its object (*room, wheels, experience* in the examples just given). Many words used as prepositions are also used as adverbs or conjunctions, and some, like *after, but, since,* serve as the three parts of speech, depending on their function in a sentence:

Preposition: The wettest summer *since* the Flood.
Conjunction: *Since* the price was so low, we took three.
Adverb: He hasn't been around *since*.

For this reason some grammarians group these three types of words as *particles* with varying functions. In this article and the ones on conjunctions and adverbs we shall not draw the lines very closely.

2. List of prepositions. The following list shows characteristic uses of the commoner prepositions. Many of them show both a concrete and an abstract meaning (*at home, at odds*). Fries estimates that nine of them (*at, by, for, from, in, of, on, to, with*) account for over 92% of prepositions used.

aboard   aboard the airliner (Formal: on board)
*about   about the town, about her, about his work
*above   above the clouds, above the average, above suspicion
according to   according to the reports, according to Hoyle
across   across the bow, across the street (Colloquial: *cross*—I'm going cross lots)
after   after dark, we all ran after him (Technical: of a drawing based on another's drawing—after Newcourt)
against   against the door, against the grain
ahead of   ahead of his generation, ahead of time
along   along the shore, along the route
alongside   alongside the dock (Colloquial: alongside of)
amid (amidst)   Formal: amid the smoke, amidst the ruins
among   among the lucky ones (used of three or more)
apart from   apart from the others, apart from his own earnings (rather formal)
apropos   Formal: apropos our discussion; or, apropos of our discussion
around   around the edge, around the town (Colloquial: around five o'clock)
as far as   as far as the door, as far as New Orleans
*as to   as to the objection, as to your interest
at   at home, at Johnstown, at his suggestion, at midnight
back of   back of the screen, back of the house, back of the proposal
because of   because of the war, because of his need
before   before the flood, before an audience, before replying
behind   behind the door, behind the pretense
below   below the surface, below our level
beneath   beneath the surface, beneath contempt (more formal than *below*)
*beside   beside the sea, beside the point, beside oneself
besides   besides those named, no other besides this
*between   between New York and Philadelphia, between life and death, between two mountains
beyond   beyond the river, beyond reach, beyond my understanding

by   by the house, by an inch, by force, by himself, by night
concerning   concerning my friend, concerning our interests
contrary to   contrary to orders, contrary to our expectation
despite   Formal: despite hostile criticism
down   down the chute, down the slope, down the list
*due to   due to an error, due to carelessness
during   during the last ten years, during the services
for   for you, for profit, for the community
from   from the attic, from the Far East, from fear
in   in the country, in the house, in the Bible, in trouble
in place of   in place of the old regulations
*inside   inside the house, inside ten minutes (Colloquial: inside of ten minutes)
in spite of   in spite of the law, in spite of his prejudices
in view of   in view of these concessions
into   into the mountains, into the street, into the subject (*in—into—in to)
like   like a horse, like a tornado
near   near the window, near the top, near exhaustion
*of   of Wisconsin, of the same color, of my opinion, of the king
*off   off the path, off the platform (Colloquial: off of the path)
on account of   on account of the weather, on account of his belief
*onto   onto the train, onto the beach (Formal: on to the beach)
out of   out of the auditorium, out of sight
over   over the fence, over the plains, over her head
owing to   owing to the emergency, owing to our inability
past   past the stores, past the mark, past the hour
*per   per day, per pound
round   round the Maypole, round the town
since   since his election, since Victorian days
through   through the first barrier, through accident
throughout   throughout the day, throughout his speech
*till   till morning, till the intermission
to   to Los Angeles, to the ocean, to Governor Smith, to the point
*toward   toward Fort Worth, toward dinner time, toward the truth
under   under the awning, under cover, under the arch
until   until dusk, until two o'clock (*till, until, 'til)
unto   Archaic: unto death, unto the last drop
up   up the slope, up the scale
upon   upon a sure foundation, upon further investigation
up to   up to this point
via   via the Nickel Plate
with   with his fellows, with caution, with the affirmative
within   within bounds, within the city, within a year

3. Use of prepositions. (a) EXACT OR IDIOMATIC PREPOSITIONS. A number of words are accompanied by certain prepositions, as contented *with* conditions, *in* my estimation. Some words have various meanings with different prepositions, as agree *with* (a person), agree *to* (a suggestion), agree *in* (principles, qualities). You can add indefinitely to the following list:

deprive *of* pleasure
eligible *for* membership
fascinated *by* this glamor
This glamor had fascination *for* him.
fear *of* fire, fear *for* his safety

hindrance *to* advancement
impressed *by* (or *with*) his ability
means *of* winning
pride *in* his college
unconscious *of* their stares

The right preposition does not give much trouble with words that we use commonly, because we learn the words by hearing or seeing them in their usual constructions. Obviously it is safer to learn words as they are actually used, to learn *acquiesce in* (acquiesce in a decision) rather than just *acquiesce*. If a person uses an unidiomatic preposition, it is probably because he is not at home with the word or is confused because usage is divided on that particular locution (as *different *from* or *than* or *to*). Dictionaries give the appropriate preposition used with particular words. This book treats a few idioms that are likely to raise questions: *ability (to); *agree to, agree with; *all (of); *compare—contrast; *different.

A special reminder is needed that when two words are used which are completed by different prepositions *both* prepositions should be used:

The first lesson learned by the sturdy Italian boy just over from the "old country" was *obedience to* and *respect for* others besides his parents. (Not: obedience and respect *for* others)
Some people cannot reconcile their *interest in* and their *fear of* snakes.
The committee acknowledged its *interest in*, but denied its *responsibility for*, housing conditions.

When both words call for the same preposition, it need not be repeated:

Observers from the North were astonished to find the slaves both *obedient* and *submissive to* their masters.
The box office refused to make any *allowance* or *refund for* tickets purchased from an agent.

b) PREPOSITIONS BULKING TOO LARGE. English has a number of group prepositions (*according to, in regard to, by means of*) that sometimes become conspicuous because they bulk too large for their purely functional work of showing relationship. They are not grammatically wrong, but used in any noticeable numbers tend to make a flatfooted style. For many of them a simple preposition can be substituted with real gain.

In these examples, sometimes one of the words can be omitted (the word in brackets) or a simple preposition (in brackets) can be substituted:

We made supper [*consisting*] *of* beans, fried potatoes, and steak.

Consumers Union attempts to furnish reliable information *in regard to* [*about*] all sorts of goods and services.

For politeness' sake the pronoun of the first person stands last when used [*in connection*] *with* other pronouns: "He, you, and I had better do it."

It has been said that in six months after graduation from college a man can pick up as much practical knowledge *connected with* [*of*] business administration as a non-graduate can in ten years.

. . . recent demonstrations *on the part of* [*by*] certain students in Columbia University . . .

Prepositions sometimes bulk too large in writing because we carry over to paper our colloquial tendency to use double prepositions when single ones would do the work: *in back of* for *back of, outside of* for *outside, off of* for *off*. . . .

These are not appropriate in formal English, which at its best makes one word do its exact duty, but may be in order in informal English if they help give an easy tone and if they do not become too noticeable. The writer should decide whether these colloquial idioms are appropriate to other traits of his style.

For further examples and discussion see the articles *as to, *of, off, *onto, and so on; *Function words.

The general advice is that prepositions should not attract particular attention or be allowed to weigh down a statement, since they are function words, but that at the same time a style should not be stiffened by trying to avoid natural phrases.

c) COLLOQUIAL OMISSION OF PREPOSITIONS. Informal and colloquial English show not only a frequent piling up of prepositions but the opposite tendency too—dropping a preposition that would be used in formal English. Prepositions, especially *of*, receive so little stress that they naturally drop out entirely in rapid speech and this same trait is now increasingly found in writers whose style is conspicuously colloquial. A few examples (with the preposition usual in formal English in brackets) will suggest the tendency:

. . . of permitting forward passing [from] any place behind the line of scrimmage.—JOHN KIERAN, *The New York Times*, Dec. 30, 1937

Malcolm Cowley . . . pointed out that the color [of] cloth we were using for the Giants faded too easily; . . .—BENNETT A. CERF, *The New Republic*, Apr. 21, 1937

The most notable piece of equipment was an apparatus which made it possible to run the presses [at] almost twice their former speed.

Just as I got my last shirt out [of] the drawer . . .—VINCENT McHUGH, *Caleb Catlum's America*, p. 85

A *couple [of] days later . . .

d) PREPOSITION AT END OF SENTENCE. It was once fashionable for textbooks to put a stigma upon prepositions standing at the end of their constructions (What did you do it *for?*). But postponing the preposition is a characteristic English idiom, even though it runs contrary to our usual tendency to keep words of a construction close together. In fact it is so generally the normal word order that the real danger is in clumsiness from trying to avoid a preposition at the end of a clause or sentence:

> Tell me what it is to which you object [Natural: what you object to].
> To whatever authority we may appeal, he will quibble over the method to be adopted [Natural: Whatever authority we may appeal to . . .].

Extreme cases are possible (like the boy's "What did you bring that book for me to be read to out of for?"), but there is no reason for hesitating to let a preposition fall at the end if natural idiom and rhythm place it there. (Compare *Verb-adverb combinations.)

Placing the preposition at the end is such a firmly fixed habit that sometimes we use one at the beginning and at the end:

> . . . in the lives of individuals *with* whom he had come in contact *with.*

Obviously such a sentence shows lack of revision.

(REFERENCES: Curme, *Syntax,* pp. 566-69; Fowler, pp. 457-59 and other index entries; Fries, ch. 7; Hall, pp. 213-17.)

Present tense *Tenses of verbs; for the "historical present" see Chapter 8, page 211.

principal—principle Associate *principal* as an adjective (the *principal* reason—the *principal* man of the town—the *principal* force involved) with other adjectives ending in *-al:* historic*al*, politic*al*, music*al*.

Principal as a noun is probably an abbreviation of a phrase in which it was originally an adjective: the *principal* that draws interest was once *the principal sum;* the *principal* of a school, *the principal teacher;* the *principal* in a legal action, the *principal party;* the *principals* in the cast of a play or movie, the *principal actors.* These are the only common uses of *principal* as a noun.

The noun meaning a general truth (the *principles* of science) or a rule of conduct (a man of high *principles*) is *principle.*

Principal clause The main or independent clause of a sentence. See *Clauses, *Complex sentences.

Prin **Principal parts of verbs** Correction: Change the verb form to the one in good use, as given in the list below or in a dictionary.

The principal parts of a verb are the infinitive (*ask*), the past tense form (*asked*), and the past participle (*asked*). Most English verbs are "regular"; that is, their past tense and past participle are formed by adding *-ed* to the infinitive. A number, most of them descended from Old English strong verbs (compare the strong verbs in modern German), make these past parts by a change in vowel (*strike, struck, struck*). Some of these are becoming regular (*shined, weaved*), and many are made regular in colloquial and vulgate usage (*blowed, growed*).

The following list includes a number of verbs with these irregular parts or with some other question of form. A form in parentheses is decidedly less common in writing, and those labeled *vulg.* (vulgate) would not ordinarily occur in current writing. A recent dictionary should be consulted for other verbs.

Infinitive	*Past tense*	*Past participle*
arise	arose	arisen
bear	bore	borne
		*born (given birth to)
begin	began (vulg. begun)	begun (vulg. began)
bid (to offer)	bid	bid
bid (order)	bade	bidden
bite	bit	bitten, bit
blow	blew (vulg. blowed)	blown (vulg. blowed)
break	broke	broken
		(colloq: broke)
*burst	burst	burst
catch	caught	caught
choose (chōōz)	chose (chôz)	chosen
come	came (vulg. come)	come
dig	dug (digged)	dug
*do	did	done
dive	*dove, dived	dived, dove
draw	drew	drawn (vulg. drawed)
dream	dreamed, dreamt	dreamed, dreamt
drink	drank (archaic and vulg. drunk)	drunk (drank—drunken)
*eat	ate (local, eat [et])	eaten (eat)
fall	fell	fallen
find	found	found
flee	fled	fled
fly	flew	flown
forget	forgot	forgotten, forgot
freeze	froze	frozen (froze)
*get	got	got, gotten
give	gave (vulg. give)	given
go	went	gone
grow	grew (vulg. growed)	grown

Infinitive	Past tense	Past participle
hang	hung, *hanged	hung, hanged
hear	heard	heard
know	knew (vulg. knowed)	known
*lay	laid	laid
lead	led	led
lend (*loan)	lent	lent
let	let	let
lie (see *lay)	*lay	lain
light	*lighted, lit	lighted, lit
lose	lost	lost
pay	*paid (of ropes: payed)	paid (payed)
plead	pleaded, plead, pled	pleaded, plead, pled
prove	proved	*proved, proven
ride	rode	ridden
ring	rang, rung	rung
rise	rose	risen
run	ran (vulg. run)	run
say	said	said
see	saw	seen
set	set	set
shine	shone, shined	shone, shined
show	showed	showed, shown
shrink	shrank, shrunk	shrunk
sing	sang, sung	sung
sink	sank, sunk	sunk
sit	sat (vulg. set)	sat (vulg. set)
slide	slid	slid (slidden)
sow	sowed	sown, sowed
speak	spoke	spoken
spit	spit, spat	spit, spat
spring	sprang, sprung	sprung
stand	stood	stood
steal	stole	stolen
stink	stunk, stank	stunk
swim	swam, swum	swum
take	took	taken
tear	tore	torn
throw	threw (vulg. throwed)	thrown
tread	trod	trodden, trod
wake	waked, woke	waked, woke (woken)
wear	wore	worn
weave	wove (weaved)	woven, wove
win	won	won
wind (wind)	wound	wound
	(nautical: winded)	
wring	wrung	wrung
write	wrote	written

(REFERENCES: Fries, pp. 59-71; Mencken, p. 430 ff.)

Verbs marked * are discussed in separate entries in this *Index*.

prior to Heavy (often journalese) for *before:*

Prior to [Before] coming here he had been at Stanford.

process, procedure, proceed We naturally spell *process* with one *e*, and *proceed* with two *e*'s; but only memory can make us spell *procedure* with one *e*. The verb is proc*eed* and the two nouns are proc*ess* and proc*edure*. The pronunciation prō′ses is British rather than American; say pros′es. Pros′ə sēz is usually an affectation for the plural; say pros′es əz.

Proceed means "to go," strictly in a rather formal fashion, and is best kept for movement (We proceeded at a decent rate of speed). "We proceeded to unpack" usually means no more than "We unpacked" or "Then we unpacked."

Profanity Styles change in the handling of cusswords and profanity. At present most writers, most editors, and most publishers are liberal, much more liberal than formerly. In fiction, where the words represent a character, simply be sure they are fitting and called for. Both cussing and cursing are primarily oral, matters of muscular release rather than of meaning, and they often attract more attention to themselves in print than they deserve. That is, you can't put on paper all the vulgarity proper to a vulgar person's speech; the effect will be suggested by an occasional bit of cussing. In biography, criticism, and miscellaneous informational articles you have less freedom. There double dashes and euphemistic blankety-blanks are more likely to be found. Such devices ordinarily give the impression of a writer who is playing at being tough or who hasn't the courage to use language he believes is really appropriate. Use the expressions the subject seriously calls for, compromising as little or as much as your temperament and circumstance demand. In matter submitted to magazines, editors will make whatever alterations their policies demand.

Professor Write:

Professor Tewksbury [or] Prof. E. W. Tewksbury [or]
E. W. Tewksbury, professor of electrical engineering.

The colloquial *prof* is a clipped word, not an abbreviation, and if it is written it should not have a period:

He said all profs were a little crazy anyway.

Strictly speaking *professor* should be confined to names of assistant professors, associate professors, and professors. Applying it to instructors is sometimes a well meant courtesy but more often carelessness. Teachers who are doctors of philosophy ("Ph.D.'s") are often addressed as *doctor*, though now that so many teachers have the degree, the title has lost its distinction. In official and business usage an *instructor* who has a doctor's degree is often addressed as *doctor*. It would be better to address all teachers as *Mr.* or *Miss* or *Mrs.*—as many professors would prefer. Students should follow the conventions of their own campus.

Progressive verb forms Those made with *to be* and the present participle: I am asking, he was asking, they have been asking.
(SEE *Tenses of verbs, *Verbs.)

Pronominal adjectives Several types of pronouns, used also as adjectives, are called pronominal adjectives:

> Interrogative: *Which* way did he go?
> Demonstrative: *that* way   *this* book   *those* boys
> Possessive: *my* hat   *his* idea   *your* dog   *their* seats
> Indefinite: *some* people   *each* person   *all* men

Pron **Pronouns, types and forms** Correction: Change the form of the pronoun marked to the one expected in the grammatical construction in which it stands.

1. The personal pronouns. 2. Relative pronouns. 3. Interrogative pronouns. 4. Reflexive pronouns. 5. Reciprocal pronouns. 6. Numeral pronouns. 7. Demonstrative pronouns. 8. Indefinite pronouns.

A pronoun is a word that represents ("means") a person or thing or idea without naming it. Usually the meaning of a pronoun is completed by referring to a noun, called its *antecedent*, that names the person or thing or idea and that has been recently used in the discussion (as the two *that's* in this sentence refer to *noun* and *its* refers to *pronoun*). For some pronouns, the "indefinites" *all, anybody, few . . .* (§ 8), the reference is either directly to the persons or things meant or it is made clear by the context in which it stands.

Pronouns are used in all the grammatical functions of nouns, as subjects, objects, appositives, and so on (*Nouns § 3). Their uses are described in *Reference of pronouns. This article lists the various types of pronouns and their case and plural forms.

1. The personal pronouns

Some of the most common grammatical problems come from the fact that the personal and relative pronouns have separate forms for the nominative and accusative cases and our nouns do not. (*between you and me, *It's me, *who, whom §§ 2, 3)

		Nomina- tive	Genitive	Accusa- tive
1st person	Singular:	*I	my, mine	me
	Plural:	we	our, ours	us
2d person	Singular:	you	your, yours	you
	Plural:	you	your, yours	you
3d person	Singular:			
	masculine:	he	his	him
	feminine:	she	her, hers	her
	neuter:	*it	its (of it)	it
	either gender:	*one	one's	one
	Plural:	they	their, theirs	them

Archaic forms of the second person singular, *thou, thy* or *thine, thee,* are used only in religious services, by the Society of Friends, and occasionally in poetry.

Mine, formerly used before words beginning with a vowel or *h* (*mine eyes, mine help*) is no longer so used: *my eyes, my help.* The emphatic form of the genitive is used without a noun:

The money is *mine* (*ours, yours, hers, theirs*).
Yours came a whole week before *mine.*

2. Relative pronouns

*who	whose	whom
*that	of that	that
*which	of which, whose	whom

Whoever, whichever, whatever (and archaic: *whosoever, whichsoever, whatsoever*) usually have an accent of surprise, irritation, or playfulness.

3. Interrogative pronouns. *who, *which, what; occasionally whoever, whatever

4. Reflexive pronouns. Reflexive or intensive pronouns are made of the personal pronouns plus the suffix *-self* or *-selves.* They are called reflexive because the action of the verb is directed toward the subject of the construction (He shaves *himself;* She bought *herself* two hats). See *himself, herself, *myself.

When used as intensives, these words are usually construed as pronouns in apposition:

The mayor himself delivered the address.   I can finish the job myself.

5. Reciprocal pronouns. See *each other; one another (formal).
6. Numeral pronouns. The *cardinal numbers (one, two, three . . .) and the ordinals (first, second, third . . .) are used as pronouns: *Three* were there; The *eighth* won.

Pronunciation

7. Demonstrative pronouns

*this, these   *that, those   (Compare *kind, sort)
the *former, the latter, the first, the second . . .
*such, *so (I told you so)
*same

8. Indefinite pronouns.

A large number of words, of greater or less indefiniteness, often function as pronouns:

all	everybody (*every § 2)	nothing
another	everyone	*one, oneself
*any	everything	other
anybody	few	several
anyone	many	*some
anything	much	somebody
*both	neither	someone
*each	*nobody	something
each one	*none	*such
*either	no one	

(Questions on the uses of pronouns are discussed in *Reference of pronouns. REFERENCES: Curme, *Parts of Speech*, ch. 10; *Syntax*, index references; Fries, index references; Kennedy, § 51 and index references.)

Pronunciation

1. Levels of pronunciation. 2. Regional differences in pronunciation. 3. Pronunciation key. 4. Special points in pronunciation. 5. Pronunciation list.

The greater part of anyone's use of language is spoken; consequently his pronunciation—the tone, the stress, the quality of particular sounds—is extremely important. A book cannot help much in this, since pronunciation is learned almost entirely by conscious or unconscious imitation of other speakers, but it can perhaps suggest an attitude toward a few of the major questions in spoken English. As with words, constructions, and other traits of language, pronunciation varies according to the level of the speech used and varies in different regions. Some principles of selection from among the various forms are needed.

1. Levels of pronunciation. From the point of view of their social standing, various types of pronunciation can be grouped under the general headings of vulgate, informal, and formal usage, each of which will differ somewhat between regions.

a) Vulgate pronunciation is the speech of people with relatively little education, used appropriately in their daily occupations but out of place in public affairs or in social groups using some other level of speech. Vulgate pronunciation is usually somewhat slower than educated speech, often being a "drawl." The local qualities of

706

sounds that are characteristic of the educated usage of a region are more conspicuous in the vulgate. Short *a* may be conspicuously "flat," as in *calf* or *laugh;* the characteristic Western *r* may be more conspicuous, and the Southern *r* may disappear altogether (as mō for *more*, where educated speakers would often have mōǝ), or a New Englander or a New Yorker may add an *r* to a word ending with a vowel (He had no idear of how to run a farm). In a good deal of New England and Western speech there is a nasal quality. Unstressed syllables may be completely lost, as kump'ni for *company*. Final consonants are often slighted and words run together. There are many individual words or groups of words that have vulgate pronunciations more or less widely current in a dialect area or throughout the whole country: rīl for *roil* (once in good use); aks for *ask;* el'ǝm for *elm;* woild for *world;* wunst for *once*. One of the results of an effective education is a dropping of the more conspicuous traits of vulgate pronunciation. This is an important social matter, since dress and speech are the principal superficial marks of class distinction in our society.

b) At the other extreme is formal pronunciation, found chiefly in the platform speaking of ministers, teachers, and of others who make public appearances, in the stage pronunciation of actors and the more consciously trained radio announcers, and sometimes in an exaggerated form in concert singing. This speech is somewhat slower than usual conversational speech, without the relaxed quality of a drawl, though it may slur certain syllables rather consciously (as the *-ary* words noted in § 4c). It is likely to give a fuller and more distinct value to individual vowel sounds, tends to use "broad" or intermediate *a* (*A § 4), and so on. The stresses are somewhat heavier than in informal speech and tend to stress individual words rather than phrase units. Dictionaries for the most part record this rather conscious platform enunciation in indicating the pronunciation of words, though more recent dictionaries tend to give more attention to informal speech.

c) Between these two extremes is informal pronunciation, usual in the conversation of educated people, and, spoken somewhat more slowly than in conversation, also in platform appearances. It shows more regional flavor than formal pronunciation but not so much as the vulgate. Its stresses are lighter than in formal speech and it is more rapid than either formal or vulgate. The stress is more a phrase or sentence stress than a presenting of individual words: *Saturday* by itself might be pronounced sat'ǝr dā, but in "I shan't be here Saturday" it would become sat'ǝr di and in rapid speech would be sat′ə di or sa′ə di (and in vulgate even sa′di). Function words (*the, and, that, there, to,* and the pronouns) rarely get their full values in typical speech and rarely need them. Vowels tend to become shorter, many become indeterminate (ə), and consonants that are hard to sound in their position are slighted or dropped or assimilated with other sounds as *t* in *sit down* (si doun′), or *th* in *clothes* (klōz). This represents the process by which *cupboard* has become kub′ərd and *Christmas* has become kris′məs. In words that are not in common use, however, such slighting of consonants is usually felt as vulgate rather than informal.

A person's pronunciation should be appropriate as far as possible to the situation in which he is speaking. Ordinarily the exactness of formal pronunciation is out of place in conversation, even in "cultivated" conversation, as are the laxities of vulgate. Too conscious attention to pronunciation in informal situations will handicap the speaker and irritate the listener. Pronunciation in appearances before groups must necessarily be somewhat slower, more distinct, but fundamentally it is a refinement of the speaker's better conversational style.

2. Regional differences in pronunciation. A single standard of English pronunciation is even more impossible than a single standard in the use of words or in grammatical constructions, which are stabilized somewhat by written literature. Since pronunciation necessarily is learned from personal associations, it naturally and unavoidably shows variety between regions. An educated Londoner, Scotsman, Bostonian, Chicagoan, Atlantan will show traits of their native speech but not enough to make them unintelligible to each other. British-made dictionaries are not satisfactory guides for pronunciation in the United States. Most American-made dictionaries have tended to represent New England and eastern pronunciation, partly because many words would have to be respelled two or three times if all parts of the country were considered.

The best that a person can do in checking his pronunciation when a real question comes up is to consult a *recent, carefully edited American* dictionary and compare its recommendations with the usage of the group with which he lives. For a person who is likely to consult a dictionary at all, this will mean the more or less educated people in his community. If the dictionary offers a choice, he should take the word he hears around him unless another is more natural to him and he wants to keep that, risking being a little different. If the one he hears consistently from fairly well educated people is not recorded in the dictionary, he is still safe in using that.

The problem of a person going to live in a different part of the country is more complex. Should he drop his native speech and do as the Romans do? If he makes a specific and hasty effort to pick up the new speech, he will be almost sure to make mistakes, that is, he will confuse the two. If he can stand off the first attacks on his speechways, he will soon find that he will attract less attention. Then he will naturally acquire, bit by bit and without forcing, many of the new ways. He need not be ashamed of honest traces remaining of his native speech. (See Chapter 2, "Variations due to place," p. 58.)

In fact, the words to worry about are not those in everyday use so much as the new ones acquired in taking up new work or a new social status or new ideas or, in college, new subjects of study. Care should be taken to get a conventional pronunciation of these new words (*acclimate, desultory, schizophrenic* . . .) as they are learned, to be at home with them from the beginning.

As Fowler puts it (p. 466), "The broad principles are: Pronounce as your neighbours do, not better." For the majority of words your neighbors are the general public. For words in more restricted use, your neighbors are the group that uses them. Consequently there will be more local flavor in informal and familiar speech, less in speaking to limited and special audiences. It is more important to avoid vulgate pronunciations than the regional pronunciations of educated people.

3. Pronunciation key. In this book the pronunciation of words is indicated by respelling them in the letters and symbols given below.

Further details of the sounds represented by each letter of the alphabet, with examples, will be found in the articles on the separate letters, *A, *B, *C, and so on in this *Index*.

The stress of syllables is represented by a ′ for a main stress and a ′ for a lighter stress, placed after the stressed syllable: ag′ri kul′chər.

A vowel sound in a stressed syllable will be more fully sounded than in one without stress (contrast the *o* of *below* [bi lō′] and of *obey* [which ranges from ō bā′ to ə bā′]).

a	apple (ap′əl), fact (fakt)
ā	age (āj), say (sā), inflate (in flāt′)
ä	far (fär), father (fä′thər)
b	back (bak), robber (rob′ər)
ch	child (chīld), church (chûrch)
d	do (do͞o), did (did)
e	bet (bet), effect (i fekt′)
ē	equal (ē′kwəl), see (sē), police (pə lēs′)
f	fat (fat), stuff (stuf)

g   go (gō), baggage (bag′ij)

h   hotel (hō tel′) boyhood (boi′hood)

hw   wheel (hwēl), whether (hweŧħ′ər)

i   if (if), pithy (pith′i)

ī   ice (īs), buy (bī)

j   jam (jam), edge (ej), age (āj)

k   king (king), back (bak), cocoa (kō′kō)

l   life (līf), silly (sil′i), fill (fil)

m   am (am), meet (mēt), sample (sam′pəl)

n   note (nōt), inner (in′ər)

ng   sing (sing), song (sông)

o   rock (rok), stop (stop)

ō   open (ō′pən), hope (hōp), go (gō)

ô   bought (bôt), ball (bôl), caught (kôt)

oi   voice (vois), boil (boil)

oo   book (book), put (poot)

o͞o   tool (to͞ol), rule (ro͞ol), move (mo͞ov)

ou   house (hous), out (out), cow (kou)

p   paper (pā′pər), cap (kap)

r   reach (rēch), try (trī), tired (tīrd), door (dōr)

s   say (sā), listen (lis′ən), yes (yes)

sh   she (shē), rush (rush), cushion (koosh′ən)

t   tie (tī), sit (sit), kitten (kit′ən)

th   thin (thin), both (bōth), bath (bath)

ŧħ   that (ŧħat), bother (boŧħ′ər), bathe (bāŧħ)

u   cup (kup), butter (but′ər)

ū   useful (ūs′fool), music (mū′zik) [Begins with a *y* sound]

û   urge (ûrge), bird (bûrd), term (tûrm)

v   very (ver′i), salve (sav or säv), save (sāv)

w   will (wil), with (wiŧħ or with), won't (wônt)

y   young (yung), yellow (yel′ō)

z   zero (zir′ō), breeze (brēz), trees (trēz)

zh   measure (mezh′ər), rouge (ro͞ozh)

ə   Called *schwa* (shwä), represents the indefinite vowel sound of many unstressed syllables. It is variously spelled: *a* in *sofa* (sō′fə), *e* in *secretary* (sek′rə ter′i), and by the other vowels and combinations of vowels.

ḷ, m̩, ṇ, ṛ Syllabic consonants, used in unstressed syllables when no vowel sound can be distinguished: little (lit′ḷ), wooden (wood′ṇ). When spoken slowly these syllables have ə, and are sometimes so respelled.

An *r* following a vowel changes the vowel's sound, as in *care, sere, core, sure,* but a separate symbol is not used to represent the change: kar, sēr, kōr, sho͞or.

    4. Special points in pronunciation. (a) THE NEUTRAL VOWEL. The naturalness of the neutral vowel (the italicized vowels in *a*gain, acad*e*my, dorm*i*tory, laboratory, circ*u*s) has been explained in the discussion of informal pronunciation (§ 1c). For suggestions on spelling these words see *Slurred vowels.

b) STRESS. In general, English is a rather strongly stressed (accented) language. The force of the stress varies a good deal among individual speakers. The stress of particular words (*detail, *address) varies with their meaning or with the frequency of their use, and according to their position in sentences. See also *Noun and verb stress.

c) SECONDARY STRESS. A word of three or especially of four syllables is likely to have a main and a secondary stress: *secondary* sek′ən der′i, *incidental* in′si den′təl. One of the differences between British and American pronunciation is that we tend to keep secondary stresses in many words in which the British have but one:

necessary: American nes′ə ser′i; British nes′əs ri
dictionary: American dik′shə ner′i; British dik′shṇ ri

A few Americans foolishly attempt to follow the British shortening of such words, in the belief that the shorter pronunciation is the more genteel.

d) PRONUNCIATION AND SPELLING. Words really live in their oral forms, and any guide to pronunciation must start with the spoken words, not the written. But our spelling represents, roughly at least, the sounds of words, or often it represents the sounds they once had. (See Chapter 6, p. 155.)

When words are acquired from reading rather than from hearing, they are very often over-pronounced, in what are known as "spelling pronunciations." *Sophomore* on most campuses is two syllables, sof′mōr, but people who see it more than they hear it are likely to sound the middle *o* slightly (sof′ə mōr); *yearling* is yûr′ling where it is regularly used, yēr′ling as a spelling pronunciation. Genuine familiarity with words is shown by using the oral rather than the spelling pronunciation.

5. Pronunciation list. The list on the following page is in part to raise questions of pronunciation. The pronunciations suggested should be tested by comparing them with those you hear. For most words that raise questions of pronunciation, consult a good recent dictionary, as suggested in § 1 of this article.

Pronunciations of other words will be found in the articles on each letter of the alphabet, *Foreign words in English, *Spelling, *Proper names, and in various articles on particular words.

When two forms are given, no choice is implied; a distinctly less common form stands in brackets. A large number of words are spoken in two or more ways in good usage.

An * means that there is a separate entry on that word.

abdomen ab′də min, ab dō′min
absorb ab sôrb′, ab zôrb′
absurd əb sûrd′ [əb zûrd′]
acclimate ə klī′mit, ak′lə māt
*adult ə dult′, ad′ult
advertisement əd vûr′tiz mənt,
    əd vûr′tis mənt,
    ad′vər tīz′mənt
ally (noun) al′ī, ə lī′; plural
    more often ə līz′; verb ə lī′
alma mater al′mə mā′ter,
    al′mə mä′tər [äl′mə mä′tər]
alternate (verb) ôl′tər nāt, al′tər nāt;
    (adjective) ôl′tər nit, al′tər nit
amateur am′ə chər, am′ə tūr′,
    am′ə tyoor, am′ə tûr′
amenable ə mē′ nə bəl,
    ə men′ ə bəl
apparatus ap′ə rā′təs, ap′ə rat′əs
applicable ap′li kə bəl, ə plik′ə bəl
Aryan ar′yən, ar i ən
atypical ə tip′ə kəl, ā tip′ə kəl (See *a-)
aviation ā′vi ā′shn̩, av′i ā′shn̩
aye (yes) ī
bade bad
*biography bī og′rə fi, bi og′rə fi
bureaucracy bū rok′rə si
business biz′nis
chauffeur shō′fər, shō fûr′
chic shēk, shik [chik]
combatant kom′bə tənt,
    kum′bə tənt
company kum′pə ni; [vulgate,
    kump′ni]
*contents kon′tents [kən tents′]
coup kōō [kōōp]
coupon kōō′pon, kū′pon
coyote kī′ōt, kī ō′ti
*data dā′tə, dat′ə, dä′tə
debut di bū′, dā′bū deb′ū
debutant deb′ū tänt, deb′ū tänt′,
    deb′yə tant
decade, dek′ād, de kād′, dek′əd
desperado des′pər ä′dō,
    des′pər ä′dō
diphtheria dif thir′i ə, dip thir′i ə
diphthong dif′thong, dip′thong
disputable dis pūt′ə bl, dis′pū tə bl
drama drä′mə, dram′ə [drā′mə]
*economics ē′kə nom′iks,
    ek′ə nom′iks
*either ē′thər [ī′thər]

electricity ə lek′tris′ə ti
Elizabethan i liz′ə bē′thn̩,
    i liz′ə beth′ n̩
err ûr [er]
exquisite eks′kwi zit, ik skwiz′it
finance fi nans′, fī′nans
formidable fôr′mə də bəl
fortnight fôrt′nīt, fôrt′nit
gibbous gib′əs
*gladiolus glad′i ō′ləs,
    glə dī′ə ləs
gunwale gun′əl
harass har′əs, hə ras′
heinous hā′nəs
*human hū′mən [ū′mən]
idea ī dē′ə [ī′di ə]
impious im′pi əs
indict in dīt′
isolate ī′sə lāt, is′ə lāt
juvenile jōō′və nil, jōō′və nīl
kimono kə mō′nə [kə mō′nō]
laugh laf, läf (*A §4)
launch lônch, länch
*leisure lē′zhər, lezh′ər
lever lev′ər, lē′vər
lilacs lī′ləks
matrix mat′riks, mā′triks
menu men′ū, mā′nū
mischievous mis′chə vəs
news nūz, nōōz
oasis ō ā′sis, ō′ə sis
orgy ôr′ji
parliament pär′lə mənt
patriot pā′tri ət
penalize pē′nəl īz, pen′əl īz
percolator pûr′kə lā′tər
*Phi Beta Kappa fī′bā′tə kap′ə
*pianist pi an′ist, pē′ə nist
pleasure plezh′ər
premier prē′mi ər pri mir′
presentation prez′n̩ tā′shn̩,
    prē′zn̩ tā′shn̩
process pros′es, prō′ses
pronunciation prə nun′si ā′shn̩
quay kē
ratio rā′shō, rā′shi ō
real rē′əl, rēl
reel rēl
research ri sûrch′, rē′sûrch
rodeo rō′di ō [rō dā′ō]
rotogravure rō′tə grə vyoor′,
    rō′tə grā′vyoor

*route root, rout
sociology sō′si ol′ə ji, sō′shi ol′ə ji
strictly strikt′li, strik′li
sumac shoo′mak, soo′mak
the thə, thi [thē]
tomato tə mä′tō, tə mä′tō,

[tə mat′ō]
usage ū′sij, ū′zij
vaudeville vôd′vil, vôd′ə vil,
vōd′vil
white hwīt, [wīt]
worsted (yarn) woos′tid

(SEE *Colloquial and written English, *Foreign words in English, *Proper names, *Rhythm, *Spelling. REFERENCES: Kenyon and Knott; Robertson, ch. 7; C. K. Thomas, *Phonetics of American English* (New York, 1947); "A Guide to Pronunciation," *Webster's New International Dictionary*, second edition, especially Part I, "Standard Pronunciation." For the International Phonetic Alphabet, used in scientific transcription of speech, see any issue of *American Speech* and most books on linguistics.)

Proofreading A check of copy is the last act before giving a manuscript to anyone for serious consideration. Proofreading the final copy of a theme for mechanical mistakes that may have slipped in while copying it, is an important part of the work in a composition course —and one that pays dividends.

After copy has been set in type it must be checked for typographical and other mistakes before it is ready to be printed. A tentative print is made on long sheets known as *galley proof*. After the type has been corrected and made up into the pages which are to be finally printed, *page proofs* are taken and read for a last check.

Corrections are indicated in proof by abbreviations and symbols placed at one side of the line to be changed, with a *caret (∧) inserted at the exact point in the line where the change is to be made. Proofreader's marks are illustrated on page 714. See publishers' stylebooks for further details.

Proper adjectives Proper nouns used as adjectives and adjectives directly derived from proper names and still referring to the place or person are capitalized. After proper adjectives lose the reference to their origins, they become simple adjectives and are no longer capitalized:

the French language   American interests
the Indian service, but india ink
a Paris (or Parisian) café, but paris green

Proper names Considerable care needs to be taken to spell and pronounce the names of people, places, companies, institutions as the people most concerned with them wish to have them spelled and pronounced. Many are rare or in some way unusual—*Thames* (temz), *Worcester* (woos tər), *San Joaquin* (san′wô kēn′). Analogy cannot be relied on: it is Waco (wā′kō), Texas, but Saco (saw′kō), Maine.

In place names the recommendation to use the pronunciation current in the place is complicated because the inhabitants often do not agree. *Chicago* is pronounced shi kô′gō and shi kä′gō, as well as with minor variants. English has tended to anglicize or even to rename many foreign places: *Paris* (pa′ris instead of pä rē′).

Many fairly common names occur in various forms: *How—Howe, Harvey—Hervey, Cohen—Cohn—Kohen, Mac-Mc-M,′* and

---

Proofreader's Marks

♋	Delete	*em*/	Insert em dash
⑨	Delete and close up	*en*/	Insert en dash
⊘	Reverse	⋏	Insert semicolon
⌒	Close up	⊙	Insert colon and en quad
#	Insert space	⊙	Insert period and en quad
⌒/#	Close up and insert space	?/	Insert interrogation point
¶	Paragraph	⑦	Query to author
☐	Indent 1 em	⌒	Use ligature
⊏	Move to left	⑤	Spell out
⊐	Move to right	*tr*	Transpose
⊔	Lower	*wf*	Wrong font
⊓	Raise	*bf*	Set in **bold face** type
∧	Insert marginal addition	*rom*	Set in roman type
⋁⋏	Space evenly	*ital*	Set in *italic* type
✗	Broken letter— used in margin	*caps*	Set in CAPITALS
		sc	Set in SMALL CAPITALS
↧	Push down space	*lc*	Set in lower case
=	Straighten line	✗	Lower-case letter
‖	Align type	*stet*	Let it stand; restore words crossed out
⋀	Insert comma		
⋁	Insert apostrophe	*no*¶	Run in same paragraph
⋎	Insert quotation mark	*ld in*	Insert lead between lines
=/	Insert hyphen	*hr#*	Hair space between letters

From *A Manual of Style*, The University of Chicago Press

so on. Special care is needed with names having silent letters or some peculiarity of spelling or phrasing: Pittsburg*h*, Lindberg*h*, the John*s* Hopkins University, the State University of Iowa, the Ohio State University.

Dictionaries and encyclopedias give the pronunciation and spelling of the best known people and places. For foreign names in current news, we can try to follow the national newscasters. They will show some variation, but they have made an effort to find a reasonable pronunciation.

Getting proper names in the right form is courtesy as well as accuracy. This is especially important in all published work.

(REFERENCES: Allen W. Read, "The Basis of Correctness in the Pronunciation of Place-Names," *American Speech*, 1933, 8:42-46; *Webster's Biographical Dictionary*, *Webster's Geographical Dictionary*, Kenyon and Knott, and recent dictionaries. *Course names.)

proposition is originally a business word for *offer, plan, proposal* which is inappropriate in general usage. "I have a proposition for you" = "I have a plan . . ."

Prosody See *Verse form.

proved—proven As the past participle of *prove, proved* is much more common than *proven* and is always acceptable (He had proved . . .). But *proven* is often used (It had proven quite satisfactory).

Proverb See *Epigrams.

provided—providing Both are used as conjunctions: He should be home soon provided (or: providing) the buses haven't been held up.

Provincialisms See *Localisms and Chapter 2, "Variations due to place," p. 58.

psychology, psychiatry Watch the spelling of these words:

psychiatry (sī kī′ə tri)   psychiatrist (sī kī′ə trist)   psychiatric (si′ki at′rik)
psychology   psychologist   psychoanalyze   psychoanalysis

public is a *collective noun and takes either a singular or plural construction according as the writer wishes to stress the whole group or the individuals:

The *public is* invited.   The *public are* invited.
His *public is made up* of the very young and the fairly old.
Consult the libraries and you will find that the ordinary public do not read poetry.—P. B. BALLARD, *Thought and Language*, p. 250

715

Pn **Punctuation** Correction: Correct the obvious error in punctuation. If the change to be made is not clear to you, consult the Index article on the particular mark.

A discussion of the function and general uses of the punctuation marks, and of differing styles of punctuation ("open" and "close") will be found in Chapter 5, page 131.

Details of the uses of the individual marks will be found in the *Index* articles on each:

'	*Apostrophe	!	*Exclamation mark
*	*Asterisk	-	*Hyphen
{ }	*Brace	....	*Leaders
[ ]	*Brackets	( )	*Parentheses
∧	*Caret	.	*Period
:	*Colon	?	*Question mark
,	*Comma	" "	*Quotation marks
—	*Dash (including the long dash ——)	;	*Semicolon
...	*Ellipsis	——	*Underlining (for italic type)

See also: *Division of words; *Letters; *Restrictive and nonrestrictive; *Series.

Puns A *pun* is a figure of speech in which a word is used in two senses at once (the nut that holds the wheel = automobile driver) or in which a word is substituted for another of similar sound but different meaning (hire education). Reasonable punning, funny or serious, is a healthy use of language. The objection often made to puns is to their overuse or to puns which involve sound and not meaning. Good puns are appropriate to colloquial and informal usage, usually giving an accent of ironic humor (as in Dorothy Parker's "a girl's best friend is her mutter") or of mild satire:

> The taking of the census makes it clear that America is still a land of opportunity. Every person, however humble, has a chance to become a national figure.—Howard Brubaker, *The New Yorker*, Apr. 8, 1950

(COMPARE *Homonyms.)

Purist A purist is a person who is overcareful in the use of language, especially one who wishes everyone to follow the rules of prescriptive grammar (*Grammar § 2) and who tries to hold words to their strictest meanings. Dictionaries and scientific grammars are descriptive and consequently more liberal. See Chapter 3, "Puristic standards," p. 75.

Purpose Adverbial clauses of purpose are most commonly introduced by *so that:*

He is packing tonight *so that* he can start early in the morning.

More formally, *that* is used; and more wordily, *in order that.*
Colloquially **so* is used alone:

He is packing tonight *so* he can start early in the morning.

put in—put across *Put in* is good informal usage for *spend* (put
in time, put in money). *Put over* (a plan, a sale), *put across* (a
scheme, an idea) are colloquial and are often objected to because
they are too frequently used.

Q is an unnecessary letter in English. It was brought into
English use in words borrowed from French, originally derived from
Latin (*question, quarter, quit*), and later borrowings directly from
Latin added to the number (*quorum, quota*). Some Old English
words with *ƙw* sound (spelled *cw*) were respelled with *qu: quick*
(from *cwic*), *queen* (from *cwen*), *quench* (from *cwencan*).

Q is always followed by *u* in English. *Qu* is ordinarily pronounced
ƙw (*quite, quill, quadrilateral*), though in a few words the French
value, *ƙ*, is kept: *coquette* (kō ket′), *quatorze* (kə tôrz′). Final *-que*
is *ƙ: antique* (an tēk′), *unique* (ū nēk′). It is not necessary to keep
the French pronunciation in words that have been anglicized:
Quebec (kwi bek′), **questionnaire.*

Qualifying statements See Chapter 7, page 178.

Question mark (?) Correction: Punctuate this sentence as a *Quest*
question.

1. The principal use of the question mark is as the end stop to a
question: What was the real reason?

2. A question mark may or may not be used after a request that
is phrased as a question, depending on the formality of the style:

Formal: Will you please return this at your earliest convenience?
Informal: Will you please return this at your earliest convenience.

3. A question mark is no longer used after an indirect question:
He wanted to know what the real reason was.

4. A question mark is used to show that a statement is approximate or questionable, as with uncertain dates:

Geoffrey Chaucer 1340?-1400 [or] Geoffrey Chaucer 1340(?)-1400

5. A question mark in parentheses as a mildly sarcastic comment or to label would-be witticisms is now out of fashion and is better omitted:

> No fashionable woman would think of going to a football game unless she looked like a giant squirrel or some other innocent(?) [Better omitted] fur-bearing animal.

6. When a question mark and quotation marks fall together, the question mark is outside if the quoting sentence is the question, inside if the quotation is the question:

> He asked, "Did you really say that?"
> Did you really say "I thought you were older than that"?

After a double question only one question mark is used.

> Did she ask, "How many are coming?"

(SEE ch. 5, "Question mark," p. 140, and *Quotation marks § 4.)

questionnaire keeps the French spelling, with two *n*'s. The English form *questionary* does not make much progress. Pronounced as an English word: kwes'chn̠ ar'.

Questions **1.** In speaking, a rising inflection usually marks a question, and in writing, a question mark at the end. But usually a question is more accurately indicated by the form of the sentence. It may be introduced by an interrogative word:

> Pronoun: *Who* was that? *What* would you do in his place?
> Adjective: *Which* way did he go? *What* book shall I read next?
> Adverb: *Where* shall we eat? *When* will you be coming back? *How much* is that one? *Why* didn't you say so in the first place?

A question may be indicated by inverted word order, the verb coming before its subject. In older English any verb could stand first (*Came* he yesterday?), but now this order is found only with *be, have, shall, will, can, may, must, need,* and *ought* (*Was* he there?) and in colloquial subjectless sentences (*Want* this one?). Ordinarily a phrasal verb is used and the auxiliary comes before the subject (*Do you think* he would go if he was asked?) as a sort of compromise inversion. A statement may be turned into a question by an inverted clause at the end (He didn't try, did he?).

A direct question that is parenthetically part of another sentence sometimes begins with a capital and sometimes not:

> He felt a strong urge—as indeed who doesn't?—to write a really good modern novel.—NOEL COWARD, *To Step Aside,* p. 9

2. Questions are useful, if sparingly used, to focus the reader's attention, either to introduce a change in subject, as in the first of the two quotations that follow, or to emphasize by the change in sentence movement an important point, as in the second:

Will it ever be possible for the middle classes to gain real individualism? To achieve the goal, they must undergo a "radical" change. The old picture of the original Babbitt, symbolized by Louis Philippe, with his cumbersome form, his pear-shaped head, his thick neck swallowing up his chin, his prominent belly, and ridiculous frock-coat tightened at the waist, must disappear. In its place must be substituted the portrait of a young man, possessing the trim build of an athlete; the eager willingness to work, produce, and share; and the sharp mentality of a scholar.—F. C. PALM, *The Middle Classes, Then and Now*, p. 409.

We are beginning to see that the ideal of a liberal education is too large to be put into four years of a college course. It is the growth of a lifetime spent in contact with the actual world. But it is not too much to ask that in a university the student should be brought into contact with different types of the intellectual life, and that each type should be kept distinct. He should learn that the human mind is a marvelous instrument and that it may be used in more than one way.

Variety in courses of study is less important than variety and individuality of mental action. How does a man of science use his mind? How does an artist feel? What makes a man a jurist, a man of business, a politician, a teacher? How does ethical passion manifest itself? What is the historical sense?

These are not questions to be answered on examination papers. But it is a reasonable hope that a young man in the formative period of his life may learn the answers through personal contacts.—SAMUEL McCHORD CROTHERS, *The Pleasures of an Absentee Landlord*, pp. 48-49.

Occasionally a question makes an effective opening for a paper, but it should be a genuine question, leading to the subject, and not a general one concocted just "to get attention."

3. An indirect question is a question that is not quoted directly but is made a subordinate member of another sentence. An indirect question is not marked with either a question mark or with quotation marks, and the tense of the verb is changed, if necessary, to fit the sentence in which it stands:

Direct: "What are our plans for tomorrow?"
Indirect: He asked what our plans for tomorrow were.
Direct: He asked, "Do you really understand what you have read?"
Indirect: He asked us if we really understood what we had read.
He always asks us whether we understand what we have read.

4. A leading question is one phrased to suggest the answer desired, as "You wouldn't do that, would you?" (contrasted with "Would you do that?").

5. For a statement cast in the form of a question see *Rhetorical question.

quite In formal English *quite* means "entirely, wholly," as in "quite gone." In informal English, it is changed in meaning to "somewhat, very, rather": "I am quite tired"; "We went quite a long way."

This meaning passes over into a number of convenient colloquial phrases: *quite a few, quite a little, quite a lot. Quite some time* is colloquial.

Quot **Quotation marks (" ")** Correction: **Make the quotation marks conform to conventional usage.**

1. Indicating quotations. 2. Principal uses. 3. Miscellaneous uses. 4. With other marks.

(The most frequent slips are: forgetting the end quotation marks; punctuation with interrupted quotations, § 4c; quotation marks combined with other marks, § 4a, b.)

1. Methods of indicating quotations. (a) Double quotes (" ") are the usual marks. The mark before the quoted matter is the *open-quote*, and the one after is the *close-quote*.

b) The use of single quotes (' ') is common in England and is increasing in the United States. The single quotes are as accurate as the double and are much less spotty on the page.

c) For quotations within quotations, double and single quotes are alternated. If you begin with the double marks: " '. . .' "; if you begin with the single: ' ". . ." '. If there are quotations within two such quotations, continue to alternate the double and single quotes.

d) Indenting is used to indicate quotations, especially in factual writing involving numerous quotations of some length, as in this book. No quotation marks are used, and in print the size of type is usually reduced. Publishing houses have rules about how long a quotation must be to be reduced and indented—that it should run to at least five lines, for example, or consist of more than one complete sentence. In double spaced typewritten manuscript, such quotations are usually indented and single spaced; in longhand copy they are simply indented.

2. Principal uses of quotation marks. (a) Quotation marks are used to indicate all passages taken from another writer, whether a phrase or a page or more (except when the quotation is indented). The quoted matter may be worked into the constructions of the quoter's sentence, or it may stand by itself:

From the enormous mass of material put at his disposal, Mr. Garnett chose those letters that would make "a book in which Lawrence's career, his intellectual development and the details of his life should be recorded, traced and documented almost entirely in his own words."—CHARLES POORE, *The New York Times*, March 10, 1939

When speeches or a short conversation are not given for their own sake but to illustrate a point, they are usually put in the body of the paragraph:

Do these instances of the beginnings of new words give us any hints in the search for those new words for which every passing month shows the urgent need? I think they do. First, simplicity and euphony—though not simplicity at all costs. Many years ago, I was chaffing an old friend about the deficiency of his native Welsh. "It's very lacking in the most ordinary scientific terms," I remarked. "For example?" "Well, what's the Welsh for *galvanometer?*" I asked. "And if it comes to that, what's the English for it?" A very proper rejoinder which, correctly interpreted, means that *gas* is preferable to *aeriform fluid*, and *drop-counter* to *stalagmometer*. All within reason, of course: does it follow, for example, that *foreword* is better than *preface?*—ALLAN FERGUSON, "The Scientist's Need for New Words," *The Listener*, April 21, 1937

b) There are no half quotes. A sentence is either an exact quotation in quotation marks, or else it isn't and so is not quoted. A speech summarized or quoted "indirectly" is not marked:

Direct quotation: The manager told me, "I work harder in one day keeping the girls busy than they work all week."
Indirect quotation: The manager told me that he worked harder in one day keeping the girls busy than they worked all week. (Not: The manager told me "that he worked harder in one day keeping the girls busy than they worked all week.")

c) Some writers of fiction—William Saroyan, William Carlos Williams (in *Life Along the Passaic River*), and others—do not use quotation marks in the dialog of their stories, but the practice is not common, and dropping them is somewhat confusing. See *Conversation for their use in dialog.

3. Miscellaneous uses of quotation marks. (a) Many magazines use quotes around titles of books and periodicals, for which formal writing uses italics:

Down on Boston's historic waterfront, a yachting-supply firm has in its window a display of books intended for the practical use of mariners. Standing between Bowditch's "New American Practical Navigator" and Dutton's "Navigation and Nautical Astronomy" is Mitchell's "Gone with the Wind."—*The New Yorker*, Dec. 4, 1937

In academic style, which uses italics for titles of books and the names of periodicals, quotes are used for titles of written works shorter than volume length, for single poems, short stories, magazine articles, but not ordinarily for chapter titles. See Chapter 13, "Form of bibliographical entries," page 378, and *Titles of articles, books, etc.

b) In formal writing words that are used as words rather than for their meaning, like the examples in this book, are put in italics (underlined in manuscript); in informal writing they would often be put in quotes:

> "Capitalism" is thus a shape, a form, which speaks, commands, fights, runs away. Asked to define it, the debater on the left introduces more abstractions: "Absentee ownership," "surplus value," "class struggle," "private ownership of the means of production," "exploitation of the masses," "imperialism," "vested interests," "proletariat," "bourgeoisie," the "profit system," and many more. The great words roll.—STUART CHASE, *The Tyranny of Words*, p. 275

c) In formal writing a word from a conspicuously different level of speech may be put in quotation marks, but this practice is less common than formerly. In informal writing there is less need for these apologetic quotes, because there is greater latitude in choice of words. If the word is appropriate, use it without apology, and if it isn't appropriate, ordinarily don't use it.

> Everybody told Bib what a sucker [not "sucker"] he was, but he still had confidence in the designer of the plane.
> After the Yale man had said his piece, the Dartmouth frosh started to blow his horn again. [The question here is whether the *said his piece, frosh,* and *blow his horn* are appropriate; if they are not, quotes will not make the sentence respectable.]

Colloquial figures of speech do not need to be quoted:

> A dirt path would be easier to walk on and at the same time wouldn't wear out so much cowhide. [Not "cowhide"]

d) Practice differs in writing single words that are spoken or thought:

> Stephen said "Yes," so we went to work at once.
> Stephen said *Yes,* so we went to work at once.
> Stephen said Yes, so we went to work at once.

Probably the first form is the most common.

4. Quotation marks and other marks. **(a)** When a question mark or an exclamation mark ends a quotation, it is placed inside the quotes:

> "Don't go near that wire!" he shouted.
> Then in a calm voice she asked, "Why couldn't you have said so in the first place?"

When a question mark or exclamation mark belongs to a sentence that includes a quotation, it is placed after the quotes:

What kind of work can a man put into "the cheapest building that will last fifteen years"?—LEWIS MUMFORD, *Sticks and Stones*, p. 172

b) Most American publishers put commas and periods inside the close-quotes, whether they belong with the quotation or not. The reason for this is that the quotes help fill the small spot of white that would be left if the comma or period came outside. Some writers follow the conventions that apply to the exclamation and question marks, putting comma or period inside the quotes if it belongs with the quotation, outside if it belongs with the quoting sentence, but this usage is much less common.

Semicolons usually stand after the quotation mark.

c) Introductory words and stage directions are set off by a comma, or by two commas if they interrupt the quotation:

Robert said, "I should think that by this time you would have learned what he expects of you."

"History," it has been said, "does not repeat itself. The historians repeat one another."—MAX BEERBOHM, *Works*, p. 43

(Note that *does* is not capitalized after the interruption because it does not begin a sentence.)

The comma with a short informal introductory phrase is really unnecessary, since the quotes keep the two elements distinct, and there is noticeable tendency to do without it:

The OED says 'The stress conte'nt is historical, & still common among the educated.'—H. W. FOWLER, p. 93

"Poetry gives most pleasure" said Coleridge "when only generally and not perfectly understood"; . . .—A. E. HOUSMAN, *The Name and Nature of Poetry*, p. 36

When quoted phrases are closely built into the construction of a sentence, they are not set off by commas:

I hurried past the zero case with its cream molds, just barely saying "Hi!" to Danny and the girls behind it.

"I give him the book" has two equally correct passives: "He is given the book" and "The book is given to him."—E. H. STURTEVANT, *Linguistic Change*, p. 138

A formal introduction to a quotation is usually followed by a colon, as in the statements introducing the examples in this article.
(SEE ch. 13, "Suggestions for taking notes," p. 382, and "The first draft," p. 386; *Conversation; *Plagiarism.)

q. v. means "which see" (from Latin *quod vide*). It is used as a cross reference label in some reference works, though now more generally replaced by the English *see*.

R (r) as in *ready, arch, arrears, car.*

The *r* sound shows wide variation, more than that of any other consonant. It varies in different English-speaking regions, from Scotch and North of England "burrs" to replacement by ə (as in dōə for *door*) or even to complete omission. In American speech, *r* is strongest in Western pronunciation, less conspicuous in New England, Southern, and metropolitan New York.

The *r* sound also varies according to its position in a word. It is strongest, in all regions, before a vowel: *real, rob, cheering, fairy.* Before a consonant sound it varies, as from bäk to bärk in *bark.* At the end of a word *r* is likely to be slighted, especially if the following word begins with a consonant sound: *are* (ä or är), *fare* (faə or far); if the following word begins with a vowel, the *r* sound is usually full, as in *far away.* In vulgate and sometimes in educated informal pronunciation *r* is intruded where none belongs to the word, as in "an idea*r* of what's right," or it is transposed ("metathesis"), as in mod'rən for *modern,* ad'ri on'daks for *Adirondacks.*

In this *Guide and Index* the *r* symbol indicates the pronunciation of words with the expectation that the speaker will render the sort of *r* that he is accustomed to.

(For further details of *r* in American pronunciation see Kenyon and Knott, §§ 26, 82-85.)

racket The spelling *racquet* is British. Write *tennis racket.*

Racket in the sense of an illegitimate way of making money, usually involving threats or violence, has made its way from slang into the informal language. Used to mean any business or particular way of making money (the baseball racket, the lumber racket), it is still slang unless used to imply illegitimate means.

radio takes the regular verb and noun endings: *radioed, radioing, radios, radio's.*

raise—rear *Rear* is now formal in the sense of *rearing* a child or of being *reared. Bring up* in this sense is current in all levels of usage. *Raised* is good informal usage: "I was born and raised in Kentucky."

724

rarely means "seldom" (or in archaic and formal English, "with rare skill," as "a rarely carved panel").

Rarely ever (I rarely ever go) is an established colloquial idiom.

ration (rations) *Ration* is pronounced rā′shən or rash′ən, the latter the more general.

re- The prefix *re-*, meaning "again," is hyphened: (1) when the word to which it is joined begins with *e*: *re-enact, re-enlist, re-enter, re-examine,* and (2) when the form with hyphen can have a different meaning from the form without:

> *reform*, to change, improve—*re-form*, to shape again
> *recover*, to regain—*re-cover*, to cover again

and (3) (rarely) for emphasis, as in "now *re-seated* in fair comfort," or in informal or humorous compounds, *re-re-married*.

Otherwise there is no hyphen: *rearrange, refine, remit.*

reaction has escaped from chemistry and the biological sciences to become a *counter word for any response of feeling or idea:

> Let me have your reaction to [often *on*] this.
> She reacted violently when he appeared.
> My reaction to this poem was on the whole favorable.

The objection to *reaction* in such use is the objection to all counter words. It tends to crowd out more appropriate or more exact words —*opinion, attitude, feeling, response, impression,* and any number of words for exact feelings and opinions.

Reading and writing We naturally read for entertainment and for instruction; our inclinations lead us to the first type and either inclination or necessity to the latter. But besides these fundamental motives for reading, anyone interested in writing has another— reading to set a goal for his own writing. This does not mean consciously imitating *Time* or *The New Yorker* or Walter Lippmann, Ernest Hemingway, or James Joyce. It means rather reading with attention and occasional analysis the writers who genuinely appeal to us and allowing what does appeal genuinely to influence casually and naturally our own way of writing.

This sort of reading influence is especially necessary in college because a student must read so much in textbooks and routine reference books and in the literature of earlier periods. This earlier literature furnishes material for thought and feeling—but very often an English major loses touch with the idiom of his own time. To counteract the effect of this college reading, a student interested in writing needs to read as widely as he can in the better current magazines and books, fiction and non-fiction, especially of the type that he hopes to write. It is not likely that he will write papers that will be better than what he reads and he has no very sure background for judging his own work except a sensitive and critical reading of the somewhat similar work of the more important writers of his time.

real—really   *Real* is not used in formal writing except as an adjective: "a real experience, a real chore." In vulgate and familiar use, *real* is an adverb, a more emphatic *very* (Write real soon; It's real pretty; It went off real well).

Really is both an informal and a formal adverb (a really successful party. It really went off well).

(REFERENCE: Pooley, pp. 161-63.)

realtor   This business coinage has an advantage not possessed by most of its class, since it is much more economical than *real estate agent*. Pronounced rē'əl tər, rē'əl tôr.

reason is because   In formal English the construction beginning "The reason is . . ." is completed by a noun or a noun clause, to balance the noun *reason:*

> The reason for my poor work in French was [noun:] my intense dislike of the subject.
> The reason for my poor work in French was [noun clause:] that I disliked the subject intensely.

But in speech not many noun clauses introduced by *that* are used and the connective that most obviously stresses the notion of reason is *because*, so that in colloquial English we should probably find:

> The reason for my poor work in French was because I didn't like the subject.

"The reason is because . . ." is frequently found in writing:

> In general it may be said that the reason why scholasticism was held to be an obstacle to truth was because it seemed to discourage further enquiry along experimental lines.—BASIL WILLEY, *The Seventeenth Century Background*, p. 7

Marckwardt and Walcott call this construction "Acceptable colloquially" (pp. 31, 112). In such use the *because* clause, in spite of its form, is a noun clause, not an adverbial.

(REFERENCES: Pooley, pp. 134-5; F. N. Cherry, "Some Evidence in the Case of 'is because,'" *American Speech*, 1933, 8: 55-60.)

receipt—recipe (ri sēt′—res′ə pi) Both words mean "a formula, directions for making something." Locally one or the other may be preferred by cooks, but they are interchangeable in meaning. *Receipt* also means "a written acknowledgment for something received."

Reciprocal pronouns *Each other*, *one another* are called reciprocal pronouns. They are used only as objects of verbs or prepositions. In formal usage some writers keep *each other* to refer to two, *one another* for more than two. General usage has *each other* for all senses.

> They had hated each other for years.
> Formal: For the first time all the members really saw one another.
> Informal: For the first time all the members really saw each other.

reckon See *calculate, guess, reckon.

Redundancy, Redundant See Chapter 10, "Repetition," page 289, *Repetition, *Wordiness.

Reference of pronouns Correction: **Change the pronoun marked** *Ref* **(or revise the sentence) so that its reference will be exact and obvious and the pronoun itself will be in the conventional form.**
1. Clear reference. 2. Agreement. 3. Indefinite reference. 4. Unnecessary pronouns. 5. Avoiding pronouns. 6. Omissions.
A pronoun refers to something without naming it, so that its meaning is usually completed by its reference to some other word or group of words, called its *antecedent*. This fact makes using pronouns accurately more complicated than the use of other words. The personal and relative pronouns are further complicated by having a separate case form for the accusative, as nouns do not. And in writing, the form and reference of pronouns can be seen clearly, so that their casual use, which does not attract attention in speech, should be made more exact and the conventions of published usage should be followed. For these reasons a writer needs to watch his pronouns especially, and in revising a paper he should make sure that they are accurate in form and in reference. Since a college student almost always knows the form that is appropriate in a given sentence, an exact use of pronouns is simply a matter of care. Testing the reference of pronouns is one of the specific jobs of revision.
    This article runs over the principal points in the use of pronouns in formal and informal English.
    1. Exact and clear reference. (a) If the meaning of a pronoun is completed by reference to a particular noun, the reference to this antecedent should be exact and obvious.

The first hundred miles, *which* we covered before lunch, were rough, but *they* seemed to go faster than the sixty we did in the afternoon. (The noun *miles* is the antecedent of *which* and of *they*.)

All purchases for the University pass through a central purchasing office. *These* include books, trucks, building materials, food, and hundreds of other items. (*These* refers to *purchases*.)

Swimming may be more fun than calisthenics, but *it* can't give such a general development. (*It* refers to *swimming*.)

On July 3 Mr. Havermeyer asked Mr. Paige to come to *his* house. (*His* refers to *Mr. Havermeyer*. Although another name has been mentioned, only a perverse reader would fail to understand the statement. *The former's* instead of *his* would be pedantic here.)

Professor Frank thought that McKinly was grateful to *him* for allowing *him* to graduate. (The first *him* refers to *Professor Frank*, the second to *McKinly*. Actually no ambiguity is possible here and the sentence would be all right in speech and informal writing.)

Confusion may arise when the pronoun seems to refer to a nearby noun to which it cannot sensibly refer or when there is no noun nearby; when it refers to a noun used subordinately in the preceding construction, perhaps to one used as a possessive or as an adjective; and when two or more pronouns are crossed so that the exact reference isn't readily clear. Usually to improve such a reference the sentence must be revised.

He isn't married and doesn't plan on *it*. (. . . and doesn't *plan to marry*.)

The next year he had an attack of acute appendicitis. *It* broke before the doctors had a chance to operate. (*It* cannot refer to *appendicitis* in the statement made. The second sentence should begin *His appendix broke*. Slips in reference are common when the pronoun refers back to a noun in the preceding sentence.)

A legislator should be a man who knows a little about law and government and he should know how to apply *them* to the best interests of his people. (For *them* put *his knowledge*.)

Bill provided more excitement one afternoon when he was skipping rocks across the swimming hole and cut open *a young girl's head who* was swimming under water. (. . . and cut open *the head of a young girl who* was swimming under water.)

To many of us the word *geology* means little in our everyday lives. Yet *it* deals with materials in use for making our homes and factories, metals of which our cars are made, and the fuel which enables us to drive them. (*It* should refer to *geology* [the science] not to *the word*. To revise, drop *the word* in the first line.)

Businessmen without regard for anyone else have exploited the mass of workers at every point, not caring whether *they* were earning a decent living wage, but only whether *they* were getting a lot of money. (The first *they* refers to *workers*, the second to *businessmen*. The sentence needs complete rewriting, but the second part could be improved somewhat by saying: . . . not caring whether they paid a decent living wage, but only whether they were getting a lot of money.)

Remember that clear reference is a matter of *meaning*, not just of the presence or position of certain words.

b) English uses *which, that, this,* and sometimes *it* to refer to the idea of a previous clause. Formal usage tends to avoid this type of reference or to limit it to *this*.

Informal: Her friend was jealous of her clothes and money and had taken this way of showing it. (*It* refers to the idea in *was jealous.*)

Formal: Her friend was jealous of her clothes and money and had taken this way of showing her feeling.

Informal: He never seemed to realize when academic tempests were brewing, which was probably a good thing.—J. R. PARKER, *Academic Procession,* p. 86 (*Which* refers to the idea of the first clause.)

Formal: He never seemed to realize when academic tempests were brewing. This was probably a good thing.

Informal: From his firm grip, piercing eyes, and stern mouth I could see that he was not to be trifled with, which was well proved a few weeks later. (*Which* refers to the *that*-clause.)

Formal: From his firm grip, piercing eyes, and stern mouth I could see that he was not to be trifled with. This was well proved a few weeks later.

c) In conversation the reference of pronouns is freer than in writing. The following colloquial examples, which would probably pass unnoticed in a conversation, show one reason why in writing we sometimes find pronouns that seem inexact or that do not conform to editorial standards.

Colloquial	*Written*
Gordon's mother asked me to take him fishing because he was so interested in *it* but had never caught *one.*	Gordon's mother asked me to take him fishing because he was so interested in *it* but had never caught *a fish.*
Everyone likes to dance and knew he would get plenty of *it* during the party weekend.	Everyone likes to dance and knew he would get plenty of *dancing* during the party weekend.
In aquaplaning the ropes should never be wound around the wrists, because if thrown *he* would be dragged along and injured.	The ropes should never be wound around *the planer's* wrists, because if thrown *he* would be dragged along and injured.

2. Agreement of pronoun with antecedent. Pronouns referring to specific antecedents agree with the antecedents in number, gender, and person.

a) AGREEMENT IN NUMBER. A pronoun agrees with its antecedent in number: singular antecedent, singular pronoun; plural antecedent, plural pronoun.

Singular: *Jimmy* tried to go quietly, but *he* couldn't keep from whistling.
Plural: *The boys* had tried to go quietly, but *they* couldn't keep from whistling.

In formal English, *each*, *every*, *everyone* are referred to by singular pronouns (*every and its compounds § 1) :

> Almost everyone has some little superstitions which *he* would not violate for love or money.

In colloquial English these words are treated as collectives and are found usually with a plural pronoun:

> Almost everyone has some little superstitions which *they* would not violate for love or money.
>
> Maugham takes anyone from a gigolo to a lord and develops them [Formal: him] with equal ease and finesse.

This colloquial agreement is sometimes found in print, but editors usually bring it in line with formal usage before publication.

(REFERENCE: Russell Thomas, "Concord Based on *Meaning* versus Concord Based on *Form*: The Indefinites," *College English*, 1939, 1: 38-45.)

A collective noun is referred to by either a singular or a plural pronoun, depending upon its meaning in the sentence (*Collective nouns) :

> Singular: When a *gang* of rabbit hunters spreads out over a field, *it* doesn't lose any time.
> Plural: When a *gang* of rabbit hunters spread out over a field, *they* don't lose any time.

Often when a pronoun does not agree with its antecedent, the antecedent could be changed rather than the pronoun:

> Putting himself in the shoes of the slave owner, Lincoln realized that they had a right to feel as they did toward emancipation. (This could be made consistent by making *slave owner* plural better than by changing *they* to *he*.)
> Labor's third and major contention is that they do not receive an adequate return for the services they render. (Here changing *Labor's* to *The workers'* would be more accurate than changing the pronouns to the singular.)

b) AGREEMENT IN PERSON. Except in indefinite pronouns (§ 3 of this article), there is little difficulty with agreement:

> First person: I wish Mr. Patterson had told *me* before.
> Second person: You should have thought of that *yourself*.
> Third person: The woman had said *she* was over twenty-one.

A relative pronoun agrees with its antecedent:

> Formal: I, *who am* your nearest relative, would help you.
> He is one of those people who do just what they want to. (*They* refers to *who*, which refers to *people*.)

c) CASE OF PRONOUNS. The case of a pronoun depends upon the construction in which it stands, not upon its antecedent. See *Case and the articles there referred to; *be § 2, *who, whom.

3. Indefinite reference. Often pronouns are used to refer to the writer's group or to the readers or to people in general instead of to specifically mentioned people. English has no such convenient pronoun as the German *man* or the French *on*. Our *one* has a definitely formal and stiffish connotation. *We* and *you* seem to be slightly more personal, more expressive, and are very generally used, as in various articles in this book. This is a question of style rather than of grammar, and whether *you* or *they* ("They say . . .") or *we* or *one* or *people* or some other noun is used depends on its fitness in the particular passage.

Care should be taken to keep indefinite pronouns consistent, not shifting from *one* to *you*, for example:

> When *you* have worked a day here *you* have really earned your money.
> Or: When *one* has worked a day here *he* has really earned his money.
> Not: When *one* has worked a day here *you* have really earned your money.

An indefinite pronoun should not be substituted for a definite personal pronoun:

> For *me* there is no fun in reading unless *I* can put myself in the position of the characters and feel that *I* am really in the scene. (Not: For *me* there is no fun in reading unless *you* can put yourself in the position of the characters and feel that *you* are really in the scene.)

The indefinite pronouns (*all, any, each, everybody, few, nobody, somebody*, and so on [*Pronouns § 8]) have no expressed antecedent, so that their use involves consistency but not agreement.

Since English has no single pronoun to mean he-or-she, the masculine *he* is conventionally used instead (*he-or-she):

> The time comes to every senior when *he* [Not: *he or she*] anxiously looks forward to that eventful day.

4. Unnecessary pronouns. Sometimes a possessive pronoun is used where *the* would be more idiomatic:

> We stopped to see the [rather than *our*] first unusual sight.

5. Avoiding pronouns. Pronouns are necessary and convenient but because they do lead sometimes to inconsistent uses (that are marked by teachers and editors), some writers tend to avoid them, using a noun instead. The result is usually unidiomatic or clumsy English:

731

That's the reason I hesitate to picture the owner of *a grip* from the appearance of *the bag*. (Better: That's the reason I hesitate to picture the owner of *the bag* from *its* appearance.)

Arrest of *the woman* yesterday followed several days of observation of *the woman's* [Better: *her*] activities by agents of the Stores Mutual Protective Association.

Pronouns are especially useful to bind together clauses and sentences. In the following paragraph each sentence seems to be a new beginning, but with pronouns instead of *Mr. Frothingham*, the paragraph would be closely connected:

Roland W. Frothingham died at his home on Commonwealth avenue on Tuesday. Mr. Frothingham [He] was born in Boston in 1846 and had lived here ever since. Mr. Frothingham's [His] ancestors came from Ipswich. Mr. Frothingham [He] was educated at Harvard College.

6. Omission of pronouns. In familiar writing and in conversation, pronouns, especially *I*, are often omitted (*I § 3; Chapter 9, "Subjectless sentences," page 259) and in colloquial and informal writing the relative pronoun is often not used in relative clauses (*Relative clauses).

The first man [*that*] I met had never heard of such a street.

(For the classes and forms of pronouns, see *Pronouns; for further instances of their use, see the articles on particular pronouns, *I, *we, *who, whom, *himself, herself, *myself. See also ch. 4, "Pronouns," p. 108. References: All grammars treat the use of pronouns. The discussions in the large grammars (Curme, Jespersen . . .) are extended and discuss many special uses.)

Reference paper   The methods and form of an academic reference paper are presented in detail in Chapter 13, page 363.

References   See Chapter 13, "The working bibliography," page 377 and "Footnote form," page 388.

Referent   (ref'ər ənt) is the object, class of objects, act, situation, quality, or fancy which a word means. The referent of *book* is either a particular book being discussed or a generalized notion based on our observation of various books. For discussion see Chapter 11, "Denotation," page 318.

Reflexive pronouns   See *Pronouns § 4, *himself, herself, *myself.

regard (regards)   Good English uses the prepositional phrase *in regard to;* vulgate and low colloquial use more often *in regards to.*

regardless   *-less* is a negative ending and makes the word mean "without regard to"; prefixing an *ir-* (*irregardless*) doubles the negative and makes a word so far regarded as unacceptable in writing but in frequent colloquial use.

Relationships between facts (material of paragraphs). See Chapter 7, page 180.

Relative clauses A relative clause is an adjective clause introduced by a relative pronoun (*that, which,* or *who*), or a relative adverb (*where, when, why*), or without connective:

The rain *that began in the morning* kept on all night.
The coach was now abused by the alumni *who two years before had worshiped him.*
The road to the left, *which looked almost impassable,* was ours.
The first place *where they camped* turned out to be impossible.
The man *I met that afternoon* has been my friend ever since. (Formal: The man *whom* I met . . .)
The ideas *we held in common* were few indeed. (Formal: The ideas *that* we held . . .)

A relative clause stands after the noun it modifies. In the first sentence above, the clause modifies *rain,* in the second *alumni,* in the third *road,* the fourth *place,* the fifth *man,* and the sixth *ideas.*

(SEE *that, *who, whom, *which, *Restrictive and nonrestrictive.)

Several relative clauses in succession make for an awkward, or at least conspicuous, house-that-Jack-built sentence that should be avoided:

People *who* buy houses *that* have been built in times *which* had conspicuous traits of architecture *which* have been since abandoned often have to remodel their purchases completely.

Relative pronouns The relative pronouns are *as, that, what, whatever, which* (*of which, whose*), *who* (*whose, whom*), *whoever.*

Somebody, *who* [or *whom*] I don't know, shouted, "Put 'em out."
The Senator, *whose* term expires next year, is already worrying.
I haven't read the same book *that* [*as*] you have.

That refers to persons or things, *who* to persons. *Which* refers to animals or objects or situations, and also to collective nouns even if they refer to persons:

The army which mobilizes first has the advantage.
The Board of Directors, which met on Saturday . . .
The Board of Directors, who are all bankers, . . .

(Particular points in the use of these relatives will be found in separate entries on each, especially those on *that, *which, *who, whom. SEE also *Restrictive and nonrestrictive.)

Relative words   See Chapter 11, page 320.

remember   In vulgate English *remember* is supported by *of* (I don't remember of doing that) and colloquially by *about* (I don't remember about that at all). In most written English the unsupported verb is used:

> I don't remember doing it.   I don't remember that at all.

Renaissance—Renascence   The long spelling is the more common. *Renaissance* is pronounced ren′ə säns′ or ren′ə zäns′, or, less commonly, ri nā′səns; *Renascence* is usually pronounced ri nas′əns. The word is capitalized when it refers to the period of history, not when referring to a revival, as "the pre-war renaissance in poetry."

Rep   **Repetition**   Correction: Revise so as to remove the ineffective repetition of word, meaning, or sound.

Repetition of word, thought, or sound may be an effective trait of style, contributing especially to emphasis. Unhappy repetition is discussed in Chapter 10, "Repetition," page 289; successful repetition is discussed in the same section, page 291. This article reviews only some unsuccessful sorts of repetition that ordinarily require revision.

1. Words and phrases.   A word that is the name of the subject of a paper or of one of its important parts must occur frequently, though pronouns and economical sentences can keep down the repetition. Unnecessary, ineffective repetition is usually a mark of carelessness or insensitiveness. An attentive reading over would have led the writers of the following to revise their sentences, removing the obvious repetitions and other deadwood too:

> The administration of the Incan government was *based* on a decimal *basis*. [. . . was on a decimal basis]
> The Indian's culture was so different from the white man's [culture] that he has done very well to change as much as he has in such a short [period of] time.
> From here on there was no trail and if there had been it would have been snowed under [by the snow of] the night before.

Especially conspicuous is repetition of a word used in a different sense:

> Our club is as much a fraternity as any house along the row. Our unity and fraternity [Substitute: *brotherhood*] have brought us real satisfaction and much success.

2. Meaning.   Meaning of single words or of longer groups is often repeated in near synonyms:

. . . *where* he did very successful work *there.* (Drop the *there.*)

In *many* books the setting [*very often*] is in some foreign country.

At eight thirty [in the morning] you punch the time clock for the start of the day.

Here comes an elderly woman whose feet and legs are harnessed into a pair of [antiquated and] almost obsolete high-button shoes.

New leg kicks are shown him, new arm stretches are demonstrated, and different ways of breathing illustrated. (He is shown new leg tricks, new arm stretches, and different ways of breathing.)

3. Sound. Jingles and rhyming words are out of place in prose and do not occur as often as repetitions of unstressed syllables, especially the *-ly* of adverbs and the endings of some abstract nouns, like *-tion,* which are unpleasant when noticeable.

Reports Business and technical reports are a form of presentation of material for easy and immediate reference. A report may contain the results of laboratory or field research, of any type of investigation, as in business and advertising surveys; it may be a more or less routine report of activity, processes, progress; or it may carry principally a recommendation for action or decision with the evidence upon which the recommendation is based. It is essentially an orderly presentation of data arranged for a specific purpose.

The typical parts of a full report are:

1. Title page, carrying the title, name of the maker of the report, the person or group to whom it is made, place and date, and any other necessary preliminary information

2. Letter of transmittal, usually a formal presentation of the report in the form of a letter from the maker to the recipient. (The letter may contain special acknowledgments and other preface matter.)

3. Table of contents, listing the main heads and usually at least one level of subheads, with page references

4. A brief preliminary summary of the most important ideas developed in the body if it is long

5. The body of the report, presenting the data, the apparatus or methods used in compiling it, necessary discussion, or recommendations

6. An appendix, if necessary, containing tables of figures, documents, bibliographies, or any matter that would be hard to work into the body of the text

7. Index, if the report is long and treats a variety of topics

In style the outstanding features of a report are clarity and ease of reference. Usually the margins are wide, the spacing generous, the headings and directions to a reader many and revealing. Data is often thrown into the form of tables of statistics, *diagrams, graphs, illustration. A report is usually compactly technical, in the vocabulary and idiom of the people to receive it, who are usually trained in the field.

The clarity, compactness, and adjustment to particular readers make a report a specialized but highly effective form of communication. Since its sole aim is presentation of data gathered for a specific purpose, it does not lend itself to amateur practice, but a student would do well to familiarize himself with the type of report likely to be used in the field in which he expects to work, and if possible to make a collection of reports for future guidance.

(Fuller discussion of the method and form of reports will be found in books on business, scientific, and technical writing, such as the following: Agg, Thomas R. and Foster, Walter L., *The Preparation of Engineering Reports* (New York, 1935). Baker, R. P. and Howell, A. C., *The Preparation of Reports* (New York), rev. ed., 1938 [The most comprehensive treatment].)

Requests See *Commands and requests.

researcher has been added to the English vocabulary as a needed shortening for *research worker:*

> Private collections of newspapers have never been many, though at least two men have earned the gratitude of generations of researchers—Burny . . . and Hope. . . .—London *Times Literary Supplement* Feb. 6, 1930

Research paper See Chapter 13, The Reference Paper, page 363.

Resolutions A resolution is a formal record of action taken by a meeting or an organization to be sent to someone. It is used typically in expression of sympathy or in recording of sentiment or in recommendation of action. The style is formal and the expression arranged in a standardized formula:

> WHEREAS, The experiences of the past few weeks have shown . . .; and
> WHEREAS, Our expectations of a more favorable attitude on the part of . . .; therefore be it
> *Resolved,* That this body feels it its duty to inform . . .; and be it further
> *Resolved,* That a copy of these resolutions be sent . . .
> John W. Appel, Secretary

rest There are two *rest*'s in English, both in good standing. *Rest*, repose, is from Old English *rest; rest*, remainder, is from French *reste*.

Rest **Restrictive and nonrestrictive** Correction: If the modifier marked is restrictive, it should not be separated from the word it modifies by a comma; if it is nonrestrictive, it should be set off by a comma or by two commas.

    1. **Restrictive, or close, modifiers.** A restrictive modifier defines, limits, identifies the word it refers to, that is, it gives a fact that sets the word off from other things of the same class. In speaking or

reading aloud, there is little pause and the voice is usually sustained. If the modifier is omitted, the statement either becomes meaningless, as in the first sentence below, or else it has a quite different meaning, as in the second:

> It was a quite different looking person *who walked out into the cold frosty air a few minutes later.*
> The right of the dictatorships *to decide how long this wholesale killing goes on* is unquestioned.

The italicized elements in the following sentences are restrictive and should stand as they are here, without commas:

> His opponent appeared at one of the really important rallies *with a drink too much in him.*
> Reform should be an application *to wider fields* of methods *with which people are already familiar* and *of which they approve.*
> In many states parole boards still persist in turning loose prisoners *who should remain behind bars.*
> Mr. Colman proves his versatility as an actor *when he philosophizes one minute and punches his brother on the nose the next.* He portrays a man of action *if the occasion requires* and at the same time a mild-mannered, soft-spoken individual *who gives the impression of being able to think.* He has to make important decisions *when his brother and Margo tell him that this Utopia is a lot of hooey.* Mr. Colman is the only actor I have ever seen *who can show that he is thinking.*

2. Nonrestrictive, or loose, modifiers. Modifiers which do not limit the meaning of a noun but add a descriptive detail are nonrestrictive and are set off by a comma or commas. In speaking or reading aloud, there is usually a slight pause and change in level of voice before and after a loose modifier. As a rule a nonrestrictive modifier can be omitted without altering the fundamental meaning of the statement.

A modifier that follows a proper noun is usually nonrestrictive, since the name itself identifies exactly the person or place mentioned:

> Josie, *aged 16*, told Ma and Pa Pansky a thing or two.
> Just below Poughkeepsie, *which we reached in a little over two hours,* we had another breakfast in a roadside lunch wagon.

3. Optional punctuation. Not all modifiers are clearly restrictive or nonrestrictive: there are degrees of closeness. Use of commas emphasizes a slight relationship, lack of commas suggests a closer relation. The difference in such sentences is more of tone, of movement than of meaning. The italicized modifiers in these sentences might or might not be set off by commas:

> These physicians *who so vigorously oppose state medicine* have definite bases for their opinion.

> They had *of course* more experience by then.
> The sound of swing music reached my ears from a room down the hall *even before I heard the tramping feet that seemed to go with it.*

In open punctuation fewer commas are used, tending to bind the parts of a sentence closer together. As a rule the safest test is reading the sentence aloud, using commas if you pause slightly and change your tone of voice before the modifier.

(SEE ch. 5, "With close and loose modifiers," p. 144. REFERENCE: W. Paul Jones, "Punctuating Nonrestrictives," *College English*, 1948, 10:158-62.)

Result Adverbial clauses of result are introduced typically by *so that, so, so . . . that, such . . . that,* and *that. So* is rather informal and colloquial, *such . . . that* and *that* likely to be formal. The most common is *so that.*

> He had been taught always to expect the worst, so that [so] he wasn't surprised.
> He was so used to suffering that one more disaster made little difference.
> The house was such an expense that they were giving it up.

Reverend is not used without the first name or initials of the person to whom it refers; the abbreviation is used in newspaper and more or less informal writing:

Reverend James Shaw Rev. James Shaw
Reverend J. T. Shaw Rev. J. T. Shaw
Not: Rev. Shaw

The Reverend before a name is rather more formal:

the Reverend James T. Shaw   the Reverend Mr. Shaw

The reverend used instead of a clergyman's name (The reverend wasn't there) is colloquial and vulgate.

In the salutation of a letter, after an inside address, write *Dear Sir:* or *Dear Mr. Shaw:*

Revision Most people, amateurs and professionals, do better work if they write a first draft rather rapidly and then revise it. In revision a writer checks his material, to see if it is sufficient for his purpose; looks at the plan, the paragraphs, the sentences from a reader's point of view, so far as he can; and he looks at the small matters, spelling, punctuation, the words, and the grammatical constructions. Most of the points taken up in this *Guide-Index* are to be applied in revision.

(For further discussion see ch. 1, "Revising," p. 16; ch. 7, "Revising paragraphs," p. 189; ch. 9, "Writing and revising sentences," p. 264; and the alphabetical articles in this book that you may need.)

Rhetoric Rhetoric is the study of the theory and practice of composition, both oral and written.

The principles of rhetoric are so liable to abuse that the terms *rhetoric* and *rhetorical* are often used in a derogatory sense to imply excessive elaborateness in style, a show of words rather than a show of meaning. Partly because of this degradation of the word *rhetoric*, *composition* is often used in its place.

Rhetorical questions are really statements in the form of questions, since no direct answer is expected and the writer does not intend to give one. In conversation they often carry some special accent, of accusation, for example: "Could you have done any better?"

> Since nearly three-fourths of your efforts are directed toward reversing this natural order of things, may I ask Your Excellency a few random questions? Why is it that of two brothers under my observation in the same environment, one entered the United States Senate, while the other all his life has conducted a fourth class, small town restaurant? Why has one of our greatest publicists an imbecile brother and a wayward sister? Why, of two brothers, reared under the same roof, with the same parental influence, does one become a village loafer and the other a philosopher? Why, out of the first fifty-one names in the Hall of Fame, are ten of them the sons and daughters of preachers? Why is one out of twelve of all the names in *Who's Who*, our most democratic roster of fame, the child of a minister? Is it necessary for me to present proof to you that ministers are on the average men of character and intelligence? Why out of the first forty-six names in the Hall of Fame, have twenty-six of them from one to three relatives of national renown? Does it not argue that they probably belong to great breeds, truly noble strains of blood? Why is it, that if you are born from certain strains of blood you have one chance in five of having a celebrated relative, and if from other strains your chance in this respect is hardly one in a thousand? Why has the Edwards family, living in thirty-three different countries, under differing environments, out of one thousand four hundred members given us one thousand four hundred social servants, many of world distinction, while the Ishmael family, studied by Eastbrook, out of approximately fifteen thousand members has given us nearly fifteen thousand social scourges?—ALBERT EDWARD WIGGAM, *The New Decalogue of Science*, p. 46

rhyme, rime The simpler spelling seems to be gaining slowly on *rhyme*. It is not only simpler but was the original spelling in English.

Rhyme is a characteristic of verse but is out of place and an unnecessary distraction in prose (As I lay in bed, I heard the *rain* in the *drain*).

Rhythm A detailed study of the rhythm of prose would belong to the study of literature, but a writer needs to remember that part of the effect even of written language comes from rhythm, from the frequency and intensity and arrangement of the stresses of his words. In reference works and news stories rhythm counts for little, but in writing that can be read aloud with pleasure it is a considerable factor and even in reading silently most people get some impression of the sound of a passage.

A rhythmical analysis of a short passage of formal and of informal prose will show some characteristic qualities of rhythm and can serve as a basis for further discussion of rhythm in prose.

And so, | when their day | is over, | when their good | and their evil | have become | eternal | by the immortality | of the past, | be it ours | to feel | that, | where they suffered, | where they failed, | no deed | of ours | was the cause; | but wherever | a spark | of the divine | fire | kindled | in their hearts, | we were | ready | with encouragement, | with sympathy, | with brave words | in which | high courage | glowed.

—BERTRAND RUSSELL, Mysticism and Logic, p. 56

Mother | used to go | to the cemetery | in Woodlawn | with her arms | full of | flowers, | and lay | the pretty things | by some | headstone, | as a sign | of remembrance. | After a while | she bought | a cast-iron | chair | and left it | out there, | inside | the square | family plot, | so that when | it took her | a long time | to arrange | her flowers | she could sit down | and rest.

—CLARENCE DAY, Life With Father, p. 257

1. Analysis of rhythm. A sensitive reading aloud is the real test of rhythm, but occasional analysis will emphasize certain traits of rhythm and perhaps of other points of style. It is best to read the passage to be analyzed aloud naturally and then to go over it again, noting and marking the stresses. Although readers will vary somewhat in their reading of certain sentences, as they do in reading lines of verse, there will be a surprising agreement among readers after a little practice. Elaborate schemes for analysis of prose have been worked out, but a simpler scheme is given here that will be sufficient to indicate the principal qualities.

a) STRESS. The stress that syllables receive varies considerably in force, but usually it is sufficient to indicate three levels, lack of stress (x), full stress (´), and an intermediate, or secondary stress (`):

x ／ x   ／ x͓ x   x ／ x   ／ x   ＾
an intermediate or secondary stress

Care needs to be taken not to exaggerate the stress in reading for analysis.

b) FEET. In prose rhythm the "feet" do not cut across words as they do in analyses of verse, but follow sense units. Feet may range from one syllable to seven or eight syllables. They are arranged and named according to the position of the main stress:

Rising, beginning with unstressed or lightly stressed syllable and ending with a fully stressed syllable:

x ／   x   x ／   x ／   ＾
and so   with her arms   when their day

Falling, beginning with a stressed syllable and ending with one of little or no stress:

／ x   ／   ／ x   ／ ／ x x
mother   high courage   stressed syllables

Waved, the foot beginning and ending with syllables of the same stress. This type may be subdivided into

Crest, in which the stressed syllables are in the middle:

x ／ x   x ／ x   x x ／ x x x
eternal   and left it   to the cemetery

Trough, in which the stressed syllables are at the ends:

／ x x ／   ／ x x ／
after a while   family plot

Level, one stressed syllable or two or more stressed syllables:

／   ／ ／
glowed   no deed

Some readers tend to make shorter feet, representing slower reading and fuller stresses, and others make longer feet with fewer full stresses:

x x x ／   x x x ／ ／
of the divine | fire   *or*   of the divine fire

x ／   ／ ／ x   x ／ ／ ／ x
in which | high courage   *or*   in which high courage

For practice work in analysis of rhythm probably the first method is better than the second and it has been followed in the passages analyzed above.

c) SUMMARIZING THE FEET. If a summary of the analysis of the paragraphs by Russell and Day quoted on the opposite page would be useful, it can be made by some such tabulation as the following:

Rising feet	*Russell*		*Day*	
x ′	5		5	
x x ′ (x ′ ′, etc.)	9		5	
Longer	1		2	
Total		15		12
Falling feet				
′ x (′ ′)	3		6	
′ x x	0		0	
′ ′ x	1		0	
Longer	0		0	
Total		4		6
Crest				
x ′ x	2		4	
x ′ x x	1		0	
x x ′ x	3		1	
Longer	2		2	
Total		8		7
Trough				
′ x ′	0		1	
′ x x ′	0		2	
Longer	0		0	
Total		0		3
Level				
′	3		1	
′ ′	1		0	
Total		4		1

2. **Comments on prose rhythm.** (a) In contrast to verse, the rhythm of prose is marked by variety of movement; passages cannot be defined in two words like "iambic pentameter" (though the importance and actual descriptiveness of such metrical labels of verse have been exaggerated). Certain contrasts, such as a series of long feet broken by a short one and vice versa, are characteristic of good prose.

b) It is generally regarded that the movement of the end of a sentence and to a less extent of the end of subordinate elements, such as clauses, are the most important feature of rhythm. The ending will either be rising, with the heavy stress last, which usually gives a vigorous conclusion, or falling, with the unstressed syllable last. The beginnings of a series of sentences usually show variety in stress.

c) Usually a sentence should not be continued after a pleasing final rhythm. This explains in part why "tacked-on" expressions often seem ineffective.

d) Although beginning and ending are the most important elements in rhythm, good English prose does not sag in the middle of sentences. Wordiness or long functional phrases contribute to weak rhythm. For instance:

The wheels that are made here vary greatly in size, because of the fact that they are made for all types of machinery. Contrast: because they are made for all types of machinery.

e) The stresses of prose as of poetry vary considerably in their intensity. The stresses in the passage from Bertrand Russell are heavier than those in the one from Clarence Day, as those in Browning's poems are heavier than those in Robert Frost's.

f) Rising and waved rhythms are most characteristic of English prose. Falling and level rhythms are less common and are often useful for gaining variety. English sentences seem rarely to begin with a strong stress. The most common opening is the x ′ foot.

These suggestions can lead to detailed observation of prose rhythm that will point out some of the characteristic differences between writers. Sometimes such an analysis can suggest some changes in revising a manuscript to improve the rhythm of the sentences.

(REFERENCES: Norton R. Tempest, *The Rhythm of English Prose* (Cambridge, 1930), is probably the best discussion of the subject; Oliver Elton, *English Prose Numbers* ("Essays and Studies by Members of the English Association," iv, 29-54); Dobrée, pp. 22, 27; Rickert, ch. 5; George Saintsbury, *A History of English Prose Rhythm* (London, 1922)

right In the sense of "very," *right* is a localism (We'll be right glad to see you).
Right along, *right away*, *right off* are colloquial and informal idioms.

rise In referring to people, *arise* is formal and poetic; *rise* is rather formal; *get up* is informal and colloquial.

role *Role* (a role in a play) is still conservatively spelled with the circumflex (rôle), but in common usage the accent has been dropped:

Any *role* that seemed heroic attracted me.—CLARENCE DAY, *Life With Father*, p. 82.

Roman numbers For the forms and uses of Roman numbers (i, ii, iii, cxlvi . . .) see *Numbers § 3.

round—around In colloquial and informal usage *round* and *around* are used interchangeably, with a definite tendency to use *round* (or to clip the *a* of *around* so short that it would be taken for *round*).

In formal English there is some tendency to keep *around* to mean "here and there" or "in every direction" and *round* for "in a circular motion" or "in a reverse motion":

I have looked all around.   There aren't any around here.
He is going round the world.   Everyone turned round.

Around is informal in the sense of "about, near":

He had around $200 in bills. Is anybody around [that is, around here]?

All-round is an informal adjective (an all-round flour, an all-round athlete), which is often *all-around* in colloquial usage.
Round has no apostrophe.

route   The pronunciation rōōt is general, but rout is in common use, especially in the Army and colloquially, as of newspaper and delivery routes.

run   In good informal use in the sense of "manage, operate" (He runs a hotel in Florida).

Run-on sentences   A run-on sentence is made up of two or more grammatically complete sentences written as one, without a connective between the statements and punctuated with a comma or with no mark at all:

The average age of a college freshman is 18 or 19, some may be a year or two younger.
You may say, "Look at Switzerland, she is always neutral."

Ineffective run-on sentences are discussed in *Comma fault, and effective ones in *Contact clauses. Both types are discussed more fully in Chapter 9, "Run-on sentences," page 253.

S represents principally two sounds, *s* and *z*: *s* as in *so, sorry, biscuit, crops; z* as in *easy, was, Jones*. In a few words *s* spells *sh*: *tension, sure, sugar;* and in some *zh*: *leisure, pleasure, measure*.

S is silent in several words, most of them from French: *aisle, debris, rendezvous, island, Arkansas, Louisville,* often in *Saint Louis,* and usually in *Illinois*.

(See *sh; for plurals in *-s* see *Plurals § 1, *Jones; for the genitive of words ending in *-s,* *Genitive case § 1a.)

said   As an adjective *said* (the said person, the said idea) is legal and is not used in general writing.

saint   The abbreviation *St.* is used with names (*St. John, St. Louis*); plural *SS.* (*SS. Peter and Paul*). Occasionally the French feminine form, *Sainte,* is used (*Sault Sainte Marie*). The abbreviation of the feminine form is *Ste.*

same   *Same* is used as an adjective (the same color) and as a pronoun in such expressions as "The same happened to me once" and popularly in "I'll take the same," "more of the same."

Same as a pronoun is also characteristic of legal and outmoded business use: "and enclose check for same" where better style would have *it* or *them* instead of *same.*

Sarcasm   Sarcasm is a quality of bitterness or reproach in a statement—ironical (that is, to be interpreted differently depending on one's point of view) or direct. The sarcasm lies in its harshness. See *Humor, and Chapter 12, "Degree of statement," page 352.

say   *Say* is the general word for speaking. *Talk* implies a continued "saying." *State* implies a formal "saying" and is better kept for this meaning (Not: "Mr. Owen stated that he was ready if we were").

In labeling the speeches of characters in a story, *said* is the best word to use, since it attracts least attention, unless there is reason for using a more specific word. See *Conversation.

Say in informal English also means "order, request" (He said to go back or we'd get in trouble).

Say in the sense of "suppose," "perhaps," "for instance" (Say they went sixteen miles) is colloquial and informal.

scarcely   See *Double negative § 3.

Schoolgirl style   The "schoolgirl style" is characterized by sentimental counter words (*lovely, cute*), by exaggeration, and by reliance on all sorts of mechanical forms of emphasis—exclamation marks, dashes, capitals, one, two, and even three underlinings. These serve as satisfying muscular release to the writer and may add a sort of glow to a letter, but they should not be transferred to the printed page, and any suggestion of the style, except of course to help portray a character, should be avoided.

Scientific and technical writing   The ideal of scientific writing was expressed very early in the modern scientific movement in Thomas Sprat's *History of the Royal Society* (1667). The members of the Society, he said, tried

> to return back to the primitive purity, and shortness, when men delivered so many things, almost in an equal number of words. They have exacted from all their members a close, naked, natural way of speaking; positive expressions; clear senses; a native easiness: bringing all things as near the

745

mathematical plainness as they can; and preferring the language of artizans, countrymen, and merchants, before that of wits or scholars.

Exactness rather than grace or variety, or even emphasis, is the goal of most scientific and scholarly writing, of most writing that is done by members of a profession to be read by other members. Occasionally it attains the ideal of "delivering so many things, almost in an equal number of words":

> A stable, stainless, organic mercury compound solution of high germicidal value, particularly in serum and other protein media.

But if Thomas Sprat could read much current scientific writing, he would find that it had departed far from "the language of artizans, countrymen, and merchants."

The chief reason for the "big words" that seem to a layman the most conspicuous trait of scientific writing is that scientists have discovered and named qualities and things of which the average person is quite unaware. Their descriptions are more detailed than people in general need. On page 13 of *Webster's New Collegiate Dictionary*, for instance, is a scientific description of the *n* sound:

> § 66. *n* as in *none, knit, canny, inn*, etc., is the voiced tongue-point alveolar nasal continuant corresponding to the voiced tongue-point stop *d* and the voiceless tongue-point stop *t*. All three sounds are made with the tongue point on the alveolar ridge (teethridge), and are hence sometimes called alveolar consonants, or, less accurately, dentals.—By permission. From *Webster's New Collegiate Dictionary*, copyright, 1949, by G. & C. Merriam Co.

In contrast to the rather loose meanings of words in general usage, scientific writers try to confine their words to a single specific meaning. Ordinary people speak of *biliousness* and *eyestrain*, though those words have no definite meaning for doctors or oculists. Some scientific words are taken from the general vocabulary and given special meanings, like *magnitude* in astronomy, *force* in physics, *complex* in psychoanalysis, *dip* and *incline* in geology. But the tendency now is to build words from Latin or more often from Greek roots that are self-explanatory (to anyone who knows their elements): *photo-micrography, beta-methyl-amido-croton-anilide.*

The sentence structure and other traits of style in scientific writing are formal, appropriately formal because its audience is specialized. The style is impersonal, completely impersonal in monographs, textbooks, and articles in the scientific journals, less impersonal in popular treatments of scientific subjects. Three levels of scientific writing are illustrated in the following quotations. The first paragraph is a simple statement of fact:

The nature of the force exerted by a wave upon any obstacle, such as a cliff or beach, depends in part upon the type of wave and its condition at the moment of collision with the obstacle. If an unbroken oscillatory wave strikes a vertical wall or cliff the base of which reaches down to deep water, the wave is reflected back. At the instant of contact the crest of the wave rises to twice its normal height and the cliff is subjected to the hydrostatic pressure of this unusually high water column. The absence of any forward thrust of the water mass under these conditions is shown by the behavior of boats which have been observed to rise and fall with successive waves without touching the vertical wall only a few feet distant. Hagen concludes that under such circumstances débris must accumulate at the base of the wall and that therefore the prejudice against vertical sea walls and harbor walls, based on the fear of undermining by wave action, is ill-founded.—DOUGLAS W. JOHNSON, *Shore Processes and Shoreline Development*, p. 57

That is part of an informative treatment of wave action, accurate and compact. It would be read, however, only by someone who was consciously looking for knowledge of the subject. The following passage is intended for a more general audience, though one limited to people of some intelligence and with a definite interest in more than the superficial appearance of their world. The facts are presented with a minimum of technical language and made more vivid by the use of familiar comparisons ("rather like relays of messengers . . .").

These molecules move with very high speeds; in the ordinary air of an ordinary room, the average molecular speed is about 500 yards a second. This is roughly the speed of a rifle-bullet, and is rather more than the ordinary speed of sound. As we are familiar with this latter speed from everyday experience, it is easy to form some conception of molecular speeds in a gas. It is not a mere accident that molecular speeds are comparable with the speed of sound. Sound is a disturbance which one molecule passes on to another when it collides with it, rather like relays of messengers passing a message on to one another, or Greek torch-bearers handing on their lights. Between collisions the message is carried forward at exactly the speed at which the molecules travel. If these all traveled with precisely the same speed and in precisely the same direction, the sound would of course travel with just the speed of molecules. But many of them travel on oblique courses, so that although the average speed of individual molecules in ordinary air is about 500 yards a second, the net forward velocity of the sound is only about 370 yards a second.—SIR JAMES JEANS, *The Universe Around Us*, p. 101

For a still more popular audience the subject matter must be further simplified and the facts made dramatic, if possible, by being presented in action. Some technical words are used, but they seem to be incidental, even decorative, rather than fundamental as in formal scientific writing. The beginning of a discussion of coal-tar dyes illustrates this popular approach to scientific discussion:

747

If you put a bit of soft coal into a test tube (or, if you haven't a test tube, into a clay tobacco pipe and lute it over with clay) and heat it you will find a gas coming out of the end of the tube that will burn with a yellow smoky flame. After all the gas comes off you will find in the bottom of the test tube a chunk of dry, porous coke. These, then, are the two main products of the destructive distillation of coal. But if you are an unusually observant person, that is, if you are a born chemist with an eye to by-products, you will notice along in the middle of the tube where it is neither too hot nor too cold some dirty drops of water and some black sticky stuff. If you are just an ordinary person, you won't pay any attention to this because there is only a little of it and because what you are after is the coke and gas. You regard the nasty, smelly mess that comes in between as merely a nuisance because it clogs up and spoils your nice, clean tube.

Now that is the way the gas-makers and coke-makers—being for the most part ordinary persons and not born chemists—used to regard the water and tar that got into their pipes. They washed it out so as to have the gas clean and then ran it into the creek. But the neighbors—especially those who fished in the stream below the gas-works—made a fuss about spoiling the water, so the gas-men gave away the tar to the boys for use in celebrating the Fourth of July and election night or sold it for roofing. —EDWIN E. SLOSSON, *Creative Chemistry*, copyright 1930, D. Appleton-Century Company.

Beyond such popularizations are the sensational treatments of scientific subjects which we associate with the magazine sections of some Sunday papers. Because of the cheapness and the inaccuracy of many of these articles, scientists and scholars have tended to scorn all popularizing of their materials. But in recent years there has been an increase of reliable and interesting scientific writing for general readers as more specialists have found a challenge in seeing how much of their subject matter they can find a way of conveying to a general reader. They are now leaving less of the work of popularizing to writers not sufficiently trained to do it accurately.

Until a person can write with authority about a specialized subject, he will most likely be doing popular or semi-popular papers. Students in college can try their hand at preparing material for a somewhat limited but non-professional group of readers. The style of such papers would be rather formal, and it has one real danger. The necessity for using genuine scientific words often leads to using *unnecessary* *big words. Writers in the social sciences especially have substituted unfamiliar words or *long variants for words of the general English vocabulary, as in "It is necessary to structure into a complex culture like ours a congruent hospitality to change in all institutional areas." If such writers would only visualize their readers, they would make more use of the general English vocabulary. Professor Ballard (p. 199) puts the general principle from the reader's point of view: "and when the common language fails in clearness, in dignity, or in freedom from ambiguity, it should be eked out by the language of the laboratory and of the study. Technical jargon is an evil, but a necessary evil. And necessary evils should be kept to a minimum." It is worth trying to see how much of your specialized information you can make available to an intelligent general reader.

An increasing number of jobs now depend on some ability to write adequately scientific or technical letters, reports, or articles. The director of research in a large corporation says:

> If you can't tell in written or oral English what your results are, it is impossible to get along in any industry. For instance, the laboratory worker must submit a condensed report of his experiments to his laboratory head. This man must in turn condense the reports of many workers and send a new report on to his superior. And so on, all the way up the line. If you can't put your thoughts and figures on paper in concise readable language, you're sunk.

(REFERENCES: Dobrée, pp. 85-94; Sam F. Trelease, *The Scientific Paper* (Baltimore 1947)—with useful bibliography, pp. 142-44.)

Seasons *Spring, summer, fall, autumn, midsummer,* and so on are not capitalized except for stylistic emphasis, as sometimes in poetry or nature essays.

seem *Seem* is often used as a counter verb, making a statement needlessly qualified or distant:

> The letters of Flaubert [seem to] bring us as near to the writing of *Madame Bovary* as we can come.

In such a use *seem* is *deadwood.

Can't seem is an illogical but useful informal and colloquial idiom for "be unable": I can't seem to learn physics.

Segregating sentences Rather short sentences, carrying typically one principal statement and its modifiers, are called *segregating,* as contrasted with longer, more elaborate *aggregating* sentences. See Chapter 10, "Sentence length," page 272.

self *Self* as a suffix forms the reflexive and intensive pronouns: *myself, yourself, himself, herself, itself, oneself, ourselves, yourselves, themselves.* These are used chiefly for emphasis (I can do that myself) or as a reflexive object (I couldn't help myself). See *himself, herself, *myself.

Self as a prefix is usually hyphened to the root word:

self-control   self-explanatory   self-made   self-respect

When *self* is the root word there is no hyphen:

selfhood   selfish   selfless   selfsame

Semantics The study of the meaning and changes in meaning of words. See Chapter 11, "Denotation," page 318.

semi- *Semi-* is a prefix meaning "half or approximately half" (*semicylindrical*), "twice within a certain period" (*semiweekly, semiannual*) or "partially, imperfectly" (*semicivilized, semiprofessional*). It is not usually hyphened except before proper names (*semi-Christian*) or words beginning with *i* (*semi-invalid*).

Semi **Semicolon** (;) Correction: Use a semicolon as the mark of separation between these sentence elements.

1. To separate elements containing commas. 2. To separate coordinate clauses. 3. Semicolon and colon. 4. Semicolons and other traits of style.

A semicolon is used to mark a degree of separation between sentence elements considerably greater than that marked by a comma, nearly as great as that marked by a period. (Professor Bonner's suggestion that we call it *semiperiod* has much to recommend it.) There are a few situations in which a semicolon is usually found, but the chief question regarding its use is of appropriateness to traits of style (§ 4):

1. **To separate units that contain smaller elements separated by commas.** These may be items in a series, enumerations, figures, scores, or clauses with commas within them:

Other periodicals not entirely dissimilar were John Harris's *The English Lucian*, 1698; Ward's *Weekly Comedy*, 1699; "Sylvester Partridge's" *The Infallible Astrologer*, 1700; and the *Merry Mercury*, 1700.—GEORGE CARVER, *Periodical Essays of the Eighteenth Century*, p. xviii

Three things which a social system can provide or withhold are helpful to mental creation: first, technical training; second, liberty to follow the creative impulse; third, at least the possibility of ultimate appreciation by some public, whether large or small.—BERTRAND RUSSELL, *Proposed Roads to Freedom*, p. 169

2. **To separate coordinate clauses not closely related.**

a) BETWEEN CONTACT CLAUSES. A semicolon is used, especially in somewhat formal writing, between two *contact clauses (clauses with no expressed connective) if the separation in thought and structure is conspicuous. Usually the two statements could stand as separate sentences but the writer wishes to have them considered part of one idea. Contrasting statements are often punctuated with semicolons, as in these examples:

Words and sentences are subjects of revision; paragraphs and whole compositions are subjects of prevision.—BARRETT WENDELL, *English Composition*, p. 117

Your religion does not promise you a perfect life on earth, nor freedom from suffering; it does guarantee you the strength to bear suffering. Your religion does not expect you to be free from sin or mistakes in judgment; it does promise you forgiveness for your mistakes. Your religion expects you to continue making the best efforts you can on behalf of others; it does not guarantee that you or anyone can arrange the lives of people as he pleases. —HENRY C. LINK, *The Return to Religion*, pp. 68-69

(SEE ch. 9, "Contact clauses," "Comma faults," pp. 253, 254.)

b) WITH HEAVY CONNECTIVES. A semicolon is used between clauses connected by the weightier conjunctive adverbs (*however, moreover, nevertheless, consequently* . . .). These are heavy connectives and usually link rather long clauses in a formal style.

This program implies better orientation of individuals to the manifold problems of adjustment; therefore, certain character traits, as well as specific abilities, should show positive change.—*The English Journal*, June 1937

In order to act properly he needs to view his act as others view it; namely, as a manifestation of a character or will which is good or bad according as it is bent upon specific things which are desirable or obnoxious.—JOHN DEWEY, *Human Nature and Conduct*, p. 121

A comma is now usually more common between clauses connected by the lighter conjunctive adverbs (*so, then, yet* . . .). See *Conjunctive adverbs.

c) WITH COORDINATING CONJUNCTIONS. A semicolon is used between clauses connected by coordinating conjunctions (*and, but, for, or* . . .) if the clauses are long or if the connection is not close, if they contain commas, or if for some reason (often for contrast) the writer wishes to show an emphatic separation between them.

History as actuality includes all that has been said, felt, done, and thought by human beings on this planet since humanity began its long career; and, if Darwin is right, since the evolution of the human organism began in the primeval dawn.—C. A. BEARD, *The Discussion of Human Affairs*, p. 69

She already had some furniture of her own, including what she could take from Truda; and Louis could let her have some of his—yes?—G. B. STERN, *The Matriarch*, p. 199

Therefore those teachers who cannot admit that they may be wrong should not teach English composition; nor should those who never suspect that their pupils may be abler than they.—L. R. BRIGGS, *To College Teachers of English Composition*, p. 19

The semicolon is used to separate parts of the sentence which are of more importance, or which show a division more distinct, than those separated by commas; or to separate sections already separated by commas.—JOHN BENBOW, *Manuscript & Proof*, p. 89

3. Semicolon and colon. Do not use a semicolon, which is a mark of *separation* as the examples in this article show, in place of a colon (:), which is a mark of *anticipation:*

> There are two principal considerations in the use of semicolons: the degree of separation to be indicated between statements and the formality of the style of the passage.

4. Semicolons and other traits of style. Except for the specific situations described in § 1, the use of semicolons is in part a stylistic matter. They are more appropriate, more necessary, in rather formal styles and in long, aggregating sentences. They tend to slow up the reading and are consequently fewer in narrative than in exposition. In informal styles commas would be used in preference, or if the distinction between the clauses is considerable two sentences would be written. In the following paragraph Mr. Cowley has chosen to rely on semicolons. In brackets are put commas and periods that might have been used in a more informal writing of the same passage.

> College students inhabit an easy world of their own; [.] except for very rich people and certain types of childless wives they form the only American class that takes leisure for granted. Many, of course, earn their board and tuition tending furnaces, waiting on table or running back kick-offs for a touchdown; what I am about to say does not apply to them. The others—almost always the ruling clique of a big university, the students who set the tone for the rest—are supported practically without efforts of their own. They write a few begging letters; [,] perhaps they study a littler harder in order to win a scholarship; [,] but usually they don't stop to think where the money comes from. Above them, the president knows the source of the hard cash that runs this great educational factory; [.] he knows that the stream of donations can be stopped by a crash in the stock market or reduced in volume by newspaper reports of a professor gone bolshevik; [.] he knows what he has to tell his trustees or the state legislators when he goes to them begging for funds. The scrubwomen in the library, the chambermaids and janitors, know how they earn their food; but the students themselves, and many of their professors, are blind to economic forces; [.] society, as the source of food and football fields and professors' salaries, is a remote abstraction.—MALCOLM COWLEY, *Exile's Return*, pp. 36-37

Students tend to use more semicolons than would be used by professional writers today in informal writing. They should consider the weight of the mark in view of the general movement of their writing and make sure that the movement of the particular sentence needs the degree of separation marked by the semicolon.

(COMPARE *Comma, *Colon; ch. 5, "Colon and semicolon," p. 146. REFERENCE: Summey, pp. 97-101 and index references.)

Sentence outline   See *Outline form § 1c.

Sentences   Correction: Correct or improve the obvious fault in the   *S*
sentence marked.

The characteristics and problems of sentences are discussed in
Chapters 9 and 10 and in the following *Index* entries that treat the
most commonly needed points:

*Agreement	*Fragmentary sentence	*Shifted constructions
*Comma fault	*Idiom and idioms	*Subject and verb
*Conjunctions, use	*Misrelated modifiers	*Wordiness
*Construction	*Parallel constructions	*Word order
*Emphasis	*Reference of pronouns	

Sequence of tense   See *Tenses of verbs § 3, *Questions § 3.

Series   Commas are used between the items of a series of three or
more short items:

> The reason Odets has gained and held a public that by & large, does not
> share his Leftish ideas is obviously not the ideas themselves but his [three
> parallel adjectives:] *rich, compassionate, angry* [three nouns:] *feeling for
> people, his tremendous dramatic punch, his dialogue,* bracing as ozone.
> —*Time,* Dec. 5, 1938
>
> The supposed contents of the physical world are *prima facie* very different
> from these: [four short clauses:] *molecules have no colour, atoms make
> no noise, electrons have no taste, and corpuscles do not even smell.*—
> Bertrand Russell, *Mysticism and Logic,* p. 145

Usage is divided over the use of a comma before the last item
of such a series. Many writers, especially in an informal style, do
not use one:

> Ministers, teachers [,] and editorial writers all united against the proposal.

If the members of the series are long, or not closely connected, or
if the members have commas within them, they are separated by
semicolons:

> Why, I am asked, do we read history and biography; what is the secret
> of their perennial charm; why is it that since almost the beginning of
> recorded time they have been the most permanent and most popular of all
> forms of literature?—W. C. Abbott, *The Bookbuyer,* Christmas 1935

(For further examples and details see ch. 5, "In series," p. 143; *Comma § 2, *Semicolon § 1. Reference: R. J. McCutcheon, "The Serial Comma Before 'and' and 'or,' "
American Speech, 1940, 15: 250-54.)

service   The verb *service* (to service a car, a refrigerator) is needed
and appropriate in general English. It means more than *repair* and
has a different connotation from *maintain* or *keep up.*

set, sit People and things *sit* (past, *sat*) or they are *set* (past *set*), that is, "placed":

> I like to sit in a hotel lobby.
> I have sat in this same seat for three semesters.
> She set the soup down with a flourish.
> The post was set three feet in the ground.

A hen, however, *sets* (on her eggs). Colloquially *set* is increasingly used for both verbs.

sh *Sh* is a digraph for a sound which has nothing to do with either *s* or *h*: *shall*, *shove*, *ash*. The *sh* sound is represented by various spellings: *machine* (mə shēn′), *tissue* (tish′ū or tish′o͞o), *conscientious* (kon′shi en′shəs). Compare *zh.

shall—will, should—would
> 1. General usage. 2. Formal usage. 3. Overuse of 'shall.' 4. Future expressing doubt. 5. Other uses of 'should' and 'would.'

Future time is expressed by a number of locutions in English:

> I am going to ask for a raise.   I'll try to be on time.
> I am asking for a raise tomorrow.   I shall try to be on time.
> There is to be a dance Friday.   I will try to be on time.
> He comes next week.

Expressions like the first four are probably more common than the last three, so that it is hardly accurate to speak of a future tense made only with *shall* and *will*. But since distinctions between these auxiliaries have been regarded as an important item of reputable usage, it is necessary to discuss them in more detail than they deserve. Their use has never been uniform in English, although some grammarians have attempted to insist on uniformity. The general practices in the common situations needing these words are as follows:

    1. General usage. (a) SIMPLE FUTURE. In speech and writing the prevailing use in the United States, and in many other parts of the English-speaking world, is *will* in all persons (*I will ask, you will ask, he will ask* ...). This usage would appear in more printed matter if editors did not revise the copy to bring it in line with their stylebooks.

    b) EMPHATIC FUTURE. In expressing determination in the future or for some special emphasis, informal and colloquial usage is divided. In speech the determination is expressed by stress, which may be used on either word: I shall′ go, I will′ go. There is some tendency to use *shall* in all persons as the emphatic form: I, you, he, she, we, you, they *shall* ask. Other words (I have to go ...) are also used.

c) Contractions. In speaking and in informal writing where contractions are used, the future becomes *I'll, you'll, he'll,* and so on, which do not discriminate between *shall* and *will. Won't* is used for *will not* (formed from an obsolete *woll* and *not*) and *shan't* for *shall not.*

d) In questions. *Shall* is likely to be used in the first and third persons, and *will* in the second in asking questions, but practice is not consistent:

Shall I go?   Will you go?
What shall we do now?   What will you do now?
What shall he do?   What will he do with it?

In the negative, *won't* is the more common:

Won't I look funny in that?   What won't he think of next?

e) Shall is usual in laws, resolutions, etc:

A permanent organization shall be set up within a year.
No singer shall receive more than $700 a performance.

2. Formal usage. Some writers and editors use *shall* in the first person, *will* in the second and third persons in making the future tense, following handbook "rules" rather than actual usage.

First person:	I shall ask	we shall ask
Second person:	you will ask	you will ask
Third person:	he, she will ask	they will ask

In the emphatic future, expressing determination on the part of the speaker, formal English theoretically reverses this use of *shall* and *will*:

First person:	I will ask	we will ask
Second person:	you shall ask	you shall ask
Third person:	he, she shall ask	they shall ask

In asking questions a few people even use the form of *shall* or *will* in a question that the answerer would use in his reply. This usage is distinctly formal and usually sounds unnatural.

Shall you go? Answer: I shall (shall not) go.

3. Overuse of 'shall.' The stress that schools have put on *shall* leads to its use when it is unnatural:

Whether or not Congress will [not: shall] favor or pass laws against lynching is not for me to guess.

4. Future expressing doubt. *Should* and *would* are used in statements that carry some doubt or uncertainty about the statement

755

that is being made. They are also used in polite or unemphatic requests:

> They should be there by Monday. (Contrast: They will be there by Monday.)
> Would you please shut the door on your way out? (Contrast: Will you please . . .)

In the first person both *should* and *would* are used:

> I would be much obliged if you could do this.
> I should be much obliged if you could do this.

Usage is so much divided on the choice between these forms that one's feeling is probably the safest guide.

5. Other uses of 'should' and 'would.' *Should* as an auxiliary used with all persons expresses a mild sense of obligation, weaker than *ought*:

> I should pay this bill. (Contrast: I ought to pay this bill.)

In indirect discourse *should* and *would* represent the future tense of the direct speech:

> Direct: "I will be ready at three," Mildred said.
> Indirect: Mildred said that she would be ready at three.

Would has some currency in a colloquial or half-humorous idiom "that would be her picture," meaning "That is her picture, isn't it?"

(REFERENCES: Much has been written about the use of these words. As a beginning: Curme, *Syntax*, pp. 362-71; Fries, pp. 150-68 (a good short summary of actual usage); C. C. Fries, "The Expression of the Future," *Language*, 3: 87-95; Jespersen, chs. 25, 26; Amos L. Herold, *The English Journal*, 1936, 25: 670-76; Robertson, pp. 516-20.)

shan't One apostrophe, in the contraction of *not*.

shape Colloquial and informal in the sense of "manner, condition": They were in good shape for the trip.

Shift **Shifted constructions** Correction: Make the constructions marked consistent (parallel) in form.

Elements of a sentence that have the same relationship to the statement being made should be expressed by words in the same grammatical construction; that is, the constructions should be parallel. Adjectives should be paralleled by adjectives, nouns by nouns; a specific verb form should be continued in a similar construction; active or passive voice should be kept consistently in a sentence or passage; and so on. (The three *should be* constructions in the preceding sentence are parallel.) Shifting from one form to another may confuse a reader and anyway it is a failure to follow conventional patterns of writing. Shifts can be removed in revision. Some commonly shifted constructions are:

Shifted	*Consistent*
1) SHIFT IN SUBJECT	
Once *the car* is started, *you* will get along all right.	Once *you* get the car started, *you* will get along all right.
2) ADJECTIVE—NOUN	
This book seems *interesting* and *an informative piece of work.*	This book seems *interesting* and *informative.*
3) PERSONAL—IMPERSONAL	
In fact going to summer school is worse than no vacation at all, for when *you* have no vacation *you* do not think about all the things *a person* could do if *he* had one.	. . . for when *you* have no vacation *you* do not think about all the things *you* could do if *you* had one.
4) ADVERB—ADJECTIVE	
Along these walks are the cottages, many of which have stood *since the founding* [adverbial phrase], and others *more recent* [adjective].	. . . many of which have stood *since the founding,* and others of which have been built *more recently.*
5) NOUN—ADVERB	
Associating [noun] with these fellows and *how to adapt myself to live with them* [adverbial phrase] will be helpful to me when I am through college.	*Associating* with these fellows and *adapting* myself to live with them will be helpful to me when I am through college.
6) NOUN—ADJECTIVE	
Anyone who has *persistence* [noun] or who is *desperate* [adjective] enough can get a job on a ship.	Anyone who is *persistent* or who is *desperate* enough . . .
7) NOUN—CLAUSE	
The most important factors are *time* and *temperature,* careful *control* at every point, and *the mechanical equipment must be in perfect operating condition at any time of the day or night.*	. . . and *mechanical equipment in perfect operating condition at any time of the day or night.*

8) PARTICIPLE—CLAUSE

> How many times have you seen a fisherman *trying* to get to his favorite fishing spot without scaring all the fish away but instead *he sends out* messages with his rhythmical squeak-splash, squeak-splash.

> . . . but instead *sending out* messages . . .

9) PHRASE—CLAUSE

> I have heard complaints *about the plot being weak* and *that the setting was played up too much.*

> . . . and *the setting being played up too much.*

For other examples see Chapter 4, "Consistent constructions," page 116.

Ships' names The names of ships are indicated in three ways. In most books and generally in formal writing they are italicized (underlined in the manuscript):

> The *Caryatid*, in ballast, was steaming down the river at half-speed . . .—WILLIAM McFEE, *Casuals of the Sea*, p. 317
> Three vessels will carry on the popular "around South America" fad—the *Columbus*, the *Rotterdam*, and the *Gripsholm*.—Business Week, Nov. 6, 1937

In newspapers and personal writing there is a growing tendency to regard the names of ships simply as proper names, capitalizing them but not otherwise setting them off:

> The Magellan weighed anchor at 9:20 A.M. and moved slowly to her berth at Pier H, Weehawken, N. J.—*The New York Times*, Feb. 3, 1950

Occasionally ships' names are found in quotation marks:

> The summer of 1926 David spent as a junior member of the American Museum Greenland Expedition, . . . on the stout little schooner "Morrissey." [Jacket of *David Goes to Greenland*. In the book *Morrissey* is italicized.]

Shoptalk *Shoptalk* is the colloquial language of people used in, or in talking about, their particular occupations. For discussion see Chapter 2, "Shoptalk," page 45.

should—would See *shall—will §§ 4, 5; *Subjunctives § 1b.

show Colloquial, or theatrical shoptalk, in the sense of "a play" and usually humorous or vulgate for a dignified public performance, as of a concert; informal when applied to the movies (short for *picture show*). Informal for "chance" (They didn't have a show of winning).

show up Informal for *appear* (He didn't show up for two hours) and colloquial for *expose* (I showed him up, all right).

sic *Sic* (Latin for *thus, so;* pronounced sik) in brackets is sometimes used to mark an error in quoted matter: The letter was headed "Danbury, Conneticut [*sic*], Jan. 2."

sick *Ill* is the more formal word. The two words mean the same, except that colloquially and in British usage *sick* is often specialized to mean "nauseated."

Silent letters Written English is particularly rich in silent letters, that is, letters which do not represent any speech sound. A few of them are the result of mistaken analogies, like the *s* of *island*, which is there from confusion with the French *isle*, though it comes from Old English *igland* and has never had a pronounced *s*. Renaissance scholars inserted a number of letters that had been in the Greek and Latin words from which the English words were descended but that had never been sounded in English: Chaucer could write *det*, but we must write *debt* because the scholars recognized the word's descent from *debitum*.

But most of our silent letters act, as Professor Lounsbury put it, "as a sort of tombstone to mark the place where lie the unsightly remains of a dead and forgotten pronunciation": the pronunciation has changed but the spelling hasn't, or hasn't changed exactly. There they stand, those final *b*'s in *bomb, comb, climb*, the initial *g*'s and *k*'s in *gnarl, gnash, knack, knave, knee, knife, knuckle*, the *p*'s in Greekish words like *pneumonia* and *psychology*, the *gh*'s in *through* and *night* and *caught* that mark former pronounced gutterals.

Silent letters are sometimes defended because they tend to keep a word in touch with its ancestry, but that fact is of use only to scholars, and there are not enough scholars to pay to spell the language for them. Some people think these spellings have an esthetic value, that *night* has a beauty not in *nite* or that the superfluous *h* gives *ghost* a special weirdness. But this reason doesn't seem very substantial, since we learn these words from hearing them, and whatever quality *ghost* has as a word comes more likely from the tone in which we heard it spoken.

These silent letters are gradually being dropped, quietly, surreptitiously almost. *Apophthegm* has recently lost its *ph*—it may sometime lose its *g* too. In familiar writing *altho* is quite common; business and familiar English use *nite* and other shortened forms. But most of the silent letters hold firm, making spelling difficult.

759

Sometimes people who are not familiar with the sound of a word are led to pronounce a silent letter, giving a "spelling pronunciation," as pronouncing *indict* in dikt′ instead of in dīt′.

(SEE ch. 6, "The difficulty of English spelling," p. 156; *Pronunciation § 4d. REFERENCE: For groupings of silent letter words see W. A. Craigie, *English Spelling*, pp. 36-39, 67-73; Kennedy, pp. 241-47.)

similar The last syllable is *-lar*. Contrast *familiar*. Note the pronunciations: sim′ə lər, fə mil′yər.

similar to A wordy way of saying *like:* It was my first wreck and I hope I may never have another similar to that one [like it].

Similes See Chapter 12, "Figures of resemblance," page 348.

Simple sentences A simple sentence contains one grammatically independent statement (The man went across the street).

Simple sentences do not need to be bare, like those in a first reader. The subject or the verb may be compound, and either or both may be modified. Here are some sentences that from a grammatical point of view are equally "simple," though they vary in the amount of meaning they carry:

There are two or three large chests, a bedstead, the inevitable cradle occupied by the latest addition to the family. The small windows are seldom curtained. There are shelves for pots and pans, spoons and forks (often wooden), jars of gherkins, bottles of this and that, loaves of bread, sacks of flour, baskets of dried fruit.—LOUIS ADAMIC, *The Native's Return*, p. 271

See *Compound predicate, *Compound subject; Chapter 10, "Segregating sentences," page 273.

since See *because.

Singular number See *Plurals, *Reference of pronouns, *Subject and verb, *Collective nouns, *Verbs.

situated is often deadwood:

I was staying with friends in a little town in Canada called Picton, [situated] in the Province of Ontario.
It was a biplane and the front cockpit was [situated] right over the lower wing.

size As an adjective, *size* (a small size hat) is colloquial, typical of shoptalk. *Sized* would usually be the written form (a small sized hat).

ski Plural *skis*, sometimes *ski*. Verb: *ski, skied, skiing*. Pronunciation skē (or sometimes, following the Scandinavian, shē).

Slang Slang includes new words used principally for their novelty or force or color. They are natural and appropriate in rather light speech and writing, especially of sports, informal social activities, and the doings of young people. They are out of place in formal writing and should not be used in informal writing unless they add a quality that is appropriate and that the writer wishes. For further discussion, see Chapter 2, "Informal English," pages 46-48.

slow, slowly Both *slow* and *slowly* are adverbs, each going back to an Old English adverb form (*slawe* and *slawlice* respectively). Use whichever sounds better in the sentence. *Slow* is rather more vigorous: *Go slow*. See *Adverbs, types and forms §3.

Slurred vowels (the neutral vowel) A good many words give spelling trouble because they contain various spellings for the vowel sound represented in this book by ə: ə kad′ə mi (*academy*). These are standard pronunciations, so that no drill in sounding the syllable can help. A number of these words are related to others in which this syllable has a stress, so that the vowel stands out. Such pairs as the following may help you to spell accurately the vowel italicized in the first word:

academy—academic
affirmative—affirmation
angel—angelic
apology—apologia
comparable—compare
competition—compete
definitely—definition
degradation—degrade
democracy—democratic
despair, desperation—desperado
dormitory—dormir (French)

extravagance, extravagant—extravaganza
fertile—fertility
hypocrisy—hypocritical
laboratory—laborious
medicine—medicinal
preparation—prepare
repetition—repeat
ridicule—ridiculous
vigilance—vigilantes

But for the great majority of words with neutral vowels either a good memory or a good dictionary is essential.

so *So* is not much used as a conjunction in formal English for two reasons: It is a word of many uses and consequently not very exact or emphatic in any one; it is overworked in colloquial English, often as a substitute for more definite words.

So is used colloquially as a subordinating conjunction to introduce clauses of purpose:

Colloquial: He started early so he could get good seats.
Written: He started early so that he could get good seats; . . . in order to get good seats; . . . to get good seats.

So is more common in clauses of result, in which written English would usually have *so that* or change to a *since* construction:

> Colloquial: I wondered what they would do with the logs, so I followed them through the woods.
> Written: Since [Because] I wondered what they would do with the logs, I followed them through the woods.
> Colloquial: He is a fast reader, so he got through before I did.
> Informal: Since he is a fast reader, he got through before I did.

As a coordinating conjunction, *so* is used in garrulous narrative, in colloquial and vulgate speech:

> So we went out the Burlington road and pretty soon we got hungry. So we stopped and got some hot dogs . . .

This overuse of *so* is known as the "*so*-habit." In tightening up such narrative most of the *so*'s can be dropped; usually the sentences need to be completely reworded.

As an intensive ("feminine *so*"), *so* is also colloquial and often suggests *schoolgirl style:

> The poetry of Morris and Swinburne reads so much faster than most of Arnold's does. (. . . reads much faster [or: can be read much faster] than most of Arnold's.)
> We were so tired. (Contrast the informal: We were so tired that we didn't know what to do; or: We were so tired we didn't know what to do.)

(REFERENCE: Fries, pp. 226-27.)

so-called If you have to use *so-called*, don't duplicate the idea by putting the name of the so-called object in quotes: Not *the so-called* "*champion*," but *the so-called champion*. The word is rather stiff, and in informal writing quotation marks would often be used instead (the "champion").

So-called is usually hyphened when it precedes its principal word but not when it follows:

> Their so-called liberal views were merely an echo of the conservative attitude. (Their "liberal" views were . . .)
> Their justice, so called, smacked of partiality.

so . . . that When several words come between *so* and *that* no comma should precede *that:*

> All strands of the story are so artfully and inextricably interwoven [ ] that anything but the author's desired effect is impossible.

Social correspondence 1. **Informal notes.** The form and tone of informal social notes—invitations, answers to invitations, thank-you letters—are those of familiar letters. (*Letters §§ 1 and 2) Giving all the necessary information of time, place, and so on, promptness in answering notes, and a tone of courtesy are more important than mechanical form. If the people concerned are not intimately acquainted, a somewhat formal tone and more details of address may be needed than when they are intimates. The first note below is written to an intimate acquaintance; the other two passed between teacher and student.

Dear Helen,

My sister will be home this weekend, and I am planning a little tea for her on Saturday afternoon at four o'clock. I should be very glad if you could join us at that time and help celebrate the homecoming. Please let me know if you can come.

Affectionately yours,
Dorothy

Dear Helen,

I am having a little supper-party for my voice students next Sunday evening, and I hope that you will be able to come. We shall eat at six o'clock and later listen to a special broadcast of fine voices that should give us some helpful pointers. The program won't be long; so if you have an engagement later in the evening this should not interfere.

Cordially yours,
Marian Hall

Dear Miss Hall,

Thank you for your invitation for Sunday evening. As luck would have it, though, our sorority is giving a Pledge Banquet that same evening and it is obligatory that I attend. Consequently I'm afraid I cannot be at your home then. I am sorry to have to miss it, for home cooking is such a treat and I wanted so much to hear the broadcast.

Very sincerely yours,
Helen James

2. Formal notes. Formal social correspondence—announcements, invitations, answers to invitations—is impersonal and standardized. It is used for social events indicating, usually, formal dress or a gathering with distinguished guests. The illustration on page 764 shows the characteristic form of a printed or engraved invitation. Names are given in full, dates and other numbers are written in words, no punctuation is used at the ends of lines. Usually a reply is requested, either by *R.S.V.P.* ("répondez, s'il vous plaît") or by *The favor of a reply is requested.* The engraver or printer will help with the style of the note.

𝔇𝔢𝔩𝔱𝔞 𝔎𝔞𝔭𝔭𝔞 𝔈𝔭𝔰𝔦𝔩𝔬𝔫

requests the pleasure of your company

at a reception

in honor of

𝔍𝔬𝔥𝔫 ℌ𝔲𝔤𝔥𝔢𝔰 ℌ𝔲𝔫𝔱𝔢𝔯

on 𝔉𝔯𝔦𝔡𝔞𝔶, the twenty-sixth of 𝔐𝔞𝔶

at eight o'clock in the evening

The favor of a reply
is requested

If the note is in longhand, the form of engraved notes is still followed:

Miss Jeanette Ames
Miss Eva Loy
request the pleasure of
Mrs. Henry Jackson's
company at a breakfast bridge
on June twenty-eighth
at the Kingston Club. Ten o'clock

In answering an invitation the form of the invitation is adopted, and the exact words are followed so far as possible. The names, dates, and place are repeated.

Mrs. Henry Jackson
accepts with pleasure
the kind invitation of
Miss Jeanette Ames and Miss Eva Loy
to a breakfast bridge
on June twenty-eighth
at the Kingston Club. Ten o'clock

Solecism An error in use of words or constructions.

some, and compounds with some 1. In formal and informal written English, *some* is usually a pronoun (Some buy ink indifferently) or an adjective (some people, some ideas).

   2. As an adverb, *some* is in good informal use with comparatives (It was some better than I expected), for the more formal *somewhat*. It is informal and colloquial when used with verbs (We traded some that afternoon). It is slang as a heavily stressed adverb (We were going some', I was some' tired).

   3. The compounds *somebody, someway, somewhat, somewhere* are written as one word. *Someone* (Someone is coming) is usually one word but may be two if the *one* is stressed (Some one of them). *Someday* is written as one word or as two.

   4. *Some place* is colloquial for *somewhere*. *Someway* and *someways* are colloquial, and *somewheres*, vulgate.
(COMPARE *any, and compounds with any.)

sooner . . . than After *no sooner* the connective used is *than*, not *when:*

   The fly had no sooner hit the water than [not *when*] a huge trout snapped at it.

sophomore In spite of the dictionaries, *sophomore* is generally pronounced as two syllables, sof'mōr. The word is both noun and adjective. The adjective *sophomoric* refers to supposed undesirable traits of sophomores, as in *a sophomoric style* or *sophomoric conduct*.

sort, sort of, sort of [a] See *kind, sort, *kind of, sort of, *kind of [a], sort of [a].

Sound See Chapter 10, "Sound and rhythm," page 295.

species *Species* has the same form in both singular and plural, though some distinguish in pronunciation: singular, spē'shiz; plural, spē'shiz or spē'shēz.

   Specie (spē'shi), meaning money in coin, is a different word, a collective noun without plural form.

Spelling Correction: **Correct the spelling of the word marked,** *Sp*
referring to a dictionary if necessary.

   Chapter 6, page 155, describes some of the general characteristics of English spelling and makes some specific suggestions for improving spelling habits. It is useful also to study groups of words that have some trait in common. The following *Index* articles treat such groups. Those marked † give the most useful rules or suggestions for mastering large groups of words.

-able, -ible (desirable, legible)
-ae-, -oe- (ameba, esthetic)
† al ly (fatal, politically)
-ance, -ence (attendance, existence)
Apostrophe (Bob's picture, the companies' charter)
-cal, -cial (musical, judicial)
Capital letters
† -ce, -ge (peaceable, courageous)
Contractions (didn't, he'll)
† Doubling final consonants (refer—referred)
† E § 5, silent or mute *e* (changeable, likeness)
-ed (exceptions to rule)
† -ei-, -ie- (achieve, feign, receive)
en-, in- (encourage, inquire)
-er, -or (debater, objector)
-er, -re (luster, scepter)
Foreign words in English (chauffeur, ersatz; accent marks)
† Homonyms (words pronounced alike but spelled differently: plain, plane; altar, alter)
Hyphen (re-enter, father-in-law)
in-, un- (incapable, unedited)
-ize, -ise (apologize, advertise)
-le words (meddle, nickel)
-or (-our) (honor, Saviour)
-ough (-augh) (although, cough)
Plurals (beauties, birches, heroes, knives)
Principal parts of verbs
Pronunciation § 5
re- (reform, re-form)
Silent letters (debt, night)
† Slurred vowels (the neutral vowel) (comparable, repetition)

The following list contains many words that give difficulty in spelling. It is not exhaustive and is by no means a substitute for a dictionary, but it can be used as the basis for a discussion of spelling. Perhaps it can be most useful if you check the particular words in it that you are not sure of and occasionally skim through those to fix them better in mind. In the margins add others that have troubled you—in every way possible make it *your* list.

* means that there is a separate article in this *Index* discussing that word.

A dash separating two words (*adviser—advisor*) means that the two forms are about equally common.

A second form in brackets (*encyclopedia* [*encyclopaedia*]) means that the form in brackets is now less common than the other.

A few words are identified by pronunciation or definition in parentheses.

The words are divided into syllables so that they can be visualized in relation to their pronunciation.

ab sence
ac cept (receive)
ac cess (admittance)
ac ces si ble
ac ci den tal ly
ac com mo date
ac cus tom
ache
ac quaint ed
ac quired
a cross
ad ap ta tion
*ad dress
ad vice (noun)
ad vise (verb)
*ad vis er—ad vis or
*af fect (to influence)
ag gra vate
ag gres sion, ag gres sor
*air plane [aeroplane]
aisle (of a theater)
al co hol
al lege
all read y
*all right
al read y
al lu sion
al ma ma ter
al tar (of a church)
al ter (to change)
*al though—al tho
al to geth er
*a lum nus, a lum ni,
     a lum na, a lum nae
am a teur
a nal o gous, a nal o gy
a nal y sis
a nal yze [analyse]
an es thet ic [anaes-
     thetic]
an gel (an jəl)
an gle (ang gəl)
an nounc er
an nu al
an swer
an te ced ent

an ti knock
anx i e ty
a pol o gy
ap pa ra tus
ap par ent
ap pear anc es
ap pre ci ate
arc tic
ar gue
ar gu ment
a roused
ar ti cle
as cent (going up)
as cer tain
as i nine
as sas sin
as sent (agreement)
as so ci a tion
*ath lete, ath let ics
at tacked
at tend ance
at tend ant
at tor ney
at trac tive
au di ence
au to bi og ra phy
aux il ia ry

bach e lor
bal ance
bar i tone [barytone]
bat tal ion
be lieve
ben e fit ed
berth (a bed)
bib li og ra phy
birth (being born)
bound a ries
breath (breth)
breathe (brē th)
brid al (of a bride)
bri dle (of a horse)
bril liant
Brit ain (Great Britain)
bu reau
bu reauc ra cy

*bus, bus es—bus ses
busi ness (biz′nis)

ca fé
ca fe te ri a
cal en dar (of days)
cal i ber [cal i bre]
can't
can vas (sailcloth)
can vass (to go about)
cap i tal (city)
cap i tol (building)
cap tain
car bu re tor [car-
     burettor]
car goes
car riage
cas u al ties
cat e go ries
ceil ing
cen ter [centre]
chal leng er
cham pagne
change a ble
*chap er on
     [chap er one]
char ac ter is tic
chauf feur
chief tain
choose, choos ing
     (present)
chose, cho sen (past)
cig a ret—cigarette
co coa
co er cion
col lar
col le gi ate
colo nel
col or
co los sal
*col umn
com e dy
com mit
com mit tee
com par a tive
com par i son

com pel, com pelled
com pet i tor
com plaint
com ple ment
  (to fill out)
com pli ment
  (to praise)
con cede
con ceive
con cer to (kən cher tō)
con nois seur (kon′ə sûr′)
con quer or
con science
con sci en tious
con scious ness
con sist ent
con tempt i ble
con trol, con trolled
con vert i ble
co op er a tive—
  co-operative
  [coöperative]
corps (kōr)
corpse (kôrps)
cor ru gat ed
cos tume
coun cil (a group)
coun ci lor—coun cil lor
coun sel (advice)
coun sel or—counsellor
cour te ous, cour te sy
crept
cur ric u lar (adjective)
*cur ric u lum (noun)
cur tain
cus tom
cy lin dri cal

dair y (dãr′i)
damned
de bat er
de ceased (də sēst′)
de ceive
de cent (dē′sənt)
de cide, de ci sion
de fend ants
def i nite, def i ni tion
de pend ent (adj. or
  noun)
de scent (də sent′)
de scend ant

de scribe, de scrip tion
de sert (də zert′, leave)
des ert (dez′ ərt, waste)
de spair, des per ate
des sert (də zert′, of a
  meal)
de vel op [rare:
  develope]
dex ter ous—dextrous
di a gram mat ic
di a phragm
di a ry (dī′ə ri)
die, dies, dy ing
die sel
di e ti tian [dietician]
di lap i dat ed
din ing room
din ning (noise)
diph ther i a
dir i gi ble
dis ap pear ance
dis ap point ment
dis as trous
dis ci pli nar y
dis cre tion
dis eased (di zēzd′)
dis gust ed
dis patch [despatch]
dis si pate
dis trib u tor
dis turb ance
di vine
doc tor
dom i nant
don't
dor mi to ry
dry, dri er, dri est
du al (two)
du el (fight)
dye, dyed, dye ing

ech o, ech oes
ec sta sies
ef fect (*affect)
el i gi bil i ty
el i gi ble
em bar rass
em pha size, em phat ic,
  em phat ic al ly
em ploy ee, em ploy ees
  [employe, employé]

en cy clo pe di a
  [encyclopaedia]
en er get ic
en force
en graved
en vi ron ment
e quip ment
e quipped
es pe cial ly
es thet ic—aesthetic
ex ag ger ate
ex am ine, ex am in ing,
  ex am i na tion
ex ceed, ex ces sive
ex cel, ex cel lence
ex cept (to omit)
ex haust ed
ex hil a rat ing
ex ist ence
ex pe di tion ar y
*ex tra cur ric u lar
ex trav a gant
ex treme ly
ex u ber ance

fac ile, fa cil i ty
fair way (golf)
fal la cy
fa mil iar
fas ci na tion
Feb ru ar y
*fi an cé, fiancée
fier y
fin an cier
fli er—fly er
fore head (for′id)
for eign
for feit
for mal ly
for mer ly
for ty four—forty-four
frame house
fran ti cal ly [franticly]
fra ter ni ties
*fresh man
ful fill—fulfil
fun da men tal
fur ni ture

gage—gauge
gel a tine—gelatin
ghost

ghost like
*grade school—graded
    school
gram mar,
    gram mat i cal
*grief [grey]
grief
grue some [grewsome]
guar an tee
guard i an
guer ril la—gue ril la
    (fighting)
guid ance

hand i cap,
    hand i capped
hand ker chief
    (hang'kər chif)
hand some (han'səm)
hang ar
*height
hei nous (hā'nəs)
hin drance
hoard
hoarse (in throat)
horde
hor i zon tal
hors d'oeu vre
    (ôr dû'vr)
huge
hu man (hū'mən)
hu mane (hū mān')
hur ried ly
hy giene
hyp no sis, hyp not ic,
    hyp no tize [hypno-
    tise]
hy poc ri sy, hyp o crite
hys ter i cal

il lit er ate
il log i cal
im ag i nar y
im ag i na tion
im me di ate ly
im ple ment
im promp tu,
    im promp tus
in ad e quate
in ces sant ly
in ci den tal ly
in cred i ble

in de pend ence
in dict ment
    (in dīt'mənt)
in dis pen sa ble
in gen ious
in gen u ous
in i ti a tion
in nu en do, innuen-
    does
in oc u late
in tel lec tu al
in tel li gent
in tern [interne]
in ter pre tive
    [interpretative]
in tol er ance
in ven tor—inventer
ir rel e vant
ir re li gious
ir re sist i ble
ir rev er ent
it self

ja lop y
john ny cake
jol li ty
judg ment [judge-
    ment]

kha ki
kid nap, kid naped
    [kid napped]
ki mo no, kimonos
kin der gar ten
kitch en ette [kitch-
    enet]
knowl edge
knuck les

lab o ra to ry
la dle (lā'dəl)
lat er (lā'tər)
lat ter (lat'ər)
lau rel
lax a tive
*lead, led
leg a cy
le git i mate
lei sure ly
li a ble
li ar
li brar i an

light en ing
    (making lighter)
*light ning (a flash)
lik a ble [likeable]
li queur
liq uor
liv a ble [liveable]
live li hood
lone li ness
loose (lōos)
*lose (lōoz)
lu na tic

mack er el
mag a zine
mag nif i cent
main tain,
    main te nance
ma neu ver
    [maneuvre]
man tel (the shelf)
man tle (the cloak)
man u al
man u fac tur er
mean, meant
me di e val
    [mediaeval]
me di o cre
Me di ter ra ne an
met al
met tle
mil lion aire
min i a ture
min ute
mis chie vous
mis spelled
mold [mould]
*mor al (mor'əl)
mo rale (mə ral', or
    mə räl')
mort gage
mot to, mottoes—
    mottos
moun tain ous
mur mur
mus cle
mus tache
mys te ri ous

*na ive—naïve
nec es sar i ly
*Ne gro, Negroes

769

nei ther

*nick el

niece

nine ty ninth—
    ninety-ninth

no tice a ble

no to ri e ty

ob bli ga to—obligato

o be di ence

o bey

o bliged

ob sta cle

*oc ca sion,
    oc ca sion al ly

oc cur, oc curred,
    oc cur ring

of fi cial

oil y

o mit, o mit ted,
    o mis sion

one self

op por tu ni ty

op ti mism

or gan i za tion
    [organisation]

or gan ize [organise]

or i gin, or i gin al

out ra geous

*paid

pa ja ma [pyjama]

pam phlet

pan to mime

par al lel, paralleled

par lia ment

pa roled

par tic i pate

par tic u lar ly

*passed, past

pas time

ped es tal

per form

per mis si ble

per se ver ance

per sist ent

per son al

per son nel

per spi ra tion

per suade, per sua sion

Phil ip pines

phy si cian

pi an o, pianos

pick le

pic nic, pic nicked

pique (pēk)

pi qué (pi kā′)

plain

plane

play wright

pneu mat ic

pneu mo ni a

pol i tics

pos si bil i ty

po ta to, potatoes

prac ti ca bil i ty

*prac ti cal

prac tice [practise]

pre ced ing

pref er ence

prej u dice

prep a ra tion

pres ence

prev a lent

prim i tive

*prin ci pal

prin ci ple

pri vi lege

prob a ble, prob a bly

pro fes sor

pro gram
    [programme]

pro nounce

pro nun ci a tion

prop a gan da

pro pel ler

pro te in

psy cho an al y sis

psy cho an a lyze

psy chol o gy

pub lic ly

pump kin

pur sue, pur suit

quan ti ty

quan tum

quar an tine

quay [quai] (kē)

qui et

quite

quix ot ic

quiz, quiz zes

re al ize

re al ly

*re ceipt, rec i pe

re ceive

re cip i ent

rec la ma tion

rec og ni tion

rec om mend

re-en ter

re fer, re ferred,
    ref er ence

re for est a tion

re gion al

rel e vant

re li gious

rem i nisce

*Ren ais sance—
    Re nas cence

ren dez vous

re pel lent

rep e ti tious

res er voir

re sist ance

re spect ful ly

re spec tive ly

res tau rant

rev er ent

rhet o ric

*rhyme, rime

rhyth mi cal

ri dic u lous

sac ri le gious

sal a ry

sand wich

sax o phone

scan dal ous

scar (skär)

scare (skar)

sce nar i o

sce nic

sched ule

sec re tar i al

seize

se mes ter

sen a tor

sen si ble

sep a rate

ser geant (sär′jənt)

se vere ly, se ver i ty

shear (verb)

sheer (adj.)

sieve

sig nif i cance
*sim i lar
sin cere ly, sin cer i ty
site (of a city)
skep ti cal [sceptical]
*ski, skis, skied,
    ski ing
slim y
slug gish
soc cer
sol u ble
so phis ti ca tion
*soph o more
speak, speech
spe cif i cal ly
spec i men, specimens
spec ter [spectre]
spic y, spic i ness
spon sor
stac ca to
sta tion ar y (fixed)
sta tion er y (paper)
stat ue
stat ure
stat ute
stom ach ache
sto ry [storey] (of a
    building)
stretched
stud y ing
sub si dize,
    sub si di za tion,
    sub si dy
sub tle [subtile]
suc ceed, suc cess
suc cess ful
*suit (so͞ot)
suite (swēt—sūt)
sul fa
sul fur—sul phur
su per in tend ent

su per sede
sup pose
sup press
sur prise
sus cep ti ble
syl la ble
sym bol
sym me try,
    sym met ri cal
syph i lis
syr up—sir up

ta boo [tabu]
tar iff
tech nique [technic]
tem per a men tal
*the a ter [theatre]
their
there
there fore
they're
thor ough [thoro]
though—tho
thou sandths
through—thru
to, too, two
to day [to-day]
to geth er
traf fic, traf fick ing
trag e dy, trag ic
tre men dous ly
tru ly
Tues day
typ i cal
tyr an ny

un doubt ed ly
un prec e dent ed
un til (*till)
u su al ly
u ten sil

vac u um
veg e ta bles
venge ance
ven ti late,
    ven ti la tion
ver ti cal
vice (evil)
vig i lance
vig i lan tes
vil i fy
vil lain
vise [vice] (the tool)
vis i bil i ty
vi ta min [vitamine]
vol ume

war fare
war rant
war ring
war ri or
weath er
weight, weight y
weird
wheth er
whis key [whisky]
whoop
who's (who is)
whose
wool en [woollen]
wool ly—wool y
write, writ ing,
    writ ten
wrought

yacht
you're (you are)

zo ol o gy [zoölogy],
    zo o log i cal

Spelling pronunciation See *Pronunciation § 4d.

Split infinitive The word order in which an adverb comes between the *to* and the infinitive (The receptionist asked them *to please sit down*) is called a split infinitive. Awkward split infinitives are to be avoided:

  Awkward: After a while I was able to, although not very accurately, distinguish the good customers from the sulky ones.

Improved: After a while I was able to distinguish—though not very accurately—the good customers from the sulky ones.

Since the adverb modifies the verb, its natural position seems to be next to the actual verb form. Changing the position of *eventually* in this sentence would result in awkwardness:

He requested the Ministry of Forests to reforest the barren mountains in Macedonia in order to eventually eliminate the mosquito-breeding swamps. —Louis Adamic, *The Native's Return*, p. 321

There is no point in rearranging a sentence just to avoid splitting an infinitive unless it is an awkward one.

(References: Curme, *Syntax*, pp. 458-65; Fowler, "Split Infinitive" (for overprecise distinctions); Fries, pp. 132, 144.)

spoonful, spoonfuls The standard plural of *spoonful, tablespoonful, teaspoonful*, is *spoonfuls, tablespoonfuls, teaspoonfuls* (similarly, *basketfuls, carfuls, cupfuls, shovelfuls, tubfuls*).

Colloquially *cupsful, carsful, shovelsful*, and so on are often heard.

Squinting modifier See *Ambiguity § 2.

Staccato style A staccato style has—as its principal characteristic —short, emphatic sentences, often exclamations or questions, usually without expressed connectives between the statements. The words, especially verbs, are likely to be vigorous. It is effective in short passages that deserve sharp stressing but is likely to be tiresome and to lose its emphasis if it is long continued.

Hindenburg was shortening his lines. He was quitting northern France and Belgium. But he was holding the Argonne. Day by day the representatives of our G. H. Q. had shown us the map with every enemy division and reserve force marked. Hindenburg had thirty-two reserve divisions at the beginning of our Argonne drive. When November began two or three remained. What had become of an army of German reserves?—George Seldes, *You Can't Print That!* p. 35

Compare *Telegraphic style.

Standard English *Standard English* is a useful term to describe the language used in the conduct of public affairs, that is used in the various types of literature, in periodicals and books, in speeches, in letters and documents. In this sense it corresponds roughly to the combined Formal and Informal levels of usage and excludes Vulgate. See Chapter 3, "The basis of Good English," page 72, for further discussion.

Statements See *Declarative sentences.

still *Still* is an adverb in the sentence "It's still raining" and a conjunction (*Conjunctive adverbs) in "I can see your point of view; still I don't agree with you."

stomach No final *-e*. But *stomach ache*.

story A *story* is a narrative of either real or imaginary happenings. Typically we think of a story as an imaginary tale, a short story or novel, though a newspaper account of actual events is a news story.

A discussion of ideas may be an editorial, an article, a critical article, a review, a treatise, but it is not a story. A poem would be referred to as a story only if it was a narrative, and though plays are stories, their special form calls for reference to them by their proper name. Try to keep *story* for its real meaning.

strata *Stratum* is the singular, *strata* its plural.

street In many newspapers and in some informal writing, *street* is not capitalized as part of an address. In general writing it would be capitalized (41 High Street).

The abbreviation *St.* or *st.* is not much used except to save space in newspapers, lists, or reference works.

Stress See *Pronunciation § 4b, c; *Rhythm; *Noun and verb stress.

Strong verbs See *Principal parts of verbs.

Style Style has been defined in a number of well-known aphorisms: "Proper words in proper places make the true definition of a style" (Jonathan Swift); "Style is the dress of thoughts" (Lord Chesterfield); "Style is this: to add to a given thought all the circumstances fitted to produce the whole effect that the thought ought to produce" (Stendhal); "Style is the ultimate morality of mind" (A. N. Whitehead); and the most often quoted of all, "The style is the man" (Comte de Buffon).

Such definitions are good starting points for discussion, and they suggest ideals that may guide a person's thought and perhaps his practice. But whatever *style* may mean to critics and philosophers, for a student or writer it is most helpfully taken, in a more concrete sense, to mean a speaker's or writer's use of language, the sources of the listener's or reader's impressions of his manner of thought and expression. The connotation of *style* is of the effectiveness of the expression (rather than of description of usage or questions of correctness). In contrast to grammar, the typical structure of the language, style refers especially to the words and expressions in

Style

which the speaker or writer has a choice among the resources his language offers. An analysis of a writer's style takes into account the qualities of words, phrases, idioms, sentences, and arrangement of material.

The following adjectives are often used in describing qualities of style. Some of them are words of general meaning that are applied to style (*flat, mature*); others are technical words for qualities of language (*allusive, archaic, precious, trite*); several of them are practically synonymous (*verbose—wordy, local—provincial*). With many of the words you will be already acquainted; the meaning of the others you can find from class discussion, from referring to a good dictionary, or from the pages given to treatments in this *Guide and Index*.

*abstract, p. 341
*academic
affected
*alliterative
allusive, p. 353
amateur
Anglo-Saxon
archaic, p. 56
awkward
careless
*clear
climactic, p. 222
*colloquial
complex
concise, p. 284
concrete, p. 341
dense
difficult
diffuse
dignified, p. 48
direct
easy
economical, p. 284
elementary
*emphatic, p. 287
*epigrammatic
euphonious, p. 295
exact, p. 326
*experimental
feeble
figurative, p. 344
flabby, p. 333
flashy, p. 46
flat
florid

fluent
formal, p. 48
graceful, p. 295
*heightened
highflown
*humorous
*idiomatic
*imagistic
*imitative
immature
impersonal, p. 79
informal, p. 39
interrupted, p. 279
involved, p. 279
ironical, p. 351
journalistic
[*Newspaper English]
juvenile
*Latinized
literal, p. 326
local, p. 58
loose
lyrical
mannered
mature
metaphorical, p. 348
monotonous, p. 278
natural, p. 84
nervous
old-fashioned, p. 55
overloaded
overmodified
[*Adjectives in use]
pedantic
pithy

plain
poetic
pompous
*precious
precise
prosaic
provincial, p. 58
purple
repetitious, p. 289
resonant
*rhythmical
riming
*schoolgirl
*scientific
self-conscious
simple
slangy, p. 46
smart
smartaleck
smooth
solid
sophisticated
*staccato
stiff
*suggestive
technical
*telegraphic
trite, p. 333
varied, p. 278
verbose
vulgate, p. 52
weak
*wordy, p. 284

774

To discuss the style of a passage, read it attentively for a general impression. Then read it slowly once or more to note the qualities of words, phrases, sentences, perhaps marking some that attract particular attention or that are good illustrations of the qualities you find. Test your original impression in the light of this analysis. Try not to let an interest in details blind you to general qualities of style.

(REFERENCES: Dobrée; Rickert; many articles in Fowler; René Wellek and Austin Warren, *Theory of Literature* (New York, 1949), chs. 12-15; works on literary criticism.)

Stylebooks For editors and printers *style* means the method of handling various mechanical matters such as capital letters, punctuation, forms of plurals, division of words, details of typography. Since usage is divided on many of these points, a publisher chooses what form will be used in his publications. Most newspapers, magazines, and publishing houses have stylebooks—documents ranging from a single page to elaborate volumes containing the particular rules to be followed in preparing copy for specific publications. They often show arbitrary choices, to attain a consistency that most publishers feel is desirable. One factor in recent changes in practices in writing and printing has been the decision of some of the book publishers to let authors' copy stand nearly as written, so long as it is consistent.

Most newspaper stylebooks are not generally available, though that of *The New York Times*, revised 1950, is for sale. The University of Chicago Press *Manual of Style*, eleventh edition (Chicago, 1949) is the most influential stylebook among book publishers. John Benbow, *Manuscript & Proof* (New York, 1937), representing the style used by the American Oxford University Press, is a briefer and more modern stylebook.

Subject and verb Correction: Make the subject and verb of this clause or sentence agree according to the principles given in § 2 below. *S&V*

1. **Subject and verb as sentence elements.** The backbone of the typical English sentence is a subject and a verb. The subject names the starting point of the action or statement, and the verb advances the statement by specifying an action, state, feeling, or the existence of whatever the subject names. Except in inverted sentence order the subject stands before the verb and we identify it as the subject because of this position, as the *object follows the verb. In the sentence "The submarine sank the cruiser" we know that the submarine and not the cruiser did the sinking because *submarine* is in the subject position in the sentence.

2. Agreement of subject and verb. A verb agrees with its subject in number and person. This usually means with the grammatical number of the subject. Since, except for the verb *be*, our verbs have one form for both numbers and for all persons except an *-s* in the third singular present, relatively few problems in agreement can arise.

> Singular: *I am* more tired than usual. *A chair was placed* in the corner. *This job takes* four weeks. *The job took* four weeks.
>
> Plural: *We are* more tired than usual. *Three chairs were placed* along the wall. *These jobs take* four weeks. *The jobs took* four weeks.

The problems that arise in agreement of the subject and verb are either from a sentence form in which the grammatical number of the subject is uncertain or is blurred by the presence of other words, or from agreement with the meaning of the subject rather than with its grammatical form.

a) COLLECTIVE NOUNS. Agreement according to meaning is seen most clearly in collective nouns, which take either a singular or plural verb, depending upon whether the speaker or writer is emphasizing the group as a whole or the individuals of which it is composed. In writing, the verbs and pronouns of a given sentence should be all plural or all singular in referring back to a collective subject.

> Emphasizing the unit: The class *is* the largest in six years.
>
> Emphasizing the individuals: The class *are* by no means all intellectual giants, but *they* have done very well.

For further examples and discussion see *Collective nouns.

b) COMPOUND SUBJECTS. Ordinarily a compound subject has a plural verb:

> Alice and Francis *were* the first to arrive.
>
> The text of the poem and the commentary *make* quite a sizable volume.

When the two elements of a compound subject refer to the same person or thing, the verb is singular:

> The best teacher and the best scholar here *is* Professor Babcock.
>
> The spirit and accomplishment of these men *speaks* for itself.

The verb is often singular when the compound subject follows:

> There *is* both health and wealth in this way of life.
>
> For the winner there *was* a large cash prize and weeks of glory.

When a second part of the subject is connected with the first by *with*, *together with*, *as well as*, the agreement varies. In formal

English such a construction is kept singular. In informal English a plural is often found if the expression is equivalent to a compound subject:

> The rudder is the only essential control in taxiing, and this together with a regulative speed *keeps* the plane going in a relatively straight line.
> The winner with the four runners-up *were* given a reception. (To make this more formal, the *with* should be changed to *and*, rather than the *were* to *was*.)
> He is not a good speaker, since his hesitating manner with long "uh's" interspersed in the address *make* [formal: *makes*] him difficult to listen to.

Subjects connected by *or* take a singular verb if both are singular, a plural verb if both are plural or if the one nearer the verb is plural:

> A novel or a biography *is* to be read outside of class.
> Novels or biographies *were* the same to him.
> A novel or five short stories *were* to be read.

In questions in colloquial usage the plural is common:

> *Are* [or: *Is*] Fred or Harry in?

c) PLURAL MODIFIER OF SINGULAR SUBJECT. When a rather long plural modifier of a singular subject comes between it and the verb, formal English has a singular verb, but informal and colloquial often have a plural verb:

> This *group* of essays *is* [not *are*] concerned with problems in sociology and philosophy as they are related to biology.
> The *form* of your bibliography and footnotes *is* not standard.
> To a beginner on the organ the array of stops and pistons, manuals, couplers, and pedals *seems* [colloquial: *seem*] at first quite bewildering.
> Two thousand dollars' *worth* of pictures *were* [formal: *was*] destroyed.

d) RELATIVE PRONOUNS. A relative pronoun referring to a singular noun has a singular verb (The person *who takes* enough pains can do it) and one referring to a plural noun has a plural verb (The people *who take* pains win in the long run). In idioms like "This is one of the most discouraging things that has come out of the situation," formal usage has *that have come*, since the antecedent of *that* is *things;* informal and colloquial usage often have *that has come*, because the central idea (of *one*) is singular.

> Formal: Jeffrey is one of those moderns *who are* making *their* money talk.
> Colloquial: Jeffrey is one of those moderns *who is* making *his* money talk.

e) SUBJECT AND COMPLEMENT OF DIFFERENT NUMBER. The verb agrees with the subject:

> A day's work is four trips.   Four trips make a day's work.

f) PLURAL SUBJECT WITH SINGULAR MEANING. When the idea conveyed by a plural subject is singular in intent, the verb is usually singular:

> Five years is a long time.

(REFERENCES: Curme, *Syntax*, ch. 4; Fries, pp. 188-90, 249-50, and index references; Pooley, pp. 78-88.)

3. Punctuation between subject and verb. Since the subject and verb are part of one construction, they should not normally be separated by a comma:

> Another example of what can happen [ ] is furnished by the experience of two young women who were staying at the hotel.

(SEE *Comma § 5. Discussion and other examples of subject and verb relations will be found in ch. 4, "Subject—verb—object," p. 104; ch. 9, "The favorite English sentence," and "Minor sentence types," pp. 247, 259; ch. 10, "Separating elements," p. 292.)

Subjective case See *Nominative case, *Subject and verb.

Subjectless sentences See Chapter 9, "Subjectless sentences," page 259.

Subjects of papers See Chapter 1, "Focusing on a subject," page 8, and, for reference papers in particular, Chapter 13, "Choosing a subject," page 367.

Subjunctives Subjunctive verb forms have been used to show some attitude of feeling or doubt of the speaker toward the statement he is making.

1. Form of subjunctives. (a) SIMPLE SUBJUNCTIVE: In current English the subjunctive form of a verb is identifiable only in certain forms of the verb *be* (If I, you, he . . . *be*, If I, he . . . *were*), and in forms, made with *be* (If he *were asking*) and in the third person singular ("If he *ask*" instead of the indicative "If he *asks*," "If he *have*" instead of "If he *has*.").

b) SUBJUNCTIVE WITH AUXILIARIES: Some grammarians include as subjunctives all the locutions that can be used in expressing ideas that may also be, or have at some time been, expressed by the subjunctive, or the forms that could be used in translating subjunctives found in other languages. Under this system several auxiliaries—*may, might, should, would, let, have to*, and others—become subjunctives. This broad interpretation makes consideration of the subjunctive more complicated than is necessary, since the meaning and connotation come from the meaning of the auxiliary or from adverbs. For that reason, in the following discussion only the simple subjunctive is considered.

(SEE ch. 4, "Subjunctives," p. 103. REFERENCES: For argument in favor of confining *subjunctive* to the simple forms, see Otto Jespersen, *The Philosophy of Grammar*, pp. 315-21, and for description of the subjunctive with auxiliaries, Curme, *Syntax*, ch. 20.)

2. Uses of the subjunctive. English makes much less use of the subjunctive mood than most of the modern European languages do. There are a number of idioms in which the subjunctive may be used in English, especially in formal English, although it is almost always possible to use other verb forms. It is common in wishes, conditions, qualified or doubtful statements, and in *that*-clauses and after expressions like *It is necessary.* The following examples illustrate typical uses of the subjunctive and give alternative idioms that would be more common in speech and most writing.

a) FORMULAS. The subjunctive is found in numerous formulas, locutions surviving from a time when the subjunctive was used freely. Most of these are no longer general idioms; that is, we do not make other sentences on the pattern of *Far be it from me. . . .*

Far be it from me	Heaven forbid	If need be	Heaven help us
Be it said	Suffice it to say	God bless you	Be that as it may

Many petty oaths have this form: *Confound it; Grades be hanged.*

Some of these formulas are used in all levels of the language; some, like *Come what may*, are rather formal, and the oaths are chiefly colloquial.

b) IN THAT-CLAUSES. The subjunctive is used in many idioms for recommendations, resolutions, demands, and so on. These idioms are usually in a formal, often legal, context. Note the following examples:

Formal: We recommend that the Commissioner *designate* for this use the land formerly belonging to Mr. Brewster.
Formal: I ask that the interested citizen *watch* closely the movements of these troops.
Informal: I ask the interested citizen to watch the movements of these troops closely.
Formal: . . . the order that he *be* dropped
Informal: . . . the order to drop him
Formal: It is necessary that every member *inform* himself of these rules.
Informal: It is necessary for every member to inform himself of these rules—It is necessary that every member should inform himself of these rules—Every member must [should] inform himself of these rules.

c) IN CONDITIONS. In formal English the subjunctive is used in *if*-clauses when there is doubt of fulfillment of the condition, or when the condition is "contrary-to-fact," that is, impossible (as in "If I *were* you . . ."):

> Formal: I had to do all this if I *were* to arrive in Hartwick by ten o'clock.
> Informal: I had to do all this if I *was* to arrive in Hartwick by ten o'clock.
> Formal: The fellow who worked next to him in the plant had been turned off, and Jim could not help wondering if that *were* [Informal and more usual: *was*] a sign that some of the rest of them would be discharged, too.—ERSKINE CALDWELL, *Kneel to the Rising Sun*, p. 129
> Formal: If the subject of a verb *be* [More usual: *is*] impersonal, the verb itself may be called impersonal.—ARTHUR G. KENNEDY, *Current English*, p. 296

The subjunctive is most common in contrary-to-fact conditions.

> If one good *were* really as good as another, no good would be any good.—IRWIN EDMAN, *Four Ways of Philosophy*, p. 80

There has recently been an increase in the use of the subjunctive in American writing, even in situations in which it has nothing to add to the meaning:

> After the booker had collected his commission, if he *were* on a salary basis, he had to pay protection money to members of the combination.—ROBERT I. CENTER, *The Atlantic Monthly*, Oct. 1937

In all of these constructions a speaker or writer has a choice between the subjunctive and the indicative (which may be an "auxiliary") or an infinitive. In speech and in informal writing some idiom with the indicative would be more usual; in formal writing the subjunctive would probably be used. Professor Fries found that in both standard and vulgate English the subjunctive was found rather seldom, in considerably less than one fifth of the locutions in which it might be used. Actually subjunctives are a trait of style rather than of grammar and are used by writers, consciously or unconsciously, to set their language a little apart from everyday usage rather than for specific meaning.

Students in foreign language courses should remember that very few French and German subjunctives can be satisfactorily translated by an English subjunctive form. They should try to find the natural, idiomatic English way of expressing the idea that is idiomatically expressed by the subjunctive in the language they are translating.

(REFERENCES: The point of view presented in this article will be found in general in Ballard, pp. 12-23; Fowler, article "Subjunctives"; Fries, pp. 103-107; Hall, pp. 311-14; Jespersen, ch. 27; Marckwardt and Walcott, pp. 30, 37, 88, 89; Pooley, pp. 55-59; Thyra J. Bevier, "American Use of the Subjunctive," *American Speech*, 1931, 6: 207-15. A different point of view will be found in Curme, *Syntax*, ch. 20, Kennedy, § 106; C. A. Lloyd, "Is the Subjunctive Dying?" *The English Journal*, 1937, 26: 369-73.)

Submitting manuscript   The conventions of submitting manuscript for publication are simple:

The manuscript should be carefully typed, double spaced, on good paper (*Typewritten copy). Generous margins should be left for editorial operations. Plenty of space should be left around the title, half a page or so. Keep a carbon copy for reference.

The writer's name and address stand in the upper left-hand corner of the first page. The approximate length in words may be put in the upper right-hand corner.

It is not necessary to inclose a letter with the manuscript, since its purpose is obvious, unless there are some useful facts to give, such as the sources of material or suggestions for illustration.

Mail in a comfortable-sized envelope. Short manuscripts can go in 9 inch envelopes, folded twice; those from 4 to 12 pages can go in envelopes about 6x9 inches, folded once; and longer ones in large envelopes, flat. Photographs or drawings should be carefully packed between stiff cardboard, and clearly labeled.

Inclose an envelope large enough to hold the manuscript as it is folded, addressed to yourself, and carrying sufficient postage for its return. The editor will probably want to use it.

Subordinating conjunctions   The most common subordinating conjunctions—words that connect subordinate clauses with the main clauses of sentences—are:

after	*because	since	unless
*although	before	*so	*when
*as	how	*so that	*where
*as if	*if	though	*while
as long as	in order that	*till	why

The relative pronouns (*who, which, that, what*) function also as subordinating conjunctions.

Subordination   Correction: Make the less important of these statements grammatically subordinate to the more important.   *Sub*

Subordinate sentence elements modify the sentence as a whole, the subject, verb, object, or some other important element. They may be single words, or phrases, or clauses; but usually an important phrase (like a *verbid phrase) or subordinate clause is meant in discussing subordination. Subordinate clauses are introduced by the connectives listed in *subordinating conjunctions or by relative pronouns. They are used as nouns, adjectives, or adverbs.

The chief point to remember is that subordination should represent or correspond to a relationship between ideas. The more important ideas should be in main clauses or principal words, the less important in subordinate constructions. The exact connective shows the thought relation to the rest of the sentence.

Problems of subordination are discussed specifically in Chapter 9, "Complex sentences," page 257, and in various articles including *Clauses, *Complex sentences, *Coordination, *Conjunctions, *and.

Substandard English See Chapter 2, "Vulgate English," page 52.

Substantive A substantive is a noun, or a word (pronoun, adjective, infinitive . . .) or a group of words used as a noun. See *Nouns, *Noun clauses.

such As an intensive, *such* is colloquial and informal (It was such a hot day; such nice people). In formal writing the construction would be avoided or completed (Such nice people as they are).

Idiomatic constructions with *such* are:

> There was such a crowd that [not: so that] we couldn't even get to the door.
> The invitation is extended to such non-members as are interested. (*As* is a relative pronoun. A more informal construction would be: The invitation is extended to all non-members who are interested.)
> A good lecturer? There's no such thing. (*No such a thing* is colloquial.)

Various possible constructions with *such* are rarely used and seem somewhat stiff and unidiomatic:

> His condition was such that he could not be moved. (More usual: His condition would not allow him to be moved.)
> Psychologists could probably find various reasons why it is regarded as such. (. . . why it is so regarded.)

As a coordinating conjunction, introducing examples, *such as* has a comma before but not after:

> He was interested in all sorts of outlandish subjects, such as palmistry, numerology, and phrenology.

Suffix A syllable that can be placed after a word or root to make a new word of different meaning or function: *-ize* (*criticize*), *-ish* (*foolish*), *-ful* (*playful*). See *Origin of words § 3a.

Suggestion Making use of the associations, the connotations of words, is called *suggestion*. The words *liberty, immemorial, mystical, butcher, homey,* and thousands of others have acquired associations from their past use that may call to a listener's or reader's mind some feeling or attitude that goes beyond their original core of meaning. Relying on suggestion may be misleading or at least may be a substitute for exactness, but a responsible use of suggestive words adds color and often pleasure and keeps writing from flatness.

For discussion see Chapter 11, "Connotation: The suggestion of words," page 322; *Heightened style.

suit, suite *Suit* is pronounced sōot or sūt; *suite* (a group of attendants, a series of rooms, and so on) is swēt or sōot, sūt. The latter pronunciation is more usual in commercial talk about a set of furniture.

Sunday school Capitalize only the *Sunday* except in names of particular Sunday schools:

Sunday school   the Methodist Sunday School

Superlative of adjectives and adverbs See *Comparison of adjectives and adverbs §§ 2, 4, and 5.

Support paragraphs See Chapter 8, page 220. For order of support in papers, see Chapter 1, page 14.

sure *Sure* is primarily an adjective (sure footing; Are you sure?). As an adverb, *sure* instead of *surely* or equivalent to *certainly* or *yes*, is slangy colloquial (Sure, I'm coming; That sure is fine of you).

swim The principal parts are *swim, swam* or *swum, swum.* "He *swam* half a mile" is more common in writing than "He *swum* half a mile."

Syllabication See *Division of words.

Synecdoche See Chapter 12, "Relationship," page 350.

Synesis (sin′ə sis) In vulgate English and to a great extent in informal English there is a tendency for constructions to follow the *meaning* rather than a custom of *grammar* that might apply. Following the meaning rather than grammatical convention is known as *synesis.* In earlier days, before so much stress had been put on correctness, this construction was pretty common and found in the best places, as in "Then Philip went down to the city of Samaria and preached Christ unto *them*" (Acts 8:5)—where the pronoun's grammatical antecedent is *city* (singular) but the meaning is plural, that is, he preached to the people of the city. A collective noun has a singular verb when the group is meant or a plural verb when the individuals are meant (The team leaves tonight—The team were completely worn out. All of his 160 pounds is bone and muscle). In *these kind of shoes*, the strict grammatical agreement would be *this kind*, but since we are talking about *shoes*, it seems natural to say *these*.

In formal English such locutions are out of place. In vulgate English they are the normal and proper expressions—and should be used in writing much dialog. Between the two extremes of style the problem of agreement is more complicated. The forces of the schools have been set firmly against some of the common idioms for so long that most educated readers will feel they are at least slipshod, even when difficult to spot (as in "one of the most important messages that *has* [for *have*] come out of Spain"). They cannot be objected to on the basis of meaning, because they make the meaning more sure than the more conventional construction. They are to be avoided in formal writing because so many readers will object to them and because a writer ordinarily intends to follow the conventions of grammar as well as make his meaning clear. Often in conspicuously informal writing they fit.

(SEE *Collective nouns, *kind, sort, *Reference of pronouns, *Subject and verb.)

Synonym A synonym is a word that means almost the same as another word. For use of synonyms see Chapter 11, "Synonyms," page 324.

Syntax *Syntax* means the relationship between the words or other locutions in a sentence. Many articles in this *Index* discuss points of syntax, as, for example, *Adjectives in use, *Subject and verb, *Word order.

T (t) as in *type, quote, attach.*
  -Ed is pronounced as t after the sound of *f, k, p,* or *s* in the same syllable: *laughed, fixed, confessed, tipped, picked.* T is silent in *Christmas, often, listen, thistle, mortgage, mustn't,* and many other words, and in ordinary speech in word groups like *sit down* (si doun'). *Ti* is pronounced ch in such words as *question* and sh in such words as *nation, notion.* (Compare *D.)

taboo—tabu *Taboo* is more generally used than *tabu,* except in anthropology. Plural *taboos;* past tense of the verb, *tabooed;* pronounced tə boo'.

Taboo in language A number of words not used in certain circles —many of them not even appearing in dictionaries—are said to be *tabooed*. Communication in the subjects to which they belong is carried on by accepted substitutes. (Compare Chapter 12, "Euphemisms," page 337.)

(REFERENCES: Kennedy, pp. 431, 462-64; Jespersen, *Language*, p. 239; Edwin R. Hunter and Bernice E. Gaines, "Verbal Taboo in a College Community," *American Speech*, 1938, 13: 97-107.)

Tabulations Series of facts can often be more clearly presented in a table systematically arranged in convenient and meaningful columns. Any group of more than three or four numbers should be tabulated (See p. 276 for an example), as should series of short items (See tabulation on page 786 in *Tenses of verbs).

Occasionally in the body of a paper it is convenient to cast a series of parallel statements in a numbered tabulated form. The device should not be overworked, but it is a good way of securing emphasis by display:

The English textbook of the future, to sum up, must recognize the social nature of language, and English in particular, by
1. acknowledging that language is the tool of the social group,
2. granting that utility is the only valid basis for the creation or perpetuity of a language form,
3. pointing out the part each individual speaker plays in the retardation or acceleration of change,
4. regarding the written language in its proper light as the secondary and partial representation of the real language.—ROBERT C. POOLEY, *Grammar and Usage in Textbooks on English*, p. 151

(REFERENCE: University of Chicago Press *Manual of Style*, pp. 158-72.)

Tandem subordination An unhappy series of subordinate clauses, each of which depends on an element in the preceding:

Tandem: He had carefully selected teachers who taught classes that had a slant that was specifically directed toward students who intended to go into business.
Improved: He had carefully selected teachers who slanted their courses toward students intending to go into business [or: toward future businessmen].

Tautology *Tautology* is unprofitable repetition of meaning (the *modern* college student *of today*). (See Chapter 10, "Repetition," page 289.)

taxi The plural of the noun *taxi* is *taxis;* as a verb, the principal parts are *taxi, taxied, taxiing* or *taxying*.

teach See *learn—teach. Principal parts: *teach, taught, taught*.

technic *Technic* (tek′nik) is a variant form of *technique*. It is also used, especially in the plural (*technics*), for *technology*.

Technical English   See *Scientific and technical writing and Chapter 2, "Shoptalk," page 45.

Telegraphic style   "Telegraphic style" refers to writing in which many *function words (especially articles and connectives) are omitted. It suggests also compact constructions and vigorous words. It is not appropriate in general writing but is used in some reference works to save space, in newspaper headlines for vigor (Gang Flees Cops; Find Loot—Ditch Guns, Stolen Cash Near River), and to a certain extent in such styled writing as occurs in *Time*.

Tense **Tenses of verbs**   Correction: Make the tense of this verb conventional in form (§ 1) or consistent with others in the passage (§§ 3, 4).
  1. Tense forms. 2. Indication of time. 3. Sequence of tenses.
  4. Consistent use of tenses.

  1. Tense forms.   Except for the simple present and past tense forms, English verbs show distinctions of time by various phrase combinations, often supported by adverbs ("he is *about* to go" as a future). The following table presents the verb phrases most commonly associated with time distinctions:

		ACTIVE	PASSIVE
PRESENT TENSE		he asks he is asking he does ask	he is asked he is being asked
PAST TENSES	*Past perfect* (Past of some time in the past)	he had asked he had been asking	he had been asked
	Past (A time in the past not extending to the present)	he asked he was asking he did ask	he was asked he was being asked
	Perfect (Past, extending to the present)	he has asked he has been asking	he has been asked
FUTURE TENSES	*Future* (Future, extending from the present)	he will ask he will be asking he is going to ask	he will be asked
	Future perfect (Past from some future time)	he will have asked he will have been asking	he will have been asked

786

"Strong verbs" show a change of vowel in the past tense instead of the *-ed* ending (he rides, he rode) and also in the past participle, usually with the ending *-en* (he has ridden). (See *Principal parts of verbs.)

(REFERENCES: Curme, *Parts of Speech and Accidence*, pp. 241-333; Fries, pp. 59-71, 128-98; Mencken, pp. 427-47; Leah Dennis, "The Progressive Tense: Frequency of Its Use in English," *PMLA*, 1940, 55: 855-65.)

2. Indication of time. The time of a verb is often made more exact by an adverb or by the context:

He had come *Tuesday.*
When Harriet comes, she will be asked to explain all this.

The "progressive phrases" (*is asking, was asking, has been asking* . . .) tend to emphasize the actual activity and are increasingly being used in English.

The present tense is used to make a statement that is generally true, without reference to time:

Oil *floats* on water.
The Captain reminded the ladies that the equator *is* an imaginary line.

With an adverb of time the present may refer to the future (He comes tomorrow). The present may also refer to a statement without specified time. For example, "He comes to us well recommended" may mean that he has come already or that he will come. For the "historical present," sometimes used in vivid narrative of past events, see page 211.

For further details of the future tense see *shall and will.

Participles and infinitives express time in relation to that of the main verb. The present infinitive expresses the same time as the main verb or, often with an adverb, a time in the future:

Our team is playing *to win.*   I hope *to go abroad* next summer.

A past infinitive expresses action prior to that of the main verb:

I am sorry *to have disappointed* you.

A present participle generally refers to the time of the main verb:

Rounding a turn in the road, he came suddenly in full view of the lake.

3. Sequence of tenses. When the verb of a main clause is in the past or past perfect tense, the verb in a subordinate clause is also past:

Frank knew that the Statlers were visiting us.
Frank knew that the Statlers would visit us the following week.

787

The old man wondered whether the train had arrived.

I have never seen Slim when he hadn't [or: *didn't have;* not *hasn't*] a wad of tobacco in his mouth.

A present infinitive is, however, usual after a past verb:

I thought you would have liked to ride [not: to have ridden] in their car.
They intended to stop [not: to have stopped] only an hour in the village.

4. Consistent use of tenses. It confuses a reader to find tenses shifted without definite reason, as in this paragraph:

I *sit* down at my desk early with intentions of spending the next four hours studying. Before many minutes *passed,* I *hear* a great deal of noise down on the floor below me; a water fight *is* in progress. Study *was forgotten* for half an hour, for it *was* quite impossible to concentrate on Spanish in the midst of all this commotion. After things *quiet* down I *begin* studying again, but I *have* hardly *started* when a magazine salesman *comes* into the room, hoping to snare a large sale. After arguing with him for several minutes I finally *got* rid of him.

Shifts of this sort should be carefully avoided.

In single sentences the inconsistency usually comes from carelessness, especially from forgetting the form of the first of two parallel verbs:

Last fall in the Brown game I saw Bill Geyer hit so hard that he was knocked five feet in the air and then land [for: landed] on his head. (The writer forgot the tense of *was knocked.*)

(REFERENCE: Curme, *Syntax,* ch. 18.)

Term paper See Chapter 13, The Reference Paper, page 363.

textbook Now usually written as one word.

th *Th* spells a voiceless sound (th) as in *path* (path), *think* (thingk), and a voiced sound (t̶h̶) as in *paths* (pathz), *the* (thə, thi, th̶ē̶), *bathe* (bāt̶h̶). *Th* is silent in *isthmus* and pronounced *t* in *Thomas* and *thyme.* (See *ye=the.)

than **1. Conjunction.** *Than* as a conjunction introduces the second member of a comparison in which the things compared are unequal:

Nobody was more aware of the need for action than he was.
You will get there earlier than I will.

Than is the idiom after *no sooner:*

He had no sooner opened the door than the flames flared up.

For other comparative idioms with *than* see *Comparison of adjectives and adverbs §§ 1, 3.

2. Preposition. *Than* is often a preposition. Since the clause with *than* is usually verbless (*than he, than I*), it appears rather as a preposition and frequently, especially in colloquial and informal usage, is followed by an accusative:

General: The second was much larger than the first.
Colloquial and informal: You are certainly faster than him.

In the formal *than whom*, it is a preposition:

We admire the power of Jack Kramer, than whom there is no greater tennis player.

(REFERENCE: Jespersen, p. 133.)

3. Confusion with 'then.' *Then* is often carelessly written for *than*. (See *then—than.)

(SEE *different. REFERENCE: Dwight L. Bolinger, "Analogical Correlatives of 'Than,'" *American Speech*, 1946, 21: 199-202.)

that

1. Conjunction. 2. Relative pronoun. 3. Clauses without 'that.' 4. That which. 5. Referring to an idea. 6. 'That' as an adverb.

1. Conjunction. (a) *That* should usually be repeated with each of a series of parallel subordinate clauses:

But he also sees *that* Lafayette was a rigorously honest and honorable man, *that* he had many of the essential talents of the political compromiser, the moderate, and *that* these very talents help explain his failure in the French Revolution.—CRANE BRINTON, *The Saturday Review of Literature*, Dec. 3, 1938

b) *That* should not be repeated within a single clause:

Many people think *that* if an article is advertised by a good joker or a good band [not: that] it is a good product to buy.

2. Relative pronoun. *That* refers to persons or things, *who* usually to persons, *which* usually to things:

The number of men *that* [or *who*] fell within the age limits of the draft was 3,500,000.
He solved in five minutes a problem *that* [or *which*] I had struggled with for five hours.

That more often introduces clauses that are restrictive, *which* usually introduces clauses that are nonrestrictive:

The book *that she selected for her report* [restrictive] was the longest on the list.

The privilege of free speech, *which we hold so dear* [nonrestrictive], is now endangered.

3. Clauses without 'that.' Clauses are often made without the introductory *that*. These constructions are not elliptical (for *that* is not "omitted" or to be "understood") but are a standard shorter idiom. They are general usage in both speech and writing:

He said he would go. *Or:* He said that he would go.
I remembered my mother's birthday fell on March 10. (Or: I remembered that my mother's birthday fell on March 10.)
The first man he met turned out to be Alexander. (Or: The first man that he met turned out to be Alexander.)

The *that* is necessary when the clause comes first (That one could be punished for such a thing had not occurred to him); in appositive clauses after such nouns as *wish, belief, desire* (My hope that he would finish today was not fulfilled); and with anticipatory *it* (It is not true that I promised to pay the whole sum at once), although in short constructions, and in rather colloquial usage it is not needed (It isn't true he likes me better than he does you). *That* is usually needed in the second of two parallel clauses: I had hoped the book would be finished by June and that it would be published by November.

(REFERENCES: Curme, index references; Jespersen, pp. 350-351.)

4. That which. *That which* is formal and archaic for *what:*

He had no clear idea of *what* [not: *that which*] he was trying to say.

5. Referring to an idea. *That* (or *this*) is used to refer to the whole idea of a preceding statement when the reference is clear:

While I was studying, he sometimes turned on the radio. That was annoying, but I didn't object.

If the *that* refers to an idea suggested but not contained in a particular word, the sentence should be revised to make the reference clear:

Vague reference: My uncle is a doctor, and that is the profession I intend to enter.
Exact: My uncle's profession is medicine and that is going to be mine too.

6. 'That' as an adverb. *That* is used colloquially or locally as an adverb:

I am that hungry I could eat shoe leather.
Formal: I am so hungry that I could eat shoe leather.

that is *That is* introduces a statement the equivalent of, or the explanation of, what precedes. It is a formal connective and is best kept to introduce series or complete statements. In such a use it is usually preceded by a semicolon and followed by a comma:

> The men worked continuously for three whole weeks to complete the dam on time; that is, they worked twenty-four hours a day in three shifts, seven days a week.

In briefer constructions, a comma would be more usual, and the *that is* would not be used:

> Formal: They used the safest explosive for the purpose, that is, dynamite
> General: They used the safest explosive for the purpose, dynamite.

(COMPARE *namely and other introductory words.)

the 1. Repetition of the article before the various nouns of a series emphasizes their distinctness:

> The color, *the* fragrance, and *the* beautiful patterns of these flowers make them universal favorites.
> The color, fragrance, and pattern of these flowers are distinctive.

2. In the idiom *the . . . the,* in which the second *the* is an adverb rather than an article, usage is divided over the punctuation. In formal writing a comma is frequently used between the phrases, in general usage not:

> General: The greater one's economic insecurity the greater the tendency to sacrifice spiritual independence.—STUART CHASE, "The Luxury of Integrity," *The Nemesis of American Business*
> Formal: The greater one's economic insecurity, the greater the tendency to sacrifice spiritual independence.

3. Keep *the* with the name of our country: *the* United States.

theater, theatre *Theater* is now the general spelling except in names established some time ago. (See *-er, -re.)

their *Their* is the genitive of *they. Theirs* is the emphatic or absolute form:

> This table is exactly like theirs.

Colloquially *their* is used to refer to the collective indefinite pronouns (*anybody, anyone, everybody, everyone*), though these are singular in form:

> Colloquial: Everybody finally found their hats and coats.
> Written: Everybody finally found his hat and coat.

(SEE *every and its compounds.)

Themes

Themes Although one of the purposes of composition courses is to improve the expression of students, merely putting grammatical sentences end to end is not a sufficient task for college students. The aim of themes, as of other sorts of writing, should be to interest and inform readers. The papers should be of a sort that, done well enough, would be suitable for publication.

The chief difficulty with themes is that their writers forget their possible readers and affect a style that is unnatural to them. They write unnaturally:

> As the early morning sun is slowly breaking through the mist and the roosters are making their way out of hen houses to crow the early hours of day, one might hear the creaking of doors and the sound of padded feet while lying in bed waiting for breakfast. Upon getting out of bed into the chilly morning air and looking out of a window into the farmyard, one could see an elderly, stout gentleman busily working about.

The writers of themes would do well to write simply and directly, like the professional writers quoted in this book. Keeping readers in mind, the class or some other group, is the best way to get over this "theme attitude."

For manuscript form of themes, see "Manuscript form," pages 20-22, and *Typewritten copy.

themselves Compare *himself, *myself.

then *Then* is an adverb of time, often used as a connective (conjunctive adverb). Often the connection between clauses is made closer by using *and then*:

> The next three hours we spent in sightseeing; then we settled down to the business of being delegates to a convention.
> He ate a good meal, and then he took a nap before starting home again.

then—than These words are often carelessly confused in writing. *Then* is an adverb of time, *than* a conjunction in clauses of comparison:

> *Then* the whole crowd went to Louie's.
> I think *The Big Sky* was better *than* any other novel I read last year.

then too is overused as a connective in amateur writing:

> A reader enjoys a fast moving story; then too he may enjoy something that will set him thinking.
> Better: A reader enjoys a fast moving story, but he may also enjoy something that will set him thinking.

Then too is an especially mechanical connective when used between paragraphs.

792

there is, there are   1. *There* and *it* are used as anticipatory subjects, with the real subject following the verb. *There is* is followed by a singular subject (often colloquially by a plural), *there are* by a plural:

There is a size for every need.
There are several ways in which this can be done.

(REFERENCE: Fries, p. 56.)

2. Frequent use of these impersonal constructions tends to give a lack of emphasis:

There was a vague feeling of discontent evident in everyone's manner.
Direct: A vague feeling of discontent was evident in everyone's manner.
There are a good many college students who are easily discouraged.
Direct: A good many college students are easily discouraged.

(SEE *it.)

therefore   *Therefore* is a conjunctive adverb, a rather heavy connective, unnecessarily formal for ordinary writing:

Formal: My experiences in preparatory school had been very unpleasant; therefore I was surprised to find college students and college teachers so agreeable.
General: My experiences in preparatory school had been so unpleasant that I was surprised to find college students and college teachers so agreeable.

therein archaic or formal for *in it, in that respect.*

these kind, these sort   See *kind, sort.

they   *They* is colloquially used as an indefinite pronoun but generally is not so used in writing:

Colloquial: They have had no serious accidents at that crossing for over two years.
Written: There have been no serious accidents . . .
Colloquial: They made the great reflector at Corning.
Written: The great reflector was made at Corning.

thing   *Thing* is often deadwood:

The other thing that I have in mind is going to France.
Improved: I am also thinking of going to France.

The first thing you do is to get a few small twigs burning.
Improved: First you get a few small twigs burning.

this   1. *This*, like *that*, is regularly used to refer to the idea of a preceding clause or sentence:

He had always had his own way at home, and this made him a poor roommate.

The company train their salesmen in their own school. This [More formally: This practice] assures them a group of men with the same sales methods.

2. Used colloquially as a sort of intensified definite article: "This old man went into this restaurant." Such a use is ordinarily out of place in writing.

thou *Thou, thy, thine, thee* are archaic pronouns for the second person, used now only in the formal language of church services. Amateur poets should avoid them except in archaic contexts.

though For use as a conjunction see *although.
Colloquially *though* is used as a word of qualification or hesitation: "I didn't think he would do it, though." This use is less common in writing. If used, it would normally be set off by a comma or commas.

Thwarted subordination Sometimes amateur writers add an *and* or *but* to a construction already sufficiently connected with the rest of the sentence by a subordinating conjunction or a relative pronoun. This has been called "thwarted subordination." It is most commonly found as *and which* and *but which* constructions (*which § 4):

The first semester of the course had used three textbooks, [not: and] which had been continued for the second semester.

Tilde A mark (~) placed over a letter, as in the Spanish *cañon*, represented in English by *ny* (*canyon*).

till, until, ['til] These three words are not distinguishable in meaning. Since *'til* in speech sounds the same as *till* and looks slightly odd on paper, it is rarely used now. Use *till* or *until* according to the stress or the feel of the phrase you want. *Until* is most often used at the beginning of sentences or clauses:

Until he went to college, he never had thought of his speech.
He had never thought of his speech till [or: until] he went to college.

Time In subordinate clauses the various time relationships are indicated by the conjunctions *after, *as, as long as, as often as, as soon as, before, since, *till, until, when, whenever, *while.
(SEE also *Tenses of verbs; *Centuries, *Dates, *Hours.)

Titles of articles, books, etc.
1. **Formal usage.** In most college writing, in most books, and in some periodicals, the titles of books and the names of magazines and newspapers are put in italics (often indicated in manuscript

by underlining). Capitals are used for the first word, for all nouns, pronouns, verbs, adjectives, and adverbs, and for prepositions that stand last or that contain more than five letters:

No Place to Hide	*You Can't Take It with You*
Wit and Its Relation to the Unconscious	*Parts of Speech and Accidence*
The Atlantic Monthly	*The Kansas City Star*

Often the *the* of magazine and newspaper titles is not regarded as a part of the title and so is not capitalized. In some periodicals the name of the city in a newspaper name is not italicized (the Milwaukee *Sentinel*). Usage is divided on this point.

If the official title of a work does not follow these conventions, references to it may use the exact title or standardize it (as, *The Story of a Novel*, which was printed as *the story of a NOVEL*). Library catalogs and some long bibliographies do not use italics and capitalize only first words and proper nouns or adjectives.

Titles of short stories and magazine articles are put in quotation marks when they are used with or near titles of books or names of periodicals. They are often italicized when used without reference to their means of publication, especially in discussion of them as works of literature. Usage is divided on the titles of poems, but academic writing tends to use italics, though the titles of short poems are often in quotation marks.

The words *Preface* and *Introduction* and the titles of chapters in books are capitalized but not italicized or quoted.

(REFERENCE: University of Chicago Press *Manual of Style*, Index references.)

2. Informal usage. In many magazines (*The New Republic*, *The Saturday Evening Post*, for example) and in most newspapers, titles of books and names of periodicals are treated as proper names, capitalized but not quoted or italicized.

In formal papers for college courses and in theses formal usage should be followed; in informal college papers either style may be used, as the instructor prefers.

3. Typed copy. In typed copy that is not going to be printed it is simpler to write titles all in capitals (to save backing up and underlining). This is the common form in publishers' letters.

(SEE ch. 13, "Form of bibliographical entries," p. 378.)

Titles of themes Since titles help interest a reader in a paper, a striking and easily remembered title is an advantage. But strained titles are often ludicrous, and if no good title comes to mind, it is better just to name the subject of the paper as exactly as possible in a few words and let it go at that. As a rule titles that give no clue to the subject, such as *The Moving Finger Writes* or *The Greeks Had a Name for It*, are better avoided. Don't postpone writing a paper (or handing one in) to hunt for a clever title. In published work the title is more often made by the editor than by the writer.

The title is not a part of the paper and the first sentence should not refer to it by a pronoun. Leave a blank line between the title and the beginning of the text.

to 1. The confusion of *to* and *too* in writing is conspicuously care-less and one of the small matters to be watched in revision of papers.

2. It is generally understood that in expressions like "pages 56 to 89" the last numbered unit is included. Hours are an exception, as in 1 to 3 p.m. *Up to* or *till* exclude the last unit.

today 1. *Today* (like *tonight* and *tomorrow*) is rarely hyphened now except by people who learned to spell when the hyphen was generally used. Recent dictionaries prefer *today*.

2. *Today*, *of today* are often deadwood, adding nothing to the meaning of a statement already placed in the present:

> Economic conditions [of today] are more unsettled than they have been for two generations.

too When *too* in the sense of *also* comes within a construction it is usually set off by commas, but in informal writing it usually is not when it comes at the end:

> "I, too, have become a philosopher," she said sadly.—IRWIN EDMAN, *Philosopher's Holiday*, p. 74
> I'm going too. (More formal: I'm going, too.)

Topic outline See *Outline form § 1b.

Topic sentences See Chapter 7, "Focusing statements," page 185.

toward—towards These words are identical in meaning. *Toward* is slightly more characteristic of formal usage, perhaps for reasons of euphony.

Trans **Transitions between paragraphs** Correction: Make the relation between the thought of these two paragraphs obvious to a reader.

For discussion of transitions see Chapter 7, "Transitions between paragraphs," page 193.

Transitive and intransitive verbs A verb is transitive when it is used with an object to complete its meaning (They fought the whole gang). A verb is intransitive when it does not have an object, when the recipient of the action is not named (The choir will sing; They hid in the tall grass). Many verbs are used in both constructions, usually with different meanings (He wrote two books [transitive]; She cannot write [intransitive]). Dictionaries note whether a verb is typically used transitively or intransitively, and in what senses. *Lie* and *sit* are intransitive, *lay and *set are transitive. *Linking verbs (*be, become, taste* . . .) are regarded as intransitive.

(REFERENCE: Curme, *Parts of Speech*, ch. 4.)

Transpose Correction: Transpose, that is, reverse the order of the elements marked for greater clearness or a more emphatic order. *Tr*

A change in the order of sentences or paragraphs in copy can be shown by using numbers in the margin opposite the elements to be changed, or by circling and drawing arrows.

The transposition of letters is shown by a curved line:

Connec̸t̸icut   rec̸i̸eve

Triads Parallel series of three units are so common in writing, especially in formal writing, that they form a definite trait of style. Such a series is called a triad:

> To delight in war is a merit in the soldier, a dangerous quality in the captain, and a positive crime in the statesman.—GEORGE SANTAYANA, *Reason in Society*, p. 84

Trite Correction: Replace the trite expression with one that is *Trite* simpler and fresher.

Trite words are usually worn out figures of speech or phrases: *the picture of health, the order of the day* (outside an army post), *reign supreme, from the face of the earth, crack of dawn.* Such expressions weigh down a style and are a mark of amateur writing or of insensitiveness to words.

For fuller discussion and examples see Chapter 12, "Trite words," page 333.

try and—try to The formal idiom is *try to* (Try to get your work done before five o'clock). The general idiom is *try and* (try and do it; Try and get your work done before five o'clock). The general idiom is old and its users include Thackeray and Matthew Arnold.

(SEE Hall, p. 309.)

Type Typography is a complex technical field, but many people make a hobby of it, and most writers have some curiosity about it. A few of the fundamental facts about type are given here:

1. Type faces. There are many different type faces, each with its characteristic appearance. Every type face is made in many standard sizes and style variations. Some popular faces for book and periodical use are set here in ten point size:

This type face is Caslon

This type face is Bodoni

This type face is Garamond

This type face is Baskerville

This type face is Granjon

This *Guide-Index* is set in the following type faces and sizes:

The text is set in 11 point Granjon.

The quotations are set in 9 point Granjon.

The footnotes and references are set in 8 point Granjon.

The entry words are set in 11 point Spartan bold.

The subheads are set in 11 point Granjon bold.

Additional information about the type used in this book can be found on the last printed page.

2. Type style variations. A given face and size of type is available in several standard variations of style. The most common are:

Name and example	Abbreviation	Indicated in manuscript by:
ROMAN CAPITALS	Caps.	Three lines underneath
roman lower case	l. c.	Unmarked manuscript
ROMAN SMALL CAPITALS	s. c.	Two lines underneath
ITALIC CAPITALS	Ital. Caps.	One line underneath and labeled "all caps"
italic lower case	ital.	One line underneath
BOLD FACE CAPITALS	b. f. caps.	Wavy line underneath and labeled "all caps"
bold face lower case	b. f.	Wavy line underneath

There are, of course, combinations of the above styles: Caps and lower case, CAPS AND SMALL CAPS, *Italic Caps and lower case*, **Bold Face Caps and lower case.**

3. Type measurement. Type is measured in *points*, a point equaling 1/72 of an inch. A square unit of type of any size is an *em.* Space is usually measured in *pica* (12 point) *ems* (1/6 of an inch).

This line is set in six point type.

This line is set in ten point type.

This line is set in fourteen point type.

(See *Proofreading. References: The University of Chicago Press *Manual of Style* contains much information about type, as do other stylebooks and books on journalism, advertising, and typography.)

type of The general idiom *type of* is being shortened colloquially by omitting the *of:* this type letter. Although the construction is beginning to appear in print, general usage should still be followed: this type of letter (and not: this type of *a* letter).

Typewritten copy Manuscript for a printer, business letters and reports, and impersonal writing should be typed. In the United States we are so accustomed to typescript (and our handwriting is on the whole so illegible) that it can be used in a good deal of personal correspondence. There is an added courtesy in longhand, and "social correspondence" should usually be handwritten. Students believe they receive better grades on course papers that are typed. The ease of reading typescript may have this result when the instructor is reading principally for content, but in English compositions that advantage may be offset in part by the clearness with which the errors stand out.

In general, typewritten copy follows the customs of good manuscript but some points need special emphasis. Use only one side of the sheet, leave wide margins (especially at the right side, since letters cannot be compressed as in longhand), and keep type clean and the ribbon in good ink. Ordinarily use a black ribbon.

Regular manuscript should be double spaced. Personal writing may be single spaced and for economy single space is generally used in business writing. If single spaced, the line should be kept fairly short to make the reading easier. Full, crowded pages are forbidding reading. In typing first drafts, leave plenty of space for revision, perhaps using triple space between lines and extra space between paragraphs.

In single spaced typing, use double space between paragraphs. For double spaced typing, make a triple space between paragraphs if you wish an open appearance or special emphasis on the paragraphs. Indent paragraph first lines from five to eight spaces.

Long quotations may be indicated in double spaced copy by indenting the number of spaces used for paragraphs and single spacing the quoted matter. No quotation marks are used with this style.

The standard typewriter keyboard has no symbol for the figure 1. Use the small l (not I). For a dash use two hyphens not spaced away from the words on each side. Use space after all other punctuation marks.

Transposed letters should be erased and retyped or corrected by the proofreader's symbol. See *Proofreading. Strikeovers are often hard to read. A few mistakes can be corrected in ink, but if there are so many that the page will look messy it should be retyped. (SEE ch. 1, "Preparing the manuscript," p. 20.)

U 1. There are two "long u" sounds: (o͞o) as in *rule* (ro͞ol), *move* (mo͞ov), *lose* (lo͞oz), *booby* (bo͞o′bi), *hoodoo* (ho͞o′do͞o); and (ū), a diphthong beginning with a *y* sound and ending with o͞o, as in *use* (ūs or ūz), *few* (fū), *cute* (kūt), *beauty* (bū′ti), *you* (ū).

After *t, d, n, s, st* usage is divided between these two sounds: *tune* (tūn, to͞on), *duty* (dū′ti, do͞o′ti), *news* (nūz, no͞oz), *stew* (stū, sto͞o). The o͞o sound is frequent and is increasing among educated speakers in spite of widespread prejudice against it. (See Knott and Kenyon, § 109 and their entries on particular words of this type.)

2. There are two "short *u*" sounds: (u) as in *cup* (kup), *fun* (fun), *under* (un′dər), *son* (sun), *love* (luv), *come* (kum), *trouble* (trub′əl), *does* (duz), *other* (uth′ər); and (oo) as in *full* (fool), *pull* (pool), *wood* (wood), *woman* (woom′ən).

3. *U* as in *burn* and *curl* is represented by û (bûrn, kûrl).

An unpronounced *u* is sometimes spelled after *g*, as in *guard*.

un- (Negative prefix) See *in-, un-.

***Und* Underlining** Correction: In longhand and typewritten copy underline words and passages to correspond to the conventions of using italic type.

These conventions are of great importance in formal manuscript and in material to be printed. Newspapers have generally abandoned italics but most magazines and books use them, and in academic writing—course papers, articles in the learned journals, monographs, dissertations, reference books—rather strict conventions are still followed. (See Chapter 5, "Underlining for italics," page 150.)

Underlining is used:

1. To indicate titles of books and periodicals. The complete title should be underlined:

```
I like Babbitt and Arrowsmith the best.
He took Time and The Reader's Digest.
```

For details of this use see *Titles of articles, books, etc. and Chapter 13, "Form of bibliographical entries," page 378. Compare *Ships' names.

(REFERENCE: University of Chicago Press *Manual of Style*, pp. 43-50.)

2. For emphasis. Words that would be heavily stressed if spoken may be underlined:

```
He was the man that night.
```

Any word a writer wishes to emphasize may be underlined (italicized in print), but this is a rather mechanical form of emphasis and loses its force if overused. Whole sentences, except in textbooks and manuals, are better not underlined, since there are more intelligent ways of securing emphasis. As Fowler (p. 305) put it: "To italicize whole sentences or large parts of them as a guarantee that some portion of what one has written is really worth attending to is a miserable confession that the rest is negligible."

(SEE *Emphasis § 7, *Schoolgirl style.)

3. To mark words and locutions considered not for their meaning but as words, a common use of underlining in this and all books on language:

If we take such a sentence as *I am hungry*, neither a grammarian nor a logician would have any difficulty in pointing out the predicate, though one would say that it was *am hungry* and the other that it was simply *hungry.*— P. B. BALLARD, *Thought and Language*, p. 88

4. To mark foreign words:

But good clothes were a *sine qua non.*

(SEE *Foreign words in English.)

Understatement Understatement is a figure of speech, the opposite of exaggeration. See Chapter 12, page 351.

unique In strict formal usage *unique* means "single, sole, unequaled," and consequently cannot be compared. In informal usage, like so many words of absolute meaning, it has become somewhat generalized to mean an emphatic *rare*, and is sometimes found compared with *more* or *most*:

. . . the more unique his nature, the more peculiarly his own will be the colouring of his language.—OTTO JESPERSEN, *Mankind, Nation and Individual from a Linguistic Point of View*, p. 204

United States We live in *the* United States. The temptation to drop *the* is greatest when *United States* is forced to do duty as an adjective: Europe needs the money from United States imports. In such a case it is better to use *American* or *of the United States*. (See *American.)

Unity Unity is a by-product of clear thinking. It is a relative quality. Gross disregard of unity, including material that is quite unrelated to a paragraph or to a paper or that distracts from its main point, can be easily discovered by a reader. But genuine unity is to be judged in the light of the writer's purpose. Any statement that he can build into his discussion, that he can relate to his subject, will be appropriate. The test of unity is found not in any general principles that can be applied in every situation but in appropriateness to the writer's view of his material and his consistent carrying out of his purpose.

Various matters related to unity are discussed in Chapter 7, Writing Paragraphs, Chapter 8, Kinds and Qualities of Paragraphs, and in Chapter 9, Sentence Form.

unquote is used orally to indicate the end of a quotation.

until See *till, until.

up *Up* is a member of many typical *verb-adverb combinations in general use (give up, grow up, sit up, use up). Colloquially it is an intensive in a number of others to which it contributes no new element of meaning (divide up, fill up, raise up, join up). The latter are appropriate in informal writing but are usually avoided in formal.

Upside-down subordination Putting the main idea in a phrase or subordinate clause instead of in the main clause is sometimes called "upside-down subordination."

Upside-down: When the lightning struck the barn with a blinding flash, she had just finished dusting the hall table.
Accurate: Just as she had finished dusting the hall table, lightning struck the barn with a blinding flash.

(SEE ch. 9, "Compound sentences," "Complex sentences," pp. 251, 257.)

Usage Most of this book discusses matters of English usage. For general principles, see Chapters 2 and 3.

used to The spelling *use to* represents what we say, but should be written *used to*.

utilize is frequently put for the simpler *use*. It means specifically "put to use."

V

(v) as in *very* (ver'i), *vivid* (viv'id), *save* (sāv), *Stephen* (stē'vən), *of* (ov).

Varieties of English For variations in English usage due to time, place, and social level see Chapter 2.

Variety Variety in expression comes principally from an active and natural way of writing, and conscious effort can do little but remove the monotonous passages that sometimes occur in tired or inattentive composition. Just keep in mind that if a passage seems flat and monotonous to the writer, it will probably be even more displeasing to anyone else.

Phases of variety in writing are treated in the following places in this book:

In material and development: A fresh and convincing treatment of a subject will usually show variety in interest and in methods of development. See Chapters 7 and 8, pages 169, 209, especially the description of different sorts of paragraphs in Chapter 8.

In sentences: Sentences can be revised in the interest of variety by seeing that they vary in length and movement, that they begin with differing first elements, and that there are not long series of simple or compound sentences of the same pattern. See Chapters 9 and 10, pages 237, 271, especially "Variety in sentence movement," page 278, "Compound sentences," page 251, and "Complex sentences," page 257.

In words: Although exactness is more important than variety in words, sometimes conscious attention in revision can add to their variety and at the same time increase their accuracy. See Chapter 11, The Meaning of Words, page 303, Chapter 12, Qualities of Words, page 331, Chapter 10, "Repetition," page 289.

varsity as the name of the first team of a college or university is in the dictionaries and needs no apostrophe or apologetic quotation marks.

vase Pronounced vās, or much less often vāz. The fad of affecting the British väz has about passed.

Verb-adverb combinations In "I looked up at the top of the tree," the verb *look* is used in its ordinary sense and is modified by the adverb *up*. In "I looked up the word in the dictionary," *looked up* is a verb meaning "investigated," a meaning not explained by a literal use of the two words. Similarly a man may *break out* (literally) of jail, or *break out* with measles; he can *stand by* a certain tree, or *stand by* as a radio listener; he can *look after* a departing car, or *look after* the children. In each of these pairs of expressions, the first has a verb modified by an adverb in its ordinary meaning, and the second is really a different verb, with a meaning of its own, composed of the verb and the adverb combined.

Besides these few samples there are hundreds of such verb-adverb combinations in use, most of them one-syllabled verbs with adverbs like *about, around, at, by, down, for, in, out, through, to, up, with*. They are used most naturally in the informal and colloquial level of the language, where they often give an emphatic rhythm differing from the more formal *investigate, sacrifice (give up), surrender (give up)*. This pattern is now the most active way of forming new verbs in English.

(SEE ch. 4, "Verb-adverb combinations," p. 103; Prepositions § 3b. REFERENCE: Kennedy, pp. 297-303.)

verbal See *oral, verbal.

Verbal nouns See *Gerunds.

Verbals The parts of a verb that function as nouns or adjectives are grouped as *verbals*. *Gerunds* (or verbal nouns) are used as nouns (though they may still have a subject or object), *participles* are used as adjectives, and *infinitives* are used as adjectives or nouns:

Gerunds: *Swimming* is better exercise than *rowing*. *Having been invited* pleased him enormously.
Infinitives: His only ambition was *to pass*. It was too good *to last*. *To have asked* for more would have wrecked the whole conference. He had plenty of money *to spend*.
Participles: He reached the float, *swimming* as easily as before he had been hurt. *Asked* to take a part, he refused at first but finally accepted. *Having been invited*, he began to make plans.

For the various uses of verbals see *Gerunds, *Infinitives, and *Participles.

Verbid In this book we are keeping the term *verbal* for gerunds, infinitives, and participles when they are used simply as nouns or

adjectives and are calling them *verbids* when they are used with some
verbal characteristics, such as taking an object:

> They had tried four times *to get him up.*
> This policy, *covering your household goods,* expires September 18.
> *Running a motel* wasn't as simple as they had expected.

These verbid constructions are regarded as phrases but in several
respects behave more like clauses and raise some questions of grammar, as discussed in Chapter 4, "Verbid phrases," page 112.
(SEE Jespersen, *Philosophy,* p. 87; Aiken, pp. 204-6.)

Verbless sentences See Chapter 9, "Verbless sentences," page 260.
and *Fragmentary sentence.

Verbs

1. Tense. 2. Verbals. 3. Voice. 4. Mood. 5. Transitive-intransitive
use. 6. Syntax of verbs.

Although verbs in English are greatly simplified from what they
formerly were, they remain the most complex of the parts of speech.
In meaning, verbs indicate action (*fight, talk, think, manufacture*),
condition (*feel, sleep, wait*), or process (*become, change, grow*)—
though placing a word in any of these categories is hardly worth
arguing about. In form, verbs may indicate person, number, tense,
voice, and mood. Such special forms in English have been reduced
typically to four (e.g: *ask, asks, asking, asked*), the other relations
being shown by phrases in standard patterns (*will ask, has been
asked*). In function, verbs (except the "verbals") make a predication, form the typical clause or sentence.

The following topics are conventionally treated in a discussion
of English verbs. They are presented more fully in the *Index* articles
indicated.

1. **Tense.** A verb form is one of the means of indicating the time
in a statement: Present, *is asking* (*asks, does ask*); past, *asked* (*did
ask, was asking*); perfect, *has asked;* past perfect, *had asked;* future,
will ask; future perfect, *will have asked;* with some other alternative
phrases and comparable expressions for the passive (*is being asked,*
etc.).

(SEE *Tenses of verbs, *Principal parts of verbs, *Auxiliary verb, and articles on particular verbs like *be, *do, *shall—will, should—would.)

2. **Verbals.** Verbals are used as parts of phrasal verbs (will *ask,*
had *asked*), or as adjectives (a *coming* man, a *locked* door), or as
nouns (*To sleep* was his only wish, *Swimming* was his favorite
sport), rather than as verbs of full predication making clauses or
sentences. These forms frequently have subjects (*Her playing was*

reckless, We wanted *him* to go) or objects (He tried to force *the door*, Loading *the car* was a hard job, Having slammed *the door*, he walked away with apparent poise).

(SEE *Gerunds, *Infinitives, *Participles.)

3. Voice. Constructions in which the subject is the actor are in the active voice (He *asked* for an extension of time); those in which the subject is "acted upon" are in the passive voice (They *were asked* to go faster). Since these various forms allow for different emphases on the subject and object in sentences, they are important for accurate statement and for stylistic emphasis.

For forms see *Tenses of verbs, and for use *Voice, and for the overuse of the passive, *Passive verbs.

4. Mood. The basic mood is the indicative, in which statements are made and questions asked. The forms of the indicative are given in *Tenses of verbs. Some languages have additional inflections that show the speaker's attitude toward his statement, but English shows only vestiges of these.

Instead of an imperative mood, for commands and emphatic requests, English uses the basic (infinitive) verb form, *ask*, or the phrases *be asking* or *do ask*. These are construed as active voice and present tense, though obviously a present extending into the future. See *Commands and requests.

The debate over the subjunctive mood is discussed in the article *Subjunctives. The only identifiable subjunctive forms are in the verb *be* and in the third person singular present of other verbs: Present—*he ask*, past—*he were asking*, and in the passive *he were being asked* or *he were asked*. The indicative forms would be used in most conditions, and in most other constructions except a few with *that* (I suggest that he *take* the early train). The shades of meaning conveyed by subjunctives in many languages are in English expressed by verb phrases with *may, might, must, can, should*, and so on. This allows for a more accurate statement of the various shades of meaning.

(SEE *Subjunctives, *Auxiliary verb, *Conditions.)

5. Transitive-intransitive use. A verb that is used with an object is said to be *transitive* (He washed the car) and without an object, intransitive (He hadn't washed for two days). This is a quality of the construction rather than of the verb. Many verbs in English are used both ways, usually with some distinction in meaning. Linking verbs, which take a complement, are regarded as intransitive.

(SEE *Transitive and intransitive verbs, *Objects, *Linking verbs, *Predicate adjective, Predicate noun.)

6. Syntax of verbs. Since verbs enter into so many constructions, their status and relations with other words are discussed in a number of entries in this book. Besides treatment in Chapter 9, Sentence Form, page 237, and Chapter 4, Problems in English Grammar, page 91, and in articles on particular verbs (such as *be, *do, *can—may, could—might, *get, *shall—will, should—would), the following entries are concerned principally with the use of verbs in speaking and writing:

*Absolute phrases	*Misrelated modifiers
*Clauses	*Objects
*Collective nouns	*Participles
*Commands and requests	*Passive verbs
*Conditions	*Predicate adjective, Predicate noun
*Fragmentary sentence	*Split infinitives
*Gerunds	*Subject and verb
*Infinitives	*Tenses of verbs
*Linking verbs	*Voice

(REFERENCES: Curme, Jespersen, and all grammars treat verbs; see especially Fries, ch 8, The Uses of Function Words: With Verbs. SEE ch. 4, "Verbs," p. 100.)

Vernacular *Vernacular* formerly referred to the native, spoken language—as opposed to the literary languages of Latin or Norman French or the language of other conquerors. It now means colloquial and vulgate English, the native homely, spoken language as contrasted with formal or literary English.

Verse A full line or more of verse quoted in a paper should be lined off and written exactly as it is in the original. It should be indented from the left margin and, if very short, far enough not to leave a conspicuous blank at its right. No quotation marks are used.

Verse form The form of a line of verse is described by telling the arrangement of the stressed syllables (the kind of "foot"), the length of the line (the number of feet), and any other qualities of movement or variation from the typical movement that it shows. This article presents the vocabulary and an outline of the facts necessary for describing verse form.

The feet:

Iambic x / (An iamb)
Trochaic / x (A trochee)
Anapestic x x / (An anapest)
Dactylic / x x (A dactyl)
Spondaic / / (A spondee)

The length of lines:

Dimeter: Two feet
Trimeter: Three feet
Tetrameter: Four feet
Pentameter: Five feet
Hexameter: Six feet

Other facts:

A line is *end-stopped* if its end corresponds with a distinct sense pause, either the end of a sentence or of a major sentence element; it is *run-on* when the construction is carried over the end of the line.

Alexandrine: A line containing six iambic feet

Anacrusis: An extra unstressed syllable at the beginning of a line

Catalexis: The dropping of the final unstressed syllable

Feminine ending: An extra unstressed syllable at the end

Refrain: A line repeated, typically at the end of each stanza of a poem

A *cesura* (*caesura*) is a rhythmic pause within a line.

Two successive lines rhyming are a *couplet.*

A four-line stanza is a *quatrain,* which may have any rhyme scheme: abab, abba; an iambic tetrameter quatrain rhyming abcb is the *ballad stanza.*

More complex stanza forms (sonnet, ode, ballade, and so on) are described in books on literature and poetry.

Blank verse is unrhymed iambic pentameter. *Free verse* is verse of varied length lines with a flexible movement, usually unrhymed.

Examples of scansion:

Iambic pentameter (feminine ending):

> x / x / x / x / x / x
> A thing of beauty is a joy forever

Anapestic tetrameter:

> x x / x x / x x / x x /
> There are brains, though they moulder, that dream in the tomb

Trochaic tetrameter (catalectic), a couplet:

> / x / x / x /
> Souls of poets dead and gone,
> / x / x x / x /
> What Elysium have ye known,

These examples show that scansion tells the typical physical characteristic of verse but does not define the rhythm, which is far more important.

(REFERENCE: For the more important qualities of poetry, such as imagery, tone, color, rhythm (not to mention meaning), see books on poetry and literature.)

vertebra The plural is either *vertebrae* (vûr′tə brē) or *vertebras,* with *vertebrae* still the more common.

very 1. **'Very' as an intensive.** *Very* has been so overused that it is of doubtful value as an intensive. A writer should make sure that it really adds to the meaning of his phrase.

The Emporia Gazette once described its war upon *very* this way:

"If you feel you must write 'very,' write 'damn.'" So when the urge for emphasis is on him, the reporter writes "It was a damn fine victory. I am damn tired but damn well—and damn excited." Then, because it is the Emporia (Kan.) Gazette, the copy desk deletes the profanity and the quotation reads: "It was a fine victory. I am tired but well—and excited." That's how the Gazette attains its restrained, simple, and forceful style. Very simple.

2. 'Very' and past participles. In formal English many people will not use *very* with a past participle (He was very excited)— because by rights *very* is an intensive, supposedly marking a high degree of a *quality*, as in *very happy*, and the verb function of the participle denotes an action rather than a quality. The formal locution would be: "He was *very much* excited."

This distinction, since it is based purely on grammatical reasoning, is too subtle for users of colloquial and informal English, who use *very* to modify such participles without any qualms (I shall be very pleased to come; We shall be very delighted to have you).

When the President and the trustees finally decided to allow the Psychology Department to sponsor a clinic, Dr. Bonham was very elated.—JAMES REID PARKER, *Academic Procession*, p. 13

viewpoint A natural and economical substitute for the clumsy *point of view*. It is not stigmatized in the dictionaries.

Before we condemn him for affectation and distortion we must realize his viewpoint.—E. M. FORSTER, *Aspects of the Novel*, p. 182

viz. *Viz.* is abbreviation of the Latin *videlicet* [vi del'ə sit], to wit, namely. *Viz.* exists only in the language of rather formal documents or reference works. It is usually read "namely."

Vocabulary See Chapter 11, page 303, especially "The supply of words," page 304, and "Increasing your vocabulary," page 307.

Vocative See *Direct address.

Voice

1. Definition and forms. 2. Use of active verbs. 3. Use of passive verbs. 4. Overuse of the passive.

1. Definition and forms. When the subject of a verb is the doer of the action or is in the condition named by its verb, the verb is said to be in the active voice:

The congregation *sang* "Abide with Me."
They *will go* swimming.   Our side *had been winning*.
Jimmy's father *gave* him a car.   We *rested* an hour.

When the subject of a verb receives the action, the verb is in the passive voice:

> "Abide with Me" *was sung* by the congregation.
> Jimmy *was given* a car by his father.
> The pit *was dug* fully eight feet deep.
> They *had been caught.*

The passive form is usually a form of the verb *be* and a past participle:

	Active	Passive
Present:	he (is asking) asks	he is asked (is being asked)
Future:	he will ask	he will be asked
Perfect:	he has asked	he has been asked
Infinitives:	to ask, to have asked	to be asked, to have been asked
Participles:	asking, having asked	being asked, asked

Get and *become* and other verbs are used to form a passive, especially in colloquial English:

> If he should get elected, we'd be lost.
> Our house is getting painted.

These different expressions of the verb give considerable flexibility in sentence word order. They allow emphasis by position of the thing that is more important to the speaker, or more often merely allow the speaker to approach the statement from the viewpoint of his thinking about it (the congregation or the hymn, for example, in the sentences above). The construction in English is more important as a matter of style than of grammar and is one of the devices that make it possible for one's expression to come close to his process of thought.

2. Use of active verbs. Active verbs are more common than passive because we are accustomed to the actor-action-goal pattern of expression. In the preceding paragraph, for example, the seven finite verbs (*give, allow, is, allow, is, is, make*) and the two infinitives (*to approach, to come*) are active.

3. Use of passive verbs. Passive verbs may be less frequent, but they have several important uses.

The recipient of the action, the goal, may be more important, in the writer's mind, than the doer:

> The well *was drilled* in solid rock.
> Our house *was painted* last year.

In indefinite statements the passive is often used when the doers may not be known or are not to be named in the statement:

Much *has been written* on both sides.

The passive allows various degrees of emphasis by placing the name of the act or of the doer at the end:

Our house *is being painted*. (Active: They *are painting* our house.)
Our house *was painted* by Joe Mead and his brother. (Active: Joe Mead and his brother *painted* our house.)
"Abide with Me" was sung by the choir [that is, not by the congregation].

Sometimes the passive shows a change in the relation between subject and verb (though the shift should not be made within a sentence unless the action is continuous):

We *drove* [active] there and *were taken out* [passive] in a dory.

For discussion of the object of a passive verb, see *Objects § 1b.
4. Overuse of the passive. For the objectionable use of passive verbs when active would be more effective, see *Passive verbs.
(REFERENCES: Curme, *Syntax*, pp. 102-103; Fries, pp. 188-93; Jespersen, ch. 12.)

Voiced sounds In voiced sounds the vocal cords vibrate, as in the vowels and *b, d, g, v, z, zh,* and *th* (th̶). *P, t, k, f, s, sh,* and *th* (th) are voiceless sounds corresponding to the voiced consonants.

Some nouns and verbs are distinguished by voicing of the consonant in the verb: *use* (noun, ūs—verb, ūz), *proof—prove* (noun, pro͞of—verb, pro͞ov), *grief—grieve* (grēf—grēv).

A few spelling errors seem to be caused by a confusion between voicing and non-voicing, as *significance* (-kəns) often appears as *signifigance* (-gəns).

Vowels See *Consonants and articles on the separate vowels, *A, *E, *I, *O, *U.

Vulgate English Correction: Change the vulgate word or form or idiom to one appropriate to educated usage. *Vulg*

For discussion of uneducated or "substandard" English see Chapter 2, "Vulgate English," page 52.

W (w) as in *wild* (wīld), *twinkle* (twing′kəl), *quick* (kwik), *choir* (kwīr). W is silent in *write* (rīt), *two* (to͞o), *sword* (sōrd), and other words, and spoken though not spelled in *one* (wun), *once* (wuns).

wake   English is oversupplied with verbs for waking from sleep (intransitive) and waking someone else from sleep (transitive). Each is used in both senses:

> *awake* (*awaked*, *awaked* or *awoke*, *awoke*). Rather formal; more commonly used intransitively (I awoke).
> *awaken* (*awakened*, *awakened*). Formal.
> *wake* (*waked* or *woke*, *waked* or *woke* [*woken*]). More widely used than the preceding.
> *waken* (*wakened*, *wakened*). Less common than *wake*.

The usual solution is the *verb-adverb combination *wake up* (*waked* or *woke up*):

> She waked up (woke up) at eleven. She waked (woke) me up at six.

want   The general idiom with *want* has an infinitive:

> General: I want you to get all you can from the year's work.
> Local: I want for you to get all you can from the year's work.
> Local: I want that you should get all you can from the year's work.

Want is colloquial for *ought, had better:* You want to review all the notes if you're going to pass his exam.

In the sense of *lack* or *need*, *want* is formal and suggests British usage: The letter, though clear, wants correcting.

The colloquial *want in*, *want out* without a complementary verb (The dog wants out) seems to be of Scotch rather than German origin and is widely used in the United States. (See Albert H. Marckwardt, "*Want* with Ellipsis of Verbs of Action," *American Speech*, 1948, 23:3-9.)

way, ways   *Way* is colloquially and informally used for *away* (way over across the valley). *Way* is used in a number of colloquial idioms (*in a bad way, out our way*, I don't see how she can act *the way* she does).

Ways is locally used for *way* in expressions like *a little ways* down the road.

we   1. Indefinite we. *We* is frequently used as an indefinite pronoun in expressions like *We find*, *We sometimes feel*, to avoid passive and impersonal constructions. (See *Reference of pronouns § 3.)

2. Editorial we. In editorial columns and in some other regular departments of periodicals, like "The Talk of the Town" in *The New Yorker*, the writer refers to himself as *we*. In some instances the *we* refers to an editorial board that determines the opinions expressed but more often it is a convention. It is less used than formerly.

The usage has passed into familiar and informal writing, especially of a light tone. Used merely to avoid *I*, *we* is usually conspicuous and to be avoided. (See *I § 2.)

well See *good—well.

wh is the English spelling for the sounds of *hw*: *what* (hwot or hwut), *when* (hwen), *wheel* (hwēl), *whether* (hweth′ər), *why* (hwī). In *who* (hōō), *whole* (hōl, hul), *whoop* (hōōp), and so on, *wh* represents h or w.

Other words spelled with *wh* are frequently pronounced with w: *white* (wīt), *whether* (weth′ər), *why* (wī). The practice seems to be increasing in the United States and is recognized in Knott and Kenyon. See that book, page xliv; Robertson, page 227; *Oxford English Dictionary*, *wh*.

when Most handbooks warn against statements like "Welding is when two pieces of metal are heated and made into one." The reason given is that it is illogical or ungrammatical to equate an "adverbial clause" with a noun. This reasoning is fallacious because a clause cannot be classified solely by its introductory word. *When* (and *where*) clauses are frequently used (1) in noun constructions, as in "Do you have any way of knowing *when she will come?*" in which the *when* clause is the object of *knowing*, and (2) as adjectives, as in "There comes a time *when a man has to be careful of his diet*," in which the clause modifies *time*.

The objection to the construction is stylistic rather than grammatical and comes from the overuse of *when* clauses in amateurish definitions (Communism is when all property is owned by all the people together or by the state). The more formal pattern would be: Communism is a system in which all property is owned by all the people together or by the state.

The construction, then, is to be discouraged rather than forbidden.

(REFERENCES: Fries, pp. 233-34; Marckwardt and Walcott, p. 115; Russell Thomas, *College English*, 1949, 10: 406-8. Compare *reason is because.)

when, as, and if Securities are advertised "when, as, and if issued," and the phrase *when and if* or *if and when* is used in talking about goods whose future is uncertain. It should not be used when the matter is certain, or in non-business contexts except when appropriate to the tone.

where *Where* clauses frequently are used as adjectives, most commonly where some notion of place is involved:

General: This is the place where the trucks stop.
General: He wants a job where he will be with people.
More formal: He wants a job in which he will be with people.

Where clauses in definitions are subject to the same objections as *when* clauses (see *when); that is, they frequently sound amateurish:

Amateurish: Etching is where you cut lines in a copper plate and then print from them.
General: Etching is the process of cutting lines in a copper plate and then printing from it.

(REFERENCES: Fries, pp. 234-35; Marckwardt and Walcott, p. 115.)

whether   *Whether* is used in indirect questions: He asked whether you could come.

In statements *whether* is used with *or* to indicate two alternatives: They have never decided whether he committed suicide or was murdered.

In formal usage *or not* is frequently used with *whether* to indicate a second alternative when it is simply the negative of the one stated: They have never decided whether or not he was murdered. But in informal usage *or not* is frequently omitted (They have never decided whether he was murdered), and should not be used if it will make an awkward statement:

General: Whether or not this was the best plan, they went ahead. *Or:* Whether this was the best plan or not, they went ahead.
General: It is a sorry state when pupils don't know whether or not to believe their teachers.
Clumsy: It is a sorry state when pupils don't know whether to believe their teachers or not [Omit the *or not*].

(REFERENCE: Fries, pp. 207, 217. See *if, § 2, *Conditions.)

which   1. *Which* refers to things and to groups of people regarded impersonally (The legislature which passed the act . . .).

2. *Which* (like *that* and *this*) frequently has as its antecedent the idea of a phrase or clause:

Relative pronouns are as troublesome to the inexpert but conscientious writer as they are useful to everyone, *which* is saying much.—H. W. FOWLER, *A Dictionary of Modern English Usage*, p. 709

The only need is that, as with other uses of pronouns, the reference should be clear.

(SEE Webster's Dictionary, article *which*. Compare *this.)

3. *Whose* is often used as the genitive of *which*, instead of the more cumbersome *of which*:

This story of the life of General Custer is *Boots and Saddles,* whose author is the General's wife.

4. And which. *And* and *but* are carelessly used to join a *which* clause, which is subordinate, to a main statement.

Inaccurate: He got the contract to install new copper work on the Post Office, and which will require 4500 pounds of lead-coated copper.

Accurate: He got the contract to install new copper work on the Post Office, which will require 4500 pounds of lead-coated copper.

while *While* most exactly is a connective of time:

While the rest were studying, he was playing cards.

While also means *though* or *but,* but rather weakly:

Magazines, newspapers, and scientific books became my chief interest, while [More exact: *but*] plays and poems were still a torture to me.

While is sometimes used for *and,* but not often:

The second number was an acrobatic exhibition, while [Better: *and*] the third was a lady trapeze artist.

Awhile is an adverb, written as one word: *Awhile ago.* In phrases in which *while* is a noun, the *a* should be written separate: *In a while; After a while.*

(REFERENCE: Fries, pp. 236-37.)

Whitespace Whitespace has the function of a punctuation mark in display matter. It has now taken the place of commas and periods at the ends of lines and envelope addresses, in letter headings, in titles of books and articles, in outlines, in lines that are spaced off in advertisements, posters, etc., in matter set in tables or columns. No punctuation marks are used at the ends of lines in formal social notes. In indented quotations whitespace has displaced the quote marks. These various uses have helped relieve the spottiness of correspondence and many printed pages.

who, whom

1. Antecedent of 'who.' 2. 'Who' versus 'whom.' 3. 'Who' separated from verb. 4. The number of the verb.

1. Antecedent of 'who.' *Who* refers to people, to personified objects (a ship, a country), and occasionally to animals:

Diogenes Checkpoints says what is needed is a list of horses who should be out of training.—AUDAX MINOR, *The New Yorker,* Aug. 27, 1938

815

Whose is commonly used as the genitive of *which*.

(REFERENCE: Hall, pp. 320-27. See *which, § 3.)

2. 'Who' versus 'whom.' Twenty-five years ago the *Oxford English Dictionary* said *whom* was "no longer current in natural colloquial speech." The struggle to make writing conform to grammatical rules of case is consequently difficult and full of problems. *Whom* consistently occurs only when it immediately follows a preposition as object (I don't know to whom I should go). But since the preposition often comes last in the expression, in general usage we find *who* (I don't know who I should go to). Three factors combine to make this construction usual: (1) the position before the verb—the "subject-territory," (2) the infrequent use of *whom* in speech, and (3) our habit of not using relative pronouns to introduce clauses (I know the man [whom] you mean).

Formal usage, no doubt largely enforced by copy editors, generally keeps the objective form:

> Formal: Whom [object of *introduce*] do you introduce to whom [object of the immediately preceding *to*]?
> General: Who do you introduce to whom?
> Formal: No matter whom [object of *meets*] one meets, the first thing one mentions is the weather.
> General: No matter who you meet, the first thing you mention is the weather.

Which you use, then, depends on the level and tone of the particular piece of writing. In formal and academic writing there will be more *whom*'s than there will be in informal narratives and personal writing.

(REFERENCES: Fries, pp. 88-96, 237; Pooley, pp. 72-77, 221; all other competent grammarians.)

3. 'Who' separated from verb. When *who* is the subject of a verb separated from it by other words, care should be taken to keep the subject form:

> He made a list of all the writers who [subject of *were*] he thought were important in the period.

Whom sometimes occurs here, probably as the result of trying to keep the formal practice of using *whom* when it is an object preceding its verb (§ 2):

> . . . factory laborers and factory owners, young conscripts and seasoned army officers, folk whom [subject of *have disappeared*] I discover have disappeared for treason against National Socialism since they wrote . . .—NORA WALN, *The Atlantic Monthly*, Jan. 1939

4. The number of the verb. A verb of which *who* is the subject has the number of the antecedent of the *who:*

> I'm one of the few people who don't [antecedent *people*] like to read many books.
> I'm one who doesn't [antecedent *one*] like to read books.

Colloquially there is a strong tendency to make the verb of the *who* clause agree with the principal subject, which would give *doesn't* in the first sentence above. This is avoided in careful writing.

will See *shall—will.

wire *Wire* is informal and colloquial for *telegram, telegraph. Live wire* (a person) is colloquial.

with There seems to be a temptation to use *with* when another preposition or a different construction would be more accurate:

> Our outfit was composed of two platoons with [Better: of] 43 men each.
> I'll never forget the farmer who, not seeing the wave, tried to get his few cows to safety and was washed away with [Better: by] the water.
> Americans believe in freedom, but with Germans it is different [Perhaps: but Germans are different].

woman See *man, woman.

woods See *falls, woods.

Word composition See *Origin of words § 3a.

Wordiness Correction: Compress this passage by replacing the *Wordy* wordy expressions with more compact and exact ones.
   1. Circumlocution. 2. Long function words. 3. Deadwood.
   4. Fuzzy writing.
   The use of unnecessary words in conveying one's ideas results in flabby writing. Unprofitable words can be removed or replaced by more economical ones in revision. The commonest types of wordiness are:
   1. Circumlocution—the use of several words instead of one exact word:

> *destroyed by fire* means *burned*
> *come in contact with* usually means *meet* or *know*
> *the necessary funds* usually means no more than *the money*
> *in this day and age* means *today*
> *the sort of metal they use for plating the shiny parts of automobiles* might mean *chromium*

(SEE ch. 10, "Direct phrasing," p. 285.)

2. Long function words—function phrases that might be replaced by one or by fewer words: *During the time that* [*while*] she was in Los Angeles she had at least six different jobs.

(SEE *Function words § 2.)

3. Deadwood—words which add nothing to the meaning:

The cars are neat and graceful [in appearance].
In the majority of cases they do not. *For:* The majority do not.
The home of my boyfriend was in a town called Hillsdale. *For:* My boyfriend's home was in Hillsdale.

(SEE ch. 10, "Sentence economy," p. 284.)

4. Formless, fuzzy writing:

Wordy	*Revised*
It has some of the best ski trails in the country and as far as the other cold weather sports are concerned, they have them too, along with one of the most fashionable hotels in the country.	They have a very fashionable hotel, all the cold weather sports, and some of the best ski trails in the country.

(SEE also ch. 10, "Long and short constructions," p. 286, "Repetition," p. 289, and specific articles like *case, *exception, *Passive verbs, *seem, *there is, there are.)

WO Word order Correction: Revise the order of words or other elements so that the meaning is more clear, or the sentence is more natural, or more effective.

1. Position changed for emphasis. 2. Interrupted constructions. 3. Misleading word order.

The order of words and of other locutions in a sentence is a fundamental part of English grammar and in addition contributes to some effects of style, especially emphasis. The work done in many languages by inflections (endings) is in English performed largely by *function words (prepositions, auxiliary verbs, and so on) and by the word order. Since we pick up the standard word order as we learn to talk, it offers little difficulty. We use naturally the subject-verb-object order of clauses and sentences (page 247), we put adjectives before their nouns and relative clauses after their nouns, and in general put modifiers near the words modified.

This article is intended to bring the fact of word order to your attention rather than to cover its large number of details. It emphasizes three instances in which the order is variable.

1. Position changed for emphasis. As a rule an element taken out of its usual position receives increased emphasis, as when the object is put before both subject and verb:

Object first: That book I read when I was sixteen. (Instead of: I read that book when I was sixteen.)

Predicate adjective first: Lucky are the ones who register early. (Instead of: The ones who register early are lucky.)

(SEE ch. 10, "Position," p. 293.)

2. Interrupted constructions. When a word or words interrupt a construction, the effect is usually unhappy unless the interrupting word deserves special emphasis:

Between subject and verb: Newspaper headlines in these trying and confused times are continually intensifying the fears of the American people. (More natural: in these trying and confused times newspaper headlines are. . . .)

Between verb and adverb: He played quietly, efficiently on. He took a pack from his pocket and she took one thoughtfully out.

More natural: He played on, quietly, efficiently. He took a pack from his pocket and she took one out thoughtfully [or: and she thoughtfully took one out].

(SEE ch. 10, "Interrupted movement," p. 279, *Split infinitive.)

3. Misleading word order. English usually has a modifier close to the word modified and care must be taken that modifiers separated from their main words are not misleading.

Misleading	Improved
I wish to order one of the machines which I saw advertised in *The Saturday Evening Post* sent to the above address.	I wish to order sent to the above address one of the machines which I saw advertised in *The Saturday Evening Post*.
Her uncle, King Leopold, was even unable to influence her.	Even her uncle, King Leopold, was unable to influence her.
This success in villages will probably be duplicated in the cities as time goes on at an accelerated rate.	As time goes on, this success in villages will probably be duplicated at an accelerated rate in cities.
Until recently the chains have been able to get special prices on the goods they buy from producers with little opposition.	Until recently the chains have been able to get with little opposition special prices on the goods they buy from manufacturers.

(SEE *Ambiguity § 2. REFERENCES: Margaret M. Bryant, *College English*, 1944, 5: 434-38; Fries, ch. 10; Curme, *Syntax*, ch. 17; Kennedy, pp. 500-508; C. Alphonso Smith, *Studies in English Syntax* (Boston, 1906), ch. 2, The Short Circuit in English Syntax.)

Words Correction: Replace the word marked by one that is more WW exact, more effective, or more appropriate.

General questions of the use of words are treated in Chapter 11, The Meaning of Words, page 303, and Chapter 12, Qualities of Words, page 331. Many specific words that are likely to raise questions have articles of their own (*contact, *drunk, *hope, *however, *notorious, *try and—try to, *ye—the . . .). Very often the solution to a question of diction can be found in a good dictionary.

Most of this book is about words. Some of the more general topics about words or their uses will be found under the following heads, in the *Index* articles marked * or in the chapters at the pages given.

worth while   Written as two words, or hyphened (especially when preceding its noun: a worth-while book), or (occasionally) as one word.

would   See *shall—will, should—would §§ 4, 5.

would of   See *have § 3.

would rather   See *had better, had rather.

Written English   See *Colloquial and written English.

X is an unnecessary letter in English. It spells several sounds represented by different phonetic symbols (ks) as in *fox* (foks), *exclusive* (eks klōō′siv), *exceed* (ek sēd′); (gz) as in *exist* (eg zist′), *exhibit* (eg zib′it); (ksh) as in *luxury* (luk′shə ri); (gzh) as in *luxurious* (lug zhoor′i əs or luk shoor′i əs); (z) in *xylophone*, *Xantippe*. In British usage *ct* is sometimes spelled *x* as in *inflexion*.

Xmas Informal, chiefly advertising; pronounced like *Christmas,* for which it stands.

X-ray Hyphened; may or may not be spelled with a capital.

Y

(y) as in *yes* (yes), *beyond* (bi yond'). Y also spells *i* sounds, as in *sky* (skī), *bloody* (blud'i).

A final *y* following a consonant is changed to *i* before a suffix beginning with a vowel except *i: duty—dutiable, try—tries, body—bodies, bodied;* but *play—played, playing, playable, fly—flying.*

ye = the In Old English *th* of *the* was represented by the letter thorn, þ. In early printing the letter *y,* which looked most like the thorn, was used to represent it. Consequently we find *ye (the), yat (that), yem (them)* in early books and even oftener find the forms in manuscript down to about 1800.

The *y* then represents *th* and is pronounced *th.* Its use in recent faking of antiquity has not changed this fact: Ye Olde Coffee Shoppe is just The Old Coffee Shop and should be so pronounced.

ye = you *Ye,* originally the nominative plural and then the nominative singular of the second person pronoun (now *you*), survived for a long time in poetry and other literature with a tendency to be archaic (sermons, florid oratory) but is now obsolete.

yes *Yes* and *no* are adverbs. They may modify a sentence (Yes, you're right) or may have the value of a coordinate clause (No; but you should have told me) or may stand as complete sentences. ("Do you really intend to go with him?" "Yes.")

Yes is principally a written form, rarely used in speech, where there are innumerable substitutes, from *ye-us* to *yop* and the "colloquial nasals," not to mention the current slang affirmatives and the longer lived ones like *OK.*

yet *Yet* is an adverb (The books haven't come yet); and in rather formal English it is also used as a *coordinating conjunction, equivalent to *but:* "His speech was almost unintelligible, yet for some unknown reason I enjoyed it."

you *You* is used as an indefinite pronoun (It's a good book, if you like detective stories) in general writing. Formal English would more often use *one* or a different construction, though the prejudice against *you* is declining. (See *one, *they.)

821

When *you* is used in an informal approach to readers or to an audience, it sometimes may be unintentionally personal (or even insulting), or seem to indicate an invidious distinction between writer and reader: "Take, for instance, *your* [better: *our* or *one's*] family problems."

In familiar English *was* is used with *you* referring to one person, and in vulgate *you is* and *you was* are both singular and plural.

you all In Southern American *you all*, contracted to *y'all*, is frequently used as the plural of *you*, as in some other regions *you folks* is used. It is also used when addressing one person regarded as one of a group, usually a family, as in Benbow's speech to Popeye, "If it's whiskey, I don't care how much you all make or sell or buy" (William Faulkner, *Sanctuary*, p. 4), in which the *you all* refers to Popeye and his household.

It is sometimes asserted that *you all* is also used as a singular, addressing one. (See almost any volume of *American Speech*, especially ii and iv.) It apparently is occasionally used as a singular but this use is regarded by educated Southerners as an error.
(REFERENCE: Mencken, pp. 449-50.)

your—you're In revision check for careless confusion of these words. *Your* is a possessive pronoun (your books); *you're* is a subject and verb (you're all right).

youth is overused in the sense of "young people" and suggests a ministerial style.

Z (z) as in *Zion* (zī'ən), *buzz* (buz), *busy* (biz'i), *shoes* (shōōz).

zh The phonetic symbol representing the sound in *rouge* (rōōzh), *measure* (mezh'ər) and so on. (See *G § 3.)

zoology In spite of several dictionaries, zoology is prevailingly spelled without the dieresis or hyphen. It is well to resist the temptation to pronounce it zōō ol'i ji and keep it zō ol'i ji.

 See *Ampersand.

Acknowledgments

The author gratefully acknowledges the kindness of authors and publishers in giving permission to reproduce their materials in *Writer's Guide and Index to English*. Where the territory rights are divided among various publishers, the acknowledgment states what permission was granted. An unqualified acknowledgment indicates that world permission was granted.

George Allen & Unwin Ltd: World exclusive of the United States and Canada for selection from *The Conquest of Happiness* by Bertrand Russell. British Empire for selections from *Individualism Old and New* by John Dewey, *Language in Thought and Action* by S. I. Hayakawa, *Prejudices: Fifth Series* by H. L. Mencken, and *Mysticism and Logic* by Bertrand Russell.

American Association of University Professors Bulletin: selection from "The Functional Bases of Appraising Academic Performance" by Logan Wilson; used by permission of the American Association of University Professors and Logan Wilson.

Eleanor Anderson: selections from "I'm a Fool" in *Horses and Men*, *The Modern Writer*, and "The Egg" in *The Triumph of the Egg* by Sherwood Anderson.

Edward Arnold & Co: World exclusive of the United States for selection from *Aspects of the Novel* by E. M. Forster.

Associated Students of the University of California at Los Angeles: selection from *The California Daily Bruin*.

The Atlantic Monthly: selections from *The Atlantic Monthly*, June 1949: "Fishing in the Rockies" by John Hodgdon Bradley, "What Is a Book Contract?" by Paul Brooks, "Gene Rhodes: Cowboy Novelist" by J. Frank Dobie, "The 'Hood' and the 'Bismarck': The Sinking of the 'Hood'" by Captain Russell Grenfell, R. N., "The Tidelands and Oil" by Robert E. Hardwicke, "Britain's Young Offenders" by Basil Henriques, "The Marital Deduction" by Lynn Lloyd, "'My Only and Last Love': Byron's Unpublished Letters to Countess Teresa Guiccioli" by Iris Origo, "The Color Line in Fraternities" by Alfred S. Romer. Selections from "Hook" by Walter Van Tilburg Clark, August 1940; and "A Coat for St. Patrick's Day" by W. B. Ready, March 1950.

Arthur Barker Ltd: British Empire for selection from *Time: The Present* by Tess Slesinger.

The Bobbs-Merrill Company Inc: selection from *The New Decalogue of Science* by Albert Edward Wiggam. Copyright 1923. Used by special permission of the publishers, The Bobbs-Merrill Company Inc.

Albert & Charles Boni Inc: World exclusive of the British Empire for selections from *The Bridge of San Luis Rey* by Thornton Wilder. Copyright, 1927, by Albert & Charles Boni Inc.

Brandt & Brandt: selections from "A Death in the Country" and "The Blood of the Martyrs" in *Thirteen O'Clock* by Stephen Vincent Benét, published by

Farrar and Rinehart, Inc. Copyright, 1932, by the Butterick Company. Copyright, 1925, 1928, 1930, 1932, 1935, 1936, 1937, by Stephen Vincent Benét. Selection from *John Brown's Body* by Stephen Vincent Benét, published by Farrar & Rinehart, Inc. Copyright, 1927, 1928, by Stephen Vincent Benét. Selection from "Farewell! Farewell! Farewell!" in *Costumes by Eros* by Conrad Aiken. Copyright, 1928, by Conrad Aiken. World exclusive of the United States and Canada for selection from *The Yearling* by Marjorie Kinnan Rawlings.

Ann Bridge: selections from *Enchanter's Nightshade* by Ann Bridge.

Gelett Burgess: selection from *Short Words Are Words of Might* by Gelett Burgess.

George T. Bye and Company: British Empire for selection from *An Almanac for Moderns* by Donald Culross Peattie. Copyright, 1935, by Donald Culross Peattie.

Cambridge University Press: selection from *The Universe Around Us* by Sir James Jeans.

H. S. Canby: selections from *Saturday Papers*, edited by H. S. Canby and others; and "War or Peace in Literature" in *Designed for Reading* by H. S. Canby, W. R. Benét and A. Loveman, published by The Macmillan Company.

Jonathan Cape Limited: World exclusive of the United States for selections from *News from Tartary* by Peter Fleming, *The Meaning of Culture* by John Cowper Powys, and *Novel on Yellow Paper* by Stevie Smith. World exclusive of the United States and Canada for selection from *The Heat of the Day* by Elizabeth Bowen. British Empire except Canada for selections from *Green Hills of Africa* by Ernest Hemingway.

Cassell & Company Ltd: British Empire (except Canada and Newfoundland) and the Continent of Europe for selection from *The Gathering Storm* by Winston S. Churchill.

Chatto & Windus: selections from *A Writer's Notes on His Trade* and *Disenchantment* by C. E. Montague. British Empire for selections from *North to the Orient* by Anne Morrow Lindbergh, and *Queen Victoria* by Lytton Strachey.

Laura Baker Cobb: selection from *A Plea for Old Cap Collier* by Irvin S. Cobb, copyright, 1921, by Doubleday, Doran & Company, Inc.

College English: from selections in *College English:* "English for Maturity" by Thomas Clark Pollock, February 1949; and "The Growth of Thoreau's Reputation" by Randall Stewart, January 1946.

Constable & Company Limited: World exclusive of the United States and Canada for selection from *Persons and Places* by George Santayana. World exclusive of the United States for selection from *Reperusals and Recollections* by Logan Pearsall Smith.

Malcolm Cowley: selection from *Exile's Return* by Malcolm Cowley.

Thomas Y. Crowell Company: selection from *Roget's International Thesaurus of English Words and Phrases*, edited by C. O. Sylvester Mawson.

Crown Publishers: selection from *The American Craftsman* by Scott Graham Williamson. Copyright, 1940, by Crown Publishers, New York. Used by permission of Crown Publishers.

Current History: selection from "The Good and Evil of the New Industrialism" by Stuart Chase in *Current History*, July 1929.

825

Oxford University Press, Inc. (New York): selection from *The Philosophy of Rhetoric* by I. A. Richards.

The Phi Delta Kappan: selection from "Poor People Have Brains, Too" by Allison Davis in *The Phi Delta Kappan,* April 1949.

Robert C. Pooley: selection from *Grammar and Usage in Textbooks on English* by Robert C. Pooley.

Prentice-Hall, Inc: selection from *A Rhetoric of Motives* by Kenneth Burke. Published by Prentice-Hall, Inc., New York, 1950.

Princeton University Press: selection from *Army Talk* by Elbridge Colby.

G. P. Putnam's Sons: selections from *Jungle Days* by William Beebe, and *From a College Window* by A. C. Benson. World exclusive of the British Empire for selections from *Individualism Old and New* by John Dewey. From *An Almanac for Moderns* by Donald Culross Peattie. Copyright, 1935, by Donald Culross Peattie. Courtesy of G. P. Putnam's Sons.

Random House, Inc: selections from *Home Is Where You Hang Your Childhood* by Leane Zugsmith. From *The Daring Young Man on the Flying Trapeze* by William Saroyan, copyright, 1934, 1941, by The Modern Library, Inc. United States and Canada for selection from *Lectures in America* by Gertrude Stein. United States for selection from *Retreat from Reason* by Lancelot Hogben.

Rinehart & Company Incorporated: selection from *The Fall of the City* by Archibald MacLeish, copyright, 1937.

Routledge and Kegan Paul Ltd: World exclusive of the United States for selection from *Happy Days, 1880-1892* by H. L. Mencken. British Empire for selection from *Patterns of Culture* by Ruth Benedict.

San Francisco Chronicle: selection from "This World" Supplement by Vance Johnson, February 5, 1950.

The Saturday Review of Literature: from selections in *The Saturday Review of Literature:* "Notes for an Autobiography" by Albert Einstein, November 26, 1949; and from an article by Christopher Morley, September 24, 1938.

Science and Mechanics: diagram "Construction of Skis" in *Science and Mechanics,* February 1939.

Charles Scribner's Sons: selections from *Enjoyment of Poetry* by Max Eastman, "Haircut" in *Roundup* by Ring Lardner, and *English Composition* by Barrett Wendell. From "An Escapade" in *A Native Argosy* by Morley Callaghan; used by permission of Charles Scribner's Sons and Morley Callaghan. World exclusive of the British Empire for selections from *Green Hills of Africa* by Ernest Hemingway. United States and Canada for selections from *The Man of Property* by John Galsworthy, *Persons and Places* by George Santayana, *The Yearling* by Marjorie Kinnan Rawlings, and *From Death to Morning* and *Look Homeward, Angel* by Thomas Wolfe. United States for selection from *News from Tartary* by Peter Fleming. Selection from *The Art of Letters* by Robert Lynd; permission granted by Charles Scribner's Sons and Gerald Duckworth & Co. Ltd.

Simon and Schuster, Inc: selections from "The Net" by Robert Coates in *Short Stories from The New Yorker,* copyright, 1940; *Reading I've Liked* by Clifton Fadiman, copyright, 1941; *Color Blind* by Margaret Halsey, copyright, 1946; and *Winter Orchard* by Josephine Johnson, copyright, 1935. World exclusive of the British Empire for selections reprinted from *With Malice Toward*

List of Writers
and Sources Quoted

List of writers and sources from whom the longer quotations in *The Writer's Guide and Index to English* were taken.

Agar, Herbert, 176, 178
Aiken, Conrad, 215
Allport, Floyd, 230
Anderson, Sherwood, 23, 65, 172-173

Bacon, Francis, 548
Ballard, P. B., 350
Barzun, Jacques, 175, 181, 471
Beard, C. A., 174
Becker, Carl L., 51
Beebe, William, 232
Benedict, Ruth, 43-44
Benét, Stephen Vincent, 36-37, 324
Benson, A. C., 659-660
Benson, Sally, 211, 215-216
Berger, Meyer, 482
Bingham, Alfred M., 275
Boswell, Peyton, Jr., 357
Bowen, Elizabeth, 204-205
Boyle, Kay, 213
Bradley, John Hodgdon, 198
Bridge, Ann, 347
Brooks, Paul, 197
Burgess, Gelett, 340
Burke, Kenneth, 361-362

The California Daily Bruin, 184
Callaghan, Morley, 218
Carmer, Carl, 194
Canby, H. S., 349, 456
Cather, Willa, 39
Chase, Mary Ellen, 510
Chase, Stuart, 344, 722
Chidsey, Donald B., 172
Childs, Marquis W., 655
Churchill, Winston S., 153
Clark, Walter Van Tilburg, 231

Cleaton, Irene and Allen, 515
Coates, Robert M., 296
Cobb, Irvin S., 7, 594
Colby, Elbridge, 361
Conrad, Joseph, 296, 586-587, 607
Cowley, Malcolm, 221-222, 342-343, 752
Crothers, Samuel McChord, 719

Daly, Maureen, 361
Davis, Allison, 356-357
Day, Clarence, 43, 246-247, 261, 740
Dewey, John, 179-180
Dobie, J. Frank, 197
Dos Passos, John, 138-139
Dryden, John, 547
Dunsany, Lord, 291-292

East, Edward M., 175
Eastman, Max, 291
Edman, Irwin, 258, 343-344
Einstein, Albert, 233
The Emporia Gazette, 809
Ernst, Morris L., 230
Etnier, Elizabeth, 273

Fadiman, Clifton, 180-181, 504
Ferguson, Allan, 721
Ferguson, Otis, 346
Fitzgerald, F. Scott, 231
Fleming, Peter, 280-281
Forster, E. M., 64
Fortune, 481
Fowler, H. W., 431, 662
Franck, Harry A., 217-218
Frank, Waldo, 483
Fries, C. C., 73, 501

Gorer, Geoffrey, 252

CONCERNING THE TYPE FACES USED IN THIS BOOK

The text matter of *Writer's Guide and Index to English* has been set on the Linotype machine in Granjon, a type face designed by George W. Jones, one of England's great printers. Though Granjon is by no means a copy of the classic sixteenth century Garamond, its basic design comes from that source. A companion face, Granjon roman bold, is used for subheads within the text matter. The other type faces used in this book—for chapter titles, initial letters, and major heads in the *Guide*, for entry words in the *Index*—are various sizes and weights of a type family generally known as Futura, after the face developed from designs of a German architect, Paul Renner. The larger sizes used here are called Twentieth Century by their manufacturer, Lanston Monotype Company; the smaller sizes used here are called Spartan by their manufacturer, Mergenthaler Linotype Company.

To the student

Your papers will be criticized by references to the alphabetical articles in the *Index* of the book, and you should revise your papers accordingly:

1. A ring around a word or phrase that you have used means that there is an article on that word or phrase, and that you should look it up.

2. Your instructor may use abbreviations for the *Index* articles listed below when he corrects your papers. Look up the article that corresponds to the abbreviation written on your paper and make the appropriate changes (suggested in boldface type right after the entry word in the *Index*). Page references are given to the *Guide* when it contains fuller information than the *Index* articles.